DRAMA

An Introductory Anthology

DRAMA

An Introductory Anthology

PN6112
R36d

Edited by

OTTO REINERT

University of Washington, Seattle

BOSTON

Little, Brown and Company

TORONTO

PREFACE

ANY SMALL SELECTION OF WORLD DRAMA may be challenged, and mine is not offered as a gathering of Western man's twelve greatest plays. But the intrinsic worth of each play is, I think, beyond argument, and collectively they represent a range of drama, in time and kind, that I hope can serve to introduce the reader to the generic study of drama as literature.

The introduction sketches a general theory of drama, defines some technical terms, and takes the reader through a close analysis of a dramatic scene. The comments on the individual plays are meant to be suggestive rather than exhaustive — to raise issues, imply questions, invite approaches. I do not think I have defeated my purpose by recording my own interpretations and evaluations in cases where not to do so would have struck me as coy. If I ever seem to interpose myself between the reader and the play, I can only say that the plays are big enough to accommodate more than one critic.

In the notes to *Everyman* and *Macbeth* the specialist will recognize my indebtedness to earlier editors: Joseph Quincy Adams and A. C. Cawley of *Everyman*; Kenneth Muir (New Arden), G. L. Kittredge, John Dover Wilson (Cambridge), Alfred Harbage (Pelican), and Louis B. Wright and Virginia A. Lamar (Folger Library) of *Macbeth*.

The biographical notes are brief but, I hope, useful. The bibliographies are obviously selective — drastically so in some cases. Among possible choices, ease of availability has sometimes determined inclusion.

Mrs. Helene Høverstad, Mrs. Phyllis Dumas, Erik Pierstorff, M.A. and Professors Paul Dietrichson and Robert Stanton have read the general introduction in manuscript at various stages. I am grateful for their criticism and encouragement. I want to thank my wife Dorothy for arresting irrelevance, obscurity, and infelicity in the early versions of the manuscript.

O. R.
Seattle

CONTENTS

Bertolt Brecht
Caucasian chalk circle
Ed. Albee
Who Afraid of Va. Woolf
Samuel Beckett — waiting
for Godot

DRAMA

An Introductory Anthology

INTRODUCTION

A Definition of Drama

Drama, like poetry and fiction, is an art of words — mainly words of dialogue. People talking is the basic dramatic situation. The talk may be interrupted by wordless activity — sword-play, love-making — but such activity will derive its significance from its context of dialogue. If not, we are dealing with pantomime and not with drama.

A performance of drama is more than just an art of words, of course. It is the joint product of many arts, such as acting, directing, and stage designing. But the performance is no more the drama than the concert is the symphony. A play is a potential but never-to-be-realized performance, inherent in the configuration of the playwright's words, independent of the artists of the theater whom it keeps challenging to produce performed drama.

Drama is distinguished from the other forms of literature by performability and by the objectivity that performability implies. The statement "She is a woman without hope" is, as stage direction, undramatic. It could become a speech by one of the characters, or it could inspire an actress to perform an electrifying gesture of fluttering futility. But as stage direction it is novelistic rather than dramatic. It does not denote anything actable, and it violates the objectivity that is a condition for the playwright's craft: the tacit agreement between him and us that for the duration of the make-believe he does not exist at all, that the characters can be known only by what they reveal of themselves in speech and action. The play must tell itself; the characters must speak for themselves. Even the play that by design expresses the playwright's inmost self can reach us only as a piece of objective, external reality, a dynamic spectacle of speakers, among whom a self-projection of the playwright's has no separate esthetic status.

Plays and movies based on novels prove there is much that is per-

1

formable in the other genres of literature as well. But the art of poet and novelist extends beyond dialogue and description of stageables. A novelist can suspend action indefinitely and discourse abstractly on any subject. He can judge and analyze human souls and, omniscient, enter into them at will. He can address his reader directly. And if he never makes use of these novelistic freedoms, he is, in effect, a dramatist, whether he calls his work a play or not.

Actually, this is a stricter definition of drama than many plays allow. Bernard Shaw, for example, often violates dramatic objectivity in stage directions that interpret his characters. The most flagrant example is perhaps the ending of *Candida*. When the heroine has sent her would-be lover, a young poet, "into the night" and turns to her husband, Shaw tells us, "They embrace. But they do not know the secret in the poet's heart." No amount of theatrical ingenuity can stage that last sentence. The point is not that Shaw's plays sometimes include bits of novels; we are concerned here with determining the quality that all plays have in common — the quality that makes them, distinctly, *drama*. Performability is that quality. The spectator is in the theater to watch and listen. Shaw's comments do not exist for him, except insofar as they may have been translated into the language of the theater: sights and sounds the audience can perceive, directly through the senses in the physical theater, imaginatively in the theater in the mind.

This is not to exclude from the genre of drama works that cannot, for technical reasons, be staged in any existing theater or which, if staged, would overtax the patience and subtlety of an audience. Not only are such pragmatic criteria obviously relative, there is also a sense in which dramatic poems like *Samson Agonistes* and *Prometheus Unbound*, though not intended for the stage and in some respects unperformable (if only by being bad box-office), are superbly dramatic. That is, their form is a system of speaking parts developing a coherent and complete action. Whatever abstracts they entail are expressed in speech, and speech is performable by impersonators of the fictitious speakers.

The mode of drama is the objectivity of the performable. Movement, directness, concreteness are its characteristics. The dramatic experience, whether in the theater or over a printed play, is one of urgent immediacy, of watching and listening to human destinies in the making, here and now, which the novelist or poet can duplicate only by being, precisely, dramatic.

Drama and the Reader

From such a definition it follows that the skillful reader of plays supplies vivid and relevant images to the dialogue, whether such images are suggested to him directly by speeches and stage directions or he translates what is unstageable in the printed play into concretes that participate in the total, complex image — words, movement, scene — of the drama being enacted in his mind.

Basic to any kind of meaningful response to literature is understanding of the author's words in context and of the underlying conditions for action in the imagined world. "Understanding" depends on more than conscientious use of footnotes and dictionary; it entails a total response: intellectual, emotional, sensory. And though all readers cannot respond equally well, they can all make the effort to engage more than the top of their minds and the shallows of their souls. Generally, in the case of plays from ages and cultures different from our own, *some* awareness of cultural background will be imperative, and *more* desirable, but the line between some and more is hard to draw in given cases. For some readers, at least, certain plays will create their own climate of understanding.

Perhaps the ideal performance of the play, the standard by which both a theatrical production and a reading of it should be judged, will be thought of as the performance the playwright himself envisioned for his play. But this is neither a practicable nor even a really reasonable formula. There are playwrights who have left no record as to how they thought their plays should be produced, or whose ideas are too vague or incomplete to be of much help, or who refuse to answer when asked. And even if we assume that the original staging realized the playwright's ideal, for most older plays we can reconstruct it only by means of more or less inferential evidence, either within the play itself or supplied by research. Nor are the playwright's views, when available, necessarily more valid than someone else's — just as composers are not necessarily the best performers of their own works or even the best critics of the performance of their works by others. Intention is not accomplishment.

There is more force to the argument that a meaningful reading of a play requires knowledge of the kind of theater for which it was written. To read Sophocles or Shakespeare, the argument goes, we must know something about Greek and Elizabethan stagecraft, see productions that try to reproduce the contemporary performance, see models or pictures or diagrams of the playhouses, or at the very least read descriptions of them.

It is certainly true that the more knowledge the reader has of the culture — including the theatrical culture — reflected in what he reads, the more significant and enjoyable his reading will be. And the impossibility of ever knowing everything about a play and the fact that knowledge alone is insufficient for recreating the sense impressions, the beliefs, attitudes, and moods of a bygone audience cannot invalidate the efforts of historians of drama and theater to know as much as possible. Though each culture, each age, each reader, even the same reader at different times, reads a literary work differently, knowledge of what can be factually known about it and its times is a protection against an anarchic subjectivity of interpretation that could eventually destroy its continuum of identity. This is part of the justification of scholarship.

But though knowledge of theatrical conditions, past or present, can discipline and enrich one's experience of a play, and though such knowledge is valuable for its own sake, it is still not a precondition for the dramatic imagination itself. The images that arise in the mind during the reading of drama can be translated into stage actualities, but they are not images of such actualities. The reader does not ordinarily imagine a staged scene but its real life counterpart — not a stage castle, crypt, or kitchen, but the real thing — Macbeth, not Orson Welles or Maurice Evans. The exceptions are the director, designer, or actor who read with a projected performance in mind and — and he is the one who concerns us — the reader who comes to his reading of the play fresh from an impressive performance of it. His reading experience will no doubt be more vivid than it otherwise would have been, but it will also be more limited. His imagination will be channeled by his memory of the hundreds of big and little details of voice and mimicry, movement and set, costume and light, that together make up any particular actualization of the ideal abstract the play is. Any one performance, however brilliant, is bound to be different from — both more and less than — the literary work that occasioned it, forever detached as the latter is from the impermanent particulars of the real. A good production may help a reader imagine what he found unimaginable as he read the play, or it may cool and contain an imagination that catches fire too easily, but a reader to whom a play is nothing but a blueprint for an evening in the theater has abdicated his rights as reader. It is only because most people *can* stage a play in their imagination, alive with the sights and sounds of reality, that drama is literature at all — that is, capable of being experienced through reading. The theater is the home of drama, and drama may be the occasion for theater, but all theater is not drama, nor is the drama lost without the theater.

Dramatic Conventions

Understanding the underlying conditions for action in the imagined world involves understanding dramatic conventions — the conditions which playwright and audience between them have implicitly (whether they are conscious of it or not) agreed to accept as reality in the play. In the sense that what is called for is a willingness to take the world of imagination as reality for the time being, acceptance of conventions enters into any kind of successful artistic experience. But because the theater makes tangible the forms of the make-believe, conventions operate with particular force in the experience of drama — most insistently in the theater, but also in reading.

Chorus, soliloquy, and aside are examples of conventions, mainly of older drama. They were no more everyday realities then than they are now, but as artistic devices they were given status as reality because they satisfied needs for dramatic expression without going beyond what the contemporary public was willing to tolerate as make-believe. Some conventions may have been means to achieve certain kinds of communication under the technically limiting conditions of older theater. For example, such "facts" of the imagined world as location and time of day, which in the modern theater can be established by sets and electric lights, were on the Elizabethan stage communicated by the dialogue itself. Hence the rather remarkable number of Shakespearean characters who mention time and place in their speeches, particularly in the opening of scenes (see, for example, *Macbeth*, II, i, first few lines). To the extent that such information is for the benefit of the audience rather than for the listeners on stage, the device is conventional: a breach of reality for the sake of establishing, economically and often beautifully, "reality" within the play.

Conventions vary with time and place. Yesterday's conventions are today's absurdities and tomorrow's brilliant innovations. No play is without them. If a modern reader finds older drama "quaint" and "unrealistic," it may be because he takes the conventions of realism too much for granted, automatically regards them as authentically life-like, since most of the drama he meets in today's mass media is realistic. Or if he is sophisticated enough to recognize the conventions of realism and the necessity for them, he may still feel they are the only "natural" conventions. But if he objects to the artificiality of the neoclassical convention of the three unities (which demanded that the action of the play be confined to a single plot, a single place, and a single day), he ought also to object to the convention of today's film and television that presents human beings as disembodied heads in facial close-ups and to the three-walled rooms of most post-Renaissance theater. And there is no reason to believe that playgoers of the past would have found a modern theater, with its artificially lighted box peeked into by a supposedly non-existent audience, any less unnatural than we presume to find the choric rituals and public unburdenings of soul in soliloquy in their plays. If the naïve or stubbornly literal-minded is bothered by the hero's apparent deafness to the villain's stage whisper, by the scarcity of actors on stage during Shakespeare's battle scenes, or by the free and flexible treatment of time and place in a contemporary play like *A View from the Bridge*, he simply fails to understand or accept dramatic convention.

Action, Plot, Conflict

Like most serious writing, drama represents man's use of words to make sense out of the myriad perplexities that befall him. The dramatist sees the world not primarily as shapes and colors and feelings, or as an object for religious or philosophical or scientific contemplation, or as a market, or as a reluctant machine that challenges his skill and ingenuity to make it run better. He sees it rather as an arena for human action manifested in speech.

The newcomer to the reading of drama may at first find confusing the conversations of unknowns, surprised in the embroilments with a life of which he knows nothing. He may miss preliminary explanations, the novelist's guiding hand. And if he has had experience with performed drama, he may also miss the aid to understanding provided by the presences and the voices of actors and by the physical spectacle in which they appear. That he can be guided by stage directions and ponder the dialogue at his leisure he may feel to be poor compensation for the absence of the sights and sounds of performance.

What the characters say and do begins to make sense only as we learn more about them, but we learn more about them only by what they say and do. Gradually they become more than a list of names. They reveal their antecedents and their present situations, their motives and purposes, they assume plot identity and "character." We learn to respond to the revealing remark or gesture, to listen to the eloquence of their silence, to sense their continuous pressure on the plot. Among them, they define and develop the dramatic action.

Dramatic action is neither physical activity nor simply the sum of everything that happens on stage: conversation, eating, people running up and down staircases, laughter, doors closing, lights going on. These are part of the action, but in the traditional (mainly Aristotelian) definition action itself is a more comprehensive concept. A set of definitions may be useful at this point.

A play is a patterning of language, character, event, and spectacle, each element a function of the other three. Its plot is the particular sequence of events that gives it the coherence and movement toward a given end that could not inhere in a random aggregate of happenings. Plot is the way the playwright has chosen to tell his story, the detailed arrangement of incidents for maximum meaning, beauty, and suspense. The action of the play is both the summation of the plot and the abstraction of its meaning, the distillation of the play's totality, the answer, in a single phrase, to the question, "What happens?" We call tragic the action that ends by exacting suffering or death from the protagonist as the price at which we (and perhaps he) are brought to new or heightened awareness of man's being and his relation to the ultimate moral or metaphysical issues in life. We call comic the action that concerns man in his mundane or social relationships, exposes vice and folly for contempt and laughter, and ends by vindicating reason, moderation, goodwill, love, virtue, or other sane and normal human values. Tragedy's domain is the infinite, its characteristic subject matter the mystery of evil and suffering. Comedy's domain is the finite, its characteristic subject matter man's triumphs and tribulations as gregarious animal.

Formally, most plots are divisible into four parts. (1) The exposition, which gives essential information about the characters' backgrounds and sets the plot in motion. (2) The complication, usually the bulk of the play, interweaving the characters' shifting fortunes and including the climax, a point of high tension and the critical juncture at which a decision or an event irretrievably determines the result of the action. (3) The reversal, or peripety, the point at which the complication culminates in the resolution of the plot: the protagonist's fortune changing from good to bad (tragedy) or from bad to good (comedy). (4) The dénouement or unraveling, which presents the consequences of the reversal, ties up loose ends, and allows the audience to regain emotional equilibrium. The plays in which the four parts of the plot are neatly distinct and laid end to end are few and not likely to be of the highest order. Much more commonly, plot is a complex, organic structure, whose parts blend into one another and overlap or alternate. To use the terms mechanically in dramatic analysis will almost certainly end in critical disaster.

For purposes of illustration, we may try to apply our terms to *Oedipus Rex*. The *story* of the play is the entire chronicle of the fulfillment of the prophecy from the time it was first announced to Laios and Iocaste till the moment Oedipus exits, blind and banished. The *plot* is the causally connected sequence of events that gradually reveals the significance of the past. The *action* is the quest for Laios's murderer, for the quest is what motivates Oedipus to initiate the plot, and the plot is over the moment the quest ends in the discovery of Oedipus himself as the murderer. In most plays the *exposition* comes early, but in *Oedipus Rex* it can be said to continue right up to the *reversal:* Oedipus' fortune changes when he sees the significance of the revealed past, that he, the seeker, is the man sought. It follows that the play's exposition and its *complication* very nearly coincide, for the exposition is defined as the communication to the audience of those facts of the pre-play past that are necessary for an understanding of the present, and such communication — simultaneously to us and to Oedipus — is precisely what occupies the interval between Oedipus's first statement of purpose and the ironic accomplishment of it in the reversal. In other words, the complication is Oedipus's unwitting movement, through his own deliberate search for truth, toward tragedy. The *climax* occurs at the last moment when Oedipus could still avoid the fatal knowledge, the moment when in his pride of good fortune and anticipated achievement he refuses to listen to Iocaste's warning not to inquire further into his parentage. The *dénouement* is what follows the reversal: the report of Iocaste's suicide and of Oedipus's blinding himself, the dialogue between Oedipus and the Choragos, Oedipus's soliloquy, Creon's taking charge, the banishment of Oedipus, and the Chorus' final statement of moral.

Plot generates and releases suspense — the feeling in the audience that keeps it wondering what happens next. One characteristic of great drama is that its suspense survives knowledge of "how things come out," because our absorbed wait for what is going to happen concerns the outcome less than it concerns the happenings themselves. We may know exactly what happens in *Oedipus Rex* and still attend, fascinated and moved, to every small step in the protagonist's gradual approach to disaster. In fact, superior plays have a way of seeming better in later readings. What we lose in mere thrill we gain in understanding and enjoyment through our intimacy with the characters and our knowledge of events to come. Familiarity also increases our appreciation and enjoyment of dramaturgy: the exercise of the playwright's craft, the manipulation of plot and character in the integrated structure of successful dramatic action. As the football fan goes to the game not just to learn who wins but to enjoy the game being played, so the lover of drama seeks vicarious experience of significant action in artistic form — not just information about a result.

Conflict is the element in plot that creates suspense; it is what the plot is about. In *Oedipus Rex* the conflict may be variously defined — perhaps most simply as man versus god or fate, or as the tragic irreconcilability of human and divine purpose. Or we may sense the conflict chiefly as irony: the distance between what Oedipus *thinks* his purpose — to purge the city — will accomplish for him personally ("By avenging the murdered king I protect myself") and what it *does* accomplish. To Oedipus himself, up until the moment when the final piece of the puzzle falls into place, the conflict appears as one between his intent and the human and circumstantial obstacles in its way.

Double or multiple conflict need not be a symptom of structural weakness. The several conflicts — or even, as in some of Shakespeare's plays, the different plots — may appear as different facets of a many-sided subject, each presenting it in a new view. A wider definition of the play's issue may subsume them all. For example, in Chekhov's *Three Sisters* most of the characters are kept from achieving happiness and self-fulfillment by some obstacle or other — some quality in themselves, other people, circumstances. These various conflicts cohere in a complex but single image of the passion of frustration, of the clash of aspiration with reality.

Conflict is opposition of forces, of whatever kind: man versus mountain, man versus God, man versus himself. It may be as simple as that of a fairy tale (bad queen versus good princess, bad guy versus good sheriff). It may be as elemental as that of *Everyman*, as preposterous as that of *The Lesson*, as dialectic and ambiguous as that of *The Wild Duck*, as grimly ethical as that of *Purgatory*, as nearly farcical as that of *Tartuffe* and *Arms and the Man*, as metaphysical as that of three such different plays as *Oedipus Rex*, *The Ghost Sonata*, and *The Good Woman of Setzuan*. Drama without conflict is unthinkable. For the essence of the dramatic experience is the fascination with the progress of clashing forces toward resolution: the hero's death or triumph, the villain's defeat, the wedding, the re-establishment of order in a private, a communal, or a universal cosmos.

The spoken word is the medium of drama, the objectivity of the performable its mode or manner of being, the surrender of our imagination to that of the playwright the condition for its existence for us, but the drama itself is the action of human conflict. This action we witness partly as safe and superior deities, enjoying the pleasure of dramatic irony at the expense of people who do not know what is happening to them; partly as sympathetic observers, commiserating with the good, relishing the downfall of the bad; and partly as fellow fools and sufferers: there but for the grace of God go we.

Anatomy of a Scene

Near the end of the second act of *Cyrano de Bergerac* by Edmond Rostand there is a scene that may profitably be studied as an example of successful dramatic plotting. When we understand exactly what goes on in Rostand's exploitation of a carefully prepared, complex situation and exactly how and why the scene affects us, we understand something about the technique of drama. We enjoy the scene for its suspense, its psychology, its humor, its implied pathos, but we enjoy all these all the more if we also delight in the spectacle of a master manipulator taking his engaging puppets through their paces. In the curious state of schizophrenia in which we enjoy a good play we are simultaneously aware of the characters as *men* and as *parts*.

Cyrano is in love with his pretty cousin Roxane, but he despairs of success because he feels his enormous nose makes his countenance ridiculous. Roxane does, in fact, love someone else, a handsome young officer, Christian de Neuvillette, who has just joined Cyrano's company of Guards. She tells Cyrano of her love and asks him to protect Christian against bullying by the other officers. To Cyrano, no sacrifice is too great where Roxane is concerned, and, though secretly heartbroken, he gives her his word. Of this interview Christian is ignorant. All he knows about Cyrano is what the other officers have just told him: that he is swift and terrible in his anger against anyone who dares make fun of his nose, even by as much as the remotest allusion. Christian takes aside Carbon de Castel-Jaloux, the Captain of the Guards, and asks him how as an outsider and a newcomer to the company he — Christian — can get himself accepted. Carbon tells him he will have to prove his courage. At this point Cyrano begins his story of the previous night's heroic adventure.

CYRANO: . . . (*All bring their stools and listen eagerly.* CHRISTIAN
  sits astride over a chair.)
  Well! When I started out for this hotch-potch,
  the moon shone round in heaven as a watch;
  then of a sudden some horologist,
  clearing the dial with a rag of mist,
  muffled the argent circle of its light,
  and the whole world was plunged in utmost night.
  There were no lamps in the streets, and I suppose
  a man could see no further than
CHRISTIAN: his nose.

  (*Silence. Everybody rises slowly, watching* CYRANO *in turn.* He
  breaks off astounded. A pause.)

CYRANO: Who is this fellow?
AN OFFICER: 'Tis a lad who came
  only this morning.
CYRANO (*advancing on* CHRISTIAN): This morning?
CARBON (*under his breath*): And his name
  Baron de Neuvill —
CYRANO (*quickly, holding himself in*): What!
  (*Goes pale and red, still moving toward* CHRISTIAN.)
  I — (*Then controlling himself, says in a low voice:*)
  Very well.
  (*He continues:*) I was saying — (*with sudden fury*) — God!
  (*Continues naturally:*) The night was black as Hell!
  And to protect this plate of warmed-up mince,
  I thought, I shall offend some peer or prince,
  Who'll pull
CHRISTIAN: your nose—

  (*Everyone rises.* CHRISTIAN *remains seated.*)

CYRANO (*choking*): Who'll pull, I said, a tooth out.
  A tooth, I said, and thought, to let the truth out,
  I'll pinch
CHRISTIAN: your nose —
CYRANO: my finger in the crack
  of the door, and when my noble answers back
  he'll trap
CHRISTIAN: your nose.
CYRANO (*mopping his brow*): my fingers in the jamb!
  But then I thought: March, Gascon that I am!
  On, Cyrano! and though 'twas growing darker,

I held my way and met
CHRISTIAN: some nosey Parker!
CYRANO: I stand on guard and find me
CHRISTIAN: — nose by nose
CYRANO (*leaping forward*): Thunder of God!

(*All the Gascons rush forward to see.* CYRANO *on nearly reaching* CHRISTIAN *masters himself and continues.*)

CYRANO: with drunken oafs in rows
   who stank
CHRISTIAN: your nose out —
CYRANO (*pale and smiling*): breathing beer at large!
   I spring to action!
CHRISTIAN: Nose upwards.
CYRANO: and I charge!
   Two disembowel, another I impale,
   spit a fourth in riposte
CHRISTIAN: A likely tale!
CYRANO (*bursting*): Out, all of you.
FIRST OFFICER: The tiger's roused. Beware!
CYRANO: Out! Leave us two alone!
SECOND OFFICER: Death's in the air!
   You'll find him chopped to mincemeat!
RAGUENEAU: Mincemeat!
ANOTHER OFFICER: Yes,
   and dished up in your kitchen.
RAGUENEAU: I confess
   I feel as limp and pale as any napkin!
CARBON: But —
ANOTHER: He'll not leave a crumb, no! not a scrapkin.
ANOTHER: I faint with terror of what is bound to happen.
ANOTHER (*closing door R.*): Most horrible!

(*Exeunt all.* CYRANO *and* CHRISTIAN *remain face to face, looking at one another.*)

CYRANO: Hither, my arms are open.
CHRISTIAN: Sir!
CYRANO: It was brave!
CHRISTIAN: But —
CYRANO: Brave. Let's know each other!
CHRISTIAN: I do not understand.
CYRANO: Embrace her brother!
CHRISTIAN: Whose?

CYRANO: Hers.
CHRISTIAN: Who's she?
CYRANO: Roxane! . . .*

What makes this effective drama? There is the almost automatic appeal of an interesting human conflict. There is the conflict between what we *expect* will happen (or, perhaps more accurately, what we *pretend* to expect will happen) and what *does* happen. First, we expect Cyrano to fly at Christian, but he doesn't. Then, when he finally does explode, we expect him and Christian to fight, but they don't.

But our interest in conflict does not fully explain the success of the scene. Conflict may account for the suspense, for our sense of plot, but it does not account for the irony or the humor, and it accounts only partly for our realization of character. We respond as we do because we know more than the characters know. Much of the drama is in our awareness of their unawareness.

Characters in literature are aware of themselves only as people in real life are aware of *them*selves. Even when we look at ourselves from the outside and try to see ourselves as others see us (as Cyrano so often in the play dramatizes himself and performs his splendid role as poet-swordsman-lover-wit for his own enjoyment), we can never, by the very nature of things, see ourselves in the detached view-in-the-round that is available to others. We are disqualified as objective and all-informed observers by our own identity: we are what we observe. Relative to fictional characters we are "the others." We have the advantage, however, over perceptive outsiders in real life that we know — or, at least, *can* know — literally all there is to be known about the characters. They have no existence outside the work in which they appear. Macbeth never was a boy, because the play knows nothing about his boyhood. Lady Macbeth has been a mother because she tells us so ("I have given suck"), but it is futile to wonder where the child or children are now. The theories we suggest may not be contradicted by anything in the play, they may even be plausible and interesting, but nothing can ever make them anything but irrelevant to Shakespeare's play. The sole function of Lady Macbeth's being a mother is to measure the fearful intensity of her royal ambition. Characters in literature are, after all, not real people, but plot mechanisms, the constituent moving parts of a dynamic situation. Only if we are aware of them in this double vision, both as human beings and as an artist's deliberate

* From *Cyrano de Bergerac*, by Edmond Rostand, translated by Humbert Wolfe. Reprinted by permission of Ann Wolfe.

artifacts, can we experience their world as literature rather than as life-substitute or daydream.

Exactly what is it we know in this scene that the characters do not know? We know, but Christian does not, that on this particular occasion Cyrano's nose can safely be made fun of. We know, but Cyrano does not (at least, not at first), what Christian's motives for insulting Cyrano are. We know, but the other officers do not, that Christian is not an impudent cad risking his neck and that there is a reason behind Cyrano's strange forbearance.

But more important than this knowledge itself are its implications. Christian's ignorance saves his character in our eyes. If he knew that Roxane's love protected him from Cyrano's wrath — that Cyrano's hands are tied the moment he learns Christian's name — he would be despicable. He must believe he runs a real risk; otherwise, the proof of his courage, however the officers might be taken in, would not be genuine, and we would see him as a malicious coward taking advantage of Cyrano in order to pass himself off as brave. And since we also realize that Christian fully expects to have to pay for his insolence by fighting a man who — as he is just finding out — last night fought off one hundred men single-handed, we can free him from any suspicion that he insults Cyrano for the mere fun of it. Similarly, the nobility of Cyrano's self-restraint, the elements of both pathos and farce in the agonizing conflict within him between jealousy, self-respect, and concern for his public dignity on the one hand and loyalty to his promise to Roxane on the other — all this would vanish if we thought for a moment that the insults did not really hurt and anger him. We enjoy the scene because we are aware of the discrepancy between appearance and reality for both men. To Christian, the danger is real, but it really isn't; to Cyrano, the insults are real, but they really aren't. The scene establishes Christian in our minds not just as a courageous young man but as an ingenious one as well, for his way of proving his courage strikes us as clever and — under the circumstances — "just right." From this point on, we are willing to find him worthy of Roxane's love and Cyrano's friendship. Similarly, we see Cyrano as nobly self-disciplined (though not, admirably enough, beyond the point where no longer just his nose but his truthfulness is being traduced, with Christian's contemptuous "A likely tale!") and as a lover so unselfish that he is willing to risk his reputation as man of honor and to spare his rival for the sake of remaining faithful to his word to the woman he loves. And we find pleasure in the unexpected twist Rostand gives the hackneyed love triangle of romantic melodrama. Here, for once, the hero's rival is not the villain.

But for all our superior knowledge, there is also something we do not know, and our ignorance heightens the suspense. The officers' failure to understand what is going on provides an amusing chorus of astonishment that reaches its climax as Cyrano thunderously clears the room and prepares to chop Christian to mincemeat — or so the officers think. But can we really be certain they may not be right? Unlike the officers, we understand the reasons for both men's seemingly inexplicable behavior, but we, too, may feel that the point has been reached where Cyrano is being taunted beyond endurance. The crescendo effect of Christian's interrupting references to noses is a provocation so outrageous that we may feel that Cyrano would be justified in butchering his tormentor. Nor is there anything in Cyrano's behavior at the moment he bursts that promises he won't do just that. And yet, though we are aware of all this, we still know exactly what has caused Cyrano's outburst, when, instead of attacking Christian as soon as they are alone, we find him making friends with him. We could hardly foresee this reaction; at least, we could not be sure of it, but when it comes we feel it to be in character. Cyrano bursts because he needs relief from being insulted in front of his friends, to whom he cannot explain his patience without revealing Roxane's and Christian's love for one another and his own role as guardian of that love. And even if by this time Cyrano has guessed that there is nothing personal in Christian's insults, that Christian is simply making use of the well-known taboo concerning Cyrano's nose in order to prove his courage (as Cyrano's "It was brave!" suggests), this hardly lessens his frustration or is a reason why he should allow himself to be insulted forever. Cyrano's psychology here proves that Rostand has the true dramatist's ability to make a character's action seem surprising and inevitable at the same time.

In addition to revealing character; furthering the plot; creating suspense, resolving it, and in resolving it creating more (What will happen when the officers return? What will follow from Cyrano's and Christian's friendship? Who wins Roxane?); and controlling the potential sentimentality in the situation by means of farce and physical action, the scene does at least one thing more: it allows us to enjoy the playwright's skill with words. It is a skill we can appreciate even without comparing Wolfe's translation with Rostand's original French. One example will suffice. Rostand has Cyrano tell his story in such a way that Christian again and again can interrupt with his references to noses without straining the naturalness of the story-telling. The joke is continually being set up anew and is funny each time. We admire the sequence of interruptions all the more for recognizing the playwright's problem: to make each interruption seem apropos without too obviously rigging Cyrano's narrative. It is a little like watching a skillful juggler. We are "sure," yet delightedly not sure, that another cup or another saucer cannot possibly go on top of the ten-foot pole. Yet they do — again and again. Here we enjoy the dramatist's display of technical mastery of his material, the triumph of form over matter. We fear the collapse of his design, not knowing how it can help collapsing, and yet not really expecting it to. That anything so artfully intricate can be made both so elegantly natural and so humanly engrossing — *that* is, in this particular instance, the art of drama.

Sophocles

OEDIPUS REX

An English Version by Dudley Fitts and Robert Fitzgerald

Persons Represented

OEDIPUS	IOCASTE
A PRIEST	MESSENGER
CREON	SHEPHERD OF LAÏOS
TEIRESIAS	SECOND MESSENGER
CHORUS OF THEBAN ELDERS	

THE SCENE: *Before the palace of Oedipus, King of Thebes. A central door and two lateral doors open onto a platform which runs the length of the façade. On the platform, right and left, are altars; and three steps lead down into the "orchestra," or chorus-ground. At the beginning of the action these steps are crowded by suppliants who have brought branches and chaplets of olive leaves and who lie in various attitudes of despair.* OEDIPUS *enters.*

PROLOGUE

OEDIPUS: My children, generations of the living
In the line of Kadmos, nursed at his ancient hearth:
Why have you strewn yourselves before these altars
In supplication, with your boughs and garlands?
The breath of incense rises from the city
With a sound of prayer and lamentation.

Children,

I would not have you speak through messengers,

And therefore I have come myself to hear you —
I, Oedipus, who bear the famous name.
(*To a* PRIEST:)
You, there, since you are eldest in the company,
Speak for them all, tell me what preys upon you,
Whether you come in dread, or crave some blessing:
Tell me, and never doubt that I will help you
In every way I can; I should be heartless
Were I not moved to find you suppliant here.

PRIEST: Great Oedipus, O powerful King of Thebes!
You see how all the ages of our people
Cling to your altar steps: here are boys
Who can barely stand alone, and here are priests
By weight of age, as I am a priest of God,
And young men chosen from those yet unmarried;
As for the others, all that multitude,
They wait with olive chaplets in the squares,
At the two shrines of Pallas, and where Apollo
Speaks in the glowing embers.
                                        Your own eyes
Must tell you: Thebes is in her extremity
And can not lift her head from the surge of death.
A rust consumes the buds and fruits of the earth;
The herds are sick; children die unborn,
And labor is vain. The god of plague and pyre
Raids like detestable lightning through the city,
And all the house of Kadmos is laid waste,
All emptied, and all darkened: Death alone
Battens upon the misery of Thebes.

You are not one of the immortal gods, we know;
Yet we have come to you to make our prayer
As to the man of all men best in adversity
And wisest in the ways of God. You saved us
From the Sphinx, that flinty singer, and the tribute
We paid to her so long; yet you were never
Better informed than we, nor could we teach you:
It was some god breathed in you to set us free.

Therefore, O mighty King, we turn to you:
Find us our safety, find us a remedy,
Whether by counsel of the gods or men.
A king of wisdom tested in the past
Can act in a time of troubles, and act well.

Noblest of men, restore
Life to your city! Think how all men call you
Liberator for your triumph long ago;
Ah, when your years of kingship are remembered,
Let them not say *We rose, but later fell* —
Keep the State from going down in the storm!
Once, years ago, with happy augury,
You brought us fortune; be the same again!
No man questions your power to rule the land:
But rule over men, not over a dead city!
Ships are only hulls, citadels are nothing,
When no life moves in the empty passageways.

OEDIPUS: Poor children! You may be sure I know
All that you longed for in your coming here.
I know that you are deathly sick; and yet,
Sick as you are, not one is as sick as I.
Each of you suffers in himself alone
His anguish, not another's; but my spirit
Groans for the city, for myself, for you.

I was not sleeping, you are not waking me.
No, I have been in tears for a long while
And in my restless thought walked many ways.
In all my search, I found one helpful course,
And that I have taken: I have sent Creon,
Son of Menoikeus, brother of the Queen,
To Delphi, Apollo's place of revelation,
To learn there, if he can,
What act or pledge of mine may save the city.
I have counted the days, and now, this very day,
I am troubled, for he has overstayed his time.
What is he doing? He has been gone too long.
Yet whenever he comes back, I should do ill
To scant whatever hint the god may give.

PRIEST: It is a timely promise. At this instant
They tell me Creon is here.

OEDIPUS: O Lord Apollo!
May his news be fair as his face is radiant!

PRIEST: It could not be otherwise: he is crowned with bay,
The chaplet is thick with berries.

OEDIPUS: We shall soon know;
He is near enough to hear us now.

(*Enter* CREON.)

O Prince:

Brother: son of Menoikeus:
What answer do you bring us from the god?
CREON: It is favorable. I can tell you, great afflictions
Will turn out well, if they are taken well.
OEDIPUS: What was the oracle? These vague words
Leave me still hanging between hope and fear.
CREON: Is it your pleasure to hear me with all these
Gathered around us? I am prepared to speak,
But should we not go in?
OEDIPUS: Let them all hear it.
It is for them I suffer, more than for myself.
CREON: Then I will tell you what I heard at Delphi.

In plain words
The god commands us to expel from the land of Thebes
An old defilement that it seems we shelter.
It is a deathly thing, beyond expiation.
We must not let it feed upon us longer.
OEDIPUS: What defilement? How shall we rid ourselves of it?
CREON: By exile or death, blood for blood. It was
Murder that brought the plague-wind on the city.
OEDIPUS: Murder of whom? Surely the god has named him?
CREON: My lord: long ago Laïos was our king,
Before you came to govern us.
OEDIPUS: I know;
I learned of him from others; I never saw him.
CREON: He was murdered; and Apollo commands us now
To take revenge upon whoever killed him.
OEDIPUS: Upon whom? Where are they? Where shall we find a clue
To solve that crime, after so many years?
CREON: Here in this land, he said.
If we make enquiry,
We may touch things that otherwise escape us.
OEDIPUS: Tell me: Was Laïos murdered in his house,
Or in the fields, or in some foreign country?
CREON: He said he planned to make a pilgrimage.
He did not come home again.
OEDIPUS: And was there no one,
No witness, no companion, to tell what happened?
CREON: They were all killed but one, and he got away
So frightened that he could remember one thing only.
OEDIPUS: What was that one thing? One may be the key

To everything, if we resolve to use it.

CREON: He said that a band of highwaymen attacked them,
Outnumbered them, and overwhelmed the King.

OEDIPUS: Strange, that a highwayman should be so daring —
Unless some faction here bribed him to do it.

CREON: We thought of that. But after Laïos' death
New troubles arose and we had no avenger.

OEDIPUS: What troubles could prevent your hunting down the killers?

CREON: The riddling Sphinx's song
Made us deaf to all mysteries but her own.

OEDIPUS: Then once more I must bring what is dark to light.
It is most fitting that Apollo shows,
As you do, this compunction for the dead.
You shall see how I stand by you, as I should,
To avenge the city and the city's god,
And not as though it were for some distant friend,
But for my own sake, to be rid of evil.
Whoever killed King Laïos might — who knows? —
Decide at any moment to kill me as well.
By avenging the murdered king I protect myself.
Come, then, my children: leave the altar steps,
Lift up your olive boughs!

One of you go
And summon the people of Kadmos to gather here.
I will do all that I can; you may tell them that.

(*Exit a* PAGE.)

So, with the help of God,
We shall be saved — or else indeed we are lost.

PRIEST: Let us rise, children. It was for this we came,
And now the King has promised it himself.
Phoibos has sent us an oracle; may he descend
Himself to save us and drive out the plague.

(*Exeunt* OEDIPUS *and* CREON *into the palace by the central door.
The* PRIEST *and the* SUPPLIANTS *disperse R and L. After a short
pause the* CHORUS *enters the orchestra.*)

PARODOS

CHORUS: What is God singing in his profound   [STROPHE 1
Delphi of gold and shadow?
What oracle for Thebes, the sunwhipped city?

Fear unjoints me, the roots of my heart tremble.
Now I remember, O Healer, your power, and wonder;
Will you send doom like a sudden cloud, or weave it
Like nightfall of the past?
Speak, speak to us, issue of holy sound:
Dearest to our expectancy: be tender!

[ANTISTROPHE 1

Let me pray to Athenê, the immortal daughter of Zeus,
And to Artemis her sister
Who keeps her famous throne in the market ring,
And to Apollo, bowman at the far butts of heaven —

O gods, descend! Like three streams leap against
The fires of our grief, the fires of darkness;
Be swift to bring us rest!

As in the old time from the brilliant house
Of air you stepped to save us, come again!

Now our afflictions have no end,   [STROPHE 2
Now all our stricken host lies down
And no man fights off death with his mind;

The noble plowland bears no grain,
And groaning mothers can not bear —

See, how our lives like birds take wing,
Like sparks that fly when a fire soars,
To the shore of the god of evening.

The plague burns on, it is pitiless,   [ANTISTROPHE 2
Though pallid children laden with death
Lie unwept in the stony ways,

And old gray women by every path
Flock to the strand about the altars

There to strike their breasts and cry
Worship of Phoibos in wailing prayers:
Be kind, God's golden child!

There are no swords in this attack by fire,   [STROPHE 3
No shields, but we are ringed with cries.
Send the besieger plunging from our homes
Into the vast sea-room of the Atlantic
Or into the waves that foam eastward of Thrace —

For the day ravages what the night spares —

Destroy our enemy, lord of the thunder!
Let him be riven by lightning from heaven!

Phoibos Apollo, stretch the sun's bowstring,   [ANTISTROPHE 3
That golden cord, until it sing for us,
Flashing arrows in heaven!
                        Artemis, Huntress,
Race with flaring lights upon our mountains!

O scarlet god, O golden-banded brow,
O Theban Bacchos in a storm of Maenads,

(*Enter* OEDIPUS, *C.*)

Whirl upon Death, that all the Undying hate!
Come with blinding cressets, come in joy!

SCENE I

OEDIPUS: Is this your prayer? It may be answered. Come,
    Listen to me, act as the crisis demands,
    And you shall have relief from all these evils.

Until now I was a stranger to this tale,
As I had been a stranger to the crime.
Could I track down the murderer without a clue?
But now, friends,
As one who became a citizen after the murder,
I make this proclamation to all Thebans:
If any man knows by whose hand Laïos, son of Labdakos,
Met his death, I direct that man to tell me everything,
No matter what he fears for having so long withheld it.
Let it stand as promised that no further trouble
Will come to him, but he may leave the land in safety.

Moreover: If anyone knows the murderer to be foreign,
Let him not keep silent: he shall have his reward from me.
However, if he does conceal it; if any man
Fearing for his friend or for himself disobeys this edict,
Hear what I propose to do:

I solemnly forbid the people of this country,
Where power and throne are mine, ever to receive that man
Or speak to him, no matter who he is, or let him

Join in sacrifice, lustration, or in prayer.
I decree that he be driven from every house,
Being, as he is, corruption itself to us: the Delphic
Voice of Zeus has pronounced this revelation.
Thus I associate myself with the oracle
And take the side of the murdered king.

As for the criminal, I pray to God —
Whether it be a lurking thief, or one of a number —
I pray that that man's life be consumed in evil and wretchedness.
And as for me, this curse applies no less
If it should turn out that the culprit is my guest here,
Sharing my hearth.
              You have heard the penalty.
I lay it on you now to attend to this
For my sake, for Apollo's, for the sick
Sterile city that heaven has abandoned.
Suppose the oracle had given you no command:
Should this defilement go uncleansed for ever?
You should have found the murderer: your king,
A noble king, had been destroyed!
                      Now I,
Having the power that he held before me,
Having his bed, begetting children there
Upon his wife, as he would have, had he lived —
Their son would have been my children's brother,
If Laïos had had luck in fatherhood!
(But surely ill luck rushed upon his reign)—
I say I take the son's part, just as though
I were his son, to press the fight for him
And see it won! I'll find the hand that brought
Death to Labdakos' and Polydoros' child,
Heir of Kadmos' and Agenor's line.
And as for those who fail me,
May the gods deny them the fruit of the earth,
Fruit of the womb, and may they rot utterly!
Let them be wretched as we are wretched, and worse!

For you, for loyal Thebans, and for all
Who find my actions right, I pray the favor
Of justice, and of all the immortal gods.
CHORAGOS: Since I am under oath, my lord, I swear
    I did not do the murder, I can not name
    The murderer. Might not the oracle

That has ordained the search tell where to find him?
OEDIPUS: An honest question. But no man in the world
  Can make the gods do more than the gods will.
CHORAGOS: There is one last expedient —
OEDIPUS: Tell me what it is.
  Though it seem slight, you must not hold it back.
CHORAGOS: A lord clairvoyant to the lord Apollo,
  As we all know, is the skilled Teiresias.
  One might learn much about this from him, Oedipus.
OEDIPUS: I am not wasting time:
  Creon spoke of this, and I have sent for him —
  Twice, in fact; it is strange that he is not here.
CHORAGOS: The other matter — that old report — seems useless.
OEDIPUS: Tell me. I am interested in all reports.
CHORAGOS: The King was said to have been killed by highwaymen.
OEDIPUS: I know. But we have no witnesses to that.
CHORAGOS: If the killer can feel a particle of dread,
  Your curse will bring him out of hiding!
OEDIPUS: No.
  The man who dared that act will fear no curse.

(*Enter the blind seer* TEIRESIAS, *led by a* PAGE.)

CHORAGOS: But there is one man who may detect the criminal.
  This is Teiresias, this is the holy prophet
  In whom, alone of all men, truth was born.
OEDIPUS: Teiresias: seer: student of mysteries,
  Of all that's taught and all that no man tells,
  Secrets of Heaven and secrets of the earth:
  Blind though you are, you know the city lies
  Sick with plague; and from this plague, my lord,
  We find that you alone can guard or save us.

  Possibly you did not hear the messengers?
  Apollo, when we sent to him,
  Sent us back word that this great pestilence
  Would lift, but only if we established clearly
  The identity of those who murdered Laïos.
  They must be killed or exiled.
                           Can you use
  Birdflight or any art of divination
  To purify yourself, and Thebes, and me
  From this contagion? We are in your hands.
  There is no fairer duty

Than that of helping others in distress.

TEIRESIAS: How dreadful knowledge of the truth can be
　When there's no help in truth! I knew this well,
　But did not act on it: else I should not have come.

OEDIPUS: What is troubling you? Why are your eyes so cold?

TEIRESIAS: Let me go home. Bear your own fate, and I'll
　Bear mine. It is better so: trust what I say.

OEDIPUS: What you say is ungracious and unhelpful
　To your native country. Do not refuse to speak.

TEIRESIAS: When it comes to speech, your own is neither temperate
　Nor opportune. I wish to be more prudent.

OEDIPUS: In God's name, we all beg you —

TEIRESIAS: 　　　　　　　　　　　You are all ignorant.
　No; I will never tell you what I know.
　Now it is my misery; then, it would be yours.

OEDIPUS: What! You do know something, and will not tell us?
　You would betray us all and wreck the State?

TEIRESIAS: I do not intend to torture myself, or you.
　Why persist in asking? You will not persuade me.

OEDIPUS: What a wicked old man you are! You'd try a stone's
　Patience! Out with it! Have you no feeling at all?

TEIRESIAS: You call me unfeeling. If you could only see
　The nature of your own feelings . . .

OEDIPUS: 　　　　　　　　　　　Why,
　Who would not feel as I do? Who could endure
　Your arrogance toward the city?

TEIRESIAS: 　　　　　　　　What does it matter!
　Whether I speak or not, it is bound to come.

OEDIPUS: Then, if "it" is bound to come, you are bound to tell me.

TEIRESIAS: No, I will not go on. Rage as you please.

OEDIPUS: Rage? Why not!
　　　　　　　　And I'll tell you what I think:
　You planned it, you had it done, you all but
　Killed him with your own hands: if you had eyes,
　I'd say the crime was yours, and yours alone.

TEIRESIAS: So? I charge you, then,
　Abide by the proclamation you have made:
　From this day forth
　Never speak again to these men or to me;
　You yourself are the pollution of this country.

OEDIPUS: You dare say that! Can you possibly think you have
　Some way of going free, after such insolence?

TEIRESIAS: I have gone free. It is the truth sustains me.

OEDIPUS: Who taught you shamelessness? It was not your craft.

TEIRESIAS: You did. You made me speak. I did not want to.

OEDIPUS: Speak what? Let me hear it again more clearly.

TEIRESIAS: Was it not clear before? Are you tempting me?

OEDIPUS: I did not understand it. Say it again.

TEIRESIAS: I say that you are the murderer whom you seek.

OEDIPUS: Now twice you have spat out infamy. You'll pay for it!

TEIRESIAS: Would you care for more? Do you wish to be really angry?

OEDIPUS: Say what you will. Whatever you say is worthless.

TEIRESIAS: I say you live in hideous shame with those
   Most dear to you. You can not see the evil.

OEDIPUS: It seems you can go on mouthing like this for ever.

TEIRESIAS: I can, if there is power in truth.

OEDIPUS: There is:
   But not for you, not for you,
   You sightless, witless, senseless, mad old man!

TEIRESIAS: You are the madman. There is no one here
   Who will not curse you soon, as you curse me.

OEDIPUS: You child of endless night! You can not hurt me
   Or any other man who sees the sun.

TEIRESIAS: True: it is not from me your fate will come.
   That lies within Apollo's competence,
   As it is his concern.

OEDIPUS: Tell me:
   Are you speaking for Creon, or for yourself?

TEIRESIAS: Creon is no threat. You weave your own doom.

OEDIPUS: Wealth, power, craft of statesmanship!
   Kingly position, everywhere admired!
   What savage envy is stored up against these,
   If Creon, whom I trusted, Creon my friend,
   For this great office which the city once
   Put in my hands unsought — if for this power
   Creon desires in secret to destroy me!

   He has bought this decrepit fortune-teller, this
   Collector of dirty pennies, this prophet fraud —
   Why, he is no more clairvoyant than I am!
                           Tell us:
   Has your mystic mummery ever approached the truth?
   When that hellcat the Sphinx was performing here,
   What help were you to these people?
   Her magic was not for the first man who came along:
   It demanded a real exorcist. Your birds —

What good were they? or the gods, for the matter of that?
But I came by,
Oedipus, the simple man, who knows nothing —
I thought it out for myself, no birds helped me!
And this is the man you think you can destroy,
That you may be close to Creon when he's king!
Well, you and your friend Creon, it seems to me,
Will suffer most. If you were not an old man,
You would have paid already for your plot.

CHORAGOS: We can not see that his words or yours
Have been spoken except in anger, Oedipus,
And of anger we have no need. How can God's will
Be accomplished best? That is what most concerns us.

TEIRESIAS: You are a king. But where argument's concerned
I am your man, as much a king as you.
I am not your servant, but Apollo's.
I have no need of Creon to speak for me.

Listen to me. You mock my blindness, do you?
But I say that you, with both your eyes, are blind:
You can not see the wretchedness of your life,
Nor in whose house you live, no, nor with whom.
Who are your father and mother? Can you tell me?
You do not even know the blind wrongs
That you have done them, on earth and in the world below.
But the double lash of your parents' curse will whip you
Out of this land some day, with only night
Upon your precious eyes.
Your cries then — where will they not be heard?
What fastness of Kithairon will not echo them?
And that bridal-descant of yours — you'll know it then,
The song they sang when you came here to Thebes
And found your misguided berthing.
All this, and more, that you can not guess at now,
Will bring you to yourself among your children.

Be angry, then. Curse Creon. Curse my words.
I tell you, no man that walks upon the earth
Shall be rooted out more horribly than you.

OEDIPUS: Am I to bear this from him? — Damnation
Take you! Out of this place! Out of my sight!

TEIRESIAS: I would not have come at all if you had not asked me.

OEDIPUS: Could I have told that you'd talk nonsense, that
You'd come here to make a fool of yourself, and of me?

TEIRESIAS: A fool? Your parents thought me sane enough.
OEDIPUS: My parents again!—Wait: who were my parents?
TEIRESIAS: This day will give you a father, and break your heart.
OEDIPUS: Your infantile riddles! Your damned abracadabra!
TEIRESIAS: You were a great man once at solving riddles.
OEDIPUS: Mock me with that if you like; you will find it true.
TEIRESIAS: It was true enough. It brought about your ruin.
OEDIPUS: But if it saved this town?
TEIRESIAS: (*To the* PAGE)
                              Boy, give me your hand.
OEDIPUS: Yes, boy; lead him away.
                              — While you are here
  We can do nothing. Go; leave us in peace.
TEIRESIAS: I will go when I have said what I have to say.
  How can you hurt me? And I tell you again:
  The man you have been looking for all this time,
  The damned man, the murderer of Laïos,
  That man is in Thebes. To your mind he is foreignborn,
  But it will soon be shown that he is a Theban,
  A revelation that will fail to please.
                              A blind man,
  Who has his eyes now; a penniless man, who is rich now;
  And he will go tapping the strange earth with his staff;
  To the children with whom he lives now he will be
  Brother and father — the very same; to her
  Who bore him, son and husband — the very same
  Who came to his father's bed, wet with his father's blood.

  Enough. Go think that over.
  If later you find error in what I have said,
  You may say that I have no skill in prophecy.

(*Exit* TEIRESIAS, led *by his* PAGE. OEDIPUS *goes into the palace.*)

ODE I

CHORUS: The Delphic stone of prophecies   [STROPHE 1
  Remembers ancient regicide
  And a still bloody hand.
  That killer's hour of flight has come.
  He must be stronger than riderless
  Coursers of untiring wind,
  For the son of Zeus armed with his father's thunder

Leaps in lightning after him;
And the Furies follow him, the sad Furies.

Holy Parnassos' peak of snow   [ANTISTROPHE 1
Flashes and blinds that secret man,
That all shall hunt him down:
Though he may roam the forest shade
Like a bull gone wild from pasture
To rage through glooms of stone.
Doom comes down on him; flight will not avail him;
For the world's heart calls him desolate,
And the immortal Furies follow, for ever follow.

But now a wilder thing is heard   [STROPHE 2
From the old man skilled at hearing Fate in the wingbeat of a bird.
Bewildered as a blown bird, my soul hovers and can not find
Foothold in this debate, or any reason or rest of mind.
But no man ever brought — none can bring
Proof of strife between Thebes' royal house,
Labdakos' line, and the son of Polybos;
And never until now has any man brought word
Of Laïos' dark death staining Oedipus the King.

Divine Zeus and Apollo hold   [ANTISTROPHE 2
Perfect intelligence alone of all tales ever told;
And well though this diviner works, he works in his own night;
No man can judge that rough unknown or trust in second sight,
For wisdom changes hands among the wise.
Shall I believe my great lord criminal
At a raging word that a blind old man let fall?
I saw him, when the carrion woman faced him of old,
Prove his heroic mind! These evil words are lies.

SCENE II

CREON: Men of Thebes:
  I am told that heavy accusations
  Have been brought against me by King Oedipus.

I am not the kind of man to bear this tamely.

If in these present difficulties
He holds me accountable for any harm to him
Through anything I have said or done — why, then,

I do not value life in this dishonor.
It is not as though this rumor touched upon
Some private indiscretion. The matter is grave.
The fact is that I am being called disloyal
To the State, to my fellow citizens, to my friends.
CHORAGOS: He may have spoken in anger, not from his mind.
CREON: But did you not hear him say I was the one
   Who seduced the old prophet into lying?
CHORAGOS: The thing was said; I do not know how seriously.
CREON: But you were watching him! Were his eyes steady?
   Did he look like a man in his right mind?
CHORAGOS: I do not know.
   I can not judge the behavior of great men.
   But here is the King himself.

   (*Enter* OEDIPUS.)

OEDIPUS: So you dared come back.
   Why? How brazen of you to come to my house,
   You murderer!
                 Do you think I do not know
   That you plotted to kill me, plotted to steal my throne?
   Tell me, in God's name: am I coward, a fool,
   That you should dream you could accomplish this?
   A fool who could not see your slippery game?
   A coward, not to fight back when I saw it?
   You are the fool, Creon, are you not? hoping
   Without support or friends to get a throne?
   Thrones may be won or bought: you could do neither.
CREON: Now listen to me. You have talked; let me talk, too.
   You can not judge unless you know the facts.
OEDIPUS: You speak well: there is one fact; but I find it hard
   To learn from the deadliest enemy I have.
CREON: That above all I must dispute with you.
OEDIPUS: That above all I will not hear you deny.
CREON: If you think there is anything good in being stubborn
   Against all reason, then I say you are wrong.
OEDIPUS: If you think a man can sin against his own kind
   And not be punished for it, I say you are mad.
CREON: I agree. But tell me: what have I done to you?
OEDIPUS: You advised me to send for that wizard, did you not?
CREON: I did. I should do it again.
OEDIPUS: Very well. Now tell me:
   How long has it been since Laïos —

CREON: What of Laïos?

OEDIPUS: Since he vanished in that onset by the road?

CREON: It was long ago, a long time.

OEDIPUS: And this prophet,
Was he practicing here then?

CREON: He was; and with honor, as now.

OEDIPUS: Did he speak of me at that time?

CREON: He never did;
At least, not when I was present.

OEDIPUS: But . . . the enquiry?
I suppose you held one?

CREON: We did, but we learned nothing.

OEDIPUS: Why did the prophet not speak against me then?

CREON: I do not know; and I am the kind of man
Who holds his tongue when he has no facts to go on.

OEDIPUS: There's one fact that you know, and you could tell it.

CREON: What fact is that? If I know it, you shall have it.

OEDIPUS: If he were not involved with you, he could not say
That it was I who murdered Laïos.

CREON: If he says that, you are the one that knows it! —
But now it is my turn to question you.

OEDIPUS: Put your questions. I am no murderer.

CREON: First, then: You married my sister?

OEDIPUS: I married your sister

CREON: And you rule the kingdom equally with her?

OEDIPUS: Everything that she wants she has from me.

CREON: And I am the third, equal to both of you?

OEDIPUS: That is why I call you a bad friend.

CREON: No. Reason it out, as I have done.
Think of this first: Would any sane man prefer
Power, with all a king's anxieties,
To that same power and the grace of sleep?
Certainly not I.
I have never longed for the king's power — only his rights.
Would any wise man differ from me in this?
As matters stand, I have my way in everything
With your consent, and no responsibilities.
If I were king, I should be a slave to policy.

How could I desire a scepter more
Than what is now mine — untroubled influence?
No, I have not gone mad; I need no honors,
Except those with the perquisites I have now.

I am welcome everywhere; every man salutes me,
And those who want your favor seek my ear,
Since I know how to manage what they ask.
Should I exchange this ease for that anxiety?
Besides, no sober mind is treasonable.
I hate anarchy
And never would deal with any man who likes it.

Test what I have said. Go to the priestess
At Delphi, ask if I quoted her correctly.
And as for this other thing: if I am found
Guilty of treason with Teiresias,
Then sentence me to death! You have my word
It is a sentence I should cast my vote for —
But not without evidence!
                              You do wrong
When you take good men for bad, bad men for good.
A true friend thrown aside — why, life itself
Is not more precious!
                         In time you will know this well:
For time, and time alone, will show the just man,
Though scoundrels are discovered in a day.
CHORAGOS: This is well said, and a prudent man would ponder it.
    Judgments too quickly formed are dangerous.
OEDIPUS: But is he not quick in his duplicity?
    And shall I not be quick to parry him?
    Would you have me stand still, hold my peace, and let
    This man win everything, through my inaction?
CREON: And you want — what is it, then? To banish me?
OEDIPUS: No, not exile. It is your death I want,
    So that all the world may see what treason means.
CREON: You will persist, then? You will not believe me?
OEDIPUS: How can I believe you?
CREON: Then you are a fool.
OEDIPUS: To save myself?
CREON: In justice, think of me.
OEDIPUS: You are evil incarnate.
CREON: But suppose that you are wrong?
OEDIPUS: Still I must rule.
CREON: But not if you rule badly.
OEDIPUS: O city, city!
CREON: It is my city, too!
CHORAGOS: Now, my lords, be still. I see the Queen,

Iocastê, coming from her palace chambers;
And it is time she came, for the sake of you both.
This dreadful quarrel can be resolved through her.

(*Enter* IOCASTE.)

IOCASTE: Poor foolish men, what wicked din is this?
With Thebes sick to death, is it not shameful
That you should rake some private quarrel up?
(*To* OEDIPUS:)
Come into the house.
— And you, Creon, go now:
Let us have no more of this tumult over nothing.
CREON: Nothing? No, sister: what your husband plans for me
Is one of two great evils: exile or death.
OEDIPUS: He is right.
Why, woman I have caught him squarely
Plotting against my life.
CREON: No! Let me die
Accurst if ever I have wished you harm!
IOCASTE: Ah, believe it, Oedipus!
In the name of the gods, respect this oath of his
For my sake, for the sake of these people here!

[STROPHE 1

CHORAGOS: Open your mind to her, my lord. Be ruled by her, I beg
you!
OEDIPUS: What would you have me do?
CHORAGOS: Respect Creon's word. He has never spoken like a fool,
And now he has sworn an oath.
OEDIPUS: You know what you ask?
CHORAGOS: I do.
OEDIPUS: Speak on, then.
CHORAGOS: A friend so sworn should not be baited so,
In blind malice, and without final proof.
OEDIPUS: You are aware, I hope, that what you say
Means death for me, or exile at the least.
CHORAGOS: No, I swear by Helios, first in Heaven! [STROPHE 2
May I die friendless and accurst,
The worst of deaths, if ever I meant that!
It is the withering fields
That hurt my sick heart:
Must we bear all these ills,
And now your bad blood as well?

OEDIPUS: Then let him go. And let me die, if I must,
  Or be driven by him in shame from the land of Thebes.
  It is your unhappiness, and not his talk,
  That touches me.

                    As for him —
  Wherever he is, I will hate him as long as I live.
CREON: Ugly in yielding, as you were ugly in rage!
  Natures like yours chiefly torment themselves.
OEDIPUS: Can you not go? Can you not leave me?
CREON: I can.
  You do not know me; but the city knows me,
  And in its eyes I am just, if not in yours.

(*Exit* CREON.)

                                            [ANTISTROPHE 1
CHORAGOS: Lady Iocastê, did you not ask the King to go to his cham-
    bers?
IOCASTE: First tell me what has happened.
CHORAGOS: There was suspicion without evidence; yet it rankled
  As even false charges will.
IOCASTE: On both sides?
CHORAGOS: On both.
IOCASTE: But what was said?
CHORAGOS: Oh let it rest, let it be done with!
  Have we not suffered enough?
OEDIPUS: You see to what your decency has brought you:
  You have made difficulties where my heart saw none.

                                            [ANTISTROPHE 2
CHORAGOS: Oedipus, it is not once only I have told you —
    You must know I should count myself unwise
  To the point of madness, should I now forsake you —
        You, under whose hand,
          In the storm of another time,
        Our dear land sailed out free.
        But now stand fast at the helm!
IOCASTE: In God's name, Oedipus, inform your wife as well:
  Why are you so set in this hard anger?
OEDIPUS: I will tell you, for none of these men deserves
  My confidence as you do. It is Creon's work,
  His treachery, his plotting against me.
IOCASTE: Go on, if you can make this clear to me.
OEDIPUS: He charges me with the murder of Laïos.

IOCASTE: Has he some knowledge? Or does he speak from hearsay?
OEDIPUS: He would not commit himself to such a charge,
   But he has brought in that damnable soothsayer
   To tell his story.
IOCASTE: Set your mind at rest.
   If it is a question of soothsayers, I tell you
   That you will find no man whose craft gives knowledge
   Of the unknowable.
                      Here is my proof:

An oracle was reported to Laïos once
(I will not say from Phoibos himself, but from
His appointed ministers, at any rate)
That his doom would be death at the hands of his own son —
His son, born of his flesh and of mine!

Now, you remember the story: Laïos was killed
By marauding strangers where three highways meet;
But his child had not been three days in this world
Before the King had pierced the baby's ankles
And left him to die on a lonely mountainside.

Thus, Apollo never caused that child
To kill his father, and it was not Laïos' fate
To die at the hands of his son, as he had feared.
This is what prophets and prophecies are worth!
Have no dread of them.
                       It is God himself
Who can show us what he wills, in his own way.
OEDIPUS: How strange a shadowy memory crossed my mind,
   Just now while you were speaking; it chilled my heart.
IOCASTE: What do you mean? What memory do you speak of?
OEDIPUS: If I understand you, Laïos was killed
   At a place where three roads meet.
IOCASTE: So it was said;
   We have no later story.
OEDIPUS: Where did it happen?
IOCASTE: Phokis, it is called: at a place where the Theban Way
   Divides into the roads towards Delphi and Daulia.
OEDIPUS: When?
IOCASTE: We had the news not long before you came
   And proved the right to your succession here.
OEDIPUS: Ah, what net has God been weaving for me?
IOCASTE: Oedipus! Why does this trouble you?

OEDIPUS: Do not ask me yet.
First, tell me how Laïos looked, and tell me
How old he was.
IOCASTE: He was tall, his hair just touched
With white; his form was not unlike your own.
OEDIPUS: I think that I myself may be accurst
By my own ignorant edict.
IOCASTE: You speak strangely.
It makes me tremble to look at you, my King.
OEDIPUS: I am not sure that the blind man can not see.
But I should know better if you were to tell me —
IOCASTE: Anything — though I dread to hear you ask it.
OEDIPUS: Was the King lightly escorted, or did he ride
With a large company, as a ruler should?
IOCASTE: There were five men with him in all: one was a herald;
And a single chariot, which he was driving.
OEDIPUS: Alas, that makes it plain enough!
                              But who —
Who told you how it happened?
IOCASTE: A household servant,
The only one to escape.
OEDIPUS: And is he still
A servant of ours?
IOCASTE: No; for when he came back at last
And found you enthroned in the place of the dead king,
He came to me, touched my hand with his, and begged
That I would send him away to the frontier district
Where only the shepherds go —
As far away from the city as I could send him.
I granted his prayer; for although the man was a slave,
He had earned more than this favor at my hands.
OEDIPUS: Can he be called back quickly?
IOCASTE: Easily.
But why?
OEDIPUS: I have taken too much upon myself
Without enquiry; therefore I wish to consult him.
IOCASTE: Then he shall come.
                     But am I not one also
To whom you might confide these fears of yours?
OEDIPUS: That is your right; it will not be denied you,
Now least of all; for I have reached a pitch
Of wild foreboding. Is there anyone
To whom I should sooner speak?

Polybos of Corinth is my father.
My mother is a Dorian: Meropê.
I grew up chief among the men of Corinth
Until a strange thing happened —
Not worth my passion, it may be, but strange.

At a feast, a drunken man maundering in his cups
Cries out that I am not my father's son!

I contained myself that night, though I felt anger
And a sinking heart. The next day I visited
My father and mother, and questioned them. They stormed,
Calling it all the slanderous rant of a fool;
And this relieved me. Yet the suspicion
Remained always aching in my mind;
I knew there was talk; I could not rest;
And finally, saying nothing to my parents,
I went to the shrine at Delphi.
The god dismissed my question without reply;
He spoke of other things.
                              Some were clear,
Full of wretchedness, dreadful, unbearable:
As, that I should lie with my own mother, breed
Children from whom all men would turn their eyes;
And that I should be my father's murderer.

I heard all this, and fled. And from that day
Corinth to me was only in the stars
Descending in that quarter of the sky,
As I wandered farther and farther on my way
To a land where I should never see the evil
Sung by the oracle. And I came to this country
Where, so you say, King Laïos was killed.

I will tell you all that happened there, my lady.

There were three highways
Coming together at a place I passed;
And there a herald came towards me, and a chariot
Drawn by horses, with a man such as you describe
Seated in it. The groom leading the horses
Forced me off the road at his lord's command;
But as this charioteer lurched over towards me
I struck him in my rage. The old man saw me
And brought his double goad down upon my head

As I came abreast.

       He was paid back, and more!
Swinging my club in this right hand I knocked him
Out of his car, and he rolled on the ground.

            I killed him.

I killed them all.
Now if that stranger and Laïos were — kin,
Where is a man more miserable than I?
More hated by the gods? Citizen and alien alike
Must never shelter me or speak to me —
I must be shunned by all.

        And I myself
Pronounced this malediction upon myself!

Think of it: I have touched you with these hands,
These hands that killed your husband. What defilement!

Am I all evil, then? It must be so,
Since I must flee from Thebes, yet never again
See my own countrymen, my own country,
For fear of joining my mother in marriage
And killing Polybos, my father.

          Ah,
If I was created so, born to this fate,
Who could deny the savagery of God?

O holy majesty of heavenly powers!
May I never see that day! Never!
Rather let me vanish from the race of men
Than know the abomination destined me!

CHORAGOS: We too, my lord, have felt dismay at this.
  But there is hope: you have yet to hear the shepherd.

OEDIPUS: Indeed, I fear no other hope is left me.

IOCASTE: What do you hope from him when he comes?

OEDIPUS: This much:
  If his account of the murder tallies with yours,
  Then I am cleared.

IOCASTE: What was it that I said
  Of such importance?

OEDIPUS: Why, "marauders," you said,
  Killed the King, according to this man's story.
  If he maintains that still, if there were several,
  Clearly the guilt is not mine: I was alone.

But if he says one man, singlehanded, did it,
Then the evidence all points to me.

IOCASTE: You may be sure that he said there were several;
And can he call back that story now? He cán not.
The whole city heard it as plainly as I.
But suppose he alters some detail of it:
He can not ever show that Laïos' death
Fulfilled the oracle: for Apollo said
My child was doomed to kill him; and my child —
Poor baby! — it was my child that died first.

No. From now on, where oracles are concerned,
I would not waste a second thought on any.

OEDIPUS: You may be right.

But come: let someone go
For the shepherd at once. This matter must be settled.

IOCASTE: I will send for him.
I would not wish to cross you in anything,
And surely not in this. — Let us go in.

(*Exeunt into the palace.*)

ODE II

CHORUS: Let me be reverent in the ways of right, [STROPHE 1
Lowly the paths I journey on;
Let all my words and actions keep
The laws of the pure universe
From highest Heaven handed down.
For Heaven is their bright nurse,
Those generations of the realms of light;
Ah, never of mortal kind were they begot,
Nor are they slaves of memory, lost in sleep:
Their Father is greater than Time, and ages not.

The tyrant is a child of Pride [ANTISTROPHE 1
Who drinks from his great sickening cup
Recklessness and vanity,
Until from his high crest headlong
He plummets to the dust of hope.
That strong man is not strong.
But let no fair ambition be denied;

May God protect the wrestler for the State
In government, in comely policy,
Who will fear God, and on His ordinance wait.

Haughtiness and the high hand of disdain   [STROPHE 2
Tempt and outrage God's holy law;
And any mortal who dares hold
No immortal Power in awe
Will be caught up in a net of pain:
The price for which his levity is sold.
Let each man take due earnings, then,
And keep his hands from holy things,
And from blasphemy stand apart —
Else the crackling blast of heaven
Blows on his head, and on his desperate heart;
Though fools will honor impious men,
In their cities no tragic poet sings.

Shall we lose faith in Delphi's obscurities,   [ANTISTROPHE 2
We who have heard the world's core
Discredited, and the sacred wood
Of Zeus at Elis praised no more?
The deeds and the strange prophecies
Must make a pattern yet to be understood.
Zeus, if indeed you are lord of all,
Throned in light over night and day,
Mirror this in your endless mind:
Our masters call the oracle
Words on the wind, and the Delphic vision blind!
Their hearts no longer know Apollo,
And reverence for the gods has died away.

SCENE III

(*Enter* IOCASTE.)

IOCASTE: Princes of Thebes, it has occurred to me
    To visit the altars of the gods, bearing
    These branches as a suppliant, and this incense.
    Our King is not himself: his noble soul
    Is overwrought with fantasies of dread,
    Else he would consider
    The new prophecies in the light of the old.

He will listen to any voice that speaks disaster,
And my advice goes for nothing.

(*She approaches the altar*, R.)

                      To you, then, Apollo,
Lycean lord, since you are nearest, I turn in prayer.
Receive these offerings, and grant us deliverance
From defilement. Our hearts are heavy with fear
When we see our leader distracted, as helpless sailors
Are terrified by the confusion of their helmsman.

(*Enter* MESSENGER.)

MESSENGER: Friends, no doubt you can direct me:
  Where shall I find the house of Oedipus,
  Or, better still, where is the King himself?
CHORAGOS: It is this very place, stranger; he is inside.
  This is his wife and mother of his children.
MESSENGER: I wish her happiness in a happy house,
  Blest in all the fulfillment of her marriage.
IOCASTE: I wish as much for you: your courtesy
  Deserves a like good fortune. But now, tell me:
  Why have you come? What have you to say to us?
MESSENGER: Good news, my lady, for your house and your husband.
IOCASTE: What news? Who sent you here?
MESSENGER: I am from Corinth.
  The news I bring ought to mean joy for you,
  Though it may be you will find some grief in it.
IOCASTE: What is it? How can it touch us in both ways?
MESSENGER: The people of Corinth, they say,
  Intend to call Oedipus to be their king.
IOCASTE: But old Polybos — is he not reigning still?
MESSENGER: No. Death holds him in his sepulchre.
IOCASTE: What are you saying? Polybos is dead?
MESSENGER: If I am not telling the truth, may I die myself.
IOCASTE (*To a* MAIDSERVANT): Go in, go quickly; tell this to your
    master.

O riddlers of God's will, where are you now!
This was the man whom Oedipus, long ago,
Feared so, fled so, in dread of destroying him —
     it was another fate by which he died.
  (*Enter*   s, C.*)

OEDIPUS: Dearest Iocastê, why have you sent for me?

IOCASTE: Listen to what this man says, and then tell me
  What has become of the solemn prophecies.

OEDIPUS: Who is this man? What is his news for me?

IOCASTE: He has come from Corinth to announce your father's death!

OEDIPUS: Is it true, stranger? Tell me in your own words.

MESSENGER: I can not say it more clearly: the King is dead.

OEDIPUS: Was it by treason? Or by an attack of illness?

MESSENGER: A little thing brings old men to their rest.

OEDIPUS: It was sickness, then?

MESSENGER: Yes, and his many years.

OEDIPUS: Ah!
  Why should a man respect the Pythian hearth, or
  Give heed to the birds that jangle above his head?
  They prophesied that I should kill Polybos,
  Kill my own father; but he is dead and buried,
  And I am here — I never touched him, never,
  Unless he died of grief for my departure,
  And thus, in a sense, through me. No. Polybos
  Has packed the oracles off with him underground.
  They are empty words.

IOCASTE: Had I not told you so?

OEDIPUS: You had; it was my faint heart that betrayed me.

IOCASTE: From now on never think of those things again.

OEDIPUS: And yet — must I not fear my mother's bed?

IOCASTE: Why should anyone in this world be afraid,
  Since Fate rules us and nothing can be foreseen?
  A man should live only for the present day.

  Have no more fear of sleeping with your mother:
  How many men, in dreams, have lain with their mothers!
  No reasonable man is troubled by such things.

OEDIPUS: That is true; only —
  If only my mother were not still alive!
  But she is alive. I can not help my dread.

IOCASTE: Yet this news of your father's death is wonderful.

OEDIPUS: Wonderful. But I fear the living woman.

MESSENGER: Tell me, who is this woman that you fear?

OEDIPUS: It is Meropê, man; the wife of King Polybos.

MESSENGER: Meropê? Why should you be afraid of her?

OEDIPUS: An oracle of the gods, a dreadful saying.

MESSENGER: Can you tell me about it or are you sworn to silence?

OEDIPUS: I can tell you, and I will.

Apollo said through his prophet that I was the man
Who should marry his own mother, shed his father's blood
With his own hands. And so, for all these years
I have kept clear of Corinth, and no harm has come —
Though it would have been sweet to see my parents again.

MESSENGER: And is this the fear that drove you out of Corinth?

OEDIPUS: Would you have me kill my father?

MESSENGER: As for that
You must be reassured by the news I gave you.

OEDIPUS: If you could reassure me, I would reward you.

MESSENGER: I had that in mind, I will confess: I thought
I could count on you when you returned to Corinth.

OEDIPUS: No: I will never go near my parents again.

MESSENGER: Ah, son, you still do not know what you are doing —

OEDIPUS: What do you mean? In the name of God tell me!

MESSENGER: — If these are your reasons for not going home.

OEDIPUS: I tell you, I fear the oracle may come true.

MESSENGER: And guilt may come upon you through your parents?

OEDIPUS: That is the dread that is always in my heart.

MESSENGER: Can you not see that all your fears are groundless?

OEDIPUS: How can you say that? They are my parents, surely?

MESSENGER: Polybos was not your father.

OEDIPUS: Not my father?

MESSENGER: No more your father than the man speaking to you.

OEDIPUS: But you are nothing to me!

MESSENGER: Neither was he.

OEDIPUS: Then why did he call me son?

MESSENGER: I will tell you:
Long ago he had you from my hands, as a gift.

OEDIPUS: Then how could he love me so, if I was not his?

MESSENGER: He had no children, and his heart turned to you.

OEDIPUS: What of you? Did you buy me? Did you find me by chance?

MESSENGER: I came upon you in the crooked pass of Kithairon.

OEDIPUS: And what were you doing there?

MESSENGER: Tending my flocks.

OEDIPUS: A wandering shepherd?

MESSENGER: But your savior, son, that day.

OEDIPUS: From what did you save me?

MESSENGER: Your ankles should tell you that.

OEDIPUS: Ah, stranger, why do you speak of that childhood pain?

MESSENGER: I cut the bonds that tied your ankles together.

OEDIPUS: I have had the mark as long as I can remember.

MESSENGER: That was why you were given the name you bear.

OEDIPUS: God! Was it my father or my mother who did it?
Tell me!

MESSENGER: I do not know. The man who gave you to me
Can tell you better than I.

OEDIPUS: It was not you that found me, but another?

MESSENGER: It was another shepherd gave you to me.

OEDIPUS: Who was he? Can you tell me who he was?

MESSENGER: I think he was said to be one of Laïos' people.

OEDIPUS: You mean the Laïos who was king here years ago?

MESSENGER: Yes; King Laïos; and the man was one of his herdsmen.

OEDIPUS: Is he still alive? Can I see him?

MESSENGER: These men here
Know best about such things.

OEDIPUS: Does anyone here
Know this shepherd that he is talking about?
Have you seen him in the fields, or in the town?
If you have, tell me. It is time things were made plain.

CHORAGOS: I think the man he means is that same shepherd
You have already asked to see. Iocastê perhaps
Could tell you something.

OEDIPUS: Do you know anything
About him, Lady? Is he the man we have summoned?
Is that the man this shepherd means?

IOCASTE: Why think of him?
Forget this herdsman. Forget it all.
This talk is a waste of time.

OEDIPUS: How can you say that,
When the clues to my true birth are in my hands?

IOCASTE: For God's love, let us have no more questioning!
Is your life nothing to you?
My own is pain enough for me to bear.

OEDIPUS: You need not worry. Suppose my mother a slave,
And born of slaves: no baseness can touch you.

IOCASTE: Listen to me, I beg you: do not do this thing!

OEDIPUS: I will not listen; the truth must be made known.

IOCASTE: Everything that I say is for your own good!

OEDIPUS: My own good
Snaps my patience, then; I want none of it.

IOCASTE: You are fatally wrong! May you never learn who you are!

OEDIPUS: Go, one of you, and bring the shepherd here.
Let us leave this woman to brag of her royal name.

IOCASTE: Ah, miserable!
    That is the only word I have for you now.
    That is the only word I can ever have.

(*Exit into the palace.*)

CHORAGOS: Why has she left us, Oedipus? Why has she gone
    In such a passion of sorrow? I fear this silence:
    Something dreadful may come of it.
OEDIPUS: Let it come!
    However base my birth, I must know about it.
    The Queen, like a woman, is perhaps ashamed
    To think of my low origin. But I
    Am a child of Luck; I can not be dishonored.
    Luck is my mother; the passing months, my brothers,
    Have seen me rich and poor.
                    If this is so,
    How could I wish that I were someone else?
    How could I not be glad to know my birth?

ODE III

CHORUS: If ever the coming time were known   [STROPHE
    To my heart's pondering,
    Kithairon, now by Heaven I see the torches
    At the festival of the next full moon,
    And see the dance, and hear the choir sing
    A grace to your gentle shade:
    Mountain where Oedipus was found,
    O mountain guard of a noble race!
    May the god who heals us lend his aid,
    And let that glory come to pass
    For our king's cradling-ground.

Of the nymphs that flower beyond the years,   [ANTISTROPHE
    Who bore you, royal child,
    To Pan of the hills or the timberline Apollo,
    Cold in delight where the upland clears,
    Or Hermês for whom Kyllenê's heights are piled?
    Or flushed as evening cloud,
    Great Dionysos, roamer of mountains,
    He — was it he who found you there,
    And caught you up in his own proud

Arms from the sweet god-ravisher
Who laughed by the Muses' fountains?

SCENE IV

OEDIPUS: Sirs: though I do not know the man,
 I think I see him coming, this shepherd we want:
 He is old, like our friend here, and the men
 Bringing him seem to be servants of my house.
 But you can tell, if you have ever seen him.

(*Enter* SHEPHERD *escorted by servants.*)

CHORAGOS: I know him, he was Laïos' man. You can trust him.
OEDIPUS: Tell me first, you from Corinth: is this the shepherd
 We were discussing?
MESSENGER: This is the very man.
OEDIPUS (*To* SHEPHERD): Come here. No, look at me. You must answer
 Everything I ask. — You belonged to Laïos?
SHEPHERD: Yes: born his slave, brought up in his house.
OEDIPUS: Tell me: what kind of work did you do for him?
SHEPHERD: I was a shepherd of his, most of my life.
OEDIPUS: Where mainly did you go for pasturage?
SHEPHERD: Sometimes Kithairon, sometimes the hills near-by.
OEDIPUS: Do you remember ever seeing this man out there?
SHEPHERD: What would he be doing there? This man?
OEDIPUS: This man standing here. Have you ever seen him before?
SHEPHERD: No. At least, not to my recollection.
MESSENGER: And that is not strange, my lord. But I'll refresh
 His memory: he must remember when we two
 Spent three whole seasons together, March to September,
 On Kithairon or thereabouts. He had two flocks;
 I had one. Each autumn I'd drive mine home
 And he would go back with his to Laïos' sheepfold. —
 Is this not true, just as I have described it?
SHEPHERD: True, yes; but it was all so long ago.
MESSENGER: Well, then: do you remember, back in those days
 That you gave me a baby boy to bring up as my own?
SHEPHERD: What if I did? What are you trying to say?
MESSENGER: King Oedipus was once that little child.
SHEPHERD: Damn you, hold your tongue!
OEDIPUS: No more of that!

It is your tongue needs watching, not this man's.

SHEPHERD: My King, my Master, what is it I have done wrong?

OEDIPUS: You have not answered his question about the boy.

SHEPHERD: He does not know . . . He is only making trouble . . .

OEDIPUS: Come, speak plainly, or it will go hard with you.

SHEPHERD: In God's name, do not torture an old man!

OEDIPUS: Come here, one of you; bind his arms behind him.

SHEPHERD: Unhappy king! What more do you wish to learn?

OEDIPUS: Did you give this man the child he speaks of?

SHEPHERD: I did.
    And I would to God I had died that very day.

OEDIPUS: You will die now unless you speak the truth.

SHEPHERD: Yet if I speak the truth, I am worse than dead.

OEDIPUS: Very well; since you insist upon delaying —

SHEPHERD: No! I have told you already that I gave him the boy.

OEDIPUS: Where did you get him? From your house? From somewhere
    else?

SHEPHERD: Not from mine, no. A man gave him to me.

OEDIPUS: Is that man here? Do you know whose slave he was?

SHEPHERD: For God's love, my King, do not ask me any more!

OEDIPUS: You are a dead man if I have to ask you again.

SHEPHERD: Then . . . Then the child was from the palace of Laïos.

OEDIPUS: A slave child? or a child of his own line?

SHEPHERD: Ah, I am on the brink of dreadful speech!

OEDIPUS: And I of dreadful hearing. Yet I must hear.

SHEPHERD: If you must be told, then . . .

                                        They said it was Laïos' child,
    But it is your wife who can tell you about that.

OEDIPUS: My wife! — Did she give it to you?

SHEPHERD: My lord, she did.

OEDIPUS: Do you know why?

SHEPHERD: I was told to get rid of it.

OEDIPUS: An unspeakable mother!

SHEPHERD: There had been prophecies . . .

OEDIPUS: Tell me.

SHEPHERD: It was said that the boy would kill his own father.

OEDIPUS: Then why did you give him over to this old man?

SHEPHERD: I pitied the baby, my King,
    And I thought that this man would take him far away
    To his own country.

                                        He saved him — but for what a fate!
    For if you are what this man says you are,
    No man living is more wretched than Oedipus.

OEDIPUS: Ah God!
It was true!
           All the prophecies!
                     — Now,
O Light, may I look on you for the last time!
I, Oedipus,
Oedipus, damned in his birth, in his marriage damned,
Damned in the blood he shed with his own hand!

(*He rushes into the palace.*)

ODE IV

CHORUS: Alas for the seed of men.   [STROPHE 1

What measure shall I give these generations
That breathe on the void and are void
And exist and do not exist?

Who bears more weight of joy
Than mass of sunlight shifting in images,
Or who shall make his thought stay on
That down time drifts away?

Your splendor is all fallen.

O naked brow of wrath and tears,
O change of Oedipus!
I who saw your days call no man blest —
Your great days like ghósts góne.

That mind was a strong bow.   [ANTISTROPHE 1

Deep, how deep you drew it then, hard archer,
At a dim fearful range,
And brought dear glory down!

You overcame the stranger —
The virgin with her hooking lion claws —
And though death sang, stood like a tower
To make pale Thebes take heart.

Fortress against our sorrow!

Divine king, giver of laws,
Majestic Oedipus!

No prince in Thebes had ever such renown,
No prince won such grace of power.

And now of all men ever known   [STROPHE 2
Most pitiful is this man's story:
His fortunes are most changed, his state
Fallen to a low slave's
Ground under bitter fate.

O Oedipus, most royal one!
The great door that expelled you to the light
Gave at night — ah, gave night to your glory:
As to the father, to the fathering son.

All understood too late.

How could that queen whom Laïos won,
The garden that he harrowed at his height,
Be silent when that act was done?

But all eyes fail before time's eye,   [ANTISTROPHE 2
All actions come to justice there.
Though never willed, though far down the deep past,
Your bed, your dread sirings,
Are brought to book at last.
Child by Laïos doomed to die,
Then doomed to lose that fortunate little death,
Would God you never took breath in this air
That with my wailing lips I take to cry:

For I weep the world's outcast.

I was blind, and now I can tell why:
Asleep, for you had given ease of breath
To Thebes, while the false years went by.

EXODOS

(*Enter, from the palace,* SECOND MESSENGER.)

SECOND MESSENGER: Elders of Thebes, most honored in this land,
What horrors are yours to see and hear, what weight
Of sorrow to be endured, if, true to your birth,
You venerate the line of Labdakos!
I think neither Istros nor Phasis, those great rivers,
Could purify this place of the corruption

It shelters now, or soon must bring to light —
Evil not done unconsciously, but willed.

The greatest griefs are those we cause ourselves.
CHORAGOS: Surely, friend, we have grief enough already;
    What new sorrow do you mean?
SECOND MESSENGER: The Queen is dead.
CHORAGOS: Iocastê? Dead? But at whose hand?
SECOND MESSENGER: Her own.
    The full horror of what happened you can not know,
    For you did not see it; but I, who did, will tell you
    As clearly as I can how she met her death.

When she had left us,
In passionate silence, passing through the court,
She ran to her apartment in the house,
Her hair clutched by the fingers of both hands.
She closed the doors behind her; then, by that bed
Where long ago the fatal son was conceived —
That son who should bring about his father's death —
We heard her call upon Laïos, dead so many years,
And heard her wail for the double fruit of her marriage,
A husband by her husband, children by her child.

Exactly how she died I do not know:
For Oedipus burst in moaning and would not let us
Keep vigil to the end: it was by him
As he stormed about the room that our eyes were caught.
From one to another of us he went, begging a sword,
Cursing the wife who was not his wife, the mother
Whose womb had carried his own children and himself.
I do not know: it was none of us aided him,
But surely one of the gods was in control!
For with a dreadful cry
He hurled his weight, as though wrenched out of himself,
At the twin doors: the bolts gave, and he rushed in.
And there we saw her hanging, her body swaying
From the cruel cord she had noosed about her neck.
A great sob broke from him, heartbreaking to hear,
As he loosed the rope and lowered her to the ground.

I would blot out from my mind what happened next!
For the King ripped from her gown the golden brooches
That were her ornament, and raised them, and plunged them down

Straight into his own eyeballs, crying, "No more,
No more shall you look on the misery about me,
The horrors of my own doing! Too long you have known
The faces of those whom I should never have seen,
Too long been blind to those for whom I was searching!
From this hour, go in darkness!" And as he spoke,
He struck at his eyes — not once, but many times;
And the blood spattered his beard,
Bursting from his ruined sockets like red hail.

So from the unhappiness of two this evil has sprung,
A curse on the man and woman alike. The old
Happiness of the house of Labdakos
Was happiness enough: where is it today?
It is all wailing and ruin, disgrace, death — all
The misery of mankind that has a name —
And it is wholly and for ever theirs.

CHORAGOS: Is he in agony still? Is there no rest for him?

SECOND MESSENGER: He is calling for someone to lead him to the gates
So that all the children of Kadmos may look upon
His father's murderer, his mother's — no,
I can not say it!
                    And then he will leave Thebes,
Self-exiled, in order that the curse
Which he himself pronounced may depart from the house.
He is weak, and there is none to lead him,
So terrible is his suffering.
                    But you will see:
Look, the doors are opening; in a moment
You will see a thing that would crush a heart of stone.

(*The central door is opened;* OEDIPUS, *blinded, is led in.*)

CHORAGOS: Dreadful indeed for men to see.
Never have my own eyes
Looked on a sight so full of fear.

Oedipus!
What madness came upon you, what daemon
Leaped on your life with heavier
Punishment than a mortal man can bear?
No: I can not even
Look at you, poor ruined one.
And I would speak, question, ponder,

If I were able. No.
You make me shudder.
OEDIPUS: God.   God.
Is there a sorrow greater?
Where shall I find harbor in this world?
My voice is hurled far on a dark wind.
What has God done to me?
CHORAGOS: Too terrible to think of, or to see.

OEDIPUS: O cloud of night,   [STROPHE 1
Never to be turned away: night coming on,
I can not tell how: night like a shroud!

My fair winds brought me here.
                              Oh God. Again
The pain of the spikes where I had sight,
The flooding pain
Of memory, never to be gouged out.
CHORAGOS: This is not strange.
You suffer it all twice over, remorse in pain,
Pain in remorse.

OEDIPUS: Ah dear friend   [ANTISTROPHE 1
Are you faithful even yet, you alone?
Are you still standing near me, will you stay here,
Patient, to care for the blind?
                              The blind man!
Yet even blind I know who it is attends me,
By the voice's tone —
Though my new darkness hide the comforter.
CHORAGOS: Oh fearful act!
What god was it drove you to rake black
Night across your eyes?

OEDIPUS: Apollo. Apollo. Dear   [STROPHE 2
Children, the god was Apollo.
He brought my sick, sick fate upon me.
But the blinding hand was my own!
How could I bear to see
When all my sight was horror everywhere?
CHORAGOS: Everywhere; that is true.
OEDIPUS: And now what is left?
Images? Love? A greeting even,
Sweet to the senses? Is there anything?

Ah, no, friends: lead me away.
Lead me away from Thebes.
　　　　　　　　　　　　　　Lead the great wreck
And hell of Oedipus, whom the gods hate.
CHORAGOS: Your fate is clear, you are not blind to that.
　Would God you had never found it out!

OEDIPUS: Death take the man who unbound　　　　[ANTISTROPHE 2
　My feet on that hillside
　And delivered me from death to life! What life?
　If only I had died,
　This weight of monstrous doom
　Could not have dragged me and my darlings down.
CHORAGOS: I would have wished the same.
OEDIPUS: Oh never to have come here
　With my father's blood upon me! Never
　To have been the man they call his mother's husband!
　Oh accurst! Oh child of evil,
　To have entered that wretched bed —
　　　　　　　　　　　　　　the selfsame one!
　More primal than sin itself, this fell to me.
CHORAGOS: I do not know how I can answer you.
　You were better dead than alive and blind.
OEDIPUS: Do not counsel me any more. This punishment
　That I have laid upon myself is just.
　If I had eyes,
　I do not know how I could bear the sight
　Of my father, when I came to the house of Death,
　Or my mother: for I have sinned against them both
　So vilely that I could not make my peace
　By strangling my own life.
　　　　　　　　　　　Or do you think my children,
　Born as they were born, would be sweet to my eyes?
　Ah never, never! Nor this town with its high walls,
　Nor the holy images of the gods.
　　　　　　　　　　　For I,
　Thrice miserable! — Oedipus, noblest of all the line
　Of Kadmos, have condemned myself to enjoy
　These things no more, by my own malediction
　Expelling that man whom the gods declared
　To be a defilement in the house of Laïos.
　After exposing the rankness of my own guilt,
　How could I look men frankly in the eyes?

No, I swear it,
If I could have stifled my hearing at its source,
I would have done it and made all this body
A tight cell of misery, blank to light and sound:
So I should have been safe in a dark agony
Beyond all recollection.

       Ah Kithairon!
Why did you shelter me? When I was cast upon you,
Why did I not die? Then I should never
Have shown the world my execrable birth.

Ah Polybos! Corinth, city that I believed
The ancient seat of my ancestors: how fair
I seemed, your child! And all the while this evil
Was cancerous within me!

        For I am sick
In my daily life, sick in my origin.

O three roads, dark ravine, woodland and way
Where three roads met: you, drinking my father's blood,
My own blood, spilled by my own hand: can you remember
The unspeakable things I did there, and the things
I went on from there to do?

       O marriage, marriage!
The act that engendered me, and again the act
Performed by the son in the same bed —

        Ah, the net
Of incest, mingling fathers, brothers, sons,
With brides, wives, mothers: the last evil
That can be known by men: no tongue can say
How evil!

    No. For the love of God, conceal me
Somewhere far from Thebes; or kill me; or hurl me
Into the sea, away from men's eyes for ever.

Come, lead me. You need not fear to touch me.
Of all men, I alone can bear this guilt.

(*Enter* CREON.)

CHORAGOS: We are not the ones to decide; but Creon here
 May fitly judge of what you ask. He only
 Is left to protect the city in your place.
OEDIPUS: Alas, how can I speak to him? What right have I

To beg his courtesy whom I have deeply wronged?
CREON: I have not come to mock you, Oedipus,
    Or to reproach you, either.
    (*To* ATTENDANTS:)   —You, standing there:
    If you have lost all respect for man's dignity,
    At least respect the flame of Lord Helios:
    Do not allow this pollution to show itself
    Openly here, an affront to the earth
    And Heaven's rain and the light of day. No, take him
    Into the house as quickly as you can.
    For it is proper
    That only the close kindred see his grief.
OEDIPUS: I pray you in God's name, since your courtesy
    Ignores my dark expectation, visiting
    With mercy this man of all men most execrable:
    Give me what I ask — for your good, not for mine.
CREON: And what is it that you would have me do?
OEDIPUS: Drive me out of this country as quickly as may be
    To a place where no human voice can ever greet me.
CREON: I should have done that before now — only,
    God's will had not been wholly revealed to me.
OEDIPUS: But his command is plain: the parricide
    Must be destroyed. I am that evil man.
CREON: That is the sense of it, yes; but things are,
    We had best discover clearly what is to be done.
OEDIPUS: You would learn more about a man like me?
CREON: You are ready now to listen to the god.
OEDIPUS: I will listen. But it is to you
    That I must turn for help. I beg you, hear me.

    The woman in there —
    Give her whatever funeral you think proper:
    She is your sister.
               — But let me go, Creon!
    Let me purge my father's Thebes of the pollution
    Of my living here, and go out to the wild hills,
    To Kithairon, that has won such fame with me,
    The tomb my mother and father appointed for me,
    And let me die there, as they willed I should.
    And yet I know
    Death will not ever come to me through sickness
    Or in any natural way: I have been preserved
    For some unthinkable fate. But let that be.

As for my sons, you need not care for them.
They are men, they will find some way to live.
But my poor daughters, who have shared my table,
Who never before have been parted from their father —
Take care of them, Creon; do this for me.
And will you let me touch them with my hands
A last time, and let us weep together?
Be kind, my lord,
Great prince, be kind!

                        Could I but touch them,
They would be mine again, as when I had my eyes.

(*Enter* ANTIGONE *and* ISMENE, *attended.*)

Ah, God!
Is it my dearest children I hear weeping?
Has Creon pitied me and sent my daughters?

CREON: Yes, Oedipus: I knew that they were dear to you
   In the old days, and know you must love them still.

OEDIPUS: May God bless you for this — and be a friendlier
   Guardian to you than he has been to me!

Children, where are you?
Come quickly to my hands: they are your brother's —
Hands that have brought your father's once clear eyes
To this way of seeing —

                    Ah dearest ones,
I had neither sight nor knowledge then, your father
By the woman who was the source of his own life!
And I weep for you — having no strength to see you —,
I weep for you when I think of the bitterness
That men will visit upon you all your lives.
What homes, what festivals can you attend
Without being forced to depart again in tears?
And when you come to marriageable age,
Where is the man, my daughters, who would dare
Risk the bane that lies on all my children?
Is there any evil wanting? Your father killed
His father; sowed the womb of her who bore him;
Engendered you at the fount of his own existence!
That is what they will say of you.

                       Then, whom
Can you ever marry? There are no bridegrooms for you,
And your lives must wither away in sterile dreaming.

O Creon, son of Menoikeus!
You are the only father my daughters have,
Since we, their parents, are both of us gone for ever.
They are your own blood: you will not let them
Fall into beggary and loneliness;
You will keep them from the miseries that are mine!
Take pity on them; see, they are only children,
Friendless except for you. Promise me this,
Great Prince, and give me your hand in token of it.

(CREON *clasps his right hand.*)

Children:
I could say much, if you could understand me,
But as it is, I have only this prayer for you:
Live where you can, be as happy as you can —
Happier, please God, than God has made your father!

CREON: Enough. You have wept enough. Now go within.
OEDIPUS: I must; but it is hard.
CREON: Time eases all things.
OEDIPUS: But you must promise —
CREON: Say what you desire.
OEDIPUS: Send me from Thebes!
CREON: God grant that I may!
OEDIPUS: But since God hates me . . .
CREON: No, he will grant your wish.
OEDIPUS: You promise?
CREON: I can not speak beyond my knowledge.
OEDIPUS: Then lead me in.
CREON: Come now, and leave your children.
OEDIPUS: No! Do not take them from me!
CREON: Think no longer
That you are in command here, but rather think
How, when you were, you served your own destruction.

(*Exeunt into the house all but the* CHORUS; *the* CHORAGOS *chants
directly to the audience.*)

CHORAGOS: Men of Thebes: look upon Oedipus.

This is the king who solved the famous riddle
And towered up, most powerful of men.
No mortal eyes but looked on him with envy,
Yet in the end ruin swept over him.

Let every man in mankind's frailty
Consider his last day; and let none
Presume on his good fortune until he find
Life, at his death, a memory without pain.

⟋⟋⟋ To AN Athenian of the fifth century B.C. a theatrical performance was simultaneously entertainment, communal service, and
religious ritual. His theater was a place for the worship of Dionysos,
god of fertility and rebirth, and participation in the Dionysiac plays
was a civic honor. During the Great or Urban Dionysia, the most
important of the festivals honoring the god, performances were
given during the daylight hours of three successive days in late
winter. Three playwrights competed every year for first prize with
four plays each — three tragedies (sometimes but not usually related in subject matter) and one satyr play, *i.e.*, a ribald dramatization
of some part of ancient myth or legend, in which the members of the
chorus were dressed as satyrs.

Not very much that is definite and certain is known about the
physical characteristics of the Athenian theater. What follows represents in part fairly well established facts, in part consensus of current scholarly hypothesis. The audience — as many as 15,000 perhaps — was seated on benches in rising concentric tiers, forming a
half circle, on the southeastern slope of the Acropolis. The plays
were enacted before a long, low, wooden building (*skene*), that
served both as dressing room and as the traditional palace setting.
Immediately in front of it was the acting area for the non-choric
characters, whose lines were spoken. Nearer the audience and perhaps
on a lower level was a circular area (*orchestra*), with the altar for Dionysos in the center. Here the chorus, a group of fifteen men (in
Sophoclean tragedy), led by the choragos and accompanied by flute-
playing, moved in slow and formal patterns while they chanted
lyric odes. The odes were divided into stanzas, called *strophe* and
antistrophe, delivered, respectively, as the chorus moved first in one
and then in the opposite direction. In the absence of a curtain, one
function of the odes was to mark divisions between the episodes (in sequence, the formal divisions of the play were: *prologue, parodos, episodes, exodos*). Both actors and chorus wore masks, long robes, and
(perhaps) elevated shoes. Women's roles were played by men.

We do not know the exact date for *Oedipus Rex*, the most famous of Sophocles' plays. The year 430 B.C., give or take a few
years, has been a common guess. We do know that the group of

plays to which it belonged did not win the prize. Aristotle's *Poetics*, the most important classical treatment of tragic theory, discusses *Oedipus Rex* as a model tragedy, the cause of the purgation (*katharsis*) of the emotions of pity and fear in the audience.

From the old myth of man's effort to circumvent the divine will Sophocles made a tautly suspenseful plot, in which pace, causality, and irony combine in a metaphor of the myth's metaphysical content. The grim facts transcend the merely horrible and sensational. The very coincidences of timing and identity that are likely to bother readers taught to treasure plausibility (*e.g.,* the arrivals of Creon and the messenger from Corinth with relevant news just when the plot calls for it) suggest divine direction of events and thus serve to vindicate Apollo against Oedipus' and Iocaste's impious slander of him and his prophet Teiresias. So do the many instances of dramatic irony of speech and event. Oedipus swears to avenge the murder of Laios "just as though I were his son." When he fears he may be Laios's killer his only hope is that the shepherd who alone survived the fight will stick to his earlier story that Laios was killed by a group rather than by a single man. But the shepherd turns out to be the one man who can prove not only that Oedipus did kill Laios but also that he is Laios's son. When Iocaste expresses her contempt for soothsayers in an effort to put Oedipus's mind at rest, she is led to tell a story that accomplishes exactly the opposite and which proves Apollo's prophecy correct.*

---

* It is proof of the play's near-perfection of form that we overlook its technical flaws, or, if we see them, are willing to permit them because of the effects they make possible. It strains belief that neither Oedipus nor Iocaste reacts when the other tells of a prophecy each ought to recognize as identical with the one that concerns him-(her-)self. In Oedipus's case it might be argued — though not very convincingly — that Iocaste's disturbing reference, almost immediately afterward, to the place "where three highways meet" preoccupies his mind, but such an argument does not work twice.

A more flagrant slip is involved in the account of how Laios' murder was reported to the Thebans. From the conversations between Oedipus and Creon in the Prologue and between Oedipus and Iocaste in Scene II the following sequence of events emerges: (1) Laios is killed. (2) His death is reported in Thebes but not vigorously investigated because (3) the Sphinx begins to plague the city. (4) Oedipus kills the Sphinx, arrives in Thebes, marries Iocaste, and is made king. (5) The shepherd, the lone survivor of the fight with Oedipus, returns to Thebes, finds Oedipus on the throne, and asks Iocaste to be sent away. But if events happened in this order, who reported the manner in which Laios was killed? And if the sequence is not correct (that is, if Iocaste for some unexplained reason lies to Oedipus in Scene II or has forgotten the order of events) and the shepherd returned to Thebes *before* Oedipus's arrival, what reason would he have for saying that a "band of highwaymen" or "marauding strangers" — rather than a single man — killed Laios?

What about Apollo's justice? Oedipus has committed the worst imaginable of human crimes: he has killed his father and slept with his mother. But since he is obviously innocent of evil intent, can the god be called just who exacts such suffering for crimes thus committed? How can Oedipus be held responsible for a destiny decreed for him before his birth, for the god's manipulation of events in such a way that the measures he and his parents take to avert the destiny become the very means by which it is fulfilled? If we assume his crime to be not the parricide and the incest but his attempts to outwit the god, then Laios is at least equally guilty and yet escapes Oedipus's fearful suffering. The meaning of Oedipus' suffering further darkens when we realize it is the result of his effort to save his city. Ignorant, he has lived happily for years after killing Laios and marrying Iocaste. A more callous witness to his people's suffering might have been spared the knowledge. And if we argue that he suffers because of his pride — that his tragic flaw (*hamartia*) is overconfidence (*hubris*) — doesn't the severity of the punishment seem far in excess of the gravity of the crime? One recognizes the quality of moral ambiguity in the myth that led the French playwright Jean Cocteau to entitle his modern version of it *The Infernal Machine*. It is as if the god has placed a time bomb under Oedipus's existence and we are listening to the last minutes ticking away.

But Oedipus blinds himself in an agony of shame and guilt and horror, and to Creon he is a pollution of which Thebes must cleanse herself. Beyond Oedipus's bewildered "What has the god done to me?" it does not occur to him or to anyone else in the play to challenge the justice of what is happening to him. Does this shock us? Or are we at the end of the play aware of law rather than of injustice, of restitution of health to the stricken city through the atonement of evil (however innocently committed) rather than of divine malice, let alone meaninglessness? That Oedipus is an abomination in the eyes of man and god alike is a matter neither of justice nor morality, but it is a fact, and it must be heeded. The universe is not obliged to fit man's sense of fair play. As the confident, well-meaning, and efficient detective changes into abject criminal, we sense how frail man's defenses are, how absolute his finitude, how ineluctable his fate.

For so comprehensive is the Sophoclean wisdom that the play without contradiction can accommodate the truth that though Oedipus' suffering is not, properly speaking, *punishment*, there is yet a sense in which it can be said that he brings disaster upon himself, that his character is his fate. He suffers because he fails to see the connection between the drunken Corinthian's taunt about his

parentage and the prophecy with which Apollo's oracle answers his
request for confirmation or refutation of the Corinthian's words. He
suffers because, having killed a man, he should have hesitated before
marrying any woman who might, theoretically, be that man's wife.
He suffers because he refuses to listen to Teiresias' and Iocaste's
warning to leave the past alone. In the Prologue, we feel he is too
much the "I, Oedipus, who bears the famous name" not to come to
a tragic end. His rash anger with Teiresias and Creon reveals how
thin the layer of rationality is in the man who answered the Sphinx's
riddle. We are not surprised to learn a little later that he killed
Laios in a rage. He diminishes in stature as a man of determination
and perseverance when we realize that he abandons his inquiry concerning the Corinthian's words and seeks instead to avert the prophecy and, later, abandons his search for Laios' murderer for the quest
for his own identity. Dramatic irony shrills in our ears as this man,
on the very edge of discovering that all his life he has been moving
toward the doom he has all his life been trying to escape, boasts of
being self-made and congratulates himself as being "a child of
luck":

> If this is so,
> How could I wish that I were someone else?
> How could I not be glad to know my birth?

All this is not quite to say that prudence and forethought could
have averted the will of the god, that the oracle only foresaw, and
did not predestine, what Oedipus brought upon himself, that,
though he may have been doomed to do what he did, he was not
doomed to find out what he had done. The ambiguities remain.

But no matter how we seek to resolve them — and a number of
different answers have been given to the problem of evil in *Oedipus
Rex* — the ironies through which Oedipus moves give him stature.
He is more than a passive victim of fate. He struggles. The metaphysical implications of his character, its very flaws, make him heroic
as well as human, and he is nowhere more fully both than in the
moment when inward illumination forever darkens his sight of the
world he thought he controlled and he fulfills his destiny in assuming the paradoxical function of the blind seer he had mocked
and accused. The act of blinding completes one cycle of Oedipus'
fate and begins another that culminates in the sober and mystical
serenity of *Oedipus at Colonus*. Hubris takes Oedipus through
tragedy and beyond. "Neither destiny nor Oedipus is acquitted or
condemned" is how one critic puts the play's affirmation of an order
that passes human understanding. For all its pain and horror, the

play reflects *sophrosyne* — moderation, due proportion, harmony — not understood, perhaps, or accepted, but overwhelmingly felt.

In the play's tissue of ironies the riddle of human suffering remains dark. It is the friendly messenger from Corinth, expecting reward for the good news he brings, who measures off Oedipus' and Iocaste's last minutes of happiness. His silence during the dialogue between Oedipus and the old shepherd is pure pathos, and at the end of it we can see him slink off, ignored, shaken. And the voice that lingers with us is our own voice, that of the chorus, the voice of common humanity, worried, ignorant, sorrowing for itself:

> What measure shall I give these generations
> That breathe on the void and are void
> And exist and do not exist?

Anonymous

EVERYMAN

Characters

GOD

MESSENGER	KNOWLEDGE
DEATH	CONFESSION
EVERYMAN	BEAUTY
FELLOWSHIP	STRENGTH
KINDRED	DISCRETION
COUSIN	FIVE WITS
GOODS	ANGEL
GOOD DEEDS	DOCTOR

Here Beginneth a Treatise how the High Father of Heaven Sendeth Death to Summon Every Creature to Come and Give Account of their Lives in this World, and is in Manner of a Moral Play.

MESSENGER: I pray you all give your audience,
And hear this matter with reverence,
By figure[1] a moral play:
The *Summoning of Everyman* called it is,
That of our lives and ending shows
How transitory we be all day.
This matter is wondrous precious,
But the intent of it is more gracious,
And sweet to bear away.
The story saith: Man, in the beginning
Look well, and take good heed to the ending,

[1] form

From the book *Everyman and Mediaeval Miracle Plays*, edited by A. C. Cawley; a Dutton Everyman Paperback. Reprinted by permission of E. P. Dutton & Co., Inc. Canadian rights granted by J. M. Dent & Sons, Ltd.

Be you never so gay!
Ye think sin in the beginning full sweet,
Which in the end causeth the soul to weep,
When the body lieth in clay.
Here shall you see how Fellowship and Jollity,
Both Strength, Pleasure, and Beauty,
Will fade from thee as flower in May;
For ye shall hear how our Heaven King
Calleth Everyman to a general reckoning:
Give audience, and hear what he doth say.   (*Exit.*)

(GOD *speaketh:*)

GOD: I perceive, here in my majesty,
How that all creatures be to me unkind,
Living without dread in worldly prosperity:
Of ghostly[2] sight the people be so blind,
Drowned in sin, they know me not for their God;
In worldly riches is all their mind,
They fear not my righteousness, the sharp rod.
My law that I showed, when I for them died,
They forget clean,[3] and shedding of my blood red;
I hanged between two, it cannot be denied;
To get them life I suffered[4] to be dead;
I healed their feet, with thorns hurt was my head.
I could do no more than I did, truly;
And now I see the people do clean forsake me:
They use the seven deadly sins damnable,
As pride, covetise, wrath, and lechery
Now in the world be made commendable;
And thus they leave of angels the heavenly company.
Every man liveth so after his own pleasure,
And yet of their life they be nothing[5] sure:
I see the more that I them forbear
The worse they be from year to year.
All that liveth appaireth[6] fast;
Therefore I will, in all the haste,
Have a reckoning of every man's person;
For, and[7] I leave the people thus alone
In their life and wicked tempests,
Verily they will become much worse than beasts;
For now one would by envy another up eat;

---

[2] spiritual   [3] completely, altogether   [4] allowed myself   [5] not at all
[6] becomes worse   [7] if

Charity they do all clean forget.
I hoped well that every man
In my glory should make his mansion,
And thereto I had them all elect;
But now I see, like traitors deject,
They thank me not for the pleasure that I to them meant,
Nor yet for their being I them have lent.
I proffered the people great multitude of mercy,
And few there be that asketh it heartily.
They be so cumbered with worldly riches
That needs on them I must do justice,
On every man living without fear.
Where art thou, Death, though mighty messenger?

(*Enter* DEATH.)

DEATH: Almighty God, I am here at your will,
    Your commandment to fulfil.
GOD: Go thou to Everyman,
    And show him, in my name,
    A pilgrimage he must on him take,
    Which he in no wise[8] may escape;
    And that he bring with him a sure reckoning
    Without delay or any tarrying.   (GOD *withdraws.*)
DEATH: Lord, I will in the world go run overall,[9]
    And cruelly outsearch both great and small;
    Every man will I beset that liveth beastly
    Out of God's laws, and dreadeth not folly.
    He that loveth riches I will strike with my dart,
    His sight to blind, and from heaven to depart[10] —
    Except that alms be his good friend —
    In hell for to dwell, world without end.
    Lo, yonder I see Everyman walking.
    Full little he thinketh on my coming;
    His mind is on fleshly lusts and his treasure,
    And great pain it shall cause him to endure
    Before the Lord, Heaven King.

(*Enter* EVERYMAN.)

Everyman, stand still! Whither art thou going
    Thus gaily? Hast thou thy Maker forget?
EVERYMAN: Why askest thou?
    Wouldest thou wit?[11]

---

[8] manner   [9] everywhere   [10] separate   [11] know

DEATH: Yea, sir; I will show you:
 In great haste I am sent to thee
 From God out of his majesty.
EVERYMAN: What, sent to me?
DEATH: Yea, certainly.
 Though thou have forget him here,
 He thinketh on thee in the heavenly sphere,
 As, ere we depart, thou shalt know.
EVERYMAN: What desireth God of me?
DEATH: That shall I show thee:
 A reckoning he will needs have
 Without any longer respite.
EVERYMAN: To give a reckoning longer leisure I crave;
 This blind [12] matter troubleth my wit.
DEATH: On thee thou must take a long journey;
 Therefore thy book of count [13] with thee thou bring,
 For turn again thou cannot by no way.
 And look thou be sure of thy reckoning,
 For before God thou shalt answer, and show
 Thy many bad deeds, and good but a few;
 How thou hast spent thy life, and in what wise,
 Before the chief Lord of paradise.
 Have ado [14] that we were in that way, [15]
 For, wit thou well, thou shalt make none [16] attorney.
EVERYMAN: Full unready I am such reckoning to give.
 I know thee not. What messenger art thou?
DEATH: I am Death, that no man dreadeth, [17]
 For every man I rest, [18] and no man spareth;
 For it is God's commandment
 That all to me shall be obedient.
EVERYMAN: O Death, thou comest when I had thee least in mind!
 In thy power it lieth me to save;
 Yet of my good will I give thee, if thou will be kind:
 Yea, a thousand pound shalt thou have,
 And defer this matter till another day.
DEATH: Everyman, it may not be, by no way.
 I set not by [19] gold, silver, nor riches,
 Ne by pope, emperor, king, duke, ne princes;
 For, and I would receive gifts great,
 All the world I might get;
 But my custom is clean contrary.

[12] obscure   [13] account   [14] see to it   [15] on that journey   [16] have no
[17] dreads no man   [18] arrest   [19] do not care for

I give thee no respite. Come hence, and not tarry.

EVERYMAN: Alas, shall I have no longer respite?
I may say Death giveth no warning!
To think on thee, it maketh my heart sick,
For all unready is my book of reckoning.
But twelve year and I might have abiding,
My counting-book I would make so clear
That my reckoning I should not need to fear.
Wherefore, Death, I pray thee, for God's mercy,
Spare me till I be provided of remedy.

DEATH: Thee availeth not to cry, weep, and pray;
But haste thee lightly[20] that thou were gone that journey,
And prove thy friends if thou can;
For, wit thou well, the tide abideth no man,
And in the world each living creature
For Adam's sin must die of nature.[21]

EVERYMAN: Death, if I should this pilgrimage take,
And my reckoning surely make,
Show me, for[22] saint charity,
Should I not come again shortly?

DEATH: No, Everyman; and thou be once there,
Thou mayst never more come here,
Trust me verily.

EVERYMAN: O gracious God in the high seat celestial,
Have mercy on me in this most need!
Shall I have no company from this vale terrestrial
Of mine acquaintance, that way me to lead?

DEATH: Yea, if any be so hardy
That would go with thee and bear thee company.
Hie[23] thee that thou were gone to God's magnificence,
Thy reckoning to give before his presence.
What, weenest[24] thou thy life is given thee,
And thy worldly goods also?

EVERYMAN: I had wend[25] so, verily.

DEATH: Nay, nay; it was but lent thee;
For as soon as thou art go,
Another a while shall have it, and then go therefro,[26]
Even as thou hast done.
Everyman, thou art mad! Thou hast thy wits five,
And here on earth will not amend thy life;
For suddenly I do come.

[20] quickly [21] as a natural thing [22] in the name of [23] hurry [24] think
[25] thought [26] from it

EVERYMAN: O wretched caitiff, whither shall I flee,
  That I might scape this endless sorrow?
  Now, gentle Death, spare me till to-morrow,
  That I may amend me
  With good advisement.[27]
DEATH: Nay, thereto I will not consent,
  Nor no man will I respite;
  But to the heart suddenly I shall smite
  Without any advisement.
  And now out of thy sight I will me hie;
  See thou make thee ready shortly,
  For thou mayst say this is the day
  That no man living may scape away.   (*Exit* DEATH.)
EVERYMAN: Alas, I may well weep with sighs deep!
  Now have I no manner of company
  To help me in my journey, and me to keep;
  And also my writing is full unready.
  How shall I do now for to excuse me?
  I would to God I had never be get! [28]
  To my soul a full great profit it had be;
  For now I fear pains huge and great.
  The time passeth. Lord, help, that all wrought!
  For though I mourn it availeth nought.
  The day passeth, and is almost ago;[29]
  I wot not well what for to do.
  To whom were I best my complaint to make?
  What and I to Fellowship thereof spake,
  And showed him of this sudden chance?
  For in him is all mine affiance;[30]
  We have in the world so many a day
  Be good friends in sport and play.
  I see him yonder, certainly.
  I trust that he will bear me company;
  Therefore to him will I speak to ease my sorrow.
  Well met, good Fellowship, and good morrow!

  (FELLOWSHIP *speaketh:*)

FELLOWSHIP: Everyman, good morrow, by this day!
  Sir, why lookest thou so piteously?
  If any thing be amiss, I pray thee me say,
  That I may help to remedy.
EVERYMAN: Yea, good Fellowship, yea;

[27] reflection   [28] been born   [29] gone   [30] trust

I am in great jeopardy.

FELLOWSHIP: My true friend, show to me your mind;
　I will not forsake thee to my life's end,
　In the way of good company.

EVERYMAN: That was well spoken, and lovingly.

FELLOWSHIP: Sir, I must needs know your heaviness;[31]
　I have pity to see you in any distress.
　If any have you wronged, ye shall revenged be,
　Though I on the ground be slain for thee —
　Though that I know before that I should die.

EVERYMAN: Verily, Fellowship, gramercy.

FELLOWSHIP: Tush! by thy thanks I set not a straw.
　Show me your grief, and say no more.

EVERYMAN: If I my heart should to you break,[32]
　And then you to turn your mind from me,
　And would not me comfort when ye hear me speak,
　Then should I ten times sorrier be.

FELLOWSHIP: Sir, I say as I will do indeed.

EVERYMAN: Then be you a good friend at need:
　I have found you true herebefore.

FELLOWSHIP: And so ye shall evermore;
　For, in faith, and thou go to hell,
　I will not forsake thee by the way.

EVERYMAN: Ye speak like a good friend; I believe you well.
　I shall deserve it, and I may.

FELLOWSHIP: I speak of no deserving, by this day!
　For he that will say, and nothing do,
　Is not worthy with good company to go;
　Therefore show me the grief of your mind,
　As to your friend most loving and kind.

EVERYMAN: I shall show you how it is:
　Commanded I am to go a journey,
　A long way, hard and dangerous,
　And give a strait count, without delay,
　Before the high Judge, Adonai.[33]
　Wherefore, I pray you, bear me company,
　As ye have promised, in this journey.

FELLOWSHIP: That is matter indeed. Promise is duty;
　But, and I should take such a voyage on me,
　I know it well, it should be to my pain;
　Also it maketh me afeard, certain.
　But let us take counsel here as well as we can,

[31] sorrow　　[32] open　　[33] Hebrew name for God

For your words would fear[34] a strong man.

EVERYMAN: Why, ye said if I had need
Ye would me never forsake, quick[35] ne dead,
Though it were to hell, truly.

FELLOWSHIP: So I said, certainly,
But such pleasures be set aside, the sooth to say;
And also, if we took such a journey,
When should we come again?

EVERYMAN: Nay, never again, till the day of doom.

FELLOWSHIP: In faith, then will not I come there!
Who hath you these tidings brought?

EVERYMAN: Indeed, Death was with me here.

FELLOWSHIP: Now, by God that all hath bought,
If Death were the messenger,
For no man that is living to-day
I will not go that loath journey —
Not for the father that begat me!

EVERYMAN: Ye promised otherwise, pardie.[36]

FELLOWSHIP: I wot well I said so, truly;
And yet if thou wilt eat, and drink, and make good cheer,
Or haunt to women the lusty company,[37]
I would not forsake you while the day is clear,[38]
Trust me verily.

EVERYMAN: Yea, thereto ye would be ready!
To go to mirth, solace, and play,
Your mind will sooner apply,
Than to bear me company in my long journey.

FELLOWSHIP: Now, in good faith, I will not that way.
But and thou will murder, or any man kill,
In that I will help thee with a good will.

EVERYMAN: O, that is a simple advice indeed.
Gentle fellow, help me in my necessity!
We have loved long, and now I need;
And now, gentle Fellowship, remember me.

FELLOWSHIP: Whether ye have loved me or no,
By Saint John, I will not with thee go.

EVERYMAN: Yet, I pray thee, take the labour, and do so much for me
To bring me forward,[39] for saint charity,
And comfort me till I come without the town.

FELLOWSHIP: Nay, and thou would give me a new gown,
I will not a foot with thee go;

[34] frighten   [35] alive   [36] by God   [37] frequent the pleasant company of women   [38] until daybreak   [39] escort me

But, and thou had tarried, I would not have left thee so.
And as now God speed thee in thy journey,
For from thee I will depart as fast as I may.
EVERYMAN: Whither away, Fellowship? Will thou forsake me?
FELLOWSHIP: Yea, by my fay! [40] To God I betake[41] thee.
EVERYMAN: Farewell, good Fellowship; for thee my heart is sore.
Adieu for ever! I shall see thee no more.
FELLOWSHIP: In faith, Everyman, farewell now at the ending;
For you I will remember that parting is mourning.

(*Exit* FELLOWSHIP.)

EVERYMAN: Alack! shall we thus depart indeed —
Ah, Lady, help! — without any more comfort?
Lo, Fellowship forsaketh me in my most need.
For help in this world whither shall I resort?
Fellowship herebefore with me would merry make,
And now little sorrow for me doth he take.
It is said, 'In prosperity men friends may find,
Which in adversity be full unkind.'
Now whither for succour shall I flee,
Sith that[42] Fellowship hath forsaken me?
To my kinsmen I will, truly,
Praying them to help me in my necessity;
I believe that they will do so,
For kind[43] will creep where it may not go.
I will go say, for yonder I see them.
Where be ye now, my friends and kinsmen?

(*Enter* KINDRED *and* COUSIN.)

KINDRED: Here be we now at your commandment.
Cousin, I pray you show us your intent
In any wise, and do not spare.[44]
COUSIN: Yea, Everyman, and to us declare
If ye be disposed to go anywhither;
For, wit you well, we will live and die together.
KINDRED: In wealth and woe we will with you hold,
For over his kin a man may be bold.[45]
EVERYMAN: Gramercy, my friends and kinsmen kind.
Now shall I show you the grief of my mind:
I was commanded by a messenger,
That is a high king's chief officer;
He bade me go a pilgrimage, to my pain,

[40] faith [41] commend [42] since [43] kinship, family [44] hold back
[45] a man may freely command the services of his family

And I know well I shall never come again;
Also I must give a reckoning strait,
For I have a great enemy[46] that hath me in wait,
Which intendeth me for to hinder.

KINDRED: What account is that which ye must render?
That would I know.

EVERYMAN: Of all my works I must show
How I have lived and my days spent;
Also of ill deeds that I have used [47]
In my time, sith life was me lent;
And of all virtues that I have refused.
Therefore, I pray you, go thither with me
To help to make mine account, for saint charity.

COUSIN: What, to go thither? Is that the matter?
Nay, Everyman, I had liefer[48] fast[49] bread and water
All this five year and more.

EVERYMAN: Alas, that ever I was bore! [50]
For now shall I never be merry,
If that you forsake me.

KINDRED: Ah, sir, what ye be a merry man!
Take good heart to you, and make no moan.
But one thing I warn you, by Saint Anne —
As for me, ye shall go alone.

EVERYMAN: My Cousin, will you not with me go?

COUSIN: No, by our Lady! I have the cramp in my toe.
Trust not to me, for, so God me speed,
I will deceive you in your most need.

KINDRED: It availeth not us to tice.[51]
Ye shall have my maid with all my heart;
She loveth to go to feasts, there to be nice,[52]
And to dance, and abroad to start:[53]
I will give her leave to help you in that journey,
If that you and she may agree.

EVERYMAN: Now show me the very effect of your mind:
Will you go with me, or abide behind?

KINDRED: Abide behind? Yea, that will I, and I may!
Therefore farewell till another day.   (*Exit* KINDRED.)

EVERYMAN: How should I be merry or glad?
For fair promises men to me make,
But when I have most need they me forsake.
I am deceived; that maketh me sad.

46 *i.e.*, the Devil   47 practiced   48 rather   49 have nothing but   50 born
51 entice   52 wanton   53 rush

COUSIN: Cousin Everyman, farewell now,
  For verily I will not go with you.
  Also of mine own an unready reckoning
  I have to account; therefore I make tarrying.
  Now God keep thee, for now I go.   (*Exit* COUSIN.)
EVERYMAN: Ah, Jesus, is all come hereto?
  Lo, fair words maketh fools fain;[54]
  They promise, and nothing will do, certain.
  My kinsmen promised me faithfully
  For to abide with me steadfastly,
  And now fast away do they flee:
  Even so Fellowship promised me.
  What friend were best me of to provide? [55]
  I lose my time here longer to abide.
  Yet in my mind a thing there is:
  All my life I have loved riches;
  If that my Good[56] now help me might,
  He would make my heart full light.
  I will speak to him in this distress —
  Where art thou, my Goods and riches?

(GOODS *speaks from a corner:*)

GOODS: Who calleth me? Everyman? What! hast thou haste?
  I lie here in corners, trussed and piled so high,
  And in chests I am locked so fast,
  Also sacked in bags. Thou mayst see with thine eye
  I cannot stir; in packs low I lie.
  What would ye have? Lightly me say.
EVERYMAN: Come hither, Good, in all the haste thou may,
  For of counsel I must desire thee.
GOODS: Sir, and ye in the world have sorrow or adversity,
  That can I help you to remedy shortly.
EVERYMAN: It is another disease that grieveth me;
  In this world it is not, I tell thee so.
  I am sent for, another way to go,
  To give a strait count general
  Before the highest Jupiter of all;
  And all my life I have had joy and pleasure in thee,
  Therefore, I pray thee, go with me;
  For, peradventure, thou mayst before God Almighty
  My reckoning help to clean and purify;
  For it is said ever among[57]

[54] glad   [55] to provide me with   [56] goods, possessions   [57] at times

That money maketh all right that is wrong.
GOODS: Nay, Everyman, I sing another song.
  I follow no man in such voyages;
  For, and I went with thee,
  Thou shouldst fare much the worse for me;
  For because on me thou did set thy mind,
  Thy reckoning I have made blotted and blind,
  That thine account thou cannot make truly;
  And that hast thou for the love of me.
EVERYMAN: That would grieve me full sore,
  When I should come to that fearful answer.
  Up, let us go thither together.
GOODS: Nay, not so! I am too brittle, I may not endure;
  I will follow no man one foot, be ye sure.
EVERYMAN: Alas, I have thee loved, and had great pleasure
  All my life-days on good and treasure.
GOODS: That is to thy damnation, without leasing,
  For my love is contrary to the love everlasting;
  But if thou had me loved moderately during,
  As to the poor to give part of me,
  Then shouldst thou not in this dolour be,
  Nor in this great sorrow and care.
EVERYMAN: Lo, now was I deceived ere I was ware,
  And all I may wite[58] misspending of time.
GOODS: What, weenest thou that I am thine?
EVERYMAN: I had wend so.
GOODS: Nay, Everyman, I say no.
  As for a while I was lent thee;
  A season thou hast had me in prosperity.
  My condition is man's soul to kill;
  If I save one, a thousand I do spill.
  Weenest thou that I will follow thee?
  Nay, not from this world, verily.
EVERYMAN: I had wend otherwise.
GOODS: Therefore to thy soul Good is a thief;
  For when thou art dead, this is my guise[59] —
  Another to deceive in this same wise
  As I have done thee, and all to his soul's reprief.[60]
EVERYMAN: O false Good, cursed may thou be,
  Thou traitor to God, that hast deceived me
  And caught me in thy snare!
GOODS: Marry, thou brought thyself in care,

---

[58] blame on   [59] practice   [60] shame

Whereof I am glad;
I must needs laugh, I cannot be sad.
EVERYMAN: Ah, Good, thou hast had long my heartly love;
I gave thee that which should be the Lord's above.
But wilt thou not go with me indeed?
I pray thee truth to say.
GOODS: No, so God me speed!
Therefore farewell, and have good day. (*Exit* GOODS.)
EVERYMAN: O, to whom shall I make my moan
For to go with me in that heavy journey?
First Fellowship said he would with me gone;
His words were very pleasant and gay,
But afterward he left me alone.
Then spake I to my kinsmen, all in despair,
And also they gave me words fair;
They lacked no fair speaking,
But all forsook me in the ending.
Then went I to my Goods, that I loved best,
In hope to have comfort, but there had I least;
For my Goods sharply did me tell
That he bringeth many into hell.
Then of myself I was ashamed,
And so I am worthy to be blamed;
Thus may I well myself hate.
Of whom shall I now counsel take?
I think that I shall never speed
Till that I go to my Good Deed.
But, alas, she is so weak
That she can neither go nor speak;
Yet will I venture on her now.
My Good Deeds, where be you?

(GOOD DEEDS *speaks from the ground:*)

GOOD DEEDS: Here I lie, cold in the ground;
Thy sins hath me sore bound,
That I cannot stir.
EVERYMAN: O Good Deeds, I stand in fear!
I must you pray of counsel,
For help now should come right well.
GOOD DEEDS: Everyman, I have understanding
That ye be summoned account to make
Before Messias, of Jerusalem King;

And you do by me,[61] that journey with you will I take.

EVERYMAN: Therefore I come to you, my moan to make;
　I pray you that ye will go with me.

GOOD DEEDS: I would full fain, but I cannot stand, verily.

EVERYMAN: Why, is there anything on you fall?

GOOD DEEDS: Yea, sir, I may thank you of[62] all;
　If ye had perfectly cheered me,
　Your book of count full ready had be.
　Look, the books of your works and deeds eke![63]
　Behold how they lie under the feet,
　To your soul's heaviness.

EVERYMAN: Our Lord Jesus help me!
　For one letter here I cannot see.

GOOD DEEDS: There is a blind reckoning in time of distress.

EVERYMAN: Good Deeds, I pray you help me in this need,
　Or else I am for ever damned indeed;
　Therefore help me to make reckoning
　Before the Redeemer of all thing,
　That King is, and was, and ever shall.

GOOD DEEDS: Everyman, I am sorry of your fall,
　And fain would I help you, and I were able.

EVERYMAN: Good Deeds, your counsel I pray you give me.

GOOD DEEDS: That shall I do verily;
　Though that on my feet I may not go,
　I have a sister that shall with you also,
　Called Knowledge, which shall with you abide,
　To help you to make that dreadful reckoning.

(*Enter* KNOWLEDGE)

KNOWLEDGE: Everyman, I will go with thee, and be thy guide,
　In thy most need to go by thy side.

EVERYMAN: In good condition I am now in every thing,
　And am wholly content with this good thing,
　Thanked be God my creator.

GOOD DEEDS: And when she hath brought you there
　Where thou shalt heal thee of thy smart,[64]
　Then go you with your reckoning and your Good Deeds together,
　For to make you joyful at heart
　Before the blessed Trinity.

EVERYMAN: My Good Deeds, gramercy!
　I am well content, certainly,
　With your words sweet.

[61] as I advise　　[62] for　　[63] also　　[64] pain

KNOWLEDGE: Now go we together lovingly
　　To Confession, that cleansing river.
EVERYMAN: For joy I weep; I would we were there!
　　But, I pray you, give me cognition
　　Where dwelleth that holy man, Confession.
KNOWLEDGE: In the house of salvation:
　　We shall find him in that place,
　　That shall us comfort, by God's grace.

(KNOWLEDGE *takes* EVERYMAN *to* CONFESSION.)

　　Lo, this is Confession. Kneel down and ask mercy,
　　For he is in good conceit[65] with God Almighty.
EVERYMAN: O glorious fountain, that all uncleanness doth clarify,
　　Wash from me the spots of vice unclean,
　　That on me no sin may be seen.
　　I come with Knowledge for my redemption,
　　Redempt with heart and full contrition;
　　For I am commanded a pilgrimage to take,
　　And great accounts before God to make.
　　Now I pray you, Shrift,[66] mother of salvation,
　　Help my Good Deeds for my piteous exclamation.
CONFESSION: I know your sorrow well, Everyman.
　　Because with Knowledge ye come to me,
　　I will you comfort as well as I can,
　　And a precious jewel I will give thee,
　　Called penance, voider of adversity;
　　Therewith shall your body chastised be,
　　With abstinence and perseverance in God's service.
　　Here shall you receive that scourge of me,
　　Which is penance strong that ye must endure,
　　To remember thy Saviour was scourged for thee
　　With sharp scourges, and suffered it patiently;
　　So must thou, ere thou scape that painful pilgrimage.
　　Knowledge, keep him in this voyage,
　　And by that time Good Deeds will be with thee.
　　But in any wise be siker[67] of mercy,
　　For your time draweth fast; and ye will saved be,
　　Ask God mercy, and he will grant truly.
　　When with the scourge of penance man doth him[68] bind,
　　The oil of forgiveness then shall he find.
EVERYMAN: Thanked be God for his gracious work!
　　For now I will my penance begin;

[65] esteem　　[66] confession　　[67] sure　　[68] himself

This hath rejoiced and lighted my heart,
Though the knots be painful and hard within.
KNOWLEDGE: Everyman, look your penance that ye fulfil,
What pain that ever it to you be;
And Knowledge shall give you counsel at will
How your account ye shall make clearly.
EVERYMAN: O eternal God, O heavenly figure,
O way of righteousness, O goodly vision,
Which descended down in a virgin pure
Because he would every man redeem,
Which Adam forfeited by his disobedience:
O blessed Godhead, elect and high divine,
Forgive my grievous offence;
Here I cry thee mercy in this presence.
O ghostly treasure, O ransomer and redeemer,
Of all the world hope and conductor,[69]
Mirror of joy, and founder of mercy,
Which enlumineth heaven and earth thereby,[70]
Hear my clamorous complaint, though it late be;
Receive my prayers, of thy benignity;
Though I be a sinner most abominable,
Yet let my name be written in Moses' table.
O Mary, pray to the Maker of all thing,
Me for to help at my ending;
And save me from the power of my enemy,
For Death assaileth me strongly.
And, Lady, that I may by mean of thy prayer
Of your Son's glory to be[71] partner,
By the means of his passion, I it crave;
I beseech you help my soul to save.
Knowledge, give me the scourge of penance;
My flesh therewith shall give acquittance:[72]
I will now begin, if God give me grace.
KNOWLEDGE: Everyman, God give you time and space!
Thus I bequeath you in the hands of our Saviour;
Now may you make your reckoning sure.
EVERYMAN: In the name of the Holy Trinity,
My body sore punished shall be:
Take this, body, for the sin of the flesh!   (*Scourges himself.*)
Also thou delightest to go gay and fresh,
And in the way of damnation thou did me bring,
Therefore suffer now strokes and punishing.

[69] guide   [70] besides   [71] be   [72] atonement

Now of penance I will wade the water clear,
To save me from purgatory, that sharp fire.

(GOOD DEEDS *rises from the ground*)

GOOD DEEDS: I thank God, now I can walk and go,
　And am delivered of my sickness and woe.
　Therefore with Everyman I will go, and not spare;
　His good works I will help him to declare.
KNOWLEDGE: Now, Everyman, be merry and glad!
　Your Good Deeds cometh now; ye may not be sad.
　Now is your Good Deeds whole and sound,
　Going upright upon the ground.
EVERYMAN: My heart is light, and shall be evermore;
　Now will I smite faster than I did before.
GOOD DEEDS: Everyman, pilgrim, my special friend,
　Blessed be thou without end;
　For thee is preparate the eternal glory.
　Ye have me made whole and sound,
　Therefore I will bide by thee in every stound.[73]
EVERYMAN: Welcome, my Good Deeds; now I hear thy voice,
　I weep for very sweetness of love.
KNOWLEDGE: Be no more sad, but ever rejoice;
　God seeth thy living in his throne above.
　Put on this garment to thy behoof,[74]
　Which is wet with your tears,
　Or else before God you may it miss,
　When ye to your journey's end come shall.
EVERYMAN: Gentle Knowledge, what do ye it call?
KNOWLEDGE: It is a garment of sorrow:
　From pain it will you borrow;[75]
　Contrition it is,
　That geteth forgiveness;
　It pleaseth God passing well.
GOOD DEEDS: Everyman, will you wear it for your heal?
EVERYMAN: Now blessed be Jesu, Mary's Son,
　For now have I on true contrition.
　And let us go now without tarrying;
　Good Deeds, have we clear our reckoning?
GOOD DEEDS: Yea, indeed, I have it here.
EVERYMAN: Then I trust we need not fear;
　Now, friends, let us not part in twain.
KNOWLEDGE: Nay, Everyman, that will we not, certain.

[73] always (or: in every attack) 　[74] advantage 　[75] take

GOOD DEEDS: Yet must thou lead with thee
  Three persons of great might.
EVERYMAN: Who should they be?
GOOD DEEDS: Discretion and Strength they hight,[76]
  And thy Beauty may not abide behind.
KNOWLEDGE: Also ye must call to mind
  Your Five Wits as for your counsellors.
GOOD DEEDS: You must have them ready at all hours.
EVERYMAN: How shall I get them hither?
KNOWLEDGE: You must call them all together,
  And they will hear you incontinent.[77]
EVERYMAN: My friends, come hither and be present,
  Discretion, Strength, my Five Wits,[78] and Beauty.

  (*Enter* BEAUTY, STRENGTH, DISCRETION, *and* FIVE WITS)

BEAUTY: Here at your will we be all ready.
  What will ye that we should do?
GOOD DEEDS: That ye would with Everyman go,
  And help him in his pilgrimage.
  Advise you, will ye with him or not in that voyage?
STRENGTH: We will bring him all thither,
  To his help and comfort, ye may believe me.
DISCRETION: So will we go with him all together.
EVERYMAN: Almighty God, lofed[79] may thou be!
  I give thee laud that I have hither brought
  Strength, Discretion, Beauty, and Five Wits. Lack I nought.
  And my Good Deeds, with Knowledge clear,
  All be in my company at my will here;
  I desire no more to[80] my business.
STRENGTH: And I, Strength, will by you stand in distress,
  Though thou would in battle fight on the ground.
FIVE WITS: And though it were through the world round,
  We will not depart for sweet ne sour.
BEAUTY: No more will I unto death's hour,
  Whatsoever thereof befall.
DISCRETION: Everyman, advise you first of all;
  Go with a good advisement and deliberation.
  We all give you virtuous monition
  That all shall be well.
EVERYMAN: My friends, harken what I will tell:
  I pray God reward you in his heavenly sphere.
  Now harken, all that be here,

[76] are called [77] immediately [78] senses [79] praised [80] for

For I will make my testament
Here before you all present:
In alms half my good I will give with my hands twain
In the way of charity, with good intent,
And the other half still shall remain
In queth,[81] to be returned there[82] it ought to be.
This I do in despite of the fiend of hell,
To go quit out of his peril
Ever after and this day.

KNOWLEDGE: Everyman, harken what I say:
    Go to priesthood, I you advise,
    And receive of him in any wise
    The holy sacrament and ointment together.
    Then shortly see ye turn again hither;
    We will all abide you here.

FIVE WITS: Yea, Everyman, hie you that ye ready were.
    There is no emperor, king, duke, ne baron,
    That of God hath commission
    As hath the least priest in the world being;
    For of the blessed sacraments pure and benign
    He beareth the keys, and thereof hath the cure[83]
    For man's redemption — it is ever sure —
    Which God for our soul's medicine
    Gave us out of his heart with great pine.
    Here in this transitory life, for thee and me,
    The blessed sacraments seven there be:
    Baptism, confirmation, with priesthood good,
    And the sacrament of God's precious flesh and blood,
    Marriage, the holy extreme unction, and penance;
    These seven be good to have in remembrance,
    Gracious sacraments of high divinity.

EVERYMAN: Fain would I receive that holy body,
    And meekly to my ghostly father I will go.

FIVE WITS: Everyman, that is the best that ye can do.
    God will you to salvation bring,
    For priesthood exceedeth all other thing:
    To us Holy Scripture they do teach,
    And converteth man from sin heaven to reach;
    God hath to them more power given
    Than to any angel that is in heaven.
    With five words[84] he may consecrate,

---

[81] bequest   [82] where   [83] charge   [84] *i.e., Hoc est enim corpus meum* (For this is my body); from the sacrament of the Eucharist

God's body in flesh and blood to make,
And handleth his Maker between his hands.
The priest bindeth and unbindeth all bands,
Both in earth and in heaven.
Thou ministers[85] all the sacraments seven;
Though we kissed thy feet, thou were worthy;
Thou art surgeon that cureth sin deadly:
No remedy we find under God
But all only[86] priesthood.
Everyman, God gave priests that dignity,
And setteth them in his stead among us to be;
Thus be they above angels in degree.

(EVERYMAN *goes to the priest to receive the last sacraments.*)

KNOWLEDGE: If priests be good, it is so,[87] surely.
But when Jesus hanged on the cross with great smart,
There he gave out of his blessed heart
The same sacrament in great torment:
He sold them not to us, that Lord omnipotent.
Therefore Saint Peter the apostle doth say
That Jesu's curse hath all they
Which God their Saviour do buy or sell,
Or they for any money do take or tell.[88]
Sinful priests giveth the sinners example bad;
Their children sitteth by other men's fires, I have heard;
And some haunteth women's company
With unclean life, as lusts of lechery:
These be with sin made blind.
FIVE WITS: I trust to God no such may we find;
Therefore let us priesthood honour,
And follow their doctrine for our souls' succour.
We be their sheep, and they shepherds be
By whom we all be kept in surety.
Peace, for yonder I see Everyman come,
Which hath made true satisfaction.
GOOD DEEDS: Methink it is he indeed.

(*Re-enter* EVERYMAN)

EVERYMAN: Now Jesu be your alder speed! [89]
I have received the sacrament for my redemption,
And then mine extreme unction:

85 administer   86 except   87 *i.e.*, "above angels in degree"   88 count
89 help to all of you

Blessed be all they that counselled me to take it!
And now, friends, let us go without longer respite;
I thank God that ye have tarried so long.
Now set each of you on this rood[90] your hand,
And shortly follow me:
I go before there I would be; God be our guide!

STRENGTH: Everyman, we will not from you go
Till ye have done this voyage long.

DISCRETION: I, Discretion, will bide by you also.

KNOWLEDGE: And though this pilgrimage be never so strong,[91]
I will never part you fro.

STRENGTH: Everyman, I will be as sure by thee
As ever I did by Judas Maccabee.[92]

(EVERYMAN *comes to his grave.*)

EVERYMAN: Alas, I am so faint I may not stand;
My limbs under me doth fold.
Friends, let us not turn again to this land,
Not for all the world's gold;
For into this cave must I creep
And turn to earth, and there to sleep.

BEAUTY: What, into this grave? Alas!

EVERYMAN: Yea, there shall ye consume, more and less.[93]

BEAUTY: And what, should I smother here?

EVERYMAN: Yea, by my faith, and never more appear.
In this world live no more we shall,
But in heaven before the highest Lord of all.

BEAUTY: I cross out all this; adieu, by Saint John!
I take my cap in my lap, and am gone.

EVERYMAN: What, Beauty, whither will ye?

BEAUTY: Peace, I am deaf; I look not behind me,
Not and thou wouldest give me all the gold in thy chest.

(*Exit* BEAUTY.)

EVERYMAN: Alas, whereto may I trust?
Beauty goeth fast away from me;
She promised with me to live and die.

STRENGTH: Everyman, I will thee also forsake and deny;
Thy game liketh me not at all.

EVERYMAN: Why, then, ye will forsake me all?

90 cross   91 hard, difficult   92 Jewish religious and national leader against Syria in the 2nd century B.C. He told his men that "the success of war is not in the multitude: but strength cometh from heaven." (Apocrypha, I Maccabees, 3:19)   93 high and low

Sweet Strength, tarry a little space.

STRENGTH: Nay, sir, by the rood of grace!
    I will hie me from thee fast,
    Though thou weep till thy heart to-brast.[94]

EVERYMAN: Ye would ever bide by me, ye said.

STRENGTH: Yea, I have you far enough conveyed.
    Ye be old enough, I understand,
    Your pilgrimage to take on hand;
    I repent me that I hither came.

EVERYMAN: Strength, you to displease I am to blame;
    Yet promise is debt, this ye well wot.

STRENGTH: In faith, I care not.
    Thou art but a fool to complain;
    You spend your speech and waste your brain.
    Go thrust thee into the ground!   (*Exit* STRENGTH.)

EVERYMAN: I had wend surer I should you have found.
    He that trusteth in his Strength
    She him deceiveth at the length.
    Both Strength and Beauty forsaketh me;
    Yet they promised me fair and lovingly.

DISCRETION: Everyman, I will after Strength be gone;
    As for me, I will leave you alone.

EVERYMAN: Why, Discretion, will ye forsake me?

DISCRETION: Yea, in faith, I will go from thee,
    For when Strength goeth before
    I follow after evermore.

EVERYMAN: Yet, I pray thee, for the love of the Trinity,
    Look in my grave once piteously.

DISCRETION: Nay, so nigh will I not come;
    Farewell, every one!   (*Exit* DISCRETION.)

EVERYMAN: O, all thing faileth, save God alone —
    Beauty, Strength, and Discretion;
    For when Death bloweth his blast,
    They all run from me full fast.

FIVE WITS: Everyman, my leave now of thee I take;
    I will follow the other, for here I thee forsake.

EVERYMAN: Alas, then may I wail and weep,
    For I took you for my best friend.

FIVE WITS: I will no longer thee keep;
    Now farewell, and there an end.   (*Exit* FIVE WITS.)

EVERYMAN: O Jesu, help! All hath forsaken me.

GOOD DEEDS: Nay, Everyman; I will bide with thee.

[94] broke to pieces

I will not forsake thee indeed;
Thou shalt find me a good friend at need.
EVERYMAN: Gramercy, Good Deeds! Now may I true friends see.
They have forsaken me, every one;
I loved them better than my Good Deeds alone.
Knowledge, will ye forsake me also?
KNOWLEDGE: Yea, Everyman, when ye to Death shall go;
But not yet, for no manner of danger.
EVERYMAN: Gramercy, Knowledge, with all my heart.
KNOWLEDGE: Nay, yet I will not from hence depart
Till I see where ye shall become.
EVERYMAN: Methink, alas, that I must be gone
To make my reckoning and my debts pay,
For I see my time is nigh spent away.
Take example, all ye that this do hear or see,
How they that I loved best do forsake me,
Except my Good Deeds that bideth truly.
GOOD DEEDS: All earthly things is but vanity:
Beauty, Strength, and Discretion do man forsake,
Foolish friends, and kinsmen, that fair spake —
All fleeth save Good Deeds, and that am I.
EVERYMAN: Have mercy on me, God most mighty;
And stand by me, thou mother and maid, holy Mary.
GOOD DEEDS: Fear not; I will speak for thee.
EVERYMAN: Here I cry God mercy.
GOOD DEEDS: Short[95] our end, and minish our pain;
Let us go and never come again.
EVERYMAN: Into thy hands, Lord, my soul I commend;
Receive it, Lord, that it be not lost.
As thou me boughtest, so me defend,
And save me from the fiend's boast,
That I may appear with that blessed host
That shall be saved at the day of doom.
In manus tuas, of mights most
For ever, *commendo spiritum meum.*[96]   (*He sinks into his grave.*)
KNOWLEDGE: Now hath he suffered that we all shall endure;
The Good Deeds shall make all sure.
Now hath he made ending;
Methinketh that I hear angels sing,
And make great joy and melody
Where Everyman's soul received shall be.
ANGEL: Come, excellent elect spouse, to Jesu!

[95] shorten   [96] into thy hands I commend my spirit (Luke, 23:46)

Hereabove thou shalt go
Because of thy singular virtue.
Now the soul is taken the body fro,
Thy reckoning is crystal-clear.
Now shalt thou into the heavenly sphere,
Unto the which all ye shall come
That liveth well before the day of doom.

(*Enter* DOCTOR)

DOCTOR: This moral men may have in mind.
Ye hearers, take it of worth,[97] old and young,
And forsake Pride, for he deceiveth you in the end;
And remember Beauty, Five Wits, Strength, and Discretion,
They all at the last do every man forsake,
Save[98] his Good Deeds there doth he take.
But beware, for and they be small
Before God, he hath no help at all;
None excuse may be there for every man.
Alas, how shall he do then?
For after death amends may no man make,
For then mercy and pity doth him forsake.
If his reckoning be not clear when he doth come,
God will say: '*Ite, maledicti, in ignem eternum.*' [99]
And he that hath his account whole and sound,
High in heaven he shall be crowned;
Unto which place God bring us all thither,
That we may live body and soul together.
Thereto help the Trinity!
Amen, say ye, for saint charity.

Thus Endeth this Moral Play of EVERYMAN.

❧ EVERYMAN is a morality play, a kind of drama that flourished in Western Europe during the later Middle Ages (fourteenth to sixteenth centuries) and in England influenced Elizabethan drama.

Though independent of the drama of antiquity, medieval drama, like the drama of the Greeks, had a religious origin. After the collapse of the Graeco-Roman civilization and during the subsequent "dark ages" in Europe, theatrical activity was largely limited to

[97] value it   [98] unless   [99] depart, ye cursed, into everlasting fire (Matthew, 25:41)

travelling troupes of jugglers, minstrels, and acrobats. The Catholic Church was cool to mimetic performance by such vagabonds and looked upon the remaining pagan theaters as temples of sin, but it was the Church itself that revived drama. From as early as the tenth century there is a record of church dramatization (the use of impersonation and dialogue) of a short Biblical scene, the meeting of the Angel and the three women at Christ's tomb on Easter morning. For such performances, given within the church itself as part of the holy service, words and melodies were added to the Biblical text. Such additions were known as *tropes*. In time, performances of tropes became more elaborate, turning into short plays called, particularly in England, "miracles" and, particularly in France, "mysteries." After the Pope instituted the Feast of Corpus Christi in 1264, tropes became part of the celebration of the Feast. In England, performance of miracles was common after celebration of the Feast of Corpus Christi had become regular in 1311. Miracles were popular with both clergy and congregation. Their language soon became the vernacular, and they thus served to make Christian lore imaginatively real for largely illiterate worshippers to whom the Latin liturgy was unintelligible. In England, by the fourteenth century, miracles and mysteries were for the most part performed outside the church and the church precincts, partly because performances were becoming quite lengthy and elaborate and partly because the growing use of comic characters introduced a worldly and unseemly element. Selected members of the various town guilds performed one of the plays of a larger cycle of plays. The sacred story given a guild to dramatize was often one that was felt to be appropriate to that guild's craft, as when the water carriers enacted the Flood and the carpenters the Crucifixion. Most frequently, the cycle plays were staged on platforms on wheels, appearing in sequence before stationary audiences along a route through the town.

Despite the obvious religious content of *Everyman*, the moralities in general represent a further secularization of the older church plays. Rather than stories from the Bible or from saints' lives, the moralities dramatize more universal moral or religious concepts, like the struggle between Good and Evil for man's soul, or man's perilous road through life to perdition or salvation. The morality is an allegory, and its characters are personified abstractions with names like Youth, Mankind, Everyman, Vice, Vanity, World, Death. This does not mean they are without individualizing, realistic traits — even comical ones, like Cousin's excuse for not going with Everyman: "No, by our Lady! I have the cramp in my toe."

Everyman is the best known of the medieval moralities. Most authorities date it about 1500 and believe the English play to be derived from a contemporary Dutch original. The earliest extant English texts were printed during the first third of the sixteenth century.

At a first reading, *Everyman* may seem like a quaint, longwinded, somewhat simpleminded statement of venerable Christian platitudes, dotted with undigested bits of theology and of church polemic against the selling of holy offices. The characters may seem wooden with abstraction, the verse so unmusical as to detract from the edifying message, and the plot uncomplicated to the point of nonexistence.

To take the last charge first: there *is* a plot in *Everyman*. With sure sense of dramatic economy the playwright gives us no view of Everyman's earlier, indulgent self, but there is nothing vague about the last phase of his life that we do see — the movement from complacency through despair and Christian regeneration to the good end of the Latin phrases he intones as he enters his grave. There is a distinct point of reversal and an unexpected complication as Everyman's fortune dips a second time. To answer why he is able to bear the second desertion better than the first is to define the nature of his growing spiritual strength, as regeneration follows despair. The formal parallelism between the two desertion scenes calls attention to their thematic link and indicates a degree of conscious literary craftsmanship in the author. The longer one contemplates the plot of *Everyman*, the more one becomes conscious of how much compressed dramatic tension, psychological truth, theological sophistication, and formal beauty are concealed beneath the surface naïveté.

Everyman himself is both individual man and mankind — both the shallow sensualist who tries to bribe Death and the collective object of God's all-embracing concern. The limits of his function are marked, at one end, by the pathetic lameness of his reply when Death asks him if he really had thought his worldly goods were his to keep:

> I had wend so, verily

and, at the other, by God's magnificent:

> I hoped well that every man
> In my glory should make his mansion,
> And thereto I had them all elect.

The personification is more than a mechanical device; the pronominal significance is the essence of the play, its key metaphor. The tension between the specific and the general meaning of the name helps to explain the play's terrifying relevance. The other characters, too, are more than abstractions. Among them, they cover a range of wryly perceived human realities. There is the irony of Fellowship's effusive protestations of undying loyalty — all the more ironic for being unsolicited; there are Death's solemn colloquialisms; there are the little touches that distinguish Cousin from Kindred; there is the sense of a human personality in God's:

> I could do no more than I did, truly.

With this last speech we are moving into the esoteric areas of the play. It raises issues concerning God's ways with men, has eschatological implications.

If it is true that the verse hobbles, it is also true that its very roughness contributes to the play's mood, to its air of homespun earnestness, its stark though childlike commitment to an urgent concern with the one thing that really matters in a Christian life. Musical lilt would have worked against its purpose. It may even be possible to show that the prosody is not quite so haphazard as it may seem at first. The shorter, three-stressed lines and the masculine endings have a way of turning up in passages of special momentousness.

And there is hardly anything trite about the play's sense of the brevity of human life, of the falling-off of the things of the world, of living under sentence of death, of wanting to warn us all. Even non-Christians will understand what the critic had in mind who said that after *Everyman* all other plays somehow seem to deal with inessentials.)⁓

William Shakespeare

MACBETH

Characters

DUNCAN, *King of Scotland*

MALCOLM
DONALBAIN } *his sons*

MACBETH
BANQUO } *generals of the King's army*

MACDUFF
LENNOX
ROSS
MENTEITH } *noblemen of Scotland*
ANGUS
CAITHNESS

FLEANCE, *son to* BANQUO

SIWARD, *earl of Northumberland, commanding the English forces*

YOUNG SIWARD, *his son*

SEYTON, *an officer attending on* MACBETH

BOY, *son to* MACDUFF

AN ENGLISH DOCTOR

A SCOTTISH DOCTOR

A CAPTAIN

A PORTER

AN OLD MAN

LADY MACBETH

LADY MACDUFF

GENTLEWOMAN, *attending on* LADY MACBETH

HECATE

THREE WITCHES

APPARITIONS

LORDS, GENTLEMEN, OFFICERS, SOLDIERS, MURDERERS, ATTENDANTS,
and MESSENGERS

SCENE: *Scotland, England*

ACT I

Scene 1 [Scotland. An open place.]

(*Thunder and lightning. Enter three* WITCHES.)

FIRST WITCH: When shall we three meet again
In thunder, lightning, or in rain?
SECOND WITCH: When the hurlyburly's[1] done,
When the battle's lost and won.
THIRD WITCH: That will be ere the set of sun.
FIRST WITCH: Where the place?
SECOND WITCH: Upon the heath.
THIRD WITCH: There to meet with Macbeth.
FIRST WITCH: I come, Graymalkin! [2]
SECOND WITCH: Paddock[2] calls.
THIRD WITCH: Anon! [3]
ALL: Fair is foul, and foul is fair.
Hover through the fog and filthy air. (*Exeunt.*)

Scene 2 [A camp near Forres.]

(*Alarum[4] within.[5] Enter* KING [DUNCAN], MALCOLM, DONALBAIN,
LENNOX, *with* ATTENDANTS, *meeting a bleeding* CAPTAIN.)

KING: What bloody man is that? He can report,
As seemeth by his plight, of the revolt
The newest state.
MALCOLM: This is the sergeant
Who like a good and hardy soldier fought
'Gainst my captivity. Hail, brave friend!
Say to the King the knowledge of the broil
As thou didst leave it.
CAPTAIN: Doubtful it stood,
As two spent swimmers that do cling together
And choke their art.[6] The merciless Macdonwald
(Worthy to be a rebel, for to that[7]
The multiplying villainies of nature
Do swarm upon him) from the Western Isles
Of kerns and gallowglasses[8] is supplied;

---

[1] *i.e.,* the battle in progress [2] the witches' attendant spirits, a cat and a toad, respectively [3] at once! (*i.e.,* we're coming!) [4] trumpet call to arms [5] off stage [6] hamper one another's skill [7] to that end [8] Irish soldiers, respectively lightly armed infantry and cavalry armed with axes

And Fortune, on his damned quarrel smiling,
Showed like a rebel's whore. But all's too weak;
For brave Macbeth (well he deserves that name),
Disdaining Fortune, with his brandished steel,
Which smoked with bloody execution
(Like valor's minion[9]), carved out his passage
Till he faced the slave;
Which ne'er shook hands nor bade farewell to him
Till he unseamed him from the nave[10] to the chops
And fixed his head upon our battlements.

KING: O valiant cousin![11] worthy gentleman!

CAPTAIN: As whence the sun 'gins his reflection[12]
Shipwracking storms and direful thunders break,
So from that spring whence comfort seemed to come
Discomfort swells. Mark, King of Scotland, mark.
No sooner justice had, with valor armed,
Compelled these skipping kerns to trust their heels
But the Norweyan lord, surveying vantage,[13]
With furbished arms and new supplies of men,
Began a fresh assault.

KING: Dismayed not this
Our captains, Macbeth and Banquo?

CAPTAIN: Yes,
As sparrows eagles, or the hare the lion.
If I say sooth, I must report they were
As cannons overcharged with double cracks, so they
Doubly redoubled strokes upon the foe.
Except[14] they meant to bathe in reeking wounds,
Or memorize another Golgotha,
I cannot tell —
But I am faint; my gashes cry for help.

KING: So well thy words become thee as thy wounds;
They smack of honor both. Go get him surgeons.

(*Exit* CAPTAIN, *attended.*)

(*Enter* ROSS *and* ANGUS.)

Who comes here?

MALCOLM: The worthy Thane of Ross.

LENNOX: What a haste looks through his eyes! So should he look
That seems to speak things strange.

---

9 darling   10 navel   11 Acc. to Holinshed, this was the relationship between Duncan and Macbeth.   12 *i.e.*, from the east   13 seeing opportunity
14 unless

ROSS: God save the King!

KING: Whence cam'st thou, worthy thane?

ROSS: From Fife, great King,
  Where the Norweyan banners flout the sky
  And fan our people cold. Norway himself,[15]
  With terrible numbers,
  Assisted by that most disloyal traitor
  The Thane of Cawdor, began a dismal[16] conflict,
  Till that Bellona's bridegroom,[17] lapped in proof,[18]
  Confronted him with self-comparisons,[19]
  Point against point, rebellious arm 'gainst arm,
  Curbing his lavish spirit; and to conclude,
  The victory fell on us.

KING: Great happiness!

ROSS: That now
  Sweno, the Norways' king, craves composition;[20]
  Nor would we deign him burial of his men
  Till he disbursed, at Saint Colme's Inch,
  Ten thousand dollars to our general use.

KING: No more that Thane of Cawdor shall deceive
  Our[21] bosom[22] interest. Go pronounce his present[23] death
  And with his former title greet Macbeth.

ROSS: I'll see it done.

KING: What he hath lost noble Macbeth hath won.   (*Exeunt.*)

Scene 3 [A heath near Forres.]

(*Thunder. Enter the three* WITCHES.)

FIRST WITCH: Where hast thou been, sister?

SECOND WITCH: Killing swine.

THIRD WITCH: Sister, where thou?

FIRST WITCH: A sailor's wife had chestnuts in her lap
  And mounched and mounched and mounched. "Give me," quoth I.
  "Aroint thee,[24] witch!" the rump-fed[25] ronyon[26] cries.
  Her husband's to Aleppo gone, master o' the "Tiger";
  But in a sieve I'll thither sail
  And, like a rat without a tail,

---

[15] the king of Norway   [16] disastrous   [17] *i.e.*, Macbeth (B. was the Roman goddess of war)   [18] clad in proven armor   [19] *i.e.*, matching skill and equipment   [20] asks for terms   [21] my (the royal we)   [22] dearest, most vital   [23] immediate   [24] begone   [25] fat-rumped   [26] scabby creature

I'll do, I'll do, and I'll do.
SECOND WITCH: I'll give thee a wind.
FIRST WITCH: Th' art kind.
THIRD WITCH: And I another.
FIRST WITCH: I myself have all the other,
    And the very ports they blow,
    All the quarters that they know
    I' the shipman's card.[27]
    I'll drain him dry as hay.
    Sleep shall neither night nor day
    Hang upon his penthouse lid.[28]
    He shall live a man forbid.[29]
    Weary sev'nights, nine times nine,
    Shall he dwindle, peak, and pine.[30]
    Though his bark cannot be lost,
    Yet it shall be tempest-tost.
    Look what I have.
SECOND WITCH: Show me! show me!
FIRST WITCH: Here I have a pilot's thumb,
    Wracked as homeward he did come.

(*Drum within.*)

THIRD WITCH: A drum, a drum!
    Macbeth doth come.
ALL: The Weird[31] Sisters, hand in hand,
    Posters[32] of the sea and land,
    Thus do go about, about,
    Thrice to thine, and thrice to mine,
    And thrice again, to make up nine.
    Peace! The charm's wound up.

(*Enter* MACBETH *and* BANQUO.)

MACBETH: So foul and fair a day I have not seen.
BANQUO: How far is't called to Forres? What are these,
    So withered, and so wild in their attire,
    That look not like the inhabitants o' the earth,
    And yet are on't? Live you? or are you aught
    That man may question? You seem to understand me,
    By each at once her choppy[33] finger laying
    Upon her skinny lips. You should be women,

[27] compass card; or: chart   [28] *i.e.*, eyelid   [29] accursed and (hence) shunned   [30] all roughly synonymous   [31] serving fate   [32] messengers [33] chapped

And yet your beards forbid me to interpret
That you are so.

MACBETH: Speak, if you can. What are you?

FIRST WITCH: All hail, Macbeth! Hail to thee, Thane of Glamis!

SECOND WITCH: All hail, Macbeth! Hail to thee, Thane of Cawdor!

THIRD WITCH: All hail, Macbeth, that shalt be King hereafter!

BANQUO: Good sir, why do you start and seem to fear
   Things that do sound so fair? I' the name of truth.
   Are ye fantastical,[34] or that indeed
   Which outwardly ye show? My noble partner
   You greet with present grace and great prediction
   Of noble having and of royal hope,
   That he seems rapt withal.[35] To me you speak not.
   If you can look into the seeds of time
   And say which grain will grow and which will not,
   Speak then to me, who neither beg nor fear
   Your favors nor your hate.

FIRST WITCH: Hail!

SECOND WITCH: Hail!

THIRD WITCH: Hail!

FIRST WITCH: Lesser than Macbeth, and greater.

SECOND WITCH: Not so happy, yet much happier.

THIRD WITCH: Thou shalt get[36] kings, though thou be none.
   So all hail, Macbeth and Banquo!

FIRST WITCH: Banquo and Macbeth, all hail!

MACBETH: Stay, you imperfect speakers, tell me more!
   By Sinel's[37] death I know I am Thane of Glamis,
   But how of Cawdor? The Thane of Cawdor lives,
   A prosperous gentleman; and to be King
   Stands not within the prospect of belief,
   No more than to be Cawdor. Say from whence
   You owe[38] this strange intelligence, or why
   Upon this blasted heath you stop our way
   With such prophetic greeting. Speak, I charge you.

   (WITCHES *vanish.*)

BANQUO: The earth hath bubbles, as the water has,
   And these are of them. Whither are they vanished?

MACBETH: Into the air, and what seemed corporal[39] melted
   As breath into the wind. Would they had stayed!

BANQUO: Were such things here as we do speak about?

[34] imaginary   [35] therewith   [36] beget   [37] Macbeth's father, acc. to
Holinshed   [38] have   [39] corporeal

Or have we eaten on the insane[40] root
That takes the reason prisoner?
MACBETH: Your children shall be kings.
BANQUO: You shall be King.
MACBETH: And Thane of Cawdor too. Went it not so?
BANQUO: To the selfsame tune and words. Who's here?

(*Enter* ROSS *and* ANGUS.)

ROSS: The King hath happily received, Macbeth,
    The news of thy success; and when he reads
    Thy personal venture in the rebels' fight,
    His wonders and his praises do contend
    Which should be thine or his. Silenced with that,[41]
    In viewing o'er the rest o' the selfsame day,
    He finds thee in the stout[42] Norweyan ranks,
    Nothing afeard of what thyself didst make,
    Strange images of death. As thick as hail
    Came post with post, and every one did bear
    Thy praises in his kingdom's great defense
    And poured them down before him.
ANGUS: We are sent
    To give thee from our royal master thanks;
    Only to herald thee into his sight,
    Not pay thee.
ROSS: And for an earnest of a greater honor,
    He bade me, from him, call thee Thane of Cawdor;
    In which addition,[43] hail, most worthy Thane!
    For it is thine.
BANQUO: What, can the devil speak true?
MACBETH: The Thane of Cawdor lives. Why do you dress me
    In borrowed robes?
ANGUS: Who was the Thane lives yet,
    But under heavy judgment bears that life
    Which he deserves to lose. Whether he was combined
    With those of Norway, or did line[44] the rebel
    With hidden help and vantage, or that with both
    He labored in his country's wrack, I know not;
    But treasons capital, confessed and proved,
    Have overthrown him.
MACBETH (*Aside*):   Glamis, and Thane of Cawdor!

[40] making insane   [41] *i.e.*, the conflict within him between his tongue-tying wonder and his desire to praise Macbeth   [42] brave   [43] additional title [44] strengthen

The greatest is behind.[45] — (*To* ROSS *and* ANGUS.) Thanks for your
   pains.
(*Aside to* BANQUO) Do you not hope your children shall be kings,
When those that gave the Thane of Cawdor to me
Promised no less to them?
BANQUO (*Aside to* MACBETH): That, trusted home,[46]
   Might yet enkindle you unto the crown,
   Besides the Thane[47] of Cawdor. But 'tis strange!
   And oftentimes, to win us to our harm,
   The instruments of darkness tell us truths,
   Win us with honest trifles, to betray's
   In deepest consequence. —
   Cousins, a word, I pray you.
MACBETH (*Aside*): Two truths are told,
   As happy prologues to the swelling act
   Of the imperial theme. — I thank you, gentlemen. —
   (*Aside*) This supernatural soliciting
   Cannot be ill; cannot be good. If ill,
   Why hath it given me earnest of success,
   Commencing in a truth? I am Thane of Cawdor.
   If good, why do I yield to that suggestion
   Whose horrid image doth unfix my hair
   And make my seated heart knock at my ribs
   Against the use[48] of nature? Present fears
   Are less than horrible imaginings.
   My thought, whose murder yet is but fantastical,
   Shakes so my single[49] state of man that function
   Is smothered in surmise and nothing is
   But what is not.
BANQUO: Look how our partner's rapt.
MACBETH (*Aside*): If chance will have me King, why, chance may
   crown me,
   Without my stir.
BANQUO: New honors come upon him,
   Like our strange garments, cleave not to their mold
   But with the aid of use.
MACBETH (*Aside*): Come what come may,
   Time and the hour runs through the roughest day.
BANQUO: Worthy Macbeth, we stay upon[50] your leisure.
MACBETH: Give me your favor.[51] My dull brain was wrought
   With things forgotten. Kind gentlemen, your pains

[45] to come   [46] all the way   [47] thanedom   [48] habit   [49] unaided;
or: undivided, whole   [50] await   [51] pardon

Are registered where every day I turn
The leaf to read them.[52] Let us toward the King.
(*Aside to* BANQUO) Think upon what hath chanced, and, at more
time,
The interim having weighed it, let us speak
Our free hearts each to other.

BANQUO (*Aside to* MACBETH):   Very gladly.

MACBETH (*Aside to* BANQUO): Till then, enough. — Come, friends.

                (*Exeunt.*)

Scene 4 [Forres. The Palace.]

(*Flourish. Enter* KING [DUNCAN], LENNOX, MALCOLM, DONALBAIN,
and ATTENDANTS.)

KING: Is execution done on Cawdor? Are not
Those in commission yet returned?

MALCOLM: My liege,
They are not yet come back. But I have spoke
With one that saw him die; who did report
That very frankly he confessed his treasons,
Implored your Highness' pardon, and set forth
A deep repentance. Nothing in his life
Became him like the leaving it. He died
As one that had been studied[53] in his death
To throw away the dearest thing he owed[54]
As 'twere a careless trifle.

KING: There's no art
To find the mind's construction[55] in[56] the face.
He was a gentleman on whom I built
An absolute trust.

(*Enter* MACBETH, BANQUO, ROSS, *and* ANGUS.)

            O worthiest cousin,
The sin of my ingratitude even now
Was heavy on me! Thou art so far before[57]
That swiftest wing of recompense is slow
To overtake thee. Would thou hadst less deserved,
That the proportion[58] both of thanks and payment
Might have been mine! Only I have left to say,
More is thy due than more than all can pay.

---

[52] *i.e.,* in my mind   [53] rehearsed   [54] owned   [55] read the mind   [56] by
means of   [57] ahead (in merit)   [58] proper adjustment

MACBETH: The service and the loyalty I owe,
In doing it pays itself. Your Highness' part
Is to receive our duties; and our duties
Are to your throne and state children and servants,
Which do but what they should by doing everything
Safe toward your love and honor.

KING: Welcome hither.
I have begun to plant thee and will labor
To make thee full of growing. Noble Banquo,
That hast no less deserved, nor must be known
No less to have done so, let me infold[59] thee
And hold thee to my heart.

BANQUO: There if I grow,
The harvest is your own.

KING: My plenteous joys,
Wanton[60] in fullness, seek to hide themselves
In drops of sorrow. Sons, kinsmen, thanes,
And you whose places are the nearest, know
We will establish our estate upon
Our eldest, Malcolm, whom we name hereafter
The Prince of Cumberland; which honor must
Not unaccompanied invest him only,
But signs of nobleness, like stars, shall shine
On all deservers. From hence to Inverness,
And bind us further to you.

MACBETH: The rest[61] is labor, which is not used for you.
I'll be myself the harbinger, and make joyful
The hearing of my wife with your approach;
So, humbly take my leave.

KING: My worthy Cawdor!

MACBETH (*Aside*): The Prince of Cumberland! That is a step
On which I must fall down, or else o'erleap,
For in my way it lies. Stars, hide your fires!
Let not light see my black and deep desires.
The eye wink at[62] the hand; yet let that be,
Which the eye fears, when it is done, to see.   (*Exit.*)

KING: True, worthy Banquo: he is full so valiant,
And in his commendations I am fed;
It is a banquet to me. Let's after him,
Whose care is gone before to bid us welcome.
It is a peerless kinsman.   (*Flourish. Exeunt.*)

---

[59] embrace   [60] unrestrained; or: perverse (since joy makes him weep)
[61] leisure   [62] deliberately ignore

Scene 5 [Inverness. Macbeth's Castle.]

(*Enter* MACBETH'S WIFE, *alone, with a letter.*)

LADY (*Reads*): "They met me in the day of success; and I have learned by the perfect'st report they have more in them than mortal knowledge. When I burned in desire to question them further, they made themselves air, into which they vanished. Whiles I stood rapt in the wonder of it, came missives from the King, who all-hailed me Thane of Cawdor, by which title, before, these Weird Sisters saluted me, and referred me to the coming on of time with 'Hail, King that shalt be!' This have I thought good to deliver thee, my dearest partner of greatness, that thou mightst not lose the dues of rejoicing by being ignorant of what greatness is promised thee. Lay it to thy heart, and farewell."

Glamis thou art, and Cawdor, and shalt be
What thou art promised. Yet do I fear thy nature.
It is too full o' the milk of human kindness
To catch the nearest way. Thou wouldst be great;
Art not without ambition, but without
The illness[63] should attend it. What thou wouldst highly,
That wouldst thou holily; wouldst not play false,
And yet wouldst wrongly win. Thou'ldst have, great Glamis,
That which cries "Thus thou must do," if thou have it;
And that[64] which rather thou dost fear to do
Than wishest should be undone.[65] Hie thee hither,
That I may pour my spirits in thine ear
And chastise with the valor of my tongue
All that impedes thee from the golden round[66]
Which fate and metaphysical[67] aid doth seem
To have thee crowned withal.[68]

(*Enter* MESSENGER.)

                              What is your tidings?
MESSENGER: The King comes here tonight.
LADY: Thou'rt mad to say it!
   Is not thy master with him? who, were't so,
   Would have informed for preparation.

---

[63] evil   [64] *i.e.,* the murder of Duncan   [65] not done. The passage is disputed. Lady Macbeth seems to think that her husband desires (or lacks) both the crown and Duncan's murder (or, perhaps, both the decisiveness to do the murder and the accomplished murder itself).   [66] *i.e.,* the crown   [67] supernatural   [68] with

MESSENGER: So please you, it is true. Our Thane is coming.
One of my fellows had the speed of him,
Who, almost dead for breath, had scarcely more
Than would make up his message.

LADY: Give him tending;
He brings great news. (*Exit* MESSENGER.)
The raven himself is hoarse
That croaks the fatal entrance of Duncan
Under my battlements. Come, you spirits
That tend on mortal thoughts, unsex me here,
And fill me, from the crown to the toe, top-full
Of direst cruelty! Make thick my blood;
Stop up the access and passage to remorse,
That no compunctious visitings of nature
Shake my fell[69] purpose nor keep peace between
The effect and it! Come to my woman's breasts
And take my milk for[70] gall, you murd'ring ministers,
Wherever in your sightless substances
You wait on nature's mischief! Come, thick night,
And pall thee in the dunnest[71] smoke of hell,
That my keen knife see not the wound it makes,
Nor heaven peep through the blanket of the dark
To cry "Hold, hold!"

(*Enter* MACBETH.)

Great Glamis! worthy Cawdor!
Greater than both, by the all-hail hereafter!
Thy letters have transported me beyond
This ignorant present, and I feel now
The future in the instant.

MACBETH: My dearest love,
Duncan comes here tonight.

LADY: And when goes hence?

MACBETH: Tomorrow, as he purposes.

LADY: O, never
Shall sun that morrow see!
Your face, my Thane, is as a book where men
May read strange matters. To beguile the time,[72]
Look like the time; bear welcome in your eye,
Your hand, your tongue; look like the innocent flower,
But be the serpent under't. He that's coming

[69] fierce, cruel   [70] in exchange for   [71] blackest   [72] *i.e.*, people, "the world"

Must be provided for; and you shall put
This night's great business into my dispatch,[73]
Which shall to all our nights and days to come
Give solely sovereign sway and masterdom.

MACBETH: We will speak further.

LADY: Only look up clear.
To alter favor ever is to fear.[74]
Leave all the rest to me.   (*Exeunt.*)

Scene 6 [The same. Before Macbeth's Castle.]

(*Hautboys*[75] *and torches. Enter* KING [DUNCAN], MALCOLM, DONALBAIN, BANQUO, LENNOX, MACDUFF, ROSS, ANGUS, *and* ATTENDANTS.)

KING: This castle hath a pleasant seat.[76] The air
Nimbly and sweetly recommends itself
Unto our gentle senses.

BANQUO: This guest of summer,
The temple-haunting martlet,[77] does approve
By his loved mansionry that the heaven's breath
Smells wooingly here. No jutty, frieze,
Buttress, nor coign[78] of vantage, but this bird
Hath made his pendent bed and procreant cradle.
Where they most breed and haunt, I have observed
The air is delicate.

(*Enter* LADY [MACBETH].)

KING: See, see, our honored hostess!
The love that follows us sometime is our trouble,
Which still we thank as love. Herein I teach you
How you shall bid God 'ield us for your pains
And thank us for your trouble.[79]

LADY: All our service
In every point twice done, and then done double,
Were poor and single business to contend
Against those honors deep and broad wherewith
Your Majesty loads our house. For those of old,

73 management   74 to change expression is dangerous; or: is to show fear
75 oboe players   76 location   77 martin (a bird of the swallow family)
78 corner   79 Duncan means something like this: Even when love is troublesome, we (or I, the King) are grateful to it for being love. Thus, though my visit may be troublesome to you, you ought to ask God to reward me for it and be grateful to me yourselves.

And the late dignities heaped up to them,
We rest your hermits.[80]

KING: Where's the Thane of Cawdor?
We coursed him at the heels and had a purpose
To be his purveyor;[81] but he rides well,
And his great love, sharp as his spur, hath holp him
To his home before us. Fair and noble hostess,
We are your guest tonight.

LADY: Your servants ever
Have theirs, themselves, and what is theirs, in compt,[82]
To make their audit[83] at your Highness' pleasure,
Still[84] to return your own.

KING: Give me your hand;
Conduct me to mine host. We love him highly
And shall continue our graces toward him.
By your leave, hostess.   (*Exeunt.*)

Scene 7 [The same. Macbeth's Castle.]

(*Hautboys. Torches. Enter a* SEWER,[85] *and divers* SERVANTS *with
dishes and service over the stage. Then enter* MACBETH.)

MACBETH: If it were done when 'tis done, then 'twere well
It were done quickly. If the assassination
Could trammel up[86] the consequence, and catch,
With his[87] surcease,[88] success, that but this blow
Might be the be-all and the end-all here,
But here, upon this bank and shoal of time,
We'ld jump the life to come. But in these cases
We still have judgment here, that[89] we but teach
Bloody instructions, which, being taught, return
To plague the inventor. This even-handed justice
Commends the ingredience[90] of our poisoned chalice
To our own lips. He's here in double trust:
First, as I am his kinsman and his subject,
Strong both against the deed; then, as his host,
Who should against his murderer shut the door,
Not bear the knife myself. Besides, this Duncan
Hath borne his faculties so meek, hath been
So clear[91] in his great office, that his virtues

[80] beadsmen (holy men who pray for others)   [81] forerunner   [82] subject to
account, in trust   [83] giving of account   [84] always   [85] chief servant, butler   [86] entangle in a net   [87] Duncan's; or: the assassination's   [88] cessa-
tion, end   [89] so that; or: in that   [90] ingredients   [91] blameless

Will plead like angels, trumpet-tongued, against
The deep damnation of his taking-off;
And pity, like a naked new-born babe,
Striding the blast, or heaven's cherubin, horsed
Upon the sightless couriers[92] of the air,
Shall blow the horrid deed in every eye,
That tears shall drown the wind. I have no spur
To prick the sides of my intent, but only
Vaulting ambition, which o'erleaps itself
And falls on the other —

(*Enter* LADY [MACBETH].)

How now? What news?
LADY: He has almost supped. Why have you left the chamber?
MACBETH: Hath he asked for me?
LADY: Know you not he has?
MACBETH: We will proceed no further in this business.
He hath honored me of late, and I have bought
Golden opinions from all sorts of people,
Which would be worn now in their newest gloss,
Not cast aside so soon.
LADY: Was the hope drunk
Wherein you dressed yourself? Hath it slept since?
And wakes it now to look so green and pale
At what it did so freely? From this time
Such I account thy love. Art thou afeard
To be the same in thine own act and valor
As thou art in desire? Wouldst thou have that
Which thou esteem'st the ornament of life,
And live a coward in thine own esteem,
Letting "I dare not" wait upon "I would,"
Like the poor cat i' the adage? [93]
MACBETH: Prithee peace!
I dare do all that may become a man.
Who dares do more is none.
LADY: What beast was't then
That made you break this enterprise to me?
When you durst do it, then you were a man;
And to be more than what you were, you would
Be so much more the man. Nor time nor place
Did then adhere,[94] and yet you would make both.

92 winds   93 "the cat would have fish but would not wet her feet"
94 were then opportune

They have made themselves, and that their fitness now
Does unmake you. I have given suck, and know
How tender 'tis to love the babe that milks me.
I would, while it was smiling in my face,
Have plucked my nipple from his boneless gums
And dashed the brains out, had I so sworn as you
Have done to this.

MACBETH: If we should fail?

LADY: We fail?
But[95] screw your courage to the sticking place,[96]
And we'll not fail. When Duncan is asleep
(Whereto the rather shall his day's hard journey
Soundly invite him), his two chamberlains
Will I with wine and wassail so convince[97]
That memory, the warder of the brain,
Shall be a fume, and the receipt[98] of reason
A limbeck[99] only. When in swinish sleep
Their drenched natures lie as in a death,
What cannot you and I perform upon
The unguarded Duncan? what not put upon
His spongy officers, who shall bear the guilt
Of our great quell? [100]

MACBETH: Bring forth men-children only,
For thy undaunted mettle should compose
Nothing but males. Will it not be received,
When we have marked with blood those sleepy two
Of his own chamber and used their very daggers,
That they have done't?

LADY: Who dares receive it other,
As we shall make our griefs and clamor roar
Upon his death?

MACBETH: I am settled and bend up
Each corporal agent to this terrible feat.
Away, and mock the time with fairest show;
False face must hide what the false heart doth know. (*Exeunt.*)

[95] only [96] notch (on a crossbow) [97] overcome [98] container [99] top
of the retort, to which the fumes rise during distillation [100] killing

ACT II

Scene 1 [The same. Court of Macbeth's Castle.]

(*Enter* BANQUO, *and* FLEANCE *with a torch before him.*)

BANQUO: How goes the night, boy?

FLEANCE: The moon is down; I have not heard the clock.

BANQUO: And she goes down at twelve.

FLEANCE: I take't, 'tis later, sir.

BANQUO: Hold, take my sword. There's husbandry[101] in heaven;
  Their candles are all out. Take thee that[102] too.
  A heavy summons lies like lead upon me,
  And yet I would not sleep. Merciful powers,
  Restrain in me the cursed thoughts that nature
  Gives way to in repose!

(*Enter* MACBETH, *and a* SERVANT *with a torch.*)

                         Give me my sword.
  Who's there?

MACBETH: A friend.

BANQUO: What, sir, not yet at rest? The King's abed.
  He hath been in unusual pleasure and
  Sent forth great largess to your offices.[103]
  This diamond he greets your wife withal
  By the name of most kind hostess, and shut up[104]
  In measureless content.

MACBETH: Being unprepared,
  Our will became the servant to defect,
  Which else should free have wrought.

BANQUO: All's well.
  I dreamt last night of the three Weird Sisters.
  To you they have showed some truth.

MACBETH: I think not of them.
  Yet when we can entreat an hour to serve,
  We would spend it in some words upon that business,
  If you would grant the time.

BANQUO: At your kind'st leisure.

MACBETH: If you shall cleave to my consent,[105] when 'tis,[106]

---

[101] thrift [102] his dagger (?) [103] household departments (*i.e.*, the servants) [104] concluded [105] support me [106] at the proper time (*i.e.*, the
time for choosing a new king after Duncan's death)

It shall make honor for you.
BANQUO: So I lose none
In seeking to augment it but still keep
My bosom franchised[107] and allegiance clear,
I shall be counseled.
MACBETH: Good repose the while!
BANQUO: Thanks, sir. The like to you! (*Exeunt* BANQUO *and* FLEANCE.)
MACBETH: Go bid thy mistress, when my drink is ready,
She strike upon the bell. Get thee to bed.   (*Exit* SERVANT.)
Is this a dagger which I see before me,
The handle toward my hand? Come, let me clutch thee!
I have thee not, and yet I see thee still.
Art thou not, fatal vision, sensible
To feeling as to sight? or art thou but
A dagger of the mind, a false creation,
Proceeding from the heat-oppressed brain?
I see thee yet, in form as palpable
As this which now I draw.
Thou marshal'st[108] me the way that I was going,
And such an instrument I was to use.
Mine eyes are made the fools o' the other senses,
Or else worth all the rest. I see thee still;
And on thy blade and dudgeon[109] gouts[110] of blood,
Which was not so before. There's no such thing.
It is the bloody business which informs
Thus to mine eyes. Now o'er the one half-world
Nature seems dead, and wicked dreams abuse[111]
The curtained sleep. Witchcraft celebrates
Pale Hecate's[112] offerings; and withered murder,
Alarumed by his sentinel, the wolf,
Whose howl's his watch, thus with his stealthy pace,
With Tarquin's[113] ravishing strides, toward his design
Moves like a ghost. Thou sure and firm-set earth,
Hear not my steps which way they walk, for fear
Thy very stones prate of my whereabout
And take the present horror[114] from the time,
Which now suits with it. Whiles I threat, he lives;
Words to the heat of deeds too cold breath gives.

(*A bell rings.*)

[107] in free tenure; or: free from guilt   [108] lead   [109] wooden handle
[110] drops   [111] deceive   [112] goddess of darkness and witchcraft   [113] in
Roman legend, the ravisher of Lucrece   [114] *i.e.,* the horror of murderous
silence

I go, and it is done. The bell invites me.
Hear it not, Duncan, for it is a knell
That summons thee to heaven, or to hell.   (*Exit.*)

Scene 2 [The same.]

(*Enter* LADY [MACBETH].)

LADY: That which hath made them drunk hath made me bold;
  What hath quenched them hath given me fire. Hark! Peace!
  It was the owl that shrieked, the fatal bellman
  Which gives the stern'st good-night. He is about it.
  The doors are open, and the surfeited grooms[115]
  Do mock their charge with snores. I have drugged their possets,[116]
  That[117] death and nature do contend about them
  Whether they live or die.
MACBETH (*Within*): Who's there? What, ho?
LADY: Alack, I am afraid they have awaked,
  And 'tis not done! The attempt, and not the deed,
  Confounds[118] us. Hark! I laid their daggers ready;
  He could not miss 'em. Had he not resembled
  My father as he slept, I had done't.

(*Enter* MACBETH.)

                     My husband!
MACBETH: I have done the deed. Didst thou not hear a noise?
LADY: I heard the owl scream and the crickets cry.
  Did not you speak?
MACBETH: When?
LADY: Now.
MACBETH: As I descended?
LADY: Ay.
MACBETH: Hark!
  Who lies i' the second chamber?
LADY: Donalbain.
MACBETH: This is a sorry sight.
LADY: A foolish thought, to say a sorry sight.
MACBETH: There's one did laugh in's sleep, and one cried "Murder!"
  That they did wake each other. I stood and heard them.
  But they did say their prayers and addressed them
  Again to sleep.

---

[115] Duncan's guards   [116] hot bedtime drinks, made of milk, ale, and spices
[117] so that   [118] ruins

LADY: There are two lodged together.

MACBETH: One cried "God bless us!" and "Amen!" the other,
    As they had seen me with these hangman's hands,
    List'ning their fear. I could not say "Amen!"
    When they did say "God bless us!"

LADY: Consider it not so deeply.

MACBETH: But wherefore could not I pronounce "Amen"?
    I had most need of blessing, and "Amen"
    Stuck in my throat.

LADY: These deeds must not be thought
    After these ways. So, it will make us mad.

MACBETH: Methought I heard a voice cry "Sleep no more!
    Macbeth does murder sleep"—the innocent sleep,
    Sleep that knits up the raveled sleave[119] of care,
    The death of each day's life, sore labor's bath,
    Balm of hurt minds, great nature's second course,
    Chief nourisher in life's feast.

LADY: What do you mean?

MACBETH: Still it cried "Sleep no more!" to all the house;
    "Glamis hath murdered sleep, and therefore Cawdor
    Shall sleep no more! Macbeth shall sleep no more!"

LADY: Who was it that thus cried? Why, worthy Thane,
    You do unbend your noble strength to think
    So brainsickly of things. Go get some water
    And wash this filthy witness[120] from your hand.
    Why did you bring these daggers from the place?
    They must lie there. Go carry them and smear
    The sleepy grooms with blood.

MACBETH: I'll go no more.
    I am afraid to think what I have done;
    Look on't again I dare not.

LADY: Infirm of purpose!
    Give me the daggers. The sleeping and the dead
    Are but as pictures. 'Tis the eye of childhood
    That fears a painted devil. If he do bleed,
    I'll gild[121] the faces of the grooms withal,
    For it must seem their guilt.   (*Exit.*)

(*Knocking within.*)

MACBETH: Whence is that knocking?
    How is't with me when every noise appals me?
    What hands are here? Ha! they pluck out mine eyes!

119 coarse silk, apt to tangle   120 evidence   121 smear

Will all great Neptune's ocean wash this blood
Clean from my hand? No. This my hand will rather
The multitudinous seas incarnadine,[122]
Making the green one red.

(*Enter* LADY [MACBETH].)

LADY: My hands are of your color, but I shame
To wear a heart so white.[123] (*Knock.*) I hear a knocking
At the south entry. Retire we to our chamber.
A little water clears us of this deed.
How easy is it then! Your constancy
Hath left you unattended.[124] (*Knock.*) Hark! more knocking.
Get on your nightgown, lest occasion call us
And show us to be watchers. Be not lost
So poorly in your thoughts.
MACBETH: To know my deed, 'twere best not know myself.

(*Knock.*)

Wake Duncan with thy knocking! I would thou couldst!   (*Exeunt.*)

Scene 3 [The same.]

(*Enter a* PORTER. *Knocking within.*)

PORTER: Here's a knocking indeed! If a man were porter of hell gate,
he should have old[125] turning the key. (*Knock.*) Knock, knock,
knock! Who's there, i' the name of Belzebub? Here's a farmer that
hanged himself on the expectation of plenty.[126] Come in time!
Have napkins[127] enow about you; here you'll sweat for't. (*Knock.*)
Knock, knock! Who's there, in the other devil's name? Faith, here's
an equivocator, that could swear in both the scales against either
scale; who committed treason enough for God's sake, yet could not
equivocate to heaven. O, come in, equivocator! (*Knock.*) Knock,
knock, knock! Who's there? Faith, here's an English tailor come
hither for stealing out of a French hose. Come in, tailor. Here you
may roast your goose.[128] (*Knock.*) Knock, knock! Never at quiet!
What are you? But this place is too cold for hell. I'll devil-porter it
no further. I had thought to have let in some of all professions that
go the primrose way to the everlasting bonfire. (*Knock.*) Anon,
anon! (*Opens the gate.*) I pray you remember the porter.

[122] make blood-red   [123] *i.e.,* cowardly   [124] *i.e.,* your loss of composure exposes you; or: your firmness has left you   [125] much   [126] *i.e.,* fearing a price-
depressing surplus crop   [127] handkerchiefs   [128] pressing iron

(*Enter* MACDUFF *and* LENNOX.)

MACDUFF: Was it so late, friend, ere you went to bed,
That you do lie so late?

PORTER: Faith, sir, we were carousing till the second cock;[129] and drink, sir, is a great provoker of three things.

MACDUFF: What three things does drink especially provoke?

PORTER: Marry, sir, nose-painting, sleep, and urine. Lechery, sir, it provokes, and unprovokes: it provokes the desire, but it takes away the performance. Therefore much drink may be said to be an equivocator with lechery: it makes him, and it mars him; it sets him on, and it takes him off; it persuades him, and disheartens him; makes him stand to, and not stand to; in conclusion, equivocates him in a sleep, and, giving him the lie, leaves him.

MACDUFF: I believe drink gave thee the lie[130] last night.

PORTER: That it did, sir, i' the very throat on me; but I requited him for his lie; and, I think, being too strong for him, though he took up my legs sometime, yet I made a shift[131] to cast[132] him.

MACDUFF: Is thy master stirring?

(*Enter* MACBETH.)

Our knocking has awaked him; here he comes.

LENNOX: Good morrow, noble sir.

MACBETH:　　　　　　　　　　Good morrow, both.

MACDUFF: Is the King stirring, worthy Thane?

MACBETH:　　　　　　　　　　Not yet.

MACDUFF: He did command me to call timely on him;
I have almost slipped the hour.

MACBETH:　　　　　　　　　I'll bring you to him.

MACDUFF: I know this is a joyful trouble to you;
But yet 'tis one.

MACBETH: The labor we delight in physics[133] pain.
This is the door.

MACDUFF:　　　　　　I'll make so bold to call,
For 'tis my limited[134] service.　　　　　　　　　　(*Exit.*)

LENNOX: Goes the King hence today?

MACBETH:　　　　　　　　　He does; he did appoint so.

LENNOX: The night has been unruly. Where we lay,
Our chimneys were blown down; and, as they say,
Lamentings heard i' the air, strange screams of death,

---

[129] conventionally thought of as crowing at 3 A.M.　　[130] (1) made you a liar, (2) forced you to lie down (as in wrestling)　　[131] managed　[132] throw
[133] heals　　[134] scheduled

And prophesying, with accents terrible,
Of dire combustion[135] and confused events
New hatched to the woeful time. The obscure bird[136]
Clamored the livelong night. Some say the earth
Was feverous and did shake.

MACBETH: 'Twas a rough night.

LENNOX: My young remembrance cannot parallel
A fellow to it.

(*Enter* MACDUFF.)

MACDUFF: O horror, horror, horror! Tongue nor heart
Cannot conceive nor name thee!

MACBETH and LENNOX: What's the matter?

MACDUFF: Confusion now hath made his masterpiece!
Most sacrilegious murder hath broke ope
The Lord's anointed temple[137] and stole thence
The life o' the building!

MACBETH: What is't you say? the life?

LENNOX: Mean you his Majesty?

MACDUFF: Approach the chamber, and destroy your sight
With a new Gorgon.[138] Do not bid me speak.
See, and then speak yourselves.   (*Exeunt* MACBETH *and* LENNOX.)
                    Awake, awake!
Ring the alarum bell. Murder and treason!
Banquo and Donalbain! Malcolm! awake!
Shake off this downy sleep, death's counterfeit,
And look on death itself! Up, up, and see
The great doom's image! Malcolm! Banquo!
As from your graves rise up and walk like sprites
To countenance this horror! Ring the bell!

(*Bell rings. Enter* LADY [MACBETH].)

LADY: What's the business,
That such a hideous trumpet calls to parley
The sleepers of the house? Speak, speak!

MACDUFF: O gentle lady,
'Tis not for you to hear what I can speak!
The repetition in a woman's ear
Would murder as it fell.

(*Enter* BANQUO.)

---

[135] political unrest   [136] the owl   [137] the King's body   [138] a monster the sight of whose head turned the beholder to stone

　　　　　　　　　O Banquo, Banquo,
Our royal master's murdered!
LADY:　　　　　　　　　　　Woe, alas!
　What, in our house?
BANQUO:　　　　　　　　Too cruel anywhere.
　Dear Duff, I prithee contradict thyself
　And say it is not so.

(*Enter* MACBETH, LENNOX, *and* ROSS.)

MACBETH: Had I but died an hour before this chance,
　I had lived a blessed time; for from this instant
　There's nothing serious in mortality;[139]
　All is but toys; renown and grace is dead;
　The wine of life is drawn, and the mere lees
　Is left this vault[140] to brag of.

(*Enter* MALCOLM *and* DONALBAIN.)

DONALBAIN: What is amiss?
MACBETH:　　　　　　　　You are, and do not know't.
　The spring, the head, the fountain of your blood
　Is stopped, the very source of it is stopped.
MACDUFF: Your royal father's murdered.
MALCOLM:　　　　　　　　　O, by whom?
LENNOX: Those of his chamber, as it seemed, had done't.
　Their hands and faces were all badged with blood;
　So were their daggers, which unwiped we found
　Upon their pillows.
　They stared and were distracted. No man's life
　Was to be trusted with them.
MACBETH: O, yet I do repent me of my fury
　That I did kill them.
MACDUFF:　　　　　　　Wherefore did you so?
MACBETH: Who can be wise, amazed,[141] temp'rate, and furious,
　Loyal and neutral, in a moment? No man.
　The expedition[142] of my violent love
　Outrun the pauser, reason. Here lay Duncan,
　His silver skin laced with his golden blood,
　And his gashed stabs looked like a breach in nature
　For ruin's wasteful entrance; there, the murderers,
　Steeped in the colors of their trade, their daggers
　Unmannerly breeched with gore. Who could refrain

[139] human life　　[140] Macbeth compares the world arched over by the heavens
to a vaulted wine cellar.　　[141] confused　　[142] haste

That had a heart to love and in that heart
Courage to make's love known?
LADY: Help me hence, ho!
MACDUFF: Look to the lady.
MALCOLM (*Aside to* DONALBAIN): Why do we hold our tongues,
That most may claim this argument for ours? [143]
DONALBAIN (*Aside to* MALCOLM): What should be spoken here,
Where our fate, hid in an auger hole,[144]
May rush and seize us? Let's away,
Our tears are not yet brewed.
MALCOLM (*Aside to* DONALBAIN): Nor our strong sorrow
Upon the foot of motion.
BANQUO: Look to the lady.

(LADY MACBETH *is carried out.*)

And when we have our naked frailties hid,
That suffer in exposure, let us meet
And question[145] this most bloody piece of work,
To know it further. Fears and scruples shake us.
In the great hand of God I stand, and thence
Against the undivulged pretense[146] I fight
Of treasonous malice.
MACDUFF: And so do I.
ALL: So all.
MACBETH: Let's briefly put on manly readiness
And meet i' the hall together.
ALL: Well contented.
                   (*Exeunt all but* MALCOLM *and* DONALBAIN.)
MALCOLM: What will you do? Let's not consort with them.
To show an unfelt sorrow is an office
Which the false man does easy. I'll to England.
DONALBAIN: To Ireland I. Our separated fortune
Shall keep us both the safer. Where we are,
There's daggers in men's smiles; the near in blood,
The nearer bloody.[147]
MALCOLM: This murderous shaft that's shot
Hath not yet lighted, and our safest way
Is to avoid the aim. Therefore to horse!
And let us not be dainty of[148] leave-taking

---

[143] *i.e.,* whom this topic concerns more than it does anyone else   [144] *i.e.,* obscure place   [145] inquire into   [146] secret schemes   [147] *i.e.,* the closer the relative the more dangerous he is   [148] particular with

But shift away. There's warrant[149] in that theft
Which steals itself when there's no mercy left.   (*Exeunt.*)

Scene 4 [The same. Without Macbeth's Castle.]

(*Enter* ROSS *with an* OLD MAN.)

OLD MAN: Threescore and ten I can remember well;
    Within the volume of which time I have seen
    Hours dreadful and things strange; but this sore night
    Hath trifled former knowings.
ROSS: Ah, good father,
    Thou seest the heavens, as troubled with man's act,
    Threaten his bloody stage. By the clock 'tis day,
    And yet dark night strangles the traveling lamp.
    Is't night's predominance, or the day's shame,
    That darkness does the face of earth entomb
    When living light should kiss it?
OLD MAN: 'Tis unnatural,
    Even like the deed that's done. On Tuesday last
    A falcon, tow'ring in her pride of place,[150]
    Was by a mousing owl hawked at and killed.
ROSS: And Duncan's horses (a thing most strange and certain),
    Beauteous and swift, the minions of their race,
    Turned wild in nature, broke their stalls, flung out,
    Contending 'gainst obedience, as they would make
    War with mankind.
OLD MAN: 'Tis said they eat[151] each other.
ROSS: They did so, to the amazement of mine eyes
    That looked upon't.

(*Enter* MACDUFF.)

            Here comes the good Macduff.
    How goes the world, sir, now?
MACDUFF: Why, see you not?
ROSS: Is't known who did this more than bloody deed?
MACDUFF: Those that Macbeth hath slain.
ROSS: Alas, the day!
    What good could they pretend? [152]
MACDUFF: They were suborned.[153]
    Malcolm and Donalbain, the King's two sons,

[149] justification   [150] summit of flight   [151] ate   [152] expect, hope
for   [153] bribed

Are stol'n away and fled, which puts upon them
Suspicion of the deed.

ROSS:　　　　　　　　　'Gainst nature still!
Thriftless ambition, that will raven up
Thine own live's means! Then 'tis most like
The sovereignty will fall upon Macbeth.

MACDUFF: He is already named, and gone to Scone
To be invested.

ROSS:　　　　　　　Where is Duncan's body?

MACDUFF: Carried to Colmekill,
The sacred storehouse of his predecessors
And guardian of their bones.

ROSS:　　　　　　　　　Will you to Scone?

MACDUFF: No, cousin, I'll to Fife.

ROSS:　　　　　　　　　Well, I will thither.

MACDUFF: Well, may you see things well done there. Adieu,
Lest our old robes sit easier than our new!

ROSS: Farewell, father.

OLD MAN: God's benison go with you, and with those
That would make good of bad, and friends of foes! (*Exeunt omnes.*)

ACT III

Scene 1 [Forres. The Palace.]

(*Enter* BANQUO.)

BANQUO: Thou hast it now — King, Cawdor, Glamis, all,
As the Weird Women promised; and I fear
Thou play'dst most foully for't. Yet it was said
It should not stand[154] in thy posterity,
But that myself should be the root and father
Of many kings. If there come truth from them
(As upon thee, Macbeth, their speeches shine),
Why, by the verities on thee made good,
May they not be my oracles as well
And set me up in hope? But, hush, no more!

(*Sennet*[155] *sounded. Enter* MACBETH, *as King;* LADY [MACBETH],
as Queen; LENNOX, ROSS, LORDS, *and* ATTENDANTS.)

[154] remain　　　[155] trumpet announcement of an important arrival

MACBETH: Here's our chief guest.

LADY: If he had been forgotten,
It had been as a gap in our great feast,
And all-thing unbecoming.

MACBETH: Tonight we hold a solemn supper, sir,
And I'll request your presence.

BANQUO: Let your Highness
Command upon me, to the which my duties
Are with a most indissoluble tie
For ever knit.

MACBETH: Ride you this afternoon?

BANQUO: Ay, my good lord.

MACBETH: We should have else desired your good advice
(Which still hath been both grave and prosperous)
In this day's council; but we'll take tomorrow.
Is't far you ride?

BANQUO: As far, my lord, as will fill up the time
'Twixt this and supper. Go not my horse the better,
I must become a borrower of the night
For a dark hour or twain.

MACBETH: Fail not our feast.

BANQUO: My lord, I will not.

MACBETH: We hear our bloody cousins are bestowed
In England and in Ireland, not confessing
Their cruel parricide, filling their hearers
With strange invention. But of that tomorrow,
When therewithal we shall have cause of state
Craving us jointly. Hie you to horse. Adieu,
Till you return at night. Goes Fleance with you?

BANQUO: Ay, my good lord. Our time does call upon's.

MACBETH: I wish your horses swift and sure of foot,
And so I do commend you to their backs.
Farewell.   (*Exit* BANQUO.)
Let every man be master of his time
Till seven at night. To make society
The sweeter welcome, we will keep ourself
Till supper time alone. While[156] then, God be with you!
          (*Exeunt* LORDS *and others. Manent* MACBETH *and a* SERVANT.)
Sirrah,[157] a word with you. Attend those men
Our pleasure?

SERVANT: They are, my lord, without the palace gate.

MACBETH: Bring them before us.   (*Exit* SERVANT.)

[156] until   [157] common form of address to inferiors

To be thus[158] is nothing,
But to be safely thus. Our fears in Banquo
Stick deep, and in his royalty of nature
Reigns that which would be feared. 'Tis much he dares,
And to that dauntless temper of his mind
He hath a wisdom that doth guide his valor
To act in safety. There is none but he
Whose being I do fear; and under him
My genius[159] is rebuked, as it is said
Mark Antony's was by Cæsar. He chid the Sisters
When first they put the name of King upon me,
And bade them speak to him. Then, prophet-like,
They hailed him father to a line of kings.
Upon my head they placed a fruitless crown
And put a barren scepter in my gripe,
Thence to be wrenched with an unlineal[160] hand,
No son of mine succeeding. If't be so,
For Banquo's issue have I filed[161] my mind;
For them the gracious Duncan have I murdered;
Put rancors in the vessel of my peace
Only for them, and mine eternal jewel[162]
Given to the common enemy of man[163]
To make them kings, the seed of Banquo kings!
Rather than so, come, Fate, into the list,
And champion me to the utterance![164] Who's there?

(*Enter* SERVANT *and two* MURDERERS.)

Now go to the door and stay there till we call.   (*Exit* SERVANT.)
Was it not yesterday we spoke together?
MURDERERS: It was, so please your Highness.
MACBETH: Well then, now
Have you considered of my speeches? Know
That it was he, in the times past, which held you
So under fortune, which you thought had been
Our innocent self. This I made good to you
In our last conference, passed in probation[165] with you
How you were borne in hand,[166] how crossed; the instruments;
Who wrought with them; and all things else that might
To half a soul and to a notion crazed
Say "Thus did Banquo."

---

[158] *i.e.*, king   [159] guardian spirit   [160] not of my descent   [161] defiled
[162] *i.e.*, my soul   [163] *i.e.*, the Devil   [164] duel to the death   [165] reviewed
the proofs   [166] manipulated

FIRST MUR.: You made it known to us.

MACBETH: I did so; and went further, which is now
Our point of second meeting. Do you find
Your patience so predominant in your nature
That you can let this go? Are you so gospeled
To pray for this good man and for his issue,
Whose heavy hand hath bowed you to the grave
And beggared yours for ever?

FIRST MUR.: We are men, my liege.

MACBETH: Ay, in the catalogue ye go for men,
As hounds and greyhounds, mongrels, spaniels, curs,
Shoughs, water-rugs,[167] and demi-wolves are clept
All by the name of dogs. The valued file[168]
Distinguishes the swift, the slow, the subtle,
The housekeeper,[169] the hunter, every one
According to the gift which bounteous nature
Hath in him closed; whereby he does receive
Particular addition, from[170] the bill
That writes them all alike; and so of men.
Now, if you have a station in the file,
Not i' the worst rank of manhood, say't;
And I will put that business in your bosoms
Whose execution takes your enemy off,
Grapples you to the heart and love of us,
Who wear our health but sickly in his life,
Which in his death were[171] perfect.

SECOND MUR.: I am one, my liege,
Whom the vile blows and buffets of the world
Have so incensed that I am reckless what
I do to spite the world.

FIRST MUR.: And I another,
So weary with disasters, tugged with fortune,
That I would set my life on any chance,
To mend it or be rid on't.

MACBETH: Both of you
Know Banquo was your enemy.

MURDERERS: True, my lord.

MACBETH: So is he mine, and in such bloody distance[172]
That every minute of his being thrusts
Against my near'st of life;[173] and though I could
With barefaced power sweep him from my sight

---

[167] breeds of dogs   [168] listing acc. to value   [169] watch dog   [170] apart from   [171] would be   [172] hostility   [173] vital parts

And bid my will avouch it, yet I must not,
For[174] certain friends that are both his and mine,
Whose loves I may not drop, but wail his fall
Who I myself struck down. And thence it is
That I to your assistance do make love,
Masking the business from the common eye
For sundry weighty reasons.

SECOND MUR.:   We shall, my lord,
Perform what you command us.

FIRST MUR.:   Though our lives —

MACBETH: Your spirits shine through you. Within this hour at most
I will advise you where to plant yourselves,
Acquaint you with the perfect spy o' the time,[175]
The moment on't; for't must be done tonight,
And something from[176] the palace (always thought[177]
That I require a clearness),[178] and with him,
To leave no rubs[179] nor botches in the work,
Fleance his son, that keeps him company,
Whose absence is no less material to me
Than is his father's, must embrace the fate
Of that dark hour. Resolve yourselves apart;
I'll come to you anon.

MURDERERS: We are resolved, my lord.

MACBETH: I'll call upon you straight. Abide within.

                              (*Exeunt* MURDERERS.)

It is concluded. Banquo, thy soul's flight,
If it find heaven, must find it out tonight.

                                     (*Exit.*)

Scene 2 [The same.]

(*Enter* MACBETH'S LADY *and a* SERVANT.)

LADY: Is Banquo gone from court?

SERVANT: Ay, madam, but returns again tonight.

LADY: Say to the King I would attend his leisure
For a few words.

SERVANT: Madam, I will.   (*Exit.*)

LADY: Naught's had, all's spent,
Where our desire is got without content.
'Tis safer to be that which we destroy
Than by destruction dwell in doubtful joy.

[174] because of   [175] *i.e.,* a lookout, who turns up in sc. 3 as 3rd Murderer;
or: the ideal time (for the murder)   [176] some distance removed from
[177] keeping in mind   [178] freedom from suspicion   [179] imperfections

(*Enter* MACBETH.)

How now, my lord? Why do you keep alone,
Of sorriest fancies your companions making,
Using those thoughts which should indeed have died
With them they think on? Things without all remedy
Should be without regard. What's done is done.

MACBETH: We have scotched[180] the snake, not killed it.
She'll close[181] and be herself, whilst our poor malice
Remains in danger of her former tooth.
But let the frame of things disjoint, both the worlds suffer,
Ere we will eat our meal in fear and sleep
In the affliction of these terrible dreams
That shake us nightly. Better be with the dead,
Whom we, to gain our peace, have sent to peace,
Than on the torture of the mind to lie
In restless ecstasy.[182] Duncan is in his grave;
After life's fitful fever he sleeps well.
Treason has done his worst: nor steel nor poison,
Malice domestic, foreign levy, nothing,
Can touch him further.

LADY: Come on.
Gentle my lord, sleek o'er your rugged looks;
Be bright and jovial among your guests tonight.

MACBETH: So shall I, love; and so, I pray, be you.
Let your remembrance apply to Banquo;
Present him eminence[183] both with eye and tongue:
Unsafe the while, that we
Must lave our honors in these flattering streams
And make our faces vizards[184] to our hearts,
Disguising what they are.[185]

LADY: You must leave this.

MACBETH: O, full of scorpions is my mind, dear wife!
Thou know'st that Banquo, and his Fleance, lives.

LADY: But in them Nature's copy's not eterne.

MACBETH: There's comfort yet; they are assailable.
Then be thou jocund. Ere the bat hath flown
His cloistered flight, ere to black Hecate's summons
The shard-borne[186] beetle with his drowsy hums
Hath rung night's yawning peal, there shall be done

---

[180] slashed   [181] heal   [182] frenzy   [183] exalt him   [184] masks   [185] *i.e.,*
we are so insecure that we need to flatter Banquo   [186] borne on hard wing;
or: dung-bred

A deed of dreadful note.

LADY: What's to be done?

MACBETH: Be innocent of the knowledge, dearest chuck,
Till thou applaud the deed. Come, seeling[187] night,
Scarf up the tender eye of pitiful day,
And with thy bloody and invisible hand
Cancel and tear to pieces that great bond[188]
Which keeps me pale! Light thickens, and the crow
Makes wing to the rooky wood.
Good things of day begin to droop and drowse,
Whiles night's black agents to their preys do rouse.
Thou marvell'st at my words; but hold thee still:
Things bad begun make strong themselves by ill.
So prithee go with me. (*Exeunt.*)

Scene 3 [The same. A park near the Palace.]

(*Enter three* MURDERERS.)

FIRST MUR.: But who did bid thee join with us?

THIRD MUR.: Macbeth.

SECOND MUR.: He needs not our mistrust, since he delivers
Our offices, and what we have to do,
To the direction just.

FIRST MUR.: Then stand with us.
The west yet glimmers with some streaks of day.
Now spurs the lated traveler apace
To gain the timely inn, and near approaches
The subject of our watch.

THIRD MUR.: Hark! I hear horses.

BANQUO (*Within*): Give us a light there, ho!

SECOND MUR.: Then 'tis he! The rest
That are within the note of expectation[189]
Already are i' the court.

FIRST MUR.: His horses go about.

THIRD MUR.: Almost a mile; but he does usually,
So all men do, from hence to the palace gate
Make it their walk.

(*Enter* BANQUO, *and* FLEANCE *with a torch.*)

SECOND MUR.: A light, a light!

[187] blinding (by sewing the eyelids together, as on a falcon)   [188] *i.e.*, that
which keeps Banquo's body and soul together; or: fate's pledge that Banquo's
descendants become kings   [189] among the expected guests

THIRD MUR.:   'Tis he.
FIRST MUR.: Stand to't.
BANQUO: It will be rain tonight.
FIRST MUR.:   Let it come down!

(*They set upon* BANQUO.)

BANQUO: O, treachery! Fly, good Fleance, fly, fly, fly!
  Thou mayst revenge. O slave!

(*Dies.* FLEANCE *escapes.*)

THIRD MUR.: Who did strike out the light?
FIRST MUR.:   Was't not the way? [190]
THIRD MUR.: There's but one down; the son is fled.
SECOND MUR.:   We have lost
  Best half of our affair.
FIRST MUR.: Well, let's away, and say how much is done.   (*Exeunt.*)

Scene 4 [The same. Hall in the Palace.]

(*Banquet prepared. Enter* MACBETH, LADY [MACBETH], ROSS, LENNOX, LORDS, *and* ATTENDANTS.)

MACBETH: You know your own degrees,[191] sit down. At first
  And last the hearty welcome.
LORDS: Thanks to your Majesty.
MACBETH: Ourself will mingle with society
  And play the humble host.
  Our hostess keeps her state,[192] but in best time
  We will require her welcome.
LADY: Pronounce it for me, sir, to all our friends,
  For my heart speaks they are welcome.

(*Enter* FIRST MURDERER [*to the door*].)

MACBETH: See, they encounter thee with their hearts' thanks.
  Both sides are even: here I'll sit i' the midst.
  Be large in mirth; anon we'll drink a measure
  The table round. (*Moves toward* MURDERER *at door.*) There's blood
    upon thy face.
MURDERER: 'Tis Banquo's then.
MACBETH: 'Tis better thee without[193] than he within.
  Is he dispatched?

[190] *i.e.*, shouldn't I have done that?   [191] ranks (hence: order of seating)
[192] remains in her chair of state   [193] on your outside

MURDERER: My lord, his throat is cut. That I did for him.

MACBETH: Thou art the best o' the cutthroats! Yet he's good
That did the like for Fleance. If thou didst it,
Thou art the nonpareil.

MURDERER: Most royal sir,
Fleance is scaped.

MACBETH (*Aside*): Then comes my fit again. I had else been perfect;
Whole as the marble, founded as the rock,
As broad and general[194] as the casing air.
But now I am cabined, cribbed, confined, bound in
To saucy doubts and fears. — But Banquo's safe?

MURDERER: Ay, my good lord. Safe in a ditch he bides,
With twenty trenched gashes on his head,
The least a death to nature.

MACBETH: Thanks for that!
There the grown serpent lies; the worm[195] that's fled
Hath nature that in time will venom breed,
No teeth for the present. Get thee gone. Tomorrow
We'll hear ourselves again.   (*Exit* MURDERER.)

LADY: My royal lord,
You do not give the cheer. The feast is sold[196]
That is not often vouched, while 'tis a-making,
'Tis given with welcome. To feed[197] were best at home.
From thence, the sauce to meat is ceremony;
Meeting were bare without it.

(*Enter the* GHOST OF BANQUO, *and sits in* MACBETH's *place.*)

MACBETH: Sweet remembrancer!
Now good digestion wait on appetite,
And health on both!

LENNOX: May't please your Highness sit.

MACBETH: Here had we now our country's honor, roofed,
Were the graced person of our Banquo present;
Who may I rather challenge for unkindness
Than pity for mischance!

ROSS: His absence, sir,
Lays blame upon his promise. Please't your Highness
To grace us with your royal company?

MACBETH: The table's full.

LENNOX: Here is a place reserved, sir.

MACBETH: Where?

194 free and unconfined   195 serpent   196 *i.e.*, is like hospitality that is for
sale (as that of inns and taverns)   197 *i.e.*, merely to eat

LENNOX: Here, my good lord. What is't that moves your Highness?

MACBETH: Which of you have done this?

LORDS: What, my good lord?

MACBETH: Thou canst not say I did it. Never shake
Thy gory locks at me.

ROSS: Gentlemen, rise. His Highness is not well.

LADY: Sit, worthy friends. My lord is often thus,
And hath been from his youth. Pray you keep seat.
The fit is momentary; upon a thought
He will again be well. If much you note him,
You shall offend him and extend his passion.[198]
Feed, and regard him not. — Are you a man?

MACBETH: Ay, and a bold one, that dare look on that
Which might appal the devil.

LADY: O proper stuff!
This is the very painting of your fear.
This is the air-drawn dagger which you said
Led you to Duncan. O, these flaws[199] and starts
(Impostors to[200] true fear) would well become
A woman's story at a winter's fire,
Authorized by her grandam. Shame itself!
Why do you make such faces? When all's done,
You look but on a stool.

MACBETH: Prithee see there! behold! look! lo! How say you?
Why, what care I? If thou canst nod, speak too.
If charnel houses and our graves must send
Those that we bury back, our monuments[201]
Shall be the maws[202] of kites.   (*Exit* GHOST.)

LADY: What, quite unmanned in folly?

MACBETH: If I stand here, I saw him.

LADY: Fie, for shame!

MACBETH: Blood hath been shed ere now, i' the olden time,
Ere humane statute purged the gentle weal; [203]
Ay, and since too, murders have been performed
Too terrible for the ear. The time has been
That, when the brains were out, the man would die,
And there an end! But now they rise again,
With twenty mortal murders on their crowns,
And push us from our stools. This is more strange
Than such a murder is.

LADY: My worthy lord,

[198] prolong his fit   [199] outbursts   [200] imitators of   [201] tombs
[202] stomachs   [203] civilized society

Your noble friends do lack you.

MACBETH: I do forget.
  Do not muse[204] at me, my most worthy friends.
  I have a strange infirmity, which is nothing
  To those that know me. Come, love and health to all!
  Then I'll sit down. Give me some wine, fill full.

(*Enter* GHOST.)

  I drink to the general joy o' the whole table,
  And to our dear friend Banquo, whom we miss.
  Would he were here! To all, and him, we thirst,
  And all to all.

LORDS: Our duties, and the pledge.

MACBETH: Avaunt, and quit my sight! Let the earth hide thee!
  Thy bones are marrowless, thy blood is cold;
  Thou hast no speculation[205] in those eyes
  Which thou dost glare with!

LADY: Think of this, good peers,
  But as a thing of custom. 'Tis no other.
  Only it spoils the pleasure of the time.

MACBETH: What man dare, I dare.
  Approach thou like the rugged Russian bear,
  The armed rhinoceros, or the Hyrcan[206] tiger;
  Take any shape but that, and my firm nerves
  Shall never tremble. Or be alive again
  And dare me to the desert with thy sword.
  If trembling I inhabit[207] then, protest me
  The baby of a girl. Hence, horrible shadow!
  Unreal mock'ry, hence!   (*Exit* GHOST.)
                    Why, so! Being gone,
  I am a man again. Pray you sit still.

LADY: You have displaced the mirth, broke the good meeting
  With most admired[208] disorder.

MACBETH: Can such things be,
  And overcome us like a summer's cloud
  Without our special wonder? You make me strange
  Even to the disposition that I owe,[209]
  When now I think you can behold such sights
  And keep the natural ruby of your cheeks
  When mine is blanched[210] with fear.

---

[204] wonder   [205] rationality   [206] of an area near the Caspian Sea   [207] live (*i.e.,* dwell in my body); or: stay home   [208] marvelled at   [209] my nature   [210] paled

ROSS: What sights, my lord?

LADY: I pray you speak not. He grows worse and worse;
Question enrages him. At once, good night.
Stand not upon the order of your going,
But go at once.

LENNOX: Good night, and better health
Attend his Majesty!

LADY: A kind good night to all!

(*Exeunt* LORDS *and* ATTENDANTS.)

MACBETH: It will have blood, they say: blood will have blood.
Stones have been known to move and trees to speak;
Augures[211] and understood relations[212] have
By maggot-pies and choughs[213] and rooks brought forth
The secret'st man of blood. What is the night?

LADY: Almost at odds with morning, which is which.

MACBETH: How say'st thou[214] that Macduff denies his person
At our great bidding?

LADY: Did you send to him, sir?

MACBETH: I hear it by the way; but I will send.
There's not a one of them but in his house
I keep a servant feed.[215] I will tomorrow
(And betimes[216] I will) to the Weird Sisters.
More shall they speak; for now I am bent to know
By the worst means the worst. For mine own good
All causes shall give way. I am in blood
Stepped in so far that, should I wade no more,
Returning were as tedious as go o'er.
Strange things I have in head, that will to hand,
Which must be acted ere they may be scanned.

LADY: You lack the season[217] of all natures, sleep.

MACBETH: Come, we'll to sleep. My strange and self-abuse[218]
Is the initiate[219] fear that wants[220] hard use.
We are yet but young in deed. (*Exeunt.*)

Scene 5 [A heath.]

(*Thunder. Enter the three* WITCHES, *meeting* HECATE.)

FIRST WITCH: Why, how now, Hecate? You look angerly.

HECATE: Have I not reason, beldams[221] as you are,

---

[211] auguries   [212] causes   [213] magpies and crows   [214] what do you say
to the fact   [215] paid (to spy)   [216] very early   [217] preservative
[218] strange self-deception   [219] *i.e.,* the beginner's   [220] lacks   [221] hags

Saucy and overbold? How did you dare
To trade and traffic with Macbeth
In riddles and affairs of death;
And I, the mistress of your charms,
The close[222] contriver of all harms,
Was never called to bear my part
Or show the glory of our art?
And, which is worse, all you have done
Hath been but for a wayward son,
Spiteful and wrathful, who, as others do,
Loves for his own ends, not for you.
But make amends now. Get you gone
And at the pit of Acheron[223]
Meet me i' the morning. Thither he
Will come to know his destiny.
Your vessels and your spells provide,
Your charms and everything beside.
I am for the air. This night I'll spend
Unto a dismal and a fatal end.
Great business must be wrought ere noon.
Upon the corner of the moon
There hangs a vap'rous drop profound.
I'll catch it ere it come to ground;
And that, distilled by magic sleights,
Shall raise such artificial sprites
As by the strength of their illusion
Shall draw him on to his confusion.[224]
He shall spurn fate, scorn death, and bear
His hopes 'bove wisdom, grace, and fear;
And you all know security[225]
Is mortals' chiefest enemy.

(*Music and a song within.* "Come away, come away," &c.)

Hark! I am called. My little spirit, see,
Sits in a foggy cloud and stays for me.   (*Exit.*)
FIRST WITCH: Come, let's make haste. She'll soon be back again.
                                                 (*Exeunt.*)

[222] secret   [223] a river in the underworld   [224] destruction   [225] overconfidence

Scene 6 [Forres. The Palace.]

(*Enter* LENNOX *and another* LORD.)

LENNOX: My former speeches have but hit your thoughts,
 Which can interpret[226] farther. Only I say
 Things have been strangely borne.[227] The gracious Duncan
 Was pitied of Macbeth. Marry,[228] he was dead!
 And the right valiant Banquo walked too late;
 Whom, you may say (if't please you) Fleance killed,
 For Fleance fled. Men must not walk too late.
 Who cannot want the thought[229] how monstrous
 It was for Malcolm and for Donalbain
 To kill their gracious father? Damned fact!
 How it did grieve Macbeth! Did he not straight,
 In pious rage, the two delinquents tear,
 That were the slaves of drink and thralls of sleep?
 Was not that nobly done? Ay, and wisely too!
 For 'twould have angered any heart alive
 To hear the men deny't. So that I say
 He has borne all things well; and I do think
 That, had he Duncan's sons under his key
 (As, an't[230] please heaven, he shall not), they should find
 What 'twere to kill a father. So should Fleance.
 But peace! for from broad[231] words, and 'cause he failed
 His presence at the tyrant's feast, I hear
 Macduff lives in disgrace. Sir, can you tell
 Where he bestows himself?
LORD: The son of Duncan,
 From whom this tyrant holds the due of birth,[232]
 Lives in the English court, and is received
 Of the most pious Edward with such grace
 That the malevolence of fortune nothing
 Takes from his high respect. Thither Macduff
 Is gone to pray the holy King upon his aid
 To wake Northumberland[233] and warlike Siward;
 That by the help of these (with Him above
 To ratify the work) we may again
 Give to our tables meat, sleep to our nights,

[226] make inferences from [227] handled (*i.e.*, by Macbeth) [228] an oath; here something like: No wonder! [229] cannot help thinking [230] if it [231] free, outspoken [232] birthright [233] *i.e.*, the people of N.

Free from our feasts and banquets bloody knives,
Do faithful homage and receive free honors —
All which we pine for now. And this report
Hath so exasperate the King that he
Prepares for some attempt of war.

LENNOX: Sent he to Macduff?

LORD: He did; and with an absolute "Sir, not I!" [234]
   The cloudy[235] messenger turns me[236] his back
   And hums, as who should say, "You'll rue the time
   That clogs[237] me with this answer."

LENNOX: And that well might
   Advise him to a caution t' hold what distance
   His wisdom can provide. Some holy angel
   Fly to the court of England and unfold
   His message ere he come, that a swift blessing
   May soon return to this our suffering country
   Under a hand accursed!

LORD: I'll send my prayers with him.   (*Exeunt.*)

ACT IV

Scene 1 [A cavern. In the middle, a boiling cauldron.]

(*Thunder. Enter the three* WITCHES.)

FIRST WITCH: Thrice the brinded[238] cat hath mewed.

SECOND WITCH: Thrice, and once the hedge-pig whined.

THIRD WITCH: Harpier[239] cries; 'tis time, 'tis time.

FIRST WITCH: Round about the cauldron go;
   In the poisoned entrails throw.
   Toad, that under cold stone
   Days and nights has thirty-one
   Swelt'red[240] venom sleeping got,[241]
   Boil thou first i' the charmed pot.

ALL: Double, double, toil and trouble;
   Fire burn, and cauldron bubble.

SECOND WITCH: Fillet of a fenny[242] snake,
   In the cauldron boil and bake;

---

[234] Macduff's answer to Macbeth's messenger
[235] sullen, gloomy
[236] turns   [237] encumbers   [238] brindled, streaked
[239] the name of
the 3rd witch's attendant spirit (?); cf. I, 1, 9-10
[240] oozed out
[241] formed during sleep   [242] swamp

Eye of newt, and toe of frog,
Wool of bat, and tongue of dog,
Adder's fork, and blindworm's[243] sting,
Lizard's leg, and howlet's[244] wing;
For a charm of pow'rful trouble
Like a hell-broth boil and bubble.
ALL: Double, double, toil and trouble;
Fire burn, and cauldron bubble.
THIRD WITCH: Scale of dragon, tooth of wolf,
Witch's mummy,[245] maw and gulf[246]
Of the ravined[247] salt-sea shark,
Root of hemlock, digged i' the dark;
Liver of blaspheming Jew,
Gall of goat, and slips of yew
Slivered in the moon's eclipse;
Nose of Turk and Tartar's lips;
Finger of birth-strangled babe
Ditch-delivered by a drab: [248]
Make the gruel thick and slab.[249]
Add thereto a tiger's chaudron
For the ingredience of our cauldron.[250]
ALL: Double, double, toil and trouble;
Fire burn, and cauldron bubble.
SECOND WITCH: Cool it with a baboon's blood,
Then the charm is firm and good.

(*Enter* HECATE *to the other three* WITCHES.)

HECATE: O, well done! I commend your pains,
And every one shall share i' the gains.
And now about the cauldron sing
Like elves and fairies in a ring,
Enchanting all that you put in.

(*Music and a song,* "Black spirit," &c.)

SECOND WITCH: By the pricking of my thumbs,
Something wicked this way comes.
                    Open locks,
                    Whoever knocks!

(*Enter* MACBETH.)

---

[243] supposedly venomous lizard   [244] owlet's   [245] mummified flesh
[246] gullet   [247] ravenous   [248] whore   [249] thick   [250] entrails

MACBETH: How now, you secret, black, and midnight hags?
　What is't you do?
ALL: 　　　　　　　　A deed without a name.
MACBETH: I conjure you by that which you profess
　(Howe'er you come to know it), answer me.
　Though you untie the winds and let them fight
　Against the churches; though the yesty[251] waves
　Confound and swallow navigation up;
　Though bladed[252] corn be lodged[253] and trees blown down;
　Though castles topple on their warders' heads;
　Though palaces and pyramids do slope
　Their heads to their foundations; though the treasure
　Of nature's germens[254] tumble all together,
　Even till destruction sicken — answer me
　To what I ask you.
FIRST WITCH: 　　　　　Speak.
SECOND WITCH: 　　　　　　　Demand.
THIRD WITCH: 　　　　　　　　　　We'll answer.
FIRST WITCH: Say, if th' hadst rather hear it from our mouths
　Or from our masters.
MACBETH: 　　　　　Call 'em! Let me see 'em.
FIRST WITCH: Pour in sow's blood, that hath eaten
　Her nine farrow;[255] grease that's sweaten
　From the murderer's gibbet throw
　Into the flame.
ALL: 　　　　　Come, high or low;
　Thyself and office deftly show!

(*Thunder.* FIRST APPARITION, *an Armed Head.*)

MACBETH: Tell me, thou unknown power —
FIRST WITCH: 　　　　　　　　　　He knows thy thought.
　Hear his speech, but say thou naught.
FIRST APPAR.: Macbeth! Macbeth! Macbeth! Beware Macduff;
　Beware the Thane of Fife. Dismiss me. Enough. 　(*He descends.*)
MACBETH: Whate'er thou art, for thy good caution thanks!
　Thou hast harped[256] my fear aright. But one word more —
FIRST WITCH: He will not be commanded. Here's another,
　More potent than the first.

(*Thunder.* SECOND APPARITION, *a Bloody Child.*)

SECOND APPAR.: Macbeth! Macbeth! Macbeth!

---

[251] foamy 　[252] ripe 　[253] beaten down 　[254] seeds (of all that has not yet been brought into existence) 　[255] litter of nine 　[256] guessed

MACBETH: Had I three ears, I'ld hear thee.

SECOND APPAR.: Be bloody, bold, and resolute; laugh to scorn
The pow'r of man, for none of woman born
Shall harm Macbeth. *(Descends.)*

MACBETH: Then live, Macduff. What need I fear of thee?
But yet I'll make assurance double sure
And take a bond of fate.[257] Thou shalt not live!
That I may tell pale-hearted fear it lies
And sleep in spite of thunder.

(Thunder. THIRD APPARITION, *a Child Crowned, with a tree in his hand.)*

What is this
That rises like the issue of a king
And wears upon his baby-brow the round
And top of sovereignty?

ALL: Listen, but speak not to't.

THIRD APPAR.: Be lion-mettled, proud, and take no care
Who chafes, who frets, or where conspirers are.
Macbeth shall never vanquished be until
Great Birnam Wood to high Dunsinane Hill
Shall come against him. *(Descends.)*

MACBETH: That will never be.
Who can impress[258] the forest, bid the tree
Unfix his earth-bound root? Sweet bodements, good!
Rebellious dead rise never till the Wood
Of Birnam rise, and our high-placed Macbeth
Shall live the lease of nature, pay his breath
To time and mortal custom.[259] Yet my heart
Throbs to know one thing. Tell me, if your art
Can tell so much — shall Banquo's issue ever
Reign in this kingdom?

ALL: Seek to know no more.

MACBETH: I will be satisfied. Deny me this,
And an eternal curse fall on you! Let me know.
Why sinks that cauldron? and what noise is this?

(Hautboys.)

FIRST WITCH: Show!

SECOND WITCH: Show!

THIRD WITCH: Show!

---

[257] make fate give a pledge   [258] draft   [259] natural death

ALL: Show his eyes, and grieve his heart!
    Come like shadows, so depart!

(A *show of eight* KINGS, *the eighth with a glass*[260] *in his hand, and* BANQUO *last.*)

MACBETH: Thou art too like the spirit of Banquo. Down!
    Thy crown does sear mine eyeballs. And thy hair,
    Thou other gold-bound brow, is like the first.
    A third is like the former. Filthy hags!
    Why do you show me this? A fourth? Start, eyes!
    What, will the line stretch out to the crack of doom?
    Another yet? A seventh? I'll see no more.
    And yet the eighth appears, who bears a glass
    Which shows me many more; and some I see
    That twofold balls and treble scepters[261] carry.
    Horrible sight! Now I see 'tis true;
    For the blood-boltered[262] Banquo smiles upon me
    And points at them for his. (APPARITIONS *descend.*) What? Is this
        so?
FIRST WITCH: Ay, sir, all this is so. But why
    Stands Macbeth thus amazedly?
    Come, sisters, cheer we up his sprites
    And show the best of our delights.
    I'll charm the air to give a sound
    While you perform your antic round,
    That this great king may kindly say
    Our duties did his welcome pay.

(*Music. The* WITCHES *dance, and vanish.*)

MACBETH: Where are they? Gone? Let this pernicious hour
    Stand aye[263] accursed in the calendar!
    Come in, without there!

(*Enter* LENNOX.)

LENNOX: What's your Grace's will?
MACBETH: Saw you the Weird Sisters?
LENNOX: No, my lord.
MACBETH: Came they not by you?
LENNOX: No indeed, my lord.

[260] magic mirror   [261] regal insignia of Great Britain. In 1604 James I, king of both England and Scotland and allegedly Banquo's descendant, claimed the title "King of Great Britain, France, and Ireland."   [262] with hair matted with blood   [263] forever

MACBETH: Infected be the air whereon they ride,
  And damned all those that trust them! I did hear
  The galloping of horse. Who was't came by?
LENNOX: 'Tis two or three, my lord, that bring you word
  Macduff is fled to England.
MACBETH: Fled to England?
LENNOX: Ay, my good lord.
MACBETH (*Aside*): Time, thou anticipat'st[264] my dread exploits.
  The flighty[265] purpose never is o'ertook
  Unless the deed go with it. From this moment
  The very firstlings of my heart shall be
  The firstlings of my hand. And even now,
  To crown my thoughts with acts, be it thought and done!
  The castle of Macduff I will surprise,
  Seize upon Fife, give to the edge o' the sword
  His wife, his babes, and all unfortunate souls
  That trace him in his line.[266] No boasting like a fool!
  This deed I'll do before this purpose cool.
  But no more sights! — Where are these gentlemen?
  Come, bring me where they are.   (*Exeunt.*)

Scene 2 [Fife. Macduff's Castle.]

(*Enter* MACDUFF'S WIFE, *her* SON, *and* ROSS.)

WIFE: What had he done to make him fly the land?
ROSS: You must have patience, madam.
WIFE: He had none.
  His flight was madness. When our actions do not,
  Our fears do make us traitors.
ROSS: You know not
  Whether it was his wisdom or his fear.
WIFE: Wisdom? To leave his wife, to leave his babes,
  His mansion, and his titles, in a place
  From whence himself does fly? He loves us not,
  He wants[267] the natural touch. For the poor wren,
  (The most diminutive of birds) will fight,
  Her young ones in her nest, against the owl.
  All is the fear, and nothing is the love,
  As little is the wisdom, where the flight
  So runs against all reason.
ROSS: My dearest coz,[268]

264 forestalls   265 fleeting   266 *i.e.,* are related to him   267 lacks
268 cousin, kinswoman

I pray you school[269] yourself. But for your husband,
He is noble, wise, judicious, and best knows
The fits o' the season.[270] I dare not speak much further;
But cruel are the times, when we are traitors
And do not know ourselves;[271] when we hold rumor
From what we fear, yet know not what we fear,
But float upon a wild and violent sea
Each way and move — I take my leave of you.
Shall not be long but I'll be here again.
Things at the worst will cease, or else climb upward
To what they were before. — My pretty cousin,
Blessing upon you!

WIFE: Fathered he is, and yet he's fatherless.

ROSS: I am so much a fool, should I stay longer,
It would be my disgrace and your discomfort.
I take my leave at once.   (*Exit.*)

WIFE: Sirrah, your father's dead;
And what will you do now? How will you live?

SON: As birds do, mother.

WIFE: What, with worms and flies?

SON: With what I get, I mean; and so do they.

WIFE: Poor bird! thou'dst never fear the net nor lime,[272]
The pitfall nor the gin.[273]

SON: Why should I, mother? Poor[274] birds they are not set for.
My father is not dead, for all your saying.

WIFE: Yes, he is dead. How wilt thou do for a father?

SON: Nay, how will you do for a husband?

WIFE: Why, I can buy me twenty at any market.

SON: Then you'll buy 'em to sell again.

WIFE: Thou speak'st with all thy wit; and yet, i' faith,
With wit enough for thee.

SON: Was my father a traitor, mother?

WIFE: Ay, that he was!

SON: What is a traitor?

WIFE: Why, one that swears, and lies.[275]

SON: And be all traitors that do so?

WIFE: Every one that does so is a traitor and must be hanged.

SON: And must they all be hanged that swear and lie?

WIFE: Every one.

SON: Who must hang them?

[269] discipline   [270] present unrest   [271] are not ourselves aware (of being so)   [272] birdlime   [273] snare   [274] insignificant   [275] breaks his oaths

WIFE: Why, the honest men.

SON: Then the liars and swearers are fools; for there are liars and swearers enow[276] to beat the honest men and hang up them.

WIFE: Now God help thee, poor monkey!
But how wilt thou do for a father?

SON: If he were dead, you'ld weep for him. If you would not, it were a good sign that I should quickly have a new father.

WIFE: Poor prattler, how thou talk'st!

(*Enter a* MESSENGER.)

MESSENGER: Bless you, fair dame! I am not to you known,
Though in your state of honor I am perfect.[277]
I doubt[278] some danger does approach you nearly.
If you will take a homely[279] man's advice,
Be not found here. Hence with your little ones!
To fright you thus methinks I am too savage;
To do worse to you were fell cruelty,
Which is too nigh your person. Heaven preserve you!
I dare abide no longer. (*Exit.*)

WIFE: 　　　　　　　　Whither should I fly?
I have done no harm. But I remember now
I am in this earthly world, where to do harm
Is often laudable, to do good sometime
Accounted dangerous folly. Why then, alas,
Do I put up that womanly defense
To say I have done no harm? — What are these faces?

(*Enter* MURDERERS.)

MURDERERS: Where is your husband?

WIFE: I hope, in no place so unsanctified
Where such as thou mayst find him.

MURDERERS: 　　　　　　　　He's a traitor.

SON: Thou liest, thou shag-eared[280] villain!

MURDERERS: 　　　　　　　　What, you egg!
(*Stabbing him.*)
Young fry of treachery!

SON: 　　　　　　He has killed me, mother.
Run away, I pray you! (*Dies.*)

(*Exit* LADY MACDUFF, *crying* "Murder!" *followed by* MURDERERS.)

---

[276] enough　　[277] *i.e.,* I know you well for a noblewoman　　[278] fear
[279] of simple rank　　[280] with shaggy hair about the ears

Scene 3 [England. Before the King's Palace.]

(*Enter* MALCOLM *and* MACDUFF.)

MALCOLM: Let us seek out some desolate shade, and there
 Weep our sad bosoms empty.

MACDUFF: Let us rather
 Hold fast the mortal[281] sword and, like good men,
 Bestride[282] our downfall'n birthdom.[283] Each new morn
 New widows howl, new orphans cry, new sorrows
 Strike heaven on the face, that it resounds
 As if it felt with Scotland and yelled out
 Like syllable of dolor.[284]

MALCOLM: What I believe, I'll wail;
 What know, believe; and what I can redress,
 As I shall find the time to friend,[285] I will.
 What you have spoke, it may be so perchance.
 This tyrant, whose sole[286] name blisters our tongues,
 Was once thought honest; you have loved him well;
 He hath not touched you yet. I am young; but[287] something
 You may discern[288] of him through me,[289] and wisdom[290]
 To offer up a weak, poor, innocent lamb
 T' appease an angry god.

MACDUFF: I am not treacherous.

MALCOLM: But Macbeth is.
 A good and virtuous nature may recoil[291]
 In an imperial charge.[292] But I shall crave your pardon.
 That which you are, my thoughts cannot transpose.[293]
 Angels are bright still, though the brightest[294] fell.
 Though all things foul would wear the brows of grace,
 Yet grace must still look so.

MACDUFF: I have lost my hopes.

MALCOLM: Perchance even there where I did find my doubts.
 Why in that rawness[295] left you wife and child,
 Those precious motives, those strong knots of love,
 Without leave-taking? I pray you,
 Let not my jealousies[296] be your dishonors,

---

[281] deadly [282] stand over protectively [283] native land [284] similar word of sorrow [285] *i.e.,* convenient time [286] mere, very [287] *i.e.,* Though I am young, I realize that [288] Corrected by most editors to: deserve [289] by means of me (*i.e.,* by betraying me) [290] *i.e.,* it is (or: would be) wisdom [291] yield [292] to a royal command [293] change [294] *i.e.,* Satan (Lucifer) [295] exposed state [296] suspicions

But mine own safeties. You may be rightly just,
Whatever I shall think.

MACDUFF: Bleed, bleed, poor country!
Great tyranny, lay thou thy basis sure,
For goodness dare not check thee! Wear thou thy wrongs;
The title is affeered! [297] Fare thee well, lord.
I would not be the villain that thou think'st
For the whole space that's in the tyrant's grasp
And the rich East to boot.

MALCOLM: Be not offended.
I speak not as in absolute[298] fear of you.
I think our country sinks beneath the yoke;
It weeps, it bleeds, and each new day a gash
Is added to her wounds. I think withal [299]
There would be hands uplifted in my right;
And here from gracious England have I offer
Of goodly thousands. But, for all this,
When I shall tread upon the tyrant's head
Or wear it on my sword, yet my poor country
Shall have more vices than it had before,
More suffer and more sundry ways than ever,
By him that shall succeed.

MACDUFF: What should he be?

MALCOLM: It is myself I mean; in whom I know
All the particulars[300] of vice so grafted [301]
That, when they shall be opened, black Macbeth
Will seem as pure as snow, and the poor state
Esteem him as a lamb, being compared
With my confineless harms.

MACDUFF: Not in the legions
Of horrid hell can come a devil more damned
In evils to top Macbeth.

MALCOLM: I grant him bloody,
Luxurious,[302] avaricious, false, deceitful,
Sudden,[303] malicious, smacking of every sin
That has a name. But there's no bottom, none,
In my voluptuousness. Your wives, your daughters,
Your matrons, and your maids could not fill up
The cistern of my lust; and my desire
All continent[304] impediments would o'erbear

[297] certified   [298] definite, complete   [299] furthermore   [300] varieties
[301] engrafted   [302] lecherous   [303] violent   [304] restraining

That did oppose my will. Better Macbeth
Than such an one to reign.

MACDUFF: Boundless intemperance
In nature[305] is a tyranny. It hath been
The untimely emptying of the happy throne
And fall of many kings. But fear not yet
To take upon you what is yours. You may
Convey[306] your pleasures in a spacious plenty,
And yet seem cold — the time you may so hoodwink.
We have willing dames enough. There cannot be
That vulture in you to devour so many
As will to greatness dedicate themselves,
Finding it so inclined.

MALCOLM: With this there grows
In my most ill-composed affection[307] such
A stanchless[308] avarice that, were I King,
I should cut off the nobles for their lands,
Desire his jewels, and this other's house,
And my more-having would be as a sauce
To make me hunger more, that I should forge
Quarrels unjust against the good and loyal,
Destroying them for wealth.

MACDUFF: This avarice
Sticks deeper, grows with more pernicious root
Than summer-seeming[309] lust; and it hath been
The sword[310] of our slain kings. Yet do not fear.
Scotland hath foisons[311] to fill up your will
Of your mere own.[312] All these are portable,[313]
With other graces weighed.

MALCOLM: But I have none. The king-becoming graces,
As justice, verity,[314] temp'rance, stableness,
Bounty, perseverance, mercy, lowliness,[315]
Devotion, patience, courage, fortitude,
I have no relish[316] of them, but abound
In the division of each several crime,
Acting it many ways. Nay, had I pow'r, I should
Pour the sweet milk of concord into hell,
Uproar the universal peace, confound
All unity on earth.

---

[305] in man's nature   [306] manage secretly   [307] character   [308] insatiable
[309] *i.e.*, of short duration, like summer   [310] *i.e.*, cause of death   [311] abun-
dance   [312] merely out of your own (royal property)   [313] endurable
[314] truthfulness   [315] humility   [316] taste, trace

MACDUFF: O Scotland, Scotland!

MALCOLM: If such a one be fit to govern, speak.
I am as I have spoken.

MACDUFF: Fit to govern?
No, not to live. O nation miserable,
With an untitled tyrant bloody-scept'red,
When shalt thou see thy wholesome days again,
Since that[317] the truest issue of thy throne
By his own interdiction[318] stands accursed
And does blaspheme his breed? Thy royal father
Was a most sainted king; the queen that bore thee,
Oft'ner upon her knees than on her feet,
Died[319] every day she lived. Fare thee well!
These evils thou repeat'st upon thyself
Have banished me from Scotland. O my breast,
Thy hope ends here!

MALCOLM: Macduff, this noble passion,
Child of integrity, hath from my soul
Wiped the black scruples, reconciled my thoughts
To thy good truth and honor. Devilish Macbeth
By many of these trains[320] hath sought to win me
Into his power; and modest wisdom plucks me
From over-credulous haste; but God above
Deal between thee and me! for even now
I put myself to thy direction and
Unspeak mine own detraction, here abjure
The taints and blames I laid upon myself
For[321] strangers to my nature. I am yet
Unknown to woman, never was forsworn,
Scarcely have coveted what was mine own,
At no time broke my faith, would not betray
The devil to his fellow, and delight
No less in truth than life. My first false speaking
Was this upon myself. What I am truly,
Is thine and my poor country's to command;
Whither indeed, before thy here-approach,
Old Siward with ten thousand warlike men
Already at a point[322] was setting forth.
Now we'll together; and the chance of goodness
Be like our warranted quarrel! [323] Why are you silent?

[317] since   [318] ban   [319] *i.e.*, renounced the world   [320] schemes   [321] as
[322] fully armed   [323] may our chance for success equal the justice of our
fight

MACDUFF: Such welcome and unwelcome things at once
    'Tis hard to reconcile.

(*Enter a* DOCTOR.)

MALCOLM: Well, more anon.[324] Comes the King forth, I pray you?
DOCTOR: Ay, sir. There are a crew of wretched souls
    That stay[325] his cure. Their malady convinces
    The great assay of art;[326] but at his touch,
    Such sanctity hath heaven given his hand,
    They presently amend.
MALCOLM: I thank you, doctor.   (*Exit* DOCTOR.)
MACDUFF: What's the disease he means?
MALCOLM: 'Tis called the evil: [327]
    A most miraculous work in this good king,
    Which often since my here-remain[328] in England
    I have seen him do. How he solicits heaven
    Himself best knows; but strangely-visited[329] people,
    All swol'n and ulcerous, pitiful to the eye,
    The mere despair of surgery, he cures,
    Hanging a golden stamp[330] about their necks,
    Put on with holy prayers; and 'tis spoken,
    To the succeeding royalty he leaves
    The healing benediction. With this strange virtue,
    He hath a heavenly gift of prophecy,
    And sundry blessings hang about his throne
    That speak him full of grace.

(*Enter* ROSS.)

MACDUFF: See who comes here.
MALCOLM: My countryman; but yet I know him not.
MACDUFF: My ever gentle cousin, welcome hither.
MALCOLM: I know him now. Good God betimes remove
    The means that makes us strangers!
ROSS: Sir, amen.
MACDUFF: Stands Scotland where it did?
ROSS: Alas, poor country,
    Almost afraid to know itself! It cannot
    Be called our mother, but our grave; where nothing,
    But who knows nothing, is once seen to smile;
    Where sighs and groans, and shrieks that rent the air,

[324] soon   [325] await   [326] effort of (medical) science   [327] scrofula (a disease of the lymph glands)   [328] stay   [329] strangely afflicted   [330] coin

Are made, not marked;[331] where violent sorrow seems
A modern ecstasy.[332] The dead man's knell
Is there scarce asked for who; and good men's lives
Expire before the flowers in their caps,
Dying or ere they sicken.

MACDUFF: O, relation
Too nice,[333] and yet too true!

MALCOLM: What's the newest grief?

ROSS: That of an hour's age doth hiss the speaker;[334]
Each minute teems a new one.

MACDUFF: How does my wife?

ROSS: Why, well.

MACDUFF: And all my children?

ROSS: Well too.

MACDUFF: The tyrant has not battered at their peace?

ROSS: No, they were well at peace when I did leave 'em.

MACDUFF: Be not a niggard of your speech. How goes't?

ROSS: When I came hither to transport the tidings
Which I have heavily borne, there ran a rumor
Of many worthy fellows that were out;[335]
Which was to my belief witnessed the rather
For that I saw the tyrant's power afoot.
Now is the time of help. Your eye in Scotland
Would create soldiers, make our women fight
To doff their dire distresses.

MALCOLM: Be't their comfort
We are coming thither. Gracious England hath
Lent us good Siward and ten thousand men.
An older and a better soldier none
That Christendom gives out.

ROSS: Would I could answer
This comfort with the like! But I have words
That would be howled out in the desert air,
Where hearing should not latch[336] them.

MACDUFF: What concern they?
The general cause? or is it a fee-grief[337]
Due to[338] some single breast?

ROSS: No mind that's honest
But in it shares some woe, though the main part
Pertains to you alone.

---

[331] noticed   [332] common frenzy   [333] precisely detailed   [334] *i.e.*, causes
him to be hissed, because it is already stale news   [335] up in arms   [336] catch
[337] the limit of grief possible for an individual to feel   [338] belonging to

MACDUFF: If it be mine,
  Keep it not from me, quickly let me have it.
ROSS: Let not your ears despise my tongue for ever,
  Which shall possess them with the heaviest sound
  That ever yet they heard.
MACDUFF: Humh! I guess at it.
ROSS: Your castle is surprised; your wife and babes
  Savagely slaughtered. To relate the manner
  Were, on the quarry of these murdered deer,
  To add the death of you.
MALCOLM: Merciful heaven!
  What, man! Ne'er pull your hat upon your brows.
  Give sorrow words. The grief that does not speak
  Whispers the o'erfraught heart and bids it break.
MACDUFF: My children too?
ROSS: Wife, children, servants, all
  That could be found.
MACDUFF: And I must be from thence?
  My wife killed too?
ROSS: I have said.
MALCOLM: Be comforted.
  Let's make us med'cines of our great revenge
  To cure this deadly grief.
MACDUFF: He has no children. All my pretty ones?
  Did you say all? O hell-kite! All?
  What, all my pretty chickens and their dam
  At one fell swoop?
MALCOLM: Dispute[339] it like a man.
MACDUFF: I shall do so;
  But I must also feel it as a man.
  I cannot but remember such things were
  That were most precious to me. Did heaven look on
  And would not take their part? Sinful Macduff,
  They were all struck for thee! Naught[340] that I am,
  Not for their own demerits, but for mine,
  Fell slaughter on their souls. Heaven rest them now!
MALCOLM: Be this the whetstone of your sword. Let grief
  Convert to anger; blunt not the heart, enrage it.
MACDUFF: O, I could play the woman with mine eyes
  And braggart with my tongue! But, gentle heavens,
  Cut short all intermission.[341] Front to front[342]

[339] confront   [340] wicked   [341] interval of delay   [342] face to
face

Bring thou this fiend of Scotland and myself.
Within my sword's length set him. If he scape,[343]
Heaven forgive him too!
MALCOLM: This tune goes manly.
  Come, go we to the King. Our power is ready;
  Our lack is nothing but our leave.[344] Macbeth
  Is ripe for shaking, and the pow'rs above
  Put on[345] their instruments. Receive what cheer you may.
  The night is long that never finds the day.   (*Exeunt.*)

ACT V

Scene 1 [Dunsinane. Macbeth's Castle.]

(*Enter a* DOCTOR OF PHYSIC *and a* WAITING GENTLEWOMAN.)

DOCTOR: I have two nights watched with you, but can perceive no truth in your report. When was it she last walked?

GENTLEWOMAN: Since his Majesty went into the field I have seen her rise from her bed, throw her nightgown upon her, unlock her closet, take forth paper, fold it, write upon't, read it, afterwards seal it, and again return to bed; yet all this while in a most fast sleep.

DOCTOR: A great perturbation in nature, to receive at once the benefit of sleep and do the effects of watching! [346] In this slumb'ry agitation, besides her walking and other actual performances, what (at any time) have you heard her say?

GENTLEWOMAN: That, sir, which I will not report after her.

DOCTOR: You may to me, and 'tis most meet[347] you should.

GENTLEWOMAN: Neither to you nor any one, having no witness to confirm my speech.

(*Enter* LADY [MACBETH], *with a taper.*)

Lo you, here she comes! This is her very guise,[348] and, upon my life, fast asleep! Observe her; stand close.[349]

DOCTOR: How came she by that light?

GENTLEWOMAN: Why, it stood by her. She has light by her continually. 'Tis her command.

DOCTOR: You see her eyes are open.

GENTLEWOMAN: Ay, but their sense is shut.

DOCTOR: What is it she does now? Look how she rubs her hands.

---

[343] escapes   [344] all we need is permission to leave; or: to say good-bye
[345] urge on   [346] being awake   [347] proper   [348] habitual appearance
[349] concealed

GENTLEWOMAN: It is an accustomed action with her, to seem thus washing her hands. I have known her continue in this a quarter of an hour.

LADY: Yet here's a spot.

DOCTOR: Hark, she speaks! I will set down what comes from her, to satisfy[350] my remembrance the more strongly.

LADY: Out, damned spot! out, I say! One; two. Why then 'tis time to do't. Hell is murky. Fie, my lord, fie! a soldier, and afeard? What need we fear who knows it, when none can call our pow'r to accompt? Yet who would have thought the old man to have had so much blood in him?

DOCTOR: Do you mark that?

LADY: The Thane of Fife had a wife. Where is she now? What, will these hands ne'er be clean? No more o' that, my lord, no more o' that! You mar all with this starting.

DOCTOR: Go to,[351] go to! You have known what you should not.

GENTLEWOMAN: She has spoke what she should not, I am sure of that. Heaven knows what she has known.

LADY: Here's the smell of the blood still. All the perfumes of Arabia will not sweeten this little hand. Oh, oh, oh!

DOCTOR: What a sigh is there! The heart is sorely charged.

GENTLEWOMAN: I would not have such a heart in my bosom for the dignity of the whole body.

DOCTOR: Well, well, well.

GENTLEWOMAN: Pray God it be, sir.

DOCTOR: This disease is beyond my practice. Yet I have known those which have walked in their sleep who have died holily in their beds.

LADY: Wash your hands, put on your nightgown, look not so pale! I tell you yet again, Banquo's buried. He cannot come out on's[352] grave.

DOCTOR: Even so?

LADY: To bed, to bed! There's knocking at the gate. Come, come, come, come, give me your hand! What's done cannot be undone. To bed, to bed, to bed! *(Exit.)*

DOCTOR: Will she go now to bed?

GENTLEWOMAN: Directly.

DOCTOR: Foul whisp'rings are abroad. Unnatural deeds
Do breed unnatural troubles. Infected minds
To their deaf pillows will discharge their secrets.
More needs she the divine than the physician.
God, God forgive us all! Look after her;

---

[350] assure, confirm   [351] an exclamation of impatience and reproof: "Come on!"   [352] of his

Remove from her the means of all annoyance,[353]
And still keep eyes upon her. So good night.
My mind she has mated,[354] and amazed my sight.
I think, but dare not speak.

GENTLEWOMAN: Good night, good doctor.   (*Exeunt.*)

Scene 2 [The country near Dunsinane.]

(*Drum and Colors. Enter* MENTEITH, CAITHNESS, ANGUS, LENNOX,
SOLDIERS.)

MENTEITH: The English pow'r is near, led on by Malcolm,
    His uncle Siward, and the good Macduff.
    Revenges burn in them; for their dear causes
    Would to the bleeding and the grim alarm[355]
    Excite the mortified[356] man.

ANGUS: Near Birnam Wood
    Shall we well meet them; that way are they coming.

CAITHNESS: Who knows if Donalbain be with his brother?

LENNOX: For certain, sir, he is not. I have a file
    Of all the gentry. There is Siward's son
    And many unrough[357] youths that even now
    Protest[358] their first of manhood.

MENTEITH: What does the tyrant?

CAITHNESS: Great Dunsinane he strongly fortifies.
    Some say he's mad; others, that lesser hate him,
    Do call it valiant fury; but for certain
    He cannot buckle his distempered[359] cause
    Within the belt of rule.[360]

ANGUS: Now does he feel
    His secret murders sticking on his hands.
    Now minutely[361] revolts upbraid his faith-breach.
    Those he commands move only in command,
    Nothing in love. Now does he feel his title
    Hang loose about him, like a giant's robe
    Upon a dwarfish thief.

MENTEITH: Who then shall blame
    His pestered senses[362] to recoil and start,
    When all that is within him does condemn
    Itself for being there?

[353] harm, injury (*i.e.,* by her own hand)   [354] bewildered, overcome
[355] *i.e.,* the battle   [356] dead   [357] not yet bearded   [358] assert
[359] swollen with disease   [360] self-government   [361] every minute
[362] tortured mind

CAITHNESS: Well, march we on
  To give obedience where 'tis truly owed.
  Meet we the med'cine[363] of the sickly weal;
  And with him pour we in our country's purge
  Each drop of us.
LENNOX: Or so much as it needs
  To dew the sovereign flower[364] and drown the weeds.
  Make we our march toward Birnam.   (*Exeunt, marching.*)

Scene 3 [Dunsinane. A room in the Castle.]

(*Enter* MACBETH, DOCTOR, *and* ATTENDANTS.)

MACBETH: Bring me no more reports. Let them fly all!
  Till Birnam Wood remove to Dunsinane,
  I cannot taint with fear. What's the boy Malcolm?
  Was he not born of woman? The spirits that know
  All mortal consequences have pronounced me thus:
  "Fear not, Macbeth. No man that's born of woman
  Shall e'er have power upon thee." Then fly, false thanes,
  And mingle with the English epicures.[365]
  The mind I sway[366] by and the heart I bear
  Shall never sag with doubt nor shake with fear.

(*Enter* SERVANT.)

  The devil damn thee black, thou cream-faced loon![367]
  Where got'st thou that goose look?
SERVANT: There is ten thousand —
MACBETH: Geese, villain?
SERVANT: Soldiers, sir.
MACBETH: Go prick thy face and over-red[368] thy fear,
  Thou lily-livered boy. What soldiers, patch?[369]
  Death of thy soul! Those linen cheeks of thine
  Are counselors to fear. What soldiers, whey-face?
SERVANT: The English force, so please you.
MACBETH: Take thy face hence.   (*Exit* SERVANT.)
          Seyton! — I am sick at heart,
  When I behold — Seyton, I say! — This push[370]
  Will cheer me ever, or disseat me now.
  I have lived long enough. My way of life

[363] *i.e.*, Malcolm   [364] *i.e.*, Malcolm   [365] people given to soft living
[366] move; or: rule myself   [367] nobody, worthless person   [368] paint red
[369] fool, clown   [370] effort

Is fallen into the sere,[371] the yellow leaf;
And that which should accompany old age,
As honor, love, obedience, troops of friends,
I must not look to have; but, in their stead,
Curses not loud but deep, mouth-honor,[372] breath,
Which the poor heart would fain deny, and dare not.
Seyton!

(*Enter* SEYTON.)

SEYTON: What's your gracious pleasure?
MACBETH: What news more?
SEYTON: All is confirmed, my lord, which was reported.
MACBETH: I'll fight, till from my bones my flesh be hacked.
   Give me my armor.
SEYTON: 'Tis not needed yet.
MACBETH: I'll put it on.
   Send out mo[373] horses, skirr[374] the country round;
   Hang those that talk of fear. Give me mine armor.
   How does your patient, doctor?
DOCTOR: Not so sick, my lord,
   As she is troubled with thick-coming fancies
   That keep her from her rest.
MACBETH: Cure her of that!
   Canst thou not minister to a mind diseased,
   Pluck from the memory a rooted sorrow,
   Raze out the written troubles of the brain,
   And with some sweet oblivious[375] antidote
   Cleanse the stuffed bosom of that perilous stuff
   Which weighs upon the heart?
DOCTOR: Therein the patient
   Must minister to himself.
MACBETH: Throw physic to the dogs, I'll none of it! —
   Come, put mine armor on. Give me my staff.
   Seyton, send out. — Doctor, the thanes fly from me. —
   Come, sir, dispatch. — If thou couldst, doctor, cast[376]
   The water[377] of my land, find her disease,
   And purge it to a sound and pristine health,
   I would applaud thee to the very echo,
   That should applaud again. — Pull't off,[378] I say. —
   What rhubarb, senna,[379] or what purgative drug,

[371] dry   [372] insincere respect and flattery   [373] more   [374] scour   [375] inducing oblivion   [376] analyze   [377] urine   [378] *i.e.*, some part of the armor that Macbeth in his hurry has put on wrong (?)   [379] a medicinal herb

Would scour these English hence? Hear'st thou of them?
DOCTOR: Ay, my good lord. Your royal preparation
  Makes us hear something.
MACBETH: Bring it[380] after me!
  I will not be afraid of death and bane[381]
  Till Birnam Forest come to Dunsinane.
DOCTOR (*Aside*): Were I from Dunsinane away and clear,
  Profit again should hardly draw me here.   (*Exeunt.*)

Scene 4 [Country near Birnam Wood.]

(*Drum and Colors. Enter* MALCOLM, SIWARD, MACDUFF, SIWARD'S
SON, MENTEITH, CAITHNESS, ANGUS, LENNOX, ROSS, *and* SOLDIERS,
marching.)

MALCOLM: Cousins, I hope the days are near at hand
  That chambers will be safe.[382]
MENTEITH: We doubt it nothing.
SIWARD: What wood is this before us?
MENTEITH: The wood of Birnam.
MALCOLM: Let every soldier hew him down a bough
  And bear't before him. Thereby shall we shadow[383]
  The numbers of our host and make discovery[384]
  Err in report of us.
SOLDIERS: It shall be done.
SIWARD: We learn no other but the confident tyrant
  Keeps still in Dunsinane and will endure
  Our setting down[385] before't.
MALCOLM: 'Tis his main hope;
  For where there is advantage to be given,[386]
  Both more and less[387] have given him the revolt;
  And none serve with him but constrained things,
  Whose hearts are absent too.
MACDUFF: Let our just censures[388]
  Attend the true event,[389] and put we on
  Industrious soldiership.
SIWARD: The time approaches
  That will with due decision make us know
  What we shall say we have, and what we owe.[390]
  Thoughts speculative their unsure hopes relate,

---

[380] *i.e.*, a piece of the armor (?)   [381] destruction   [382] *i.e.*, when we can
sleep securely   [383] hide   [384] reconnaissance   [385] *i.e.*, to a siege
[386] where opportunity offers itself   [387] high and low   [388] judgments
[389] actual outcome   [390] possess

But certain issue strokes must arbitrate;[391]
Toward which advance the war.   (*Exeunt, marching.*)

Scene 5 [Dunsinane. Within the Castle.]

(*Enter* MACBETH, SEYTON, *and* SOLDIERS, *with Drum and Colors.*)

MACBETH: Hang out our banners on the outward walls.
  The cry is still, "They come!" Our castle's strength
  Will laugh a siege to scorn. Here let them lie
  Till famine and the ague[392] eat them up.
  Were they not forced[393] with those that should be ours,
  We might have met them dareful, beard to beard,
  And beat them backward home.

(*A cry within of women.*)

                    What is that noise?
SEYTON: It is the cry of women, my good lord.   (*Exit.*)
MACBETH: I have almost forgot the taste of fears.
  The time has been, my senses would have cooled
  To hear a night-shriek, and my fell[394] of hair
  Would at a dismal treatise[395] rouse and stir
  As life were in't. I have supped full with horrors.
  Direness, familiar to my slaughterous thoughts,
  Cannot once start me.

(*Enter* SEYTON.)

                 Wherefore was that cry?
SEYTON: The Queen, my lord, is dead.
MACBETH: She should have died hereafter;[396]
  There would have been a time for such a word.
  Tomorrow, and tomorrow, and tomorrow
  Creeps in this petty pace from day to day
  To the last syllable of recorded time;
  And all our yesterdays have lighted fools
  The way to dusty death. Out, out, brief candle!
  Life's but a walking shadow, a poor player,
  That struts and frets his hour upon the stage
  And then is heard no more. It is a tale

---

[391] strokes (of battle) are needed to settle the issue with certainty   [392] pestilence   [393] reinforced   [394] fleece, "head"   [395] horror story   [396] she would have died sooner or later; or: she should have picked a more convenient time for dying

Told by an idiot, full of sound and fury,
Signifying nothing.

(*Enter a* MESSENGER.)

Thou com'st to use thy tongue. Thy story quickly!
MESSENGER: Gracious my lord,
   I should report that which I say I saw,
   But know not how to do't.
MACBETH: Well, say, sir!
MESSENGER: As I did stand my watch upon the hill,
   I looked toward Birnam, and anon methought
   The wood began to move.
MACBETH: Liar and slave!
MESSENGER: Let me endure your wrath if't be not so.
   Within this three mile may you see it coming;
   I say, a moving grove.
MACBETH: If thou speak'st false,
   Upon the next tree shalt thou hang alive,
   Till famine cling[397] thee. If thy speech be sooth,
   I care not if thou dost for me as much.
   I pull in[398] resolution, and begin
   To doubt the equivocation of the fiend,
   That lies like truth. "Fear not, till Birnam Wood
   Do come to Dunsinane!" and now a wood
   Comes toward Dunsinane. Arm, arm, and out!
   If this which he avouches does appear,
   There is nor flying hence nor tarrying here.
   I 'gin to be aweary of the sun,
   And wish the estate o' the world were now undone.
   Ring the alarum bell! Blow wind, come wrack,
   At least we'll die with harness[399] on our back!   (*Exeunt.*)

Scene 6 [Dunsinane. Before the Castle.]

(*Drum and Colors. Enter* MALCOLM, SIWARD, MACDUFF, *and their Army, with boughs.*)

MALCOLM: Now near enough. Your leavy screens throw down
   And show like those you are. You, worthy uncle,
   Shall with my cousin, your right noble son,
   Lead our first battle.[400] Worthy Macduff and we
   Shall take upon's what else remains to do,

---

[397] shrivel   [398] rein   [399] armor   [400] front battalion

According to our order.[401]

SIWARD: Fare you well.
Do we but find the tyrant's power tonight,
Let us be beaten if we cannot fight.

MACDUFF: Make all our trumpets speak, give them all breath,
Those clamorous harbingers of blood and death.

                              (*Exeunt. Alarums continued.*)

Scene 7 [Another part of the field.]

(*Enter* MACBETH.)

MACBETH: They have tied me to a stake. I cannot fly,
But bearlike I must fight the course.[402] What's he
That was not born of woman? Such a one
Am I to fear, or none.

(*Enter* YOUNG SIWARD.)

YOUNG SIWARD: What is thy name?

MACBETH: Thou'lt be afraid to hear it.

YOUNG SIWARD: No; though thou call'st thyself a hotter name
Than any is in hell.

MACBETH: My name's Macbeth.

YOUNG SIWARD: The devil himself could not pronounce a title
More hateful to mine ear.

MACBETH: No, nor more fearful.

YOUNG SIWARD: Thou liest, abhorred tyrant! With my sword
I'll prove the lie thou speak'st.

(*Fight, and* YOUNG SIWARD *slain.*)

MACBETH: Thou wast born of woman.
But swords I smile at, weapons laugh to scorn,
Brandished by man that's of a woman born.   (*Exit.*)

(*Alarums. Enter* MACDUFF.)

MACDUFF: That way the noise is. Tyrant, show thy face!
If thou beest slain and with no stroke of mine,
My wife and children's ghosts will haunt me still.
I cannot strike at wretched kerns, whose arms
Are hired to bear their staves.[403] Either thou, Macbeth,
Or else my sword with an unbattered edge
I sheathe again undeeded. There thou shouldst be.

---

[401] battle plan   [402] bout   [403] spears

By this great clatter one of greatest note
Seems bruited.[404] Let me find him, Fortune!
And more I beg not.   (*Exit.*)

(*Alarums. Enter* MALCOLM *and* SIWARD.)

SIWARD: This way, my lord. The castle's gently rendered: [405]
    The tyrant's people on both sides do fight;
    The noble thanes do bravely in the war;
    The day almost itself professes yours,
    And little is to do.
MALCOLM: We have met with foes
    That strike beside us.[406]
SIWARD: Enter, sir, the castle.   (*Exeunt. Alarum.*)

Scene 8 [Another part of the field.]

(*Enter* MACBETH.)

MACBETH: Why should I play the Roman fool and die
    On mine own sword? Whiles I see lives,[407] the gashes
    Do better upon them.

(*Enter* MACDUFF.)

MACDUFF: Turn, hellhound, turn!
MACBETH: Of all men else I have avoided thee.
    But get thee back! My soul is too much charged
    With blood of thine already.
MACDUFF: I have no words;
    My voice is in my sword, thou bloodier villain
    Than terms can give thee out! [408]

(*Fight. Alarum.*)

MACBETH: Thou losest labor.
    As easy mayst thou the intrenchant[409] air
    With thy keen sword impress[410] as make me bleed.
    Let fall thy blade on vulnerable crests.
    I bear a charmed life, which must not yield
    To one of woman born.
MACDUFF: Despair thy charm!
    And let the angel whom thou still hast served

---

[404] reported   [405] surrendered   [406] *i.e.,* deliberately missing; or: on our
side   [407] *i.e.,* living enemies   [408] report you   [409] invulnerable
[410] mark

Tell thee, Macduff was from his mother's womb
Untimely ripped.

MACBETH: Accursed be that tongue that tells me so,
For it hath cowed my better part of man!
And be these juggling fiends no more believed,
That palter[411] with us in a double sense,
That keep the word of promise to our ear
And break it to our hope! I'll not fight with thee!

MACDUFF: Then yield thee, coward,
And live to be the show and gaze o' the time!
We'll have thee, as our rarer monsters are,
Painted upon a pole, and underwrit
"Here may you see the tyrant."

MACBETH: I will not yield,
To kiss the ground before young Malcolm's feet
And to be baited with the rabble's curse.
Though Birnam Wood be come to Dunsinane,
And thou opposed, being of no woman born,
Yet I will try the last. Before my body
I throw my warlike shield. Lay on, Macduff,
And damned be him that first cries "Hold, enough!"

                    (*Exeunt fighting. Alarums.*)

Scene 9 [The same.]

(*Retreat and flourish. Enter, with Drum and Colors,* MALCOLM,
SIWARD, ROSS, THANES, *and* SOLDIERS.)

MALCOLM: I would the friends we miss were safe arrived.

SIWARD: Some must go off;[412] and yet, by[413] these I see,
So great a day as this is cheaply bought.

MALCOLM: Macduff is missing, and your noble son.

ROSS: Your son, my lord, has paid a soldier's debt.
He only lived but till he was a man,
The which no sooner had his prowess confirmed
In the unshrinking station[414] where he fought
But like a man he died.

SIWARD: Then he is dead?

ROSS: Ay, and brought off the field. Your cause of sorrow
Must not be measured by his worth, for then
It hath no end.

---

[411] quibble   [412] die   [413] to judge by   [414] *i.e.,* place where he stood his ground

SIWARD: Had he his hurts before?

ROSS: Ay, on the front.

SIWARD: Why then, God's soldier be he!
  Had I as many sons as I have hairs,
  I would not wish them to a fairer death.
  And so his knell is knolled.

MALCOLM: He's worth more sorrow,
  And that I'll spend for him.

SIWARD: He's worth no more.
  They say he parted well and paid his score,
  And so, God be with him! Here comes newer comfort.

(*Enter* MACDUFF, *with* MACBETH's *head.*)

MACDUFF: Hail, King! for so thou art. Behold where stands
  The usurper's cursed head. The time is free.[415]
  I see thee compassed[416] with thy kingdom's pearl,[417]
  That speak my salutation in their minds;
  Whose voices I desire aloud with mine —
  Hail, King of Scotland!

ALL: Hail, King of Scotland!   (*Flourish.*)

MALCOLM: We shall not spend a large expense of time
  Before we reckon with[418] your several loves
  And make us even with[419] you. My Thanes and kinsmen,
  Henceforth be Earls, the first that ever Scotland
  In such an honor named. What's more to do
  Which would[420] be planted newly[421] with the time[422] —
  As calling home our exiled friends abroad
  That fled the snares of watchful tyranny,
  Producing forth the cruel ministers
  Of this dead butcher and his fiendlike queen,
  Who (as 'tis thought) by self and violent hands
  Took off her life — this, and what needful else
  That calls upon us, by the grace of Grace[423]
  We will perform in measure,[424] time, and place.
  So thanks to all at once and to each one,
  Whom we invite to see us crowned at Scone.

(*Flourish. Exeunt omnes.*)

[415] liberated   [416] surrounded   [417] *i.e.*, her best men   [418] appraise
[419] *i.e.*, reward   [420] needs to   [421] begun anew; or: begun quickly
[422] *i.e.*, my reign   [423] divine grace   [424] properly

Shakespeare's theater, the Globe, was a small, octagonal building of three levels of galleries surrounding a center space, almost half of which was occupied by the stage. This, the "apron," was a low, wooden platform, partly covered by a roof and adjoining a recessed inner stage in the building itself. Above the apron there may have been an upper inner stage. The open area surrounding the apron on three sides was called the pit. Here stood the poorer spectators; their social betters were seated in the galleries. Costumes were elaborate but historically unauthentic for plays set in non-Elizabethan times. Props were used to a limited extent, but hardly any effort was made to create stage verisimilitude. It was an intimate theater, in which actor and audience were physically close, and in which the absence of elaborate sets or stage machinery invited an imaginative and fluid dramatic form.

Like many of Shakespeare's plays, *Macbeth* cannot be accurately dated, but the evidence points to 1606. The basis for the text is the Folio of 1623, the first collected edition of Shakespeare, published by Heminge and Condell, Shakespeare's colleagues in the acting company, the King's Servants. Although *Macbeth* is the second shortest of all Shakespeare's plays (the early *The Comedy of Errors* is the shortest), it probably contains non-Shakespearean interpolations, notably the two scenes in which Hecate appears. Shakespeare's source was Raphael Holinshed's *Chronicles of England, Scotland, and Ireland* (1578). As usual, Shakespeare has treated his historical (or semi-historical) source material quite freely — Holinshed's Banquo, for example, is Macbeth's accomplice. Shakespeare probably altered his character as a compliment to King James II of England and Scotland, whose ancestor Banquo was said to be.

For all its brutality of incident, the play's chief interest is psychological and poetic. Its action is the hero's corruption by "vaulting ambition, which o'erleaps itself," Scotland's savior becoming her murderous usurper. Macbeth's nature raises a question about his fitness as a tragic hero. Why is it that he not only fascinates but evokes sympathy as well? The answer may lie in the quality of his consciousness. With a statement that violates the play's integrity as imagined reality but nevertheless illuminates an aspect of tragedy, it may be said about Macbeth — as about so many of Shakespeare's erring heroes — that his language redeems him. Throughout his darkening career we feel that what he does is a mounting horror to himself — that he pays for his evil with agony of soul, and knows that he pays. The imagination and sensibility at work in the "To-morrow, and tomorrow, and tomorrow" soliloquy reveal the waste of potential goodness and greatness in Macbeth. The tragic feeling the play elicits may be due to our awareness of that waste. It is one of Shakespeare's major triumphs of characterization that we can see Macbeth as a tragic character, that he transcends the inconsistency that would attach to him in a mere outline, in which he would appear as a man who knows and feels one thing and does the exact opposite.

Who is responsible for Macbeth's destiny? In one sense it is himself. What he does he does with open eyes, deliberately choosing evil as his good, aware that though he is *tempted* by visions of the crown he is not *compelled* by them. Nowhere does he blame forces outside of himself for what he does.

Yet, it would not have seemed altogether unreasonable if he had done so. It is difficult to read the last scenes of Act I without feeling that but for his wife Macbeth would not have killed Duncan — at least, not on that particular occasion. But though Lady Macbeth's guilt is clear, she does not continue to motivate her husband's evil. His remark to her as he plots the murder of Banquo,

> Be innocent of the knowledge, dearest chuck,

suggests in a flash both his love for her and his understanding of her nature. Her absence from the play after the banquet scene (III, iv) prepares us (we see in retrospect) for her final psychological collapse. Macbeth has no word of blame for his wife (his epitaph on her, "She should have died hereafter," is perhaps obscure, but it hardly bespeaks resentment), and to see her as her husband's evil genius, a figure like the Dark Angel in the old morality play, is to reduce a character as complex as Macbeth himself to a moral abstraction. One can do so only by ignoring the sleepwalking scene.

What role, then, do the three witches play in Macbeth's tragedy? How do they relate to Lady Macbeth? Are they the representatives of fate, as the adjective "weird" (derived from Old Norse *wyrd* = "fate") suggests? Or are they rather forces of evil, damning Macbeth's soul by means of equivocal promises? Carried far enough, such an interpretation makes of Macbeth a pawn manipulated by malicious forces. And yet, the argument that there is an element of fatalism in the play could be supported by its ironies: the seeds of destruction that lie in Macbeth's very triumph; the unexpected moral similarity between the two thanes of Cawdor; the unsuspected truth in Duncan's words as he sets out for Macbeth's castle:

> From hence to Inverness,
> And bind us further to you.

our recollection during the sleepwalking scene of Lady Macbeth's confidence after the murder of Duncan:

> A little water clears us of this deed.
> How easy is it then!

the philosophical paradoxes (again in retrospect) involved in Macbeth's early pondering of the witches' prophecy:

> If chance will have me King, why, chance may crown me,
> Without my stir.

But does the suggestion of fate's guiding hand in such ironies amount to a fatalistic premise for the play? In another view, the weird sisters may appear as secret wishes and desires in Macbeth and the play keep its ethical import — the hero's flaw still determining the action. That the witches appear to Banquo as well and haunt his dreams (II, i) need not destroy this interpretation; it could simply mean that though both men are tempted only Macbeth yields. Perhaps the wisdom in Banquo's lines to Macbeth accounts for the difference in their responses to temptation:

> And oftentimes, to win us to our harm,
> The instruments of darkness tell us truths,
> Win us with honest trifles, to betray's
> In deepest consequence.

And if the questions about ultimate guilt and responsibility in *Macbeth* prove as unanswerable as such questions are in *Oedipus Rex*, the reason may be that metaphysical inconclusiveness is the context of all great tragedy.

Another approach to the play — supplementary rather than alternative to that just suggested — is through consideration of its imagery. Critics have shown how sets of images concerning blood, clothes, and farm husbandry stipple the dialogue, making abstracts concrete and visible, defining values. If language itself registers values, it becomes significant how often the words "man" and "manly" occur in *Macbeth*. There are moments when one feels the play's real subject matter to be the proper definition of manliness. To Lady Macbeth, manliness is courage and resoluteness. But Macbeth at one point knows:

> I dare do all that may become a man,
> Who dares do more is none.

Lady Macbeth's sarcasm, that in that case it was a "beast" who first thought of killing Duncan, turns out in the end to have been almost literally true. For by doing more than becomes man to do Macbeth is seen time and again as something other than man: "devilish," a "hell-kite," a fruit "ripe for the shaking," a dwarf dressed in giant's robes. His wife is a "she-wolf." The nature of Macbeth's relationship to his three major victims — Duncan, Banquo, Macduff's family — suggests the qualities of true manhood — loyalty, friendship, mercy, respectively — that he rejects in committing the three murders. False manliness becomes cruelty. It is the excess of the virtues that enable him to save Scotland that destroys him.

Consider one final image, since it defines the nature of Macbeth's evil in a wider context. What happens to sanctified kingship in Macbeth's hands? The King of England, a true king, has the power to cure disease, but Macbeth is himself his country's malady, "pestering," a grotesque freak, fit to be shown in a cage. When he asks the doctor to

> cast
> The water of my land, find her disease,
> And purge it to a sound and pristine health,

don't we feel that what he really is asking for is his own destruction? The rule of the Macbeths represents the temporary triumph of unreason over reason, unnature over nature, chaos over cosmos — as again images will testify. And one reason why the ending of the play is so strongly cathartic is that Macbeth's death, like the banishment of Oedipus, signifies the restoration of health and sanity to the sick land. As the forces of goodness and justice assemble and move, Macbeth ceases to dominate the play; he is absent between IV, ii and V, iii. Health is about to be restored to the body politic. At the moment of his triumph, King Malcolm, like his father Duncan, speaks of "planting" his loyal servants in the fruitful soil of his kingly trust and favor. The metaphor is unthinkable in Macbeth's mouth.

Molière

TARTUFFE

Translated by Renée Waldinger

Characters

> MADAME PERNELLE, *Orgon's mother*
> ORGON, *Elmire's husband*
> ELMIRE, *Orgon's wife*
> DAMIS, *Orgon's son*
> MARIANE, *Orgon's daughter*
> VALÈRE, *Mariane's admirer*
> CLÉANTE, *Orgon's brother-in-law*
> TARTUFFE, *a hypocrite*
> DORINE, *Mariane's maid*
> MONSIEUR LOYAL, *a sergeant*
> AN OFFICER
> FLIPOTE, *Madame Pernelle's maid*

SCENE: *The action takes place in Paris.*

ACT I

Scene 1 [MADAME PERNELLE, FLIPOTE, *her maid*, ELMIRE, MARIANE, DORINE, DAMIS, CLÉANTE]

MADAME PERNELLE: Come, Flipote, come, let's get rid of them.
ELMIRE: You are walking so fast that I can hardly follow you.
MADAME PERNELLE: Don't bother, daughter, don't bother; don't go any further; there is no need for all this ceremony.

ELMIRE: We are only doing what is due to you. But, mother, what makes you leave so quickly?

MADAME PERNELLE: Because I cannot bear to see such goings on, and no one tries to please me. Yes, I leave your house, very little impressed; all my instructions are contradicted here; nothing is respected, everyone has his say, and it's just like a circus.

DORINE: If . . .

MADAME PERNELLE: You are, my girl, somewhat of a loud-mouth and very fresh; you're mighty free with your advice.

DAMIS: But . . .

MADAME PERNELLE: You are a fool, my boy, to put it bluntly. I, your own grandmother, tell you so, and I have told my son, your father, a hundred times, that you were fast becoming a good-for-nothing, and that you would not give him anything but trouble.

MARIANE: I think . . .

MADAME PERNELLE: My goodness, granddaughter, you seem so modest, and to look at you, butter would not melt in your mouth. But, as they say, still waters run deep, and you do secretly things I dislike very much.

ELMIRE: But, mother . . .

MADAME PERNELLE: If you don't mind, daughter, your behavior is completely wrong: you should set them a good example and their late mother managed them much better. You are extravagant and it offends me to see you dressed like a princess. The woman who wants to please her husband only, daughter, does not need so much finery.

CLÉANTE: But after all, Madame . . .

MADAME PERNELLE: As for you, sir, who are her brother, I esteem you very much, I like you and respect you; nevertheless, if I were my son, her husband, I would entreat you not to come into our house. You are always advocating a way of life that should not be followed by decent people. I am speaking very frankly, but that's the way I am, and I do not mince words when I have something on my mind.

DAMIS: Your Mr. Tartuffe is a blessed soul, no doubt.

MADAME PERNELLE: He is a very worthy man to whom one ought to pay attention, and I cannot allow, without getting angry, to have him attacked by a fool like you.

DAMIS: What! should I allow a censorious bigot to usurp an absolute authority in this house? And shall we not be permitted the least amusement unless that dear gentleman gives us his consent?

DORINE: If we were to listen to him and believe in his maxims, we could not do anything without committing a sin; for he controls everything, this zealous critic.

MADAME PERNELLE: And whatever he controls is very well controlled.

He wishes to show you the way to Heaven, and my son ought to make all of you love him.

DAMIS: No, really, grandmother, neither father nor anything else will ever induce me to look kindly upon him. I would betray my heart were I to speak differently. His manner constantly enrages me; I can foresee that, at one time or another, I shall come to a real quarrel with that boor.

DORINE: To be sure, it's downright scandalous to see a stranger take over such authority in this house; to see a beggar, who had no shoes when he came, and whose clothes were not worth sixpence, so far forget himself that he contradicts everything and plays the master.

MADAME PERNELLE: Mercy on me! Matters would be far better if everything were managed according to his pious directions.

DORINE: He passes for a saint in your imagination. Believe me, all he does is nothing but hypocrisy.

MADAME PERNELLE: What a tongue!

DORINE: I would not trust him without good security, any more than I would his man Laurent.

MADAME PERNELLE: I do not know what the servant may be at heart, but I shall vouch that the master is a worthy man. You bear him ill-will and reject him only because he tells you the truth. It's against sin that his heart rises in anger, and he does everything in the interests of Heaven.

DORINE: Yes, but why, especially lately, can't he endure that anyone come into this house? In what way does an honest visit offend Heaven to such an extent that we must have such a fuss about it that our ears are splitting? Among ourselves, do you want me to be frank? Upon my word I believe him to be jealous of my mistress.

MADAME PERNELLE: Hold your tongue and mind what you are saying. He is not the only one who condemns these visits. All the bustle that attends the people you frequent, these carriages forever stationed at the door, the noisy company of so many footmen, cause a great disturbance in the whole neighborhood. I am willing to believe that there is really no harm; but then people do talk of it, and that is not right.

CLÉANTE: Alas, Madame, will you prevent people from talking? It would be a very unhappy thing in life, if, for the foolish stories that can be told about us, we had to renounce our best friends, and even if we could resolve to do so, do you think we would oblige everyone to keep his tongue? There is no protection against slander. Let us therefore pay no attention to all that silly chatter, let us endeavor to live innocently and leave the gossips to say what they please.

DORINE: May not Daphné, our neighbor, and her little husband, be the

persons who speak ill of us? Those whose own conduct is most ridiculous are always the first to slander others. They never fail to catch
eagerly the slightest rumor of a love-affair, to spread the news of it
with the greatest joy and to give it the turn they want. By coloring
other people's actions like their own, they think they can justify their
own to society; and in the false hope of some resemblance, give an
air of innocence to their own intrigues; or shift elsewhere part of the
public blame with which they are too heavily burdened.

MADAME PERNELLE: All these arguments have nothing to do with this.
Everyone knows that Orante leads an exemplary life; all her cares
tend to Heaven; and I have heard it said that she strongly condemns
the company that comes here.

DORINE: An admirable example, indeed, and this lady is very kind! It
is true that she lives very austerely; but it is age that has put this
ardent zeal into her heart, and everyone knows that she is a prude
against her true wishes. As long as she was able to make conquests
she enjoyed her advantages well enough. But seeing the lustre of her
eyes diminish, she wishes to renounce the world which is on the
point of leaving her; and under the pompous cloak of lofty wisdom
conceals the decay of her worn-out charms. These are the vicissitudes
of former coquettes. It is hard for them to see their admirers desert
them. Thus forsaken, their gloomy anxiety sees no other recourse
but that of prudery; and the severity of these good women censures
everything and forgives nothing. Loudly they find fault with everyone's life, not through charity, but through envy which cannot bear
that another enjoy those pleasures for which their age makes them
no longer yearn.

MADAME PERNELLE: These are the fancy stories that are told to please
you, daughter. We all have to keep quiet in your house for my lady
keeps chattering all day. But I intend to have my say in my turn. Let
me tell you that my son never did anything wiser than to take this
devout man into his family; that Heaven, as a matter of fact, has
sent him here to reclaim your lost souls; that for your salvation you
ought to listen to him; and that he censures nothing that is not cen-
surable. These visits, these balls, these conversations are all inventions
of the wicked spirit. Pious words are never heard at any of them;
only idle chatter, songs and nonsense. Quite often your neighbor
comes in for his share of it and everyone knows how to slander right
and left. In short, sensible people become completely mixed up by
the confusion of such get-togethers. A thousand different idle stories
are started in no time and, as a certain preacher said so well the
other day, it's a perfect tower of Babel, for everyone chatters away
without interruption. And to tell you the story which brought this

up . . . (*Pointing to* CLÉANTE.) But here is this young man giggling already. Go and look for the fools that make you laugh, and without . . . goodbye, daughter, I will say no more. Let me tell you that I have lost a good deal of my respect for your home and that it will be a long time before I set foot in it again. (*Slapping* FLIPOTE'S *face*.) Let's go, you! You're dreaming and your head is lost in the clouds. By my word, I'll know how to warm your ears. Let's go, you slut, let's go!

Scene 2 [CLÉANTE, DORINE]

CLÉANTE: I don't want to go there, for fear she should start arguing again; that this old lady . . .

DORINE: Ah! It is too bad she does not hear you talk this way; she would soon tell you that you have some nerve and that she is not old enough to be called that.

CLÉANTE: How excited she got with us for nothing, and how infatuated she seems with her Tartuffe!

DORINE: Oh! really, all this is nothing compared with the son; and if you had seen him you would say: "It's much worse." During our troubles[1] he acted like a man of sense and showed courage in the service of the king, but he has become a perfect dolt since he got so fond of his Tartuffe. He calls him brother and loves him in his heart a hundred times more than his mother, his son, his daughter or his wife. He is the sole confidant of all his secrets and the wise director of all his actions. He caresses him, embraces him; and it seems to me, he couldn't show more tenderness to a mistress. He wants him to be seated at the head of the table; he is delighted to see him eat more than half a dozen men; the choicest morsels of everything must be given to him, and if he happens to belch, he tells him: "May God preserve you!" In short he is crazy about him; he means everything to him, he's his hero; he admires all he does, quotes him on all occasions; he looks upon his most trifling actions as miracles, and every word he utters is considered an oracle. The other who knows his dupe and wishes to make the most of him, understands the art of dazzling him by a hundred deceitful tricks. His pretended devotions draw constantly large sums from our master and he assumes the right of commenting upon the conduct of every one of us. Even the conceited ass who is his valet takes it upon himself to lec-

[1] The troubles of the Fronde, when members of the nobility who wanted to retain their feudal privileges and opposed the ever-increasing centralization of power, revolted against the King and the court party during the minority of Louis XIV. Orgon had remained loyal to the King.

ture us; he comes preaching to us with fierce looks and throws away our ribbons, our rouge and beauty patches. The rascal, the other day, tore with his own hands a fine handkerchief he had found in a prayer book, saying that it was a dreadful sin to mix the finery of the devil with holy things.

Scene 3 [ELMIRE, MARIANE, DAMIS, CLÉANTE, DORINE]

ELMIRE: You are very fortunate not to have been present at the speech she made at the door. But I just saw my husband; since he didn't see me I want to go upstairs to await his coming.

CLÉANTE: I'll wait for him here to waste less time, and merely to say hello.

DAMIS: Hint something about my sister's marriage. I suspect that Tartuffe is opposed to it and that he is forcing my father to make so many evasions; and you are not unaware of the great interest I take in it. If one passion fills my sister's and Valère's heart, his sister, as you know, is dear to me; and if it were necessary . . .

DORINE: He is coming.

Scene 4 [ORGON, CLÉANTE, DORINE]

ORGON: Ah! brother, good day.

CLÉANTE: I was leaving and I am glad to see you back. The country is not very cheerful at present.

ORGON: Dorine . . . (*To* CLÉANTE.) Brother, pray, stay. Allow me to inquire what news there is here, to ease my mind. (*To* DORINE.) Has everything gone on well these two days? What has happened here? How is everyone?

DORINE: The day before yesterday, my mistress was feverish the whole day and had a terrible headache.

ORGON: And Tartuffe?

DORINE: Tartuffe? He's fine, stout and fat, with a good complexion and a rosy mouth.

ORGON: Poor man!

DORINE: The whole night she did not close her eyes for a moment; she was so feverish that she could not sleep and we had to sit up with her till the morning.

ORGON: And Tartuffe?

DORINE: Feeling pleasantly sleepy, he went to his room when he left the table, and jumped into his warm bed where he slept undisturbed till the next day.

ORGON: Poor man!

DORINE: Finally, giving in to our arguments, she resolved to let herself be bled,[2] and she was immediately relieved.

ORGON: And Tartuffe?

DORINE: He revived his courage, as he should, and fortifying his soul against all misfortunes, drank four large cups of wine to make up for the blood that our mistress had lost.

ORGON: Poor man!

DORINE: At present both are fine; I shall go and inform our mistress how glad you are of her recovery.

Scene 5 [ORGON, CLÉANTE]

CLÉANTE: She is laughing at you, to your face, brother, and without wishing to make you angry I shall tell you quite frankly that she is right. Have you ever heard of such a whim? And can it be that a man has such magic power in our day to make you forget everything for him? That after having relieved his indigence in your house, you should go so far as to . . .

ORGON: Stop right there, brother; you do not know the man of whom you are speaking.

CLÉANTE: I do not know him, if you like; but, after all, to know what kind of man he must be . . .

ORGON: Brother, you would be delighted to know him and there would be no end to your raptures. He is a man . . . who . . . ha! . . . a man . . . in short, a man. Whoever follows his precepts enjoys a deep peace and looks at everyone as so much dirt. Yes, I am becoming quite different since I am in contact with him. He teaches not to be attached to anything, he detaches my soul from all friendships, and were I to see my brother, children, mother, and wife die, it wouldn't bother me any more than that.

CLÉANTE: Humane sentiments, these, my brother!

ORGON: Ah! if you had seen how I met him you would have liked him as much as I do. Every day he came to church, looking so gentle, and kneeled right opposite me. He attracted the eyes of the whole congregation by the fervor with which he sent his prayers to Heaven; he sighed, was enraptured, and humbly kissed the ground every few moments. And, when I went out, he swiftly ran before me to offer me holy water at the door. Informed by his servant, who imitated him in everything, of his poverty and his station in life, I made him some presents; but, with great modesty, he always wanted to return some of them. "It's too much," he said to me, "it's too much by half. I do not deserve to arouse your pity." And when I refused to

2 Bloodletting was a common remedy at that time.

take them back, he would go and give them to the poor, right in my presence. Finally the Heavens moved me to bring him into my house and, since then, everything seems to prosper here. I see that he corrects everything and that, for my sake, he even takes a great interest in my wife; he warns me about the people who flirt with her and he is far more jealous of her than I am. But you won't believe how far his religious zeal goes; he considers a sin every little trifle in himself; a mere nothing is all that is needed to shock him; so much so that the other day he accused himself of having caught a flea, while praying, and having killed it in anger.

CLÉANTE: My goodness! I believe you are mad, brother. Are you making fun of me with such a speech? And what do you mean with all that foolishness? . . .

ORGON: Brother, these words have the tone of free-thinking. You are somewhat tainted with it, and, as I have told you several times, you will get yourself into some unpleasant business.

CLÉANTE: This is the usual speech of people like you. They want everyone to be blind as they are. To be clear-sighted is to be a free-thinker; and whoever does not worship these empty affectations has neither respect nor faith for sacred things. Come, all your speeches do not frighten me; I know what I am saying and the Heavens see my heart. We are not slaves of all your affected demonstrations; there are hypocrites in religion as well as in courage; and, as we never see truly brave men make a lot of noise wherever honor leads them, so the good and truly pious whom we ought to imitate are not the ones who make such demonstrations. What! won't you make any distinction between hpyocrisy and true devotion. You want to treat in the same way and give the same honor to the mask as to the face; put artifice on a level with sincerity, confound appearance with reality, value the shadow as much as the person, and counterfeit money as much as good money? Men, for the most part, are strange creatures! They never keep the golden mean. The bounds of reason are too narrow for them; in every characteristic they go beyond its limitations and they often spoil the noblest action because they want to exaggerate it and push it too far. These are just a few comments I am making, brother.

ORGON: Yes, you are no doubt a revered doctor of theology; you possess all the knowledge in the world; you are the only wise man and the only enlightened one; the oracle, the Cato, of the present age, and compared to you all men are fools.

CLÉANTE: I am not, brother, a revered doctor of theology and I do not possess all the wisdom in the world; but, to make it short, I know enough to differentiate between truth and falsehood. And just as I see no type of person more worthy of praise than the truly devout, for nothing in the world is nobler and more beautiful than true devotion; so I see nothing more hateful than the put-on expression of a pretended zeal, than those downright charlatans, those public devotees, whose sacrilegious and deceitful grimace abuse with impunity, and according to their fancy, make a jest of what is most venerable and sacred among men; those people who, motivated by self-interest, make a trade of piety, and want to buy honor and reputation at the cost of hypocritical looks to Heaven and affected raptures; these people, let me tell you, whom we see show an uncommon zeal for the next world in order to make their fortunes in this; who, with great affectation and much prayer, daily beg for and preach solitude, while remaining in the midst of the court; who know how to reconcile their zeal with their vices; who are passionate, revengeful, faithless and full of artifice, and who, in order to destroy a man, insolently cover their private resentment under the cloak of Heaven's interests. They are the more dangerous in their wrath because they use against us the weapons we revere and because their passion, for which they are commended, prompts them to assassinate us with a consecrated blade. There are too many of this vile character. But the sincerely devout are easily recognized. Our age has shown us some, brother, who may serve as glorious examples. Look at Ariston, look at Périandre, Oronte, Alcidamas, Polydore, Clitandre: no one contests their title. They are not at all braggarts of virtue; we see none of this insufferable ostentation in them and their devotion is humane and manageable. They do not censure all our actions; they think there is too much pride in all these corrections; and leaving big words to others, reprove our actions by their own. They do not consider something evil just because it seems so, and they are always ready to judge others favorably. They have no cabals, no intrigues to carry on; all their desire is to live well themselves. They never persecute a sinner, they hate sin only, nor do they exert a keener zeal for the interests of Heaven, than Heaven itself does. These are the men for me; this is the way to act, this is, in short, the example to be followed. Your man is indeed not of that type. You vaunt his zeal with the best intention, but I believe you are dazzled by a false lustre.

ORGON: My dear brother-in-law, have you had your say?

CLÉANTE: Yes.

ORGON: Then I am your humble servant. (*He tries to leave.*)

CLÉANTE: Pray, one word more, brother. Let's stop this discussion. You know you promised to take Valère for your son-in-law.

ORGON: Yes.

CLÉANTE: You had chosen a date for this wedding.

ORGON: That is true.

CLÉANTE: Why then postpone the ceremony?

ORGON: I don't know.

CLÉANTE: Could you have some other intention?

ORGON: Perhaps.

CLÉANTE: Will you break your word?

ORGON: I am not saying that.

CLÉANTE: There is no obstacle, I think, to prevent you from fulfilling your promise.

ORGON: That depends.

CLÉANTE: Why so much fuss about a single word. Valère sent me to ask you about it.

ORGON: Heaven be praised!

CLÉANTE: But what shall I tell him?

ORGON: Anything you wish.

CLÉANTE: But I have to know your intentions. What are they?

ORGON: To do what Heaven ordains.

CLÉANTE: But to the point. Valère has your word. Will you keep it, or not?

ORGON: Good-bye.

CLÉANTE (*Alone*): I fear some misfortune for his love. I must warn him of what is going on.

ACT II

Scene 1 [ORGON, MARIANE]

ORGON: Mariane.

MARIANE: Father.

ORGON: Come here. I have something to tell you in secret.

MARIANE: What are you looking for?

ORGON (*Who is looking into a closet*): I want to see whether there is anyone who could overhear us because this little place is fit for such a purpose. Now we are all right. I have always, Mariane, found you of sweet disposition, and you have always been very dear to me.

MARIANE: I am very much obliged to you for this fatherly affection.

ORGON: That is well said, daughter; and to deserve it, your only care should be to please me.

MARIANE: That is indeed the height of my ambition.

ORGON: Very well. What do you think of Tartuffe, our guest?

MARIANE: Who, I?

ORGON: You. Take care how you answer.

MARIANE: Alas! I'll say whatever you wish.

ORGON: That is sensibly spoken. Tell me then, daughter, that he is a man of the highest merit, that he touches your heart, and that it would be pleasant to you to have him, with my consent, become your husband. Eh?

MARIANE (*Drawing back in surprise*): What?

ORGON: What is the matter?

MARIANE: Excuse me?

ORGON: What?

MARIANE: I must have misunderstood?

ORGON: How?

MARIANE: Who, would you have me say, touches my heart, and whom would it be pleasant to have for a husband with your consent?

ORGON: Tartuffe.

MARIANE: That is not so, father, I assure you. Why do you wish me to tell you such a falsehood?

ORGON: But I want it to be the truth; and it is sufficient for you that I have resolved it.

MARIANE: What! You wish, father . . .

ORGON: Yes, daughter, I intend to join Tartuffe to my family through your marriage. He will be your husband. I have decided that I have a right to . . .

Scene 2 [DORINE, ORGON, MARIANE]

ORGON: What are you doing here? Your curiosity is very great, my girl, to bring you to listen in such a way.

DORINE: In truth, I do not know whether it is a rumor which arises from some conjecture or from chance, but I have heard the news of this marriage and I treated it as a pure joke.

ORGON: Why, is the thing so incredible?

DORINE: So much so, sir, that I don't even believe you when you say it.

ORGON: I know how to make you believe it.

DORINE: Oh, come, sir, you are telling us a funny story.

ORGON: I'm only telling you what you will soon see.

DORINE: Nonsense!

ORGON: What I say, daughter, is no joke.

DORINE: Come, don't believe your father! he is joking.

ORGON: I am telling you . . .

DORINE: No, it's in vain, we won't believe you.

ORGON: At last, my anger . . .

DORINE: Well, then, we'll believe you and it's too bad for you. What, can it be, sir, what with that air of common sense and this beard in the middle of the face, you are mad enough to want . . .

ORGON: Listen here: you have taken certain liberties here that quite displease me; I am telling you that, my girl.

DORINE: Let's talk without getting angry, I beg you, sir. Are you making fun of us, sir, in making this scheme? Your daughter is not cut out for a bigot, he has other things to think about. And besides, what will such an alliance bring you? Why should you, with all your wealth, go and choose a beggar for a son-in-law . . .

ORGON: Hold your tongue. If he has nothing, know that we ought to esteem him for it. His poverty is no doubt an honest poverty. It ought to raise him above all honors because he has allowed himself to be deprived of his wealth by his little care of things temporal and his great attachment to things eternal. But my help will give him the means of getting out of his troubles and of recovering his property. His lands are well-known in his province and, as poor as he is, he is indeed a nobleman.

DORINE: Yes, he says so, and this vanity does not agree very well with piety. Whoever embraces the innocence of a holy life should not boast so much of his name and his lineage; and the humble ways of piety cannot endure the glare of that ambition. What is the good of this pride? . . . But this talk offends you. Let us speak of his person and let's leave his lineage alone. Would you, without any compunction, give a girl like her to a man like him? Shouldn't you think of propriety and foresee the consequences of such a marriage? Remember that a girl's virtue is in danger when her wishes are thwarted in her marriage; that her intention of living virtuously depends upon the qualities of the husband who has been chosen for her, and those men who are always pointed at for having unfaithful wives,[3] often make their wives what they are. In short it's very difficult to be faithful to certain types of husbands and whoever gives his daughter to a man she hates is responsible to Heaven for the mistakes she makes. Consider to what perils your plan exposes you.

ORGON: I can tell you that I need her to teach me how to live!

DORINE: You cannot do better but follow my advice.

ORGON: Let's not waste any more time with this nonsense, daughter. I know what you need and I am your father. I had promised you to Valère; but besides his liking to gamble, or so I heard, I suspect him of being somewhat of a free-thinker. I don't notice that he goes to church very much.

---

[3] The literal translation is: those men at whose forehead people point.

DORINE: Do you want him to run there just when you go, like those who go there only to be seen?

ORGON: I am not asking your advice about this. In short, the other one is on the best terms with Heaven, and that is a treasure second to none. This union will gratify your wishes to the full; it will be replete with sweetness and delight. You will live together, faithful in your love, really like two children, like turtle-doves. There will never be any unhappy fights between you and you will do with him whatever you may wish.

DORINE: She? She won't make anything but a fool out of him, I assure you.

ORGON: Hey! What language!

DORINE: I say that he has the look of one and that his destiny, sir, will be stronger than all your daughter's virtue.

ORGON: Stop interrupting me and try to hold your tongue without poking your nose into what does not concern you.

DORINE: I am only talking, sir, in your interest. (*She always interrupts him when he turns around to talk to his daughter.*)

ORGON: You take too much interest; hold your tongue, if you please.

DORINE: If I didn't care for you . . .

ORGON: I don't want you to care for me.

DORINE: But I wish to care for you, sir, in spite of yourself!

ORGON: Ah!

DORINE: I have your reputation much at heart and I cannot bear to have you made the subject of everyone's gossip.

ORGON: Won't you keep quiet?

DORINE: It's against my conscience to let you make such an alliance.

ORGON: Will you hold your tongue, you serpent, whose impudence . . .

DORINE: Ah! you are so pious and yet you fly into a rage!

ORGON: Yes, I get very angry at all that impertinence and I am resolved that you shall hold your tongue.

DORINE: Be it so. But even though I do not say a word, I still think so.

ORGON: Think, if you wish; but take care not to talk to me about it, or . . . Enough. (*Turning to his daughter.*) As a wise man I have carefully weighed everything.

DORINE (*Aside*): I am so furious that I can't talk.

ORGON: Without being a fop, Tartuffe looks like . . .

DORINE: Yes, he has some mug!

ORGON: That even if you have no relish for his other gifts . . . (*He turns to* DORINE *and looks at her.*)

DORINE: She has some bargain! If I were in her shoes, a man would surely not marry me against my will without impunity. I would show him, soon after the ceremony, that a wife has a revenge always at hand.

ORGON: Then you won't pay any attention to what I say?

DORINE: What are you complaining about? I am not talking to you.

ORGON: Then what are you doing?

DORINE: I am talking to myself.

ORGON: Very well. To punish her extreme insolence, I'll have to give her a slap in the face. (*He gets into position to give her a slap; and every time he looks around,* DORINE *stands straight without talking.*) You must approve my plan, daughter . . . You must believe that the husband . . . whom I have chosen for you . . . (*To* DORINE.) Why aren't you talking to yourself?

DORINE: I have nothing to say to myself.

ORGON: Just another little word.

DORINE: I don't feel like it.

ORGON: Of course, I was watching you.

DORINE: I am not such a fool.

ORGON: In short, daughter, you must obey and show a complete deference for my choice.

DORINE (*As she runs away*): I would scorn to take such a husband. (*He wants to slap her, but misses.*)

ORGON: You have a cursed hussy with you, daughter, with whom I couldn't live any longer without forgetting myself. I am not in a condition to continue this conversation; her insolent remarks have made me boiling mad and I am going to take some air to recover a little.

Scene 3 [DORINE, MARIANE]

DORINE: Pray tell me, have you lost your tongue? And must I act your part in this affair? Will you allow such a senseless proposal to be made to you without saying the least word against it?

MARIANE: What do you want me to do against a tyrannical father?

DORINE: What you have to do to ward off such a menace.

MARIANE: What?

DORINE: Tell him that a heart cannot love by proxy; that you are getting married for yourself, not for him; that since you are the one for whom the whole transaction is made, it is you, not he, who must like the husband; and that if he finds his Tartuffe so charming, he can marry him without any interference.

MARIANE: A father, I confess, has so much authority over us that I never had the strength to answer him.

DORINE: But let's talk about this. Valère has made advances to you; do you love him, pray, or don't you?

MARIANE: Ah! you do great injustice to my love, Dorine! Do you have to ask me that? Haven't I opened my heart to you a hundred times about that, and don't you know how much in love I am with him?

DORINE: How do I know whether your lips have spoken of the true feelings of your heart and whether you are really taken with this admirer?

MARIANE: You do me great wrong, Dorine, when you doubt it, and my true feelings have but been shown too clearly.

DORINE: You really love him, then?

MARIANE: Yes, passionately.

DORINE: And, to all appearance, he loves you as well?

MARIANE: I think so.

DORINE: And you are equally anxious to be married to each other?

MARIANE: Of course.

DORINE: What do you expect from this other match, then?

MARIANE: To kill myself if they force me to do it.

DORINE: Very well. That's a recourse that hadn't occurred to me. You only have to die to get out of trouble. No doubt this remedy is marvelous. I get furious when I hear that kind of language.

MARIANE: My goodness, Dorine, how angry you are getting! You don't sympathize at all with anyone's unhappiness.

DORINE: I do not sympathize with anyone who talks nonsense, and gives in as you do at a decisive moment.

MARIANE: But what do you want? If I am timid . . .

DORINE: Love requires firmness.

MARIANE: But have I wavered in my affection for Valère? And isn't it his business to obtain my father's consent?

DORINE: But what! If your father is a churlish fool who is entirely bewitched by his Tartuffe, and will break up a match he had agreed on, is that your lover's fault?

MARIANE: But shall I, by a flat refusal and scornful disdain, show everyone how much in love I am? However great my love may be, shall I, for Valère's sake, forget the modesty of my sex and my filial duty? And do you want me to display my passion to everyone . . .

DORINE: No, no, I don't want anything. I see that you want to belong to Monsieur Tartuffe; and now I think of it, I would be in the wrong to turn you away from such a union. Why should I oppose your wishes? The match in itself is very advantageous. Monsieur Tartuffe! Oh! oh! is this a trifling offer? Certainly Monsieur Tartuffe, all things considered, is not a man to be sneezed at, and it's no small honor to be his better half. Everyone is already crowning him with glory. He belongs to the nobility in his part of the country, he is good-looking. He has red ears and a florid complexion; you'll be only too happy with such a husband.

MARIANE: Good gracious . . .

DORINE: You can't imagine how happy you will be when you are the wife of such a handsome husband!

MARIANE: Ah! stop such talk, I beg you, and give me your help against this match. I give up. I am ready to do anything.

DORINE: No; a daughter has to obey her father, were he to give her an ape for a husband. Yours is an enviable fate, what are you complaining of? You will drive in a stagecoach to his provincial town which will abound in uncles and cousins, and you will enjoy entertaining them. First you will be introduced to the best society. You will go and visit, by way of welcome, the bailiff's lady and the magistrate's wife, who will do you the honor of giving you a folding-chair. There, at carnival time, you may expect a ball, with a large band, to wit, two bagpipes, and sometimes you may see Fagotin and his marionettes. If your husband, however . . .

MARIANE: Ah, you are killing me! Try rather to help with your advice.

DORINE: I am your servant.

MARIANE: Ah! Dorine, have pity . . .

DORINE: To punish you, this match must take place.

MARIANE: Dear girl, please!

DORINE: No.

MARIANE: If I declare to you that . . .

DORINE: No. Tartuffe is your man and you shall have a taste of him.

MARIANE: You know that I have always confided in you. Do me . . .

DORINE: No. You shall be Tartuffed.

MARIANE: Well! since my fate cannot move you, leave me from now on entirely to my despair. My heart will seek help there and I know an infallible remedy for all my suffering. (*She wants to leave.*)

DORINE: Hey there! come back, I'll forget my anger. After all, I must take pity on you.

MARIANE: Look here, if they expose me to this cruel torment, let me tell you, Dorine, I shall die.

DORINE: Don't worry; it can cleverly be prevented . . . But here comes Valère, your beloved.

Scene 4 [VALÈRE, MARIANE, DORINE]

VALÈRE: I have just been told some news, my dear, that I didn't know and which is certainly very pretty.

MARIANE: What's that?

VALÈRE: That you are marrying Tartuffe.

MARIANE: There is no doubt that my father has taken this idea into his head.

VALÈRE: Your father, my dear . . .

MARIANE: Has altered his mind. He has just proposed this to me.

VALÈRE: What! Seriously?

MARIANE: Yes, seriously; he has openly declared himself for this match.

VALÈRE: And what, my dear, are your intentions?

MARIANE: I don't know.

VALÈRE: The answer is honest. You don't know?

MARIANE: No.

VALÈRE: No?

MARIANE: What would you advise me?

VALÈRE: I? I'll advise you to take this husband.

MARIANE: That is your advice?

VALÈRE: Yes.

MARIANE: Seriously?

VALÈRE: Of course. The choice is glorious and well worth consideration.

MARIANE: Well, sir, this is an advice that I shall accept.

VALÈRE: You will have no trouble in following it, it seems to me.

MARIANE: No more than it cost you to give it.

VALÈRE: I? I gave it to you to please you.

MARIANE: And I shall take it to please you.

DORINE (*Aside*): Let's see what this will come to.

VALÈRE: This, then, is how you love? And it was all deceit when you . . .

MARIANE: Let us not speak of that, pray. You have told me frankly that I should accept the husband selected for me; and I declare that I intend to do it since you give me this wholesome advice.

VALÈRE: Don't use my advice as your excuse. You had already made your decision, and you are grasping any frivolous pretext to justify the breaking of your word.

MARIANE: That is true, and it's well said.

VALÈRE: No doubt about it; and you have never had any real love for me.

MARIANE: Alas! you may think so, if you please.

VALÈRE: Yes, yes; I may think so; but my offended feelings will perhaps forestall you in such a design; and I know where to offer both my heart and my hand.

MARIANE: Ah! I don't doubt it; the love that merit arouses . . .

VALÈRE: For Heaven's sake, let's drop merit. No doubt I have very little of that and you prove it. But I hope much from the kindness another will show me; and I know someone who will welcome me and will not be ashamed to consent to repair my loss.

MARIANE: The loss is not so great, and you easily enough console yourself of this change . . .

VALÈRE: I'll do my best, you may depend on that. A heart that forgets us wounds our reputation; we must do our best to forget it also. If we do not succeed we must at least pretend to do so; for the cowardice of continuing to love the one who abandoned us is never forgiven.

MARIANE: This sentiment is certainly noble and sublime.

VALÈRE: It is so; and everyone must approve it. What! would you have me keep my love for you forever and see you before my very eyes pass into the arms of another without bestowing elsewhere a heart which you reject?

MARIANE: On the contrary; as for me, that is what I hope for and I wish it were already done.

VALÈRE: You wish it?

MARIANE: Yes.

VALÈRE: You have insulted me enough, madam; and I am going to satisfy you this very instant. (*He is about to leave, but comes back.*)

MARIANE: Very well.

VALÈRE: Remember, at least, that you yourself drive me to this extremity.

MARIANE: Yes.

VALÈRE: And that my intention only follows your example.

MARIANE: Very well, my example.

VALÈRE: Enough; you will be obeyed on the spot.

MARIANE: So much the better.

VALÈRE: This is the last time you will ever see me.

MARIANE: So much the better.

VALÈRE (*Leaves, but turns back at the door*): Hey?

MARIANE: What?

VALÈRE: Didn't you call me?

MARIANE: I? You are dreaming.

VALÈRE: Well then, I'll keep on going. Farewell, madam.

MARIANE: Farewell, sir.

DORINE: I think that you are losing your senses with all that folly, and I let you quarrel so long to see how far you would go. Come here, Monsieur Valère. (*She takes hold of his arm and* VALÈRE *makes a show of resistance.*)

VALÈRE: Hey! What do you want, Dorine?

DORINE: Come here.

VALÈRE: No, no; I am too indignant. Don't hinder me from what she wants.

DORINE: Stop.

VALÈRE: No, look here, I have made up my mind.

DORINE: Ah!

MARIANE: He cannot bear to see me, my presence drives him away; I would do much better to leave him here alone.

DORINE (*Leaving* VALÈRE *and running to* MARIANE): Now the other. Where are you going?

MARIANE: Leave me.

DORINE: You must come back.

MARIANE: No, no, Dorine; you are trying to detain me in vain.

VALÈRE: I see indeed that the sight of me is a torture to her; and I had no doubt better free her from it.

DORINE (*Leaving* MARIANE *and running to* VALÈRE): Again? The devil take you! Stop this nonsense and come here both of you. (*She holds them both.*)

VALÈRE: But what are your intentions?

MARIANE: What do you want to do?

DORINE: To get you together again and rescue you. (*To* VALÈRE.) Are you mad to have such an argument?

VALÈRE: Didn't you hear how she spoke to me?

DORINE: Are you out of your senses to get so angry?

MARIANE: Didn't you see the whole thing, and how he treated me?

DORINE (*To* VALÈRE): Nonsense on both sides. She has no other wish than to remain yours, I can vouch for that. (*To* MARIANE.) He loves no one but you, and has no other desire but to be your husband, I answer for it upon my life.

MARIANE: Why give me such advice, then?

VALÈRE: Why ask me for advice on such a subject?

DORINE: You are a couple of fools. Come, give me your hand, both of you. (*To* VALÈRE.) Come, you.

VALÈRE (*Giving his hand to* DORINE): What's the good of my hand?

DORINE (*To* MARIANE): Come now, yours.

MARIANE (*Also giving her hand*): What's the use of all that?

DORINE: Goodness me! Come here, quickly. You love each other more than you may think.

VALÈRE (*To* MARIANE): Don't do things with such bad grace and try to look at me without anger. (MARIANE *looks at* VALÈRE *and smiles faintly.*)

DORINE: To tell the truth, lovers are all crazy.

VALÈRE: Now really! have I no cause for complaint? And, not wanting to lie, weren't you mean to take pleasure in telling me such painful things.

MARIANE: But aren't you the most ungrateful man . . .

DORINE: Let's leave this whole discussion for another time and let us think about averting this confounded marriage.

MARIANE: Tell us what we should do.

DORINE: We shall do all kinds of things. Your father is making fun of us, and all of this is nonsense. But, as for you, it would be better that you pretend to comply quietly with his extravagance so that, in case of need, it will be easier for you to delay this proposed marriage. In gaining time we shall remedy everything. Sometimes you'll pretend an illness which will overcome you suddenly and will require delay; sometimes you'll pretend some ill omen; you, unluckily, met a corpse, broke a mirror, or dreamed of muddy water. In short, the best of this is that they cannot unite you to anyone else but him unless you say yes. But, the better to succeed, it would be wise, it seems to me, that we are not seen talking together. (*To* VALÈRE.) Leave now, and without delay urge your friends to make Orgon keep his promise. We are going to interest her brother and enlist her stepmother on our side. Farewell.

VALÈRE (*To* MARIANE): Whatever efforts we may be all making, my greatest hope, to tell the truth, lies in you.

MARIANE (*To* VALÈRE): I cannot answer for the wishes of a father, but I shall belong to no one but to Valère.

VALÈRE: How happy you make me! and whatever they may try . . .

DORINE: Ah! lovers never get tired of talking. Go, I tell you.

VALÈRE (*Takes a step and comes back*): Finally . . .

DORINE: What chattering! (*Pushing each of them by the shoulder.*) Go this way, and you, the other.

ACT III

Scene 1 [DAMIS, DORINE]

DAMIS: May lightning strike me dead this very instant, may everyone treat me as the greatest of scoundrels, if any respect or authority shall stop me from doing something rash.

DORINE: For pity's sake, curb this temper. Your father has only talked about it. We do not always carry out what we propose and the road is long between the plan and the deed.

DAMIS: I must stop the plots of this conceited ass and whisper a few words into his ear.

DORINE: Gently, pray! Let your mother-in-law deal with him as well as with your father. She has some influence with Tartuffe; he agrees to all that she says and he could even have some tender feelings for her. Would to Heaven that this were true! A pretty thing it would be! In short, the interest she takes in you forces her to send for him; she wants to sound him out about this marriage that troubles you, to know his intentions, and to acquaint him with the sad consequences which it may cause, if he entertains any hope on this subject. His servant told me that he was praying and I wasn't able to see him; but he also told me that he was coming down. Leave then, if you please, and let me wait for him.

DAMIS: I may be present at this interview.

DORINE: No: they must be alone.

DAMIS: I shall not say anything to him.

DORINE: You are joking; we know your usual outbursts and that's the perfect way to spoil everything. Go.

DAMIS: No, I want to see without getting angry.

DORINE: How annoying you are! He is coming; go away.

Scene 2 [TARTUFFE, LAURENT, DORINE]

TARTUFFE (*Noticing* DORINE): Laurent, put away my hair shirt and my scourge and pray that Heaven may ever enlighten you. If anyone comes to see me tell them that I have gone to the prisoners to share the alms that I have received.

DORINE: What affectation and what boasting!

TARTUFFE: What do you want?

DORINE: To tell you . . .

TARTUFFE (*Taking a handkerchief from his pocket*): Ah! For Heaven's sake! Before you say anything, take this handkerchief, I beg you.

DORINE: What?

TARTUFFE: Cover this bosom which I cannot bear to see. The soul is offended by such sights and they give rise to sinful thoughts.

DORINE: You are, then, very susceptible to temptation, and the flesh makes a strong impression on your senses! Of course I do not know what heat inflames you, but my desires are not so quickly aroused; and I could see you naked from head to toe without being tempted in the least by that whole hide of yours.

TARTUFFE: Show a little modesty in your conversation or I shall leave you on the spot.

DORINE: No, no, I am the one who will leave you alone. I have only two words to say to you. My mistress is going to come down to this room and she wishes the favor of a moment's conversation.

TARTUFFE: Alas! with pleasure.

DORINE (*Aside*): How he softens up! Upon my word, I stick to what I've said of him.

TARTUFFE: Is she coming soon?

DORINE: I think I hear her. Yes, it is she, and I leave you together.

Scene 3 [ELMIRE, TARTUFFE]

TARTUFFE: May Heaven, with its great kindness, forever give you health, both of soul and body; and bless your days as much as the humblest of its votaries desires!

ELMIRE: I am much obliged for this pious wish; but let us take a seat to be more comfortable.

TARTUFFE: Are you completely recovered from your illness?

ELMIRE: Completely; my fever soon left me.

TARTUFFE: My prayers have not sufficient merit to have brought about this grace from above; but I did not make any vows to Heaven that did not concern your recovery.

ELMIRE: Your zeal for me has been too solicitous.

TARTUFFE: Your dear health cannot be overrated and I would have given mine to make it well again.

ELMIRE: That is carrying Christian charity very far, and I am much indebted to you for all this kindness.

TARTUFFE: I do far less for you than you deserve.

ELMIRE: I wanted to talk to you in private about a certain matter, and I am very glad that no one is here to observe us.

TARTUFFE: I am also overjoyed at it, and you may be sure that it is very pleasant to me, Madam, to find myself alone with you. It is an opportunity that I have often requested from Heaven without having it granted before this.

ELMIRE: What I wish is a few words with you in which you bare your heart and conceal nothing from me.

TARTUFFE: And I too, as a rare favor, wish only to show you my entire soul, and to swear to you that the criticisms I have made about the visits you receive in homage of your charms, do not come from any hatred towards you, but rather from a passionate zeal that carries me away, and from a pure motive . . .

ELMIRE: That is how I understand it; and I believe that it is my salvation that gives you this concern.

TARTUFFE (*Pressing her fingertips*): Yes, Madam, without doubt; and my fervor is such . . .

ELMIRE: Ow! you squeeze me too hard.

TARTUFFE: It's from excessive zeal. I never had any intention of hurting you, and I would much rather . . . (*He puts his hand on her knee.*)

ELMIRE: What is your hand doing there?

TARTUFFE: I am feeling your dress; its material is very soft.

ELMIRE: Ah! I beg you, let go of me! I am very ticklish. (*She pulls back her chair and* TARTUFFE *draws nearer with his.*)

TARTUFFE: Gracious me! How marvellous is the workmanship of this lace! They work in a miraculous way today; never has anything been so beautifully made.

ELMIRE: That is true. But let us talk a little of what concerns us. I have heard that my husband wants to retract his promise and give his daughter to you. Tell me, is that true?

TARTUFFE: He has briefly mentioned it to me; but to tell you the truth, Madam, that is not the happiness for which I am sighing, and I behold elsewhere the marvellous attractions of the felicity which would satisfy all my wishes.

ELMIRE: That is because you have no love for earthly things.

TARTUFFE: My breast does not contain a heart of stone.

ELMIRE: As for me, I believe that all your sighs tend towards Heaven and that nothing here below rouses your desires.

TARTUFFE: The love which attaches us to eternal beauties does not extinguish in us the love of temporal ones. Our senses can easily be charmed with the perfect works that Heaven has created. Its reflected charms shine forth in such as you; but in your person it displays its rarest wonders. It has poured out on your face such beauty that eyes are dazzled and the heart enraptured; and I could not look at you, perfect creature, without admiring in you the author of nature, and without feeling my heart touched with an ardent love at the sight of the fairest of portraits in which he painted himself. At first I feared that this secret ardor was a clever snare of the dark spirit, and my heart even resolved to flee from your eyes, thinking that you might be an obstacle to my salvation. But finally I perceived, oh most charming beauty, that my passion could be not guilty; that I could reconcile it with modesty, and that is what has made me give in to it. It is, I confess, a great presumption on my part to dare to offer you this heart; but I expect, in my hopes, everything from your kindness, and nothing from the vain efforts of my weakness. In you are my hope, my happiness, my peace; on you depend my torment or beatitude. And it is by your decision solely, that I shall be happy, if you wish it, or miserable, if it pleases you.

ELMIRE: The declaration is extremely gallant; but it is, to tell the truth, somewhat surprising. It seems to me that you should protect your heart better, and reflect upon a design of this nature. A pious man like you, whom everyone speaks of as . . .

TARTUFFE: Ah! although I am a pious man, I am not the less a man; and when it beholds your celestial charms, a heart lets itself be conquered and reasons not. I know that such words coming from me seem strange; but after all, Madam, I am no angel, and if you condemn the declaration I make, you must lay the blame upon your bewitching charms. From the moment I first set eyes upon your more than human splendor, you became the queen of my being. The ineffable sweetness of your divine glances broke down the resistance of my obstinate heart; it surmounted everything, fastings, prayers, tears, and turned all my desires to your charms. My eyes and my sighs have told you so a thousand times; and to explain myself better, I am now using my voice. If you should look with some kindness upon the tribulations of your unworthy slave, if your goodness will console me, and will condescend to stoop to my nothingness, I shall always have for you, oh sweet miracle, a devotion, which nothing can equal. Your honor does not run any risk with me and need fear no disgrace on my part. All these court gallants whom women idolize are noisy in their doings and vain in their talk; they are constantly boasting of their successes and they receive no favors without divulging them; and their indiscreet tongues, in which people confide, desecrate the altar on which their hearts offer sacrifice. But people like us burn with a discreet flame and with them a secret is always kept. The care we take of our own reputation is a complete guarantee for the person beloved, and it is only with us, when our heart is accepted, that love is found without scandal and pleasure without fear.

ELMIRE: I am listening to what you say, and your rhetoric explains in rather strong terms to me. But aren't you afraid that I might feel like telling my husband of this gallant ardor; and that the prompt knowledge of that kind of love might well alter the friendship he has for you?

TARTUFFE: I know that you are too kind and that you will forgive my temerity; that you will excuse, under the score of human frailty, the violent outbursts of a love that offends you; and will consider, by looking at yourself, that I am not blind, and that a man is made of flesh and blood.

ELMIRE: Some might, perhaps, take this in another manner; but I shall show my discretion. I shall not tell the matter to my husband; but in return I want something from you; that is to forward honestly and without any quibbling the marriage of Valère and Mariane; to renounce the unjust power which would enrich you with what belongs to another; and . . .

Scene 4 [ELMIRE, DAMIS, TARTUFFE]

DAMIS (*Emerging from a closet in which he had hidden*): No, Madam, no; this must be made public. I was in there and I heard everything; and Providence seems to have led me there to confound the pride of a traitor who wrongs me; to show me a way of taking my revenge of his hypocrisy and insolence; to undeceive my father and bare fully the heart of a villain who talks to you of love.

ELMIRE: No, Damis, it is enough that he reforms and tries to deserve my forgiveness. Since I have promised it, do not make me break my word. I do not feel like provoking a scandal; a woman laughs at such foolishness and never troubles her husband's ears with it.

DAMIS: You have your reasons for acting in this manner, and I have mine too for acting otherwise. To wish to spare him is ridiculous; and the insolent pride of his bigotry has already triumphed too much over my rightful anger and created too many disorders among us. The scoundrel has governed my father too long and has plotted against my affections as well as Valère's. My father must be undeceived about this perfidious scoundrel; and Heaven offers me an easy means. I am indebted to It for this opportunity and it is too favorable a one to be neglected. I would deserve to have it taken from me if, having it in hand, I did not make use of it.

ELMIRE: Damis . . .

DAMIS: No, if you please, I must do what I think best. My heart is filled with joy now, and whatever you may say will never dissuade me from the pleasure of taking my revenge. Without going any further I shall make an end to the affair; and here is just the perfect opportunity.

Scene 5 [ORGON, DAMIS, TARTUFFE, ELMIRE]

DAMIS: We are going to entertain you, father, with a completely fresh incident which will surprise you greatly. You are well repaid for all your caresses and this gentleman rewards your tenderness handsomely. His great zeal for you has just come to light. He aims at nothing less than at dishonoring you; and I have surprised him here making to your wife the insulting confession of a guilty passion. She has a sweet disposition and her too-discreet heart wanted absolutely to keep this secret from you; but I cannot encourage such impudence and think that to have been silent about it would have been to do you an injury.

ELMIRE: Yes, I believe that we should never break in upon a husband's peace with such foolish stories; that our honor does not depend upon that and that it is enough for us to know how to defend ourselves. These are my feelings; and you would have said nothing, Damis, if I had any credit with you.

Scene 6 [ORGON, DAMIS, TARTUFFE]

ORGON: What have I just heard, oh Heavens! is it credible?

TARTUFFE: Yes, brother, I am a wicked, guilty, unhappy sinner, full of iniquity, the greatest villain that ever breathed. Every moment of my life is filled with blemishes; it is only a mass of crimes and corruption and I see that Heaven, in order to punish me, wants to mortify me on this occasion. Whatever great offence may be levelled at me, I will not dare to have the pride to deny it. Believe what you are told, arm your resentment, and like a criminal, drive me from your house. No shame could be great enough that I would not deserve more.

ORGON (*To his son*): Ah, traitor, do you dare, by this falsehood, try to tarnish the purity of his virtue?

DAMIS: What! the feigned meekness of this hypocrite will make you deny . . .

ORGON: Hold your tongue, accursed plague!

TARTUFFE: Ah! Let him talk; you accuse him wrongly, and you had much better believe what he tells you. Why be so favorable to me after hearing such a fact? Are you aware, after all, of what I am capable? Do you trust my outward appearance, brother? And because of what you see, believe me to be better? No, no, you let appearances deceive you, and I am nothing less, alas, than what they think of me. Everyone takes me for a respectable man; but the truth is that I am worthless. (*Turning to* DAMIS.) Yes, my dear son, speak up, call me a treacherous infamous lost scoundrel, a thief, a murderer; crush me with even more hateful names; I am not contradicting you, I have deserved them; and am willing to endure disgrace on my knees, as shame brought about by the crimes of my life.

ORGON (*To* TARTUFFE): Brother, that is too much. (*To his son.*) Doesn't your heart relent, traitor?

DAMIS: What? His words beguile you so far as to . . .

ORGON: Hold your tongue, rascal! (*To* TARTUFFE.) Brother, hey! Rise, I beg you. (*To his son.*) Infamous scoundrel!

DAMIS: He can . . .

ORGON: Hold your tongue!

DAMIS: I am beside myself! What! I pass . . .

ORGON: If you say one more word, I'll break your arm.

TARTUFFE: Brother, in the name of Heaven, do not forget yourself. I would much rather suffer the greatest hardship than have him receive the slightest scratch because of me.

ORGON (*To his son*): Ungrateful monster!

TARTUFFE: Leave him be. If I have to ask you, on both knees, to forgive him . . .

ORGON (*To* TARTUFFE): Alas! you must be jesting? (*To his son.*) Behold his kindness, scoundrel.

DAMIS: Then . . .

ORGON: Peace!

DAMIS: What, I . . .

ORGON: Peace, I tell you! I know well what motive goads you to attack him. All of you hate him and I now see wife, children and servants all let loose against him. Every trick is impudently used to remove this pious person from my house; but the more you strive to get him out, the greater care I shall take to keep him here; and I shall hasten to give him my daughter to confound the pride of my whole family.

DAMIS: Do you mean to compel her to accept him?

ORGON: Yes, traitor, and this very evening to make you really furious. Ah! I defy you all and shall let you know that I must be obeyed and that I am the master. Come, retract; and right now, scoundrel, throw yourself at his feet to ask his forgiveness.

DAMIS: Who, I? forgiveness of this rascal who, by his impostures . . .

ORGON: Ah! you resist, you tramp, and insult him to boot? A stick, a stick! (*To* TARTUFFE.) Don't hold me back. (*To his son.*) Out of my house, this very instant, and never dare set foot into it again.

DAMIS: Yes, I shall leave, but . . .

ORGON: Quickly, leave this place. I deprive you of your inheritance, rascal, and give you my curse, besides.

Scene 7 [ORGON, TARTUFFE]

ORGON: To offend a holy person that way!

TARTUFFE: Oh Heaven! forgive him the anguish he has given me. (*To* ORGON.) If you could understand my grief at seeing myself blackened in my brother's sight . . .

ORGON: Alas!

TARTUFFE: The very thought of this ingratitude wounds me so terribly . . . The horror I conceive of it . . . My heart is so oppressed that I cannot speak and think that it will be my death.

ORGON (*Running, in tears, towards the door through which he has sent away his son*): Scoundrel! I am sorry that my hand has spared you and that I have not knocked you down on the spot. Compose yourself, brother, and don't be troubled.

TARTUFFE: Let us put an end to these unhappy discussions. I realize what uneasiness I have brought into this house and I think, brother, that I have to leave it.

ORGON: What? Are you jesting?

TARTUFFE: They hate me and I see that they are trying to make you suspect my integrity.

ORGON: What does it matter? Do you see me listening to them?

TARTUFFE: They will not fail to continue, you may be sure, and these same stories, which you are rejecting now, will perhaps be listened to another time.

ORGON: No, brother, never.

TARTUFFE: Ah! brother, a wife can easily deceive a husband.

ORGON: No, no.

TARTUFFE: Allow me, by removing myself from here promptly, to deprive them of any cause for attacking me thus.

ORGON: No, you will stay; my life depends on it.

TARTUFFE: Well, then I shall have to mortify myself. However, if you would . . .

ORGON: Ah!

TARTUFFE: So be it, let us not talk about it any more. But I know how I must behave on this occasion. Honor is a delicate thing and friendship obliges me to prevent rumors and not to give any room for suspicion. I shall avoid your wife and you will not see me . . .

ORGON: No, in spite of everybody, you will see her often. To drive everyone mad is my greatest joy, and I want you to be seen with her at all times. And that isn't all; the better to brave them all, I wish to have no other heir but you, and I am going right now to sign you a deed of gift for my whole estate. A true and honest friend whom I take for my son-in-law is far dearer to me than son, wife, and relatives. Wouldn't you accept what I propose?

TARTUFFE: The will of Heaven be done in all things!

ORGON: Poor man! Let us quickly have a draft drawn up and let all envy burst with spite!

ACT IV

Scene 1 [CLÉANTE, TARTUFFE]

CLÉANTE: Yes, everyone talks about it. and you can believe me, the scandal caused by this news is not to your credit. And I have met you, sir, quite opportunely, to tell you my opinion in two words. I am not examining these reports very thoroughly; I shall pass over that and take the thing at its worst. Let us suppose that Damis has not acted well and that you have been wrongly accused; is it not the part of a good Christian to forgive the offense to smother all desire of vengeance in your heart? And should you allow that, because of a quarrel with you, a son be driven from his father's house? I am telling you again and I am talking frankly, that great and small are scandalized by it; and if you will take my advice you will make peace and not push matters to extremes. Make a sacrifice of your anger to God, and restore a son to his father's favor.

TARTUFFE: Alas! as far as I am concerned I would like that with all my heart. I, sir, do not bear him any ill-will; I forgive him everything, I blame him for nothing and I should like to serve him with my best capacities. But the interests of Heaven could not consent to that, and if he returns into this house, I shall have to leave. After his unparalleled action any relationship between us would give rise to scandal. Heaven knows what everyone would immediately think of it. They would ascribe it to shrewd policy, and they would say everywhere that, feeling guilty, I pretend a charitable zeal for my accuser; that I am afraid and wish to conciliate him in order to bribe him, in a sly manner, into silence.

CLÉANTE: You put us off here with sham excuses and all your reasons, sir, are too farfetched. Why do you take into your hands the interests of Heaven? Does It need us to punish the guilty? Leave the care of Its own vengeance to itself; think only of the forgiveness of all offenses It prescribes, and do not consider the judgment of men when you follow the sovereign orders of Heaven. What! the trivial regard for what men may think will hinder the glory of a good action? No, no, let us always do what Heaven prescribes and let us not perplex our heads with any other cares.

TARTUFFE: I have told you already that in my heart I forgive him; and that, sir, is doing what Heaven ordains; but after the scandal and the affront of today, Heaven does not require me to live with him.

CLÉANTE: And does it require you, sir, to lend an ear to what mere caprice dictates to his father; and to accept the gift of an estate to which, in justice, you have no claim whatever?

TARTUFFE: Those who know me will not think that this proceeds from self-interest. All the riches of this world have little attraction for me; I am not dazzled by their false glare; and if I should decide to accept from his father this donation that he wished to make me, it is only, to tell the truth, because I fear that all that wealth might fall into wicked hands; lest it may be divided among people who would make a bad use of it in this world and would not use it, as I intend to do, for the glory of Heaven and the good of my fellow-men.

CLÉANTE: Hey, sir, you need not have such delicate scruples which may occasion the complaints of a rightful heir. Allow him, without worrying about anything, to become the owner of his estate at his own perils, and consider that it is even better that he misuses it than that you should be accused of defrauding him of it. I am only surprised that you could have accepted such a proposal without embarrassment; for, after all, has true piety any maxim which shows how to rob a legitimate heir of his property? And, if it is true that Heaven has put into your heart an invincible obstacle to your living with Damis, wouldn't it be better that, as a discreet person, you should make a civil retreat from this house, than to allow that, contrary to all reason, the son be turned away from it because of you. Believe me, sir, this would be giving a proof of your probity . . .

TARTUFFE: It is half past three, sir; certain pious duties call me upstairs, and you will excuse my leaving you so soon.

CLÉANTE: Ah!

Scene 2 [ELMIRE, MARIANE, DORINE, CLÉANTE]

DORINE: For Heaven's sake, sir, try to help her as we do. She is in mortal grief; and the marriage contract that her father resolved upon for tonight drives her every moment to despair. He is just coming. Pray let us unite our efforts and try, by force or cunning, to frustrate this unfortunate design that has caused us all so much trouble.

Scene 3 [ORGON, ELMIRE, MARIANE, CLÉANTE, DORINE]

ORGON: Ah! I am glad to see you all assembled. (*To* MARIANE.) There is something in this contract to make you laugh and you know already what that means.

MARIANE (*On her knees*): Father, in the name of Heaven that is a witness to my grief and by everything that can move your heart, forego somewhat your paternal rights and dispense my true desires from obedience. Do not compel me, by this harsh rule, to complain to Heaven for what I owe you; and this life, alas, that you have given me, do not make it wretched, father. If, contrary to the tender hopes that I have formed, you forbid me to belong to the one I dared love, at least out of your kindness that I implore on my knees, save me from the torment of belonging to the man I abhor; and do not drive me to despair by exerting your full power over me.

ORGON (*Touched*): Come, be firm, my heart! Let there be no human weakness!

MARIANE: Your kindness for him does not hurt me: show it to its full extent; give him your estate and should it not be enough, add all of mine to it. I consent with all my heart and I leave you to dispose of it. But at least do not go as far as my own person, and allow me to end, in the austerity of a convent, the sad days that Heaven has allotted to me.

ORGON: Ah! there we have it! All girls want to become nuns when their father opposes their love affairs. Get up. The more repugnance you feel in accepting it, the greater will be your merit. Mortify your senses by this marriage and do not bother me any further.

DORINE: But what! . . .

ORGON: Hold your tongue, you. Meddle only in what concerns you. I absolutely forbid you to say another word.

CLÉANTE: If you allow me to answer you and give you some advice . . .

ORGON: Brother, your advice is the best in the world: it is very rational and I set great store by it. But you will allow me not to avail myself of it.

ELMIRE (*To her husband*): Upon seeing what I see, I no longer know what to say, and I quite admire your blindness. You must be very bewitched, and prepossessed in his favor to deny to us the incident of today.

ORGON: I am your servant and judge by appearances. I know your indulgence for my rascal of a son, and you were afraid to disavow the nasty trick he wanted to play on that poor man. For you were too unexcited to be believed and you would have appeared much more upset.

ELMIRE: Must our honor bluster so vehemently at the simple confession of an amorous outburst? And can we reply to all that concerns it only with fury in our eyes and insults in our mouth? As for me, I simply laugh at such talk, and scandal about this does not please me in the least. I like to show my discreetness quietly and am not at all in favor of these savage prudes, whose honor is armed with claws and teeth, and who, at the least word, would disfigure a man's face. Heaven preserve me from such good discretion! I prefer a virtue that is not diabolical, and believe that a discreet and cold refusal is not less effective in discouraging an admirer.

ORGON: Well, I know the whole affair and will not alter my course of action.

ELMIRE: Once more I am surprised at your strange weakness. But what answer would your credulity make if I should let you see that you have been told the truth?

ORGON: See?

ELMIRE: Yes.

ORGON: Nonsense!

ELMIRE: But if I found the means to let you see it clearly? . . .

ORGON: Idle stories!

ELMIRE: What a man! Answer me at least. I am not asking you to believe us; but suppose that a place could be found where you might see and overhear everything; what would you say then of your honest man?

ORGON: In that case, I would say that . . I wouldn't say anything, because this couldn't be.

ELMIRE: Your delusion has lasted long enough and I have been accused too much of imposture. I must, for my gratification, and without going any further, make you a witness to all I have told you.

ORGON: So be it; I take you at your word. We shall see your dexterity and how you will make good this promise.

ELMIRE (*To* DORINE): Ask him to see me.

DORINE: He is crafty and perhaps it will be difficult to catch him.

ELMIRE: No; we are easily duped by those we love, and conceit drives us to deceive ourselves. Ask him to come down. (*Turning to* CLÉANTE *and to* MARIANE.) And you, go now.

Scene 4 [ELMIRE, ORGON]

ELMIRE: Come over to this table and hide under it.

ORGON: What!

ELMIRE: It's essential that you be well concealed.

ORGON: Why under this table!

ELMIRE: For Heaven's sake! let me do what I want. I have thought about my plan, and you will judge. Get under there, I tell you, and when you are there, be careful that you are neither seen nor heard.

ORGON: I confess that I am very complaisant; but I want to see the end of your enterprise.

ELMIRE: I believe that you will have nothing to reply to me. (*To her husband who is hidden under the table.*) Mind! I am going to touch upon a strange subject of conversation; do not be shocked in any way. I must be permitted to say whatever I may like, for it is to convince you as I have promised. Since I am reduced to it, I am going to make this hypocrite drop his mask by addressing sweet words to him, by flattering the shameless desires of his passion and giving him full scope for his boldness. As it is for your sake alone, and the better to confound him, that I pretend to yield to his wishes, I shall cease as soon as you show yourself, and things will go only as far as you wish. It is for you to stop his mad passion when you think matters have gone far enough, to spare your wife, and not to expose me any more than is necessary to disabuse you. It is your concern, you can control it, and . . . He is coming. Keep still and take care not to come out.

Scene 5 [TARTUFFE, ELMIRE, ORGON (*under the table*)]

TARTUFFE: I have been told that you wish to speak to me here.

ELMIRE: Yes. I have secrets to reveal to you. But close this door before I tell them to you and look everywhere for fear of being overheard. A scene like the one we had before is surely not one we want here. I was never so startled in my life. Damis frightened me terribly for you, and you saw indeed that I did my utmost to change his intentions and moderate his outbursts. My confusion, it is true, was so great that I did not have the idea of contradicting him; but thank Heaven, because of that, everything has turned out for the best and is upon a much surer footing. The esteem in which you are held has dispelled the storm and my husband cannot take offense at you. The better to brave the scandal of people's nasty comments he wants us to be together at all times; and that is why I can, without fear of incurring blame, be together alone with you; and this justifies me in opening to you my heart, a little too ready, perhaps, to listen to your passion.

TARTUFFE: This language is somewhat difficult to understand, Madam, and a little while ago, you spoke in a quite different manner.

ELMIRE: Ah! if such a refusal makes you angry, how little you know the heart of a woman! How little you understand what it tries to convey when it defends itself so feebly. Our modesty will always combat, in these moments, those tender sentiments with which we may be inspired. Whatever reason we may find for the passion that subdued us, we shall always feel a little ashamed to confess it. We deny it at first, but in such a way as to give you sufficiently to understand that our heart surrenders; that for the sake of honor, words oppose our wishes, and that such refusals promise everything. Without doubt, this is making a rather daring confession to you, and showing little regard for our modesty; but since these words have at last escaped me, would I have tried so hard to restrain Damis? Would I, pray, have so complacently listened, for such a long time, to the offer of your heart? Would I have taken the matter as I have done, if the offer of your heart had had nothing in it to please me? And when I myself tried to force you to refuse the match which had just been proposed, what should such insistence have given you to understand, but the interest I was inclined to take in you, and the vexation it would have given me that this marriage should in the least divide a heart that I wish all to myself.

TARTUFFE: It is indeed an extreme pleasure, Madam, to hear these words from the lips one loves; their honey plentifully diffuses throughout every sense a sweetness I have never before tasted. The happiness of pleasing you is my supreme study, and my heart will find its beatitude in fulfilling your wishes; but, you must excuse this heart if it dares still to have some doubt in its own felicity. I may look upon these words as a sort of stratagem to compel me to break off a match that is on the point of being concluded; and if I may explain myself frankly to you, I shall not rely upon these tender words, until some of your favors, for which I sigh, have assured me of the sincerity they have expressed, and fixed in my heart a firm belief in the bewitching kindness that you have for me.

ELMIRE (*Coughs to warn her husband*): What! Would you proceed so fast and exhaust the tenderness of a heart at once? We take the greatest pains to make the sweetest declarations; meanwhile that is not enough for you, and we cannot go so far as to satisfy you, unless we push the affair to the ultimate favors?

TARTUFFE: The less we deserve a blessing, the less we dare hope for it. Our love can hardly rely upon words. We suspect easily a fate filled with happiness and we wish to enjoy it before believing in it. As for me, who knows I deserve your favors so little, I doubt the success of my rashness; and shall believe nothing, Madam, until you have convinced my passion by tangible proof.

ELMIRE: Good Heavens! how tyrannically your love acts! And into what strange confusion it throws me! With what a fierce sway it governs our hearts, and with what violence it pushes for what it desires! What! Can I find not protection from your pursuit, and will you hardly give me time to breathe? Is it decent to persist with such rigor and to insist upon your demands being satisfied immediately; and to take advantage thus, by your pressing efforts, of the weakness, which you see one has for you?

TARTUFFE: But if you look upon my addresses with a favorable eye, why do you refuse me convincing proofs?

ELMIRE: But how can I consent to what you wish without offending the Heaven of which you are always speaking?

TARTUFFE: If it is only Heaven that is opposed to my desires, it is a trifle for me to remove such an obstacle; and that need be no restraint upon your love.

ELMIRE: But they terrify us so with the judgment of Heaven!

TARTUFFE: I can dissipate these ridiculous fears for you, Madam, and I know the art of easing scruples. Heaven forbids, it is true, certain gratifications (*a scoundrel is speaking*), but there are ways of compounding those matters. According to different wants, there is a science which stretches the strings of our conscience, and which rectifies the immorality of our action with the purity of our intentions. We shall be able to initiate you into these secrets, Madam; you have only to let yourself be led by me. Satisfy my desires and have no fear; I shall be responsible for everything and shall take the sin upon myself. (ELMIRE *coughs hard.*) You are coughing very much, Madam.

ELMIRE: Yes, I am very uncomfortable.

TARTUFFE: Would you like a piece of this licorice?

ELMIRE: It's an obstinate cold, no doubt; and I know that all the licorice in the world will do nothing for it.

TARTUFFE: That is, to be sure, very annoying.

ELMIRE: Yes, more than I can say.

TARTUFFE: In short, your scruples are easily overcome. You may be sure of complete secrecy with me and the harm lies only in the stir it arouses. The scandal it creates is what constitutes the offense, and sinning in secret is not sinning at all.

ELMIRE (*After having coughed once more*): In short I see that I must resolve to yield, that I must consent to grant you everything; and that with less than this I should not expect that you be satisfied and give in. It is indeed very hard to go to that extreme and it is quite against my will that I venture this far; but since you are obstinately bent upon reducing me to this, since you will not believe anything I say, but ask for more convincing proofs, I must resolve to do it and satisfy you. If this gratification offends, so much the worse for those who force me to it: the fault certainly ought not to be mine.

TARTUFFE: Yes, Madam; I take it upon myself; and the thing in itself . . .

ELMIRE: Open the door a little and look, pray, if my husband is not in that gallery.

TARTUFFE: What need is there to take so much care about him? Between ourselves, he is a man to be led by the nose. He is likely to take pride in all our conversations and I have brought him so far that he will see everything without believing anything.

ELMIRE: It does not matter. Go out, pray, for a moment, and look carefully everywhere outside.

Scene 6 [ORGON, ELMIRE]

ORGON (*Coming from under the table*): This is, I admit to you, an abominable man! I can't get over it, and all of this stuns me completely.

ELMIRE: What! You come out so soon? You must be jesting. Get under the tablecloth again; it isn't time yet. Stay to the end to make sure of everything and do not trust mere conjectures.

ORGON: No, nothing more wicked ever came out of hell.

ELMIRE: Good Heavens! You should not believe too lightly; let yourself be fully convinced before giving in; and don't be hasty for fear of making a mistake. (*She pushes her husband behind her.*)

Scene 7 [TARTUFFE, ELMIRE, ORGON]

TARTUFFE: Everything conspires, Madam, to my satisfaction. I have surveyed this whole apartment; no one is there, and my delighted soul . . .

ORGON (*Stopping him*): Gently! you are too eager in your amorous desires, and you should not abandon yourself to your passion. Ah! ah! my good man, you wished to deceive me! How your soul gives in to temptation! You would marry my daughter and covet my wife! I have doubted for a long time that all of this was really true and I always expected that you would change your tone; but this is pushing the proof far enough: I am satisfied and wish for no more.

ELMIRE (*To* TARTUFFE): It is against my inclinations that I have done all this; but I have been reduced to the necessity of treating you thus.

TARTUFFE: What! you believe . . .

ORGON: Come, pray, no protests; get out of here, and without more ado.

TARTUFFE: My intention . . .

ORGON: These speeches are no longer of any use, you must get out of this house this very instant.

TARTUFFE: It's for you to get out, you who speak as if you were the master. The house belongs to me, I will make you realize it, and will show you plainly that it is useless to have recourse to these base tricks to pick a quarrel with me; that you are not as safe as you may

think when you insult me; that I have the means of confounding
and punishing imposture, of avenging offended Heaven and making
those repent, who talk of turning me out of here.

Scene 8 [ELMIRE, ORGON]

ELMIRE: What kind of language is this, and what does he mean?

ORGON: To tell you the truth I am very embarrassed and this is no
laughing matter.

ELMIRE: How so?

ORGON: I see my fault by what he says and the deed of gift troubles
my mind.

ELMIRE: The deed of gift? . . .

ORGON: Yes, the thing is done. But I have something else that disturbs
me too.

ELMIRE: What is that?

ORGON: You will know everything; but first let us see whether a certain
casket is still upstairs.

ACT V

Scene 1 [ORGON, CLÉANTE]

CLÉANTE: Where would you run?

ORGON: Alas! how would I know?

CLÉANTE: It seems to me that we should begin by consulting together
what can be done in this emergency.

ORGON: This casket troubles me terribly; it makes me despair more
than all the rest.

CLÉANTE: This casket is then an important mystery?

ORGON: It is a deposit that Argas, this friend for whom I feel so sorry,
has himself put into my hands in the greatest secrecy. He selected
me for this when he fled; and from what he told me these are the
papers upon which his life and fortune depend.

CLÉANTE: Why then did you entrust it into other hands?

ORGON: Merely out of a scruple of my conscience. I went straight to
confide the secret to my traitor; and his arguments persuaded me
to give him this casket to keep, so that, in case of any inquiry, I
might be able to deny it by a ready subterfuge, whereby my conscience might be fully secure, when taking an oath contrary to the
truth.

CLÉANTE: This is very bad, at least to judge from appearances; and the deed of gift and this confidence have been, to tell you my sentiments, steps which you have taken too inconsiderately. You can be carried far with such pledges; and this fellow having these advantages over you, it is a great imprudence on your part to drive him to extremities; and you ought to seek some gentler method.

ORGON: What! Under the fair appearance of such touching zeal to hide such a double-dealing heart and so wicked a soul! And I, who received him in my house poor and indigent . . . It is all over. I renounce all pious people . . . I shall henceforth hold them in utter abhorrence and shall become worse towards them, than the very devil.

CLÉANTE: Well! now you exaggerate again! You never preserve a moderate temper in anything; you never keep within reason's bounds, and always rush from one extreme to another. You see your error and realize that you have been imposed upon by a hypocritical zeal. But, in order to reform, what reason is there that you should be guilty of a worse mistake, and that you should make no difference between the heart of that perfidious rascal and those of all pious people? What! because a rascal has audaciously deceived you, under the pompous show of apparent austerity, will you insist that everyone is like him and that there is no really pious man to be found nowadays? Leave these foolish deductions to free-thinkers, distinguish between real virtue and the appearance of it; never bestow your esteem too hastily and keep it in the necessary middle course. Beware, if possible, of doing honor to imposture; but at the same time, do not attack true piety; and if you must fall into an extreme, rather offend again on the other side.

Scene 2 [DAMIS, ORGON, CLÉANTE]

DAMIS: What! father, is it true that this scoundrel threatens you, that he has forgotten all the favors that he has received and that his cowardly and too-contemptible pride turns your kindness for him against yourself?

ORGON: Yes, my son; and it causes me inconceivable grief.

DAMIS: Leave him to me, I want to cut off both his ears. Such insolence must not be tolerated; I must free you from him at once; and, to put an end to this affair, I have to strike him down.

CLÉANTE: That is spoken just like a young fellow; moderate, if you please, these violent outbursts; we live under a government, and in an age, in which violence only makes matters worse.

Scene 3 [MADAME PERNELLE, MARIANE, ELMIRE, DORINE, DAMIS, ORGON, CLÉANTE]

MADAME PERNELLE: What is this? What dreadful things do I hear?

ORGON: Some news that my own eyes have witnessed, and you see how I am repaid for my care. I harbor piously a man in his misery; I shelter him and treat him as my own brother; daily I heap favors on him; I give him my daughter and my whole fortune; and at that very moment, the perfidious, infamous wretch forms the wicked design of seducing my wife; and, not content even with these base attempts, he dares to threaten me with my own favors; and to ruin me, wants to use the advantages that my indiscreet good nature have given him; to turn me out of my estate which I have made over to him and reduce me to that condition from which I rescued him.

DORINE: Poor man!

MADAME PERNELLE: I can never believe, my son, that he wanted to commit such a black deed.

ORGON: What!

MADAME PERNELLE: Good people are always envied.

ORGON: What do you mean by this talk, mother?

MADAME PERNELLE: That there are strange doings in your house and that we know but too-well the hatred they bear him.

ORGON: What has this hatred to do with what I have told you?

MADAME PERNELLE: I have told you a hundred times when you were a little boy: virtue is always persecuted in this world; the envious will die, but envy never.

ORGON: But in what way does this bear on today's events?

MADAME PERNELLE: They may have made up a hundred idle stories against him.

ORGON: I have already told you that I saw everything myself.

MADAME PERNELLE: The malice of slanderers is very great.

ORGON: You will make me swear, mother. I have already told you that I saw this audacious crime with my own eyes.

MADAME PERNELLE: Evil tongues have always venom to scatter about, and nothing here below can guard against it.

ORGON: This is a very senseless argument. I have seen it, I tell you, seen it with my own eyes, seen, what you call seen. Must I din it a hundred times into your ears and shout like four people.

MADAME PERNELLE: My goodness! most of the time, appearances deceive; you must not always judge by what you see.

ORGON: I am getting furious.

MADAME PERNELLE: Human nature is liable to false suspicions and good is often construed as evil.

ORGON: Must I construe as a charitable design the desire to kiss my wife?

MADAME PERNELLE: It is necessary to have good reasons when you accuse people; and you should have waited until you were quite certain of the thing.

ORGON: How the devil could I be more certain? Should I have waited, mother, till before my very eyes, he had . . . You will make me say some foolish thing.

MADAME PERNELLE: In short his soul burns with too-pure a flame, and I cannot conceive at all that he would have attempted the things that have been mentioned.

ORGON: Come, I am so angry that if you were not my mother, I don't know what I might say to you.

DORINE: A just punishment, sir, for what happens in this world; you would not believe anyone and now no one will believe you.

CLÉANTE: We are wasting in mere trifles the time that should be spent in taking other measures. One must not sleep while a scoundrel threatens.

DAMIS: What! would his impudence go to that extreme?

ELMIRE: As for me, I do not believe that this is possible, and his ingratitude is too visible here.

CLÉANTE: Do not depend on that; he will be cunning enough to justify his doings against you, and for less than this, a powerful clique has involved people in a dismal maze. I tell you once more that armed with what he has you should never have urged him that far.

ORGON: That is true; but what could I do? At the presumption of that traitor, I was unable to master my resentment.

CLÉANTE: I wish with all my heart that we could patch up even an appearance of peace between you two.

ELMIRE: If I had known how he was armed against us I would have avoided bringing things to such a crisis, and my . . .

ORGON (*To* DORINE): What does this man want? Go and see quickly. I am in a fine condition to have someone come to see me.

Scene 4 [MONSIEUR LOYAL, MADAME PERNELLE, ORGON, DAMIS, MARIANE, DORINE, ELMIRE, CLÉANTE]

MONSIEUR LOYAL: Good morning, dear sister. Pray, let me speak to your master.

DORINE: He is busy, and I doubt whether he can see anyone at present.

MONSIEUR LOYAL: I have no intention of intruding in this house. I believe that my visit will have nothing to displease him, and I have come about a matter of which he will be very glad.

DORINE: Your name?

MONSIEUR LOYAL: Tell him only that I come on the part of Monsieur Tartuffe, for his good.

DORINE (*To* ORGON): This is a man who comes, in a civil way, from Monsieur Tartuffe, for some business about which, he says, you will be very glad.

CLÉANTE: You must see who this man is and what he wants.

ORGON: Perhaps he comes to reconcile us. How shall I behave towards him?

CLÉANTE: Your anger must not burst out; and if he speaks of an agreement, you must listen to him.

MONSIEUR LOYAL: Good day, sir. May Heaven punish those who would wrong you, and may it be as favorable to you as I wish!

ORGON: This mild beginning confirms my conjecture and already foretells some reconciliation.

MONSIEUR LOYAL: Your whole family has always been dear to me and I was servant to your father.

ORGON: Sir, I am very ashamed, and beg your pardon for not knowing your name.

MONSIEUR LOYAL: My name is Loyal, I am a native of Normandy; I am a bailiff of the upper court, in spite of envy. For forty years, thank Heaven, I have had the good fortune to fill that office with great honor; and I have come, with your leave, sir, to serve you with the writ of a certain decree.

ORGON: What! you are here . . .

MONSIEUR LOYAL: Please, no excitement, sir. This is nothing but a summons, an order to leave this house, you and yours, to take out your furniture and make room for others, without delay or remission, as required hereby.

ORGON: I! Leave this house.

MONSIEUR LOYAL: Yes, sir, if you please. The house at present, as you well know, belongs incontestably to good Monsieur Tartuffe. He is henceforth lord and master of your whole estate, by virtue of a contract of which I am the bearer. It is in due form, and cannot be contested.

DAMIS: This impudence is certainly enormous, and I admire it.

MONSIEUR LOYAL: Sir, my business is not with you; it is with this gentleman; he is both reasonable and mild; and he knows too well the duty of an honest man to oppose the law in any way.

ORGON: But . . .

MONSIEUR LOYAL: Yes, sir, I know that you would not rebel for a million in gold, and that, like a gentleman, you will allow me to execute here the orders I have received.

DAMIS: Mister bailiff, you could easily get the feel of a stick on your black gown here.

MONSIEUR LOYAL: Sir, either make your son hold his tongue or leave the room; I should be very sorry to be obliged to write this down and to see your name figure in my official report.

DORINE (*Aside*): This Mister Loyal looks very disloyal.

MONSIEUR LOYAL: I have great sympathy, sir, for all honest people, and I have charged myself with these writs only to oblige and please you, only to prevent the choice of those who, not having the same consideration for you that inspires me, might have proceeded in a less gentle way.

ORGON: And what can be worse than to order people to leave their own house?

MONSIEUR LOYAL: You are given time and I shall suspend until tomorrow the execution of the warrant, sir. I shall only come to spend the night here with ten of my helpers without a scandal and without noise. As a formality you will have to bring me the keys to your door before you go to bed, please. I shall take care not to disturb your rest and to permit nothing improper. But early tomorrow morning you must do your best to clear the house of even the least utensil. My helpers will assist you and I have picked out strong fellows to help you remove everything. One cannot act better than I do, I think; and as I am treating you with great indulgence, I beg you also, sir, to make good use of it, so that I may not be annoyed in the execution of my duty.

ORGON (*Aside*): I would willingly give just now the best hundred gold pieces I have left for the pleasure of striking on his snout the soundest blow that ever was dealt.

CLÉANTE (*Softly to* ORGON): Leave well alone. Let us not spoil anything further.

DAMIS: I can hardly restrain myself at this strange impertinence, and my hand is itching.

DORINE: Upon my word, Monsieur Loyal, with such a broad back, a few blows of a strong stick would do you no harm.

MONSIEUR LOYAL: We might easily punish these infamous words, my girl; and there are laws against women too.

CLÉANTE: Let's stop all this, sir; we've had enough. Give us this paper right now, pray, and leave us.

MONSIEUR LOYAL: Till we see you again. May Heaven bless you all!

ORGON: And may it confound you, and the one who sent you.

Scene 5 [ORGON, CLÉANTE, MARIANE, ELMIRE, MADAME PERNELLE, DORINE, DAMIS]

ORGON: Well! mother, do you see now whether I am right; and you may judge of the rest from this performance. Do you at last see his treacheries?

MADAME PERNELLE: I am stunned and feel as if dropped from the clouds.

DORINE: You are wrong to complain, you are wrong to blame him, and his pious intentions are confirmed by this. His virtue is made perfect in the love for his neighbor. He knows that riches often corrupt man, and, out of true charity, he wants to take everything away from you that might become an obstacle to your salvation.

ORGON: Hold your tongue! these are the words I must always repeat to you.

CLÉANTE: Let's go and see what course of action you should choose.

ELMIRE: Go and expose the audacity of this ungrateful wretch. This proceeding invalidates the contract; and his treachery will appear too black to allow him to have the success which we surmise.

Scene 6 [VALÈRE, ORGON, CLÉANTE, ELMIRE, MARIANE]

VALÈRE: It is with great regret, sir, that I come to bother you; but I am constrained to it by a pressing danger. A very intimate and faithful friend of mine, who knows the interest which I take in what concerns you, has for my sake, by a most delicate step, violated the secrecy due to the affairs of State, and has just sent me advice, the consequence of which reduces you to the expedient of sudden flight. The scoundrel who has long imposed upon you, has accused you to the King an hour ago, and among other charges which he brings against you, has put into his hands the important casket of a state criminal, of which, he says, contrary to the duty of a subject, you have kept the guilty secret. I do not know the details of the crime laid to your charge; but a warrant has been issued against you; and to execute it better, he himself is to accompany the person who is to arrest you.

CLÉANTE: Now his rights are armed; and this is how the traitor seeks to make himself master of your estate.

ORGON: The man is, I confess, a wicked beast.

VALÈRE: The least delay may be fatal to you. I have my coach at the door to carry you off with a thousand louis which I bring you. Let us not waste any time, the blow is terrible, and is one of those that are best parried by flight. I offer myself to conduct you to a place of safety, and will accompany you to the end of your flight.

ORGON: Alas! what do I not owe to your obliging care! To thank you I must wait for another time; and I ask Heaven to be so propitious to me that I may one day acknowledge this generous service. Farewell; be careful, the rest of you.

CLÉANTE: Go quickly. We will try, brother, to do what is proper.

Scene 7 [A POLICE OFFICER, TARTUFFE, VALÈRE, ORGON, ELMIRE, MARIANE, *etc.*]

TARTUFFE: Slowly, sir, slowly, do not run so fast. You will not have to go far to find a lodging; we take you prisoner in the King's name.

ORGON: Traitor! You have reserved this blow for the last! That is the stroke, villain, by which you ruin me completely; and this crowns all your perfidies.

TARTUFFE: Your insults cannot make me angry; Heaven has taught me to suffer everything.

CLÉANTE: Your moderation is great, I confess!

DAMIS: How impudently the villain makes fun of Heaven!

TARTUFFE: All your outbursts cannot move me in the least; and I think of nothing but my duty.

MARIANE: You may glorify yourself very much upon this; and this task is very honorable for you to undertake.

TARTUFFE: A task cannot but be glorious when it proceeds from the power that sends me here.

ORGON: But did you remember, ungrateful scoundrel, that my charitable hand rescued you from a wretched condition?

TARTUFFE: Yes, I know what help I received from you; but the King's interest is my first duty. The just obligation of this sacred duty stifles all gratitude in my heart; and I would sacrifice to such a powerful consideration, friends, wife, relatives, and myself with them.

ELMIRE: The hypocrite!

DORINE: How well he knows how to make himself a cloak of all that is sacred!

CLÉANTE: But if it is as perfect as you say, this zeal which inspires you and upon which you pride yourself, why hasn't it shown itself until Orgon caught you trying to seduce his wife; and why did you not think of denouncing him until his honor obliged him to drive you from his house. I am not saying that the gift of his whole estate which he had made to you should have turned you from your duty;

but, intending to treat him as a criminal today, why did you consent
to take anything from him?

TARTUFFE (*To the officer*): Pray, sir, free me from this clamor, and be
good enough to execute your orders.

OFFICER: Yes, we have indeed delayed too long to discharge them;
your words remind me of this just in time; and to execute them,
follow me at once to the prison which is destined to be your abode.

TARTUFFE: Who? I, sir?

OFFICER: Yes, you.

TARTUFFE: Why to prison?

OFFICER: I have no intention of giving you the reason. (*To* ORGON.)
Compose yourself, sir, after so great an alarm. We live under a King
who is an enemy of fraud, a King whose eyes penetrate into the
heart and whom the art of impostors cannot deceive. His great soul
is blessed with sharp discernment, and always looks clearly at things;
it is never betrayed by exaggeration, and his solid reason falls into
no excess. He bestows lasting glory on men of worth; but he shows
this zeal without blindness, and his love for sincerity does not fore-
close his heart to the horror which falsehood must inspire. Even
this person was not able to deceive him and he has kept clear of
more artful snares. From the very beginning he has perceived, because of his great enlightenment, all the vileness concealed within
his heart. In coming to accuse you, he betrayed himself, and by a
just stroke of supreme justice, has shown himself to the King as
a notorious rogue against whom he had received information under
another name; and his life is a long series of wicked actions, of
which whole volumes might be written. Our monarch, in short, has
defeated his vile ingratitude and disloyalty towards you; he has
added this affair to his other misdeeds, and has placed me under
his orders, only to see his impertinence carried out to the end, and
to oblige him to give you full satisfaction. Yes, he wishes me to strip
this traitor of all your papers which he claims to possess, and to give
them to you. By his sovereign power he annuls the obligation of the
contract which gave him all your estate and lastly, he forgives you
this secret offense in which the flight of a friend has involved you;
and this is the reward of your former zeal in upholding his rights;
to show that his heart knows how to recompense a good action when
you least expect it; that merit with him is never lost; and that he
remembers good much better than evil.

DORINE: Heaven be praised!

MADAME PERNELLE: Now I can breathe.

ELMIRE: Happy ending!

MARIANE: Who would have dared say so?

ORGON (*To* TARTUFFE): Well, there you are, traitor . . .

CLÉANTE: Ah! brother, stop; and do not descend to indignities. Leave the wretch to his unhappy fate and do not add to the remorse that overwhelms him. Rather wish that his heart, on this day, may return to virtue; and that he may reform his life, by detesting his vice, and may soften the justice of our great King; while you throw yourself at his knees to render thanks for his kindness, which has treated you so leniently.

ORGON: Yes, this is well said. Let us throw ourselves joyfully at his feet, to praise the kindness which his heart displays to us. Then, having acquitted ourselves of this first duty, we must apply ourselves to the just cares of another, and by a sweet union crown in Valère the flame of a generous and sincere lover.

TARTUFFE belongs with the neoclassical drama of seventeenth-century France. From Italian stagecraft of the Renaissance the French theater during the reign of Louis XIV developed most of the features of the conventional modern theater: a deep box stage framed by a proscenium arch, with the audience seated in front; a curtain; wings for movable sets; artificial light; elaborate painted scenery and backstage mechanical devices for special effects; actresses in female roles. It also took over some of the dramatic conventions of the Italian theater, particularly the three unities and — in comedy — the characters of the *commedia dell'arte*, semi-farces in which characters and plot were given but the dialogue improvised during performance. In *Tartuffe*, we recognize Orgon, the foolish and tyrannical father, Valère and Mariane, the nice if somewhat bland young lovers, and Dorine, the pert and clever maid, as descendants from their stock Italian prototypes.

Tartuffe had a complicated birth. An early version of its present first three acts made up the whole play when it was first given at Versailles in 1664. King Louis himself was amused, but the religious bigots at court took offense and prevailed upon him to ban the play. "The King," says a contemporary, "could not in his delicate carefulness for the things that concern religion suffer vice to be made so like virtue, that one might be taken for the other." The play was, however, given private readings and even performances during the next few years, probably in a five-act version. For a public performance of the play (in five acts) in 1667 Molière had changed his title to *The Impostor*, to leave no one in doubt that he was attacking only false piety, and dressed Tartuffe as a fop rather than in priest-like black, but again he drew the ire of the religious authorities. Only in 1669 did the King permit the play, with its original title restored and in its present form, to be freely performed.

For us, living in a more liberal — or indifferent — age, the implications of Tartuffe's hypocrisy are likely to be less controversial, though hardly less meaningful. Tartuffe threatens a family with ruin, almost disrupts the basic social unit, breaks natural bonds. He is himself a solitary outsider, familyless, friendless, loveless, without any social context. But the fact that he is not related to anybody or anything before Orgon picks him up is not, somehow, a cause for pity. Rather, it makes him a sinister, antisocial figure, lone evil against the vital group.

Formally, what is most striking about the play is the delay of Tartuffe's appearance for more than two acts. The delay represents a daring piece of dramaturgy, for though the gain in audience suspense is obvious, there is also the risk of anticlimax when the title character *does* appear. But his first speech, "Laurent, put away my hair shirt and my scourge and pray that Heaven may enlighten you" brilliantly justifies the device. False unction is on display forever in this penitent ascetic with a valet.

The little scene reveals a major characteristic of Molière's comic art. What his characters are they are with an intensity and thoroughness and sharpness of outline that establish their identity once and for all. We are dealing with blacks and whites. There are no complexities or ambiguities or subtle depths. Virtue and wisdom exist less for their own sake than as antitheses to vice and folly, and if the gulls appear as stereotypes that is no more than their own doing. They are diminishers of their own humanity. The opening dialogue between old Madame Pernelle and the various members of the household, in which they all take turns trying to interrupt the old lady's harangue but only succeed in drawing her fire, represents a patterning of speech that is obviously unnatural but which nevertheless justifies itself not only as a certain rhythm of dialogue but also as a method by which human attitudes are clearly defined and contrasted. Molière is not interested in photographic realism or in doing justice to the infinite complexities of the human soul, in discovering the good that surely must reside somewhere even in a bigot. He is interested in providing us with a memorable spectacle of hypocrisy, gullibility, and obstinacy in action. The long, stilted speeches, the alternating passages of fast, cut-and-thrust dialogue, the exaggerations and oversimplifications and contrivances of situation and character, these are all deliberate formalizations of the dramatist's art, devices that both heighten the comedy — or farce, if one likes — and extend the anatomy of basic human attitudes. Take a famous scene that presents some characteristic difficulties in the way of enjoying Molière — scene 4 in Act I. Orgon has just returned from a trip to the country and asks the maid Dorine how everyone has been during his absence. Dorine tells him his wife has had an attack of fever, Orgon asks about Tartuffe, Dorine says he is comfortable and in excellent health, Orgon exclaims, "Poor man." This sequence of four speeches is repeated three times. Again a pattern is established, and we gather an impression of Orgon's perversion of values.

But is it funny? Does it reflect actual human behavior, even allowing the playwright the privilege of exaggeration for heightened effect? What does it *mean* to say "Poor man" about someone you have just been told is perfectly well and content? Why is the speech repeated?

The exchange is, obviously, a shortcut to characterization as well as a piece of verbal slapstick. But if it were only that, we would not be dealing with great comedy. We are, though, and the reason is that we can feel the unnaturalness and idiocy of Orgon's replies to be functional to Molière's theme. Orgon's affection for Tartuffe, to the point of ignoring and even injuring his own family, *is* a form of lunacy. His response to the news of his wife's illness is no more insane than his later decision to give his daughter in marriage to a man who is hateful to her or to disinherit his son in favor of that man and of entrusting him with a friend's secrets. While Dorine's speeches in the scene are full and flavorful, vivid with concrete detail, Orgon's are limited to four words, two set phrases, the expression of a small and frozen attitude. He listens and yet does not listen. What Dorine tells him about Tartuffe does not reach him as meaning; it only triggers a piece of pious cant; he answers automatically, totally inadequate to the human situation. He speaks like a man hypnotized, or under a spell. There is poetic justice (as Dorine points out) in the scene in which Madame Pernelle obstinately refuses to believe that Tartuffe could have designs on Elmire, even after her son has been convinced by the evidence of his own eyes. If, after the spell has been broken, Orgon is frustrated by his equally rigorous mother into contemplating the absurdity of his own previous behavior, this is precisely Molière's point. Orgon has only himself to blame for his troubles and for his flatness of character. In a sense, the play is about inflexibility of spirit as much as it is about hypocrisy.

Against Orgon's obstinate stupidity and unnaturalness of feeling and against the increasingly sinister presence of Tartuffe (consider the function and effect of M. Loyal in this connection), the play asserts the primary value of sane moderation in human relationships. Three characters represent these values: Cléante, the voice of wisdom and restraint, whose most significant speech is the one in which he objects to Orgon's vow never again to trust a pious man; Dorine, who constantly deflates stuffiness and pretension and who saves Valère and Mariane from their own foolish pride; and Elmire, who refuses to become hysterical over Tartuffe's advances and succeeds in opening Orgon's eyes by using herself as bait to lure Tartuffe into giving himself away. These three combine goodness with intelligence and strength. In contrast, there are the good characters who suffer because of some excess of feeling: Damis' rashness ends in his discomfiture and the temporary strengthening of Tartuffe's hand, and Mariane has to be rescued from her own despair. Valère's character is ambivalent in this respect. He and Mariane are too stubbornly proud to manage their own romance, but at the very end of the play he passes from folly to a kind of heroism and becomes Tartuffe's contrast (*foil,* in the technical term): Tartuffe repays Orgon's kindness with ingratitude; Valère repays Orgon's injustice with kindness.

If Cléante is Molière's spokesman (*raisonneur*), it becomes significant that he and his allies are rendered helpless against the efficacy of evil at the end. The best they can hope for is some way of coming to terms with Tartuffe. To recover what Orgon's error has cost them appears impossible. For a moment in Act V, the play seems about to turn into a kind of tragedy — the family to be destroyed by the evil intruder. At this point Molière does something that courses in writing drama warn against; he introduces a *deus ex machina,* a person (or fact) who has not entered the action before and who steps in to resolve an otherwise impossible situation. In this case, the god from the wings is King Louis XIV, represented by the Officer who arrests Tartuffe. Nothing earlier in the play has led us to expect this development. Is it, therefore, more than fulsome flattery of Molière's patron and an awkward way out of a plot that threatened to master the supposed writer of comedy? It is certainly not playing the game according to the rules of detective fiction.

Again one must keep in mind Molière's artistic end — not plausibility but communication of wisdom in effective drama. The fact that outside help is needed, that the all-powerful hand of the king must interfere to keep evil from succeeding against innocence, becomes a plot metaphor for the simple truth that discovery of one's error and sincere remorse for it do not necessarily rectify its consequences. We are moving here on the very edge of comedy, where the forces of stupidity and evil somehow seem more substantial than those of reason and goodness. Religious hypocrisy may be laughable, but it is also dangerous. The comedy turns serious. Innocent, gullible, well-meaning man is unable to cope with evil alone. He needs kingly help.)⌇

Henrik Ibsen

THE WILD DUCK

A New Translation by Otto Reinert

Characters

WERLE, *a manufacturer and merchant*
GREGERS WERLE, *his son*
OLD EKDAL
HJALMAR EKDAL, *his son, a photographer*
GINA EKDAL, *Hjalmar's wife*
HEDVIG, *their daughter, fourteen years old*
MRS. SØRBY, *Werle's housekeeper*
RELLING, *a physician*
MOLVIK, *a former student of theology*
GRÅBERG, *a bookkeeper in Werle's office*
PETTERSEN, *Werle's servant*
JENSEN, *a hired waiter*
A FLABBY GENTLEMAN
A THIN-HAIRED GENTLEMAN
A NEARSIGHTED GENTLEMAN
SIX OTHER GENTLEMEN, *Werle's dinner guests*
OTHER HIRED WAITERS

SCENE: *The first act takes place at* WERLE'S; *the other four, in* HJALMAR EKDAL'S *studio.*

ACT I

An expensive-looking and comfortable study in WERLE'S *house; bookcases and upholstered furniture; in the middle of the room a desk with papers and ledgers; lamps with green shades give the room a soft, subdued light. In the rear, open double doors with portieres pulled apart reveal a large, elegant drawing room, brightly illuminated by lamps and candles. Front right, a small door to the office wing. Front left, a fireplace with glowing coals in it. Farther back on the left wall, double doors to the dining room.*

PETTERSEN, WERLE'S *servant, in livery, and the hired waiter* JENSEN, *in black, are setting the study in order for the guests. In the drawing room, two or three other hired waiters are lighting candles, moving chairs, etc. Sounds of conversation and laughter of many people come from the dining room. Someone signals he wishes to make a speech by touching his glass with his knife. Silence follows, a short speech is made, there are noises of approval, then again conversation.*

PETTERSEN (*lights a lamp by the fireplace and puts a shade on it*): Just listen to that, Jensen. There's the old man now, proposing a long toast to Mrs. Sørby.

JENSEN (*moving an armchair*): Do you think it's true what people say, that the two of 'em — y'know — ?

PETTERSEN: Couldn't say.

JENSEN: I bet he used to be quite a goat in the old days.

PETTERSEN: Maybe so.

JENSEN: They say this dinner is for his son.

PETTERSEN: That's right. He came home yesterday.

JENSEN: It's the first I've heard Werle has a son.

PETTERSEN: He has a son, all right. But he's up at the works at Høydal all the time. He hasn't been home as long as I've been here.

A HIRED WAITER (*in the drawing room doorway*): Pst, Pettersen, there's an old fellow here, says he —

PETTERSEN (*under his breath*): Dammit! Can't have anybody in here now!

(OLD EKDAL *appears from the right in the drawing room. He is dressed in a shabby old coat with a high collar. Wool mittens. He carries a walking stick and a fur cap in his hand. Under his arm a parcel in thick paper. Dirty, reddish brown wig. Small, gray mustache.*)

PETTERSEN (*going towards him*): Good Lord! What are *you* doing here?

EKDAL (*in the doorway*): Got to get into the office, Pettersen.

PETTERSEN: The office closed an hour ago, and —

EKDAL: They told me that downstairs. But Gråberg is still in there. Be a good boy, Pettersen; let me in this way. (*Points to the small office door.*) Been through here before.

PETTERSEN: Oh well, all right. (*Opens the door.*) But see you go out the other way. We're having guests tonight.

EKDAL: I know, I know — h'm! Thanks a lot, Pettersen, old boy. Good old friend. Thanks. (*Mutters.*) Ass!

(*He enters the office.* PETTERSEN *closes the door behind him.*)

JENSEN: Is he one of them office people, too?

PETTERSEN: Oh no. He just does some extra copying for them, when they need it. But he's been a fine enough fellow in his day, old Ekdal has.

JENSEN: You know, he sort of looked like that.

PETTERSEN: Oh yes. He used to be a lieutenant.

JENSEN: I'll be damned! A lieutenant!

PETTERSEN: Yessir: Then he got mixed up in some forest deal or something. They say he pretty near ruined Werle once. The two of 'em were partners — owned the Høydal works together. Oh yes, Ekdal and I are good friends. We've had many a drink together at Madam Eriksen's place, we have.

JENSEN: Didn't look to me like he'd have much to buy people drinks with.

PETTERSEN: Good Lord, Jensen. It's my treat, of course. I always say one should be nice to people who've seen better days.

JENSEN: So he went bankrupt?

PETTERSEN: Worse than that. He went to prison.

JENSEN: Prison!

PETTERSEN: Or something. — (*Listens.*) Shhh. They are getting up from the table.

(*Servants open the doors to the dining room.* MRS. SØRBY *appears, in conversation with a couple of the dinner guests. The rest of the company follows in small groups.* WERLE *is among them. The last to appear are* HJALMAR EKDAL *and* GREGERS WERLE.)

MRS. SØRBY (*to the servant, in passing*): Pettersen, tell them to serve the coffee in the music room, will you?

PETTERSEN: Very well, Mrs. Sørby.

(*She and the two guests go into the drawing room and disappear, right.* PETTERSEN *and* JENSEN *follow them out.*)

A FLABBY GENTLEMAN (*to* A THIN-HAIRED *one*): Phew! That dinner — It was almost too much for me.

THE THIN-HAIRED GENTLEMAN: Oh, I don't know. With a little bit of good will, it's amazing what one can accomplish in three hours.

THE FLABBY GENTLEMAN: Yes, but afterwards, afterwards, my dear chamberlain!

A THIRD GENTLEMAN: I am told the coffee and liqueurs will be served in the music room.

THE FLABBY GENTLEMAN: Wonderful! Then maybe Mrs. Sørby will play something for us.

THE THIN-HAIRED GENTLEMAN (*in a low voice*): If only she doesn't play us a different tune one of these days.

THE FLABBY GENTLEMAN: Don't worry. Bertha isn't one to let old friends down.

(*They laugh and enter the drawing room.*)

WERLE (*in a low and troubled voice*): I don't think anybody noticed, Gregers.

GREGERS (*looks at him*): Noticed what?

WERLE: You didn't either?

GREGERS: What?

WERLE: We were thirteen at the table.

GREGERS: Really? Were we thirteen?

WERLE (*with a glance at* HJALMAR EKDAL): Usually we are only twelve. (*To the other guests:*) Gentlemen!

(*He and the remaining guests, except* HJALMAR *and* GREGERS, *leave through the drawing room, rear right.*)

HJALMAR (*who has overheard the conversation*): You shouldn't have invited me, Gregers.

GREGERS: Nonsense! This is supposed to be a party for *me*. Shouldn't I invite my one and only friend?

HJALMAR: But I don't think your father approves. I never come to this house.

GREGERS: So I hear. But I wanted to see you and talk to you. — Well, well, we two old school fellows have certainly drifted apart. It must be sixteen — seventeen years since we saw each other.

HJALMAR: Is it really that long?

GREGERS: It is indeed. And how are you? You look fine. You're almost stout.

HJALMAR: Stout is hardly the word, but I suppose I look a little more manly than I used to.

GREGERS: Yes, you do. Your appearance hasn't suffered any all these years.

HJALMAR (*gloomily*): But the inner man — ! Believe me, that's a different story. You know, of course, how utterly everything has collapsed for me and mine since we last met.

GREGERS (*in a lower voice*): How is your father these days?

HJALMAR: I'd just as soon not talk about him. My poor, unfortunate father lives with me, of course. He has no one else in the whole world to turn to. But it is so terribly difficult for me to talk about these things. Tell me rather how you have been — up there at the works.

GREGERS: Lonely — blissfully lonely. I've had all the time in the world to think over all sorts of things. — Here. Let's make ourselves comfortable.

(*He sits down in an armchair near the fireplace and gets* HJALMAR *to take another chair beside him.*)

HJALMAR (*softly*): All the same, I do want to thank you, Gregers, for inviting me to your father's table. It proves to me you no longer bear me a grudge.

GREGERS (*surprised*): Grudge? What makes you think I ever did?

HJALMAR: You did at first, you know.

GREGERS: When?

HJALMAR: Right after the tragedy. Of course, that was only natural. After all, your own father only escaped by the skin of his teeth. Oh, that terrible old business!

GREGERS: And so I bore you a grudge? Who told you that?

HJALMAR: I know you did, Gregers. Your father said so himself.

GREGERS (*startled*): Father! Really? H'm. So that's why you've never written — not a single word.

HJALMAR: Yes.

GREGERS: Not even when you decided to become a photographer?

HJALMAR: Your father thought it would be better if I didn't write about anything at all.

GREGERS (*looking straight ahead*): Oh well, maybe he was right, at that. — But tell me, Hjalmar — do you feel you have adjusted pretty well to your situation?

HJALMAR (*with a small sigh*): Oh yes, I think I have. Can't say I haven't, anyway. At first, of course, things seemed very strange. My circumstances were so completely different. But then, everything had changed. Father's great, ruinous tragedy — The shame — The disgrace —

GREGERS (*feelingly*): Yes, yes. I see.

HJALMAR: Of course there was no way in which I could pursue my studies. There wasn't a penny left. Rather the opposite; there was debt. Mainly to your father, I think.

GREGERS: H'm —

HJALMAR: Well — then I thought it best to take the bull by the horns and make a clean break with the past — you know, all at once. Your father thought so, too, and since he had been so helpful, and —

GREGERS: Father helped you?

HJALMAR: Yes, surely you know that? Where do you think I got the money to learn photography and to set up my own studio? Things like that are expensive, I can tell you.

GREGERS: And father paid for all that?

HJALMAR: Yes, didn't you know? I understood him to say he had written to you about it.

GREGERS: Not a word that it was *he*. He must have forgotten. We only write business letters. So it was father — !

HJALMAR: It certainly was. But he has never wanted people to know that. It was he who made it possible for me to get married, too. Or maybe — maybe you didn't know that, either?

GREGERS: No! How could I? (*Shakes* HJALMAR's *arm.*) My dear Hjalmar, I can't tell you how happy all this makes me — and pains me, too. Perhaps I have been unfair to father. In some respects, anyway. For this shows he has a heart, you know. A kind of conscience —

HJALMAR: Conscience?

GREGERS: Or whatever you want to call it. No, really, I can't tell you how glad I am to hear this about father. — So you are married, Hjalmar. That's more than I ever will be. I trust you find yourself happy as a married man?

HJALMAR: Yes, I certainly do. She is as good and competent a wife as any man could ask for. And she is by no means without culture.

GREGERS (*a little taken aback*): No, of course not.

HJALMAR: Life itself is an education, you see. Being with me every day — And then there are a couple of remarkable men we see quite a lot of. I assure you, you'd hardly recognize Gina.

GREGERS: Gina?

HJALMAR: Yes. Surely you remember her name was Gina?

GREGERS: Whose name? I haven't the slightest idea —

HJALMAR: But don't you remember she was here in the house for a while?

GREGERS (*looks at him*): Is it Gina Hansen — ?

HJALMAR: Of course it is Gina Hansen.

GREGERS: — who kept house for us the last year of mother's illness?

HJALMAR: That's it. But my dear friend, I know for a fact that your father wrote you about my marriage.

GREGERS (*who has risen*): Yes, so he did, that's true, but not that — (*paces the floor*). Wait a minute — Yes, he did — now when I think back. But father always writes such short letters. (*Sits down on the arm of the chair.*) Listen, Hjalmar — this interests me — how did you make Gina's acquaintance — your wife, I mean?

HJALMAR: Quite simply. You remember she didn't stay here very long. Everything was so unsettled during your mother's illness. Gina couldn't take that, so she gave notice and moved out. That was the year before your mother died. Or maybe it was the same year.

GREGERS: It was the same year. I was up at Høydal at the time. Then what happened?

HJALMAR: Well, Gina moved in with her mother, Madam Hansen, an excellent, hardworking woman, who ran a small eating place. And she had a room for rent, too. A nice, comfortable room.

GREGERS: Which you were lucky enough to get?

HJALMAR: Yes. Through your father, in fact. And it was there I really learned to know Gina.

GREGERS: And then you got engaged?

HJALMAR: Yes. It's easy for young people to fall in love, you know. H'm —

GREGERS (*gets up, walks up and down*): Tell me — after you'd become engaged, was that when father — I mean, was that when you took up photography?

HJALMAR: That's right. Naturally, I wanted to get married and have a place of my own, the sooner the better. And both your father and I agreed that photography was the best thing I could get into. Gina thought so, too. Oh yes, that was another reason. It so happened that Gina had learned how to retouch.

GREGERS: What a wonderful coincidence.

HJALMAR (*smiling contentedly*): Yes, wasn't it? Don't you think it worked out very well?

GREGERS: Remarkably well, I should say. So father has really been a kind of Providence for you, Hjalmar; hasn't he?

HJALMAR (*moved*): He did not abandon his old friend's son in his days of need. That's one thing about your father: he does have a heart.

MRS. SØRBY (*enters on* WERLE's *arm*): I don't want to hear another word, my dear sir. You are not to stay in there staring at all those bright lights. It isn't good for you.

WERLE (*letting go of her arm and moving his hand across his eyes*): I almost think you are right.

(PETTERSEN *and* JENSEN *enter carrying trays with glasses of punch.*)

MRS. SØRBY (*to the guests in the drawing room*): Gentlemen, if you want a glass of punch, you'll have to take the trouble to come in here.

THE FLABBY GENTLEMAN (*to* MRS. SØRBY): Dear Mrs. Sørby, please tell me it isn't so. You have not withdrawn your cherished permission to smoke?

MRS. SØRBY: Yes, Chamberlain. No smoking here in Mr. Werle's own sanctum.

THE THIN-HAIRED GENTLEMAN: And when did you append these harsh paragraphs to the tobacco regulations, Mrs. Sørby?

MRS. SØRBY: After the last dinner, Chamberlain, when certain persons abused their liberties.

THE THIN-HAIRED GENTLEMAN: And will not even the smallest infraction be tolerated, Mrs. Sørby? Really none at all?

MRS. SØRBY: None whatsoever, Chamberlain.

(*Most of the guests are gathered in the study. The servants are serving punch.*)

WERLE (*to* HJALMAR, *over by a table*): Well, Ekdal, what is that you are looking at?

HJALMAR: Oh, just an album, sir.

THE THIN-HAIRED GENTLEMAN (*moving about*): Ah yes! Photographs! That's your line, of course.

THE FLABBY GENTLEMAN (*seated*): Haven't you brought some of your own along?

HJALMAR: No, I haven't.

THE FLABBY GENTLEMAN: Too bad. Looking at pictures is good for the digestion, you know.

THE THIN-HAIRED GENTLEMAN: And then it would have contributed a mite to the general entertainment.

A NEARSIGHTED GENTLEMAN: And all contributions are gratefully received.

MRS. SØRBY: The chamberlains think that when one has been invited to dinner, one ought to work for one's food, Mr. Ekdal.

THE FLABBY GENTLEMAN: With a cuisine like this that's only a pleasure.

THE THIN-HAIRED GENTLEMAN: Oh well, if it's a question of the struggle for existence —

MRS. SØRBY: You are so right!

(*They continue their conversation, laughing and joking.*)

GREGERS (*in a low voice*): You must join in, Hjalmar.

HJALMAR (*with a twist of his body*): What am I to say?

THE FLABBY GENTLEMAN: Don't you believe, sir, that Tokay may be considered relatively beneficial to the stomach?

WERLE (*by the fireplace*): I'll guarantee the Tokay you were served to-night, at any rate. It is one of the very best years. I am sure you noticed that yourself.

THE FLABBY GENTLEMAN: Yes, it really was unusually delicate-tasting.

HJALMAR (*hesitantly*): Do the years differ?

THE FLABBY GENTLEMAN (*laughs*): Ah, Mr. Ekdal! Splendid!

WERLE (*with a smile*): I see it is hardly worth while to serve you fine wine.

THE THIN-HAIRED GENTLEMAN: Tokay is like photographs, Mr. Ekdal. Both need sunshine. Or isn't that so?

HJALMAR: Yes, sunshine has something to do with it.

MRS. SØRBY: Just the same with chamberlains. They need sunshine, too — royal sunshine, as the saying goes.

THE THIN-HAIRED GENTLEMAN: Ouch! That's a tired old joke, Mrs. Sørby.

THE NEARSIGHTED GENTLEMAN: The lady will have her fun —

THE FLABBY GENTLEMAN: — and at our expense. (*Wagging his finger.*) Madam Bertha! Madam Bertha!

MRS. SØRBY: But it is true that vintages differ widely sometimes. The older the better.

THE NEARSIGHTED GENTLEMAN: Do you count me among the older vintages?

MRS. SØRBY: Far from it.

THE THIN-HAIRED GENTLEMAN: Well, well! But what about me, Mrs. Sørby?

THE FLABBY GENTLEMAN: And me? What vintages do we belong to?

MRS. SØRBY: I reckon you among the sweet vintages, gentlemen.

(*She sips a glass of punch. The chamberlains laugh and flirt with her.*)

WERLE: Mrs. Sørby always finds a way out — when she wants to. But gentlemen, you aren't drinking! Pettersen, please see to it that — ! Gregers, let's have a glass together.

(GREGERS *does not move.*)

Won't you join us, Ekdal? I had no opportunity at the table —

(GRÅBERG *comes in through the office door.*)

GRÅBERG: Beg your pardon, Mr. Werle, but I can't get out.

WERLE: They've locked you in again, eh?

GRÅBERG: Yes, they have, sir. And Flakstad has left with the keys.

WERLE: That's all right. You just come through here.

GRÅBERG: But there is somebody else —

WERLE: Doesn't matter. Come on, both of you.

(GRÅBERG *and* OLD EKDAL *enter from the office.*)

WERLE (*involuntarily*): Damn!

(*Laughter and talk among the guests cease.* HJALMAR *gives a start when he sees his father, puts down his glass, and turns away toward the fireplace.*)

EKDAL (*does not look up but makes quick little bows to both sides, as he mutters*): Beg pardon. Came the wrong way. Gate's locked. Gate's locked. Beg pardon. (*He and* GRÅBERG *go out, rear right.*)

WERLE (*between his teeth*): That idiot Gråberg!

GREGERS (*staring, his mouth hanging open, to* HJALMAR): Don't tell me that was — !

THE FLABBY GENTLEMAN: What is it? Who was that?

GREGERS: Nothing. Just the bookkeeper and somebody else.

THE NEARSIGHTED GENTLEMAN (*to* HJALMAR): Did *you* know that man?

HJALMAR: I don't know — I didn't notice —

THE FLABBY GENTLEMAN (*getting up*): What the devil has gotten into everybody? (*He walks over to some other guests, who are talking in low voices.*)

MRS. SØRBY (*whispers to the servant*): Give him something from the kitchen to take home. Something good.

PETTERSEN (*nods his head*): I'll do that, ma'am. (*Goes out.*)

GREGERS (*shocked, in a low voice to* HJALMAR): Then it really was he?

HJALMAR: Yes.

GREGERS: And you stood there and denied him!

HJALMAR (*in a fierce whisper*): But how *could* I — ?

GREGERS: — acknowledge your own father?

HJALMAR (*pained*): Oh, if you had been in my place, maybe —

(*The low conversation among the guests changes to forced gaiety.*)

THE THIN-HAIRED GENTLEMAN (*approaching* HJALMAR *and* GREGERS, *in a friendly mood*): Aha! Reminiscing about university days, gentlemen? — Don't you smoke, Mr. Ekdal? Can I give you a light? Oh that's right. We are not allowed —

HJALMAR: Thanks, I don't smoke.

THE FLABBY GENTLEMAN: Don't you have a nice little poem you could recite for us, Mr. Ekdal? You used to do that so beautifully.

HJALMAR: I am sorry. I don't remember any.

THE FLABBY GENTLEMAN: That's a shame. Well, in that case, Balle, what do we do?

(*They both walk into the drawing room.*)

HJALMAR (*gloomily*): Gregers — I am leaving! You see, when a man has felt Fate's crushing blow — Say goodbye to your father for me.
GREGERS: Yes, of course. Are you going straight home?
HJALMAR: Yes. Why?
GREGERS: I thought I might come up and see you a little later.
HJALMAR: No, don't do that. Not to my home. My home is a gloomy one, Gregers, particularly after a brilliant banquet such as this. We can meet somewhere in town.
MRS. SØRBY (*has come up to them; in a low voice*): Are you leaving, Ekdal?
HJALMAR: Yes.
MRS. SØRBY: Say hello to Gina.
HJALMAR: Thank you. I'll do that.
MRS. SØRBY: Tell her I'll be up to see her one of these days.
HJALMAR: Fine. (*To* GREGERS) You stay here. I'll slip out without anybody noticing. (*Drifts off. A little later he goes into the drawing room and out right.*)
MRS. SØRBY (*in a low voice to the servant who has returned*): Well, did you give the old man something?
PETTERSEN: Oh yes. A bottle of brandy.
MRS. SØRBY: Oh dear. Couldn't you have found something better?
PETTERSEN: But Mrs. Sørby, there's nothing he likes better than brandy.
THE FLABBY GENTLEMAN (*in the doorway to the drawing room, with a sheet of music in his hand*): Will you play a duet, Mrs. Sørby?
MRS. SØRBY: Yes, gladly.
THE GUESTS: Good! Good!

(*She and all the guests go out rear right.* GREGERS *remains standing by the fireplace.* WERLE *is looking for something on the desk and appears to wish to be left alone. Since* GREGERS *does not leave,* WERLE *walks towards the drawing room door.*)

GREGERS: Father, do you have a moment?
WERLE (*stops*): What is it?
GREGERS: I'd like a word with you.
WERLE: Couldn't it wait till we're alone?
GREGERS: No, it can't, for maybe we'll never be alone again.
WERLE (*coming closer*): What does that mean?

(*During the following scene, the sound of a piano is faintly heard from the music room.*)

GREGERS: How is it that that family has been allowed to go to ruin so miserably?

WERLE: I suppose you refer to the Ekdals?

GREGERS: Yes, I do mean the Ekdals. Lieutenant Ekdal was once your close friend.

WERLE: Yes, unfortunately. Too close. I have felt that keenly enough for many years. It was his fault that my good name and reputation, too, were — somewhat tarnished.

GREGERS (*in a low voice*): Was he the only one who was guilty?

WERLE: Who else, do you mean?

GREGERS: The two of you were together on that big purchase of forest land, weren't you?

WERLE: But it was Ekdal who surveyed the area — surveyed it fraudulently. It was he who felled all that timber on state property. He was responsible for everything that went on up there. I didn't know what he was doing.

GREGERS: I doubt that Lieutenant Ekdal himself knew what he was doing.

WERLE: That may well be. The fact remains that he was convicted and I was not.

GREGERS: Yes, I know there were no proofs.

WERLE: Acquittal is acquittal. Why do you want to bring back that miserable old business that gave me gray hairs before my time? Is that what has been on your mind all these years up there? I can assure you, Gregers, here in town that whole story has been forgotten long ago, as far as I am concerned.

GREGERS: But what about that unfortunate family?

WERLE: Well, now, exactly what do you want me to do for those people? When Ekdal got out, he was a broken man, beyond help altogether. Some people go to the bottom as soon as they've got some buckshot in them and never come up again. Believe me, Gregers, I've done all I possibly could do, if I didn't want to put myself in a false light and give people occasion for all sorts of talk and suspicion —

GREGERS: Suspicion? I see.

WERLE: I have given Ekdal copying work to do for the office, and I pay him far, far more than he is worth.

GREGERS (*without looking at him*): H'm. I don't doubt that.

WERLE: You are laughing? Don't you think I am telling you the truth?

Oh, to be sure, you won't find it in my books. I never enter expenses like that.

GREGERS (*with a cold smile*): No, I suppose there are certain expenses that are better not entered.

WERLE (*puzzled*): What do you mean?

GREGERS (*being brave*): Have you entered what it cost you to let Hjalmar Ekdal learn photography?

WERLE: I? What do you mean — entered?

GREGERS: I know now it was you who paid for it. And I also know it was you who set him up in business — quite comfortably, too.

WERLE: All right! And you still say I have done nothing for the Ekdals! I assure you, Gregers, those people have cost me a pretty penny!

GREGERS: Have you entered those expenses?

WERLE: Why do you ask?

GREGERS: I have my reasons. Listen — at the time you were providing so kindly for your old friend's son, wasn't that just when he was getting married?

WERLE: Damn it, Gregers! How can I remember — ! After so many years — !

GREGERS: You wrote me a letter at the time. A business letter, of course. And in a postscript you mentioned very briefly that Hjalmar Ekdal had married one Miss Hansen.

WERLE: That's right. That was her name.

GREGERS: But you did not say anything about Miss Hansen being Gina Hansen, our ex-housekeeper.

WERLE (*with scornful but forced laughter*): No, to tell the truth, it didn't occur to me that you were particularly interested in our ex-housekeeper.

GREGERS: I wasn't. But — (*Lowers his voice.*) somebody else in this house was.

WERLE: What do you mean? (*Flaring up.*) Don't tell me you're referring to me!

GREGERS (*in a low but firm voice*): Yes, I am referring to you.

WERLE: And you dare — ! You have the audacity — ! How can that ingrate, that — that photographer fellow — how dare he make accusations like that!

GREGERS: Hjalmar hasn't said a word. I don't think he has the faintest suspicion of anything like this.

WERLE: Then where do you get it from? Who could have said a thing like that?

GREGERS: My poor, unfortunate mother. The last time I saw her.

WERLE: Your mother! I might have thought so! You and she — you always stood together. It was she who first turned you against me.

GREGERS: No, it was all she had to go through, till things became too much for her and she died in sheer misery.

WERLE: Oh, nonsense! She didn't have to go through anything! No more than what others have had to, anyway. There's just no way of getting on with morbid, hysterical people — that's something *I* have had to learn! And here you are, with a suspicion like that — dabbling in old rumors and gossip against your own father. Listen here, Gregers. It really seems to me that at your age you might find something more useful to do.

GREGERS: Yes, it is about time.

WERLE: Then maybe your mind would be more at ease than it seems to be now. What is the point of working away, year in and year out, as just an ordinary clerk up there at Høydal, with not so much as a penny beyond regular wages? It's plain silly!

GREGERS: I wish I could believe that.

WERLE: Not that I don't understand, mind you. You want to be independent, don't want to be obliged to me for anything. But right now there is a chance for you to become independent, to be on your own in everything.

GREGERS: Oh? How so?

WERLE: When I wrote you that I needed you here in town right away — h'm —

GREGERS: Yes, what is it you want of me? I've been waiting to hear all day.

WERLE: I am offering you a partnership in the firm.

GREGERS: I! In your firm? As a partner?

WERLE: Yes. That doesn't mean we have to be together all the time. You could take over the business here in town and I could go up to Høydal.

GREGERS: You would want to do that?

WERLE: Well, you see, Gregers. I can't work as well as I used to. I'll have to save my eyes. They are getting weaker.

GREGERS: You have always had weak eyes.

WERLE: Not as bad as now. Besides — there are other things, too, that may make it advisable for me to live up there — for a while, anyway.

GREGERS: Nothing like this has ever even occurred to me.

WERLE: Look here, Gregers. I know there are many things that stand between us. But after all, we are father and son. It seems to me we ought to be able to come to some sort of understanding.

GREGERS: For appearance's sake, I suppose you mean.

WERLE: Well, that would be something, anyway. Think it over, Gregers. Wouldn't that be possible? What do you say?

GREGERS (*looks at him coldly*): There is something behind this.

WERLE: I don't understand.

GREGERS: You want to use me for something.

WERLE: In a relationship as close as ours I suppose one person can always be of use to the other.

GREGERS: Yes. So they say.

WERLE: I want to have you at home with me for a while. I am a lonely man, Gregers. I have always been lonely, but mostly now, when I am getting older. I need somebody around me.

GREGERS: You have Mrs. Sørby.

WERLE: So I do, and she has become almost indispensable to me. She is bright, she has an even temper, she brings life into the house — and I badly need that.

GREGERS: Well, then, everything is just as you want it.

WERLE: Yes, but I am afraid it won't last. A woman in her circumstances can easily have her position misconstrued in the eyes of the world. I'll almost go so far as to say it does a man no good either.

GREGERS: Oh, I don't know. When a man gives the kind of dinner parties you do he can take quite a few liberties.

WERLE: Yes, but what about *her*, Gregers? I am afraid she will not put up with it much longer. And even if she did, even if she ignored what people are saying and all that sort of thing, out of devotion to me — Do you really think, Gregers, you with your strong sense of justice, do you feel it would be —

GREGERS (*interrupting*): Just tell me this: are you going to marry her?

WERLE: What if I did? What then?

GREGERS: That's what I am asking. What then?

WERLE: Would it displease you very much?

GREGERS: No, not at all.

WERLE: Well, you see, I didn't know — I thought perhaps out of regard for your mother —

GREGERS: I am not given to melodramatics.

WERLE: Well, whether you are or not, you have lifted a stone from my heart. I can't tell you how pleased I am that I can count on your support in this matter.

GREGERS (*looks intently at him*): Now I see what you want to use me for.

WERLE: Use you for? What an expression!

GREGERS: Let's not be particular in our choice of words — not as long as we're by ourselves, at any rate. (*Laughs.*) So that's it. That's why I had to come to town at all costs. Because of Mrs. Sørby, there are arrangements being made for family life in this house. Touching scene between father and son! That would indeed be something new!

WERLE: I won't have you use that tone!

GREGERS: When were we ever a family here? Never in my memory. But now, of course, there is need for a display of domestic affection. It will look very well to have the son hastening home on wings of filial feeling to attend the aging father's marriage feast. What happens then to all the talk of what the poor, deceased mother had to suffer? It evaporates. Her son takes care of that.

WERLE: Gregers, I don't believe there is anyone you detest as much as me.

GREGERS (*in a low voice*): I have seen too much of you.

WERLE: You've seen me with your mother's eyes. (*Lowers his voice a little.*) But don't forget that those eyes were — clouded at times.

GREGERS (*his voice trembles*): I know what you have in mind. But who's to blame for mother's tragic weakness? You and all those — ! The last one was that female you palmed off on Hjalmar Ekdal, when you yourself no longer — !

WERLE (*shrugs his shoulders*): Word for word as if I were hearing your mother.

GREGERS (*paying no attention*): — and there he is now, with his great, trusting child's soul in the middle of all this deceit — sharing his roof with a woman like that, unaware that what he calls his home is based on a lie! (*Steps closer to* WERLE.) When I look back upon all you have done, I seem to see a battlefield strewn with mangled human destinies.

WERLE: I almost think the gap between us is too wide.

GREGERS (*with a formal bow*): So I have observed. That is why I take my hat and leave.

WERLE: You're leaving? The house?

GREGERS: Yes. For now at last I see a mission to live for.

WERLE: What mission is that?

GREGERS: You'd only laugh if I told you.

WERLE: A lonely man doesn't laugh so easily, Gregers.

GREGERS (*pointing to the rear*): Look, father. The chamberlains are playing blindman's buff with Mrs. Sørby. — Goodnight and goodbye.

(*He goes out rear right. The sound of people talking, laughing, and playing games can be heard from the drawing room, where the guests are now coming into view.*)

WERLE (*mutters scornfully*): Hah — ! The fool! And he says he is not melodramatic!

ACT II

(HJALMAR EKDAL's *studio, a large attic room. To the right, a slant-
ing roof with skylights, half covered by blue cloth. The entrance
door from the hallway is in the far right corner; the door to the
living room farther forward on the same wall. There are two doors
to the left, as well, with an iron stove between them. In the rear,
wide, sliding, double doors. The studio is unpretentious but cozy.
Between the two doors on the right and a little out from the wall
is a sofa with a table and some chairs in front of it. On the table is
a lighted lamp with a shade. Near the wall by the stove is an old
armchair. Various pieces of photographic equipment here and
there in the room. In the rear, to the left of the sliding doors, a
shelf with a few books, bottles with chemical solutions, tools, and
some other objects. Photographs, brushes, paper, etc., are lying on
the table.*

GINA EKDAL *sits by the table, sewing.* HEDVIG *sits on the sofa, reading, her hands shading her eyes, her thumbs in her ears.*)

GINA (*glances at* HEDVIG *a few times, as if secretly anxious*): Hedvig!
HEDVIG (*does not hear.*)
GINA (*louder*): Hedvig!
HEDVIG (*takes away her hands and looks up*): Yes, mother?
GINA: Hedvig, be a good girl. Don't read any more tonight.
HEDVIG: Please, mother, just a little bit longer? Can't I?
GINA: No. I want you to put that book away. Your father doesn't like
you to read so much. He never reads at night.
HEDVIG (*closing her book*): Well, father doesn't care much for reading,
anyway.
GINA (*puts her sewing aside and picks up a pencil and a small notebook
from the table*): Do you remember how much we spent for the
butter today?
HEDVIG: One crown and sixty-five øre.
GINA: That's right. (*Writes it down.*) We're using an awful lot of
butter in this family. Then there was the sausage and the cheese —
let me see — (*writing*) — and the ham — (*mumbles figures while
adding up*). Goodness! it does add up —
HEDVIG: And the beer.
GINA: Right. (*Writes.*) It gets terrible expensive, but it can't be helped.
HEDVIG: And you and I didn't need anything hot for supper since
father was out.

GINA: No, that's right. That helps some. And I did get eight crowns and fifty øre for the pictures.

HEDVIG: Was it that much?

GINA: Eight-fifty, exactly.

(*Silence.* GINA *picks up her sewing.* HEDVIG *takes paper and pencil and starts drawing, her left hand shading her eyes.*)

HEDVIG: Isn't it nice to think that father is at that big dinner party at Mr. Werle's?

GINA: Can't rightly say he's *his* guest. It was the son who invited him. (*After a pause.*) We have nothing to do with the old man.

HEDVIG: I can't wait till father comes home. He promised to ask Mrs. Sørby if he could take home something good for me.

GINA: Why yes, you can be sure there are plenty of good things in *that* house.

HEDVIG (*still drawing*): Besides, I think I am a little bit hungry, too.

(OLD EKDAL *enters right rear, the brown paper parcel under his arm, another parcel in his coat pocket.*)

GINA: So late you are today, Grandpa.

EKDAL: They'd locked the office. Had to wait for Gråberg. And then I had to go through — h'm —

HEDVIG: Did they give you any more copying to do, Grandpa?

EKDAL: This whole parcel. Look.

GINA: That's nice.

HEDVIG: And you've got another one in your pocket.

EKDAL: What? Oh never mind. That's nothing. (*Puts his walking stick away in the corner.*) This will keep me busy a long time, Gina. (*Slides one of the double doors half open.*) Shhh! (*Peeks into the attic for a while, then he cautiously slides the door shut. Chuckling.*) They're sound asleep the whole lot of 'em. And she herself's in the basket.

HEDVIG: Are you sure she won't be cold in that basket, Grandpa?

EKDAL: Cold? With all that straw? Don't you worry about *that.* (*Goes towards the door left rear.*) There are matches, aren't there?

GINA: On the dresser.

(EKDAL *goes into his room.*)

HEDVIG: It's nice that he got all that new work to do.

GINA: Yes, poor old thing. It will give him a little spending money.

HEDVIG: And he won't be able to stay down at that awful Madam Eriksen's all morning.

GINA: No; there's that, too.

HEDVIG: Do you think they're still at the table?

GINA: Lord knows. Could be.

HEDVIG: Just think of all that delicious food. I'm sure he'll be in a good mood when he comes home. Don't you think so, mother?

GINA: Yes, but what if we could tell him we'd rented the room. Wouldn't that be nice?

HEDVIG: But we don't need that tonight.

GINA: Oh yes we do. We could always use the money. The room is no good to us as it is.

HEDVIG: No, I mean that father will be in a good mood tonight, anyway. It's better to have the room for some other time.

GINA (*looking at her*): You like it when you have something nice to tell father when he comes home nights, don't you?

HEDVIG: It makes things more pleasant.

GINA (*reflectively*): Yes, I guess you're right about that.

(OLD EKDAL *enters from his room, heads for the kitchen door, left front.*)

GINA (*turning half around in her chair*): Do you need anything in the kitchen, Grandpa?

EKDAL: Yes. But don't you get up. (*Goes out.*)

GINA: I hope he isn't fooling around with the fire out there. (*After a while.*) Hedvig, go out and see what he's doing.

(OLD EKDAL *enters with a pitcher of hot water.*)

HEDVIG: Getting hot water, Grandpa?

EKDAL: That's right. Got some writing to do, but the ink's as thick as gruel. H'm —

GINA: But hadn't you better have supper first? It's all ready for you in your room.

EKDAL: Never mind supper, Gina. I tell you I'm busy. I don't want anybody coming in to me. Not anybody. H'm.

(*He goes into his room.* GINA *and* HEDVIG *look at each other.*)

GINA (*in a low voice*): I can't think where he got the money from. Can you?

HEDVIG: From Gråberg, maybe.

GINA: No, it wouldn't be that. Gråberg always gives me the money.

HEDVIG: Maybe he got a bottle on credit.

GINA: Him! Who'd give him credit?

(HJALMAR EKDAL, *in overcoat and gray hat, enters right.*)

GINA (*throws down her sewing, gets up*): Heavens, Ekdal! Home already?

HEDVIG (*getting up at the same time*): Father? So soon!

HJALMAR (*lays down his hat*): Most of them seemed to be leaving now.

HEDVIG: Already?

HJALMAR: Well, it was a dinner party, you know. (*Takes his coat off.*)

GINA: Let me help you.

HEDVIG: Me too. (*They help him off with his coat.* GINA *hangs it up in the rear.*) Were there many there, father?

HJALMAR: Not too many. About twelve or fourteen at the table.

GINA: Did you get to talk to all of them?

HJALMAR: Oh yes, a little. Though Gregers kept me engaged most of the evening.

GINA: Is he as ugly as he used to be?

HJALMAR: Well — I suppose nobody would call him handsome. Is father back?

HEDVIG: Yes, he is in there writing.

HJALMAR: Did he say anything?

GINA: No. About what?

HJALMAR: He didn't mention — ? I thought I heard he'd been with Gråberg. I think I'll go in to him for a moment.

GINA: No, you'd better not.

HJALMAR: Why not? Did he say he didn't want to see me?

GINA: He doesn't want to see anybody.

HEDVIG (*making signs to her*): Ahem!

GINA (*doesn't notice*): He's gotten himself some hot water.

HJALMAR: Ah! So he is —

GINA: Looks that way.

HJALMAR: Ah yes — my poor old white-haired father. Let him enjoy his little pleasures as best he can.

(OLD EKDAL, *a lighted pipe in his mouth, enters in an old smoking jacket.*)

EKDAL: Home again? Thought it was you I heard talking.

HJALMAR: Yes. I just came back.

EKDAL: Guess you didn't see me, did you?

HJALMAR: No, but they told me you'd gone through, so I thought I'd catch up with you.

EKDAL: H'm. That's good of you, Hjalmar. Who were they — all those people?

HJALMAR: Oh — all sorts. Chamberlain Flor and Chamberlain Balle and Chamberlain Kaspersen and chamberlain this and that. I don't know —

EKDAL (*nodding his head*): Hear that, Gina? He's been with nothing but chamberlains all evening.

GINA: Yes, I hear as they've become quite fancy in that house now.

HEDVIG: Did the chamberlains sing, father? Or recite poetry?

HJALMAR: No. They just talked nonsense. They wanted *me* to recite, though, but I didn't want to.

EKDAL: They couldn't get you to, eh?

GINA: Seems to me you might have done that.

HJALMAR: No. I don't see any reason why one has to oblige every Tom, Dick, and Harry all the time. (*Walks up and down.*) At any rate, I won't.

EKDAL: No point in being too obliging, you know. That's Hjalmar for you.

HJALMAR: I don't see why *I* always have to be the one who provides entertainment on the rare occasions when I am out for dinner. Let the others exert themselves for a change. Those fellows go from one big meal to the next, stuffing themselves day in and day out. Let *them* do something for all the food they are getting!

GINA: You didn't tell them that though, did you?

HJALMAR (*humming a little*): Well, I don't know about that. They were told a thing or two.

EKDAL: The chamberlains?

HJALMAR: Mmm — (*Casually.*) Then we had a little controversy over Tokay wine.

EKDAL: Tokay, no less! Say, that's a fine wine!

HJALMAR (*stops his walking*): It *may* be a fine wine. But let me tell you: not all the vintages are equally fine. It depends on how much sunshine the grapes get.

GINA: If you don't know everything — !

EKDAL: And they quarreled with that?

HJALMAR: They tried to, but then it was pointed out to them that it was the same way with chamberlains. Not all vintages are equally fine among chamberlains, either — so they were told.

GINA: Goodness! What you don't think of!

EKDAL: Heh-heh! So they got that to put in their pipe.

HJALMAR: Right to their face. That's how they got it.

EKDAL: Gina, d'ye hear that? He gave it to them right to their face!

GINA: Right to their face! Imagine!

HJALMAR: Yes, but I don't want you to talk about it. One doesn't talk about such things. Of course, the whole thing was done in the friendliest possible way. They are all of them pleasant, easy-going people. Why should I hurt them? No!

EKDAL: Right to their face, though —

HEDVIG (*ingratiatingly*): It's so nice to see you all dressed up, father. You look very well in tails.

HJALMAR: Yes, don't you think so? And it really fits me perfectly. As if it were tailor-made. Possibly a trifle tight in the armpits, that's all. Help me, Hedvig. (*Takes his dinner jacket off.*) I'd rather wear my own coat. Where is it, Gina?

GINA: Here it is. (*Helps him on with it.*)

HJALMAR: There now! Be sure to have Molvik get his suit back first thing in the morning.

GINA (*putting the clothes away*): I'll take care of it.

HJALMAR (*stretching*): Aaahh. This feels cozier after all. And this kind of loose-fitting, casual wear is really more in keeping with my whole appearance; don't you think so, Hedvig?

HEDVIG: Oh yes, father!

HJALMAR: Especially when I tie my neckcloth with loose, flying ends — like this? What do you think?

HEDVIG: Yes, it goes extremely well with your mustache. And with your curls, too.

HJALMAR: I'd hardly call my hair curly. Wavy, rather.

HEDVIG: Yes, for the curls are so large.

HJALMAR: Waves, really.

HEDVIG (*after a moment, pulling his sleeve*): Father?

HJALMAR: What is it?

HEDVIG: Oh, you know very well what it is!

HJALMAR: I certainly don't.

HEDVIG (*laughing and pleading*): Oh come on, father! Don't tease me!

HJALMAR: But what is it?

HEDVIG (*shaking him*): Father! Give it to me! You know, you promised me. Something good to eat.

HJALMAR: Oh, dear! I completely forgot!

HEDVIG: You are only teasing, father. Shame on you! Where is it?

HJALMAR: No, honest, I really did forget. But wait a moment. I have something else for you, Hedvig. (*Goes and searches his coat pockets.*)

HEDVIG (*jumps up and down, clapping her hands*): Oh mother, mother!

GINA: See what I mean? If you just give him time —

HJALMAR (*with a piece of paper*): Here it is.

HEDVIG: That? But that's just a piece of paper.

HJALMAR: It's the menu, Hedvig, the entire menu. Look here. It says "Menu." That means what you get to eat.

HEDVIG: Haven't you anything else for me?

HJALMAR: I tell you, I forgot all about it. But take my word for it: it's not such a great treat, all that rich food. You just sit down and read the menu, now, and I'll tell you later what the things taste like. Here you are, Hedvig.

HEDVIG (*swallowing her tears*): Thank you.

(*She sits down but doesn't read.* GINA *signals to her.* HJALMAR *notices.*)

HJALMAR (*pacing the floor*): It is really unbelievable all the things a father is supposed to keep in mind. And if he forgets the smallest item — ! Long faces right away. Oh well. One gets used to that, too. (*Stops by the stove where* OLD EKDAL *is sitting.*) Have you looked at them tonight, father?

EKDAL: I certainly have! She's in the basket!

HJALMAR: No! Really? In the basket? She is getting used to it then, I guess.

EKDAL: Didn't I tell you she would? But look, Hjalmar, there are still a few things —

HJALMAR: — improvements, yes, I know.

EKDAL: They've got to be done.

HJALMAR: Right. Let's talk about it now, father. Come over here to the sofa.

EKDAL: All right. H'm. Guess I want to fill my pipe first, though. Need to clean it, too — h'm — (*Goes into his room.*)

GINA (*with a smile, to* HJALMAR): Cleaning his pipe —

HJALMAR: Oh well, Gina — let him. The poor shipwrecked old man. — About those improvements — We'd better get to them tomorrow.

GINA: You won't have time tomorrow, Ekdal.

HEDVIG (*interrupting*): Oh, yes, mother.

GINA: For remember those prints you were going to retouch? They came for 'em again today.

HJALMAR: I see. It's those prints again, is it? Well, they'll get done. You can be sure of that. Perhaps there are some new orders come in, too?

GINA: Not a thing, worse luck. Tomorrow I've got only those two portraits I told you about.

HJALMAR: Is that all? Well, if one doesn't exert oneself, what can you expect?

GINA: But what can I do? I advertise in the papers all I can, seems to me.

HJALMAR: The papers, the papers — you see yourself how far that gets us. I suppose there hasn't been anyone to look at the room, either?

GINA: No, not yet.

HJALMAR: Just as I thought. Well, no — if one doesn't *do* anything — One has to make a real effort, Gina!

HEDVIG (*going to him*): Shall I get your flute, father?

HJALMAR: No, not the flute. *I* need no pleasures. (*Paces up and down.*) You'll see if I don't work tomorrow! You don't need to worry about *that!* You can be sure I shall work as long as my strength holds out —

GINA: But Ekdal, dear — I didn't mean it that way.

HEDVIG: How about a bottle of beer, father?

HJALMAR: Not at all. I don't need anything — (*Stops.*) Beer? Did you say beer?

HEDVIG (*brightly*): Yes, father; lovely, cool beer.

HJALMAR: Oh well — all right — since you insist, I suppose you may bring me a bottle.

GINA: Yes, do that. That'll be nice and cozy.

(HEDVIG *runs towards the kitchen door.*)

HJALMAR (*by the stove, stops her, looks at her, takes her by the head and presses her to him*): Hedvig! Hedvig!

HEDVIG (*happy, in tears*): Oh father! You are so sweet and good!

HJALMAR: No, no, don't say that. There I was — seated at the rich man's table — gorging myself on his ample fare — and I couldn't even remember · —

GINA (*seated by the table*): Nonsense, Ekdal.

HJALMAR: It is not nonsense. But you must not reckon too strictly. You know I love you, regardless.

HEDVIG (*throwing her arms around him*): And we love you, father, so much, so much!

HJALMAR: And if I am unreasonable at times, remember — God forgive me — remember I am a man beset by a host of sorrows. Well, well! (*Drying his eyes.*) No beer at such a moment. Give me my flute.

(HEDVIG *runs to the shelf and fetches it.*)

HJALMAR: Thank you. There now. With my flute in my hand and you two around me — ah!

(HEDVIG *sits down by the table next to* GINA. HJALMAR *walks back and forth, playing a Bohemian folk dance. He plays loudly but in slow tempo and with pronounced sentiment.*)

HJALMAR (*interrupts his playing, gives his left hand to* GINA, *and says with strong emotion*): Our home may be mean and humble, Gina. But it is our home. And I say to you both: here dwells contentment!

(*He resumes his playing. Presently there is a knock on the door.*)

GINA (*getting up*): Shh, Ekdal. I think somebody's coming.

HJALMAR (*putting the flute back on the shelf*): Yes, yes of course. Somebody would —

(GINA *goes to open the door.*)

GREGERS WERLE (*out in the hall*): I beg your pardon —

GINA (*taking a step back*): Oh!

GREGERS: — isn't this where Mr. Ekdal lives, the photographer?

GINA: Yes, it is.

HJALMAR (*going to the door*): Gregers! So you did come, after all. Come in.

GREGERS (*entering*): I told you I wanted to see you.

HJALMAR: But tonight — ? Have you left the party?

GREGERS: Both party and home. Good evening, Mrs. Ekdal. I don't know if you recognize me.

GINA: Oh yes. Young Mr. Werle isn't hard to recognize.

GREGERS: No, for I look like my mother, and you remember her, I am sure.

HJALMAR: You have left your home?

GREGERS: Yes. I have taken a room at a hotel.

HJALMAR: Really? — Well, since you're here, take off your coat and sit down.

GREGERS: Thanks. (*Removes his overcoat. He has changed clothes and is now dressed in a plain, gray suit, of somewhat unfashionable cut.*)

HJALMAR: Here on the sofa. Make yourself comfortable.

(GREGERS *sits down on the sofa,* HJALMAR *on a chair by the table.*)

GREGERS (*looking around*): So this is your residence, Hjalmar. This is where you live.

HJALMAR: This is the studio, as you can see.

GINA: It's roomier in here, so this is where we mostly keep ourselves.

HJALMAR: The apartment we had before was really nicer than this, but there is one big advantage here: we have plenty of space.

GINA: And we have a room across the hallway that we're renting out.

GREGERS (*to* HJALMAR): You have lodgers, too?

HJALMAR: No, not yet. These things take time, you see. One has to be on the lookout. (*To* HEDVIG.) What about that beer?

(HEDVIG *nods her head and goes out into the kitchen.*)

GREGERS: So that's your daughter.

HJALMAR: Yes, that's Hedvig.

GREGERS: Your only child, isn't she?

HJALMAR: Our only one. Our greatest joy in the world, and (*lowers his voice*) our greatest sorrow, as well.

GREGERS: What are you saying!

HJALMAR: Yes, Gregers, for there is every probability that she'll lose her sight.

GREGERS: Becoming blind!

HJALMAR: Yes. So far, there are only early symptoms, and things may be well with her for some time yet. But the doctor has warned us. It is coming, irresistibly.

GREGERS: But this is nothing less than a tragedy! How do you account for it?

HJALMAR (*with a sigh*): Heredity, most likely.

GREGERS (*struck*): Heredity?

GINA: Ekdal's mother had weak eyes.

HJALMAR: That's what father says. I of course don't remember her.

GREGERS: Poor child. How does she take it?

HJALMAR: Oh, we can't bring ourselves to tell her — I'm sure you can understand that. She suspects nothing. Joyous and carefree, chirping like a little bird, she'll flutter into life's endless night. (*Overcome by emotion.*) Oh Gregers, this is such a terrible burden for me.

(HEDVIG *enters with a tray with beer and glasses. She puts it down on the table.*)

HJALMAR (*stroking her hair*): Thanks. Thank you, Hedvig.

HEDVIG (*puts her arms around his neck and whispers something in his ear.*)

HJALMAR: No. No sandwiches now. (*Looks off.*) That is — unless Gregers wants some?

GREGERS (*with a gesture of refusal*): No. No thanks.

HJALMAR (*still in a melancholic mood*): Oh well, you might as well bring in some, all the same. A crust, if you have one. And plenty of butter, please.

GREGERS (*who has followed her with his eyes*): Otherwise she seems healthy enough.

HJALMAR: Yes, thank God, there is nothing else wrong with her.

GREGERS: I think she is going to look like you, Mrs. Ekdal. How old is she?

GINA: Hedvig is just about fourteen. Her birthday is day after tomorrow.

GREGERS: Quite big for her age, isn't she?

GINA: Yes, she has grown a lot lately.

GREGERS: It's by the children we tell we're growing older ourselves. How long have you two been married now?

GINA: We've been married for — let's see — fifteen years, pretty near.

GREGERS: Just imagine! Has it really been that long?

GINA (*taking notice, looks at him*): It certainly has.

HJALMAR: That's right. Fifteen years, less a few months. (*Changing topic.*) Those must have been long years for you up there at the works, Gregers.

GREGERS: They were long while they lasted. Now afterwards I hardly know where they went.

(OLD EKDAL *enters from his room, without his pipe, but with his old-fashioned lieutenant's cap on his head. His walk is a trifle unsteady.*)

EKDAL: I'm ready for you now, Hjalmar. Let's talk about this — h'm — What was it again?

HJALMAR (*going towards him*): Father, there's someone here. Gregers Werle. I don't know if you remember him?

EKDAL (*looks at* GREGERS, *who has stood up*): Werle? That's the son, isn't it? What does he want from me?

HJALMAR: Nothing. He has come to see me.

EKDAL: Then there's nothing wrong?

HJALMAR: Of course not.

EKDAL (*swinging one arm back and forth*): Not that I am scared, mind you, but —

GREGERS (*goes up to him*): I just wanted to bring you greetings from your old hunting grounds, Lieutenant Ekdal.

EKDAL: Hunting grounds?

GREGERS: Yes, the woods up around the Høydal works.

EKDAL: Oh yes, up there. Yes, I used to know that country quite well in the old days.

GREGERS: You were quite a hunter then, weren't you?

EKDAL: Could be. Maybe I was. You're looking at my get-up. I don't ask anybody's permission to wear it in the house. Just as long as I don't go outside —

(HEDVIG *brings a plate with open-faced sandwiches, which she puts down on the table.*)

HJALMAR: You sit down, father, and have a glass of beer. Help yourself, Gregers.

(EKDAL *mutters something and shuffles over to the sofa.* GREGERS *sits down on a chair next to him;* HJALMAR *is on the other side of* GREGERS. GINA *sits some distance from the table, sewing.* HEDVIG *is standing by her father.*)

GREGERS: Do you remember, Lieutenant Ekdal, when Hjalmar and I used to come up and visit you summers and Christmas?

EKDAL: You did? No; can't say as I do. But it's true I used to be a good hunter, if I do say so myself. I've killed bears, too. Nine of 'em.

GREGERS (*looks at him with compassion*): And now your hunting days are over.

EKDAL: Oh — I wouldn't say that. I still go hunting once in a while. Well, yes, not in the old way, of course. For you see, the woods — the woods — the woods —! (*Drinks.*) Nice-looking woods up there now?

GREGERS: Not as in your time. They have cut a great deal.

EKDAL: Cut? (*In a lower voice and as if afraid.*) That's risky business, that is. It has consequences. The woods are vengeful.

HJALMAR (*filling his glass*): Here, father. Have some more.

GREGERS: How can a man like you — such an outdoors man as you used to be — how can you stand living here in the middle of a musty city, within four walls?

EKDAL (*chuckles, glancing at* HJALMAR): Oh, it's not so bad here. Not bad at all.

GREGERS: But surely — all the things your soul grew used to up there — ? The cool, invigorating breezes? The free life in woods and mountains, among beasts and birds — ?

EKDAL (*smiling*): Hjalmar, shall we show it to him?

HJALMAR (*quickly, a little embarrassed*): Oh no, father. Not tonight.

GREGERS: What is it he wants to show me?

HJALMAR: Oh, it's just — something. You can see it some other time.

GREGERS (*continues addressing* OLD EKDAL): You see, this is what I had in mind, Lieutenant. Why don't you come up to Høydal with me? I'll probably be going back shortly. I'm sure you could get some copying work to do up there as well. For down here you can't have a thing to cheer you up and keep you occupied.

EKDAL (*looks at him in astonishment*): Don't *I* have — !

GREGERS: Yes, of course, you have Hjalmar. But then he has his own family. And a man like you, who have always loved the outdoors —

EKDAL (*striking the table*): Hjalmar, he *shall* see it!

HJALMAR: But father, do you really think so? It's dark and —

EKDAL: Nonsense. There's a moon. (*Getting up.*) I say he's got to see it. Let me out. Come and help me, Hjalmar!

HEDVIG: Oh yes, father! Do!

HJALMAR (*getting up*): Oh well, all right.

GREGERS (*to* GINA): What is it?

GINA: Oh, don't expect anything much.

(EKDAL *and* HJALMAR *have gone to the rear of the room. Each of them slides one of the double doors back.* HEDVIG *is helping the old man.* GREGERS *remains standing by the sofa.* GINA *keeps on sewing, paying no attention. Through the opened doors can be seen a big, elongated, irregular-shaped attic, with nooks and corners and a couple of chimneys standing free from the wall. Moonlight falls through several skylights, illuminating some parts of the room, while others are in deep shadow.*)

EKDAL (*to* GREGERS): You are welcome to come closer, sir.

GREGERS (*goes up to them*): What is this really?

EKDAL: See for yourself. H'm.

HJALMAR (*somewhat embarrassed*): This is all father's, you understand.

GREGERS (*at the door, peering into the attic*): Do you keep chickens, Lieutenant?

EKDAL: Should say we do. They're roosting now. But you ought to see those chickens in daylight!

HEDVIG: And there is —

EKDAL: Hush, don't say anything yet.

GREGERS: And I see you've got pigeons, too.

EKDAL: Could be we have. We've got pigeons, all right! The roosts are up on the rafters, for pigeons like to be up high, you know.

HJALMAR: They aren't all of them just ordinary pigeons.

EKDAL: Ordinary! I should say not! We've got tumblers and even a couple of pouters. But come over here. Do you see that pen over by the wall?

GREGERS: Yes. What do you use that for?

EKDAL: That's where the rabbits are at night.

GREGERS: Oh? You have rabbits, too, do you?

EKDAL: Damn right we have rabbits! He asks if we have rabbits, Hjalmar! H'm. But now we're coming to the *real* thing. Here we are. Move, Hedvig. You stand here and look down — there; that's right. Now, do you see a basket with straw in it?

GREGERS: Yes, I do. And I see a bird.

EKDAL: H'm — A "bird."

GREGERS: Isn't it a duck?

EKDAL (*offended*): I'd say it's a duck!

HJALMAR: But what kind of duck, do you think?

HEDVIG: It's not just an ordinary duck.

EKDAL: Hush!

GREGERS: And it's not a muscovy duck, either.

EKDAL: No, Mr. — Werle; it's not a muscovy, for it's a wild duck!

GREGERS: Is it really? A wild duck?

EKDAL: That's what it is. The — "bird," as you called it. A wild duck. It's our wild duck.

HEDVIG: *My* wild duck. For it belongs to me.

GREGERS: And it lives here in the attic? It's thriving?

EKDAL: What's so odd about that? She's got a big pail of water to splash around in.

HJALMAR: Fresh water every other day.

GINA (*turning to* HJALMAR): Ekdal, please. I'm freezing.

EKDAL: H'm. All right; let's close up. Just as well not to disturb their night's rest, anyway. Help me Hedvig.

(HJALMAR *and* HEDVIG *slide the double doors shut.*)

EKDAL: You can have a good look at her some other time. (*Sits down in the armchair by the stove.*) I'm telling you, they are strange birds, those wild ducks.

GREGERS: But how did you ever catch it, Lieutenant?

EKDAL: I didn't. There's a certain man in this town we can thank for her.

GREGERS (*struck by a thought*): Would that man be my father?

EKDAL: Indeed it is. It's your father, sure enough. H'm.

HJALMAR: Funny you'd guess that, Gregers.

GREGERS: You told me before that you owed a great deal to my father, so I thought that perhaps —

GINA: But we didn't get the duck from Werle himself.

EKDAL: It's Håkon Werle we have to thank for her all the same, Gina. (*To* GREGERS.) He was out in a boat, see, and took a shot at her. But he doesn't see so well, your father doesn't. H'm. Anyway, she was only wounded.

GREGERS: I see. She got some buckshot in her.

HJALMAR: Yes. A little.

HEDVIG: Right under the wing, so she couldn't fly.

GREGERS: Then she went to the bottom, I suppose.

EKDAL (*sleepily, his voice muffled*): So it did. Always do that, wild ducks. Dive straight to the bottom — far as they can, sir. Bite themselves fast in the grasses and roots and weeds and all the other damn stuff down there. And never come up again.

GREGERS: But, Lieutenant, *your* wild duck did.

EKDAL: He had such a wonderfully clever dog, your father. And that dog — it went down and got the duck up.

GREGERS (*to* HJALMAR): And so it came to you?

HJALMAR: Not right away. First your father took it home with him, but it didn't seem to get on too well there, and then he told Pettersen to get rid of it.

EKDAL (*half asleep*): H'm — Pettersen — Ass —

HJALMAR: That's how we got it, for father knows Pettersen a little, and when he heard about the wild duck, he asked Pettersen to give it to him.

GREGERS: And now it seems perfectly contented in there in the attic.

HJALMAR: Yes, you would hardly believe how well it gets on. It's becoming fat. I think perhaps it's been in there so long that it has forgotten what wild life is like. And that makes all the difference.

GREGERS: I am sure you are right, Hjalmar. The thing to do is never to let it look at sea and sky again. — But I don't think I should stay any longer. I believe your father is asleep.

HJALMAR: Oh, as far as that is concerned —

GREGERS: Oh yes, one thing more. You said you had a room for rent? A vacant room?

HJALMAR: We do. What of it? Do you know anyone who — ?

GREGERS: Could I get it?

HJALMAR: You?

GINA: Oh, Mr. Werle, I'm sure *you* don't want to —

GREGERS: Couldn't I have it? If I can, I'll move in first thing in the morning.

HJALMAR: Yes, indeed, with the greatest pleasure.

GINA: No, but Mr. Werle, that's not a room for you.

HJALMAR: Gina! How can you say that?

GINA: It's not large enough or light enough, and —

GREGERS: That doesn't matter, Mrs. Ekdal.

HJALMAR: I think it's quite a nice room myself, and decently furnished, too.

GINA: But remember those two downstairs.

GREGERS: Who are they?

GINA: There's one who used to be a private tutor.

HJALMAR: Molvik is his name. He studied to be a minister once.

GINA: And then there's a doctor, name of Relling.

GREGERS: Relling? I know him slightly. He used to practice up at Høydal.

GINA: They are a couple of real wild characters those two. Out all hours of the night, and when they come home they aren't always — y'know —

GREGERS: One gets used to that sort of thing. I hope I'll be like the wild duck.

GINA: H'm. Well, I think you ought to sleep on it first.

GREGERS: I take it you don't really want me in the house, Mrs. Ekdal.

GINA: Good Lord! How can you say a thing like that?

HJALMAR: Yes, Gina. It really does seem very odd of you. (*To* GREGERS.) Does this mean you'll be staying in town for a while?

GREGERS (*putting on his overcoat*): Yes, I think I'll stay.

HJALMAR: But not with your father? What do you intend to do?

GREGERS: If I knew that, Hjalmar, I'd be much better off. But when you're cursed with a name like "Gregers" — and then "Werle" after that — Did you ever hear of an uglier name?

HJALMAR: I don't think it's ugly at all.

GREGERS: Ugh! I feel like spitting in the face of anybody with a name like that. But since it's my cross in life to be Gregers Werle, such as I am —

HJALMAR: Ha-ha! If you weren't Gregers Werle, what would you like to be?

GREGERS: If I could choose, I'd like to be a really clever dog.

GINA: A dog!

HEDVIG (*involuntarily*): Oh no!

GREGERS: Yes, an exceptionally skillful dog — the kind that goes down to the bottom after wild ducks when they've dived down among the weeds and the grass down there in the mud.

HJALMAR: Honestly, Gregers. This makes no sense whatever.

GREGERS: I suppose it doesn't. But tomorrow morning, then, I'll be moving in. (*To* GINA.) You won't have any trouble with me; I'll do everything myself. (*To* HJALMAR.) The other things we can talk about tomorrow. — Goodnight, Mrs. Ekdal. (*Nods to* HEDVIG.) Goodnight!

GINA: Goodnight, Mr. Werle.

HEDVIG: Goodnight.

HJALMAR (*who has lighted a candle*): Wait a moment. I'll see you down. I'm sure it's all dark on the stairs.

(GREGERS *and* HJALMAR *go out through the entrance door, right rear.*)

GINA (*staring ahead, her sewing lowered in her lap*): Wasn't it funny all that talk about wanting to be a dog?

HEDVIG: Do you know, mother — I think he really meant something else.

GINA: What would that be?

HEDVIG: No, I couldn't say, but it was just like he had something else in mind all the time.

GINA: You think so? It sure was funny, though.

HJALMAR (*returning*): The lamp was still burning. (*Blows out the candle and sits down.*) Ah, at last it's possible to get a bite to eat. (*Starts on the sandwiches.*) Now do you see what I mean, Gina — about seizing the opportunity?

GINA: What opportunity?

HJALMAR: Well — it was lucky, wasn't it, that we got the room rented? And then to somebody like Gregers, a dear old friend.

GINA: Well, I don't know what to say to that.

HEDVIG: Oh mother, you'll see it will be fun.

HJALMAR: I must say you are strange. First you wanted nothing more than to get a lodger; then when we do, you don't like it.

GINA: I know, Ekdal. If only it had been somebody else. What do you think old Werle will say?

HJALMAR: He? It's none of his business.

GINA: But don't you see that something's bound to be wrong between the two of 'em, since the young one is moving out. Sure you know how those two are.

HJALMAR: That may be so, but —

GINA: And maybe Werle will think you are behind it!

HJALMAR: All right! Let him think that. Oh, by all means, Werle has done a great deal for me — I'm the first to admit it. But that doesn't mean I everlastingly have to let him run my life.

GINA: But Ekdal, dear, it could hurt Grandpa. Perhaps he'll lose what little he's making from working for Gråberg.

HJALMAR: I almost wish he would! Is it not humiliating for a man like me to see his gray-haired father treated like dirt? Ah, but soon now the time will be ripe. I feel it. (*Takes another sandwich.*) As sure as I have a mission in life, it shall be accomplished!

HEDVIG: Oh yes, father!

GINA: Shhh! Don't wake him up.

HJALMAR (*in a lower voice*): I say it again: I *will* accomplish it! The day will come, when — That's why it's such a good thing we got the room rented out, for that makes me more independent. And that's necessary for a man with a mission in life. (*Over by the armchair, with feeling.*) Poor old white-haired father. Trust your Hjalmar. He has broad enough shoulders — powerful shoulders, at any rate. Some day you'll wake up, and — (*to* GINA.) Or don't you believe that?

GINA (*getting up*): Sure I do, but let's first get him to bed.
HJALMAR: Yes, let us.

(*They tenderly lift the old man.*)

ACT III

(*The studio. It is morning. Daylight comes in through the sky-light, the blue cloth having been pulled aside.*

HJALMAR *sits at the table, retouching a photograph. Several other photographs are lying in front of him. After a while,* GINA, *in coat and hat, enters from outside. She is carrying a covered basket.*)

HJALMAR: Back already, Gina?
GINA: Yes. I'm in a hurry. (*Puts the basket down on a chair and takes off her coat and hat.*)
HJALMAR: Did you look in at Gregers's?
GINA: I did. It looks real nice in there. He fixed up the place real pretty, soon as he moved in.
HJALMAR: Oh?
GINA: Remember, he was to take care of everything himself? Well, he built a fire in the stove, but he hadn't opened the flue, so the whole room got filled with smoke. Phew! It smelled like —
HJALMAR: Oh dear —
GINA: Then do you know what he does? This really beats everything. He wanted to put out the fire, so he pours the water from the wash basin into the stove. The whole floor is sloppy with filth!
HJALMAR: I am sorry.
GINA: I've got the janitor's wife to clean up after him, pig as he is, but the room can't be lived in till this afternoon.
HJALMAR: Where is he now?
GINA: He said he was going out for a while.
HJALMAR: I went in there for a moment, too — right after you had left.
GINA: He told me. You've asked him for breakfast.
HJALMAR: Just a bit of a late morning meal. It's the first day and all. We can hardly do less. I am sure you have something.
GINA: I'll have to find something, at any rate.
HJALMAR: Be sure it's plenty, though. I think Relling and Molvik are coming, too. I ran into Relling on the stairs just now, and so of course I had to —

GINA: So we are to have those two as well.

HJALMAR: Good heavens, one or two more or less — can that make any difference?

EKDAL (*opens his door and looks in*): Listen, Hjalmar — (*Sees* GINA.) Well, never mind.

GINA: Do you want something, Grandpa?

EKDAL: No. It doesn't matter. H'm! (*Goes back inside his room.*)

GINA (*picking up her basket*): Make sure he doesn't go out.

HJALMAR: Yes, I will. — Say, Gina — how about some herring salad? I believe Relling and Molvik made a night of it again last night.

GINA: If only they don't get here too soon.

HJALMAR: I'm sure they won't. Just take your time.

GINA: Well, all right. Then you can work some in the meantime.

HJALMAR: I *am* working! I'm working as hard as I can!

GINA: All I mean is you'd have it out of the way for later. (*Goes into the kitchen.*)

(HJALMAR *picks up the photograph and the brush and works for a while — slowly and with evident distaste.*)

EKDAL (*peeks in, looks around, says in a low voice*): Pst! Are you busy?

HJALMAR: Yes. I am struggling with these everlasting pictures —

EKDAL: All right, all right. If you're busy, then you're busy. H'm! (*Goes back inside his room. The door remains open.*)

HJALMAR (*works in silence for a while, puts his brush down, walks over to* EKDAL's *door*): Are *you* busy, father?

EKDAL (*grumbling inside his room*): When *you* are busy, *I* am busy! H'm!

HJALMAR: Oh all right. (*Returns to his work.*)

EKDAL (*appears in his door again after a while*): H'm, Hjalmar, listen — I'm not so *terribly* busy, you know.

HJALMAR: I thought you were writing.

EKDAL: Dammit all! Can't that Gråberg wait a day or two? Didn't think it was a matter of life and death.

HJALMAR: Of course not. And you aren't a slave, after all.

EKDAL: And there is this other job in there —

HJALMAR: Just what I was thinking. Do you want to go in there now? Shall I open the door for you?

EKDAL: Good idea.

HJALMAR (*getting up*): Then we'd have that job out of the way.

EKDAL: Exactly. It has to be ready for tomorrow, anyway. It *is* tomorrow, isn't it?

HJALMAR: Sure it's tomorrow.

(*They slide the double doors open. The morning sun is shining through the skylight. Some pigeons are flying around; others are cooing on their perches. From farther inside the room the chickens are heard clucking once in a while.*)

HJALMAR: All right, father. Guess you can go ahead.

EKDAL (*entering the attic*): Aren't you coming?

HJALMAR: Yes, do you know — I almost think I will. (*Notices* GINA *in the kitchen door.*) I? No, I don't have the time. I have to work. But then there is this thing —

(*He pulls a cord. A curtain comes down from within the attic. Its lower part is made out of a strip of old sailcloth; its upper part is a piece of stretched-out fish net. The attic floor is now no longer visible.*)

HJALMAR (*returns to the table*): Now! Maybe I can have peace for a few minutes.

GINA: Is he fooling around in there again?

HJALMAR: Would you rather he went down to Madam Eriksen? (*Sitting down.*) Do you want anything? I thought you said —

GINA: I just wanted to ask you if you think we can set the table in here?

HJALMAR: Yes. There aren't any appointments this early, are there?

GINA: No — only those two sweethearts who want their picture taken.

HJALMAR: Damn! Couldn't they come some other time!

GINA: Goodness, Ekdal, they'll be here after dinner, when you're asleep.

HJALMAR: Oh, in that case it's all right. Yes, let's eat in here.

GINA: Fine. But there's no hurry with the table. You're welcome to use it some more.

HJALMAR: Can't you see I *am* using it?

GINA: Then you'll be all done for afterwards, you know. (*Goes into the kitchen.*)

(*Brief silence.*)

EKDAL (*in the door to the attic, inside the fish net*): Hjalmar!

HJALMAR: What?

EKDAL: Afraid we'll have to move the pail, after all.

HJALMAR: What else have I been saying all along?

EKDAL: H'm — h'm — h'm! (*Disappears inside again.*)

HJALMAR (*keeps on working for a moment, glances over towards the attic, half rises, as* HEDVIG *enters from the kitchen. He quickly sits down again*): What do you want?

HEDVIG: Just to be with you, father.

HJALMAR (*after a short while*): Seems to me like you're snooping around. Have you been told to watch me, perhaps?

HEDVIG: No, of course not.

HJALMAR: What is mother doing?

HEDVIG: Mother is in the middle of the herring salad. (*Comes over to the table.*) Isn't there any little thing I can help you with, father?

HJALMAR: Oh no. It is better I do it all alone — as long as my strength lasts. There is no need for you to worry about anything, Hedvig, as long as your father is allowed to keep his health.

HEDVIG: Oh father. I won't have you talk that horrid way. (*She walks around a bit, stops by the opening to the inner room and looks in.*)

HJALMAR: What is he doing in there?

HEDVIG: Looks like a new ladder up to the water pail.

HJALMAR: He'll never manage that by himself! And here I am condemned to sit — !

HEDVIG (*goes to him*): Give me the brush, father. I can do it.

HJALMAR: I won't hear of it. You'll just be ruining your eyes.

HEDVIG: No, I won't. Give me the brush.

HJALMAR (*getting up*): It would only be for a minute or two —

HEDVIG: What possible harm could that do? (*Takes the brush.*) There now. (*Sits down.*) And here is one I can use as model.

HJALMAR: But don't ruin your eyes! Do you hear me? I will not take the responsibility. It's all yours. I'm just telling you.

HEDVIG (*working*): Yes, of course.

HJALMAR: You are really very good at it, Hedvig. It will only be for a few minutes, you understand.

(*He slips into the attic by the edge of the curtain.* HEDVIG *keeps on working.* HJALMAR *and* EKDAL *can be heard talking behind the curtain.*)

HJALMAR (*appearing inside the net*): Hedvig, please give me the pliers on the shelf. And the chisel. (*Turns around.*) See here, father. Just let me show you what I have in mind first.

(HEDVIG *fetches the tools from the shelf and gives them to him.*)

HJALMAR: Thank you. It was a good thing I went in.

(*He leaves the doorway. Sounds of carpentering and conversation are heard from inside.* HEDVIG *remains watching them. After a while there is a knock on the entrance door. She does not notice.*)

GREGERS (*bareheaded and coatless, enters, stops near the door*): H'm!

HEDVIG (*turns around and walks towards him*): Good morning! Won't you please come in?

GREGERS: Thank you. (*Looks towards the attic.*) You seem to have workmen in the house.

HEDVIG: Oh no. It's just father and Grandpa. I'll tell them you're here.

GREGERS: Please don't. I'd rather wait a while. (*Sits down on the sofa.*)

HEDVIG: It's such a mess in here — (*Begins removing the photographs.*)

GREGERS: Never mind. Are they pictures you are retouching?

HEDVIG: Yes. It is something I help father with.

GREGERS: I hope you won't let me disturb you.

HEDVIG: I won't.

(*She moves the things more within her reach and resumes work.* GREGERS *watches her in silence.*)

GREGERS: Did the wild duck sleep well last night?

HEDVIG: Yes, thank you. I think so.

GREGERS (*turning towards the attic*): In daylight it looks quite different from last night when there was a moon.

HEDVIG: Yes, it varies so. In the morning it looks different than in the afternoon, and when it rains it looks different than when the sun is shining.

GREGERS: You have noticed that?

HEDVIG: Yes, of course.

GREGERS: Do you too spend much time with the wild duck?

HEDVIG: Yes, when I can.

GREGERS: I suppose you don't have much spare time, though. You are going to school, of course?

HEDVIG: Not any more. Father is afraid I'll ruin my eyes.

GREGERS: Then he reads with you himself?

HEDVIG: He has promised to, but he hasn't had the time yet.

GREGERS: But isn't there anyone else who can help you?

HEDVIG: Well, yes, there is Mr. Molvik, but he isn't always — you know — quite —

GREGERS: You mean he is drunk sometimes.

HEDVIG: I think so.

GREGERS: Well, in that case you have time for many things. And in there, I suppose, it's like a world all its own?

HEDVIG: Yes, quite. And there are so many strange things in there.

GREGERS: There are?

HEDVIG: Yes, there are big closets with books in them, and in many of the books there are pictures.

GREGERS: I see.

HEDVIG: And there is an old desk with drawers and drop-down leaves and a big clock with figures that come out. But the clock doesn't run any more.

GREGERS: So time has stopped in there where the wild duck lives?

HEDVIG: Yes. And there are old coloring sets and that sort of thing, and then all the books.

GREGERS: I expect you read the books.

HEDVIG: Yes, whenever I have a chance. But most of them are in English and I can't read that. But I look at the pictures. There is a great, big book that's called "Harrison's History of London." I think it is a hundred years old. There are ever so many pictures in it. In front it shows a picture of Death with an hourglass and a girl. I think that is horrible. But then there are all the pictures of churches and castles and streets and big ships that sail the seas.

GREGERS: Tell me — where do all those strange things come from?

HEDVIG: There was an old sea captain who used to live here. He brought them home. They called him The Flying Dutchman. And that's odd, I think, for he wasn't a Dutchman at all.

GREGERS: No?

HEDVIG: No. But finally he disappeared at sea, and all the things were left here.

GREGERS: Listen — when you sit in there looking at the pictures, don't you ever want to travel and see the real, big world for yourself?

HEDVIG: Oh no. I want to stay here at home always and help father and mother.

GREGERS: With the photographs?

HEDVIG: Not just with that. Best of all I'd like to learn how to engrave pictures like those in the English books.

GREGERS: H'm. And what does your father say to that?

HEDVIG: I don't think father likes the idea very much. He is funny about things like that. You know, he says I ought to learn basket-weaving and straw-plaiting. But I don't think that sounds like much of anything at all.

GREGERS: No, I don't think it does either.

HEDVIG: Though of course father is quite right in saying that if I had learned basket-weaving I could have made the new basket for the wild duck.

GREGERS: That's true. And that really ought to have been your job, you know.

HEDVIG: Yes. Because it is my wild duck.

GREGERS: So I hear.

HEDVIG: Oh yes. I own it. But father and Grandpa get to borrow it as often as they like.

GREGERS: So? And what do they do with it?

HEDVIG: Oh — they take care of it and build things for it and that sort of thing.

GREGERS: I see. For of course the wild duck is the noblest of all the animals in there.

HEDVIG: Yes, she is, for she is a real, wild bird. And then I feel sorrier for her than for any of the others, because she's all alone, poor thing.

GREGERS: No family, like the rabbits.

HEDVIG: No. And the chickens, they have so many they were little chicks together with. But she is all alone, with none of her own near by. And there is the strange thing about the wild duck. Nobody knows her and nobody knows where she is from.

GREGERS: And she has been down to the depths of the sea.

HEDVIG (*glances quickly at him, suppresses a smile, asks*): Why do you say "the depths of the sea"?

GREGERS: What should I say?

HEDVIG: You could say "the sea bottom" or "the bottom of the sea."

GREGERS: Can't I just as well say "the depths of the sea"?

HEDVIG: Yes, but I think it sounds so strange when other people say "the depths of the sea."

GREGERS: Why is that? Tell me.

HEDVIG: No, I won't, for it is so silly.

GREGERS: I don't think so. Please tell me why you smiled.

HEDVIG: It's because every time I think of what's in there — when it comes into my head all of a sudden, I mean — I always feel that the whole room and everything that's in it are the depths of the sea. But that's silly.

GREGERS: Don't say that.

HEDVIG: Yes, for it's just an old attic, you know.

GREGERS (*looking intently at her*): Are you sure?

HEDVIG (*surprised*): That it's an attic?

GREGERS: Yes. Are you sure it is?

(HEDVIG *stares at him in silence, her mouth open in astonishment.* GINA *enters from the kitchen with linen, silverware, etc., to set the table.*)

GREGERS (*getting up*): I am afraid I am too early for you.

GINA: Oh well. You have to be somewhere. Things are almost ready now, anyway. Clear the table, Hedvig.

(*During the next scene* HEDVIG *clears the table and* GINA *sets it.* GREGERS *seats himself in the armchair and starts leafing through an album of photographs.*)

GREGERS: I understand you know how to retouch, Mrs. Ekdal.

GINA (*looks at him out of the corner of her eye*): That's right.

GREGERS: That was fortunate.

GINA: How — fortunate?

GREGERS: I mean since Ekdal is a photographer.

HEDVIG: Mother knows how to take pictures, too.

GINA: Oh yes, I've had to learn *that* business, all right.

GREGERS: Perhaps it is you who are responsible for the daily routine?

GINA: Yes, when Ekdal himself doesn't have the time —

GREGERS: I suppose he busies himself a great deal with his old father?

GINA: Yes, and then it's not for a man like Ekdal to waste his time taking pictures of everybody and his grandmother.

GREGERS: I quite agree, but since he did choose this as his profession, shouldn't he — ?

GINA: You know just as well as I do, Mr. Werle, that Ekdal isn't just one of your common, ordinary photographers.

GREGERS: Of course not, but — nevertheless —

(*A shot is heard from the attic.*)

GREGERS (*jumps up*): What was that?

GINA: Ugh! There they go, firing away again!

GREGERS: They shoot, too?

HEDVIG: They go hunting.

GREGERS: What? (*Over by the door to the attic.*) Do you go hunting, Hjalmar?

HJALMAR (*inside the curtain*): Have you arrived? I didn't know — I've been so busy — (*To* HEDVIG.) And you — not letting us know — ! (*Comes into the studio.*)

GREGERS: Do you go shooting in the attic?

HJALMAR (*showing him a double-barreled pistol*): Oh, it's only this old thing.

GINA: You and Grandpa are going to have an accident with that pestol of yours one of these days.

HJALMAR (*irritated*): I believe I have told you that this kind of firearm is called a pistol.

GINA: I don't see that that makes it any better.

GREGERS: So you have taken up hunting, too, Hjalmar?

HJALMAR: Only a little rabbit hunting now and then. It's mostly for father's sake, you understand.

GINA: Menfolks are strange. They always need something to diverge themselves with.

HJALMAR (*grimly*): That's right. We always need something to divert ourselves with.

GINA: That's exactly what I'm saying.

HJALMAR: Oh well — ! H'm! (*To* GREGERS.) Well, you see, we're fortunate in that the attic is situated so that nobody can hear the shots.

(*Puts the pistol on the top shelf.*) Don't touch the pistol, Hedvig! Remember, one barrel is loaded!

GREGERS (*peering through the net*): You have a hunting rifle, too, I see.

HJALMAR: That's father's old gun. It doesn't work any more. There's something wrong with the lock. But it's rather fun to have it around all the same, for we take it apart and clean it once in a while and grease it and put it back together again. It's mostly father, of course, who amuses himself with things like that.

HEDVIG (*standing next to* GREGERS): Now you can get a good look at the wild duck.

GREGERS: I was just looking at it. One wing is drooping a bit, isn't it?

HJALMAR: Well that's not so strange. She was hit, you know.

GREGERS: And she drags her foot a little. Or doesn't she?

HJALMAR: Perhaps a little bit.

HEDVIG: Yes, for that is the foot the dog seized her by.

HJALMAR: But aside from that she has no other hurt or defect, and that's really quite remarkable when you consider that she has a charge of buckshot in her and has been between the teeth of a dog.

GREGERS (*with a glance at* HEDVIG): Yes, and been to the depths of the sea — for so long.

HEDVIG (*smiles*): Yes.

GINA (*busy at the table*): Oh yes, that precious wild duck. There sure is enough circumstance made over it.

HJALMAR: H'm. Will you be done setting the table soon?

GINA: In a minute. Hedvig, I need your help. (GINA *and* HEDVIG *go into the kitchen.*)

HJALMAR (*in a low voice*): You had better not watch father. He doesn't like it.

GREGERS (*leaves the attic door.*)

HJALMAR: And I ought to close this before the others arrive. (*Shoos the birds away with his hands.*) Shoo! Shoo — you! (*Raising the curtain and sliding the doors back.*) This arrangement is my own invention. It is really quite amusing to fool around with these things and to fix them when they get broken. And it's absolutely necessary to have something like it, for Gina won't stand for rabbits and chickens in the studio.

GREGERS: No, I suppose not. And perhaps the studio is your wife's department?

HJALMAR: I generally leave the daily run of the business to her. That gives me a chance to retire into the living room and give my thoughts to more important things.

GREGERS: What things, Hjalmar?

HJALMAR: I have been wondering why you haven't asked me that before. Or maybe you haven't heard about the invention?

GREGERS: Invention? No.

HJALMAR: Really? You haven't? Oh well — up there in the woods and wilderness —

GREGERS: So you have invented something!

HJALMAR: Not quite yet, but I am working on it. As you can well imagine, when I decided to devote myself to photography it was not my intent to do nothing but take portraits of all sorts of ordinary people.

GREGERS: I suppose not. Your wife just said the same thing.

HJALMAR: I made a pledge to myself that if I were to give my powers to this profession, I would raise it so high that it would become both an art and a science. That is how I decided to make some remarkable invention.

GREGERS: What is it? What does it do?

HJALMAR: Well, Gregers, you must not ask for details just yet. You see, it takes time. And don't think I am driven by vanity. I can truthfully say I am not working for my own sake. Far from it. It is my life's mission that is in my thoughts night and day.

GREGERS: What mission?

HJALMAR: The old man with the silver hair — can you forget him?

GREGERS: Yes, your poor father. But what exactly do you think you can do for him?

HJALMAR: I can resurrect his respect for himself by once again raising the name of Ekdal to fame and honor.

GREGERS: So that is your life's mission.

HJALMAR: Yes. I will rescue that shipwrecked man. For he was shipwrecked the moment the storm broke. During those terrible inquiries he was not himself. The pistol over yonder — the one we use to shoot rabbits with — it has played its part in the tragedy of the Ekdal family.

GREGERS: The pistol? Really?

HJALMAR: When sentence had been pronounced and he was to be confined — he had that pistol in his hand —

GREGERS: He tried to — !

HJALMAR: Yes, but didn't dare. He was a coward. So much of a wreck, so spiritually ruined was he already then. Can you understand it? He, an officer, the killer of nine bears, descended from two lieutenant colonels — I mean one after the other, of course — Can you understand it, Gregers?

GREGERS: I can indeed.

HJALMAR: Not I. — But the pistol came to figure in our family chronicle a second time. When he had begun to wear the garb of gray and sat there behind bolt and bar — oh, those were terrible days for me, believe me. I kept the shades down on both windows. When I looked out, I saw the sun shining as usual. I saw people in the street laughing and talking about nothing. I could not understand it. It seemed to me that all of existence ought to come to a standstill, as during an eclipse of the sun.

GREGERS: I felt that way when mother died.

HJALMAR: In such an hour Hjalmar Ekdal turned the pistol against himself —

GREGERS: You too were thinking of — ?

HJALMAR: Yes.

GREGERS: But you did not pull the trigger?

HJALMAR: No. In the decisive moment I won a victory over myself. I remained alive. Take my word for it: it requires courage to go on living in a situation like that.

GREGERS: That depends on how you look at it.

HJALMAR: No, it doesn't. At any rate, it all turned out to be for the best. For soon now I will finish my invention, and when I do, Doctor Relling thinks, as I do myself, that father will be allowed to wear his uniform again. I shall claim that as my only reward.

GREGERS: So it is this business with the uniform that mostly —

HJALMAR: Yes, to be able to wear it again is what he dreams of and longs for. You have no idea how it cuts me to the quick to see him. Whenever we have a little family celebration here, like Gina's and my wedding anniversary or whatever it may be, then the old man appears in his lieutenant's uniform from happier days. But no sooner is there a knock on the door than he scuttles back to his own little room as fast as his old legs will carry him. He doesn't dare to show himself to strangers, you know. A sight like that lacerates a son's heart, Gregers!

GREGERS: About when do you think the invention will be ready?

HJALMAR: Heavens, you must not ask for details like that. An invention, you see, is something you don't altogether control yourself. It is very largely a matter of inspiration — a sudden idea — and it is next to impossible to tell beforehand when that may come.

GREGERS: But it is progressing?

HJALMAR: Certainly, it is progressing. It occupies my thoughts every day. It fills me. Every afternoon, after dinner, I shut myself up in the living room to ponder in peace. I just can't be hurried; it won't do any good. That is what Relling says, too.

GREGERS: And you don't think that all this business in the attic interferes too much, distracts you from your work?

HJALMAR: No, no, no. Quite the contrary. You must not say a thing like that. After all, I cannot everlastingly be pursuing the same exhausting train of thought. I need something else, something to occupy me during the waiting period. The inspiration, the sudden flash of insight, don't you see? — when it comes, it comes.

GREGERS: My dear Hjalmar, I almost think there is something of the wild duck in you.

HJALMAR: The wild duck? How do you mean?

GREGERS: You have plunged down through the sea and got yourself entangled in the grasses on the bottom.

HJALMAR: Are you perhaps referring to the well-nigh fatal shot that lodged in father's wing and hit me, too?

GREGERS: Not to that so much. I won't say you are crippled. But you are in a poisonous marsh, Hjalmar. You have contracted an insidious disease and gone to the bottom to die in the dark.

HJALMAR: I? Die in the dark? Honestly, Gregers. You really shouldn't say such things.

GREGERS: Don't you worry. I'll get you up again. For I, too, have got a mission in life. I found it yesterday.

HJALMAR: That may well be, but I shall ask you kindly to leave me out of it. I assure you that — aside from my easily explainable melancholia, of course — I am as contented a man as anybody could wish to be.

GREGERS: The fact that you are — that is one of the symptoms of the poisoning.

HJALMAR: No, really, Gregers. Please don't talk to me any more about disease and poison. I am not used to that sort of talk. In my house we never discuss unpleasant topics.

GREGERS: That I can well believe.

HJALMAR: No, for it isn't good for me. And there is no marshy air here, as you call it. The roof may be low in the poor photographer's home — I know very well it is — and my lot is lowly. But I am an inventor, and a provider as well. That is what raises me above my humble circumstances. — Ah! Here's lunch!

(GINA *and* HEDVIG *enter with bottles of beer, a decanter of brandy, glasses, and other appurtenances. At the same moment,* RELLING *and* MOLVIK *come through the entrance door. Neither one wears hat or coat.* MOLVIK *is dressed in black.*)

GINA (*putting the things down on the table*): Well, you two arrive just in time.

RELLING: Molvik thought he could smell herring salad, and then there was no holding him. — Good morning again, Ekdal.

HJALMAR: Gregers, may I introduce you to Mr. Molvik — And Doctor — that's right, you two already know each other, don't you.

GREGERS: Slightly.

RELLING: Oh yes, young Mr. Werle. We used to do some skirmishing up at the Høydal works. I take it you have just moved in?

GREGERS: This morning.

RELLING: Well, Molvik and I live downstairs, so you don't have far to go for doctor and minister if you need them.

GREGERS: Thank you; maybe I shall. We were thirteen at the table yesterday.

HJALMAR: Come now! Please don't start any of that unpleasantness again!

RELLING: Calm down, Ekdal. You are immune.

HJALMAR: I hope so, for my family's sake. — Sit down. Let's eat, drink, and be merry.

GREGERS: Aren't we going to wait for your father?

HJALMAR: No, he'll eat later in his own room. Do sit down!

(*The men seat themselves and begin eating and drinking.* GINA *and* HEDVIG *wait on them.*)

RELLING: Molvik got pretty high last night, Mrs. Ekdal.

GINA: Again?

RELLING: Didn't you hear me bring him home?

GINA: Can't say I did.

RELLING: That's good, for Molvik was awful last night.

GINA: Is that true, Molvik?

MOLVIK: Let us consign last night's events to oblivion. They do not represent my better self.

RELLING (*to* GREGERS): It comes over him like an irresistible impulse. Then he has to go out and get drunk. You see, Molvik is demonic.

GREGERS: Demonic?

RELLING: That's right. Molvik is demonic.

GREGERS: H'm.

RELLING: And demonic natures aren't made to follow the straight and narrow path. They have to take off for the fields once in a while. — So you still stick it out up at that filthy old place?

GREGERS: So far.

RELLING: Did you ever collect on that claim you went around presenting?

GREGERS: Claim? (*Looks at him and understands.*) Oh I see.

HJALMAR: Have you been a bill collector, Gregers?

GREGERS: Oh nonsense.

RELLING: Oh yes, he has. He went around to all the cottages up there, trying to collect on something he called "the claim of the ideal."

GREGERS: I was young.

RELLING: You're right. You were very young. And the claim of the ideal — you never collected as long as I was up there.

GREGERS: Not since then, either.

RELLING: In that case, I suppose you have been wise enough to reduce the amount somewhat.

GREGERS: Never when I have to do with a real and genuine human being.

HJALMAR: I think that is reasonable enough. — Some butter, Gina.

RELLING: And a piece of bacon for Molvik.

MOLVIK: Ugh! Not bacon!

(*There is a knock from inside the door to the attic.*)

HJALMAR: Go and open, Hedvig. Father wants to get out.

(HEDVIG *opens the door a little.* OLD EKDAL *enters with the skin of a freshly flayed rabbit.* HEDVIG *closes the door after him.*)

EKDAL: Good morning, gentlemen! Good hunting today. Got me a big one.

HJALMAR: And you skinned it yourself, I see.

EKDAL: Salted it, too. It's nice, tender meat, rabbit is. It's sweet, y'know. Tastes like sugar. Good appetite, gentlemen! (*Goes into his room.*)

MOLVIK (*getting up*): Excuse me — I can't — Got to get downstairs —

RELLING: Drink soda water, you idiot!

MOLVIK: Uh — Uh — (*Hurries out, right rear.*)

RELLING (*to* HJALMAR): Let us drink to the old hunter.

HJALMAR (*touching* RELLING'S *glass with his own*): For the sportsman on the brink of the grave — yes.

RELLING: For the gray-haired — (*Drinks.*) Tell me, is his hair gray or is it white?

HJALMAR: In between, I think. Though I don't think there are many hairs left on his head at all.

RELLING: Oh well. One can live happily with a wig, too. Ah, yes, Ekdal. You are really a very happy man. You have this beautiful ambition of yours to strive for —

HJALMAR: Believe me, I am striving.

RELLING: Then you have your excellent wife, shuffling about in slippered feet with that comfortable waddle of hers, making things nice and pleasant for you.

HJALMAR: Yes, Gina — (*Nods to her.*) — you are a good companion on life's journey.

GINA: Aw, you don't need to sit there and dissectate me!

RELLING: And your Hedvig, Ekdal.

HJALMAR (*moved*): Ah yes, the child! The child above all. Hedvig, come to me. (*Stroking her hair.*) What day is tomorrow?

HEDVIG (*playfully shaking him*): Oh, stop it, father!

HJALMAR: It's like a knife through my heart, when I consider how little we can do. Just a small celebration here in the attic.

HEDVIG: But that's just the way I like it!

RELLING: You wait till the invention is all done, Hedvig.

HJALMAR: Yes! Then you'll see, Hedvig. I have decided to secure your future. You shall be made comfortable for as long as you live. I will ask for something for you, something or other. That will be the impecunious inventor's sole reward.

HEDVIG (*whispers, her arms around his neck*): Oh you good, sweet father!

RELLING (*to* GREGERS): Well, now, don't you think it's nice for a change to sit down to a good table in a happy family circle?

HJALMAR: Yes, I really relish these hours at the table.

GREGERS: I, for one, don't like to breathe marsh air.

RELLING: Marsh air?

HJALMAR: Oh, don't start all that again!

GINA: I'll have you know there is no marsh air here, Mr. Werle. The place is aired every single day.

GREGERS (*leaving the table*): The stench I have in mind you don't get rid of by opening windows.

HJALMAR: Stench!

GINA: Yes, how do you like that, Ekdal!

RELLING: Begging your pardon — it wouldn't by any chance be you yourself who bring the stench with you from the Høydal mines?

GREGERS: It's just like you to call stench what I bring to this house.

RELLING (*walks over to* GREGERS): Listen here, Mr. Werle junior. I strongly suspect that you still carry the claim of the ideal around in your rear pocket.

GREGERS: I carry it in my heart.

RELLING: I don't care where the hell you carry it as long as you don't go bill collecting here while *I* am around.

GREGERS: And if I do so, nevertheless?

RELLING: Then you'll go head first down the stairs. Now you know!

HJALMAR: No, really, Relling — !

GREGERS: Go ahead! Throw me out!

GINA (*interposing*): No, we won't have any of that, Relling. But I will say this to you, Mr. Werle, that it seems like you are not the right person to come here and talk about stench after what you did to the stove in your room this morning.

(*There is a knock on the door.*)

HEDVIG: Mother, someone's knocking.

HJALMAR: Oh yes, let's have customers on top of everything else — !

GINA: I'll handle it. (*Opens the door, gives a start, steps back*): Oh dear!

(WERLE, *in a fur coat, steps inside.*)

WERLE: I beg your pardon, but I am told my son is here.

GINA (*swallowing hard*): Yes sir.

HJALMAR (*closer*): Sir, wouldn't you like to — ?

WERLE: Thanks. I just want a word with my son.

GREGERS: Well. Here I am.

WERLE: I want to talk with you in your room.

GREGERS: In my room — ? Oh, all right. (*Is about to leave.*)

GINA: Good Lord, no! That's not a fit place!

WERLE: All right; out here in the hall, then. I want to see you alone.

HJALMAR: You may do that right here, Mr. Werle. Relling, come into the living room with me.

(HJALMAR *and* RELLING *go out, right front.* GINA *takes* HEDVIG *with her into the kitchen, left front.*)

GREGERS (*after a brief silence*): Well. We are alone.

WERLE: You dropped some hints last night. And since you have moved in with the Ekdals, I can only assume that you are planning something or other against me.

GREGERS: I plan to open Hjalmar Ekdal's eyes. He is to see his position as it really is. That's all.

WERLE: Is that the life mission you mentioned yesterday?

GREGERS: Yes. You have left me no other.

WERLE: So you feel it is I who have twisted your mind, Gregers?

GREGERS: You have twisted my whole life. I am not thinking of all that with mother. But it is you I can thank for the fact that I am being haunted and driven by a guilty conscience.

WERLE: Ah, I see. So your conscience is ailing.

GREGERS: I should have opposed you the time you were laying traps for Lieutenant Ekdal. I should have warned him, for I suspected how things were going.

WERLE: Yes, in that case you certainly ought to have said something.

GREGERS: I didn't have the courage. I was a coward — frightened. I felt an unspeakable fear of you — both then and for a long, long time afterwards.

WERLE: That fear appears to have left you now.

GREGERS: Yes, fortunately. What has been done to Old Ekdal, both by me and by — others, for that there is no remedy. But Hjalmar I can rescue from the web of lies and deceit in which he is suffocating.

WERLE: Do you think that is a good thing to do?

GREGERS: I am sure it is.

WERLE: I take it you think Mr. Photographer Ekdal is the kind of man who will be grateful for your friendly services?

GREGERS: Yes! He is that kind of man.

WERLE: H'm. We'll see.

GREGERS: Besides, if I am to continue living, I have to find a way to heal my sick conscience.

WERLE: It will never get well. Your conscience has been sickly from the time you were a child. It's hereditary, Gregers. You have it from your mother. The only inheritance she left you.

GREGERS (*with a contemptuous half smile*): I see you still haven't forgotten your disappointment when you found out mother wasn't rich.

WERLE: Let's not change the subject. Am I to think, then, that you are firmly resolved to guide Hjalmar Ekdal into the path you consider the right one?

GREGERS: Yes. That is my firm intent.

WERLE: In that case I could have saved myself coming all the way up here. For then I suppose there is no point in my asking you to move back home again?

GREGERS: No.

WERLE: And you don't want to join the firm?

GREGERS: No.

WERLE: Very well. But since I am to marry again, your part of the estate will have to be paid you.

GREGERS (*quickly*): No, I don't want that.

WERLE: You don't want it?

GREGERS: I dare not, for my conscience's sake.

WERLE (*after a brief pause*): Are you going back up to Høydal?

GREGERS: No. I consider myself released from your service.

WERLE: But what do you want to do with yourself?

GREGERS: Accomplish my mission. Nothing else.

WERLE: But afterwards? What are you going to live on?

GREGERS: I have saved some of my salary.

WERLE: How long do you think that will last?

GREGERS: I think it will do for the time I have left.

WERLE: What is that supposed to mean?

GREGERS: I won't answer any more questions.
WERLE: Well, goodbye, Gregers.
GREGERS: Goodbye.

(WERLE *leaves.*)

HJALMAR (*looks in*): Did he leave?
GREGERS: Yes.

(HJALMAR *and* RELLING *enter from the living room,* GINA *and* HEDVIG *from the kitchen.*)

RELLING: Now that was a very successful breakfast.
GREGERS: Put on your coat, Hjalmar. I want you to take a long walk with me.
HJALMAR: Gladly. What did your father want? Did it have to do with me?
GREGERS: Just come. We'll talk. I'll go and get my coat. (*Goes out.*)
GINA: You shouldn't go with him, Ekdal.
RELLING: No, don't. Stay here.
HJALMAR (*taking his hat and coat*): What! When an old friend feels the need to open his heart for me in private — !
RELLING: But goddamit! Can't you see that the fellow is mad, cracked, insane!
GINA: Yes, listen to Relling. His mother used to have physicological fits, too.
HJALMAR: All the more reason why he needs a friend's alert eyes. (*To* GINA.) Be sure to have dinner ready at the usual time. Goodbye. (*Goes out.*)
RELLING: It's nothing less than a disaster that that man didn't go straight to hell down one of the shafts up at Høydal.
GINA: Heavens — ! Why do you say that?
RELLING (*mutters*): I have my reasons.
GINA: Do you really think young Werle is crazy?
RELLING: No, unfortunately. He is no madder than most people. He is sick, though.
GINA: What do you think is wrong with him?
RELLING: That I can tell you, Mrs. Ekdal. He suffers from an acute attack of moral integrity.
GINA: Moral integrity?
HEDVIG: Is that a disease?
RELLING: Yes, it is a national disease, but it occurs only sporadically. (*Nods to* GINA.) That was a good meal, thank you. (*Goes out.*)
GINA (*troubled, walks up and down*): Ugh! That Gregers Werle — he's always been a weird fish.

HEDVIG (*by the table, looks at her searchingly*): I think this is very strange.

ACT IV

(*The studio. Photographs have just been taken. A cloth-covered camera on a tripod, a couple of chairs, and a small table are standing about in the middle of the floor. Afternoon light. The sun is about to disappear. After a while darkness begins to fall.*

GINA *stands in the open entrance door with a small box and a wet glass plate in her hand. She is talking to someone not in sight.*)

GINA: Absolutely. When I promise something, I keep it. I'll have the first dozen ready for you on Monday. — Goodbye.

(*Sounds of someone descending the stairs.* GINA *closes the door, puts the plate inside the box and the box into the camera.*)

HEDVIG (*enters from the kitchen*): Did they leave?
GINA (*putting things in order*): Yes, thank goodness. I finally got rid of them.
HEDVIG: Can you understand why father isn't back yet?
GINA: You're sure he is not down at Relling's?
HEDVIG: No, he is not there. I just went down the kitchen stairs to ask.
GINA: His food is getting cold and everything.
HEDVIG: Yes. And father who is always so particular about having dinner on time.
GINA: Oh well. You'll see he'll be back soon.
HEDVIG: I wish he'd come. Everything seems so strange.

(HJALMAR *enters from outside.*)

HEDVIG (*towards him*): Father! If you knew how we've been waiting for you!
GINA (*glancing at him*): You've been gone quite some time.
HJALMAR (*without looking at her*): Yes, I suppose I have.

(*He starts taking his coat off.* GINA *and* HEDVIG *both go to help him. He turns them away.*)

GINA: Maybe you and Werle had something to eat some place?
HJALMAR (*hanging up his coat*): No.
GINA (*towards the kitchen door*): I'll get your dinner.
HJALMAR: Never mind. I don't feel like eating now.

HEDVIG (*coming closer*): Are you sick, father?

HJALMAR: Sick? No, I'm not sick — exactly. We had a strenuous walk, Gregers and I.

GINA: You shouldn't do that, Ekdal. You aren't used to it.

HJALMAR: H'm. There are many things in life a man has to get used to. (*Paces up and down.*) Anybody here while I've been gone?

GINA: Only that engaged couple.

HJALMAR: No new appointments?

GINA: No, not today.

HEDVIG: There will be some tomorrow, father, I am sure.

HJALMAR: I hope you are right, for tomorrow I plan to go to work in earnest.

HEDVIG: Tomorrow! But don't you remember what day is tomorrow?

HJALMAR: That's right. Well, then, the day after tomorrow. From now on I'll do everything myself. I want to assume the entire work load.

GINA: Whatever for, Ekdal? That's only making yourself miserable. I'll manage the pictures. You just go on with the invention.

HEDVIG: And the wild duck, father. And the chickens and the rabbits and —

HJALMAR: Don't ever mention all that junk to me again! Starting tomorrow, I'll never more set foot in the attic.

HEDVIG: But father, you promised that tomorrow we're having a celebration —

HJALMAR: H'm. That's right. Day after tomorrow then. That damn wild duck! I'd like to wring its neck!

HEDVIG (*with a cry*): The wild duck!

GINA: Now I've heard everything!

HEDVIG (*shaking him*): But father — it's *my* wild duck!

HJALMAR: That's why I won't do it. I don't have the heart — for your sake, Hedvig. But deep down I feel I ought to do it. I shouldn't harbor under my roof a creature that has been in those hands.

GINA: For heaven's sake! Even if Grandpa *did* get it from that awful Pettersen.

HJALMAR (*walking up and down*): There are certain demands — what shall I call them? Let me say ideal demands — certain claims, that a man disregards only at the peril of his soul.

HEDVIG (*following after him*): But think — the wild duck! That poor wild duck!

HJALMAR (*halts*): Didn't I tell you I'll spare it — for your sake? Not a hair on its head will be — h'm. Well, as I said, I'll spare it. After all, there are bigger tasks awaiting me. But you ought to go out for a little walk, Hedvig. The twilight is just right for you.

HEDVIG: I don't care to go out now.

HJALMAR: Yes, do. Seems to me you are squinting. The fumes in here aren't good for you. The air is close under this roof.

HEDVIG: All right. I'll run down the kitchen stairs and walk around a bit. My hat and coat? Oh yes, in my room. Father, please — don't do anything bad to the wild duck while I'm gone!

HJALMAR: Not a feather shall be plucked from its head. (*Clutches her to him.*) You and I, Hedvig — we two! Be on your way now.

(HEDVIG *nods goodbye to her parents and goes out through the kitchen door.*)

HJALMAR (*pacing back and forth*): Gina.

GINA: Yes?

HJALMAR: Starting tomorrow — or let's say the day after tomorrow — I'd like to keep account of the housekeeping expenses myself.

GINA: So you want to keep the accounts too, now?

HJALMAR: Keep track of what we take in, at any rate.

GINA: Lord knows, that's easily done!

HJALMAR: One wouldn't think so. It seems to me you make the money go incredibly far. (*Stops and looks at her.*) How do you do it?

GINA: It's because Hedvig and I need so little.

HJALMAR: Is it true that father is overpaid for the copying work he does for Werle?

GINA: I couldn't say about that. I don't know the rates.

HJALMAR: Well, what *does* he get? In round figures. — I want to know.

GINA: It differs. I guess it comes to about what he costs us, plus a little extra in spending money.

HJALMAR: What he costs us! And you haven't told me that!

GINA: No, I couldn't, for you were so happy because he got everything from you.

HJALMAR: And it has really been Werle all the time!

GINA: Oh well. He can afford it.

HJALMAR: Light the lamp!

GINA (*lighting the lamp*): And as far as that is concerned, how do we know it is Werle himself? It may be Gråberg —

HJALMAR: Really, Gina. You know that isn't so. Why do you say a thing like that?

GINA: I don't know. I just thought —

HJALMAR: H'm!

GINA: It wasn't me who got Grandpa all that copying to do. It was Bertha, when she took service there.

HJALMAR: It sounds to me like your voice is trembling.

GINA (*putting the shade on the lamp*): Does it?

HJALMAR: And your hands are shaking. Aren't they?

GINA (*firmly*): You might as well tell me straight, Ekdal. What has he been saying about me?

HJALMAR: Is it true — *can* it be true — that there was some kind of affair between you and Werle while you were in his house?

GINA: That's not so. Not then. He was after me, though. And Mrs. Werle thought there was something going on, and she made a fuss and a big hullaballoo about it, and she beat me and pulled me around — and so I quit.

HJALMAR: But afterwards — !

GINA: Well, then I went to live with mother. And you see — mother — she wasn't all the woman you thought she was, Ekdal. She talked to me about this, that, and the other. For Werle was a widower by that time —

HJALMAR: And then — ?

GINA: You might as well know it, I guess. He didn't give up till he had his way.

HJALMAR (*striking his hands together*): And this is the mother of my child! How could you keep a thing like this from me?

GINA: Yes, I know it was wrong. I should have told you long ago, I suppose.

HJALMAR: You should have told me right away; that's what you should have. Then I would have known what sort of woman you were.

GINA: But would you have married me, irregardless?

HJALMAR: Of course, I wouldn't!

GINA: I didn't think so, and that's why I didn't dare to tell you. I had come to care for you, you know — a whole lot I cared for you. And I just couldn't see making myself as unhappy as all that —

HJALMAR (*walking about*): And this is my Hedvig's mother! And to know that everything I lay my eyes on here (*Kicks a chair.*) — my whole home — I owe to a favored predecessor! Oh, that seducer, that damn Werle!

GINA: Do you regret the fourteen-fifteen years we've had together?

HJALMAR (*fronting her*): Tell me if you haven't felt every day and every hour to be one long agony of repentance for that web of deceitful silence you have woven around me, like a spider? Answer me! Haven't you lived here in perpetual torture of guilt and remorse?

GINA: Bless you, Ekdal! I've been plenty busy with the house and the pictures —

HJALMAR: So you never cast a probing glance at your past?

GINA: No, to tell the truth, I had almost forgotten all those old stories.

HJALMAR: Oh, this dull, apathetic calm! There is something shocking about it. Not even repentant — !

GINA: Just tell me this, Ekdal. What do you think would have become of you if you hadn't got yourself a wife like me?

HJALMAR: Like you — !

GINA: Yes, for you know I have always been more practical and able to cope with things than you. Of course, I am a couple of years older —

HJALMAR: What would have become of me!

GINA: For you've got to admit you weren't living exactly right when you first met me.

HJALMAR: So you call that living wrong! Oh, what do you know about a man's feelings when he sorrows and despairs — especially a man of my fiery temperament.

GINA: No, I guess I don't know. And I don't mean to execrete you for it, either, for you turned into as decent a man as they come as soon as you got a house and a family of your own to take care of. And now we were getting on so nicely here, and Hedvig and I were just thinking that pretty soon we might spend some money on clothes for ourselves.

HJALMAR: Yes, in the swamp of deceit!

GINA: That that fellow ever poked his nose inside here!

HJALMAR: I, too, thought our home a pleasant one. That was a mistake. Where now do I gather the necessary inner resilience to bring my invention into the world of reality? Perhaps it will die with me. If it does, it will be your past, Gina, that has killed it.

GINA (*on the verge of tears*): Please, Ekdal — don't be saying such things! I that have all my days only tried to make things nice and pleasant for you!

HJALMAR: I ask — what happens now to the breadwinner's dream? As I reclined in there on the sofa, pondering the invention, it came to me that it was going to drain me of my last drop of vitality. I knew that the day the patent was issued and in my hands — that day would be my — my day of farewell. And then it was my dream that you were to live on as the late inventor's well-to-do widow.

GINA (*wiping her tears*): I won't have you talk that way, Ekdal. May the good Lord never let me live the day when I'm your widow!

HJALMAR: Oh what difference does it all make! It is all over now, anyway. Everything!

(GREGERS *cautiously opens the entrance door and peers in.*)

GREGERS: May I come in?

HJALMAR: Yes, do.

GREGERS (*goes up to them with a beaming, happy face, reaches out his hands to them*): Now, then — you dear people — ! (*Looks from one to the other, whispers to* HJALMAR:) It hasn't happened yet?

HJALMAR (*loud*): It has happened.

GREGERS: It has?

HJALMAR: I have lived through the bitterest moment of my life.

GREGERS: But also, I trust, its most exalted one.

HJALMAR: Anyway, it's done and over with.

GINA: May God forgive you, Mr. Werle.

GREGERS (*greatly bewildered*): But I don't understand — !

HJALMAR: What don't you understand?

GREGERS: As crucial a conversation as this — a conversation that is to be the foundation for a whole new way of life — a life, a partnership, in truth and frankness —

HJALMAR: I know. I know it very well.

GREGERS: I was so sure that when I came in here now I would be met with a splendor of revelation shining from both husband and wife. But all I see is this dull, heavy gloom —

GINA: So that's it. (*Removes the lamp shade.*)

GREGERS: You refuse to understand me, Mrs. Ekdal. Well, I suppose you need time. But you, Hjalmar? Surely, you must have felt a higher consecration in this great crisis.

HJALMAR: Of course I did. That is, in a way.

GREGERS: For surely nothing in the world can be compared to finding forgiveness in one's heart for her who has erred and lovingly lifting her up to one's own heights.

HJALMAR: Do you think a man so easily forgets the draught of wormwood I just drained?

GREGERS: An ordinary man, maybe not. But a man like you — !

HJALMAR: Oh, I know. But you must not rush me, Gregers. It takes time.

GREGERS: There is much of the wild duck in you, Hjalmar.

(RELLING *has entered.*)

RELLING: Ah! Here we go with the wild duck again!

HJALMAR: Mr. Werle's crippled prey — yes.

RELLING: Werle? Is it him you're talking about?

HJALMAR: About him — and about ourselves.

RELLING (*in a low voice, to* GREGERS): Damn you to hell!

HJALMAR: What are you saying?

RELLING: I am just expressing an ardent wish that this quack here would betake himself home. If he stays around he is likely to ruin both of you.

GREGERS: Those two cannot be ruined, Mr. Relling. Of Hjalmar I need say nothing. Him we know. But she, too, has surely in the depths of her being something reliable, something of integrity —

GINA (*almost crying*): Why didn't you leave me alone then?

RELLING (*to* GREGERS): Is it impertinent to ask exactly what you want in this house?

GREGERS: I want to lay the foundation for a true marriage.

RELLING: So you don't think the Ekdals' marriage is good enough as it is?

GREGERS: I daresay it is as good a marriage as most, unfortunately. But a true marriage it has yet to become.

HJALMAR: You have never had an eye for the claim of the ideal, Relling!

RELLING: Nonsense, boy! — Begging your pardon, Mr. Werle — how many — roughly — how many true marriages have you observed in your life?

GREGERS: Hardly a single one.

RELLING: Nor have I.

GREGERS: But I have seen a number of the other kind. And I have had occasion to witness what havoc a marriage like that can work in a pair of human beings.

HJALMAR: A man's whole moral foundation may crumble under his feet; that's the terrible thing.

RELLING: Well, I can't say I've ever been exactly married, so I can't judge about that. But I do know this, that the child belongs to marriage too. And you had better leave the child alone.

HJALMAR: Oh, Hedvig! My poor Hedvig!

RELLING: Yes — keep Hedvig out of it, you two! You are grown-ups. In God's name, do whatever fool things you like to your marriage. But I am warning you: be careful what you do to Hedvig. If you're not, there is no telling what may happen to her.

HJALMAR: Happen to her!

RELLING: Yes, she may bring a disaster upon herself — and perhaps on others, too.

GINA: But how can you tell about that, Relling?

HJALMAR: Are you saying there is some immediate danger to her eyes?

RELLING: This has nothing whatever to do with her eyes. Hedvig is in a difficult age. She may do all sorts of crazy things.

GINA: I know — she does already. She's taken to fooling around with the woodstove in the kitchen. Playing fire, she calls it. Sometimes I'm scared she'll burn the whole house down.

RELLING: There you are. I knew it.

GREGERS (*to* RELLING): But how do you explain a thing like that?

RELLING (*sullenly*): Her voice is changing, sir.

HJALMAR: As long as the child has *me* — ! As long as *my* head is above the ground!

(*There is a knock on the door.*)

GINA: Shhh, Ekdal. There are people outside.

(MRS. SØRBY *enters, wearing hat and coat.*)

MRS. SØRBY: Good evening!

GINA (*going to her*): Goodness! Is it you, Bertha!

MRS. SØRBY: So it is. Maybe it's inconvenient — ?

HJALMAR: Oh by no means! A messenger from *that* house — !

MRS. SØRBY (*to* GINA): Frankly, I had hoped you'd be without your menfolks this time of day. I've just dropped in to have a word with you about something and say goodbye.

GINA: You're going away?

MRS. SØRBY: Tomorrow morning — to Høydal. Mr. Werle left this afternoon. (*Casually, to* GREGERS.) He asked me to say hello.

GINA: Imagine — !

HJALMAR: So Mr. Werle has left? And you are going after him?

MRS. SØRBY: Yes. What do you say to that, Ekdal?

HJALMAR: Look out, is all I say.

GREGERS: I can explain. Father and Mrs. Sørby are getting married.

GINA: Oh Bertha! At long last!

RELLING (*his voice trembling a little*): Surely, this cannot be true?

MRS. SØRBY: Yes, my dear Relling, true it is.

RELLING: You want to get married again?

MRS. SØRBY: That's what it amounts to. Werle has got the license. We'll have a quiet little party up at the works.

GREGERS: I suppose I should tender my felicitations like a good stepson.

MRS. SØRBY: Thank you, if you really mean it. I hope this will be for the best for both Werle and myself.

RELLING: I am sure you have every reason to think it will. Mr. Werle never gets drunk — at least not to my knowledge. Nor do I believe he is in the habit of beating up his wife, like the late lamented horse doctor.

MRS. SØRBY: Let Sørby rest quietly in his grave. He had his good sides, too.

RELLING: Mr. Industrialist Werle has better ones, I am sure.

MRS. SØRBY: At least he has not thrown away what is best in himself. The man who does that must take the consequences.

RELLING: Tonight I'll go out with Molvik.

MRS. SØRBY: Don't do that, Relling. Don't — for my sake.

RELLING: There's nothing else to do. (*To* HJALMAR.) Want to come along?

GINA: No, thank you. Ekdal doesn't go in for excapades like that.

HJALMAR (*angrily, in a half whisper*): For heaven's sake! Keep your mouth shut!

RELLING: Goodbye — Mrs. Werle! (*Goes out.*)

GREGERS (*to* MRS. SØRBY): It appears that you and Doctor Relling know each other quite well?

MRS. SØRBY: Yes, we've known each other for a good many years. At one time it looked as if we might have made a match of it.

GREGERS: I'm sure it was lucky for you that you didn't.

MRS. SØRBY: You may well say that. But I've always been wary of acting on impulse. A woman can't just throw herself away, you know.

GREGERS: Aren't you afraid I'll let my father know about this old acquaintanceship?

MRS. SØRBY: Do you really believe I haven't told him myself?

GREGERS: Oh?

MRS. SØRBY: Your father knows every little thing people might say about me with any show of truth at all. I have told him everything. That was the first thing I did when I realized what his intentions were.

GREGERS: It seems to me you are more than usually frank.

MRS. SØRBY: I have always been frank. For us women that's the best policy.

HJALMAR: What do you say to that, Gina?

GINA: Oh, women differ. Some do it one way, others do it different.

MRS. SØRBY: Well, Gina, in my opinion I have followed the wiser course. And Werle hasn't kept back anything either. You see, that's what mainly brought us together. Now he can sit and talk to me as openly as a child. He has never been able to do that before. A healthy, vigorous man like him — all through his youth and all the best years of his life he had his ears drummed full with angry sermons. And very often sermons about sins he hadn't even committed — according to what I have been told.

GINA: That's the truth.

GREGERS: If you ladies want to pursue that topic any further, I had better absent myself.

MRS. SØRBY: You may just as well stay as far as that's concerned. I won't say another word. I just wanted you to know I haven't kept anything back or played him false in any way. Maybe people will say I am a very fortunate woman, and in a way of course that's true. But I don't think I am getting any more than I am giving. I'll certainly never desert him. And I can be of more service and use to him than anybody else, now that he'll soon be helpless.

HJALMAR: Will he be helpless?

GREGERS (*to* MRS. SØRBY): Don't say anything about that here.

MRS. SØRBY: It can't be kept secret any longer, much as he'd like to. He is going blind.

HJALMAR (*struck*): Blind? That's strange. He, too?

GINA: Lots of people go blind.

MRS. SØRBY: And I'm sure you can tell yourself what that must mean to a businessman. Well, I'll try to be his eyes, the best I know how. — But I can't stay any longer. I have so much to do right now. — Oh yes, What I wanted to tell you, Ekdal, is that if Werle can be of any service to you, all you need to do is to get in touch with Gråberg.

GREGERS: That is an offer I am sure Hjalmar Ekdal will decline.

MRS. SØRBY: Really? It seems to me he hasn't always been so —

GINA: Yes, Bertha. Ekdal doesn't need to accept anything more from Mr. Werle.

HJALMAR (*slowly, with weight*): Tell your husband-to-be from me, that in the very near future I intend to go to Mr. Gråberg —

GREGERS: What! You want to do that!

HJALMAR: — I say, go to Mr. Gråberg, and demand an account of the sum I owe his employer. I desire to pay this debt of honor — ha-ha-ha! — let us call it a debt of honor! Enough! I shall pay it all, with five per cent interest.

GINA: But Ekdal — goodness! We don't have that kind of money!

HJALMAR: Be so good as to inform your fiancé that I am working incessantly on my invention. Please tell him that what sustains my mind during this exhausting enterprise is my ambition to free myself from a painful burden of debt. This is why I am an inventor. The entire proceeds from my invention are to be devoted to liberating myself from the obligation to remunerate your husband-to-be for his expenses on behalf of my family.

MRS. SØRBY: Something has happened here.

HJALMAR: Indeed, something has.

MRS. SØRBY: Well, goodbye. I had something else I wanted to talk to you about, Gina, but that will have to wait till some other time. Goodbye.

(HJALMAR *and* GREGERS *return her greeting silently.* GINA *sees her to the door.*)

HJALMAR: Not beyond the threshold, Gina!

(MRS. SØRBY *leaves.* GINA *closes the door.*)

HJALMAR: There, now, Gregers. I have that burdensome debt off my chest.

GREGERS: You soon will, at any rate.

HJALMAR: I believe my attitude must be deemed the proper one.

GREGERS: You are the man I have always taken you to be.

HJALMAR: In certain cases it is impossible to disregard the claims of the ideal. As provider for my family, I am bound, of course, to find my course of action difficult and painful. Believe me, it is no joke for a man situated as I am, without means, to assume a debt of many years' standing — a debt, you might say, covered by the sands of oblivion. But never mind. The man in me demands his rights.

GREGERS (*placing his hand on his shoulder*): Dear Hjalmar — wasn't it a good thing that I came?

HJALMAR: Yes.

GREGERS: That your whole situation was made clear to you — wasn't that a good thing?

HJALMAR (*a bit impatiently*): Of course it was. But there is one thing that shocks my sense of justice.

GREGERS: What is that?

HJALMAR: It is this that — But I don't know that I ought to speak so freely about your father —

GREGERS: Don't let that worry you. Say what you want.

HJALMAR: All right. Well, you see, there is something shocking in the notion that now it's he and not I who realizes the true marriage.

GREGERS: How can you say a thing like that!

HJALMAR: Well, it is. For your father and Mrs. Sørby are about to solemnify a union built on full mutual confidence, on complete, unconditional frankness on both sides. They conceal nothing from each other, there are no deceitful silences, there has been declared, if I may put it so, mutual absolution between them.

GREGERS: Well, what of it?

HJALMAR: Well, then — it's all there! All the difficult conditions you yourself said are prerequisites for the building of a true marriage.

GREGERS: But that's in quite a different way, Hjalmar. Surely, you won't compare either yourself or Gina with those two — ? Oh I am sure you know what I mean.

HJALMAR: Yet I can't get away from the thought that in all this there is something that offends my sense of justice. It looks exactly as if there were no just order in the universe.

GINA: Ekdal, for God's sake, don't talk like that!

GREGERS: H'm. Let's not get involved in those issues.

HJALMAR: Though, on the other hand, I do in a way discern fate's ruling finger, too. He is going blind.

GINA: We don't know that yet.

HJALMAR: There is no doubt about it. At least, we ought not to doubt it, for in that very fact lies the proof of just retribution. He did once hoodwink a trusting fellow being.

GREGERS: I am afraid he has hoodwinked many.

HJALMAR: And here comes the inexorable, the inscrutable, claiming Werle's own eyes.

GINA: How you talk! I think it's scary.

HJALMAR: It is salutary at times to contemplate the night side of existence.

(HEDVIG, *dressed for the outside, enters. She is happy, breathless.*)

GINA: Back so soon?

HEDVIG: Yes. I didn't feel like walking any farther. It was a good thing, too, for I met somebody as I was coming in.

HJALMAR: Mrs. Sørby, I suppose.

HEDVIG: Yes.

HJALMAR (*pacing the floor*): I hope you have seen her for the last time.

(*Silence.* HEDVIG, *troubled, looks from one to the other in order to gauge their mood.*)

HEDVIG (*approaching* HJALMAR, *ingratiatingly*): Father?

HJALMAR: All right — what is it, Hedvig?

HEDVIG: Mrs. Sørby had something for me.

HJALMAR (*halts*): For you?

HEDVIG: Yes. Something for tomorrow.

GINA: Bertha always brings you a little something for your birthday.

HJALMAR: What is it?

HEDVIG: No, you're not to find out now. Mother is to give it to me in the morning, when she brings me breakfast in bed.

HJALMAR: What is all this mystification that I am to be kept in the dark about!

HEDVIG (*quickly*): I'll be glad to let you see it, father. It's a big letter. (*Takes the letter out of her coat pocket.*)

HJALMAR: A letter too?

HEDVIG: The letter is all there is. I suppose the other thing will come later. Just think — a letter! I never got a letter before. And it says "Miss" on the outside of it. (*Reads.*) "Miss Hedvig Ekdal." Just think — that's me!

HJALMAR: Let me see that letter.

HEDVIG: Here you are. (*Hands it to him.*)

HJALMAR: It's Werle's handwriting.

GINA: Are you sure, Ekdal?

HJALMAR: See for yourself.

GINA: How would I know?

HJALMAR: Hedvig? May I open the letter? Read it?

HEDVIG: If you like.

GINA: Not tonight, Ekdal. It's supposed to be for tomorrow.

HEDVIG (*in a low voice*): Please let him read it! It's bound to be something nice, and then father will be in a good mood, and everything will be pleasant again.

HJALMAR: You say I may open it?

HEDVIG: Yes, please, father. I'd like to know what it is about, too.

HJALMAR: Good. (*Opens the envelope, reads the letter inside. Appears confused.*) What *is* this — ?

GINA: What does it say?

HEDVIG: Please, father — tell us!

HJALMAR: Be quiet. (*Reads the letter again. He is pale, but his voice is controlled.*) It is a gift letter, Hedvig.

HEDVIG: Imagine! What is it I get?

HJALMAR: Read for yourself.

(HEDVIG *goes over to the lamp and reads.*)

HJALMAR (*in a low voice, clenches his fists*): The eyes, the eyes! And now that letter!

HEDVIG (*interrupting his reading*): Seems to me like it's Grandpa who gets it.

HJALMAR (*taking the letter away from her*): You, Gina — can you make any sense out of this?

GINA: I don't know a blessed thing about it. Why don't you just tell me?

HJALMAR: Werle writes to Hedvig that her old grandfather no longer needs to trouble himself with the copying work he has been doing, but that he may go to the office every month and draw one hundred crowns —

GREGERS: Aha!

HEDVIG: One hundred crowns, mother! I read that.

GINA: That will be nice for Grandpa.

HJALMAR: — one hundred crowns for as long as he needs it. That means, of course, till he closes his eyes.

GINA: So *he* is all taken care of, poor soul.

HJALMAR: Then it comes. You can't have read that far, Hedvig. After his death, that money will be yours.

HEDVIG: Mine? All of it?

HJALMAR: He writes that the same amount has been set aside for you for the rest of your life. Are you listening, Gina?

GINA: Yes, I hear.

HEDVIG: Just think — all the money I'll be getting! (*Shaking* HJALMAR's *arm*.) Father! Father! But aren't you glad?

HJALMAR (*going away from her*): Glad! (*Walking about*.) Oh what vistas, what perspectives, open up before me! It is Hedvig he is so generous to!

GINA: Well, she's the one with the birthday.

HEDVIG: And of course you will get it anyway, father! Don't you know I'll give it all to you and mother?

HJALMAR: To mother, yes! That's just it!

GREGERS: Hjalmar, this is a trap being prepared for you.

HJALMAR: You think this may be another trap?

GREGERS: When he was here this morning, he said, "Hjalmar Ekdal is not the man you think he is."

HJALMAR: Not the man — !

GREGERS: "You just wait and see," he said.

HJALMAR: You were to see me selling myself for money — !

HEDVIG: Mother, what *is* all this?

GINA: Go out and take your wraps off.

(HEDVIG, *about to cry, goes out into the kitchen*.)

GREGERS: Well, Hjalmar — now we shall see who is right — he or I.

HJALMAR (*slowly tearing the letter in two, putting the pieces down on the table*): Here is my answer.

GREGERS: Just as I thought.

HJALMAR (*to* GINA, *who is standing near the stove; in a low voice*): No more concealment now. If everything was over between you and him when you — came to care for me, as you call it, then why did he make it possible for us to get married?

GINA: I guess he thought he'd make free of the house.

HJALMAR: Just that? He wasn't worried about a certain possibility?

GINA: I don't know what you're talking about.

HJALMAR: I want to know — if your child has the right to live under my roof.

GINA (*drawing herself up, her eyes flashing*): You ask me that!

HJALMAR: Just tell me one thing. Is Hedvig mine or — ? — Well?

GINA (*looks at him with cold defiance*): I don't know.

HJALMAR (*with a slight tremble*): You don't know!

GINA: How can I? A woman like me!

HJALMAR (*quietly, turning away from her*): In that case I have nothing more to do in this house.

GREGERS: Think it over, Hjalmar!

HJALMAR (*putting his overcoat on*): For a man like me there is nothing to think over.

GREGERS: Yes, there is ever so much to think over. You three must stay together if you are to attain to the sacrificial spirit of sublime forgivingness.

HJALMAR: I don't want to attain it! Never! Never! My hat! (*Takes his hat.*) My house is in ruins about me. (*Bursts out crying.*) Gregers! I have no child!

HEDVIG (*who has opened the kitchen door*): Father! What are you saying!

GINA: Oh dear!

HJALMAR: Don't come near me, Hedvig! Go far away from me. I can't stand looking at you. Oh those eyes — ! Goodbye. (*Is about to go out.*)

HEDVIG (*clings to him, cries*): No! No! Don't leave me!

GINA: Look at the child, Ekdal! Look at the child!

HJALMAR: I will not! I cannot! I must get out — away from all this! (*He tears himself loose from* HEDVIG *and exits.*)

HEDVIG (*her eyes desperate*): He's leaving us, mother! He's leaving us! He'll never come back!

GINA: Just don't cry, Hedvig. Father will be back. You wait.

HEDVIG (*throws herself sobbing down on the sofa*): No! No! He'll never come back to us any more!

GREGERS: Do you believe I meant all for the best, Mrs. Ekdal?

GINA: Yes, I suppose you did, but God forgive you all the same.

HEDVIG (*on the sofa*): I want to die! What have I done to him, mother? You just have to get him back again!

GINA: Yes, yes, yes; only be quiet. I'll go out and look for him. (*Putting on her coat.*) Perhaps he's gone down to Relling's. But you're not to lie there, bawling like that. Promise?

HEDVIG (*sobbing convulsively*): All right, I'll stop, if only father comes home again.

GREGERS (*to* GINA, *who is leaving*): But would it not be better to let him fight his agony through by himself?

GINA: He can do that afterwards. First we've got to get the child quieted down. (*Goes out.*)

HEDVIG (*sitting up, drying her eyes*): Now you have to tell me what this is all about. Why doesn't father want me any more?

GREGERS: You must not ask that till you're big and grown-up.

HEDVIG (*sobbing*): But I just can't stay as miserable as this all the time till I'm grown up. — But I know what it is. Maybe I'm not really father's child.

GREGERS (*uneasily*): How could that be?

HEDVIG: Mother might have found me. And now perhaps father has found out about it. I have read about things like that.

GREGERS: Well, if it really were so —

HEDVIG: I think he could love me just as much, regardless. More, almost. The wild duck is a gift, too, and I love her very, very much.

GREGERS (*glad to turn the conversation*): Oh yes, the wild duck. Let's talk about the wild duck, Hedvig.

HEDVIG: That poor wild duck. He can't stand the sight of her, either. Just think, he wants to wring her neck!

GREGERS: Oh, I don't think he'll do that.

HEDVIG: No, but he said it. And I think that was horrid of father, for I pray for the wild duck every night, that she may be kept safe from death and all that's evil.

GREGERS (*looks at her*): Do you usually say prayers at night?

HEDVIG: Yes, I do.

GREGERS: Who taught you that?

HEDVIG: Myself, for father was terribly sick once and had leeches on his neck, and then he said that death was his dread companion.

GREGERS: And — ?

HEDVIG: So I prayed for him when I went to bed. And I have done so ever since.

GREGERS: And now you pray for the wild duck, too?

HEDVIG: I thought it was best to mention her as well, for she was so sickly when we first got her.

GREGERS: Do you say morning prayers, too?

HEDVIG: Of course not.

GREGERS: Why is that so of course?

HEDVIG: Because it's light in the morning. There's not so much to be afraid of then.

GREGERS: And the wild duck you love so much — your father said he'd like to wring her neck?

HEDVIG: No, he said it would be better for him if he did, but he was going to spare her for my sake. And that was good of him.

GREGERS (*closer to her*): How would it be if you decided to sacrifice the wild duck for *his* sake?

HEDVIG (*getting up*): The wild duck!

GREGERS: What if you willingly gave up the dearest thing in the whole world for him?

HEDVIG: Do you think that would help?

GREGERS: Try it, Hedvig.

HEDVIG (*softly, with shining eyes*): Yes. I want to.

GREGERS: Do you think you have the right kind of strength for doing it?

HEDVIG: I shall ask Grandpa to shoot the wild duck for me.

GREGERS: Yes, do that. But not a word to your mother about this!

HEDVIG: Why not?

GREGERS: She doesn't understand us.

HEDVIG: The wild duck? I'll try it in the morning!

(GINA *enters from the hall.*)

HEDVIG (*towards her*): Did you find him, mother?

GINA: No, but I found out he's got Relling with him.

GREGERS: Are you sure?

GINA: Yes, the janitor's wife said so. Molvik's with them also.

GREGERS: Just now, when his soul so sorely needs to struggle in solitude — !

GINA (*taking off her coat*): Yes, men are funny. God knows where Relling is taking him! I ran over to Madam Eriksen's, but they aren't there.

HEDVIG (*struggling with her tears*): What if he never comes back!

GREGERS: He'll come back. I'll get word to him tomorrow, and then you'll see *how* he comes back. You count on that, Hedvig, and get a good night's sleep. Goodnight. (*Goes out.*)

HEDVIG (*throws herself sobbing on* GINA's *neck*): Mother! Mother!

GINA (*patting her back, sighing*): Yes, Relling was right. This is what happens when crazy people come around pestering us with the claim of the ordeal.

ACT V

(*The studio. Cold, gray morning light. There is wet snow on the big panes of the skylight.*

GINA, *aproned, with broom and dust cloth in her hand, enters from the kitchen and goes towards the living room door.* HEDVIG *hurries in from the outside at the same moment.*)

GINA (*stops*): Well?

HEDVIG: Yes, mother, I almost think he's down at Relling's —

GINA: What did I tell you!

HEDVIG: — for the janitor's wife said she heard Relling bring two others home with him last night.

GINA: I knew it.

HEDVIG: But what good does it do, if he doesn't come up here to us?

GINA: I want to go down and have a talk with him, anyway.

(OLD EKDAL, *in dressing gown and slippers and with his lighted pipe, appears in the door to his room.*)

EKDAL: Eh — Hjalmar — ? Isn't Hjalmar here?

GINA: No, he is out, Grandpa.

EKDAL: So early? In this blizzard? Well, I can walk by myself in the morning, I can, if it comes to that.

(*He slides the attic door open.* HEDVIG *helps him. He enters. She closes the door behind him.*)

HEDVIG (*in a low voice*): Mother, what do you think will happen when poor Grandpa hears that father has left us?

GINA: Silly! Grandpa mustn't hear anything about it, of course. It was a good thing he wasn't home last night, during all that hullaballoo.

HEDVIG: Yes, but —

(GREGERS *enters.*)

GREGERS: Well? Have you traced him yet?

GINA: They say he's down at Relling's.

GREGERS: At Relling's! Has he really been out with those two?

GINA: It looks like it.

GREGERS: But he is so badly in need of solitude — to find himself in earnest —

GINA: Yes. I should think so, too.

(RELLING *enters.*)

HEDVIG (*goes towards him*): Is father with you?

GINA (*at the same time*): Is he down there?

RELLING: He certainly is.

HEDVIG: And you haven't told us!

RELLING: I know. I am a big, bad beast. But I had this other big, bad beast to take care of, too — I mean the demonic one. And after that, I just fell asleep — sound asleep —

GINA: What does Ekdal say today?

RELLING: Not a thing.

HEDVIG: Doesn't he say anything at all?

RELLING: Not a blessed word.

GREGERS: I think I understand that.

GINA: But what is he doing?

RELLING: He is on the sofa, snoring.

GINA: Oh. Yes, Ekdal does snore a lot.

HEDVIG: He's asleep? Can he sleep now?

RELLING: It certainly looks that way.

GREGERS: That's reasonable enough, after the spiritual turmoil he's just been through —

GINA: And he isn't used to be out revelling nights, either.

HEDVIG: It may be a good thing that he is sleeping, mother.

GINA: That's what I am thinking. Anyway, we'd better not wake him up too soon. Thank you, Relling. First of all I've got to clean things up a bit and make the place look nice. Come and help me, Hedvig. (*They go into the living room.*)

GREGERS (*turning to* RELLING): Can you account for the present spiritual unrest in Hjalmar Ekdal?

RELLING: To tell you the truth, I haven't noticed any spiritual unrest in him.

GREGERS: What? At such a turning point — When his whole life is acquiring a new basis? How can you think that a personality like Hjalmar Ekdal — ?

RELLING: Personality? He? If he ever had any tendency to sprout the kind of abnormal growth you call personality, I can assure you that all roots and tendrils were thoroughly extirpated in his boyhood.

GREGERS: That would indeed be strange, considering the loving upbringing he enjoyed.

RELLING: By those two crackpot, hysterical spinster aunts of his, you mean?

GREGERS: Let me tell you that they were women who never forgot the claim of the ideal — though I suppose you'll just be making fun of me again.

RELLING: No, I'm not in the mood. I do know about them, though. He has often enough held forth about "his soul's two mothers." Personally, I don't think he has much to be grateful to them for. Ekdal's misfortune is that he has always been looked upon as a shining light in his own circle.

GREGERS: And you don't think he is that? I mean, when it comes to depth of soul?

RELLING: I have never noticed it. That his father thought so is one thing. The old lieutenant has been an idiot all his days.

GREGERS: He has all his days been a man with a childlike mind. That is what you don't understand.

RELLING: All right. But after dear, sweet Hjalmar had taken up studying — after a fashion — right away he was the light of the future among his friends, too. He was handsome enough, the rascal — red and white, just the way little shop-girls like the fellows. And he had this sentimental temperament and this warm-hearted voice, and he could give such pretty declamations of other people's poetry and other people's thoughts —

GREGERS (*indignantly*): Is this Hjalmar Ekdal you are describing?

RELLING: Yes, if you please. For this is what he looks like on the inside, the idol you are prostrating yourself for.

GREGERS: I didn't know I was as blind as all that.

RELLING: Well — not far from it. For you are sick, too, you see.

GREGERS: That is true.

RELLING: Yes it is. And yours is a complicated case. First, there is this pesky integrity fever you're suffering from, and then something worse — you are forever walking around in a delirium of adoration, always looking for something to admire outside of yourself.

GREGERS: Yes, there certainly wouldn't be much point in looking for it within myself.

RELLING: But you are always so hideously wrong about all those big, wonderful flies you see and hear buzzing around you. Once again you have entered a cottage with your claim of the ideal. People here just can't pay.

GREGERS: If this is the way you think of Hjalmar Ekdal, what sort of pleasure can you derive from your constant association with him?

RELLING: Oh well. I am supposed to be a kind of doctor, believe it or not, so the least I can do is to look after the poor patients I share quarters with.

GREGERS: Ah, I see. Hjalmar Ekdal is sick, too?

RELLING: Most people are, worse luck.

GREGERS: And what treatment do you apply in Hjalmar's case?

RELLING: My usual one. I see to it that his vital lie is kept up.

GREGERS: Vital — lie? I am not sure I heard what you said.

RELLING: That's right. I said the vital lie. You see, that's the stimulating principle.

GREGERS: May I ask with what vital lie you have infected Hjalmar?

RELLING: You may not. I never reveal professional secrets to quacks. You are capable of messing him up for me even more than you have. But the method is proven. I have used it with Molvik, too. I have made him demonic. That's the suppurative I have applied to *his* neck.

GREGERS: But *isn't* he demonic?

RELLING: What the hell does it mean — being demonic? It's just some nonsense I thought of to save his life. If I hadn't, the poor, pitiful swine would have succumbed to self-hatred and despair many a year ago. Not to mention the old lieutenant! Though he has found his own cure.

GREGERS: Lieutenant Ekdal? What about him?

RELLING: What do you think? There he is, the old slayer of bears, chasing rabbits in a dark attic. And yet, there isn't a happier hunter alive than that old man when he is playing with all that junk. The four or five dried-out Christmas trees he has saved are the whole big, wild Høydal forest to him. The rooster and the chickens are wild fowl in the tree tops, and the rabbits bouncing about on the floor are bears he's grappling with — the frisky old sportsman.

GREGERS: Ah, yes — that unfortunate old Lieutenant Ekdal. He has certainly had to compromise the ideals of his youth.

RELLING: While I think of it, Mr. Werle — don't use the foreign word "ideals." We have available a good native one: "lies."

GREGERS: You think the two things are related?

RELLING: About as closely as typhus and putrid fever.

GREGERS: Doctor Relling! I won't give up till I have rescued Hjalmar from your clutches!

RELLING: That might be his bad luck. Take his vital lie away from the average person, and you take his happiness, too. (*To* HEDVIG, *who enters from the living room.*) Well, now, little duck mother. I am going down to see if papa is still in bed pondering that wonderful invention of his. (*Goes out.*)

GREGERS (*approaching* HEDVIG): I can tell from looking at you that it has not yet been accomplished.

HEDVIG: What? Oh, that about the wild duck? No.

GREGERS: Your strength of purpose deserted you, I suppose, when the time for action had come.

HEDVIG: No, it wasn't that. But when I woke up this morning and remembered what we had talked about, it all seemed so strange.

GREGERS: Strange?

HEDVIG: Yes, I don't know — Last night, just at the time — I thought there was something very wonderful about it, but when I had slept and I thought about it again, it didn't seem like anything much.

GREGERS: I see. I could hardly expect you to grow up in this environment without injury to your soul.

HEDVIG: I don't care about that, if only father would come home again.

GREGERS: If only your eyes were opened to what gives life its worth — if only you possessed the true, joyful, brave, sacrificial spirit, then you'd see he'll return. But I still have faith in you, Hedvig. (*Goes out.*)

(HEDVIG *walks around aimlessly. She is about to enter the kitchen, when there is a knock on the inside of the door to the attic.* HEDVIG *opens the doors wide enough for* OLD EKDAL *to come out. She shuts them again.*)

EKDAL: H'm. Not much fun taking a walk by yourself, y'know.

HEDVIG: Wouldn't you like to go hunting, Grandpa?

EKDAL: It isn't hunting weather today. Too dark. Can hardly see a thing.

HEDVIG: Don't you ever want to shoot something beside rabbits?

EKDAL: Aren't the rabbits good enough, perhaps?

HEDVIG: Yes, but what about the wild duck?

EKDAL: Haw! So you're scared I'll shoot your wild duck? I'll never do that, Hedvig. Never.

HEDVIG: No, for I bet you don't know how. I've heard it's difficult to shoot wild ducks.

EKDAL: Don't know how! Should say I do!

HEDVIG: How would you do it, Grandpa? — I don't mean *my* wild duck, but another one.

EKDAL: Would try to get a shot in just below the breast; that's the best place. And try to shoot *against* the feathers, not *with*.

HEDVIG: Then they die?

EKDAL: Damn right they do — if you shoot right. — Well, better go in and dress up. H'm. Y'know. H'm — (*Goes into his own room.*)

(HEDVIG *waits a moment, glances towards the living room door, stands on tiptoe, takes the double-barreled pistol down from the shelf, looks at it.* GINA, *with broom and dust cloth, enters from the living room.* HEDVIG *quickly puts the pistol back, without* GINA'S *noticing.*)

GINA: Don't fool with father's things, Hedvig.

HEDVIG (*leaving the shelf*): I just wanted to straighten up some.

GINA: Why don't you go into the kitchen and see if the coffee is keeping hot? I am taking a tray with me when I go down.

(HEDVIG *goes into the kitchen.* GINA *starts putting the studio in order. After a short while, the door to the outside is hesitantly opened and* HJALMAR *looks in. He is wearing a coat but no hat. He looks unkempt and unwashed. His eyes are dull and luster-less.*)

GINA (*stands staring at him, still with the broom in her hand*): Bless you, Ekdal — so you did come back, after all!

HJALMAR (*enters, answers in a dull voice*): I return — only to leave.

GINA: Yes, yes, I suppose. But good Lord! how you look!

HJALMAR: Look?

GINA: And your nice winter coat? I'd say that's done for.

HEDVIG (*in the kitchen door*): Mother, don't you want me to — (*sees* HJALMAR, *gives a shout of joy and runs towards him.*) Father! Father!

HJALMAR (*turning away, with a gesture*): Go away! Go away! (*To* GINA.) Get her away from me, I say!

GINA (*in a low voice*): Go into the living room, Hedvig.

(HEDVIG *leaves silently.*)

HJALMAR (*busy, pulling out the table drawer*): I need my books with me. Where are my books?

GINA: Which books?

HJALMAR: My scientific works, of course — the technical journals I need for my invention.

GINA (*looking on the shelf*): Do you mean these over here, with no covers on them?

HJALMAR: Yes, yes, of course.

GINA (*puts a pile of journals down on the table*): Don't you want me to get Hedvig to cut them open for you?

HJALMAR: No. Nobody needs to cut any pages for me.

(*Brief silence.*)

GINA: So you *are* going to leave us, Ekdal?

HJALMAR (*rummaging among the books*): That goes without saying, I should think.

GINA: All right.

HJALMAR (*violently*): For you can hardly expect me to want to stay where my heart is pierced every single hour of the day!

GINA: God forgive you for thinking so bad of me!

HJALMAR: Proof — !

GINA: Seems to me, you're the one who should bring proof.

HJALMAR: After a past like yours? There are certain claims — I might call them the claims of the ideal —

GINA: What about Grandpa? What is *he* going to do, poor man?

HJALMAR: I know my duty. The helpless one goes with me. I'll go out and make arrangements — H'm (*Hesitantly.*) Has anybody found my hat on the stairs?

GINA: No. Have you lost your hat?

HJALMAR: I most certainly had it on when I came home last night; there isn't the slightest doubt about that. But now I can't find it.

GINA: Good Lord! Where did you go with those two drunks?

HJALMAR: Oh, don't ask about inessentials. Do you think I'm in a mood for remembering details?

GINA: I only hope you haven't got a cold, Ekdal (*Goes into the kitchen.*)

HJALMAR (*speaking to himself, in a low voice, angrily, as he empties the drawer*): You're a scoundrel, Relling! — A villain is what you are! — Miserable traitor! — I'd gladly see you assassinated — !

(*He puts aside some old letters, discovers the torn gift letter from the day before, picks it up and looks at the two pieces, puts them down quickly as* GINA *enters.*)

GINA (*putting a tray with food down on the table*): Here's a drop of coffee, if you want it. And some salt meat sandwiches.

HJALMAR (*glancing at the tray*): Salt meat? Never under this roof! True it is, I haven't taken solid nourishment for almost twenty-four hours, but that can't be helped. — My notes! My incipient memoirs! Where is my diary — all my important papers! (*Opens the door to the living room, but steps back.*) If she isn't there, too!

GINA: Heavens, Ekdal. She's got to be somewhere.

HJALMAR: Leave! (*He makes room.* HEDVIG, *scared, enters the studio. With his hand on the door knob; to* GINA.) During the last moments I spend in my former home I wish to be spared the sight of intruders — (*Enters the living room.*)

HEDVIG (*starts, asks her mother in a low and trembling voice*): Does that mean me?

GINA: Stay in the kitchen, Hedvig, or no — go to your own room. (*To* HJALMAR, *as she enters the living room.*) Wait a minute, Ekdal. Don't make such a mess in the dresser. I know where everything is.

HEDVIG (*remains motionless for a moment, in helpless fright, presses her lips together not to cry, clenches her hands, whispers*): The wild duck!

(*She tiptoes over to the shelf and takes the pistol down, opens the doors to the inner attic, goes inside, closes behind her.* HJALMAR *and* GINA *are heard talking in the living room.*)

HJALMAR (*appears with some notebooks and a pile of old papers, which he puts down on the table*): The bag obviously won't be enough. There are thousands of things I need to take with me!

GINA (*entering with the bag*): Can't you leave most of it behind for the time being and just pick up a clean shirt and some underwear?

HJALMAR: Phew — ! These exhausting preparations — ! (*Takes off his overcoat and throws it on the sofa.*)

GINA: And there's the coffee getting cold too.

HJALMAR: H'm. (*Without thinking, he takes a sip, and then another one.*)

GINA (*dusting off the back of chairs*): How are you ever going to find a large enough attic for the rabbits?

HJALMAR: You mean I have to drag all those rabbits along, too?

GINA: Grandpa can't do without his rabbits — you know that as well as I do.

HJALMAR: He'll have to get used to that. I shall have to give up higher values in life than a bunch of rabbits.

GINA (*dusting off the shelf*): Shall I put the flute in for you?

HJALMAR: No. No flute for me. But give me my pistol.

GINA: You want that old pestol?

HJALMAR: Yes. My loaded pistol.

GINA (*looking for it*): It's gone. He must have taken it inside with him.

HJALMAR: Is he in the attic?

GINA: Sure, he's in the attic.

HJALMAR: H'm. The lonely grayhead — (*He eats a sandwich, empties his cup of coffee.*)

GINA: If only we hadn't rented that room, you could have moved in there.

HJALMAR: And stay under the same roof as — ! Never! Never again!

GINA: But couldn't you stay in the living room for a day or two? There you'd have everything to yourself.

HJALMAR: Not within these walls!

GINA: How about down at Relling's and Molvik's, then?

HJALMAR: Don't mention their names to me! I get sick just thinking about them. Oh no — it's out into the wind and the snowdrifts for me — to walk from house to house seeking shelter for father and myself.

GINA: But you have no hat, Ekdal! You've lost your hat, remember?

HJALMAR: Oh, those two abominations! Rich in nothing but every vice! A hat must be procured. (*Takes another sandwich.*) Arrangements must be made. After all, I don't intend to catch my death. (*Looks for something on the tray.*)

GINA: What are you looking for?

HJALMAR: Butter.

GINA: Just a moment. (*Goes out into the kitchen.*)

HJALMAR (*shouting after her*): Oh never mind. Dry bread is good enough for me.

GINA (*bringing a plate with butter*): Here. This is supposed to be freshly churned.

(*She pours him another cup of coffee. He sits down on the sofa, puts more butter on his bread, eats and drinks in silence.*)

HJALMAR (*after a pause*): Could I, without being disturbed by anyone — and I mean *anyone* — stay in the living room for a day or two?

GINA: You certainly can, if you want to.

HJALMAR: You see, I don't know how to get all of father's things moved out on such short notice.

GINA: And there is this, too, that first you'd have to tell him that you don't want to live together with the rest of us any more.

HJALMAR (*pushing his cup away*): Yes, yes — that, too. I shall have to go into all those intricate relationships once again, to explain — I must think, I must have air to breathe, I can't bear all the burdens in one single day.

GINA: Of course not. And in such awful weather too —

HJALMAR (*moving* WERLE'S *letter*): I notice this piece of paper still lying around.

GINA: Well, I haven't touched it.

HJALMAR: Not that it concerns *me* —

GINA: I'm sure I don't expect to make use of it —

HJALMAR: Nevertheless, I suppose we shouldn't let it get completely lost. In all the fuss of moving, something might easily —

GINA: I'll take care of it, Ekdal.

HJALMAR: For the gift letter belongs to father, first of all. It's his affair whether he wants to make use of it or not.

GINA (*with a sigh*): Yes, poor old Grandpa —

HJALMAR: Just to make sure — Is there any glue?

GINA (*walks over to the shelf*): Here's a bottle.

HJALMAR: And a brush?

GINA: Here. (*Brings him both.*)

HJALMAR (*picks up a pair of scissors*): Just a strip of paper on the back — (*Cuts and glues.*) Far be it from me to lay hands on somebody else's property — least of all the property of a poverty-stricken old man. — Well — not on — that other one's, either. — There, now! Leave it to dry for a while. And when it's dry, remove it. I don't want to see that document again — ever!

(GREGERS *enters.*)

GREGERS (*a little surprised*): What? So this is where you are, Hjalmar!

HJALMAR (*quickly gets up*): Sheer exhaustion drove me to sit down.

GREGERS: And I see you've had breakfast.

HJALMAR: The body, too, makes demands at times.

GREGERS: Well, what have you decided to do?

HJALMAR: For a man like me, there is only one way open. I am in the process of gathering up my most important possessions. Obviously, that takes time.

GINA (*a trifle impatient*): Do you want me to make the living room ready for you, or do you want me to pack the bag?

HJALMAR (*after an irritated glance at* GREGERS): Pack — and make the room ready.

GINA (*picking up the bag*): All right. I'll just put in the shirts and those other things. (*She goes into the living room, closing the door behind her.*)

GREGERS (*after a short silence*): I had no idea this would be the end of it. Is it really necessary for you to leave house and home?

HJALMAR (*paces restlessly up and down*): What do you want me to do? I am not made to be unhappy, Gregers. I require peace and security and comfort around me.

GREGERS: But you can have all that, Hjalmar. Just try. It seems to me there is a firm foundation to build upon now. Start all over again. And remember, you still have your invention to live for.

HJALMAR: Oh don't talk about that invention. It may take a long time yet.

GREGERS: So?

HJALMAR: Well, yes, for heaven's sake, what do you expect me to invent, anyway? The others have invented most of it already. It's getting more difficult every day.

GREGERS: But all the labor you have put into it — ?

HJALMAR: It was that dissipated Relling who got me started on it.

GREGERS: Relling?

HJALMAR: Yes, it was he who first called attention to my talent for making some fabulous invention or other in photography.

GREGERS: I see. It was Relling — !

HJALMAR: Ah — I have been so wonderfully happy about it. Not so much about the invention itself, but because Hedvig believed in it — believed with all the strength and power of a child's soul. — That is, I *thought* she did — fool as I was.

GREGERS: Can you really think that Hedvig would be false to you?

HJALMAR: I can believe anything now. It is Hedvig who is in the way. She it is who is shutting the sun out of my entire life.

GREGERS: Hedvig? You mean Hedvig? How in the world is she going to be an obstacle?

HJALMAR (*without answering*): I have loved that child more than I can ever say. You have no idea how happy I was whenever I came back to my humble dwelling and she rushed towards me with her sweet, squinting eyes. Ha, credulous fool that I was! She was so unspeakably dear to me — and so I lulled myself into the dream that I was equally dear to her.

GREGERS: You call that a dream?

HJALMAR: How can I tell? I can't get anything out of Gina. Besides, she completely lacks any sense of the ideal aspects of the issue. But

to you I can open up, Gregers. It is this terrible doubt — perhaps
Hedvig has never really loved me.

GREGERS: Maybe you'll receive proof — (*Listens.*) Shh! What's that?
The wild duck?

HJALMAR: It's just quacking. Father's in the attic.

GREGERS: He is! (*Joy lights his face.*) I tell you again, Hjalmar —
maybe you will find proof that your poor, misunderstood Hedvig has
always loved you!

HJALMAR: Pah! What proof could she give? I dare not trust to mere
asseverations.

GREGERS: Surely, Hedvig doesn't know what deceit is.

HJALMAR: Ah, Gregers — that is just what I cannot be certain of.
Who knows what Gina and this Mrs. Sørby may have been whispering and scheming? And Hedvig's ears are big enough, believe you
me. Maybe that gift letter didn't come as such a surprise to her. It
seemed to me I noticed something like that.

GREGERS: Good heavens, Hjalmar! What kind of spirit is this that's
taken possession of you!

HJALMAR: I have had my eyes opened. You just wait. It may turn out
that the gift letter was just the beginning. Mrs. Sørby has always
been very fond of Hedvig, and now, of course, it's in her power to
do anything she likes for the child. They can take her away from me
what day and hour they choose.

GREGERS: Hedvig will never leave you, Hjalmar. Never.

HJALMAR: Don't be too sure. If they beckon her with their arms
full — ? And I who have loved her so infinitely much! I, whose
greatest joy it was to take her tenderly by the hand and lead her, as
one leads a frightened child through a dark and deserted room! Now
I feel this painful certainty that the poor photographer in his attic
has never really meant very much to her. She has only cleverly managed to keep on good terms with him while she bided her time.

GREGERS: You don't believe this, Hjalmar.

HJALMAR: That is just what is so terrible — I don't know what to believe — I'll never be able to find out! But do you really doubt that I
am right? Ah, Gregers, you put too much trust in the claim of the
ideal! If those others were to come now, with their ample offerings,
and called to the child: Leave him; life awaits you here with us —

GREGERS (*quickly*): Yes, what then — ?

HJALMAR: If then I were to ask her: Hedvig, are you willing to give
your life for me? (*Laughs scornfully.*) Oh yes — you'd find out soon
enough what answer I'd get!

(*A pistol shot is heard from within the attic.*)

GREGERS (*with a shout of joy*): Hjalmar!

HJALMAR: Must he go shooting today — !

GINA (*enters*): Can't say I like this, Ekdal — Grandpa in there all by himself, banging away.

HJALMAR: I'll take a look —

GREGERS (*agitated, feelingly*): Wait! Do you know what that was?

HJALMAR: Yes, of course, I do.

GREGERS: No, you don't. But *I* know. It was the proof!

HJALMAR: What proof?

GREGERS: It was a child's sacrifice. She has got your father to shoot the wild duck.

HJALMAR: Shoot the wild duck!

GINA: Heavens — !

HJALMAR: Whatever for?

GREGERS: She wanted to sacrifice to you what she held dearest in the whole world. For then she thought you'd love her again.

HJALMAR (*softly, moved*): Oh that child!

GINA: What she thinks of!

GREGERS: All she wanted was your love, Hjalmar. Without it, life didn't seem possible to her.

GINA (*struggling with tears*): Now, do you see, Ekdal?

HJALMAR: Gina, where is she?

GINA (*sniffling*): Poor thing. She is sitting out in the kitchen, I guess.

HJALMAR (*walks to the kitchen door, flings it open, says*): Hedvig — come! Come to me! (*Looks around.*) No. She isn't here.

GINA: Then she must be in her own room.

HJALMAR (*offstage*): No, she isn't there, either. (*Re-entering the studio.*) She must have gone out.

GINA: Yes, for you know you didn't want to see hide nor hair of her in the house.

HJALMAR: If only she'd come back soon — so I can tell her — Now I feel that everything will be all right, Gregers. Now I think we can start life over again.

GREGERS (*quietly*): I knew it. Restitution would come through the child.

(*Old* EKDAL *appears in the door to his room. He is in full uniform and is buckling on his sabre.*)

HJALMAR (*surprised*): Father! You're in there!

GINA: Do you go shooting in your room, now, Grandpa?

EKDAL (*approaches indignantly*): So you're off hunting by yourself, are you Hjalmar?

HJALMAR (*tense, confused*): You mean it wasn't you who fired that shot in the attic just now?

EKDAL: I? Fired? H'm.

GREGERS (*shouts to* HJALMAR): She has shot the wild duck herself!

HJALMAR: What *is* this? (*He hurriedly slides the attic doors open, looks in, gives a loud cry.*) Hedvig!

GINA (*runs to the door*): Oh God! What is it?

HJALMAR (*going inside*): She is lying on the floor!

GREGERS: Lying — ! (*Follows* HJALMAR *inside.*)

GINA (*at the same time*): Hedvig! (*Enters the attic.*) No! No! No!

EKDAL: Ho-ho! So *she* has taken to hunting too, now!

(HJALMAR, GINA, *and* GREGERS *drag* HEDVIG *into the studio. Her trailing right hand clasps the pistol tightly.*)

HJALMAR (*beside himself*): The pistol went off! She's hit! Call for help! Help!

GINA (*running out into the hallway, shouts down*): Relling! Relling! Doctor Relling! Hurry up here, fast as you can!

(HJALMAR *and* GREGERS *put* HEDVIG *down on the sofa.*)

EKDAL (*quietly*): The woods avenge themselves.

HJALMAR (*on his knees beside* HEDVIG): She's coming to now. She is coming to. Oh yes, yes, yes —

GINA (*having returned*): Where's she hit? I can't see a thing.

(RELLING *enters hurriedly, followed by* MOLVIK. *The latter is without vest and tie, his tailcoat thrown open.*)

RELLING: What's the matter?

GINA: They say Hedvig has shot herself.

HJALMAR: Come and help us!

RELLING: Shot herself! (*He pulls the table back and begins to examine her.*)

HJALMAR (*still on his knees, looking anxiously at* RELLING): It can't be dangerous, can it, Relling? What, Relling? She hardly bleeds at all. It can't possibly be dangerous?

RELLING: How did this happen?

HJALMAR: Oh, I don't know —

GINA: She was going to shoot the wild duck.

RELLING: The wild duck?

HJALMAR: The pistol must have gone off.

RELLING: H'm. I see.

EKDAL: The woods avenge themselves. But I'm not afraid. (*Enters the attic and closes the doors behind him.*)

HJALMAR: Relling — why don't you say anything?

RELLING: The bullet has entered her chest.

HJALMAR: Yes, but she's coming to!

RELLING: Can't you see that Hedvig is dead?

GINA (*bursts into tears*): Oh, the child, the child — !

GREGERS (*hoarsely*): In the depths of the sea —

HJALMAR (*jumps to his feet*): She must live! I want her to live! For God's sake, Relling — just for a moment — just so I can tell her how unspeakably much I have loved her all the time!

RELLING: Her heart has been pierced. Internal hemorrhage. She died instantly.

HJALMAR: And I who chased her away from me like an animal! Frightened and lonely she crawled into the attic and died for love of me. (*Sobbing.*) Never to be able to make up for it! Never to tell her — ! (*Shakes his fists upwards.*) You! You above! If thou art at all — ! Why hast thou done this unto me?

GINA: Shhh, shhh. You mustn't make such a fuss. We had no right to keep her, I suppose.

MOLVIK: The child is not dead. It sleepeth.

RELLING: Rubbish!

HJALMAR (*quieting down, walks over to the sofa, looks at* HEDVIG, *his arms crossed*): There she lies, so stiff and still.

RELLING (*trying to release the pistol*): She holds on so tightly, I can't —

GINA: No, no, Relling. Don't break her fingers. Let the pestol be.

HJALMAR: Let her have it with her.

GINA: Yes, let her. But the child isn't going to lie out here for a show. She is going into her own little room, right now. Give me a hand, Ekdal.

(HJALMAR *and* GINA *carry* HEDVIG *between them.*)

HJALMAR (*carrying*): Gina, Gina — do you think you can bear this?

GINA: The one has to help the other. Seems to me like now we both have a share in her.

MOLVIK (*raising his arms, muttering*): Praise be the Lord, to dust thou returnest, to dust thou returnest —

RELLING (*whispers*): Shut up, man! You're drunk.

(HJALMAR *and* GINA *carry* HEDVIG *through the kitchen door.* REL-LING *closes the door behind them.* MOLVIK *slinks quietly out into the hall.*)

RELLING (*goes up to* GREGERS): Nobody is going to tell me this was an accident.

GREGERS (*who has remained stunned, moving convulsively*): Who is to say how this terrible thing happened?

RELLING: There were powder burns on her dress. She must have placed the muzzle against her chest and pulled the trigger.

GREGERS: Hedvig has not died in vain. Did you notice how grief released what is great in him?

RELLING: There is a touch of greatness in most of us when we stand in sorrow by a corpse. How long do you think that will last with him?

GREGERS: As if it won't last and grow throughout the rest of his days!

RELLING: Within a year little Hedvig won't be anything to him but an occasion for spouting pretty sentiments.

GREGERS: And you dare say that about Hjalmar Ekdal!

RELLING: Let's talk about this again when the first grass has withered on her grave. You'll hear all about "the child so early taken from the father's heart." You'll see him wallow in sentimentality and self-admiration and self-pity. You just wait!

GREGERS: If you are right and I am wrong, life isn't worth living.

RELLING: Oh, life would be fairly tolerable if only we'd be spared these blasted bill collectors who come around pestering us paupers with the claim of the ideal.

GREGERS (*staring ahead*): In that case I am glad my destiny is what it is.

RELLING: Beg your pardon — what *is* your destiny?

GREGERS (*about to leave*): To be the thirteenth man at the table.

RELLING: The hell it is.

LIKE ALL of Ibsen's later plays, *The Wild Duck* appeared in book form (in 1884) before it was staged. Its earliest readers and audiences found it obscure and morbid, but its reputation has since risen. Today it is generally considered one of Ibsen's greatest plays in prose. Though for some critics this is not saying very much, the play's status is nevertheless remarkable, in view of its technical imperfections. The old romance between Mrs. Sørby and Dr. Relling is a plot excrescence, and Old Ekdal's vengeful woods introduce a note of irrelevant melodrama, but its gravest defect is Hjalmar Ekdal's character. Splendid though he is with beer and chamberlains, at times he lapses into mere caricature. So, one might say, do Molière's Tartuffe and Orgon, but Molière can get away with what Ibsen cannot, for Ibsen, unlike Molière, writes in the naturalistic convention which puts a premium on plausibility of character and incident. It is hard to accept Gregers Werle's continuing faith in the greatness of a man who almost without stop reveals his phoniness (sincere phoniness though it is). Gregers may be sick, but he is not stupid.

For most critics, however, the play survives its imperfections. It may illuminate the sources of strength of naturalistic drama in general to try to answer why.

The Wild Duck stays close to Ibsen's usual pattern. A friend (sometimes a member) of a middle-class family returns after long absence and by his return triggers disastrous revelations. The action is nearly all exposition — the gradual discovery of the painful truth about the past concealed in the family's decorous and complacent present. We recognize the pattern from *Oedipus Rex*, and *The Wild Duck* does in fact share with Sophocles' play a tightness of structure, a concentration of meaningful events in small compass of time and space, made possible by the playwright's seizure of his story near its climax. The plot is a looking-back on the past responsible for the crisis in the present. It is drama of ripe condition, a "fifth act play" compared with the panoramic, expansive, chronologically developed Shakespearean drama.

But aside from its retrospective structure, *The Wild Duck* has little in common with classical tragedy. No kingdom trembles when Hjalmar Ekdal is in agony. He is too negligible to be the concern of gods, too meanly petty to be even wicked. Beside the language of traditional tragedy, dialogue here is small talk indeed and Hjalmar's eloquence merely absurd. The Ekdal studio is a small and shrunken world — banal, pathetic, ridiculous. But can it not be argued that the inapplicability of the yardstick of great tragedy to *The Wild Duck* is less a comment on the play than on modern man and his values?

If *The Wild Duck* is not in the tragic tradition, neither does it belong with those pat, once shocking, now commonplace, social messages that date such a large part of naturalistic drama of the last and this century, exposés of skeletons, today more dead than fearful, in Victorian closets. In the plays immediately preceding *The Wild Duck* Ibsen had dramatized the damage that contemporary institutions and attitudes were doing to the individual's self-realization, happiness, and integrity. But most people resented what they took to be Ibsen's attack on the entrenched sanctities of religion and marriage and majority rule and were scandalized by his reference (in *Ghosts*) to venereal disease. *The Wild Duck* records, with deceptive blandness, the meaning of the public reaction to its author's crusade for freedom and truth: most people not only don't want the truth about themselves; they are much better off with comfortable lies. Its mood is delicately balanced between two contrasting statements of the same single fact about man: Swift's virulent irony (in *A Tale of a Tub*) in defining "the sublime and refined point of felicity" as "the possession of being well deceived" and the compassionate excuse for the grieving women of Canterbury that T. S. Eliot puts into the mouth of Saint Thomas à Becket in *Murder in the Cathedral:* "Human kind cannot bear very much reality." Together with *An Enemy of the People, The Wild Duck* demonstrates Ibsen's near compulsive habit of seeing every issue from opposite sides. In the earlier play he had put much of himself into Dr. Stockman, the hearty, indomitable fighter for truth. Here he seems to parody his own reforming self in the character of the gloomy, neurotic Gregers Werle, whose officious mission of truth ends in a child's death.

But the play never surrenders the ambiguities of its precarious poise between tragedy and farce, pathos and cynicism, pity and laughter. It is skeptical and relativistic, not doctrinaire. For if it existed for the sake of telling us that everyman's happiness depends on illusion, then its spokesman appears oddly chosen. Dr. Relling, the common-sensical realist, is pretty much of a human wreck. To Mrs. Sørby, the play's most sensible character, he is a man who has "thrown away what is best in himself." He does not enter the play till it is more than half over — a late entrance for a protagonist. Though the action may be defined as the conflict between Relling and Gregers Werle for control over Hjalmar Ekdal, Relling never really occupies the center of the play; he remains a commentator rather than participant — chorus, not hero. The principle of "the vital lie," with which he is associated, is not a major plot issue, for only incidentally does Hedvig kill herself in order to restore her father's faith in his invention. In short, to see Relling as protagonist opposite Gregers's antagonist and to equate the play with his much-quoted piece of psychological wisdom, "Take his vital lie away from the average person, and you take his happiness, too," is to shatter the ambiguities inherent in his flawed personality and inferior plot position and, for that matter, in the shoddiness of his well intentioned formula for adjustment. The fact that he has the last word hardly settles any issues. At stake between him and Gregers is the Ekdal happiness. Truth conquers the protective lie, and the result, ironically, is disaster for the one innocent and wholly lovable character in the entire household. And as if to keep us from extracting any ulterior significance from these sordid events, Ibsen ends his play by having Relling's profanity explode the pretentious melodramatics of Gregers's belief — *his* vital lie — that he is the superfluous man, tragically chosen by destiny to bring bad luck to others. The play insists on its own meaninglessness.

Nor is its symbolism reducible to some simple formula for social or mental health. It teases. It doesn't teach. The wild duck, the play's major symbol, offers endless game for interpretive ingenuity.

What does it stand for? Escape from reality? Wounded innocence? The guilty past? Whom does it represent — and *for* whom? Gregers thinks Hjalmar is a wild duck, but aren't there ways in which the duck could be said to symbolize not only Molvik and Old Ekdal, but Hedvig and even Gregers himself, as well? May we ignore Relling's reference to Gina's "comfortable waddle?"

Perhaps all this is only to say that "meaning" in *The Wild Duck* is not to be sought in a concept but in such realities as Old Ekdal's reluctance to use the pronoun "I," in Hjalmar's uncut technical journals, in Gina's infinitely patient and competent housekeeping. Before the wild duck is anything else it is part of the Ekdal establishment — an object as real as the photographs and the flute and the herring salad. It presides in the attic world of fantasy and escape, a denizen of the depths of the sea, content among the shipwrecked skipper's assorted belongings. It is one of Ibsen's triumphs that the whole unlikely contrivance of the barnyard attic is both believable as solid fact and rich and beautiful in its suggestiveness. It convinces because it is comical and pitiful, haunting and bizarre, all at the same time. By defining the attitudes of the different members of the household to the attic one can both grasp the play's major unifying image and go a long way toward understanding the characters and their position vis à vis the issue of reality versus illusion. There is a poetry of naturalism, generated when human feeling impinges upon the commonplace. The Ekdal attic is an instance.

And it is not true that the stage language of naturalism banished poetry from the theater. There is in *The Wild Duck* careful organization of words for esthetic purposes. In addition to having a utilitarian value in suggesting milieu and in setting off Hjalmar's excursions into oratory, the drab dialogue also reveals subterranean levels of imagery that bear upon theme and character. The allusions to sight and blindness, darkness and light, that weave in and out of Hjalmar's and Gregers' speeches, reinforce the blindness motif in the plot and achieve effects of mordant irony: Gregers rejecting Relling's accurate estimate of Hjalmar's character with the words, "I didn't know I was as blind as all that"; Hjalmar refusing to "look at the child" after "he has had his eyes opened."

By visual imagination and verbal ironies *The Wild Duck* transcends the triviality of a snapshot of middle-class life and the simpleminded shrillness of a social tract. What it attains is neither tragedy's sublime affirmation of man's significance in a dark world, nor the proved lesson of the documentary thesis play, but a compassionate, unsentimental vision of small people suffering under the high price of truth.)

Bernard Shaw

ARMS AND THE MAN

A Pleasant Play

Characters

RAINA PETKOFF, *a young Bulgarian lady*
CATHERINE PETKOFF, *her mother*
LOUKA, *the Petkoffs' maid*
CAPTAIN BLUNTSCHLI, *a Swiss officer in the Serbian army*
A RUSSIAN OFFICER *in the Bulgarian army*
NICOLA, *the Petkoffs' butler*
PETKOFF, *Raina's father, a major in the Bulgarian army*
SERGIUS SARANOFF, *Raina's fiancé, a major in the Bulgarian army*

ACT I

(*Night: A lady's bedchamber in Bulgaria, in a small town near the Dragoman Pass, late in November in the year 1885. Through an open window with a little balcony a peak of the Balkans, wonderfully white and beautiful in the starlit snow, seems quite close at hand, though it is really miles away. The interior of the room is not like anything to be seen in the west of Europe. It is half rich Bulgarian, half cheap Viennese. Above the head of the bed, which stands against a little wall cutting off the left hand corner of the room, is a painted wooden shrine, blue and gold, with an ivory image of Christ, and a light hanging before it in a pierced metal ball suspended by three chains. The principal seat, placed towards the other side of the room and opposite the window, is a Turkish ottoman. The counterpane and hangings of the bed, the window curtains, the little carpet, and all the ornamental textile fabrics in the room are oriental and gorgeous; the paper on the walls is occidental and paltry. The washstand, against the wall on the side nearest the ottoman and window, consists of an enamelled iron basin with a pail beneath it in a painted metal frame, and a single towel on the rail at the side. The dressing table, between the bed and the window, is a common pine table, covered with a cloth of many colours, with an expensive toilet mirror on it. The door is on the side nearest the bed; and there is a chest of drawers between. This chest of drawers is also covered by a variegated native cloth; and on it there is a pile of paper backed novels, a box of chocolate creams, and a miniature easel with a large photograph of an extremely handsome officer, whose lofty bearing and magnetic glance can be felt even from the portrait. The room is lighted by a candle on the chest of drawers, and another on the dressing table with a box of matches beside it.*

The window is hinged doorwise and stands wide open. Outside, a pair of wooden shutters, opening outwards, also stand open. On the balcony a young lady, intensely conscious of the romantic beauty of the night, and of the fact that her own youth and beauty are part of it, is gazing at the snowy Balkans. She is in her nightgown, well covered by a long mantle of furs, worth, on a moderate estimate, about three times the furniture of the room.

Her reverie is interrupted by her mother, CATHERINE PETKOFF, *a woman over forty, imperiously energetic, with magnificent black hair and eyes, who might be a very splendid specimen of the wife of a mountain farmer, but is determined to be a Viennese lady, and to that end wears a fashionable tea gown on all occasions.)*

CATHERINE (*entering hastily, full of good news*): Raina! (*She pronounces it Rah-eena, with the stress on the ee.*) Raina! (*She goes to the bed, expecting to find* RAINA *there.*) Why, where — ?

(RAINA *looks into the room.*)

Heavens, child! are you out in the night air instead of in your bed? Youll catch your death. Louka told me you were asleep.

RAINA (*dreamily*): I sent her away. I wanted to be alone. The stars are so beautiful! What is the matter?

CATHERINE: Such news! There has been a battle.

RAINA (*her eyes dilating*): Ah! (*She comes eagerly to* CATHERINE.)

CATHERINE: A great battle at Slivnitza! A victory! And it was won by Sergius.

RAINA (*with a cry of delight*): Ah! (*They embrace rapturously.*) Oh, mother! (*Then, with sudden anxiety*) is father safe?

CATHERINE: Of course! he sends me the news. Sergius is the hero of the hour, the idol of the regiment.

RAINA: Tell me, tell me. How was it? (*Ecstatically*) Oh, mother! mother! mother! (*She pulls her mother down on the ottoman; and they kiss one another frantically.*)

CATHERINE (*with surging enthusiasm*): You cant guess how splendid it is. A cavalry charge! think of that! He defied our Russian commanders — acted without orders — led a charge on his own responsibility — headed it himself — was the first man to sweep through their guns. Cant you see it, Raina: our gallant splendid Bulgarians with their swords and eyes flashing, thundering down like an avalanche and scattering the wretched Serbs and their dandified Austrian officers like chaff. And you! you kept Sergius waiting a year before you would be betrothed to him. Oh, if you have a drop of Bulgarian blood in your veins, you will worship him when he comes back.

RAINA: What will he care for my poor little worship after the acclamations of a whole army of heroes? But no matter: I am so happy! so proud! (*She rises and walks about excitedly.*) It proves that all our ideas were real after all.

CATHERINE (*indignantly*): Our ideas real! What do you mean?

RAINA: Our ideas of what Sergius would do. Our patriotism. Our heroic ideals. I sometimes used to doubt whether they were anything but dreams. Oh, what faithless little creatures girls are! When I buckled on Sergius's sword he looked so noble: it was treason to think of disillusion or humiliation or failure. And yet — and yet — (*She sits down again suddenly.*) Promise me youll never tell him.

CATHERINE: Dont ask me for promises until I know what I'm promising.

RAINA: Well, it came into my head just as he was holding me in his arms and looking into my eyes, that perhaps we only had our heroic ideas because we are so fond of reading Byron and Pushkin, and because we were so delighted with the opera that season at Bucharest. Real life is so seldom like that! indeed never, as far as I knew it then. (*Remorsefully*) Only think, mother: I doubted him: I wondered whether all his heroic qualities and his soldiership might not prove mere imagination when he went into a real battle. I had an uneasy fear that he might cut a poor figure there beside all those clever officers from the Tsar's court.

CATHERINE: A poor figure! Shame on you! The Serbs have Austrian officers who are just as clever as the Russians; but we have beaten them in every battle for all that.

RAINA (*laughing and snuggling against her mother*): Yes: I was only a prosaic little coward. Oh, to think that it was all true! that Sergius is just as splendid and noble as he looks! that the world is really a glorious world for women who can see its glory and men who can act its romance! What happiness! what unspeakable fulfillment!

(*They are interrupted by the entry of* LOUKA, *a handsome proud girl in a pretty Bulgarian peasant's dress with double apron, so defiant that her servility to* RAINA *is almost insolent. She is afraid of* CATHERINE, *but even with her goes as far as she dares.*)

LOUKA: If you please, madam, all the windows are to be closed and the shutters made fast. They say there may be shooting in the streets.

(RAINA *and* CATHERINE *rise together, alarmed.*)

The Serbs are being chased right back through the pass; and they say they may run into the town. Our cavalry will be after them; and our people will be ready for them, you may be sure, now theyre running away. (*She goes out on the balcony, and pulls the outside shutters to; then steps back into the room.*)

CATHERINE (*businesslike, housekeeping instincts aroused*): I must see that everything is made safe downstairs.

RAINA: I wish our people were not so cruel. What glory is there in killing wretched fugitives?

CATHERINE: Cruel! Do you suppose they would hesitate to kill you — or worse?

RAINA (*to* LOUKA): Leave the shutters so that I can just close them if I hear any noise.

CATHERINE (*authoritatively, turning on her way to the door*): Oh no, dear: you must keep them fastened. You would be sure to drop off to sleep and leave them open. Make them fast, Louka.

LOUKA: Yes, madam. (*She fastens them.*)

RAINA: Dont be anxious about me. The moment I hear a shot, I shall blow out the candles and roll myself up in bed with my ears well covered.

CATHERINE: Quite the wisest thing you can do, my love. Goodnight.

RAINA: Goodnight. (*Her emotion comes back for a moment.*) Wish me joy. (*They kiss.*) This is the happiest night of my life — if only there are no fugitives.

CATHERINE: Go to bed, dear; and dont think of them. (*She goes out.*)

LOUKA (*secretly to* RAINA): If you would like the shutters open, just give them a push like this. (*She pushes them: they open: she pulls them to again.*) One of them ought to be bolted at the bottom; but the bolt's gone.

RAINA (*with dignity, reproving her*): Thanks, Louka; but we must do what we are told.

(LOUKA *makes a grimace.*)

Goodnight.

LOUKA (*carelessly*): Goodnight. (*She goes out, swaggering.*)

(RAINA, *left alone, takes off her fur cloak and throws it on the ottoman. Then she goes to the chest of drawers, and adores the portrait there with feelings that are beyond all expression. She does not kiss it or press it to her breast, or shew it any mark of bodily affection; but she takes it in her hands and elevates it, like a priestess.*)

RAINA (*looking up at the picture*): Oh, I shall never be unworthy of you any more, my soul's hero: never, never, never. (*She replaces it reverently. Then she selects a novel from the little pile of books. She turns over the leaves dreamily; finds her page; turns the book inside out at it; and, with a happy sigh, gets into bed and prepares to read herself to sleep. But before abandoning herself to fiction, she raises her eyes once more, thinking of the blessed reality, and murmurs.*) My hero! my hero!

(*A distant shot breaks the quiet of the night. She starts, listening; and two more shots, much nearer, follow, startling her so that she scrambles out of bed, and hastily blows out the candle on the chest of drawers. Then, putting her fingers in her ears, she runs to the dressing table, blows out the light there, and hurries back to bed in the dark, nothing being visible but the glimmer of the light in the pierced ball before the image, and the starlight seen through the slits at the top of the shutters. The firing breaks out again: there is a startling fusillade quite close at hand. Whilst it is still echoing, the shutters disappear, pulled open from without; and for an instant the rectangle of snowy starlight flashes out with the figure of a man silhouetted in black upon it. The shutters close immediately; and the room is dark again. But the silence is now broken by the sound of panting. Then there is a scratch; and the flame of a match is seen in the middle of the room.*)

RAINA (*crouching on the bed*): Who's there? (*The match is out instantly.*) Who's there? Who is that?

A MAN'S VOICE (*in the darkness, subduedly, but threateningly*): Sh — sh! Dont call out; or youll be shot. Be good; and no harm will happen to you.

(*She is heard leaving her bed, and making for the door.*)

Take care: it's no use trying to run away.

RAINA: But who —

THE VOICE (*warning*): Remember: if you raise your voice my revolver will go off. (*Commandingly*) Strike a light and let me see you. Do you hear?

(*Another moment of silence and darkness as she retreats to the chest of drawers. Then she lights a candle; and the mystery is at an end. He is a man of about 35, in a deplorable plight, bespattered with mud and blood and snow, his belt and the strap of his revolver case keeping together the torn ruins of the blue tunic of a Serbian artillery officer. All that the candlelight and his unwashed unkempt condition make it possible to discern is that he is of middling stature and undistinguished appearance, with strong neck and shoulders, roundish obstinate looking head covered with short crisp bronze curls, clear quick eyes and good brows and mouth, hopelessly prosaic nose like that of a strong minded baby, trim soldierlike carriage and energetic manner, and with all his wits about him in spite of his desperate predicament: even with a sense of the humor of it, without, however, the least intention of trifling with it or throwing away a chance. Reckoning up what he can guess about* RAINA: *her age, her social position, her character, and the extent to which she is frightened, he continues, more politely but still most determinedly.*)

Excuse my disturbing you; but you recognize my uniform? Serb! If I'm caught I shall be killed. (*Menacingly*) Do you understand that?

RAINA: Yes.

THE MAN: Well, I dont intend to get killed if I can help it. (*Still more formidably*) Do you understand that? (*He locks the door quickly but quietly.*)

RAINA (*disdainfully*): I suppose not. (*She draws herself up superbly, and looks him straight in the face, adding, with cutting emphasis*) Some soldiers, I know, are afraid to die.

THE MAN (*with grim goodhumor*): All of them, dear lady, all of them, believe me. It is our duty to live as long as we can. Now, if you raise an alarm —

RAINA (*cutting him short*): You will shoot me. How do you know that I am afraid to die?

THE MAN (*cunningly*): Ah; but suppose I dont shoot you, what will happen then? A lot of your cavalry will burst into this pretty room of yours and slaughter me here like a pig; for I'll fight like a demon:

they shant get me into the street to amuse themselves with: I know what they are. Are you prepared to receive that sort of company in your present undress?

(RAINA, *suddenly conscious of her nightgown, instinctively shrinks and gathers it more closely about her neck. He watches her and adds pitilessly*)

Hardly presentable, eh?

(*She turns to the ottoman. He raises his pistol instantly, and cries*)

Stop!

(*She stops.*)

Where are you going?

RAINA (*with dignified patience*): Only to get my cloak.

THE MAN (*passing swiftly to the ottoman and snatching the cloak*): A good idea! I'll keep the cloak; and youll take care that nobody comes in and sees you without it. This is a better weapon than the revolver: eh? (*He throws the pistol down on the ottoman.*)

RAINA (*revolted*): It is not the weapon of a gentleman!

THE MAN: It's good enough for a man with only you to stand between him and death. (*As they look at one another for a moment, RAINA hardly able to believe that even a Serbian officer can be so cynically and selfishly unchivalrous, they are startled by a sharp fusillade in the street. The chill of imminent death hushes the man's voice as he adds*) Do you hear? If you are going to bring those blackguards in on me you shall receive them as you are.

(*Clamor and disturbance. The pursuers in the street batter at the house door, shouting,* Open the door! Open the door! Wake up, will you! *A man servant's voice calls to them angrily from within,* This is Major Petkoff's house: you cant come in here; *but a renewal of the clamor, and a torrent of blows on the door, end with his letting a chain down with a clank, followed by a rush of heavy footsteps and a din of triumphant yells, dominated at last by the voice of* CATHERINE, *indignantly addressing an officer with* What does this mean, sir? Do you know where you are? *The noise subsides suddenly.*)

LOUKA (*outside, knocking at the bedroom door*): My lady! my lady! get up quick and open the door. If you dont they will break it down.

(*The fugitive throws up his head with the gesture of a man who sees that it is all over with him, and drops the manner he has been assuming to intimidate* RAINA.)

THE MAN (*sincerely and kindly*): No use, dear: I'm done for. (*Flinging the cloak to her*) Quick! wrap yourself up: they're coming.

RAINA: Oh, thank you. (*She wraps herself up with intense relief.*)

THE MAN (*between his teeth*): Dont mention it.

RAINA (*anxiously*): What will you do?

THE MAN (*grimly*): The first man in will find out. Keep out of the way; and dont look. It wont last long; but it will not be nice. (*He draws his sabre and faces the door, waiting.*)

RAINA (*impulsively*): I'll help you. I'll save you.

THE MAN: You cant.

RAINA: I can. I'll hide you. (*She drags him towards the window.*) Here! behind the curtains.

THE MAN (*yielding to her*): There's just half a chance, if you keep your head.

RAINA (*drawing the curtain before him*): S-sh! (*She makes for the ottoman.*)

THE MAN (*putting out his head*): Remember —

RAINA (*running back to him*): Yes?

THE MAN: — nine soldiers out of ten are born fools.

RAINA: Oh! (*She draws the curtain angrily before him.*)

THE MAN (*looking out at the other side*): If they find me, I promise you a fight: a devil of a fight.

(*She stamps at him. He disappears hastily. She takes off her cloak, and throws it across the foot of the bed. Then, with a sleepy, disturbed air, she opens the door.* LOUKA *enters excitedly.*)

LOUKA: One of those beasts of Serbs has been seen climbing up the waterpipe to your balcony. Our men want to search for him; and they are so wild and drunk and furious. (*She makes for the other side of the room to get as far from the door as possible.*) My lady says you are to dress at once and to — (*She sees the revolver lying on the ottoman, and stops, petrified.*)

RAINA (*as if annoyed at being disturbed*): They shall not search here. Why have they been let in?

CATHERINE (*coming in hastily*): Raina, darling, are you safe? Have you seen anyone or heard anything?

RAINA: I heard the shooting. Surely the soldiers will not dare come in here?

CATHERINE: I have found a Russian officer, thank Heaven: he knows

Sergius. (*Speaking through the door to someone outside*) Sir: will you come in now. My daughter will receive you.

(*A young Russian officer, in Bulgarian uniform, enters, sword in hand.*)

OFFICER (*with soft feline politeness and stiff military carriage*): Good evening, gracious lady. I am sorry to intrude; but there is a Serb hiding on the balcony. Will you and the gracious lady your mother please to withdraw whilst we search?

RAINA (*petulantly*): Nonsense, sir: you can see that there is no one on the balcony. (*She throws the shutters wide open and stands with her back to the curtain where the man is hidden, pointing to the moonlit balcony. A couple of shots are fired right under the window; and a bullet shatters the glass opposite* RAINA, *who winks and gasps, but stands her ground; whilst* CATHERINE *screams, and* THE OFFICER, *with a cry of* Take care! *rushes to the balcony.*)

THE OFFICER (*on the balcony, shouting savagely down to the street*): Cease firing there, you fools: do you hear? Cease firing, damn you! (*He glares down for a moment; then turns to* RAINA, *trying to resume his polite manner.*) Could anyone have got in without your knowledge? Were you asleep?

RAINA: No: I have not been to bed.

THE OFFICER (*impatiently, coming back into the room*): Your neighbors have their heads so full of runaway Serbs that they see them everywhere. (*Politely*) Gracious lady: a thousand pardons. Goodnight. (*Military bow, which* RAINA *returns coldly. Another to* CATHERINE, *who follows him out.*)

(RAINA *closes the shutters. She turns and sees* LOUKA, *who has been watching the scene curiously.*)

RAINA: Don't leave my mother, Louka, until the soldiers go away.

(LOUKA *glances at* RAINA, *at the ottoman, at the curtain; then purses her lips secretively, laughs insolently, and goes out.* RAINA, *highly offended by this demonstration, follows her to the door, and shuts it behind her with a slam, locking it violently. The man immediately steps out from behind the curtain, sheathing his sabre. Then, dismissing the danger from his mind in a businesslike way, he comes affably to* RAINA.)

THE MAN: A narrow shave; but a miss is as good as a mile. Dear young lady: your servant to the death. I wish for your sake I had joined the Bulgarian army instead of the other one. I am not a native Serb.

RAINA (*haughtily*): No: you are one of the Austrians who set the Serbs on to rob us of our national liberty, and who officer their army for them. We hate them!

THE MAN: Austrian! not I. Dont hate me, dear young lady. I am a Swiss, fighting merely as a professional soldier. I joined the Serbs because they came first on the road from Switzerland. Be generous: youve beaten us hollow.

RAINA: Have I not been generous?

THE MAN: Noble! Heroic! But I'm not saved yet. This particular rush will soon pass through; but the pursuit will go on all night by fits and starts. I must take my chance to get off in a quiet interval. (*Pleasantly*) You dont mind my waiting just a minute or two, do you?

RAINA (*putting on her most genteel society manner*): Oh, not at all. Wont you sit down?

THE MAN: Thanks. (*He sits on the foot of the bed.*)

(RAINA *walks with studied elegance to the ottoman and sits down. Unfortunately she sits on the pistol, and jumps up with a shriek. The man, all nerves, shies like a frightened horse to the other side of the room.*)

THE MAN (*irritably*): Dont frighten me like that. What is it?

RAINA: Your revolver! It was staring that officer in the face all the time. What an escape!

THE MAN (*vexed at being unnecessarily terrified*): Oh, is that all?

RAINA (*staring at him rather superciliously as she conceives a poorer and poorer opinion of him, and feels proportionately more and more at her ease*): I am sorry I frightened you. (*She takes up the pistol and hands it to him.*) Pray take it to protect yourself against me.

THE MAN (*grinning wearily at the sarcasm as he takes the pistol*): No use, dear young lady; there's nothing in it. It's not loaded. (*He makes a grimace at it, and drops it despairingly into his revolver case.*)

RAINA: Load it by all means.

THE MAN: Ive no ammunition. What use are cartridges in battle? I always carry chocolate instead; and I finished the last cake of that hours ago.

RAINA (*outraged in her most cherished ideals of manhood*): Chocolate! Do you stuff your pockets with sweets — like a schoolboy — even in the field?

THE MAN (*grinning*): Yes: isnt it contemptible? (*Hungrily*) I wish I had some now.

RAINA: Allow me. (*She sails away scornfully to the chest of drawers,*

and returns with the box of confectionery in her hand.) I am sorry
I have eaten them all except these. (*She offers him the box.*)

THE MAN (*ravenously*): Youre an angel! (*He gobbles the contents.*)
Creams! Delicious! (*He looks anxiously to see whether there are any
more. There are none: he can only scrape the box with his fingers
and suck them. When that nourishment is exhausted he accepts the
inevitable with pathetic goodhumor, and says, with grateful emotion*) Bless you, dear lady! You can always tell an old soldier by the
inside of his holsters and cartridge boxes. The young ones carry
pistols and cartridges: the old ones, grub. Thank you. (*He hands
back the box. She snatches it contemptuously from him and throws
it away. He shies again, as if she had meant to strike him.*) Ugh!
Dont do things so suddenly, gracious lady. It's mean to revenge
yourself because I frightened you just now.

RAINA (*loftily*): Frighten me! Do you know, sir, that though I am only
a woman, I think I am at heart as brave as you.

THE MAN: I should think so. You havnt been under fire for three days
as I have. I can stand two days without shewing it much; but no
man can stand three days: I'm as nervous as a mouse. (*He sits down
on the ottoman, and takes his head in his hands.*) Would you like
to see me cry?

RAINA (*alarmed*): No.

THE MAN: If you would, all you have to do is to scold me just as if I
were a little boy and you my nurse. If I were in camp now, theyd
play all sorts of tricks on me.

RAINA (*a little moved*): I'm sorry. I wont scold you. (*Touched by the
sympathy in her tone, he raises his head and looks gratefully at her:
she immediately draws back and says stiffly*) You must excuse me:
our soldiers are not like that. (*She moves away from the ottoman.*)

THE MAN: Oh yes they are. There are only two sorts of soldiers: old
ones and young ones. Ive served fourteen years: half of your fellows
never smelt powder before. Why, how is it that youve just beaten
us? Sheer ignorance of the art of war, nothing else. (*Indignantly*) I
never saw anything so unprofessional.

RAINA (*ironically*): Oh! was it unprofessional to beat you?

THE MAN: Well, come! is it professional to throw a regiment of cavalry
on a battery of machine guns, with the dead certainty that if the
guns go off not a horse or man will ever get within fifty yards of the
fire? I couldn't believe my eyes when I saw it.

RAINA (*eagerly turning to him, as all her enthusiasm and her dreams of
glory rush back on her*): Did you see the great cavalry charge? Oh,
tell me about it. Describe it to me.

THE MAN: You never saw a cavalry charge, did you?

RAINA: How could I?

THE MAN: Ah, perhaps not. No: of course not! Well, it's a funny sight. It's like slinging a handful of peas against a window pane: first one comes; then two or three close behind him; and then all the rest in a lump.

RAINA (*her eyes dilating as she raises her clasped hands ecstatically*): Yes, first One! the bravest of the brave!

THE MAN (*prosaically*): Hm! you should see the poor devil pulling at his horse.

RAINA: Why should he pull at his horse?

THE MAN (*impatient of so stupid a question*): It's running away with him, of course: do you suppose the fellow wants to get there before the others and be killed? Then they all come. You can tell the young ones by their wildness and their slashing. The old ones come bunched up under the number one guard: they know that theyre mere projectiles, and that it's no use trying to fight. The wounds are mostly broken knees, from the horses cannoning together.

RAINA: Ugh! But I dont believe the first man is a coward. I know he is a hero!

THE MAN (*goodhumoredly*): Thats what youd have said if youd seen the first man in the charge today.

RAINA (*breathless, forgiving him everything*): Ah, I knew it! Tell me. Tell me about him.

THE MAN: He did it like an operatic tenor. A regular handsome fellow, with flashing eyes and lovely moustache, shouting his war-cry and charging like Don Quixote at the windmills. We did laugh.

RAINA: You dared to laugh!

THE MAN: Yes; but when the sergeant ran up as white as a sheet, and told us theyd sent us the wrong ammunition, and that we couldnt fire a round for the next ten minutes, we laughed at the other side of our mouths. I never felt so sick in my life; though Ive been in one or two very tight places. And I hadnt even a revolver cartridge: only chocolate. We'd no bayonets: nothing. Of course, they just cut us to bits. And there was Don Quixote flourishing like a drum major, thinking he'd done the cleverest thing ever known, whereas he ought to be courtmartialled for it. Of all the fools ever let loose on a field of battle, that man must be the very maddest. He and his regiment simply committed suicide; only the pistol missed fire: thats all.

RAINA (*deeply wounded, but steadfastly loyal to her ideals*): Indeed! Would you know him again if you saw him?

THE MAN: Shall I ever forget him!

(*She again goes to the chest of drawers. He watches her with a vague hope that she may have something more for him to eat. She takes the portrait from its stand and brings it to him.*)

RAINA: That is a photograph of the gentleman — the patriot and hero — to whom I am betrothed.

THE MAN (*recognizing it with a shock*): I'm really very sorry. (*Looking at her*) Was it fair to lead me on? (*He looks at the portrait again.*) Yes: thats Don Quixote: not a doubt of it. (*He stifles a laugh.*)

RAINA (*quickly*): Why do you laugh?

THE MAN (*apologetic, but still greatly tickled*): I didnt laugh, I assure you. At least I didnt mean to. But when I think of him charging the windmills and imagining he was doing the finest thing — (*He chokes with suppressed laughter.*)

RAINA (*sternly*): Give me back the portrait, sir.

THE MAN (*with sincere remorse*): Of course. Certainly. I'm really very sorry. (*He hands her the picture. She deliberately kisses it and looks him straight in the face before returning to the chest of drawers to replace it. He follows her, apologizing.*) Perhaps I'm quite wrong, you know: no doubt I am. Most likely he had got wind of the cartridge business somehow, and knew it was a safe job.

RAINA: That is to say, he was a pretender and a coward! You did not dare say that before.

THE MAN (*with a comic gesture of despair*): It's no use, dear lady: I cant make you see it from the professional point of view. (*As he turns away to get back to the ottoman, a couple of distant shots threaten renewed trouble.*)

RAINA (*sternly, as she sees him listening to the shots*): So much the better for you!

THE MAN (*turning*): How?

RAINA: You are my enemy; and you are at my mercy. What would I do if I were a professional soldier?

THE MAN: Ah, true, dear young lady: youre always right. I know how good youve been to me: to my last hour I shall remember those three chocolate creams. It was unsoldierly; but it was angelic.

RAINA (*coldly*): Thank you. And now I will do a soldierly thing. You cannot stay here after what you have just said about my future husband; but I will go out on the balcony and see whether it is safe for you to climb down into the street. (*She turns to the window.*)

THE MAN (*changing countenance*): Down that waterpipe! Stop! Wait! I cant! I darent! The very thought of it makes me giddy. I came up it fast enough with death behind me. But to face it now in cold blood —! (*He sinks on the ottoman.*) It's no use: I give up: I'm beaten. Give the alarm. (*He drops his head on his hands in the deepest dejection.*)

RAINA (*disarmed by pity*): Come: dont be disheartened. (*She stoops over him almost maternally: he shakes his head.*) Oh, you are a very poor soldier: a chocolate cream soldier! Come, cheer up! it takes less courage to climb down than to face capture: remember that.

THE MAN (*dreamily, lulled by her voice*): No: capture only means death; and death is sleep: oh, sleep, sleep, sleep, undisturbed sleep! Climbing down the pipe means doing something — exerting myself — thinking! Death ten times over first.

RAINA (*softly and wonderingly, catching the rhythm of his weariness*): Are you as sleepy as that?

THE MAN: Ive not had two hours undisturbed sleep since I joined. I havnt closed my eyes for forty-eight hours.

RAINA (*at her wit's end*): But what am I to do with you?

THE MAN (*staggering up, roused by her desperation*): Of course. I must do something. (*He shakes himself; pulls himself together; and speaks with rallied vigor and courage.*) You see, sleep or no sleep, hunger or no hunger, tired or not tired, you can always do a thing when you know it must be done. Well, that pipe must be got down: (*he hits himself on the chest*) do you hear that, you chocolate cream soldier? (*He turns to the window.*)

RAINA (*anxiously*): But if you fall?

THE MAN: I shall sleep as if the stones were a feather bed. Goodbye. (*He makes boldly for the window; and his hand is on the shutter when there is a terrible burst of firing in the street beneath.*)

RAINA (*rushing to him*): Stop! (*She seizes him recklessly, and pulls him quite round.*) Theyll kill you.

THE MAN (*coolly, but attentively*): Never mind: this sort of thing is all in my day's work. I'm bound to take my chance. (*Decisively*) Now do what I tell you. Put out the candle; so that they shant see the light when I open the shutters. And keep away from the window, whatever you do. If they see me theyre sure to have a shot at me.

RAINA (*clinging to him*): Theyre sure to see you: it's bright moonlight. I'll save you. Oh, how can you be so indifferent! You want me to save you, dont you?

THE MAN: I really dont want to be troublesome.

(*She shakes him in her impatience.*)

I am not indifferent, dear young lady, I assure you. But how is it to be done?

RAINA: Come away from the window. (*She takes him firmly back to the middle of the room. The moment she releases him he turns mechanically towards the window again. She seizes him and turns him back, exclaiming*) Please!

(*He becomes motionless, like a hypnotized rabbit, his fatigue gaining fast on him. She releases him, and addresses him patronizingly.*)

Now listen. You must trust to our hospitality. You do not yet know in whose house you are. I am a Petkoff.

THE MAN: A pet what?

RAINA (*rather indignantly*): I mean that I belong to the family of the Petkoffs, the richest and best known in our country.

THE MAN: Oh, yes, of course. I beg your pardon. The Petkoffs, to be sure. How stupid of me!

RAINA: You know you never heard of them until this moment. How can you stoop to pretend!

THE MAN: Forgive me: I'm too tired to think; and the change of subject was too much for me. Dont scold me.

RAINA: I forgot. It might make you cry.

(*He nods, quite seriously. She pouts and then resumes her patronizing tone.*)

I must tell you that my father holds the highest command of any Bulgarian in our army. He is (*proudly*) a Major.

THE MAN (*pretending to be deeply impressed*): A Major! Bless me! Think of that!

RAINA: You shewed great ignorance in thinking that it was necessary to climb up to the balcony because ours is the only private house that has two rows of windows. There is a flight of stairs inside to get up and down by.

THE MAN: Stairs! How grand! You live in great luxury indeed, dear young lady.

RAINA: Do you know what a library is?

THE MAN: A library? A roomful of books?

RAINA: Yes. We have one, the only one in Bulgaria.

THE MAN: Actually a real library! I should like to see that.

RAINA (*affectedly*): I tell you these things to shew you that you are not in the house of ignorant country folk who would kill you the moment they saw your Serbian uniform, but among civilized people. We go to Bucharest every year for the opera season; and I have spent a whole month in Vienna.

THE MAN: I saw that, dear young lady. I saw at once that you knew the world.

RAINA: Have you ever seen the opera of Ernani?

THE MAN: Is that the one with the devil in it in red velvet, and a soldiers' chorus?

RAINA (*contemptuously*): No!

THE MAN (*stifling a heavy sigh of weariness*): Then I dont know it.

RAINA: I thought you might have remembered the great scene where Ernani, flying from his foes just as you are tonight, takes refuge in the castle of his bitterest enemy, an old Castilian noble. The noble refuses to give him up. His guest is sacred to him.

THE MAN (*quickly, waking up a little*): Have your people got that notion?

RAINA (*with dignity*): My mother and I can understand that notion, as you call it. And if instead of threatening me with your pistol as you did you had simply thrown yourself as a fugitive on our hospitality, you would have been as safe as in your father's house.

THE MAN: Quite sure?

RAINA (*turning her back on him in disgust*): Oh, it is useless to try to make you understand.

THE MAN: Dont be angry: you see how awkward it would be for me if there was any mistake. My father is a very hospitable man: he keeps six hotels; but I couldnt trust him as far as that. What about your father?

RAINA: He is away at Slivnitza fighting for his country. I answer for your safety. There is my hand in pledge of it. Will that reassure you? (*She offers him her hand.*)

THE MAN (*looking dubiously at his own hand*): Better not touch my hand, dear young lady. I must have a wash first.

RAINA (*touched*): That is very nice of you. I see that you are a gentleman.

THE MAN (*puzzled*): Eh?

RAINA: You must not think I am surprised. Bulgarians of really good standing — people in our position — wash their hands nearly every day. So you see I can appreciate your delicacy. You may take my hand. (*She offers it again.*)

THE MAN (*kissing it with his hands behind his back*): Thanks, gracious young lady: I feel safe at last. And now would you mind breaking the news to your mother? I had better not stay here secretly longer than is necessary.

RAINA: If you will be so good as to keep perfectly still whilst I am away.

THE MAN: Certainly. (*He sits down on the ottoman.*)

(RAINA *goes to the bed and wraps herself in the fur cloak. His eyes close. She goes to the door. Turning for a last look at him, she sees that he is dropping off to sleep.*)

RAINA (*at the door*): You are not going asleep, are you?

(*He murmurs inarticulately: she runs to him and shakes him.*)

Do you hear? Wake up: you are falling asleep.

THE MAN: Eh? Falling aslee — ? Oh no: not the least in the world: I was only thinking. It's all right: I'm wide awake.

RAINA (*severely*): Will you please stand up while I am away.

(*He rises reluctantly.*)

All the time, mind.

THE MAN (*standing unsteadily*): Certainly. Certainly: you may depend on me.

(RAINA *looks doubtfully at him. He smiles weakly. She goes reluctantly, turning again at the door, and almost catching him in the act of yawning. She goes out.*)

THE MAN (*drowsily*): Sleep, sleep, sleep, sleep, slee — (*The words trail off into a murmur. He wakes again with a shock on the point of falling.*) Where am I? Thats what I want to know: where am I? Must keep awake. Nothing keeps me awake except danger: remember that: (*intently*) danger, danger, danger, dan — (*trailing off again: another shock*) Wheres danger? Mus' find it. (*He starts off vaguely round the room in search of it.*) What am I looking for? Sleep — danger — dont know. (*He stumbles against the bed.*) Ah yes: now I know. All right now. I'm to go to bed, but not to sleep. Be sure not to sleep, because of danger. Not to lie down either, only sit down. (*He sits on the bed. A blissful expression comes into his face.*) Ah! (*With a happy sigh he sinks back at full length; lifts his boots into the bed with a final effort; and falls fast asleep instantly.*)

(CATHERINE *comes in, followed by* RAINA.)

RAINA (*looking at the ottoman*): He's gone! I left him here.

CATHERINE: Here! Then he must have climbed down from the —

RAINA (*seeing him*): Oh! (*She points.*)

CATHERINE (*scandalized*): Well! (*She strides to the bed,* RAINA *following until she is opposite her on the other side.*) He's fast asleep. The brute!

RAINA (*anxiously*): Sh!

CATHERINE (*shaking him*): Sir! (*Shaking him again, harder*) Sir!! (*Vehemently, shaking very hard*) Sir!!!

RAINA (*catching her arm*): Dont, mamma; the poor darling is worn out. Let him sleep.

CATHERINE (*letting him go, and turning amazed to* RAINA): The poor darling! Raina!!! (*She looks sternly at her daughter.*)

(*The man sleeps profoundly.*)

ACT II

(*The sixth of March, 1886. In the garden of* MAJOR PETKOFF'S *house. It is a fine spring morning: the garden looks fresh and pretty. Beyond the paling the tops of a couple of minarets can be seen, shewing that there is a valley there, with the little town in it. A few miles further the Balkan mountains rise and shut in the landscape. Looking towards them from within the garden, the side of the house is seen on the left, with a garden door reached by a little flight of steps. On the right the stable yard, with its gateway, encroaches on the garden. There are fruit bushes along the paling and house, covered with washing spread out to dry. A path runs by the house, and rises by two steps at the corner, where it turns out of sight. In the middle, a small table, with two bent wood chairs at it, is laid for breakfast with Turkish coffee pot, cups, rolls, etc.; but the cups have been used and the bread broken. There is a wooden garden seat against the wall on the right.*

LOUKA, *smoking a cigaret, is standing between the table and the house, turning her back with angry disdain on a man servant who is lecturing her. He is a middle-aged man of cool temperament and low but clear and keen intelligence, with the complacency of the servant who values himself on his rank in servitude, and the imperturbability of the accurate calculator who has no illusions. He wears a white Bulgarian costume: jacket with embroidered border, sash, wide knickerbockers, and decorated gaiters. His head is shaved up to the crown, giving him a high Japanese forehead. His name is* NICOLA.)

NICOLA: Be warned in time, Louka: mend your manners. I know the mistress. She is so grand that she never dreams that any servant could dare be disrespectful to her; but if she once suspects that you are defying her, out you go.

LOUKA: I do defy her. I will defy her. What do I care for her?

NICOLA: If you quarrel with the family, I never can marry you. It's the same as if you quarrelled with me!

LOUKA: You take her part against me, do you?

NICOLA (*sedately*): I shall always be dependent on the good will of the family. When I leave their service and start a shop in Sofia, their custom will be half my capital: their bad word would ruin me.

LOUKA: You have no spirit. I should like to catch them saying a word against me!

NICOLA (*pityingly*): I should have expected more sense from you, Louka. But youre young: youre young!

LOUKA: Yes; and you like me the better for it, dont you? But I know some family secrets they wouldnt care to have told, young as I am. Let them quarrel with me if they dare!

NICOLA (*with compassionate superiority*): Do you know what they would do if they heard you talk like that?

LOUKA: What could they do?

NICOLA: Discharge you for untruthfulness. Who would believe any stories you told after that? Who would give you another situation? Who in this house would dare be seen speaking to you ever again? How long would your father be left on his little farm?

(*She impatiently throws away the end of her cigaret, and stamps on it.*)

Child: you dont know the power such high people have over the like of you and me when we try to rise out of our poverty against them. (*He goes close to her and lowers his voice.*) Look at me, ten years in their service. Do you think I know no secrets? I know things about the mistress that she wouldnt have the master know for a thousand levas. I know things about him that she wouldnt let him hear the last of for six months if I blabbed them to her. I know things about Raina that would break off her match with Sergius if —

LOUKA (*turning on him quickly*): How do you know? I never told you!

NICOLA (*opening his eyes cunningly*): So thats your little secret, is it? I thought it might be something like that. Well, you take my advice and be respectful; and make the mistress feel that no matter what you know or dont know, she can depend on you to hold your tongue and serve the family faithfully. Thats what they like; and thats how youll make most out of them.

LOUKA (*with searching scorn*): You have the soul of a servant, Nicola.

NICOLA (*complacently*): Yes: thats the secret of success in service.

(*A loud knocking with a whip handle on a wooden door is heard from the stable yard.*)

MALE VOICE OUTSIDE: Hollo! Hollo there! Nicola!

LOUKA: Master! back from the war!

NICOLA (*quickly*): My word for it, Louka, the war's over. Off with you and get some fresh coffee. (*He runs out into the stable yard.*)

LOUKA (*as she collects the coffee pot and cups on the tray, and carries it into the house*): Youll never put the soul of a servant into me.

(MAJOR PETKOFF *comes from the stable yard, followed by* NICOLA. *He is a cheerful, excitable, insignificant, unpolished man of about fifty, naturally unambitious except as to his income and his importance in local society, but just now greatly pleased with the military rank which the war has thrust on him as a man of consequence in his town. The fever of plucky patriotism which the Serbian attack roused in all the Bulgarians has pulled him through the war; but he is obviously glad to be home again.*)

PETKOFF (*pointing to the table with his whip*): Breakfast out here, eh?

NICOLA: Yes, sir. The mistress and Miss Raina have just gone in.

PETKOFF (*sitting down and taking a roll*): Go in and say Ive come; and get me some fresh coffee.

NICOLA: It's coming, sir. (*He goes to the house door.* LOUKA, *with fresh coffee, a clean cup, and a brandy bottle on her tray, meets him.*) Have you told the mistress?

LOUKA: Yes: she's coming.

(NICOLA *goes into the house.* LOUKA *brings the coffee to the table.*)

PETKOFF: Well: the Serbs havnt run away with you, have they?

LOUKA: No, sir.

PETKOFF: Thats right. Have you brought me some cognac?

LOUKA (*putting the bottle on the table*): Here, sir.

PETKOFF: Thats right. (*He pours some into his coffee.*)

(CATHERINE, *who, having at this early hour made only a very perfunctory toilet, wears a Bulgarian apron over a once brilliant but now half worn-out dressing gown, and a colored handkerchief tied over her thick black hair, comes from the house with Turkish slippers on her bare feet, looking astonishingly handsome and stately under all the circumstances.* LOUKA *goes into the house.*)

CATHERINE: My dear Paul: what a surprise for us! (*She stoops over the back of his chair to kiss him.*) Have they brought you fresh coffee?

PETKOFF: Yes: Louka's been looking after me. The war's over. The treaty was signed three days ago at Bucharest; and the decree for our army to demobilize was issued yesterday.

CATHERINE (*springing erect, with flashing eyes*): Paul: have you let the Austrians force you to make peace?

PETKOFF (*submissively*): My dear: they didnt consult me. What could I do?

(*She sits down and turns away from him.*)

But of course we saw to it that the treaty was an honorable one. It declares peace —

CATHERINE (*outraged*): Peace!

PETKOFF (*appeasing her*): — but not friendly relations: remember that. They wanted to put that in; but I insisted on its being struck out. What more could I do?

CATHERINE: You could have annexed Serbia and made Prince Alexander Emperor of the Balkans. Thats what I would have done.

PETKOFF: I dont doubt it in the least, my dear. But I should have had to subdue the whole Austrian Empire first; and that would have kept me too long away from you. I missed you greatly.

CATHERINE (*relenting*): Ah! (*She stretches her hand affectionately across the table to squeeze his.*)

PETKOFF: And how have you been, my dear?

CATHERINE: Oh, my usual sore throats: thats all.

PETKOFF (*with conviction*): That comes from washing your neck every day. Ive often told you so.

CATHERINE: Nonsense, Paul!

PETKOFF (*over his coffee and cigaret*): I dont believe in going too far with these modern customs. All this washing cant be good for the health; it's not natural. There was an Englishman at Philippopolis who used to wet himself all over with cold water every morning when he got up. Disgusting! It all comes from the English: their climate makes them so dirty that they have to be perpetually washing themselves. Look at my father! he never had a bath in his life; and he lived to be ninety-eight, the healthiest man in Bulgaria. I dont mind a good wash once a week to keep up my position; but once a day is carrying the thing to a ridiculous extreme.

CATHERINE: You are a barbarian at heart still, Paul. I hope you behaved yourself before all those Russian officers.

PETKOFF: I did my best. I took care to let them know that we have a library.

CATHERINE: Ah; but you didnt tell them that we have an electric bell in it? I have had one put up.

PETKOFF: Whats an electric bell?

CATHERINE: You touch a button; something tinkles in the kitchen; and then Nicola comes up.

PETKOFF: Why not shout for him?

CATHERINE: Civilized people never shout for their servants. Ive learnt that while you were away.

PETKOFF: Well, I'll tell you something Ive learnt too. Civilized people dont hang out their washing to dry where visitors can see it: so youd better have all that (*indicating the clothes on the bushes*) put somewhere else.

CATHERINE: Oh, thats absurd, Paul: I don't believe really refined people notice such things.

SERGIUS (*knocking at the stable gates*): Gate, Nicola!

PETKOFF: Theres Sergius. (*Shouting*) Hollo, Nicola!

CATHERINE: Oh, dont shout, Paul: it really isnt nice.

PETKOFF: Bosh! (*He shouts louder than before.*) Nicola!

NICOLA (*appearing at the house door*): Yes, sir.

PETKOFF: Are you deaf? Dont you hear Major Saranoff knocking? Bring him round this way. (*He pronounces the name with the stress on the second syllable:* SARAHNOFF.)

NICOLA: Yes, Major. (*He goes into the stable yard.*)

PETKOFF: You must talk to him, my dear, until Raina takes him off our hands. He bores my life out about our not promoting him. Over my head, if you please.

CATHERINE: He certainly ought to be promoted when he marries Raina. Besides, the country should insist on having at least one native general.

PETKOFF: Yes; so that he could throw away whole brigades instead of regiments. It's no use, my dear: he hasnt the slightest chance of promotion until we're quite sure that the peace will be a lasting one.

NICOLA (*at the gate, announcing*): Major Sergius Saranoff! (*He goes into the house and returns presently with a third chair, which he places at the table. He then withdraws.*)

(MAJOR SERGIUS SARANOFF, *the original of the portrait in* RAINA'S *room, is a tall romantically handsome man, with the physical hardihood, the high spirit, and the susceptible imagination of an untamed mountaineer chieftain. But his remarkable personal distinction is of a characteristically civilized type. The ridges of his eyebrows, curving with an interrogative twist round the projections at the outer corners; his jealously observant eye; his nose, thin, keen, and apprehensive in spite of the pugnacious high bridge and large nostril; his assertive chin would not be out of place in a Parisian salon, shewing that the clever imaginative barbarian has an acute critical faculty which has been thrown into intense activity by the arrival of western civilization in the Balkans. The result is precisely what the advent of nineteenth century thought first produced in England: to wit, Byronism. By his brooding on the perpetual failure, not only of others, but of himself, to live up to his ideals; by his consequent cynical scorn for humanity; by his jejune credulity as to the absolute validity of his concepts and the unworthiness of the world in disregarding them; by his wincings and mockeries under the sting of the petty disillusions which every hour spent among men brings to his sensitive observation, he has acquired the half tragic, half ironic air, the mysterious moodiness, the suggestion of a strange and terrible history that has left nothing but undying remorse, by which Childe Harold fascinated the grandmothers of his English contemporaries. It is clear that here or nowhere is* RAINA'S *ideal hero.* CATHERINE *is hardly less enthusiastic about him than her daughter, and much less reserved in shewing her enthusiasm. As he enters from the stable gate, she rises effusively to greet him.* PETKOFF *is distinctly less disposed to make a fuss about him.)*

PETKOFF: Here already, Sergius! Glad to see you.

CATHERINE: My dear Sergius! (*She holds out both her hands.*)

SERGIUS (*kissing them with scrupulous gallantry*): My dear mother, if I may call you so.

PETKOFF (*drily*): Mother-in-law, Sergius: mother-in-law! Sit down; and have some coffee.

SERGIUS: Thank you: none for me. (*He gets away from the table with a certain distaste for* PETKOFF'S *enjoyment of it, and posts himself with conscious dignity against the rail of the steps leading to the house.*)

CATHERINE: You look superb. The campaign has improved you, Sergius. Everybody here is mad about you. We were all wild with enthusiasm about that magnificent cavalry charge.

SERGIUS (*with grave irony*): Madam: it was the cradle and the grave of my military reputation.

CATHERINE: How so?

SERGIUS: I won the battle the wrong way when our worthy Russian generals were losing it the right way. In short, I upset their plans, and wounded their self-esteem. Two Cossack colonels had their regiments routed on the most correct principles of scientific warfare. Two major-generals got killed strictly according to military etiquette. The two colonels are now major-generals; and I am still a simple major.

CATHERINE: You shall not remain so, Sergius. The women are on your side; and they will see that justice is done you.

SERGIUS: It is too late. I have only waited for the peace to send in my resignation.

PETKOFF (*dropping his cup in his amazement*): Your resignation!

CATHERINE: Oh, you must withdraw it!

SERGIUS (*with resolute measured emphasis, folding his arms*): I never withdraw.

PETKOFF (*vexed*): Now who could have supposed you were going to do such a thing?

SERGIUS (*with fire*): Everyone that knew me. But enough of myself and my affairs. How is Raina; and where is Raina?

RAINA (*suddenly coming round the corner of the house and standing at the top of the steps in the path*): Raina is here.

(*She makes a charming picture as they turn to look at her. She wears an underdress of pale green silk, draped with an overdress of thin ecru canvas embroidered with gold. She is crowned with a dainty eastern cap of gold tinsel.* SERGIUS *goes impulsively to meet her. Posing regally, she presents her hand: he drops chivalrously on one knee and kisses it.*)

PETKOFF (*aside to* CATHERINE, *beaming with parental pride*): Pretty, isnt it? She always appears at the right moment.

CATHERINE (*impatiently*): Yes; she listens for it. It is an abominable habit.

(SERGIUS *leads* RAINA *forward with splendid gallantry. When they arrive at the table, she turns to him with a bend of the head: he bows; and thus they separate, he coming to his place and she going behind her father's chair.*)

RAINA (*stooping and kissing her father*): Dear father! Welcome home!

PETKOFF (*patting her cheek*): My little pet girl. (*He kisses her. She goes to the chair left by* NICOLA *for* SERGIUS, *and sits down.*)

CATHERINE: And so youre no longer a soldier, Sergius.

SERGIUS: I am no longer a soldier. Soldiering, my dear madam, is the coward's art of attacking mercilessly when you are strong, and keeping out of harm's way when you are weak. That is the whole secret of successful fighting. Get your enemy at a disadvantage; and never, on any account, fight him on equal terms.

PETKOFF: They wouldnt let us make a fair stand-up fight of it. However, I suppose soldiering has to be a trade like any other trade.

SERGIUS: Precisely. But I have no ambition to shine as a tradesman; so I have taken the advice of that bagman of a captain that settled the exchange of prisoners with us at Pirot, and given it up.

PETKOFF: What! that Swiss fellow? Sergius: I've often thought of that exchange since. He over-reached us about those horses.

SERGIUS: Of course he over-reached us. His father was a hotel and livery stable keeper; and he owed his first step to his knowledge of horse-dealing. (*With mock enthusiasm*) Ah, he was a soldier: every inch a soldier! If only I had bought the horses for my regiment instead of foolishly leading it into danger, I should have been a field-marshal now!

CATHERINE: A Swiss? What was he doing in the Serbian army?

PETKOFF: A volunteer, of course: keen on picking up his profession. (*Chuckling*) We shouldnt have been able to begin fighting if these foreigners hadnt shewn us how to do it: we knew nothing about it; and neither did the Serbs. Egad, there'd have been no war without them!

RAINA: Are there many Swiss officers in the Serbian Army?

PETKOFF: No. All Austrians, just as our officers were all Russians. This was the only Swiss I came across. I'll never trust a Swiss again. He humbugged us into giving him fifty ablebodied men for two hundred worn out chargers. They werent even eatable!

SERGIUS: We were two children in the hands of that consummate soldier, Major: simply two innocent little children.

RAINA: What was he like?

CATHERINE: Oh, Raina, what a silly question!

SERGIUS: He was like a commercial traveller in uniform. Bourgeois to his boots!

PETKOFF (*grinning*): Sergius: tell Catherine that queer story his friend told us about how he escaped after Slivnitza. You remember. About his being hid by two women.

SERGIUS (*with bitter irony*): Oh yes: quite a romance! He was serving in the very battery I so unprofessionally charged. Being a thorough soldier, he ran away like the rest of them, with our cavalry at his heels. To escape their sabres he climbed a waterpipe and made his way into the bedroom of a young Bulgarian lady. The young lady was enchanted by his persuasive commercial traveller's manners. She very modestly entertained him for an hour or so, and then called in her mother lest her conduct should appear unmaidenly. The old lady was equally fascinated; and the fugitive was sent on his way in the morning, disguised in an old coat belonging to the master of the house, who was away at the war.

RAINA (*rising with marked stateliness*): Your life in the camp has made you coarse, Sergius. I did not think you would have repeated such a story before me. (*She turns away coldly.*)

CATHERINE (*also rising*): She is right, Sergius. If such women exist, we should be spared the knowledge of them.

PETKOFF: Pooh! nonsense! what does it matter?

SERGIUS (*ashamed*): No, Petkoff: I was wrong. (*To* RAINA, *with earnest humility*) I beg your pardon. I have behaved abominably. Forgive me, Raina.

(*She bows reservedly.*)

And you too, madam.

(CATHERINE *bows graciously and sits down. He proceeds solemnly, again addressing* RAINA.)

The glimpses I have had of the seamy side of life during the last few months have made me cynical; but I should not have brought my cynicism here: least of all into your presence, Raina. I — (*Here, turning to the others, he is evidently going to begin a long speech when the Major interrupts him.*)

PETKOFF: Stuff and nonsense, Sergius! Thats quite enough fuss about nothing: a soldier's daughter should be able to stand up without flinching to a little strong conversation. (*He rises.*) Come: it's time for us to get to business. We have to make up our minds how those three regiments are to get back to Philippopolis: theres no forage for them on the Sofia route. (*He goes towards the house.*) Come along.

(SERGIUS *is about to follow him when* CATHERINE *rises and intervenes.*)

CATHERINE: Oh, Paul, cant you spare Sergius for a few moments? Raina has hardly seen him yet. Perhaps I can help you to settle about the regiments.

SERGIUS (*protesting*): My dear madam, impossible: you —

CATHERINE (*stopping him playfully*): You stay here, my dear Sergius: theres no hurry. I have a word or two to say to Paul.

(SERGIUS *instantly bows and steps back.*)

Now, dear (*taking* PETKOFF's *arm*): come and see the electric bell.

PETKOFF: Oh, very well, very well.

(*They go into the house together affectionately.* SERGIUS, *left alone with* RAINA, *looks anxiously at her, fearing that she is still offended. She smiles, and stretches out her arms to him.*)

SERGIUS (*hastening to her*): Am I forgiven?

RAINA (*placing her hands on his shoulders as she looks up at him with admiration and worship*): My hero! My king!

SERGIUS: My queen! (*He kisses her on the forehead.*)

RAINA: How I have envied you, Sergius! You have been out in the world, on the field of battle, able to prove yourself there worthy of any woman in the world; whilst I have had to sit at home inactive — dreaming — useless — doing nothing that could give me the right to call myself worthy of any man.

SERGIUS: Dearest: all my deeds have been yours. You inspired me. I have gone through the war like a knight in a tournament with his lady looking down at him!

RAINA: And you have never been absent from my thoughts for a moment. (*Very solemnly*) Sergius: I think we two have found the higher love. When I think of you, I feel that I could never do a base deed, or think an ignoble thought.

SERGIUS: My lady and my saint! (*He clasps her reverently.*)

RAINA (*returning his embrace*): My lord and my —

SERGIUS: Sh — sh! Let me be the worshipper, dear. You little know how unworthy even the best man is of a girl's pure passion!

RAINA: I trust you. I love you. You will never disappoint me, Sergius.

(LOUKA *is heard singing within the house. They quickly release each other.*)

I cant pretend to talk indifferently before her: my heart is too full.

(LOUKA *comes from the house with her tray. She goes to the table, and begins to clear it, with her back turned to them.*)

I will get my hat; and then we can go out until lunch time. Wouldnt you like that?

SERGIUS: Be quick. If you are away five minutes, it will seem five hours.

(RAINA *runs to the top of the steps, and turns there to exchange looks with him and wave him a kiss with both hands. He looks after her with emotion for a moment; then turns slowly away, his face radiant with the loftiest exaltation. The movement shifts his field of vision, into the corner of which there now comes the tail of* LOUKA's *double apron. His attention is arrested at once. He takes a stealthy look at her, and begins to twirl his moustache mischievously, with his left hand akimbo on his hip. Finally, striking the ground with his heels in something of a cavalry swagger, he strolls over to the other side of the table, opposite her, and says*)

Louka: do you know what the higher love is?

LOUKA (*astonished*): No, sir.

SERGIUS: Very fatiguing thing to keep up for any length of time, Louka. One feels the need of some relief after it.

LOUKA (*innocently*): Perhaps you would like some coffee, sir? (*She stretches her hand across the table for the coffee pot.*)

SERGIUS (*taking her hand*): Thank you, Louka.

LOUKA (*pretending to pull*): Oh, sir, you know I didnt mean that. I'm surprised at you!

SERGIUS (*coming clear of the table and drawing her with him*): I am surprised at myself, Louka. What would Sergius, the hero of Slivnitza, say if he saw me now? What would Sergius, the apostle of the higher love, say if he saw me now? What would the half dozen Sergiuses who keep popping in and out of this handsome figure of mine say if they caught us here? (*Letting go her hand and slipping his arm dexterously round her waist*) Do you consider my figure handsome, Louka?

LOUKA: Let me go, sir. I shall be disgraced. (*She struggles: he holds her inexorably.*) Oh, will you let go?

SERGIUS (*looking straight into her eyes*): No.

LOUKA: Then stand back where we cant be seen. Have you no common sense?

SERGIUS: Ah! thats reasonable. (*He takes her into the stable yard gateway, where they are hidden from the house.*)

LOUKA (*plaintively*): I may have been seen from the windows: Miss Raina is sure to be spying about after you.

SERGIUS (*stung: letting her go*): Take care, Louka. I may be worthless enough to betray the higher love; but do not you insult it.

LOUKA (*demurely*): Not for the world, sir, I'm sure. May I go on with my work, please, now?

SERGIUS (*again putting his arm round her*): You are a provoking little witch, Louka. If you were in love with me, would you spy out of windows on me?

LOUKA: Well, you see, sir, since you say you are half a dozen different gentlemen all at once, I should have a great deal to look after.

SERGIUS (*charmed*): Witty as well as pretty. (*He tries to kiss her.*)

LOUKA (*avoiding him*): No: I dont want your kisses. Gentlefolk are all alike: you making love to me behind Miss Raina's back; and she doing the same behind yours.

SERGIUS (*recoiling a step*): Louka!

LOUKA: It shews how little you really care.

SERGIUS (*dropping his familiarity, and speaking with freezing polite-*

ness): If our conversation is to continue, Louka, you will please remember that a gentleman does not discuss the conduct of the lady he is engaged to with her maid.

LOUKA: It's so hard to know what a gentleman considers right. I thought from your trying to kiss me that you had given up being so particular.

SERGIUS (*turning from her and striking his forehead as he comes back into the garden from the gateway*): Devil! devil!

LOUKA: Ha! ha! I expect one of the six of you is very like me, sir; though I am only Miss Raina's maid. (*She goes back to her work at the table, taking no further notice of him.*)

SERGIUS (*speaking to himself*): Which of the six is the real man? thats the question that torments me. One of them is a hero, another a buffoon, another a humbug, another perhaps a bit of a blackguard. (*He pauses, and looks furtively at* LOUKA *as he adds, with deep bitterness*) And one, at least, is a coward: jealous, like all cowards. (*He goes to the table.*) Louka.

LOUKA: Yes?

SERGIUS: Who is my rival?

LOUKA: You shall never get that out of me, for love or money.

SERGIUS: Why?

LOUKA: Never mind why. Besides, you would tell that I told you; and I should lose my place.

SERGIUS (*holding out his right hand in affirmation*): No! on the honor of a — (*He checks himself; and his hand drops, nerveless, as he concludes sardonically*) — of a man capable of behaving as I have been behaving for the last five minutes. Who is he?

LOUKA: I dont know. I never saw him. I only heard his voice through the door of her room.

SERGIUS: Damnation! How dare you?

LOUKA (*retreating*): Oh, I mean no harm: youve no right to take up my words like that. The mistress knows all about it. And I tell you that if that gentleman ever comes here again, Miss Raina will marry him, whether he likes it or not. I know the difference between the sort of manner you and she put on before one another and the real manner.

(SERGIUS *shivers as if she had stabbed him. Then, setting his face like iron, he strides grimly to her, and grips her above the elbows with both hands.*)

SERGIUS: Now listen you to me.

LOUKA (*wincing*): Not so tight: youre hurting me.

SERGIUS: That doesnt matter. You have stained my honor by making me a party to your eavesdropping. And you have betrayed your mistress.

LOUKA (*writhing*): Please —

SERGIUS: That shews that you are an abominable little clod of common clay, with the soul of a servant. (*He lets her go as if she were an unclean thing, and turns away, dusting his hands of her, to the bench by the wall, where he sits down with averted head, meditating gloomily.*)

LOUKA (*whimpering angrily with her hands up her sleeves, feeling her bruised arms*): You know how to hurt with your tongue as well as with your hands. But I dont care, now Ive found out that whatever clay I'm made of, youre made of the same. As for her, she's a liar; and her fine airs are a cheat; and I'm worth six of her. (*She shakes the pain off hardily; tosses her head; and sets to work to put the things on the tray.*)

(*He looks doubtfully at her. She finishes packing the tray, and laps the cloth over the edges, so as to carry all out together. As she stoops to lift it, he rises.*)

SERGIUS: Louka!

(*She stops and looks defiantly at him.*)

A gentleman has no right to hurt a woman under any circumstances. (*With profound humility, uncovering his head*) I beg your pardon.

LOUKA: That sort of apology may satisfy a lady. Of what use is it to a servant?

SERGIUS (*rudely crossed in his chivalry, throws it off with a bitter laugh, and says slightingly*): Oh! you wish to be paid for the hurt! (*He puts on his shako, and takes some money from his pocket.*)

LOUKA (*her eyes filling with tears in spite of herself*): No: I want my hurt made well.

SERGIUS (*sobered by her tone*): How?

(*She rolls up her left sleeve; clasps her arm with the thumb and fingers of her right hand; and looks down at the bruise. Then she raises her head and looks straight at him. Finally, with a superb gesture, she presents her arm to be kissed. Amazed, he looks at her; at the arm; at her again; hesitates; and then, with shuddering intensity, exclaims* Never! *and gets away as far as possible from her.*

Her arm drops. Without a word, and with unaffected dignity, she takes her tray, and is approaching the house when RAINA *re-*

turns, wearing a hat and jacket in the height of the Vienna fashion of the previous year, 1885. LOUKA *makes way proudly for her, and then goes into the house.*)

RAINA: I'm ready. Whats the matter? (*Gaily*) Have you been flirting with Louka?

SERGIUS (*hastily*): No, no. How can you think such a thing?

RAINA (*ashamed of herself*): Forgive me, dear: it was only a jest. I am so happy today.

(*He goes quickly to her, and kisses her hand remorsefully.* CATHERINE *comes out and calls to them from the top of the steps.*)

CATHERINE (*coming down to them*): I am sorry to disturb you, children; but Paul is distracted over those three regiments. He doesnt know how to send them to Philippopolis; and he objects to every suggestion of mine. You must go and help him, Sergius. He is in the library.

RAINA (*disappointed*): But we are just going out for a walk.

SERGIUS: I shall not be long. Wait for me just five minutes. (*He runs up the steps to the door.*)

RAINA (*following him to the foot of the steps and looking up at him with timid coquetry*): I shall go round and wait in full view of the library windows. Be sure you draw father's attention to me. If you are a moment longer than five minutes, I shall go in and fetch you, regiments or no regiments.

SERGIUS (*laughing*): Very well. (*He goes in.*)

(RAINA *watches him until he is out of her sight. Then, with a perceptible relaxation of manner, she begins to pace up and down the garden in a brown study.*)

CATHERINE: Imagine their meeting that Swiss and hearing the whole story! The very first thing your father asked for was the old coat we sent him off in. A nice mess you have got us into!

RAINA (*gazing thoughtfully at the gravel as she walks*): The little beast!

CATHERINE: Little beast! What little beast?

RAINA: To go and tell! Oh, if I had him here, I'd cram him with chocolate creams til he couldnt ever speak again!

CATHERINE: Dont talk such stuff. Tell me the truth, Raina. How long was he in your room before you came to me?

RAINA (*whisking round and recommencing her march in the opposite direction*): Oh, I forget.

CATHERINE: You cannot forget! Did he really climb up after the soldiers were gone: or was he there when that officer searched the room?

RAINA: No. Yes: I think he must have been there then.

CATHERINE: You think! Oh, Raina! Raina! Will anything ever make you straightforward? If Sergius finds out, it will be all over between you.

RAINA (*with cool impertinence*): Oh, I know Sergius is your pet. I sometimes wish you could marry him instead of me. You would just suit him. You would pet him, and spoil him, and mother him to perfection.

CATHERINE (*opening her eyes very widely indeed*): Well, upon my word!

RAINA (*capriciously: half to herself*): I always feel a longing to do or say something dreadful to him — to shock his propriety — to scandalize the five senses out of him. (*To* CATHERINE, *perversely*) I dont care whether he finds out about the chocolate cream soldier or not. I half hope he may. (*She again turns and strolls flippantly away up the path to the corner of the house.*)

CATHERINE: And what should I be able to say to your father, pray?

RAINA (*over her shoulder, from the top of the two steps*): Oh, poor father! As if he could help himself! (*She turns the corner and passes out of sight.*)

CATHERINE (*looking after her, her fingers itching*): Oh, if you were only ten years younger!

(LOUKA *comes from the house with a salver, which she carries hanging down by her side.*)

Well?

LOUKA: Theres a gentleman just called, madam. A Serbian officer.

CATHERINE (*flaming*): A Serb! And how dare he — (*checking herself bitterly*) Oh, I forgot. We are at peace now. I suppose we shall have them calling every day to pay their compliments. Well: if he is an officer why dont you tell your master? He is in the library with Major Saranoff. Why do you come to me?

LOUKA: But he asks for you, madam. And I dont think he knows who you are: he said the lady of the house. He gave me this little ticket for you. (*She takes a card out of her bosom; puts it on the salver; and offers it to* CATHERINE.)

CATHERINE (*reading*): "Captain Bluntschli"? Thats a German name.

LOUKA: Swiss, madam, I think.

CATHERINE (*with a bound that makes* LOUKA *jump back*): Swiss! What is he like?

LOUKA (*timidly*): He has a big carpet bag, madam.

CATHERINE: Oh Heavens! he's come to return the coat. Send him away: say we're not at home: ask him to leave his address and I'll write to him. Oh stop: that will never do. Wait! (*She throws herself into a chair to think it out.* LOUKA *waits.*) The master and Major Saranoff are busy in the library, arent they?

LOUKA: Yes, madam.

CATHERINE (*decisively*): Bring the gentleman out here at once. (*Peremptorily*) And be very polite to him. Dont delay. Here (*impatiently snatching the salver from her*): leave that here; and go straight back to him.

LOUKA: Yes, madam (*going*).

CATHERINE: Louka!

LOUKA (*stopping*): Yes, madam.

CATHERINE: Is the library door shut?

LOUKA: I think so, madam.

CATHERINE: If not, shut it as you pass through.

LOUKA: Yes, madam (*going*).

CATHERINE: Stop.

(LOUKA *stops.*)

He will have to go that way (*indicating the gate of the stable yard*). Tell Nicola to bring his bag here after him. Dont forget.

LOUKA (*surprised*): His bag?

CATHERINE: Yes: here: as soon as possible. (*Vehemently*) Be quick!

(LOUKA *runs into the house.* CATHERINE *snatches her apron off and throws it behind a bush. She then takes up the salver and uses it as a mirror, with the result that the handkerchief tied round her head follows the apron. A touch to her hair and a shake to her dressing gown make her presentable.*)

Oh, how? how? how can a man be such a fool! Such a moment to select!

(LOUKA *appears at the door of the house, announcing* CAPTAIN BLUNTSCHLI. *She stands aside at the top of the steps to let him pass before she goes in again. He is the man of the midnight adventure in* RAINA's *room, clean, well brushed, smartly uniformed, and out of trouble, but still unmistakably the same man. The moment* LOUKA's *back is turned,* CATHERINE *swoops on him with impetuous, urgent, coaxing appeal.*)

Captain Bluntschli: I am very glad to see you; but you must leave this house at once.

(*He raises his eyebrows.*)

My husband has just returned with my future son-in-law; and they know nothing. If they did, the consequences would be terrible. You are a foreigner: you do not feel our national animosities as we do. We still hate the Serbs: the effect of the peace on my husband has been to make him feel like a lion baulked of his prey. If he discovers our secret, he will never forgive me; and my daughter's life will hardly be safe. Will you, like the chivalrous gentleman and soldier you are, leave at once before he finds you here?

BLUNTSCHLI (*disappointed, but philosophical*): At once, gracious lady. I only came to thank you and return the coat you lent me. If you will allow me to take it out of my bag and leave it with your servant as I pass out, I need detain you no further. (*He turns to go into the house.*)

CATHERINE (*catching him by the sleeve*): Oh, you must not think of going back that way. (*Coaxing him across to the stable gates*) This is the shortest way out. Many thanks. So glad to have been of service to you. Goodbye.

BLUNTSCHLI: But my bag?

CATHERINE: It shall be sent on. You will leave me your address.

BLUNTSCHLI: True. Allow me. (*He takes out his cardcase, and stops to write his address, keeping* CATHERINE *in an agony of impatience. As he hands her the card,* PETKOFF, *hatless, rushes from the house in a fluster of hospitality, followed by* SERGIUS.)

PETKOFF (*as he hurries down the steps*): My dear Captain Bluntschli —

CATHERINE: Oh Heavens! (*She sinks on the seat against the wall.*)

PETKOFF (*too preoccupied to notice her as he shakes* BLUNTSCHLI'S *hand heartily*): Those stupid people of mine thought I was out here, instead of in the — haw! — library (*he cannot mention the library without betraying how proud he is of it*). I saw you through the window. I was wondering why you didnt come in. Saranoff is with me: you remember him, dont you?

SERGIUS (*saluting humorously, and then offering his hand with great charm of manner*): Welcome, our friend the enemy!

PETKOFF: No longer the enemy, happily. (*Rather anxiously*) I hope youve called as a friend, and not about horses or prisoners.

CATHERINE: Oh, quite as a friend, Paul. I was just asking Captain Bluntschli to stay to lunch; but he declares he must go at once.

SERGIUS (*sardonically*): Impossible, Bluntschli. We want you here badly. We have to send on three cavalry regiments to Philippopolis; and we dont in the least know how to do it.

BLUNTSCHLI (*suddenly attentive and businesslike*): Philippopolis? The forage is the trouble, I suppose.

PETKOFF (*eagerly*): Yes: thats it. (*To* SERGIUS) He sees the whole thing at once.

BLUNTSCHLI: I think I can shew you how to manage that.

SERGIUS: Invaluable man! Come along! (*Towering over* BLUNTSCHLI, *he puts his hand on his shoulder and takes him to the steps,* PETKOFF *following.*)

(RAINA *comes from the house as* BLUNTSCHLI *puts his foot on the first step.*)

RAINA: Oh! The chocolate cream soldier!

(BLUNTSCHLI *stands rigid.* SERGIUS, *amazed, looks at* RAINA, *then at* PETKOFF, *who looks back at him and then at his wife.*)

CATHERINE (*with commanding presence of mind*): My dear Raina, dont you see that we have a guest here? Captain Bluntschli: one of our new Serbian friends.

(RAINA *bows.* BLUNTSCHLI *bows.*)

RAINA: How silly of me! (*She comes down into the centre of the group, between* BLUNTSCHLI *and* PETKOFF.) I made a beautiful ornament this morning for the ice pudding; and that stupid Nicola has just put down a pile of plates on it and spoilt it. (*To* BLUNTSCHLI, *winningly*) I hope you didnt think that you were the chocolate cream soldier, Captain Bluntschli.

BLUNTSCHLI (*laughing*): I assure you I did. (*Stealing a whimsical glance at her*) Your explanation was a relief.

PETKOFF (*suspiciously, to* RAINA): And since when, pray, have you taken to cooking?

CATHERINE: Oh, whilst you were away. It is her latest fancy.

PETKOFF (*testily*): And has Nicola taken to drinking? He used to be careful enough. First he shews Captain Bluntschli out here when he knew quite well I was in the library; and then he goes downstairs and breaks Raina's chocolate soldier. He must —

(NICOLA *appears at the top of the steps with the bag. He descends; places it respectfully before* BLUNTSCHLI; *and waits for further orders. General amazement.* NICOLA, *unconscious of the effect he is producing, looks perfectly satisfied with himself. When* PETKOFF *recovers his power of speech, he breaks out at him with*)

Are you mad, Nicola?

NICOLA (*taken aback*): Sir?

PETKOFF: What have you brought that for?

NICOLA: My lady's orders, major. Louka told me that —

CATHERINE (*interrupting him*): My orders! Why should I order you to bring Captain Bluntschli's luggage out here? What are you thinking of, Nicola?

NICOLA (*after a moment's bewilderment, picking up the bag as he addresses* BLUNTSCHLI *with the very perfection of servile discretion*): I beg your pardon, captain, I am sure. (*To* CATHERINE) My fault, madam: I hope youll overlook it. (*He bows, and is going to the steps with the bag, when* PETKOFF *addresses him angrily.*)

PETKOFF: Youd better go and slam that bag, too, down on Miss Raina's ice pudding!

(*This is too much for* NICOLA. *The bag drops from his hand almost on his master's toes, eliciting a roar of*)

Begone, you butter-fingered donkey.

NICOLA (*snatching up the bag, and escaping into the house*): Yes, Major.

CATHERINE: Oh, never mind. Paul: dont be angry.

PETKOFF (*blustering*): Scoundrel! He's got out of hand while I was away. I'll teach him. Infernal blackguard! The sack next Saturday! I'll clear out the whole establishment — (*He is stifled by the caresses of his wife and daughter, who hang round his neck, petting him.*)

CATHERINE	(*together*):	Now, now, now, it
RAINA		Wow, wow, wow:

mustnt be angry. He meant
not on your first day at home.

no harm. Be good to please
I'll make another ice pudding.

me, dear. Sh-sh-sh-sh!
Tch-ch-ch!

PETKOFF (*yielding*): Oh well, never mind. Come, Bluntschli: lets have no more nonsense about going away. You know very well youre not going back to Switzerland yet. Until you do go back youll stay with us.

RAINA: Oh, do, Captain Bluntschli.

PETKOFF (*to* CATHERINE): Now, Catherine: it's of you he's afraid. Press him: and he'll stay.

CATHERINE: Of course I shall be only too delighted if (*appealingly*) Captain Bluntschli really wishes to stay. He knows my wishes.

BLUNTSCHLI (*in his driest military manner*): I am at madam's orders.

SERGIUS (*cordially*): That settles it!

PETKOFF (*heartily*): Of course!

RAINA: You see you must stay.

BLUNTSCHLI (*smiling*): Well, if I must, I must.

(*Gesture of despair from* CATHERINE.)

ACT III

(*In the library after lunch. It is not much of a library. Its literary equipment consists of a single fixed shelf stocked with old paper covered novels, broken backed, coffee stained, torn and thumbed; and a couple of little hanging shelves with a few gift books on them: the rest of the wall space being occupied by trophies of war and the chase. But it is a most comfortable sitting room. A row of three large windows shews a mountain panorama, just now seen in one of its friendliest aspects in the mellowing afternoon light. In the corner next the right hand window a square earthenware stove, a perfect tower of glistening pottery, rises nearly to the ceiling and guarantees plenty of warmth. The ottoman is like that in* RAINA'S *room, and similarly placed; and the window seats are luxurious with decorated cushions. There is one object, however, hopelessly out of keeping with its surroundings. This is a small kitchen table, much the worse for wear, fitted as a writing table with an old canister full of pens, an eggcup filled with ink, and a deplorable scrap of heavily used pink blotting paper.*

At the side of this table, which stands to the left of anyone facing the window, BLUNTSCHLI *is hard at work with a couple of maps before him, writing orders. At the head of it sits* SERGIUS, *who is supposed to be also at work, but is actually gnawing the feather of a pen, and contemplating* BLUNTSCHLI'S *quick, sure, businesslike progress with a mixture of envious irritation at his own incapacity and awestruck wonder at an ability which seems to him almost miraculous, though its prosaic character forbids him to esteem it.* THE MAJOR *is comfortably established on the ottoman, with a newspaper in his hand and the tube of his hookah within easy reach.* CATHERINE *sits at the stove, with her back to them, embroidering.* RAINA, *reclining on the divan, is gazing in a day-*

dream out at the Balkan landscape, with a neglected novel in her lap.

The door is on the same side as the stove, further from the window. The button of the electric bell is at the opposite side, behind BLUNTSCHLI.)

PETKOFF (*looking up from his paper to watch how they are getting on at the table*): Are you sure I cant help in any way, Bluntschli?

BLUNTSCHLI (*without interrupting his writing or looking up*): Quite sure, thank you. Saranoff and I will manage it.

SERGIUS (*grimly*): Yes: we'll manage it. He finds out what to do; draws up the orders; and I sign em. Division of labor! (BLUNTSCHLI *passes him a paper.*) Another one? Thank you. (*He plants the paper squarely before him; sets his chair carefully parallel to it; and signs with his cheek on his elbow and his protruded tongue following the movements of his pen.*) This hand is more accustomed to the sword than to the pen.

PETKOFF: It's very good of you, Bluntschli: it is indeed, to let yourself be put upon in this way. Now are you quite sure I can do nothing?

CATHERINE (*in a low warning tone*): You can stop interrupting, Paul.

PETKOFF (*starting and looking round at her*): Eh? Oh! Quite right, my love: Quite right. (*He takes his newspaper up again, but presently lets it drop.*) Ah, you havent been campaigning, Catherine: you dont know how pleasant it is for us to sit here, after a good lunch, with nothing to do but enjoy ourselves. Theres only one thing I want to make me thoroughly comfortable.

CATHERINE: What is that?

PETKOFF: My old coat. I'm not at home in this one: I feel as if I were on parade.

CATHERINE: My dear Paul, how absurd you are about that old coat! It must be hanging in the blue closet where you left it.

PETKOFF: My dear Catherine, I tell you Ive looked there. Am I to believe my own eyes or not?

(CATHERINE *rises and crosses the room to press the button of the electric bell.*)

What are you shewing off that bell for?

(*She looks at him majestically, and silently resumes her chair and her needlework.*)

My dear: if you think the obstinacy of your sex can make a coat out of two old dressing gowns of Raina's, your waterproof, and my mackintosh, youre mistaken. Thats exactly what the blue closet contains at present.

(NICOLA *presents himself.*)

CATHERINE: Nicola: go to the blue closet and bring your master's old coat here: the braided one he wears in the house.

NICOLA: Yes, madam. (*He goes out.*)

PETKOFF: Catherine.

CATHERINE: Yes, Paul.

PETKOFF: I bet you any piece of jewellery you like to order from Sofia against a week's housekeeping money that the coat isnt there.

CATHERINE: Done, Paul!

PETKOFF (*excited by the prospect of a gamble*): Come: heres an opportunity for some sport. Wholl bet on it? Bluntschli: I'll give you six to one.

BLUNTSCHLI (*imperturbably*): I would be robbing you, Major. Madam is sure to be right. (*Without looking up, he passes another batch of papers to* SERGIUS.)

SERGIUS (*also excited*): Bravo, Switzerland! Major: I bet my best charger against an Arab mare for Raina that Nicola finds the coat in the blue closet.

PETKOFF (*eagerly*): Your best char —

CATHERINE (*hastily interrupting him*): Don't be foolish, Paul. An Arabian mare will cost you 50,000 levas.

RAINA (*suddenly coming out of her picturesque revery*): Really, mother, if you are going to take the jewellery, I don't see why you should grudge me my Arab.

(NICOLA *comes back with the coat, and brings it to* PETKOFF, *who can hardly believe his eyes.*)

CATHERINE: Where was it, Nicola?

NICOLA: Hanging in the blue closet, madam.

PETKOFF: Well, I am d —

CATHERINE (*stopping him*): Paul!

PETKOFF: I could have sworn it wasnt there. Age is beginning to tell on me. I'm getting hallucinations. (*To* NICOLA) Here: help me to change. Excuse me, Bluntschli. (*He begins changing coats,* NICOLA *acting as valet.*) Remember: I didnt take that bet of yours, Sergius. Youd better give Raina that Arab steed yourself, since youve roused her expectations. Eh, Raina? (*He looks round at her; but she is again rapt in the landscape. With a little gush of parental affection and pride, he points her out to them, and says*) She's dreaming, as usual.

SERGIUS: Assuredly she shall not be the loser.

PETKOFF: So much the better for her. *I* shant come off so cheaply, I expect.

(*The change is now complete.* NICOLA *goes out with the discarded coat.*)

Ah, now I feel at home at last. (*He sits down and takes his newspaper with a grunt of relief.*)

BLUNTSCHLI (*to* SERGIUS, *handing a paper*): Thats the last order.

PETKOFF (*jumping up*): What! Finished?

BLUNTSCHLI: Finished.

PETKOFF (*with childlike envy*): Havnt you anything for me to sign?

BLUNTSCHLI: Not necessary. His signature will do.

PETKOFF (*inflating his chest and thumping it*): Ah well, I think weve done a thundering good day's work. Can I do anything more?

BLUNTSCHLI: You had better both see the fellows that are to take these. (SERGIUS *rises.*) Pack them off at once; and shew them that Ive marked on the orders the time they should hand them in by. Tell them that if they stop to drink or tell stories — if theyre five minutes late, theyll have the skin taken off their backs.

SERGIUS (*stiffening indignantly*): I'll say so. (*He strides to the door.*) And if one of them is man enough to spit in my face for insulting him, I'll buy his discharge and give him a pension. (*He goes out.*)

BLUNTSCHLI (*confidentially*): Just see that he talks to them properly, Major, will you?

PETKOFF (*officiously*): Quite right, Bluntschli, quite right. I'll see to it. (*He goes to the door importantly, but hesitates on the threshold.*) By the bye, Catherine, you may as well come too. Theyll be far more frightened of you than of me.

CATHERINE (*putting down her embroidery*): I daresay I had better. You would only splutter at them. (*She goes out,* PETKOFF *holding the door for her and following her.*)

BLUNTSCHLI: What an army! They make cannons out of cherry trees; and the officers send for their wives to keep discipline! (*He begins to fold and docket the papers.*)

(RAINA, *who has risen from the divan, marches slowly down the room with her hands clasped behind her, and looks mischievously at him.*)

RAINA: You look ever so much nicer than when we last met.

(*He looks up, surprised.*)

What have you done to yourself?

BLUNTSCHLI: Washed; brushed; good night's sleep and breakfast. Thats all.

RAINA: Did you get back safely that morning?

BLUNTSCHLI: Quite, thanks.

RAINA: Were they angry with you for running away from Sergius's charge?

BLUNTSCHLI (*grinning*): No: they were glad; because theyd all just run away themselves.

RAINA (*going to the table, and leaning over it towards him*): It must have made a lovely story for them: all that about me and my room.

BLUNTSCHLI: Capital story. But I only told it to one of them: a particular friend.

RAINA: On whose discretion you could absolutely rely?

BLUNTSCHLI: Absolutely.

RAINA: Hm! He told it all to my father and Sergius the day you exchanged the prisoners. (*She turns away and strolls carelessly across to the other side of the room.*)

BLUNTSCHLI (*deeply concerned, and half incredulous*): No! You dont mean that, do you?

RAINA (*turning, with sudden earnestness*): I do indeed. But they dont know that it was in this house you took refuge. If Sergius knew, he would challenge you and kill you in a duel.

BLUNTSCHLI: Bless me! then dont tell him.

RAINA: Please be serious, Captain Bluntschli. Can you not realize what it is to me to deceive him? I want to be quite perfect with Sergius: no meanness, no smallness, no deceit. My relation to him is the one really beautiful and noble part of my life. I hope you can understand that.

BLUNTSCHLI (*sceptically*): You mean that you wouldnt like him to find out that the story about the ice pudding was a — a — a — You know.

RAINA (*wincing*): Ah, dont talk of it in that flippant way. I lied: I know it. But I did it to save your life. He would have killed you. That was the second time I ever uttered a falsehood.

(BLUNTSCHLI *rises quickly and looks doubtfully and somewhat severely at her.*)

Do you remember the first time?

BLUNTSCHLI: I! No. Was I present?

RAINA: Yes; and I told the officer who was searching for you that you were not present.

BLUNTSCHLI: True. I should have remembered it.

RAINA (*greatly encouraged*): Ah, it is natural that you should forget it first. It cost you nothing: it cost me a lie! A lie!

(*She sits down on the ottoman, looking straight before her with her hands clasped round her knee.* BLUNTSCHLI, *quite touched, goes to the ottoman with a particularly reassuring and considerate air, and sits down beside her.*)

BLUNTSCHLI: My dear young lady, dont let this worry you. Remember: I'm a soldier. Now what are the two things that happen to a soldier so often that he comes to think nothing of them? One is hearing people tell lies (RAINA *recoils*) the other is getting his life saved in all sorts of ways by all sorts of people.

RAINA (*rising in indignant protest*): And so he becomes a creature incapable of faith and of gratitude.

BLUNTSCHLI (*making a wry face*): Do you like gratitude? I dont. If pity is akin to love, gratitude is akin to the other thing.

RAINA: Gratitude! (*Turning on him*) If you are incapable of gratitude you are incapable of any noble sentiment. Even animals are grateful. Oh, I see now exactly what you think of me! You were not surprised to hear me lie. To you it was something I probably did every day! every hour! That is how men think of women. (*She paces the room tragically.*)

BLUNTSCHLI (*dubiously*): Theres reason in everything. You said youd told only two lies in your whole life. Dear young lady: isnt that rather a short allowance? I'm quite a straightforward man myself; but it wouldn't last me a whole morning.

RAINA (*staring haughtily at him*): Do you know, sir, that you are insulting me?

BLUNTSCHLI: I cant help it. When you strike that noble attitude and speak in that thrilling voice, I admire you; but I find it impossible to believe a single word you say.

RAINA (*superbly*): Captain Bluntschli!

BLUNTSCHLI (*unmoved*): Yes?

RAINA (*standing over him, as if she could not believe her senses*): Do you mean what you said just now? Do you know what you said just now?

BLUNTSCHLI: I do.

RAINA (*gasping*): I! I!!! (*She points to herself incredulously, meaning* "I, Raina Petkoff tell lies!" *He meets her gaze unflinchingly. She suddenly sits down beside him, and adds, with a complete change of manner from the heroic to a babyish familiarity*) How did you find me out?

BLUNTSCHLI (*promptly*): Instinct, dear young lady. Instinct, and experience of the world.

RAINA (*wonderingly*): Do you know, you are the first man I ever met who did not take me seriously?

BLUNTSCHLI: You mean, dont you, that I am the first man that has ever taken you quite seriously?

RAINA: Yes: I suppose I do mean that. (*Cosily, quite at her ease with him*) How strange it is to be talked to in such a way! You know, Ive always gone on like that.

BLUNTSCHLI: You mean the — ?

RAINA: I mean the noble attitude and the thrilling voice.

(*They laugh together.*)

I did it when I was a tiny child to my nurse. She believed in it. I do it before my parents. They believe in it. I do it before Sergius. He believes in it.

BLUNTSCHLI: Yes: he's a little in that line himself, isnt he?

RAINA (*startled*): Oh! Do you think so?

BLUNTSCHLI: You know him better than I do.

RAINA: I wonder — I wonder is he? If I thought that — ! (*Discouraged*) Ah, well; what does it matter? I suppose, now youve found me out, you despise me.

BLUNTSCHLI (*warmly, rising*): No, my dear young lady, no, no, no a thousand times. It's part of your youth: part of your charm. I'm like all the rest of them: the nurse, your parents, Sergius: I'm your infatuated admirer.

RAINA (*pleased*): Really?

BLUNTSCHLI (*slapping his breast smartly with his hand, German fashion*): Hand aufs Herz! Really and truly.

RAINA (*very happy*): But what did you think of me for giving you my portrait?

BLUNTSCHLI (*astonished*): Your portrait! You never gave me your portrait.

RAINA (*quickly*): Do you mean to say you never got it?

BLUNTSCHLI: No. (*He sits down beside her, with renewed interest, and says, with some complacency*) When did you send it to me?

RAINA (*indignantly*): I did not send it to you. (*She turns her head away, and adds, reluctantly*) It was in the pocket of that coat.

BLUNTSCHLI (*pursing his lips and rounding his eyes*): Oh-o-oh! I never found it. It must be there still.

RAINA (*springing up*): There still! for my father to find the first time he puts his hand in his pocket! Oh, how could you be so stupid?

BLUNTSCHLI (*rising also*): It doesnt matter: I suppose it's only a photograph: how can he tell who it was intended for? Tell him he put it there himself.

RAINA (*bitterly*): Yes: that is so clever! isnt it? (*Distractedly*) Oh! what shall I do?

BLUNTSCHLI: Ah, I see. You wrote something on it. That was rash.

RAINA (*vexed almost to tears*): Oh, to have done such a thing for you, who care no more — except to laugh at me — oh! Are you sure nobody has touched it?

BLUNTSCHLI: Well, I cant be quite sure. You see, I couldnt carry it about with me all the time: one cant take much luggage on active service.

RAINA: What did you do with it?

BLUNTSCHLI: When I got through to Pirot I had to put it in safe keeping somehow. I thought of the railway cloak room; but thats the surest place to get looted in modern warfare. So I pawned it.

RAINA: Pawned it!!!

BLUNTSCHLI: I know it doesnt sound nice: but it was much the safest plan. I redeemed it the day before yesterday. Heaven only knows whether the pawnbroker cleared out the pockets or not.

RAINA (*furious: throwing the words right into his face*): You have a low shopkeeping mind. You think of things that would never come into a gentleman's head.

BLUNTSCHLI (*phlegmatically*): Thats the Swiss national character, dear lady. (*He returns to the table.*)

RAINA: Oh, I wish I had never met you. (*She flounces away, and sits at the window fuming.*)

(LOUKA *comes in with a heap of letters and telegrams on her salver, and crosses, with her bold free gait, to the table. Her left sleeve is looped up to the shoulder with a brooch, shewing her naked arm, with a broad gilt bracelet covering the bruise.*)

LOUKA (*to* BLUNTSCHLI): For you. (*She empties the salver with a fling on to the table.*) The messenger is waiting. (*She is determined not to be civil to an enemy, even if she must bring him his letters.*)

BLUNTSCHLI (*to* RAINA): Will you excuse me: the last postal delivery that reached me was three weeks ago. These are the subsequent accumulations. Four telegrams: a week old. (*He opens one.*) Oho! Bad news!

RAINA (*rising and advancing a little remorsefully*): Bad news?

BLUNTSCHLI: My father's dead. (*He looks at the telegram with his lips pursed, musing on the unexpected change in his arrangements.* LOUKA *crosses herself hastily.*)

RAINA: Oh, how very sad!

BLUNTSCHLI: Yes: I shall have to start for home in an hour. He has left a lot of big hotels behind him to be looked after. (*He takes up a fat letter in a long blue envelope.*) Here's a whacking letter from the family solicitor. (*He puts out the enclosures and glances over them.*) Great Heavens! Seventy! Two hundred! (*In a crescendo of dismay*) Four hundred! Four thousand!! Nine thousand six hundred!!! What on earth am I to do with them all?

RAINA (*timidly*): Nine thousand hotels?

BLUNTSCHLI: Hotels nonsense. If you only knew! Oh, it's too ridiculous! Excuse me: I must give my fellow orders about starting. (*He leaves the room hastily, with the documents in his hand.*)

LOUKA (*knowing instinctively that she can annoy RAINA by disparaging BLUNTSCHLI*): He has not much heart, that Swiss. He has not a word of grief for his poor father.

RAINA (*bitterly*): Grief! A man who has been doing nothing but killing people for years! What does he care? What does any soldier care? (*She goes to the door, restraining her tears with difficulty.*)

LOUKA: Major Saranoff has been fighting too; and he has plenty of heart left.

(RAINA, *at the door, draws herself up haughtily and goes out.*)

Aha! I thought you wouldnt get much feeling out of your soldier.

(*She is following* RAINA *when* NICOLA *enters with an armful of logs for the stove.*)

NICOLA (*grinning amorously at her*): Ive been trying all the afternoon to get a minute alone with you, my girl. (*His countenance changes as he notices her arm.*) Why, what fashion is that of wearing your sleeve, child?

LOUKA (*proudly*): My own fashion.

NICOLA: Indeed! If the mistress catches you, she'll talk to you. (*He puts the logs down, and seats himself comfortably on the ottoman.*)

LOUKA: Is that any reason why you should take it on yourself to talk to me?

NICOLA: Come! dont be contrary with me. Ive some good news for you.

(*She sits down beside him. He takes out some paper money.* LOUKA, *with an eager gleam in her eyes, tries to snatch it; but he shifts it quickly to his left hand, out of her reach.*)

See! a twenty leva bill! Sergius gave me that, out of pure swagger. A fool and his money are soon parted. Theres ten levas more. The Swiss gave me that for backing up the mistress' and Raina's lies

about him. He's no fool, he isnt. You should have heard old Catherine downstairs as polite as you please to me, telling me not to mind
the Major being a little impatient; for they knew what a good servant I was — after making a fool and a liar of me before them all!
The twenty will go to our savings; and you shall have the ten to
spend if youll only talk to me so as to remind me I'm a human being. I get tired of being a servant occasionally.

LOUKA: Yes: sell your manhood for 30 levas, and buy me for 10! (*Rising scornfully*) Keep your money. You were born to be a servant. I
was not. When you set up your shop you will only be everybody's
servant instead of somebody's servant. (*She goes moodily to the
table and seats herself regally in* SERGIUS's *chair.*)

NICOLA (*picking up his logs, and going to the stove*): Ah, wait til you
see. We shall have our evenings to ourselves; and I shall be master
in my own house, I promise you. (*He throws the logs down and
kneels at the stove.*)

LOUKA: You shall never be master in mine.

NICOLA (*turning, still on his knees, and squatting down rather forlornly
on his calves, daunted by her implacable disdain*): You have a great
ambition in you, Louka. Remember: if any luck comes to you, it
was I that made a woman of you.

LOUKA: You!

NICOLA (*scrambling up and going to her*): Yes, me. Who was it made
you give up wearing a couple of pounds of false black hair on your
head and reddening your lips and cheeks like any other Bulgarian
girl! I did. Who taught you to trim your nails, and keep your hands
clean, and be dainty about yourself, like a fine Russian lady! Me: do
you hear that? me!

(*She tosses her head defiantly; and he turns away, adding more
coolly*)

Ive often thought that if Raina were out of the way, and you just a
little less of a fool and Sergius just a little more of one, you might
come to be one of my grandest customers, instead of only being my
wife and costing me money.

LOUKA: I believe you would rather be my servant than my husband.
You would make more out of me. Oh, I know that soul of yours.

NICOLA (*going closer to her for greater emphasis*): Never you mind my
soul; but just listen to my advice. If you want to be a lady, your
present behaviour to me wont do at all, unless when we're alone.
It's too sharp and impudent; and impudence is a sort of familiarity:
it shews affection for me. And dont you try being high and mighty
with me, either. Youre like all country girls: you think it's genteel to

treat a servant the way I treat a stableboy. Thats only your ignorance; and dont you forget it. And dont be so ready to defy everybody. Act as if you expected to have your own way, not as if you expected to be ordered about. The way to get on as a lady is the same
as the way to get on as a servant: youve got to know your place:
thats the secret of it. And you may depend on me to know my place
if you get promoted. Think over it, my girl. I'll stand by you: one
servant should always stand by another.

LOUKA (*rising impatiently*): Oh, I must behave in my own way. You
take all the courage out of me with your coldblooded wisdom. Go
and put those logs in the fire: thats the sort of thing you understand.

(*Before* NICOLA *can retort,* SERGIUS *comes in. He checks himself a
moment on seeing* LOUKA; *then goes to the stove.*)

SERGIUS (*to* NICOLA): I am not in the way of your work, I hope.

NICOLA (*in a smooth, elderly manner*): Oh no, sir: thank you kindly.
I was only speaking to this foolish girl about her habit of running up
here to the library whenever she gets a chance, to look at the books.
Thats the worst of her education, sir: it gives her habits above her
station. (*To* LOUKA) Make that table tidy, Louka, for the Major.
(*He goes out sedately.*)

(LOUKA, *without looking at* SERGIUS, *pretends to arrange the papers on the table. He crosses slowly to her, and studies the arrangement of her sleeve reflectively.*)

SERGIUS: Let me see: is there a mark there? (*He turns up the bracelet
and sees the bruise made by his grasp. She stands motionless, not
looking at him: fascinated, but on her guard.*) Ffff! Does it hurt?

LOUKA: Yes.

SERGIUS: Shall I cure it?

LOUKA (*instantly withdrawing herself proudly, but still not looking at
him*): No. You cannot cure it now.

SERGIUS (*masterfully*): Quite sure? (*He makes a movement as if to
take her in his arms.*)

LOUKA: Dont trifle with me, please. An officer should not trifle with a
servant.

SERGIUS (*indicating the bruise with a merciless stroke of his fore-
finger*): That was no trifle, Louka.

LOUKA (*flinching; then looking at him for the first time*): Are you
sorry?

SERGIUS (*with measured emphasis, folding his arms*): I am never sorry.

LOUKA (*wistfully*): I wish I could believe a man could be as unlike a
woman as that. I wonder are you really a brave man?

SERGIUS (*unaffectedly, relaxing his attitude*): Yes: I am a brave man. My heart jumped like a woman's at the first shot; but in the charge I found that I was brave. Yes: that at least is real about me.

LOUKA: Did you find in the charge that the men whose fathers are poor like mine were any less brave than the men who are rich like you?

SERGIUS (*with bitter levity*): Not a bit. They all slashed and cursed and yelled like heroes. Psha! the courage to rage and kill is cheap. I have an English bull terrier who has as much of that sort of courage as the whole Bulgarian nation, and the whole Russian nation at its back. But he lets my groom thrash him, all the same. Thats your soldier all over! No, Louka: your poor men can cut throats; but they are afraid of their officers; they put up with insults and blows; they stand by and see one another punished like children: aye, and help to do it when they are ordered. And the officers!!! Well (*with a short harsh laugh*) I am an officer. Oh (*fervently*), give me the man who will defy to the death any power on earth or in heaven that sets itself up against his own will and conscience: he alone is the brave man.

LOUKA: How easy it is to talk! Men never seem to me to grow up: they all have schoolboy's ideas. You dont know what true courage is.

SERGIUS (*ironically*): Indeed! I am willing to be instructed. (*He sits on the ottoman, sprawling magnificently.*)

LOUKA: Look at me! How much am I allowed to have my own will? I have to get your room ready for you: to sweep and dust, to fetch and carry. How could that degrade me if it did not degrade you to have it done for you? But (*with subdued passion*) if I were Empress of Russia, above everyone in the world, then!! Ah then, though according to you I could shew no courage at all, you should see, you should see.

SERGIUS: What would you do, most noble Empress?

LOUKA: I would marry the man I loved, which no other queen in Europe has the courage to do. If I loved you, though you would be as far beneath me as I am beneath you, I would dare to be the equal of my inferior. Would you dare as much if you loved me? No: if you felt the beginnings of love for me you would not let it grow. You would not dare: you would marry a rich man's daughter because you would be afraid of what other people would say of you.

SERGIUS (*bounding up*): You lie: it is not so, by all the stars! If I loved you, and I were the Tsar himself, I would set you on the throne by my side. You know that I love another woman, a woman as high above you as heaven is above earth. And you are jealous of her.

LOUKA: I have no reason to be. She will never marry you now. The man I told you of has come back. She will marry the Swiss.

SERGIUS (*recoiling*): The Swiss!

LOUKA: A man worth ten of you. Then you can come to me; and I will refuse you. You are not good enough for me. (*She turns to the door.*)

SERGIUS (*springing after her and catching her fiercely in his arms*): I will kill the Swiss; and afterwards I will do as I please with you.

LOUKA (*in his arms, passive and steadfast*): The Swiss will kill you, perhaps. He has beaten you in love. He may beat you in war.

SERGIUS (*tormentedly*): Do you think I believe that she — she! whose worst thoughts are higher than your best ones, is capable of trifling with another man behind my back?

LOUKA: Do you think she would believe the Swiss if he told her now that I am in your arms?

SERGIUS (*releasing her in despair*): Damnation! Oh, damnation! Mockery! mockery everywhere! everything I think is mocked by everything I do! (*He strikes himself frantically on the breast.*) Coward! liar! fool! Shall I kill myself like a man, or live and pretend to laugh at myself?

(*She again turns to go.*)

Louka!

(*She stops near the door.*)

Remember: you belong to me.

LOUKA (*turning*): What does that mean? An insult?

SERGIUS (*commandingly*): It means that you love me, and that I have had you here in my arms, and will perhaps have you there again. Whether that is an insult I neither know nor care: take it as you please. But (*vehemently*) I will not be a coward and a trifler. If I choose to love you, I dare marry you, in spite of all Bulgaria. If these hands ever touch you again, they shall touch my affianced bride.

LOUKA: We shall see whether you dare keep your word. And take care. I will not wait long.

SERGIUS (*again folding his arms and standing motionless in the middle of the room*): Yes: we shall see. And you shall wait my pleasure.

(BLUNTSCHLI, *much preoccupied, with his papers still in his hand, enters, leaving the door open for* LOUKA *to go out. He goes across to the table, glancing at her as he passes.* SERGIUS, *without altering his resolute attitude, watches him steadily.* LOUKA *goes out, leaving the door open.*)

BLUNTSCHLI (*absently, sitting at the table as before, and putting down his papers*): Thats a remarkable-looking young woman.

SERGIUS (*gravely, without moving*): Captain Bluntschli.

BLUNTSCHLI: Eh?

SERGIUS: You have deceived me. You are my rival. I brook no rivals. At six o'clock I shall be in the drilling-ground on the Klissoura road, alone, on horseback, with my sabre. Do you understand?

BLUNTSCHLI (*staring, but sitting quite at his ease*): Oh, thank you: thats a cavalry man's proposal. I'm in the artillery; and I have the choice of weapons. If I go, I shall take a machine gun. And there shall be no mistake about the cartridges this time.

SERGIUS (*flushing, but with deadly coldness*): Take care, sir. It is not our custom in Bulgaria to allow invitations of that kind to be trifled with.

BLUNTSCHLI (*warmly*): Pooh! dont talk to me about Bulgaria. You dont know what fighting is. But have it your own way. Bring your sabre along. I'll meet you.

SERGIUS (*fiercely delighted to find his opponent a man of spirit*): Well said, Switzer. Shall I lend you my best horse?

BLUNTSCHLI: No: damn your horse! thank you all the same, my dear fellow.

(RAINA *comes in, and hears the next sentence.*)

I shall fight you on foot. Horseback's too dangerous; I dont want to kill you if I can help it.

RAINA (*hurrying forward anxiously*): I have heard what Captain Bluntschli said, Sergius. You are going to fight. Why?

(SERGIUS *turns away in silence, and goes to the stove, where he stands watching her as she continues, to* BLUNTSCHLI)

What about?

BLUNTSCHLI: I don't know: he hasn't told me. Better not interfere, dear young lady. No harm will be done: Ive often acted as sword instructor. He wont be able to touch me; and I'll not hurt him. It will save explanations. In the morning I shall be off home; and youll never see me or hear of me again. You and he will then make it up and live happily ever after.

RAINA (*turning away deeply hurt, almost with a sob in her voice*): I never said I wanted to see you again.

SERGIUS (*striding forward*): Ha! That is a confession.

RAINA (*haughtily*): What do you mean?

SERGIUS: You love that man!

RAINA (*scandalized*): Sergius!

SERGIUS: You allow him to make love to you behind my back, just as you treat me as your affianced husband behind his. Bluntschli: you knew our relations; and you deceived me. It is for that that I call you to account, not for having received favors I never enjoyed.

BLUNTSCHLI (*jumping up indignantly*): Stuff! Rubbish! I have received no favors. Why, the young lady doesnt even know whether I'm married or not.

RAINA (*forgetting herself*): Oh! (*Collapsing on the ottoman*) Are you?

SERGIUS: You see the young lady's concern, Captain Bluntschli. Denial is useless. You have enjoyed the privilege of being received in her own room, late at night —

BLUNTSCHLI (*interrupting him pepperily*): Yes, you blockhead! she received me with a pistol at her head. Your cavalry were at my heels. I'd have blown out her brains if she'd uttered a cry.

SERGIUS (*taken aback*): Bluntschli! Raina: is this true?

RAINA (*rising in wrathful majesty*): Oh, how dare you, how dare you?

BLUNTSCHLI: Apologize, man: apologize. (*He resumes his seat at the table.*)

SERGIUS (*with the old measured emphasis, folding his arms*): I never apologize!

RAINA (*passionately*): This is the doing of that friend of yours, Captain Bluntschli. It is he who is spreading this horrible story about me. (*She walks about excitedly.*)

BLUNTSCHLI: No: he's dead. Burnt alive.

RAINA (*stopping, shocked*): Burnt alive!

BLUNTSCHLI: Shot in the hip in a woodyard. Couldnt drag himself out. Your fellows' shells set the timber on fire and burnt him, with a half a dozen other poor devils in the same predicament.

RAINA: How horrible!

SERGIUS: And how ridiculous! Oh, war! war! the dream of patriots and heroes! A fraud, Bluntschli. A hollow sham, like love.

RAINA (*outraged*): Like love! You say that before me!

BLUNTSCHLI: Come, Saranoff: that matter is explained.

SERGIUS: A hollow sham, I say. Would you have come back here if nothing had passed between you except at the muzzle of your pistol? Raina is mistaken about your friend who was burnt. He was not my informant.

RAINA: Who then? (*Suddenly guessing the truth*) Ah, Louka! my maid! my servant! You were with her this morning all that time after — after — Oh, what sort of god is this I have been worshipping!

(He meets her gaze with sardonic enjoyment of her disenchantment. Angered all the more, she goes closer to him, and says, in a lower, intenser tone)

Do you know that I looked out of the window as I went upstairs, to have another sight of my hero; and I saw something I did not understand then. I know now that you were making love to her.

SERGIUS *(with grim humor)*: You saw that?

RAINA: Only too well. *(She turns away, and throws herself on the divan under the centre window, quite overcome.)*

SERGIUS *(cynically)*: Raina: our romance is shattered. Life's a farce.

BLUNTSCHLI *(to* RAINA, *whimsically)*: You see: he's found himself out now.

SERGIUS *(going to him)*: Bluntschli: I have allowed you to call me a blockhead. You may now call me a coward as well. I refuse to fight you. Do you know why?

BLUNTSCHLI: No; but it doesnt matter. I didnt ask the reason when you cried on; and I dont ask the reason now that you cry off. I'm a professional soldier! I fight when I have to, and am very glad to get out of it when I havent to. Youre only an amateur: you think fighting's an amusement.

SERGIUS *(sitting down at the table, nose to nose with him)*: You shall hear the reason all the same, my professional. The reason is that it takes two men — real men — men of heart, blood and honor — to make a genuine combat. I could no more fight with you than I could make love to an ugly woman. Youve no magnetism: youre not a man: youre a machine.

BLUNTSCHLI *(apologetically)*: Quite true, quite true. I always was that sort of chap. I'm very sorry.

SERGIUS: Psha!

BLUNTSCHLI: But now that youve found that life isnt a farce, but something quite sensible and serious, what further obstacle is there to your happiness?

RAINA *(rising)*: You are very solicitous about my happiness and his. Do you forget his new love — Louka? It is not you that he must fight now, but his rival, Nicola.

SERGIUS: Rival!! *(Bouncing half across the room.)*

RAINA: Dont you know that theyre engaged?

SERGIUS: Nicola! Are fresh abysses opening? Nicola!

RAINA *(sarcastically)*: A shocking sacrifice, isnt it? Such beauty! such intellect! such modesty! wasted on a middle-aged servant man. Really, Sergius, you cannot stand by and allow such a thing. It would be unworthy of your chivalry.

SERGIUS (*losing all self-control*): Viper! Viper! (*He rushes to and fro, raging.*)

BLUNTSCHLI: Look here, Saranoff: youre getting the worst of this.

RAINA (*getting angrier*): Do you realize what he has done, Captain Bluntschli? He has set this girl as a spy on us; and her reward is that he makes love to her.

SERGIUS: False! Monstrous!

RAINA: Monstrous! (*Confronting him*) Do you deny that she told you about Captain Bluntschli being in my room?

SERGIUS: No; but —

RAINA (*interrupting*): Do you deny that you were making love to her when she told you?

SERGIUS: No; but I tell you —

RAINA (*cutting him short contemptuously*): It is unnecessary to tell us anything more. That is quite enough for us. (*She turns away from him and sweeps majestically back to the window.*)

BLUNTSCHLI (*quietly, as* SERGIUS, *in an agony of mortification, sinks on the ottoman, clutching his averted head between his fists*): I told you you were getting the worst of it, Saranoff.

SERGIUS: Tiger cat!

RAINA (*running excitedly to* BLUNTSCHLI): You hear this man calling me names, Captain Bluntschli?

BLUNTSCHLI: What else can he do, dear lady? He must defend himself somehow. Come (*very persuasively*): dont quarrel. What good does it do?

(RAINA, *with a gasp, sits down on the ottoman, and after a vain effort to look vexedly at* BLUNTSCHLI, *falls a victim to her sense of humor, and actually leans back babyishly against the writhing shoulder of* SERGIUS.)

SERGIUS: Engaged to Nicola! Ha! ha! Ah well, Bluntschli, you are right to take this huge imposture of a world coolly.

RAINA (*quaintly to* BLUNTSCHLI, *with an intuitive guess at his state of mind*): I daresay you think us a couple of grown-up babies, dont you?

SERGIUS (*grinning savagely*): He does: he does. Swiss civilization nurse-tending Bulgarian barbarism, eh?

BLUNTSCHLI (*blushing*): Not at all, I assure you. I'm only very glad to get you two quieted. There! there! let's be pleasant and talk it over in a friendly way. Where is this other young lady?

RAINA: Listening at the door, probably.

SERGIUS (*shivering as if a bullet had struck him, and speaking with quiet but deep indignation*): I will prove that that, at least, is a calumny. (*He goes with dignity to the door and opens it. A yell of fury bursts from him as he looks out. He darts into the passage, and returns dragging in* LOUKA, *whom he flings violently against the table, exclaiming*) Judge her, Bluntschli. You, the cool impartial one: judge the eavesdropper.

(LOUKA *stands her ground, proud and silent.*)

BLUNTSCHLI (*shaking his head*): I mustnt judge her. I once listened myself outside a tent when there was a mutiny brewing. It's all a question of the degree of provocation. My life was at stake.

LOUKA: My love was at stake. I am not ashamed.

RAINA (*contemptuously*): Your love! Your curiosity, you mean.

LOUKA (*facing her and returning her contempt with interest*): My love, stronger than anything you can feel, even for your chocolate cream soldier.

SERGIUS (*with quick suspicion, to* LOUKA): What does that mean?

LOUKA (*fiercely*): It means —

SERGIUS (*interrupting her slightingly*): Oh, I remember: the ice pudding. A paltry taunt, girl!

(MAJOR PETKOFF *enters, in his shirtsleeves.*)

PETKOFF: Excuse my shirtsleeves, gentlemen. Raina: somebody has been wearing that coat of mine: I'll swear it. Somebody with a differently shaped back. It's all burst open at the sleeve. Your mother is mending it. I wish she'd make haste: I shall catch cold. (*He looks more attentively at them.*) Is anything the matter?

RAINA: No. (*She sits down at the stove, with a tranquil air.*)

SERGIUS: Oh no. (*He sits down at the end of the table, as at first.*)

BLUNTSCHLI (*who is already seated*): Nothing. Nothing.

PETKOFF (*sitting down on the ottoman in his old place*): Thats all right. (*He notices* LOUKA.) Anything the matter, Louka?

LOUKA: No, sir.

PETKOFF (*genially*): Thats all right. (*He sneezes.*) Go and ask your mistress for my coat, like a good girl, will you?

(NICOLA *enters with the coat.* LOUKA *makes a pretence of having business in the room by taking the little table with the hookah away to the wall near the windows.*)

RAINA (*rising quickly as she sees the coat on* NICOLA'S *arm*): Here it is papa. Give it to me Nicola; and do you put some more wood on the fire. (*She takes the coat, and brings it to* THE MAJOR, *who stands up to put it on.* NICOLA *attends to the fire.*)

PETKOFF (*to* RAINA, *teasing her affectionately*): Aha! Going to be very good to poor old papa just for one day after his return from the wars, eh?

RAINA (*with solemn reproach*): Ah, how can you say that to me, father?

PETKOFF: Well, well, only a joke, little one. Come: give me a kiss.

(*She kisses him.*)

Now give me the coat.

RAINA: No: I am going to put it on for you. Turn your back.

(*He turns his back and feels behind him with his arms for the sleeves. She dexterously takes the photograph from the pocket and throws it on the table before* BLUNTSCHLI, *who covers it with a sheet of paper under the very nose of* SERGIUS, *who looks on amazed, with his suspicions roused in the highest degree. She then helps* PETKOFF *on with his coat.*)

There, dear! Now are you comfortable?

PETKOFF: Quite, little love. Thanks. (*He sits down; and* RAINA *returns to her seat near the stove.*) Oh, by the bye, Ive found something funny. Whats the meaning of this? (*He puts his hand into the picked pocket.*) Eh? Hallo! (*He tries the other pocket.*) Well, I could have sworn — ! (*Much puzzled, he tries the breast pocket.*) I wonder — (*trying the original pocket*) Where can it — ? (*He rises, exclaiming*) Your mother's taken it!

RAINA (*very red*): Taken what?

PETKOFF: Your photograph, with the inscription: "Raina, to her Chocolate Cream Soldier: a Souvenir." Now you know theres something more in this than meets the eye; and I'm going to find it out. (*Shouting*) Nicola!

NICOLA (*coming to him*): Sir!

PETKOFF: Did you spoil any pastry of Miss Raina's this morning?

NICOLA: You heard Miss Raina say that I did, sir.

PETKOFF: I know that, you idiot. Was it true?

NICOLA: I am sure Miss Raina is incapable of saying anything that is not true, sir.

PETKOFF: Are you? Then I'm not. (*Turning to the others*) Come: do you think I dont see it all? (*He goes to* SERGIUS, *and slaps him on the shoulder.*) Sergius: youre the chocolate cream soldier, arent you?

SERGIUS (*starting up*): I! A chocolate cream soldier! Certainly not.

PETKOFF: Not! (*He looks at them. They are all very serious and very conscious.*) Do you mean to tell me that Raina sends things like that to other men?

SERGIUS (*enigmatically*): The world is not such an innocent place as we used to think, Petkoff.

BLUNTSCHLI (*rising*): It's all right, Major. I'm the chocolate cream soldier.

(PETKOFF *and* SERGIUS *are equally astonished.*)

The gracious young lady saved my life by giving me chocolate creams when I was starving: shall I ever forget their flavour! My late friend Stolz told you the story at Pirot. I was the fugitive.

PETKOFF: You! (*He gasps.*) Sergius: do you remember how those two women went on this morning when we mentioned it?

(SERGIUS *smiles cynically.* PETKOFF *confronts* RAINA *severely.*)

Youre a nice young woman, arent you?

RAINA (*bitterly*): Major Saranoff has changed his mind. And when I wrote that on the photograph, I did not know that Captain Bluntschli was married.

BLUNTSCHLI (*startled into vehement protest*): I'm not married.

RAINA (*with deep reproach*): You said you were.

BLUNTSCHLI: I did not. I positively did not. I never was married in my life.

PETKOFF (*exasperated*): Raina: will you kindly inform me, if I am not asking too much, which of these gentlemen you are engaged to?

RAINA: To neither of them. This young lady (*introducing* LOUKA, *who faces them all proudly*) is the object of Major Saranoff's affections at present.

PETKOFF: Louka! Are you mad, Sergius? Why, this girl's engaged to Nicola.

NICOLA: I beg your pardon, sir. There is a mistake. Louka is not engaged to me.

PETKOFF: Not engaged to you, you scoundrel! Why, you had twenty-five levas from me on the day of your betrothal; and she had that gilt bracelet from Miss Raina.

NICOLA (*with cool unction*): We gave it out so, sir. But it was only to give Louka protection. She had a soul above her station; and I have been no more than her confidential servant. I intend, as you know, sir, to set up a shop later on in Sofia; and I look forward to her custom and recommendation should she marry into the nobility. (*He goes out with impressive discretion, leaving them all staring after him.*)

PETKOFF (*breaking the silence*): Well, I am — hm!

SERGIUS: This is either the finest heroism or the most crawling baseness. Which is it, Bluntschli?

BLUNTSCHLI: Never mind whether it's heroism or baseness. Nicola's the ablest man Ive met in Bulgaria. I'll make him manager of a hotel if he can speak French and German.

LOUKA (*suddenly breaking out at* SERGIUS): I have been insulted by everyone here. You set them the example. You owe me an apology.

(SERGIUS, *like a repeating clock of which the spring has been touched, immediately begins to fold his arms.*)

BLUNTSCHLI (*before he can speak*): It's no use. He never apologizes.

LOUKA: Not to you, his equal and his enemy. To me, his poor servant, he will not refuse to apologize.

SERGIUS (*approvingly*): You are right. (*He bends his knee in his grandest manner.*) Forgive me.

LOUKA: I forgive you. (*She timidly gives him her hand, which he kisses.*) That touch makes me your affianced wife.

SERGIUS (*springing up*): Ah! I forgot that.

LOUKA (*coldly*): You can withdraw if you like.

SERGIUS: Withdraw! Never! You belong to me. (*He puts his arm about her.*)

(CATHERINE *comes in and finds* LOUKA *in* SERGIUS' *arms, with all the rest gazing at them in bewildered astonishment.*)

CATHERINE: What does this mean?

(SERGIUS *releases* LOUKA.)

PETKOFF: Well, my dear, it appears that Sergius is going to marry Louka instead of Raina.

(*She is about to break out indignantly at him: he stops her by exclaiming testily*)

Dont blame me: Ive nothing to do with it. (*He retreats to the stove.*)

CATHERINE: Marry Louka! Sergius: you are bound by your word to us!

SERGIUS (*folding his arms*): Nothing binds me.

BLUNTSCHLI (*much pleased by this piece of common sense*): Saranoff: your hand. My congratulations. These heroics of yours have their practical side after all. (*To* LOUKA) Gracious young lady: the best wishes of a good Republican! (*He kisses her hand, to* RAINA'S *great disgust, and returns to his seat.*)

CATHERINE: Louka: you have been telling stories.

LOUKA: I have done Raina no harm.

CATHERINE (*haughtily*): Raina!

(RAINA, *equally indignant, almost snorts at the liberty.*)

LOUKA: I have a right to call her Raina: she calls me Louka. I told Major Saranoff she would never marry him if the Swiss gentleman came back.

BLUNTSCHLI (*rising, much surprised*): Hallo!

LOUKA (*turning to* RAINA): I thought you were fonder of him than of Sergius. You know best whether I was right.

BLUNTSCHLI: What nonsense! I assure you, my dear Major, my dear Madame, the gracious young lady simply saved my life, nothing else. She never cared two straws for me. Why, bless my heart and soul, look at the young lady and look at me. She, rich, young, beautiful, with her imagination full of fairy princes and noble natures and cavalry charges and goodness knows what! And I, a commonplace Swiss soldier who hardly knows what a decent life is after fifteen years of barracks and battles: a vagabond, a man who has spoiled all his chances in life through an incurably romantic disposition, a man —

SERGIUS (*starting as if a needle had pricked him and interrupting* BLUNTSCHLI *in incredulous amazement*): Excuse me, Bluntschli: what did you say had spoiled your chances in life?

BLUNTSCHLI (*promptly*): An incurably romantic disposition. I ran away from home twice when I was a boy. I went into the army instead of into my father's business. I climbed the balcony of this house when a man of sense would have dived into the nearest cellar. I came sneaking back here to have another look at the young lady when any other man of my age would have sent the coat back —

PETKOFF: My coat!

BLUNTSCHLI: — yes: thats the coat I mean — would have sent it back and gone quietly home. Do you suppose I am the sort of fellow a young girl falls in love with? Why, look at our ages! I'm thirty-four! I dont suppose the young lady is much over seventeen. (*This estimate produces a marked sensation, all the rest turning and staring at one another. He proceeds innocently.*) All that adventure which was life or death to me, was only a schoolgirl's game to her — chocolate creams and hide and seek. Heres the proof! (*He takes the photograph from the table.*) Now, I ask you, would a woman who took the affair seriously have sent me this and written on it "Raina, to her Chocolate Cream Soldier: a Souvenir"? (*He exhibits the photograph triumphantly, as if it settled the matter beyond all possibility of refutation.*)

PETKOFF: Thats what I was looking for. How the deuce did it get there? (*He comes from the stove to look at it, and sits down on the ottoman.*)

BLUNTSCHLI (*to* RAINA, *complacently*): I have put everything right, I hope, gracious young lady.

RAINA (*going to the table to face him*): I quite agree with your account of yourself. You are a romantic idiot.

(BLUNTSCHLI *is unspeakably taken back.*)

Next time, I hope you will know the difference between a schoolgirl of seventeen and a woman of twenty-three.

BLUNTSCHLI (*stupefied*): Twenty-three!

(RAINA *snaps the photograph contemptuously from his hand; tears it up; throws the pieces in his face; and sweeps back to her former place.*)

SERGIUS (*with grim enjoyment of his rival's discomfiture*): Bluntschli: my one last belief is gone. Your sagacity is a fraud, like everything else. You have less sense than even I!

BLUNTSCHLI (*overwhelmed*): Twenty-three! Twenty-three!! (*He considers.*) Hm! (*Swiftly making up his mind and coming to his host*) In that case, Major Petkoff, I beg to propose formally to become a suitor for your daughter's hand, in place of Major Saranoff retired.

RAINA: You dare!

BLUNTSCHLI: If you were twenty-three when you said those things to me this afternoon, I shall take them seriously.

CATHERINE (*loftily polite*): I doubt, sir, whether you quite realize either my daughter's position or that of Major Sergius Saranoff, whose place you propose to take. The Petkoffs and the Saranoffs are known as the richest and most important families in the country. Our position is almost historical: we can go back for twenty years.

PETKOFF: Oh, never mind that, Catherine. (*To* BLUNTSCHLI) We should be most happy, Bluntschli, if it were only a question of your position; but hang it, you know, Raina is accustomed to a very comfortable establishment. Sergius keeps twenty horses.

BLUNTSCHLI: But who wants twenty horses? We're not going to keep a circus.

CATHERINE (*severely*): My daughter, sir, is accustomed to a first-rate stable.

RAINA: Hush, mother: youre making me ridiculous.

BLUNTSCHLI: Oh well, if it comes to a question of an establishment, here goes! (*He darts impetuously to the table; seizes the papers in the blue envelope; and turns to* SERGIUS.) How many horses did you say?

SERGIUS: Twenty, noble Switzer.

BLUNTSCHLI: I have two hundred horses.

(*They are amazed.*)

How many carriages?

SERGIUS: Three.

BLUNTSCHLI: I have seventy. Twenty-four of them will hold twelve inside, besides two on the box, without counting the driver and conductor. How many tablecloths have you?

SERGIUS: How the deuce do I know?

BLUNTSCHLI: Have you four thousand?

SERGIUS: No.

BLUNTSCHLI: I have. I have nine thousand six hundred pairs of sheets and blankets, with two thousand four hundred eider-down quilts. I have ten thousand knives and forks, and the same quantity of dessert spoons. I have three hundred servants. I have six palatial establishments, besides two livery stables, a tea garden, and a private house. I have four medals for distinguished services; I have the rank of an officer and the standing of a gentleman; and I have three native languages. Shew me any man in Bulgaria that can offer as much!

PETKOFF (*with childish awe*): Are you Emperor of Switzerland?

BLUNTSCHLI: My rank is the highest known in Switzerland: I am a free citizen.

CATHERINE: Then, Captain Bluntschli, since you are my daughter's choice —

RAINA (*mutinously*): He's not.

CATHERINE (*ignoring her*): — I shall not stand in the way of her happiness.

(PETKOFF *is about to speak.*)

That is Major Petkoff's feeling also.

PETKOFF: Oh, I shall be only too glad. Two hundred horses! Whew!

SERGIUS: What says the lady?

RAINA (*pretending to sulk*): The lady says that he can keep his tablecloths and his omnibuses. I am not here to be sold to the highest bidder. (*She turns her back on him.*)

BLUNTSCHLI: I wont take that answer. I appealed to you as a fugitive, a beggar, and a starving man. You accepted me. You gave me your hand to kiss, your bed to sleep in, and your roof to shelter me.

RAINA: I did not give them to the Emperor of Switzerland.

BLUNTSCHLI: Thats just what I say. (*He catches her by the shoulders and turns her face-to-face with him.*) Now tell us whom you did give them to.

RAINA (*succumbing with a shy smile*): To my chocolate cream soldier.

BLUNTSCHLI (*with a boyish laugh of delight*): Thatll do. Thank you. (*He looks at his watch and suddenly becomes businesslike.*) Time's up, Major. Youve managed those regiments so well that youre sure to be asked to get rid of some of the infantry of the Timok division. Send them home by way of Lom Palanka. Saranoff: dont get married until I come back: I shall be here punctually at five in the evening on Tuesday fortnight. Gracious ladies (*his heels click*) good evening. (*He makes them a military bow, and goes.*)

SERGIUS: What a man! Is he a man!

⌇⫏ WHEN *Arms and the Man*, Shaw's fourth play, appeared on the London stage in 1894, its success was both qualified and ambiguous. Some took it to be just another funny farce, but the majority took offense at Shaw's ridicule of military heroism — not a proper subject for frivolity in imperial England. In 1898 the play appeared in a volume of seven plays by Shaw, entitled *Plays Pleasant and Unpleasant*, in which it belongs with the plays pleasant. The label suggests Shavian mischievousness.

Its setting is Bulgaria, to the Victorian Englishman a distant, exotic, and somewhat comical country, forever engaged in small and colorful wars with her equally semi-civilized neighbors. Shaw has considerable fun with the backwardness, sanitary and cultural, of the Petkoffs. The setting further makes the farce more acceptable, for anything might happen among these picturesque people, and it allows Shaw to satirize Western institutions and attitudes indirectly. Also, in Act I it introduces some key images. The view through Raina's bedroom window with the mountain peak "wonderfully white and beautiful in the starlit snow" and apparently "quite close at hand, though it is really miles away" parallels Raina's view of human ideals. The room's interior, "half rich Bulgarian, half cheap Viennese" with the "ornamental textile fabrics," "oriental and gorgeous," contrasting with the "occidental and paltry" wallpaper, anticipates a central conflict in the play and renders its opposing values ambiguous. Is the point that in the process of Westernization Bulgaria loses something of rich beauty? Or do the impending marriages at the end symbolize the union of East and West (though Louka is Bulgarian, her attitude to love resembles that of the Westerner Bluntschli more than it does Sergius's and Raina's) in a way that contrasts with the arbitrary and tasteless mixture of styles in the still-romantic Raina's room?

The room's appearance, at any rate, suggests the play's two poles of action. What is chronicled is the conversion, on the issues of war and love, of Raina and Sergius from romantic idealism to healthy realism. The Swiss Bluntschli, representing the sanity and practicality and egalitarianism of the West, serves as a kind of catalyst for the process. The conversion results in realignment of partners in love.

More is involved here than a clever game of musical chairs, kept going by such old-fashioned props of intrigue as Petkoff's coat and Raina's photograph. The regrouping of the four lovers is a dramatic metaphor of Sergius' and Raina's self-discovery. Before their conversion, they speak of love as a pure and noble feeling, far exalted above lust and infidelity, either in thought or deed. Raina "adores" Sergius' portrait in Act I, but "she does not kiss it or press it to her breast, or shew it any mark of bodily affection" (though it is a question if she would not have seemed more, not less, silly if she had done so). After Sergius' return, Raina waits for "the right moment" to appear, and the reunion of the lovers becomes, both in movement and in speech, a royal ceremony, splendid but completely unspontaneous. In obvious contrast is the earthy sensualism in the scene between Sergius and Louka that follows, but it is sensualism attended by cool, calm, hard-headed thinking. Sergius puts his arm around Louka.

LOUKA: Let me go, sir. I shall be disgraced. (*She struggles: he holds her inexorably.*) Oh, will you let me go?
SERGIUS (*looking straight into her eyes*): No.
LOUKA: Then stand back where we cant be seen. Have you no common sense?

Their encounter begins when Sergius observes that "the higher love" is a "very fatiguing thing to keep up," and a little later, Raina, in a similar mood, "undergoes a perceptible relaxation of manner" as soon as Sergius leaves her. Both change their attitude to love — and, therefore, to one another — as soon as they admit to themselves how artificial and exhausting their conventionally lofty attitudes have been and how deeply the two realists touch their true nature. That the alliances at the end represent a victory of egalitarian republicanism over aristocratic snobbery is part of the general pattern of change. They experience a similar change of attitude vis à vis war. Raina begins as a sententious idealist ("Some soldiers, I know, are afraid to die"), Sergius as the leader of a mad cavalry charge ("Suicide; only the pistol missed fire"). But from the fact that Sergius fails of promotion both learn that war is a business for unheroic professionals, and from Bluntschli they learn that it is, on the one hand, suffering (good friends get burned alive) and, on the other, a craft. A soldier's first duty is to survive, food is more important than arms, the best soldier is he who can get a cavalry regiment to Phillipopolis when there is no provender. The heroic connotations of the play's allusive title ply their ironies here.

But we should not oversimplify Shaw's theme. The play deflates impossibly idealistic attitudes toward love and war, but the realism it substitutes is not a "cheap" and "paltry" prosaic practical-mindedness. If Bluntschli is something as unromantic as hotel owner, his hotel is epically equipped. He is a realist, but he is distinguished from Nicola, the realist-in-excess. Bluntschli is, if only for a moment, "Emperor of Switzerland," whose "incurably romantic disposition" is directly responsible for almost every single plot development. One realizes with astonishment that the phrase is not coy, does not serve some paradox of Shaw's; testing it against what happens in the play proves it quite true. Nicola, on the other hand, has a servant's soul, whether he serves a single master or (as he intends some day) the general public. He is the cold-blooded shopkeeper, to whom Louka is more attractive as rich customer than as penniless wife. And what saves Sergius from the cynicism that besets him after his double disillusionment (war is a "fraud, . . . a hollow sham, like love") and restores him to his magnificently mannered old self is his engagement to Louka. The point is unmistakable — not that true love is unromantic, but that romantic love is unrealistic. The most significant dialogue in the entire play follows immediately upon Raina's peripety. When Bluntschli has exposed her sham attitudes, she says, "Do you know, you are the first man I ever met who did not take me seriously?" Bluntschli replies, "You mean, dont you, that I am the first man that has ever taken you quite seriously?" And Raina happily agrees that she does indeed mean that.)~~

Anton Chekhov

THREE SISTERS

Translated by Elisaveta Fen

Characters

PROZOROV, *Andrey Serghyeevich*
NATASHA (*Natalia Ivanovna*), *his fiancée, afterwards his wife*
OLGA (*Olga Serghyeevna, Olia*) ⎫
MASHA (*Maria Serghyeevna*) ⎬ *his sisters*
IRENA (*Irena Serghyeevna*) ⎭
KOOLYGHIN, *Fiodor Ilyich, master at the High School for boys, husband of Masha*
VERSHININ, *Alexandr Ignatyevich, Lieutenant-Colonel, Battery Commander*
TOOZENBACH, *Nikolai Lvovich, Baron, Lieutenant in the Army*
SOLIONY, *Vassily Vassilich, Captain*
CHEBUTYKIN, *Ivan Romanych, Army Doctor*
FEDOTIK, *Aleksey Petrovich, Second Lieutenant*
RODÉ, *Vladimir Karlovich, Second Lieutenant*
FERAPONT (*Ferapont Spiridonych*), *an old porter from the County Office*
ANFISA, *the Prozorovs' former nurse, an old woman of 80*

SCENE: *The action takes place in a county town.*

ACT I

(*A drawing-room in the Prozorovs' house; it is separated from a large ballroom*[1] *at the back by a row of columns. It is midday;*

[1] A large room, sparsely furnished, used for receptions and dances in Russian houses.

there is cheerful sunshine outside. In the ballroom the table is be-ing laid for lunch. OLGA, *wearing the regulation dark-blue dress of a secondary school mistress, is correcting her pupils' work, stand-ing or walking about as she does so.* MASHA, *in a black dress, is sit-ting reading a book, her hat on her lap.* IRENA, *in white, stands lost in thought.*)

OLGA: It's exactly a year ago that Father died, isn't it? This very day, the fifth of May — your Saint's day, Irena. I remember it was very cold and it was snowing. I felt then as if I should never survive his death; and you had fainted and were lying quite still, as if you were dead. And now — a year's gone by, and we talk about it so easily. You're wearing white, and your face is positively radiant. . . .

(*A clock strikes twelve.*)

The clock struck twelve then, too. (*A pause.*) I remember when Father was being taken to the cemetery there was a military band, and a salute with rifle fire. That was because he was a general, in command of a brigade. And yet there weren't many people at the funeral. Of course, it was raining hard, raining and snowing.

IRENA: Need we bring up all these memories?

(*Baron* TOOZENBACH, CHEBUTYKIN *and* SOLIONY *appear behind the columns by the table in the ballroom.*)

OLGA: It's so warm to-day that we can keep the windows wide open, and yet there aren't any leaves showing on the birch trees. Father was made a brigadier eleven years ago, and then he left Moscow and took us with him. I remember so well how everything in Moscow was in blossom by now, everything was soaked in sunlight and warmth. Eleven years have gone by, yet I remember everything about it, as if we'd only left yesterday. Oh, Heavens! When I woke up this morning and saw this flood of sunshine, all this spring sun-shine, I felt so moved and so happy! I felt such a longing to get back home to Moscow!

CHEBUTYKIN (*to* TOOZENBACH): The devil you have!

TOOZENBACH: It's nonsense, I agree.

MASHA (*absorbed in her book, whistles a tune under her breath*).

OLGA: Masha, do stop whistling! How can you? (*A pause.*) I suppose I must get this continual headache because I have to go to school every day and go on teaching right into the evening. I seem to have the thoughts of someone quite old. Honestly, I've been feeling as if my strength and youth were running out of me drop by drop, day after day. Day after day, all these four years that I've been working at the school. . . . I just have one longing and it seems to grow stronger and stronger. . . .

IRENA: If only we could go back to Moscow! Sell the house, finish with our life here, and go back to Moscow.

OLGA: Yes, Moscow! As soon as we possibly can.

(CHEBUTYKIN *and* TOOZENBACH *laugh.*)

IRENA: I suppose Andrey will soon get a professorship. He isn't likely to go on living here. The only problem is our poor Masha.

OLGA: Masha can come and stay the whole summer with us every year in Moscow.

MASHA (*whistles a tune under her breath*).

IRENA: Everything will settle itself, with God's help. (*Looks through the window.*) What lovely weather it is to-day! Really, I don't know why there's such joy in my heart. I remembered this morning that it was my Saint's day, and suddenly I felt so happy, and I thought of the time when we were children, and Mother was still alive. And then such wonderful thoughts came to me, such wonderful stirring thoughts!

OLGA: You're so lovely to-day, you really do look most attractive. Masha looks pretty to-day, too. Andrey could be good-looking, but he's grown so stout. It doesn't suit him. As for me, I've just aged and grown a lot thinner. I suppose it's through getting so irritated with the girls at school. But to-day I'm at home, I'm free, and my headache's gone, and I feel much younger than I did yesterday. I'm only twenty-eight, after all. . . . I suppose everything that God wills must be right and good, but I can't help thinking sometimes that if I'd got married and stayed at home, it would have been a better thing for me. (*A pause.*) I would have been very fond of my husband.

TOOZENBACH (*to* SOLIONY): Really, you talk such a lot of nonsense, I'm tired of listening to you. (*Comes into the drawing-room.*) I forgot to tell you: Vershinin, our new battery commander, is going to call on you to-day. (*Sits down by the piano.*)

OLGA: I'm very glad to hear it.

IRENA: Is he old?

TOOZENBACH: No, not particularly. Forty, forty-five at the most. (*Plays quietly.*) He seems a nice fellow. Certainly not a fool. His only weakness is that he talks too much.

IRENA: Is he interesting?

TOOZENBACH: He's all right, only he's got a wife, a mother-in-law and two little girls. What's more, she's his second wife. He calls on everybody and tells them that he's got a wife and two little girls.

He'll tell you about it, too, I'm sure of that. His wife seems to be a bit soft in the head. She wears a long plait like a girl, she is always philosophizing and talking in high-flown language, and then she often tries to commit suicide, apparently just to annoy her husband. I would have run away from a wife like that years ago, but he puts up with it, and just grumbles about it.

SOLIONY (*enters the drawing-room with* CHEBUTYKIN): Now I can only lift sixty pounds with one hand, but with two I can lift two hundred pounds, or even two hundred and forty. So I conclude from that that two men are not just twice as strong as one, but three times as strong, if not more.

CHEBUTYKIN (*reads the paper as he comes in*): Here's a recipe for falling hair . . . two ounces of naphthaline, half-a-bottle of methylated spirit . . . dissolve and apply once a day. . . . (*Writes it down in a notebook.*) Must make a note of it. (*To* SOLIONY.) Well, as I was trying to explain to you, you cork the bottle and pass a glass tube through the cork. Then you take a pinch of ordinary powdered alum, and . . .

IRENA: Ivan Romanych, dear Ivan Romanych!

CHEBUTYKIN: What is it, my child, what is it?

IRENA: Tell me, why is it I'm so happy to-day? Just as if I were sailing along in a boat with big white sails, and above me the wide, blue sky, and in the sky great white birds floating around?

CHEBUTYKIN (*kisses both her hands, tenderly*): My little white bird!

IRENA: You know, when I woke up this morning, and after I'd got up and washed, I suddenly felt as if everything in the world had become clear to me, and I knew the way I ought to live. I know it all now, my dear Ivan Romanych. Man must work by the sweat of his brow whatever his class, and that should make up the whole meaning and purpose of his life and happiness and contentment. Oh, how good it must be to be a workman, getting up with the sun and breaking stones by the roadside — or a shepherd — or a schoolmaster teaching the children — or an engine-driver on the railway. Good Heavens! it's better to be a mere ox or horse, and work, than the sort of young woman who wakes up at twelve, and drinks her coffee in bed, and then takes two hours dressing. . . . How dreadful! You know how you long for a cool drink in hot weather? Well, that's the way I long for work. And if I don't get up early from now on and really work, you can refuse to be friends with me any more, Ivan Romanych.

CHEBUTYKIN (*tenderly*): So I will, so I will. . . .

OLGA: Father taught us to get up at seven o'clock and so Irena always wakes up at seven — but then she stays in bed till at least nine, thinking about something or other. And with such a serious expression on her face, too! (*Laughs.*)

IRENA: You think it's strange when I look serious because you always think of me as a little girl. I'm twenty, you know!

TOOZENBACH: All this longing for work. . . . Heavens! how well I can understand it! I've never done a stroke of work in my life. I was born in Petersburg, an unfriendly, idle city — born into a family where work and worries were simply unknown. I remember a valet pulling off my boots for me when I came home from the cadet school. . . . I grumbled at the way he did it, and my mother looked on in admiration. She was quite surprised when other people looked at me in any other way. I was so carefully protected from work! But I doubt whether they succeeded in protecting me for good and all — yes, I doubt it very much! The time's come: there's a terrific thunder-cloud advancing upon us, a mighty storm is coming to freshen us up! Yes, it's coming all right, it's quite near already, and it's going to blow away all this idleness and indifference, and prejudice against work, this rot of boredom that our society is suffering from. I'm going to work, and in twenty-five or thirty years' time every man and woman will be working. Every one of us!

CHEBUTYKIN: I'm not going to work.

TOOZENBACH: You don't count.

SOLIONY: In twenty-five years' time you won't be alive, thank goodness. In a couple of years you'll die from a stroke — or I'll lose my temper with you and put a bullet in your head, my good fellow. (*Takes a scent bottle from his pocket and sprinkles the scent over his chest and hands.*)

CHEBUTYKIN (*laughs*): It's quite true that I never have done any work. Not a stroke since I left the university. I haven't even read a book, only newspapers. (*Takes another newspaper out of his pocket.*) For instance, here. . . . I know from the paper that there was a person called Dobroliubov, but what he wrote about I've not the faintest idea. . . . God alone knows. . . . (*Someone knocks on the floor from downstairs.*) There! They're calling me to come down: there's someone come to see me. I'll be back in a moment. . . . (*Goes out hurriedly, stroking his beard.*)

IRENA: He's up to one of his little games.

TOOZENBACH: Yes. He looked very solemn as he left. He's obviously going to give you a present.

IRENA: I do dislike that sort of thing. . . .

OLGA: Yes, isn't it dreadful? He's always doing something silly.

MASHA: "A green oak grows by a curving shore, And round that oak hangs a golden chain" . . . (*Gets up as she sings under her breath.*)

OLGA: You're sad to-day, Masha.

MASHA (*puts on her hat, singing*).

OLGA: Where are you going?

MASHA: Home.

IRENA: What a strange thing to do.

TOOZENBACH: What! Going away from your sister's party?

MASHA: What does it matter? I'll be back this evening. Good-bye, my darling. (*Kisses* IRENA.) And once again — I wish you all the happiness in the world. In the old days when Father was alive we used to have thirty or forty officers at our parties. What gay parties we had! And to-day — what have we got to-day? A man and a half, and the place is as quiet as a tomb. I'm going home. I'm depressed to-day, I'm sad, so don't listen to me. (*Laughs through her tears.*) We'll have a talk later, but good-bye for now, my dear. I'll go somewhere or other. . . .

IRENA (*displeased*): Really, you are a . . .

OLGA (*tearfully*): I understand you, Masha.

SOLIONY: If a man starts philosophizing, you call that philosophy, or possibly just sophistry, but if a woman or a couple of women start philosophizing you call that . . . what would you call it, now? Ask me another!

MASHA: What are you talking about? You are a disconcerting person!

SOLIONY: Nothing.

"He had no time to say 'Oh, oh!'
Before that bear had struck him low" . . .

(*A pause.*)

MASHA (*to* OLGA, *crossly*): Do stop snivelling!

(*Enter* ANFISA *and* FERAPONT, *the latter carrying a large cake.*)

ANFISA: Come along, my dear, this way. Come in, your boots are quite clean. (*To* IRENA.) A cake from Protopopov, at the Council Office.

IRENA: Thank you. Tell him I'm very grateful to him. (*Takes the cake.*)

FERAPONT: What's that?

IRENA (*louder*): Tell him I sent my thanks.

OLGA: Nanny, will you give him a piece of cake? Go along, Ferapont, they'll give you some cake.

FERAPONT: What's that?

ANFISA: Come along with me, Ferapont Spiridonych, my dear. Come along. (*Goes out with* FERAPONT.)

MASHA: I don't like that Protopopov fellow, Mihail Potapych, or Ivanych, or whatever it is. It's best not to invite him here.

IRENA: I haven't invited him.

MASHA: Thank goodness.

(*Enter* CHEBUTYKIN, *followed by a soldier carrying a silver samovar. Murmurs of astonishment and displeasure.*)

OLGA (*covering her face with her hands*): A samovar! But this is dreadful! (*Goes through to the ballroom and stands by the table.*)

IRENA: My dear Ivan Romanych, what are you thinking about?

TOOZENBACH (*laughs*): Didn't I tell you?

MASHA: Ivan Romanych, you really ought to be ashamed of yourself!

CHEBUTYKIN: My dear, sweet girls, I've no one in the world but you. You're dearer to me than anything in the world! I'm nearly sixty, I'm an old man, a lonely, utterly unimportant old man. The only thing that's worth anything in me is my love for you, and if it weren't for you, really I would have been dead long ago. (*To* IRENA.) My dear, my sweet little girl, haven't I known you since the very day you were born? Didn't I carry you about in my arms? . . . didn't I love your dear mother?

IRENA: But why do you get such expensive presents?

CHEBUTYKIN (*tearfully and crossly*): Expensive presents! . . . Get along with you! (*To the orderly.*) Put the samovar over there. (*Mimics* IRENA.) Expensive presents!

(*The orderly takes the samovar to the ballroom.*)

ANFISA (*crosses the drawing-room*): My dears, there's a strange colonel just arrived. He's taken off his coat and he's coming up now. Irenushka, do be nice and polite to him, won't you? (*In the doorway.*) And it's high time we had lunch, too. . . . Oh, dear! (*Goes out.*)

TOOZENBACH: It's Vershinin, I suppose.

(*Enter* VERSHININ.)

TOOZENBACH: Lieutenant-Colonel Vershinin!

VERSHININ (*to* MASHA *and* IRENA): Allow me to introduce myself — Lieutenant-Colonel Vershinin. I'm so glad, so very glad to be here at last. How you've changed! Dear, dear, how you've changed!

IRENA: Please, do sit down. We're very pleased to see you, I'm sure.

VERSHININ (*gaily*): I'm so glad to see you, so glad! But there were three of you, weren't there? — three sisters. I remember there were three little girls. I don't remember their faces, but I knew your father, Colonel Prozorov, and I remember he had three little girls.

Oh, yes, I saw them myself. I remember them quite well. How time flies! Dear, dear, how it flies!

TOOZENBACH: Alexandr Ignatyevich comes from Moscow.

IRENA: From Moscow? You come from Moscow?

VERSHININ: Yes, from Moscow. Your father was a battery commander there, and I was an officer in the same brigade. (*To* MASHA.) I seem to remember your face a little.

MASHA: I don't remember you at all.

IRENA: Olia, Olia! (*Calls toward the ballroom.*) Olia, do come!

(OLGA *enters from the ballroom.*)

IRENA: It seems that Lieutenant-Colonel Vershinin comes from Moscow.

VERSHININ: You must be Olga Serghyeevna, the eldest. And you are Maria. . . . And you are Irena, the youngest. . . .

OLGA: You come from Moscow?

VERSHININ: Yes. I studied in Moscow and entered the service there. I stayed there quite a long time, but then I was put in charge of a battery here — so I moved out here, you see. I don't really remember you, you know, I only remember that there were three sisters. I remember your father, though, I remember him very well. All I need to do is to close my eyes and I can see him standing there as if he were alive. I used to visit you in Moscow.

OLGA: I thought I remembered everybody, and yet . . .

VERSHININ: My Christian names are Alexandr Ignatyevich.

IRENA: Alexandr Ignatyevich, and you come from Moscow! Well, what a surprise!

OLGA: We're going to live there, you know.

IRENA: We hope to be there by the autumn. It's our home town, we were born there. . . . In Staraya Basmannaya Street.

(*Both laugh happily.*)

MASHA: Fancy meeting a fellow townsman so unexpectedly! (*Eagerly.*) I remember now. Do you remember, Olga, there was someone they used to call "the lovesick Major"? You were a Lieutenant then, weren't you, and you were in love with someone or other, and everyone used to tease you about it. They called you "Major" for some reason or other.

VERSHININ (*laughs*): That's it, that's it. . . . "The lovesick Major," that's what they called me.

MASHA: In those days you only had a moustache. . . . Oh, dear, how much older you look! (*Tearfully.*) How much older!

VERSHININ: Yes, I was still a young man in the days when they called me "the lovesick Major." I was in love then. It's different now.

OLGA: But you haven't got a single grey hair! You've aged, yes, but you're certainly not an old man.

VERSHININ: Nevertheless, I'm turned forty-two. Is it long since you left Moscow?

IRENA: Eleven years. Now what are you crying for, Masha, you funny girl? . . . (*Tearfully.*) You'll make me cry, too.

MASHA: I'm not crying. What was the street you lived in?

VERSHININ: In the Staraya Basmannaya.

OLGA: We did, too.

VERSHININ: At one time I lived in the Niemietzkaya Street. I used to walk from there to the Krasny Barracks, and I remember there was such a gloomy bridge I had to cross. I used to hear the noise of the water rushing under it. I remember how lonely and sad I felt there. (*A pause.*) But what a magnificently wide river you have here! It's a marvellous river!

OLGA: Yes, but this is a cold place. It's cold here, and there are too many mosquitoes.

VERSHININ: Really? I should have said you had a really good healthy climate here, a real Russian climate. Forest, river . . . birch-trees, too. The dear, unpretentious birch-trees — I love them more than any of the other trees. It's nice living here. But there's one rather strange thing, the station is fifteen miles from the town. And no one knows why.

SOLIONY: I know why it is. (*Everyone looks at him.*) Because if the station were nearer, it wouldn't be so far away, and as it is so far away, it can't be nearer. (*An awkward silence.*)

TOOZENBACH: You like your little joke, Vassily Vassilich.

OLGA: I'm sure I remember you now. I know I do.

VERSHININ: I knew your mother.

CHEBUTYKIN: She was a good woman, God bless her memory!

IRENA: Mamma was buried in Moscow.

OLGA: At the convent of Novo-Dievichye.

MASHA: You know, I'm even beginning to forget what she looked like. I suppose people will lose all memory of us in just the same way. We'll be forgotten.

VERSHININ: Yes, we shall all be forgotten. Such is our fate, and we can't do anything about it. And all the things that seem serious, important and full of meaning to us now will be forgotten one day — or anyway they won't seem important any more. (*A pause.*) It's strange to think that we're utterly unable to tell what will be re-

garded as great and important in the future and what will be
thought of as just paltry and ridiculous. Didn't the great discoveries
of Copernicus — or of Columbus, if you like — appear useless and
unimportant to begin with? — whereas some rubbish, written up by
an eccentric fool, was regarded as a revelation of great truth? It may
well be that in time to come the life we live to-day will seem strange
and uncomfortable and stupid and not too clean, either, and perhaps
even wicked. . . .

TOOZENBACH: Who can tell? It's just as possible that future generations will think that we lived our lives on a very high plane and remember us with respect. After all, we no longer have tortures and
public executions and invasions, though there's still a great deal of
suffering!

SOLIONY (*in a high-pitched voice as if calling to chickens*): Cluck,
cluck, cluck! There's nothing our good Baron loves as much as a
nice bit of philosophizing.

TOOZENBACH: Vassily Vassilich, will you kindly leave me alone?
(*Moves to another chair.*) It's becoming tiresome.

SOLIONY (*as before*): Cluck, cluck, cluck! . . .

TOOZENBACH (*to* VERSHININ): The suffering that we see around us —
and there's so much of it — itself proves that our society has at
least achieved a level of morality which is higher. . . .

VERSHININ: Yes, yes, of course.

CHEBUTYKIN: You said just now, Baron, that our age will be called
great; but people are small all the same. . . . (*Gets up.*) Look how
small I am.

(*A violin is played off stage.*)

MASHA: That's Andrey playing the violin; he's our brother, you know.

IRENA: We've got quite a clever brother. . . . We're expecting him
to be a professor. Papa was a military man, but Andrey chose an
academic career.

OLGA: We've been teasing him to-day. We think he's in love, just a
little.

IRENA: With a girl who lives down here. She'll be calling in to-day
most likely.

MASHA: The way she dresses herself is awful! It's not that her clothes
are just ugly and old-fashioned, they're simply pathetic. She'll put
on some weird-looking, bright yellow skirt with a crude sort of fringe
affair, and then a red blouse to go with it. And her cheeks look as
though they've been scrubbed, they're so shiny! Andrey's not in love
with her — I can't believe it; after all, he has got some taste. I
think he's just playing the fool, just to annoy us. I heard yesterday

that she's going to get married to Protopopov, the chairman of the local council. I thought it was an excellent idea. (*Calls through the side door.*) Andrey, come here, will you? Just for a moment, dear.

(*Enter* ANDREY.)

OLGA: This is my brother, Andrey Serghyeevich.

VERSHININ: Vershinin.

ANDREY: Prozorov. (*Wipes the perspiration from his face.*) I believe you've been appointed battery commander here?

OLGA: What do you think, dear? Alexandr Ignatyevich comes from Moscow.

ANDREY: Do you, really? Congratulations! You'll get no peace from my sisters now.

VERSHININ: I'm afraid your sisters must be getting tired of me already.

IRENA: Just look, Andrey gave me this little picture frame to-day. (*Shows him the frame.*) He made it himself.

VERSHININ (*looks at the frame, not knowing what to say*): Yes, it's . . . it's very nice indeed. . . .

IRENA: Do you see that little frame over the piano? He made that one, too.

(ANDREY *waves his hand impatiently and walks off.*)

OLGA: He's awfully clever, and he plays the violin, and he makes all sorts of things, too. In fact, he's very gifted all round. Andrey, please, don't go. He's got such a bad habit — always going off like this. Come here!

(MASHA *and* IRENA *take him by the arms and lead him back, laughing.*)

MASHA: Now just you come here!

ANDREY: Do leave me alone, please do!

MASHA: You are a silly! They used to call Alexandr Ignatyevich "the lovesick Major," and he didn't get annoyed.

VERSHININ: Not in the least.

MASHA: I feel like calling you a "lovesick fiddler."

IRENA: Or a "lovesick professor."

OLGA: He's fallen in love! Our Andriusha's in love!

IRENA (*clapping her hands*): Three cheers for Andriusha! Andriusha's in love!

CHEBUTYKIN (*comes up behind* ANDREY *and puts his arms round his waist*): "Nature created us for love alone." . . . (*Laughs loudly, still holding his paper in his hand.*)

ANDREY: That's enough of it, that's enough. . . . (*Wipes his face.*)

I couldn't get to sleep all night, and I'm not feeling too grand just now. I read till four o'clock, and then I went to bed, but nothing happened. I kept thinking about one thing and another . . . and it gets light so early; the sun just pours into my room. I'd like to translate a book from the English while I'm here during the summer.

VERSHININ: You read English, then?

ANDREY: Yes. My father — God bless his memory — used to simply wear us out with learning. It sounds silly, I know, but I must confess that since he died I've begun to grow stout, as if I'd been physically relieved of the strain. I've grown quite stout in a year. Yes, thanks to Father, my sisters and I know French and German and English, and Irena here knows Italian, too. But what an effort it all cost us!

MASHA: Knowing three languages in a town like this is an unnecessary luxury. In fact, not even a luxury, but just a sort of useless encumbrance . . . it's rather like having a sixth finger on your hand. We know a lot of stuff that's just useless.

VERSHININ: Really! (*Laughs.*) You know a lot of stuff that's useless! It seems to me that there's no place on earth, however dull and depressing it may be, where intelligence and education can be useless. Let us suppose that among the hundred thousand people in this town, all of them, no doubt, very backward and uncultured, there are just three people like yourselves. Obviously, you can't hope to triumph over all the mass of ignorance around you; as your life goes by, you'll have to keep giving in little by little until you get lost in the crowd, in the hundred thousand. Life will swallow you up, but you'll not quite disappear, you'll make some impression on it. After you've gone, perhaps six more people like you will turn up, then twelve, and so on, until in the end most people will have become like you. So in two or three hundred years life on this old earth of ours will have become marvellously beautiful. Man longs for a life like that, and if it isn't here yet, he must imagine it, wait for it, dream about it, prepare for it, he must know and see more than his father and his grandfather did. (*Laughs.*) And you're complaining because you know a lot of stuff that's useless.

MASHA (*takes off her hat*): I'll be staying to lunch.

IRENA (*with a sigh*): Really, someone should have written all that down.

(ANDREY *has left the room, unnoticed.*)

TOOZENBACH: You say that in time to come life will be marvellously beautiful. That's probably true. But in order to share in it now, at a distance so to speak, we must prepare for it and work for it.

VERSHININ (*gets up*): Yes. . . . What a lot of flowers you've got here! (*Looks round.*) And what a marvellous house! I do envy you! All my life I seem to have been pigging it in small flats, with two chairs and a sofa and a stove which always smokes. It's the flowers that I've missed in my life, flowers like these! . . . (*Rubs his hands.*) Oh, well, never mind!

TOOZENBACH: Yes, we must work. I suppose you're thinking I'm a sentimental German. But I assure you I'm not — I'm Russian. I don't speak a word of German. My father was brought up in the Greek Orthodox faith. (*A pause.*)

VERSHININ (*walks up and down the room*): You know, I often wonder what it would be like if you could start your life over again — deliberately, I mean, consciously. . . . Suppose you could put aside the life you'd lived already, as though it was just a sort of rough draft, and then start another one like a fair copy. If that happened, I think the thing you'd want most of all would be not to repeat yourself. You'd try at least to create a new environment for yourself, a flat like this one, for instance, with some flowers and plenty of light. . . . I have a wife, you know, and two little girls; and my wife's not very well, and all that. . . . Well, if I had to start my life all over again, I wouldn't marry. . . . No, no!

(*Enter* KOOLYGHIN, *in the uniform of a teacher.*)

KOOLYGHIN (*approaches* IRENA): Congratulations, dear sister — from the bottom of my heart, congratulations on your Saint's day. I wish you good health and everything a girl of your age ought to have! And allow me to present you with this little book. . . . (*Hands her a book.*) It's the history of our school covering the whole fifty years of its existence. I wrote it myself. Quite a trifle, of course — I wrote it in my spare time when I had nothing better to do — but I hope you'll read it nevertheless. Good morning to you all! (*To* VERSHININ.) Allow me to introduce myself. Koolyghin's the name; I'm a master at the secondary school here. And a town councillor. (*To* IRENA.) You'll find a list in the book of all the pupils who have completed their studies at our school during the last fifty years. *Feci quod potui, faciant meliora potentes.* (*Kisses* MASHA.)

IRENA: But you gave me this book last Easter!

KOOLYGHIN (*laughs*): Did I really? In that case, give it me back — or no, better give it to the Colonel. Please do take it, Colonel. Maybe you'll read it some time when you've nothing better to do.

VERSHININ: Thank you very much. (*Prepares to leave.*) I'm so very glad to have made your acquaintance. . . .

OLGA: You aren't going are you? . . . Really, you mustn't.

IRENA: But you'll stay and have lunch with us! Please do.

OLGA: Please do.

VERSHININ (*bows*): I see I've intruded on your Saint's day party. I didn't know. Forgive me for not offering you my congratulations. (*Goes into the ballroom with* OLGA.)

KOOLYGHIN: To-day is Sunday, my friends, a day of rest; let us rest and enjoy it, each according to his age and position in life! We shall have to roll up the carpets and put them away till the winter. . . . We must remember to put some naphthaline on them, or Persian powder. . . . The Romans enjoyed good health because they knew how to work *and* how to rest. They had *mens sana in corpore sano.* Their life had a definite shape, a form. . . . The director of the school says that the most important thing about life is form. . . . A thing that loses its form is finished — that's just as true of our ordinary, everyday lives. (*Takes* MASHA *by the waist and laughs.*) Masha loves me. My wife loves me. Yes, and the curtains will have to be put away with the carpets, too. . . . I'm cheerful to-day, I'm in quite excellent spirits. . . . Masha, we're invited to the director's at four o'clock to-day. A country walk has been arranged for the teachers and their families.

MASHA: I'm not going.

KOOLYGHIN (*distressed*): Masha, darling, why not?

MASHA: I'll tell you later. . . . (*Crossly.*) All right, I'll come, only leave me alone now. . . . (*Walks off.*)

KOOLYGHIN: And after the walk we shall all spend the evening at the director's house. In spite of weak health, that man is certainly sparing no pains to be sociable. A first-rate, thoroughly enlightened man! A most excellent person! After the conference yesterday he said to me: "I'm tired, Fiodor Ilyich. I'm tired!" (*Looks at the clock, then at his watch.*) Your clock is seven minutes fast. Yes, "I'm tired," he said.

(*The sound of the violin is heard off stage.*)

OLGA: Will you all come and sit down, please! Lunch is ready. There's a pie.

KOOLYGHIN: Ah, Olga, my dear girl! Last night I worked up to eleven o'clock, and I felt tired, but to-day I'm quite happy. (*Goes to the table in the ballroom.*) My dear Olga!

CHEBUTYKIN (*puts the newspaper in his pocket and combs his beard*): A pie? Excellent!

MASHA (*sternly to* CHEBUTYKIN): Remember, you mustn't take anything to drink to-day. Do you hear? It's bad for you.

CHEBUTYKIN: Never mind. I've got over that weakness long ago! I

haven't done any heavy drinking for two years. (*Impatiently.*) Anyway, my dear, what does it matter?

MASHA: All the same, don't you dare to drink anything. Mind you
don't now! (*Crossly, but taking care that her husband does not
hear.*) So now I've got to spend another of these damnably boring
evenings at the director's!

TOOZENBACH: I wouldn't go if I were you, and that's that.

CHEBUTYKIN: Don't you go, my dear.

MASHA: Don't go, indeed! Oh, what a damnable life! It's intolerable.
. . . (*Goes into the ballroom.*)

CHEBUTYKIN (*follows her*): Well, well! . . .

SOLIONY (*as he passes* TOOZENBACH *on the way to the ballroom*):
Cluck, cluck, cluck!

TOOZENBACH: Do stop it, Vassily Vassilich. I've really had enough of
it. . . .

SOLIONY: Cluck, cluck, cluck! . . .

KOOLYGHIN (*gaily*): Your health, Colonel! I'm a schoolmaster . . .
and I'm quite one of the family here, as it were. I'm Masha's husband. She's got a sweet nature, such a very sweet nature!

VERSHININ: I think I'll have a little of this dark vodka. (*Drinks.*) Your
health! (*To* OLGA.) I do feel so happy with you people!

(*Only* IRENA *and* TOOZENBACH *remain in the drawing-room.*)

IRENA: Masha's a bit out of humour to-day. You know, she got married
when she was eighteen, and then her husband seemed the cleverest
man in the world to her. It's different now. He's the kindest of men,
but not the cleverest.

OLGA (*impatiently*): Andrey, will you please come?

ANDREY (*off stage*): Just coming. (*Enters and goes to the table.*)

TOOZENBACH: What are you thinking about?

IRENA: Oh, nothing special. You know, I don't like this man Soliony,
I'm quite afraid of him. Whenever he opens his mouth he says
something silly.

TOOZENBACH: He's a strange fellow. I'm sorry for him, even though he
irritates me. In fact, I feel more sorry for him than irritated. I think
he's shy. When he's alone with me, he can be quite sensible and
friendly, but in company he's offensive and bullying. Don't go over
there just yet, let them get settled down at the table. Let me stay
beside you for a bit. Tell me what you're thinking about. (*A pause.*)
You're twenty . . . and I'm not thirty yet myself. What years and
years we still have ahead of us, a whole long succession of years, all
full of my love for you! . . .

IRENA: Don't talk to me about love, Nikolai Lvovich.

TOOZENBACH (*not listening*): Oh, I long so passionately for life, I long to work and strive so much, and all this longing is somehow mingled with my love for you, Irena. And just because you happen to be beautiful, life appears beautiful to me! What are you thinking about?

IRENA: You say that life is beautiful. Maybe it is — but what if it only seems to be beautiful? Our lives, I mean the lives of us three sisters, haven't been beautiful up to now. The truth is that life has been stifling us, like weeds in a garden. I'm afraid I'm crying. . . . So unnecessary. . . . (*Quickly dries her eyes and smiles.*) We must work, work! The reason we feel depressed and take such a gloomy view of life is that we've never known what it is to make a real effort. We're the children of parents who despised work. . . .

(*Enter* NATALIA IVANOVNA. *She is wearing a pink dress with a green belt.*)

NATASHA: They've gone in to lunch already. . . . I'm late. . . . (*Glances at herself in a mirror, adjusts her dress.*) My hair seems to be all right. . . . (*Catches sight of* IRENA.) My dear Irena Serghye-evna, congratulations! (*Gives her a vigorous and prolonged kiss.*) You've got such a lot of visitors. . . . I feel quite shy. . . . How do you do, Baron?

OLGA (*enters the drawing-room*): Oh, there you are, Natalia Ivanovna! How are you, my dear?

(*They kiss each other.*)

NATASHA: Congratulations! You've such a lot of people here, I feel dreadfully shy. . . .

OLGA: It's all right, they're all old friends. (*Alarmed, dropping her voice.*) You've got a green belt on! My dear, that's surely a mistake!

NATASHA: Why, is it a bad omen, or what?

OLGA: No, but it just doesn't go with your dress . . . it looks so strange. . . .

NATASHA (*tearfully*): Really? But it isn't really green, you know, it's a sort of dull colour. . . . (*Follows* OLGA *to the ballroom.*)

(*All are now seated at the table; the drawing-room is empty.*)

KOOLYGHIN: Irena, you know, I do wish you'd find yourself a good husband. In my view it's high time you got married.

CHEBUTYKIN: You ought to get yourself a nice little husband, too, Natalia Ivanovna.

KOOLYGHIN: Natalia Ivanovna already has a husband in view.

MASHA (*strikes her plate with her fork*): A glass of wine for me, please!

Three cheers for our jolly old life! We keep our end up, we do!

KOOLYGHIN: Masha, you won't get more than five out of ten for good conduct!

VERSHININ: I say, this liqueur's very nice. What is it made of?

SOLIONY: Black beetles!

IRENA: Ugh! ugh! How disgusting!

OLGA: We're having roast turkey for dinner to-night, and then apple tart. Thank goodness, I'll be here all day to-day . . . this evening, too. You must all come this evening.

VERSHININ: May I come in the evening, too?

IRENA: Yes, please do.

NATASHA: They don't stand on ceremony here.

CHEBUTYKIN: "Nature created us for love alone." . . . (*Laughs.*)

ANDREY (*crossly*): Will you stop it, please? Aren't you tired of it yet?

(*FEDOTIK and RODÉ come in with a large basket of flowers.*)

FEDOTIK: Just look here, they're having lunch already!

RODÉ (*in a loud voice*): Having their lunch? So they are, they're having lunch already.

FEDOTIK: Wait half a minute. (*Takes a snapshot.*) One! Just one minute more! . . . (*Takes another snapshot.*) Two! All over now.

(*They pick up the basket and go into the ballroom where they are greeted uproariously.*)

RODÉ (*loudly*): Congratulations, Irena Serghyeevna! I wish you all the best, everything you'd wish for yourself! Gorgeous weather to-day, absolutely marvellous. I've been out walking the whole morning with the boys. You do know that I teach gym at the high school, don't you? . . .

FEDOTIK: You may move now, Irena Serghyeevna, that is, if you want to. (*Takes a snapshot.*) You do look attractive to-day. (*Takes a top out of his pocket.*) By the way, look at this top. It's got a wonderful hum.

IRENA: What a sweet little thing!

MASHA: "A green oak grows by a curving shore, And round that oak hangs a golden chain." . . . A green chain around that oak. . . . (*Peevishly.*) Why do I keep on saying that? Those lines have been worrying me all day long!

KOOLYGHIN: Do you know, we're thirteen at table?

RODÉ (*loudly*): You don't really believe in these old superstitions, do you? (*Laughter.*)

KOOLYGHIN: When thirteen people sit down to table, it means that some of them are in love. Is it you, by any chance, Ivan Romanych?

CHEBUTYKIN: Oh, I'm just an old sinner. . . . But what I can't make out is why Natalia Ivanovna looks so embarrassed.

(*Loud laughter.* NATASHA *runs out into the drawing-room,* ANDREY *follows her.*)

ANDREY: Please, Natasha, don't take any notice of them! Stop . . . wait a moment. . . . Please!

NATASHA: I feel so ashamed. . . . I don't know what's the matter with me, and they're all laughing at me. It's awful of me to leave the table like that, but I couldn't help it. . . . I just couldn't. . . . (*Covers her face with her hands.*)

ANDREY: My dear girl, please, please don't get upset. Honestly, they don't mean any harm, they're just teasing. My dear, sweet girl, they're really good-natured folks, they all are, and they're fond of us both. Come over to the window, they can't see us there. . . . (*Looks round.*)

NATASHA: You see, I'm not used to being with a lot of people.

ANDREY: Oh, how young you are, Natasha, how wonderfully, beautifully young! My dear, sweet girl, don't get so upset! Do believe me, believe me. . . . I'm so happy, so full of love, of joy. . . . No, they can't see us here! They can't see us! How did I come to love you, when was it? . . . I don't understand anything. My precious, my sweet, my innocent girl, please — I want you to marry me! I love you, I love you as I've never loved anybody. . . . (*Kisses her.*)

(*Enter two officers and, seeing* NATASHA *and* ANDREY *kissing, stand and stare in amazement.*)

ACT II

(*The scene is the same as in Act I. It is eight o'clock in the evening. The faint sound of an accordion is heard coming from the street.*

The stage is unlit. Enter NATALIA IVANOVNA *in a dressing-gown, carrying a candle. She crosses the stage and stops by the door leading to* ANDREY's *room.*)

NATASHA: What are you doing, Andriusha? Reading? It's all right, I only wanted to know. . . . (*Goes to another door, opens it, looks inside and shuts it again.*) No one's left a light anywhere. . . .

ANDREY (*enters with a book in his hand*): What is it, Natasha?

NATASHA: I was just going round to see if anyone had left a light anywhere. It's carnival week, and the servants are so excited about it

. . . anything might happen! You've got to watch them. Last night about twelve o'clock I happened to go into the dining-room, and — would you believe it? — there was a candle alight on the table. I've not found out who lit it. (*Puts the candle down.*) What time is it?

ANDREY (*glances at his watch*): Quarter past eight.

NATASHA: And Olga and Irena still out. They aren't back from work yet, poor things! Olga's still at some teachers' conference, and Irena's at the post office. (*Sighs.*) This morning I said to Irena: "Do take care of yourself, my dear." But she won't listen. Did you say it was a quarter past eight? I'm afraid Bobik is not at all well. Why does he get so cold? Yesterday he had a temperature, but to-day he feels quite cold when you touch him. . . . I'm so afraid!

ANDREY: It's all right, Natasha. The boy's well enough.

NATASHA: Still, I think he ought to have a special diet. I'm so anxious about him. By the way, they tell me that some carnival party's supposed to be coming here soon after nine. I'd rather they didn't come, Andriusha.

ANDREY: Well, I really don't know what I can do. They've been asked to come.

NATASHA: This morning the dear little fellow woke up and looked at me, and then suddenly he smiled. He recognized me, you see. "Good morning, Bobik," I said, "good morning, darling precious!" And then he laughed. Babies understand everything, you know, they understand us perfectly well. Anyway, Andriusha, I'll tell the servants not to let that carnival party in.

ANDREY (*irresolutely*): Well . . . it's really for my sisters to decide, isn't it? It's their house, after all.

NATASHA: Yes, it's their house as well. I'll tell them, too. . . . They're so kind. . . . (*Walks off.*) I've ordered sour milk for supper. The doctor says you ought to eat nothing but sour milk, or you'll never get any thinner. (*Stops.*) Bobik feels cold. I'm afraid his room is too cold for him. He ought to move into a warmer room, at least until the warm weather comes. Irena's room, for instance — that's just a perfect room for a baby: it's dry, and it gets the sun all day long. We must tell her: perhaps she'd share Olga's room for a bit. . . . In any case, she's never at home during the day, she only sleeps there. . . . (*A pause.*) Andriusha, why don't you say anything?

ANDREY: I was just day-dreaming. . . . There's nothing to say, anyway. . . .

NATASHA: Well. . . . What was it I was going to tell you? Oh, yes! Ferapont from the Council Office wants to see you about something.

ANDREY (*yawns*): Tell him to come up.

(NATASHA *goes out.* ANDREY, *bending over the candle which she has left behind, begins to read his book. Enter* FERAPONT *in an old shabby overcoat, his collar turned up, his ears muffled in a scarf.*)

ANDREY: Hullo, old chap! What did you want to see me about?

FERAPONT: The chairman's sent you the register and a letter or something. Here they are. (*Hands him the book and the letter.*)

ANDREY: Thanks. That's all right. Incidentally, why have you come so late? It's gone eight already.

FERAPONT: What's that?

ANDREY (*raising his voice*): I said, why have you come so late? It's gone eight already.

FERAPONT: That's right. It was still daylight when I came first, but they wouldn't let me see you. The master's engaged, they said. Well, if you're engaged, you're engaged. I'm not in a hurry. (*Thinking that* ANDREY *has said something.*) What's that?

ANDREY: Nothing. (*Turns over the pages of the register.*) Tomorrow's Friday, there's no meeting, but I'll go to the office just the same . . . do some work. I'm so bored at home! . . . (*A pause.*) Yes, my dear old fellow, how things do change, what a fraud life is! So strange! To-day I picked up this book, just out of boredom, because I hadn't anything to do. It's a copy of some lectures I attended at the University. . . . Good Heavens! Just think — I'm secretary of the local council now, and Protopopov's chairman, and the most I can ever hope for is to become a member of the council myself! I — a member of the local council! I, who dream every night that I'm a professor in Moscow University, a famous academician, the pride of all Russia!

FERAPONT: I'm sorry, I can't tell you. I don't hear very well.

ANDREY: If you could hear properly I don't think I'd be talking to you like this. I must talk to someone, but my wife doesn't seem to understand me, and as for my sisters . . . I'm afraid of them for some reason or other, I'm afraid of them laughing at me and pulling my leg. . . . I don't drink and I don't like going to pubs, but my word! how I'd enjoy an hour or so at Tyestov's, or the Great Moscow Restaurant! Yes, my dear fellow, I would indeed!

FERAPONT: The other day at the office a contractor was telling me about some business men who were eating pancakes in Moscow. One of them ate forty pancakes and died. It was either forty or fifty, I can't remember exactly.

ANDREY: You can sit in some huge restaurant in Moscow without knowing anyone, and no one knowing you; yet somehow you don't feel that you don't belong there. . . . Whereas here you know everybody, and everybody knows you, and yet you don't feel you belong here, you feel you don't belong at all. . . . You're lonely and you feel a stranger.

FERAPONT: What's that? (*A pause.*) It was the same man that told me — of course, he may have been lying — he said that there's an enormous rope stretched right across Moscow.

ANDREY: Whatever for?

FERAPONT: I'm sorry, I can't tell you. That's what he said.

ANDREY: What nonsense! (*Reads the book.*) Have you ever been to Moscow?

FERAPONT (*after a pause*): No. It wasn't God's wish. (*A pause.*) Shall I go now?

ANDREY: Yes, you may go. Good-bye. (FERAPONT *goes out.*) Good-bye. (*Reading.*) Come in the morning to take some letters. . . . You can go now. (*A pause.*) He's gone. (*A bell rings.*) Yes, that's how it is. . . . (*Stretches and slowly goes to his room.*)

(*Singing is heard off stage; a nurse is putting a baby to sleep. Enter* MASHA *and* VERSHININ. *While they talk together, a maid lights a lamp and candles in the ballroom.*)

MASHA: I don't know. (*A pause.*) I don't know. Habit's very important, of course. For instance, after Father died, for a long time we couldn't get accustomed to the idea that we hadn't any orderlies to wait on us. But, habit apart, I think it's quite right what I was saying. Perhaps it's different in other places, but in this town the military certainly do seem to be the nicest and most generous and best-mannered people.

VERSHININ: I'm thirsty. I could do with a nice glass of tea.

MASHA (*glances at her watch*): They'll bring it in presently. You see, they married me off when I was eighteen. I was afraid of my husband because he was a school-master, and I had only just left school myself. He seemed terribly learned then, very clever and important. Now it's quite different, unfortunately.

VERSHININ: Yes. . . . I see. . . .

MASHA: I don't say anything against my husband — I'm used to him now — but there are such a lot of vulgar and unpleasant and offensive people among the other civilians. Vulgarity upsets me, it makes me feel insulted, I actually suffer when I meet someone who lacks refinement and gentle manners, and courtesy. When I'm with the other teachers, my husband's friends, I just suffer.

VERSHININ: Yes, of course. But I should have thought that in a town like this the civilians and the army people were equally uninteresting. There's nothing to choose between them. If you talk to any educated person here, civilian or military, he'll generally tell you that he's just worn out. It's either his wife, or his house, or his estate, or his horse, or something. . . . We Russians are capable of such elevated thoughts — then why do we have such low ideals in practical life? Why is it, why?

MASHA: Why?

VERSHININ: Yes, why does his wife wear him out, why do his children wear him out? And what about *him* wearing out his wife and children?

MASHA: You're a bit low-spirited to-day, aren't you?

VERSHININ: Perhaps. I haven't had any dinner to-day. I've had nothing to eat since morning. One of my daughters is a bit off colour, and when the children are ill, I get so worried. I feel utterly conscience-stricken at having given them a mother like theirs. Oh, if only you could have seen her this morning! What a despicable woman! We started quarrelling at seven o'clock, and at nine I just walked out and slammed the door. (*A pause.*) I never talk about these things in the ordinary way. It's a strange thing, but you're the only person I feel I dare complain to. (*Kisses her hand.*) Don't be angry with me. I've nobody, nobody but you. . . . (*A pause.*)

MASHA: What a noise the wind's making in the stove! Just before Father died the wind howled in the chimney just like that.

VERSHININ: Are you superstitious?

MASHA: Yes.

VERSHININ: How strange. (*Kisses her hand.*) You really are a wonderful creature, a marvellous creature! Wonderful, marvellous! It's quite dark here, but I can see your eyes shining.

MASHA (*Moves to another chair*): There's more light over here.

VERSHININ: I love you, I love you, I love you. . . . I love your eyes, I love your movements. . . . I dream about them. A wonderful, marvellous being!

MASHA (*Laughing softly*): When you talk to me like that, somehow I can't help laughing, although I'm afraid at the same time. Don't say it again, please. (*Half-audibly.*) Well, no . . . go on. I don't mind. . . . (*Covers her face with her hands.*) I don't mind. . . . Someone's coming. . . . Let's talk about something else. . . .

(*Enter* IRENA *and* TOOZENBACH *through the ballroom.*)

TOOZENBACH: I have a triple-barrelled name — Baron Toozenbach-Krone-Alschauer — but actually I'm a Russian. I was baptized in the Greek-Orthodox faith, just like yourself. I haven't really got any German characteristics, except maybe the obstinate patient way I keep on pestering you. Look how I bring you home every evening.

IRENA: How tired I am!

TOOZENBACH: And I'll go on fetching you from the post office and bringing you home every evening for the next twenty years — unless you send me away. . . . (*Noticing* MASHA *and* VERSHININ, *with pleasure.*) Oh, it's you! How are you?

IRENA: Well, here I am, home at last! (*To* MASHA.) A woman came into the post office just before I left. She wanted to send a wire to her brother in Saratov to tell him her son had just died, but she couldn't remember the address. So we had to send the wire without an address, just to Saratov. She was crying and I was rude to her, for no reason at all. "I've no time to waste," I told her. So stupid of me. We're having the carnival crowd to-day, aren't we?

MASHA: Yes.

IRENA (*sits down*): How nice it is to rest! I am tired!

TOOZENBACH (*smiling*): When you come back from work, you look so young, so pathetic, somehow. . . . (*A pause.*)

IRENA: I'm tired. No, I don't like working at the post office, I don't like it at all.

MASHA: You've got thinner. . . . (*Whistles.*) You look younger, too, and your face looks quite boyish.

TOOZENBACH: It's the way she does her hair.

IRENA: I must look for another job. This one doesn't suit me. It hasn't got what I always longed for and dreamed about. It's the sort of work you do without inspiration, without even thinking.

(*Someone knocks at the floor from below.*)

That's the Doctor knocking. (*To* TOOZENBACH.) Will you answer him, dear? . . . I can't. . . . I'm so tired.

TOOZENBACH (*knocks on the floor.*)

IRENA: He'll be up in a moment. We must do something about all this. Andrey and the Doctor went to the club last night and lost at cards again. They say Andrey lost two hundred roubles.

MASHA (*with indifference*): Well, what are we to do about it?

IRENA: He lost a fortnight ago, and he lost in December, too. I wish to goodness he'd lose everything we've got, and soon, too, and then perhaps we'd move out of this place. Good Heavens, I dream of Moscow every night. Sometimes I feel as if I were going mad. (*Laughs.*) We're going to Moscow in June. How many months are there till June? . . . February, March, April, May . . . nearly half-a-year!

MASHA: We must take care that Natasha doesn't get to know about him losing at cards.

IRENA: I don't think she cares.

(*Enter* CHEBUTYKIN. *He has been resting on his bed since dinner and has only just got up. He combs his beard, then sits down at the table and takes out a newspaper.*)

MASHA: There he is. Has he paid his rent yet?

IRENA (*laughs*): No. Not a penny for the last eight months. I suppose he's forgotten.

MASHA (*laughs*): How solemn he looks sitting there!

(*They all laugh. A pause.*)

IRENA: Why don't you say something, Alexandr Ignatyevich?

VERSHININ: I don't know. I'm just longing for some tea. I'd give my life for a glass of tea! I've had nothing to eat since morning. . . .

CHEBUTYKIN: Irena Serghyeevna!

IRENA: What is it?

CHEBUTYKIN: Please come here. V*enez ici!* (IRENA *goes over to him and sits down at the table.*) I can't do without you.

(IRENA *lays out the cards for a game of patience.*)

VERSHININ: Well, if we can't have any tea, let's do a bit of philosophizing, anyway.

TOOZENBACH: Yes, let's. What about?

VERSHININ: What about? Well . . . let's try to imagine what life will be like after we're dead, say in two or three hundred years.

TOOZENBACH: All right, then. . . . After we're dead, people will fly about in balloons, the cut of their coats will be different, the sixth sense will be discovered, and possibly even developed and used, for all I know. . . . But I believe, life itself will remain the same; it will still be difficult and full of mystery and full of happiness. And in a thousand years' time people will still be sighing and complaining: "How hard this business of living is!" — and yet they'll still be scared of death and unwilling to die, just as they are now.

VERSHININ (*after a moment's thought*): Well, you know . . . how shall I put it? I think everything in the world is bound to change gradually — in fact, it's changing before our very eyes. In two or three hundred years, or maybe in a thousand years — it doesn't matter how long exactly — life will be different. It will be happy. Of course, we shan't be able to enjoy that future life, but all the same, what we're living for now is to create it, we work and . . . yes, we suffer in order to create it. That's the goal of our life, and you might say that's the only happiness we shall ever achieve.

MASHA (*laughs quietly.*)

TOOZENBACH: Why are you laughing?

MASHA: I don't know. I've been laughing all day to-day.

VERSHININ (*to* TOOZENBACH): I went to the same cadet school as you did but I never went on to the Military Academy. I read a great deal, of course, but I never know what books I ought to choose, and probably I read a lot of stuff that's not worth anything. But the longer I live the more I seem to long for knowledge. My hair's going grey and I'm getting on in years, and yet how little I know, how little! All the same, I think I do know one thing which is not only true but also most important. I'm sure of it. Oh, if only I could convince you that there's not going to be any happiness for our own generation, that there mustn't be and won't be. . . . We've just got to work and work. All the happiness is reserved for our descendants, our remote descendants. (*A pause.*) Anyway, if I'm not to be happy, then at least my children's children will be.

(FEDOTIK *and* RODÉ *enter the ballroom; they sit down and sing quietly, one of them playing on a guitar.*)

TOOZENBACH: So you won't even allow us to dream of happiness! But what if I *am* happy?

VERSHININ: You're not.

TOOZENBACH (*flinging up his hands and laughing*): We don't understand one another, that's obvious. How can I convince you?

MASHA (*laughs quietly.*)

TOOZENBACH (*holds up a finger to her*): Show a finger to her and she'll laugh! (*To* VERSHININ.) And life will be just the same as ever not merely in a couple of hundred years' time, but in a million years. Life doesn't change, it always goes on the same; it follows its own laws, which don't concern us, which we can't discover anyway. Think of the birds that migrate in the autumn, the cranes, for instance: they just fly on and on. It doesn't matter what sort of thoughts they've got in their heads, great thoughts or little thoughts, they just fly on and on, not knowing where or why. And they'll go on flying no matter how many philosophers they happen to have flying with them. Let them philosophize as much as they like, as long as they go on flying.

MASHA: Isn't there some meaning?

TOOZENBACH: Meaning? . . . Look out there, it's snowing. What's the meaning of that? (*A pause.*)

MASHA: I think a human being has got to have some faith, or at least he's got to seek faith. Otherwise his life will be empty, empty. . . . How can you live and not know why the cranes fly, why children are born, why the stars shine in the sky! . . . You must either know why you live, or else . . . nothing matters . . . everything's just wild grass. . . . (*A pause.*)

VERSHININ: All the same, I'm sorry my youth's over.

MASHA: "It's a bore to be alive in this world, friends," that's what Gogol says.

TOOZENBACH: And I feel like saying: it's hopeless arguing with you, friends! I give you up.

CHEBUTYKIN (*reads out of the paper*): Balsac's marriage took place at Berdichev.[1]

IRENA (*sings softly to herself.*)

CHEBUTYKIN: Must write this down in my notebook. (*Writes.*) Balsac's marriage took place at Berdichev. (*Reads on.*)

IRENA (*playing patience, pensively*): Balsac's marriage took place at Berdichev.

TOOZENBACH: Well, I've thrown in my hand. Did you know that I'd sent in my resignation, Maria Serghyeevna?

MASHA: Yes, I heard about it. I don't see anything good in it, either. I don't like civilians.

TOOZENBACH: Never mind. (*Gets up.*) What sort of a soldier do I make, anyway? I'm not even good-looking. Well, what does it matter? I'll work. I'd like to do such a hard day's work that when I came home in the evening I'd fall on my bed exhausted and go to sleep at once. (*Goes to the ballroom.*) I should think working men sleep well at nights!

FEDOTIK (*to* IRENA): I've got you some coloured crayons at Pyzhikov's, in Moscow Street. And this little penknife, too. . . .

IRENA: You still treat me as if I were a little girl. I wish you'd remember I'm grown up now. (*Takes the crayons and the penknife, joyfully.*) They're awfully nice!

FEDOTIK: Look, I bought a knife for myself, too. You see, it's got another blade here, and then another . . . this thing's for cleaning your ears, and these are nail-scissors, and this is for cleaning your nails. . . .

RODÉ (*in a loud voice*): Doctor, how old are you?

CHEBUTYKIN: I? Thirty-two.

(*Laughter.*)

FEDOTIK: I'll show you another kind of patience. (*Sets out the cards.*)

(*The samovar is brought in, and* ANFISA *attends to it. Shortly afterwards* NATASHA *comes in and begins to fuss around the table.*)

---

[1] A town in Western Russia well known for its almost exclusively Jewish population.

SOLIONY (*enters, bows to the company and sits down at the table.*)

VERSHININ: What a wind, though!

MASHA: Yes. I'm tired of winter! I've almost forgotten what summer is like.

IRENA (*playing patience*): I'm going to go out. We'll get to Moscow!

FEDOTIK: No, it's not going out. You see, the eight has to go on the two of spades. (*Laughs.*) That means you won't go to Moscow.

CHEBUTYKIN (*reads the paper*): Tzitzikar. Smallpox is raging. . . .

ANFISA (*goes up to* MASHA): Masha, the tea's ready, dear. (*To* VERSHININ.) Will you please come to the table, your Excellency? Forgive me, your name's slipped my memory. . . .

MASHA: Bring it here, Nanny. I'm not coming over there.

IRENA: Nanny!

ANFISA: Comi-ing!

NATASHA (*to* SOLIONY): You know, even tiny babies understand what we say perfectly well! "Good morning, Bobik," I said to him only today, "Good morning, my precious!" — and then he looked at me in such a special sort of way. You may say it's only a mother's imagination, but it isn't, I do assure you. No, no! He really is an extraordinary child!

SOLIONY: If that child were mine, I'd cook him up in a frying pan and eat him. (*Picks up his glass, goes into the drawing-room and sits down in a corner.*)

NATASHA (*covers her face with her hands*): What a rude, ill-mannered person!

MASHA: People who don't even notice whether it's summer or winter are lucky! I think I'd be indifferent to the weather if I were living in Moscow.

VERSHININ: I've just been reading the diary of some French cabinet minister — he wrote it in prison. He got sent to prison in connection with the Panama affair. He writes with such a passionate delight about the birds he can see through the prison window — the birds he never even noticed when he was a cabinet minister. Of course, now he's released he won't notice them any more. . . . And in the same way, you won't notice Moscow once you live there again. We're not happy and we can't be happy: we only want happiness.

TOOZENBACH (*picks up a box from the table*): I say, where are all the chocolates?

IRENA: Soliony's eaten them.

TOOZENBACH: All of them?

ANFISA (*serving* VERSHININ *with tea*): Here's a letter for you, Sir.

VERSHININ: For me? (*Takes the letter.*) From my daughter. (*Reads it.*) Yes, of course. . . . Forgive me, Maria Serghyeevna, I'll just leave quietly. I won't have any tea. (*Gets up, agitated.*) Always the same thing. . . .

MASHA: What is it? Secret?

VERSHININ (*in a low voice*): My wife's taken poison again. I must go. I'll get away without them seeing me. All this is so dreadfully unpleasant. (*Kisses* MASHA's *hand.*) My dear, good, sweet girl. . . . I'll go out this way, quietly. . . . (*Goes out.*)

ANFISA: Where's he off to? And I've just brought him some tea! What a queer fellow!

MASHA (*flaring up*): Leave me alone! Why do you keep worrying me? Why don't you leave me in peace? (*Goes to the table, cup in hand.*) I'm sick and tired of you, silly old woman!

ANFISA: Why. . . . I didn't mean to offend you, dear.

ANDREY'S VOICE (*off stage*): Anfisa!

ANFISA (*mimics him*): Anfisa! Sitting there in his den! . . . (*Goes out.*)

MASHA (*by the table in the ballroom, crossly*): Do let me sit down somewhere! (*Jumbles up the cards laid out on the table.*) You take up the whole table with your cards! Why don't you get on with your tea?

IRENA: How bad-tempered you are, Mashka!

MASHA: Well, if I'm bad-tempered, don't talk to me, then. Don't touch me!

CHEBUTYKIN (*laughs*): Don't touch her! . . . Take care you don't touch her!

MASHA: You may be sixty, but you're always gabbling some damn nonsense or other, just like a child. . . .

NATASHA (*sighs*): My dear Masha, need you use such expressions? You know, with your good looks you'd be thought so charming, even by the best people — yes, I honestly mean it — if only you wouldn't use these expressions of yours! Je vous prie, pardonnez moi, Marie, mais vous avez des manières un peu grossières.

TOOZENBACH (*with suppressed laughter*): Pass me . . . I say, will you please pass me. . . . Is that cognac over there, or what? . . .

NATASHA: Il parait que mon Bobik déjà ne dort pas. . . . I think he's awake. He's not been too well to-day. I must go and see him . . . excuse me. (*Goes out.*)

IRENA: I say, where has Alexandr Ignatyevich gone to?

MASHA: He's gone home. His wife's done something queer again.

TOOZENBACH (*goes over to* SOLIONY *with a decanter of cognac*): You always sit alone brooding over something or other — though what it's all about nobody knows. Well, let's make it up. Let's have cognac together. (*They drink.*) I suppose I'll have to play the piano all night to-night — a lot of rubbishy tunes, of course. . . . Never mind!

SOLIONY: Why did you say "let's make it up"? We haven't quarrelled.

TOOZENBACH: You always give me the feeling that there's something wrong between us. You're a strange character, no doubt about it.

SOLIONY (*recites*): "I am strange, but who's not so? Don't be angry, Aleko!"

TOOZENBACH: What's Aleko got to do with it? . . . (*A pause.*)

SOLIONY: When I'm alone with somebody I'm all right, I'm just like other people. But in company, I get depressed and shy, and . . . I talk all sorts of nonsense. All the same, I'm a good deal more honest and well-intentioned than plenty of others. I can prove I am.

TOOZENBACH: You often make me angry because you keep on pestering me when we're in company — but all the same, I do like you for some reason. . . . I'm going to get drunk to-night, whatever happens! Let's have another drink!

SOLIONY: Yes, let's. (*A pause.*) I've never had anything against you personally, Baron. But my temperament's rather like Lermontov's. (*In a low voice.*) I even look a little like Lermontov, I've been told. . . . (*Takes a scent bottle from his pocket and sprinkles some scent on his hands.*)

TOOZENBACH: I have sent in my resignation! Finished! I've been considering it for five years, and now I've made up my mind at last. I'm going to work.

SOLIONY (*recites*): "Don't be angry, Aleko. . . . Away, away with all your dreams!"

(*During the conversation* ANDREY *enters quietly with a book in his hand and sits down by the candle.*)

TOOZENBACH: I'm going to work!

CHEBUTYKIN (*comes into the drawing-room with* IRENA): And the food they treated me to was the genuine Caucasian stuff: onion soup, followed by chehartma — that's a meat dish, you know.

SOLIONY: Chereshma isn't meat at all; it's a plant, something like an onion.

CHEBUTYKIN: No-o, my dear friend. Chehartma isn't an onion, it's roast mutton.

SOLIONY: I tell you chereshma is a kind of onion.

CHEBUTYKIN: Well, why should I argue about it with you? You've never been to the Caucasus and you've never tasted chehartma.

SOLIONY: I haven't tasted it because I can't stand the smell of it. Chereshma stinks just like garlic.

ANDREY (*imploringly*): Do stop it, friends! Please stop it!

TOOZENBACH: When's the carnival crowd coming along?

IRENA: They promised to be here by nine — that means any moment now.

TOOZENBACH (*embraces* ANDREY *and sings*): "Ah, my beautiful porch, my lovely new porch, my . . ." [2]

ANDREY (*dances and sings*): "My new porch all made of maple-wood. . . ."

CHEBUTYKIN (*dances*): "With fancy carving over the door. . . ." (*Laughter.*)

TOOZENBACH (*kisses* ANDREY): Let's have a drink, the devil take it! Andriusha, let's drink to eternal friendship. I'll come with you when you go back to Moscow University.

SOLIONY: Which university? There are two universities in Moscow.

ANDREY: There's only one.

SOLIONY: I tell you there are two.

ANDREY: Never mind, make it three. The more the merrier.

SOLIONY: There are two universities in Moscow.

(*Murmurs of protest and cries of "Hush!"*)

There are two universities in Moscow, an old one and a new one. But if you don't want to listen to what I'm saying, if my conversation irritates you, I can keep silent. In fact I can go to another room. . . . (*Goes out through one of the doors.*)

TOOZENBACH: Bravo, bravo! (*Laughs.*) Let's get started, my friends, I'll play for you. What a funny creature that Soliony is! . . . (*Sits down at the piano and plays a waltz.*)

MASHA (*dances alone*): The Baron is drunk, the Baron is drunk, the Baron is drunk. . . .

(*Enter* NATASHA.)

NATASHA (*to* CHEBUTYKIN): Ivan Romanych! (*Speaks to him, then goes out quietly.* CHEBUTYKIN *touches* TOOZENBACH *on the shoulder and whispers to him.*)

IRENA: What is it?

CHEBUTYKIN: It's time we were going. Good-night.

IRENA: But really. . . . What about the carnival party?

ANDREY (*embarrassed*): The carnival party's not coming. You see, my dear, Natasha says that Bobik isn't very well, and so . . . Anyway, I don't know . . . and certainly don't care. . . .

IRENA (*shrugs her shoulders*): Bobik's not very well! . . .

MASHA: Never mind, we'll keep our end up! If they turn us out, out

---

[2] A traditional Russian dance-song.

we must go! (*To* IRENA.) It isn't Bobik who's not well, it's her. . . .
There! . . . (*Taps her forehead with her finger.*) Petty little
bourgeois housewife!

(ANDREY *goes to his room on the right.* CHEBUTYKIN *follows him.
The guests say good-bye in the ballroom.*)

FEDOTIK: What a pity! I'd been hoping to spend the evening here, but
of course, if the baby's ill. . . . I'll bring him some toys to-morrow.

RODÉ (*in a loud voice*): I had a good long sleep after lunch to-day on
purpose, I thought I'd be dancing all night. I mean to say, it's only
just nine o'clock.

MASHA: Let's go outside and talk it over. We can decide what to do
then.

(*Voices are heard saying* "Good-bye! God bless you!" *and* TOOZEN-
BACH *is heard laughing gaily. Everyone goes out.* ANFISA *and a
maid clear the table and put out the lights. The nurse sings to the
baby off stage. Enter* ANDREY, *wearing an overcoat and hat, followed by* CHEBUTYKIN. *They move quietly.*)

CHEBUTYKIN: I've never found time to get married, somehow . . .
partly because my life's just flashed past me like lightning, and
partly because I was always madly in love with your mother and she
was married. . . .

ANDREY: One shouldn't marry. One shouldn't marry because it's so
boring.

CHEBUTYKIN: That may be so, but what about loneliness? You can
philosophize as much as you like, dear boy, but loneliness is a dreadful thing. Although, really . . . well, it doesn't matter a damn, of
course! . . .

ANDREY: Let's get along quickly.

CHEBUTYKIN: What's the hurry? There's plenty of time.

ANDREY: I'm afraid my wife may try to stop me.

CHEBUTYKIN: Ah!

ANDREY: I won't play cards to-night, I'll just sit and watch. I'm not
feeling too well. . . . What ought I to do for this breathlessness,
Ivan Romanych?

CHEBUTYKIN: Why ask me, dear boy? I can't remember — I simply
don't know.

ANDREY: Let's go through the kitchen.

(*They go out. A bell rings. The ring is repeated, then voices and
laughter are heard.*)

IRENA (*coming in*): What's that?

ANFISA (*in a whisper*): The carnival party.

(*The bell rings again.*)

IRENA: Tell them there's no one at home, Nanny. Apologize to them.

(ANFISA *goes out.* IRENA *walks up and down the room, lost in thought. She seems agitated. Enter* SOLIONY.)

SOLIONY (*puzzled*): There's no one here. . . . Where is everybody?
IRENA: They've gone home.
SOLIONY: How strange! Then you're alone here?
IRENA: Yes, alone. (*A pause.*) Well . . . good-night.
SOLIONY: I know I behaved tactlessly just now, I lost control of myself. But you're different from the others, you stand out high above them — you're pure, you can see where the truth lies. . . . You're the only person in the world who can possibly understand me. I love you. . . . I love you with a deep, infinite . . .
IRENA: Do please go away. Good-night!
SOLIONY: I can't live without you. (*Follows her.*) Oh, it's such a delight just to look at you! (*With tears.*) Oh, my happiness! Your glorious, marvellous, entrancing eyes — eyes like no other woman's I've ever seen. . . .
IRENA (*coldly*): Please stop it, Vassily Vassilich!
SOLIONY: I've never spoken to you of my love before . . . it makes me feel as if I were living on a different planet. . . . (*Rubs his forehead.*) Never mind! I can't force you to love me, obviously. But I don't intend to have any rivals — successful rivals, I mean. . . . No, no! I swear to you by everything I hold sacred that if there's anyone else, I'll kill him. Oh, how wonderful you are!

(*Enter* NATASHA *carrying a candle.*)

NATASHA (*pokes her head into one room, then into another, but passes the door leading to her husband's room*): Andrey's reading in there. Better let him read. Forgive me, Vassily Vassilich, I didn't know you were here. I'm afraid I'm not properly dressed.
SOLIONY: I don't care. Good-bye. (*Goes out.*)
NATASHA: You must be tired, my poor dear girl. (*Kisses* IRENA.) You ought to go to bed earlier.
IRENA: Is Bobik asleep?
NATASHA: Yes, he's asleep. But he's not sleeping peacefully. By the way, my dear, I've been meaning to speak to you for some time but there's always been something . . . either you're not here, or I'm too busy. . . . You see, I think that Bobik's nursery is so cold and

damp. . . . And your room is just ideal for a baby. Darling, do you think you could move into Olga's room?

IRENA (*not understanding her*):Where to?

(*The sound of bells is heard outside, as a "troika" is driven up to the house.*)

NATASHA: You can share a room with Olia for the time being, and Bobik can have your room. He is such a darling! This morning I said to him: "Bobik, you're my very own! My very own!" And he just gazed at me with his dear little eyes. (*The door bell rings.*) That must be Olga. How late she is!

(*A maid comes up to* NATASHA *and whispers in her ear.*)

NATASHA: Protopopov! What a funny fellow! Protopopov's come to ask me to go for a drive with him. In a troika! (*Laughs.*) Aren't these men strange creatures! . . .

(*The door bell rings again.*)

Someone's ringing. Shall I go for a short drive? Just for a quarter of an hour? (*To the maid.*) Tell him I'll be down in a minute. (*The door bell rings.*) That's the bell again. I suppose it's Olga. (*Goes out.*)

(*The maid runs out;* IRENA *sits lost in thought. Enter* KOOLYGHIN *and* OLGA, *followed by* VERSHININ.)

KOOLYGHIN: Well! What's the meaning of this? You said you were going to have a party.

VERSHININ: It's a strange thing. I left here about half an hour ago, and they were expecting a carnival party then.

IRENA: They've all gone.

KOOLYGHIN: Masha's gone, too? Where has she gone to? And why is Protopopov waiting outside in a troika? Who's he waiting for?

IRENA: Please don't ask me questions. I'm tired.

KOOLYGHIN: You . . . spoilt child!

OLGA: The conference has only just ended. I'm quite worn out. The headmistress is ill and I'm deputizing for her. My head's aching, oh, my head, my head. . . . (*Sits down.*) Andrey lost two hundred roubles at cards last night. The whole town's talking about it. . . .

KOOLYGHIN: Yes, the conference exhausted me, too. (*Sits down.*)

VERSHININ: So now my wife's taken it into her head to try to frighten me. She tried to poison herself. However, everything's all right now, so I can relax, thank goodness. . . . So we've got to go away? Well, good-night to you, all the best. Fiodor Illych, would you care to come along with me somewhere or other? I can't stay at home to-night, I really can't. . . . Do come!

KOOLYGHIN: I'm tired. I don't think I'll come. (*Gets up.*) I'm tired. Has my wife gone home?

IRENA: I think so.

KOOLYGHIN (*kisses* IRENA'S *hand*): Good-night. We can rest to-morrow and the day after to-morrow, two whole days! Well, I wish you all the best. (*Going out.*) How I long for some tea! I reckoned on spending the evening in congenial company, but — *o, fallacem hominum spem!* Always use the accusative case in exclamations.

VERSHININ: Well, it looks as if I'll have to go somewhere by myself. (*Goes out with* KOOLYGHIN, *whistling.*)

OLGA: My head aches, oh, my head. . . . Andrey lost at cards . . . the whole town's talking. . . . I'll go and lie down. (*Going out.*) To-morrow I'm free. Heavens, what a joy! To-morrow I'm free, and the day after to-morrow I'm free. . . . My head's aching, oh, my poor head. . . .

IRENA (*alone*): They've all gone. No one's left.

(*Someone is playing an accordion in the street. The nurse sings in the next room.*)

NATASHA (*crosses the ballroom, wearing a fur coat and cap. She is followed by the maid*): I'll be back in half an hour. I'm just going for a little drive. (*Goes out.*)

IRENA (*alone, with intense longing*): Moscow! Moscow! Moscow!

ACT III

(*A bedroom now shared by* OLGA *and* IRENA. *There are two beds, one on the right, the other on the left, each screened off from the center of the room. It is past two o'clock in the morning. Off stage the alarm is being sounded on account of a fire which has been raging for some time. The inmates of the house have not yet been to bed.* MASHA *is lying on a couch, dressed, as usual, in black.* OLGA *and* ANFISA *come in.*)

ANFISA: Now they're sitting down there, under the stairs. . . . I keep telling them to come upstairs, that they shouldn't sit down there, but they just cry. "We don't know where our Papa is," they say, "perhaps he's got burned in the fire." What an idea! And there are people in the yard, too . . . half dressed. . . .

OLGA (*takes a dress out of a wardrobe*): Take this grey frock, Nanny.

. . . And this one. . . . This blouse, too. . . . And this skirt. Oh, Heavens! what is happening! Apparently the whole of the Kirsanovsky Streets' been burnt down. . . . Take this . . . and this, too. . . . (*Throws the clothes into* ANFISA'S *arms.*) The poor Vershinins had a fright. Their house only just escaped being burnt down. They'll have to spend the night here . . . we mustn't let them go home. Poor Fedotik's lost everything, he's got nothing left. . . .

ANFISA: I'd better call Ferapont, Oliushka, I can't carry all this.

OLGA (*rings*): No one takes any notice when I ring. (*Calls through the door.*) Is anyone there? Will someone come up, please!

(*A window, red with the glow of fire, can be seen through the open door. The sound of a passing fire engine is heard.*)

How dreadful it all is! And how tired of it I am! (*Enter* FERAPONT.) Take this downstairs please. . . . The Kolotilin girls are sitting under the stairs . . . give it to them. And this, too. . . .

FERAPONT: Very good, Madam. Moscow was burned down in 1812 just the same. Mercy on us! . . . Yes, the French were surprised all right.

OLGA: Go along now, take this down.

FERAPONT: Very good. (*Goes out.*)

OLGA: Give it all away, Nanny, dear. We won't keep anything, give it all away. . . . I'm so tired, I can hardly keep on my feet. We mustn't let the Vershinins go home. The little girls can sleep in the drawing-room, and Alexandr Ignatyevich can share the downstairs room with the Baron. Fedotik can go in with the Baron, too, or maybe he'd better sleep in the ballroom. The doctor's gone and got drunk — you'd think he'd done it on purpose; he's so hopelessly drunk that we can't let anyone go into his room. Vershinin's wife will have to go into the drawing-room, too.

ANFISA (*wearily*): Don't send me away, Oliushka, darling! Don't send me away!

OLGA: What nonsense you're talking, Nanny! No one's sending you away.

ANFISA (*leans her head against* OLGA'S *breast*): My dearest girl! I do work, you know, I work as hard as I can. . . . I suppose now I'm getting weaker, I'll be told to go. But where can I go? Where? I'm eighty years old. I'm over eighty-one!

OLGA: You sit down for a while, Nanny. . . . You're tired, you poor dear. . . . (*Makes her sit down.*) Just rest a bit. You've turned quite pale.

(*Enter* NATASHA.)

NATASHA: They're saying we ought to start a subscription in aid of the victims of the fire. You know — form a society or something for the purpose. Well, why not? It's an excellent idea! In any case it's up to us to help the poor as best we can. Bobik and Sofochka are fast asleep as if nothing had happened. We've got such a crowd of people in the house; the place seems full of people whichever way you turn. There's 'flu about in the town. . . . I'm so afraid the children might catch it.

OLGA (*without listening to her*): You can't see the fire from this room; it's quiet in here.

NATASHA: Yes. . . . I suppose my hair is all over the place. (*Stands in front of the mirror.*) They say I've got stouter, but it's not true! I'm not a bit stouter. Masha's asleep . . . she's tired, poor girl. . . . (*To* ANFISA, *coldly.*) How dare you sit down in my presence? Get up! Get out of here! (ANFISA *goes out. A pause.*) I can't understand why you keep that old woman in the house.

OLGA (*taken aback*): Forgive me for saying it, but I can't understand how you . . .

NATASHA: She's quite useless here. She's just a peasant woman, her right place is in the country. You're spoiling her. I do like order in the home, I don't like having useless people about. (*Strokes* OLGA's *cheek.*) You're tired, my poor dear! Our headmistress is tired! You know, when my Sofochka grows up and goes to school, I'll be frightened of you.

OLGA: I'm not going to be a headmistress.

NATASHA: You'll be asked to, Olechka. It's settled.

OLGA: I'll refuse. I couldn't do it. . . . I wouldn't be strong enough. (*Drinks water.*) You spoke so harshly to Nanny just now. . . . You must forgive me for saying so, but I just can't stand that sort of thing . . . it made me feel quite faint. . . .

NATASHA (*agitated*): Forgive me, Olia, forgive me. I didn't mean to upset you.

(MASHA *gets up, picks up a pillow and goes out in a huff.*)

OLGA: Please try to understand me, dear. . . . It may be that we've been brought up in a peculiar way, but anyway I just can't bear it. When people are treated like that, it gets me down, I feel quite ill. . . . I simply get unnerved. . . .

NATASHA: Forgive me, dear, forgive me! . . . (*Kisses her.*)

OLGA: Any cruel or tactless remark, even the slightest discourtesy, upsets me. . . .

NATASHA: It's quite true, I know I often say things which would be

better left unsaid — but you must agree with me, dear, that she'd
be better in the country somewhere.

OLGA: She's been with us for thirty years.

NATASHA: But she can't do any work now, can she? Either I don't understand you, or you don't want to understand me. She can't work,
she just sleeps or sits about.

OLGA: Well, let her sit about.

NATASHA (*in surprise*): What do you mean, let her sit about? Surely
she is a servant! (*Tearfully.*) No, I don't understand you, Olia! I
have a nurse for the children and a wet nurse and we share a maid
and a cook. Whatever do we want this old woman for? What for?

(*The alarm is sounded again.*)

OLGA: I've aged ten years to-night.

NATASHA: We must sort things out, Olia. You're working at your
school, and I'm working at home. You're teaching and I'm running
the house. And when I say anything about the servants, I know what
I'm talking about. . . . That old thief, that old witch must get out
of this house to-morrow! . . . (*Stamps her feet.*) How dare you
vex me so? How dare you? (*Recovering her self-control.*) Really, if
you don't move downstairs, we'll always be quarrelling. This is quite
dreadful!

(*Enter* KOOLYGHIN.)

KOOLYGHIN: Where's Masha? It's time we went home. They say the
fire's getting less fierce. (*Stretches.*) Only one block got burnt down,
but to begin with it looked as if the whole town was going to be set
on fire by that wind. (*Sits down.*) I'm so tired, Olechka, my dear.
You know, I've often thought that if I hadn't married Masha, I'd
have married you, Olechka. You're so kind. I'm worn out. (*Listens.*)

OLGA: What is it?

KOOLYGHIN: The doctor's got drunk just as if he'd done it on purpose.
Hopelessly drunk. . . . As if he'd done it on purpose. (*Gets up.*)
I think he's coming up here. . . . Can you hear him? Yes, he's
coming up. (*Laughs.*) What a fellow, really! . . . I'm going to hide
myself. (*Goes to the wardrobe and stands between it and the wall.*)
What a scoundrel!

OLGA: He's been off drinking for two years, and now suddenly he goes
and gets drunk. . . . (*Walks with* NATASHA *towards the back of
the room.*)

(CHEBUTYKIN *enters; walking firmly and soberly he crosses the
room, stops, looks round, then goes to the wash-stand and begins
to wash his hands.*)

CHEBUTYKIN (*glumly*): The devil take them all . . . all the lot of them! They think I can treat anything just because I'm a doctor, but I know positively nothing at all. I've forgotten everything I used to know. I remember nothing, positively nothing. . . . (OLGA *and* NATASHA *leave the room without his noticing.*) The devil take them! Last Wednesday I attended a woman at Zasyp. She died, and it's all my fault that she did die. Yes. . . . I used to know a thing or two twenty-five years ago, but now I don't remember anything. Not a thing! Perhaps I'm not a man at all, but I just imagine that I've got hands and feet and a head. Perhaps I don't exist at all, and I only imagine that I'm walking about and eating and sleeping. (*Weeps.*) Oh, if only I could simply stop existing! (*Stops crying, glumly.*) God knows. . . . The other day they were talking about Shakespeare and Voltaire at the club. . . . I haven't read either, never read a single line of either, but I tried to make out by my expression that I had. The others did the same. How petty it all is! How despicable! And then suddenly I thought of the woman I killed on Wednesday. It all came back to me, and I felt such a swine, so sick of myself that I went and got drunk. . . .

(*Enter* IRENA, VERSHININ *and* TOOZENBACH. TOOZENBACH *is wearing a fashionable new civilian suit.*)

IRENA: Let's sit down here for a while. No one will come in here.

VERSHININ: The whole town would have been burnt down but for the soldiers. They're a fine lot of fellows! (*Rubs his hands with pleasure.*) Excellent fellows! Yes, they're a fine lot!

KOOLYGHIN (*approaches them*): What's the time?

TOOZENBACH: It's gone three. It's beginning to get light.

IRENA: Everyone's sitting in the ballroom and nobody thinks of leaving. That man Soliony there, too. . . . (*To* CHEBUTYKIN.) You ought to go to bed, Doctor.

CHEBUTYKIN: I'm all right. . . . Thanks. . . . (*Combs his beard.*)

KOOLYGHIN (*laughs*): Half seas over, Ivan Romanych! (*Slaps him on the shoulder.*) You're a fine one! *In vino veritas*, as they used to say in Rome.

TOOZENBACH: Everyone keeps asking me to arrange a concert in aid of the victims of the fire.

IRENA: Well, who'd you get to perform in it?

TOOZENBACH: It could be done if we wanted to. Maria Serghyeevna plays the piano wonderfully well, in my opinion.

KOOLYGHIN: Yes, wonderfully well!

IRENA: She's forgotten how to. She hasn't played for three years. . . . or maybe it's four.

TOOZENBACH: Nobody understands music in this town, not a single person. But I do — I really do — and I assure you quite definitely that Maria Serghyeevna plays magnificently. She's almost a genius for it.

KOOLYGHIN: You're right, Baron. I'm very fond of Masha. She's such a nice girl.

TOOZENBACH: Fancy being able to play so exquisitely, and yet having nobody, nobody at all, to appreciate it!

KOOLYGHIN (*sighs*): Yes. . . . But would it be quite proper for her to play in a concert? (*A pause.*) I don't know anything about these matters, my friends. Perhaps it'll be perfectly all right. But you know, although our director is a good man, a very good man indeed, and most intelligent, I know that he does hold certain views. . . . Of course, this doesn't really concern him, but I'll have a word with him about it, all the same, if you like.

CHEBUTYKIN (*picks up a china clock and examines it.*)

VERSHININ: I've got my clothes in such a mess helping to put out the fire, I must look like nothing on earth. (*A pause.*) I believe they were saying yesterday that our brigade might be transferred to somewhere a long way away. Some said it was to be Poland, and some said it was Cheeta, in Siberia.

TOOZENBACH: I heard that, too. Well, the town will seem quite deserted.

IRENA: We'll go away, too!

CHEBUTYKIN (*drops clock and breaks it*): Smashed to smithereens!

(*A pause. Everyone looks upset and embarrassed.*)

KOOLYGHIN (*picks up the pieces*): Fancy breaking such a valuable thing! Ah, Ivan Romanych, Ivan Romanych! You'll get a bad mark for that!

IRENA: It was my mother's clock.

CHEBUTYKIN: Well, supposing it was. If it was your mother's, then it was your mother's. Perhaps I didn't smash it. Perhaps it only appears that I did. Perhaps it only appears to us that we exist, whereas in reality we don't exist at all. I don't know anything, no one knows anything. (*Stops at the door.*) Why are you staring at me? Natasha's having a nice little affair with Protopopov, and you don't see it. You sit here seeing nothing, and meanwhile Natasha's having a nice little affair with Protopopov. . . . (*Sings.*) Would you like a date? . . . (*Goes out.*)

VERSHININ: So. . . . (*Laughs.*) How odd it all is, really. (*A pause.*) When the fire started, I ran home as fast as I could. When I got near, I could see that our house was all right and out of danger, but the two little girls were standing there, in the doorway in their night clothes. Their mother wasn't there. People were rushing about, horses, dogs . . . and in the kiddies' faces I saw a frightened, anxious, appealing look, I don't know what! . . . My heart sank when I saw their faces. My God, I thought, what will these children have to go through in the course of their poor lives? And they may live a long time, too! I picked them up and ran back here with them, and all the time I was running, I was thinking the same thing: what will they have to go through? (*The alarm is sounded. A pause.*) When I got here, my wife was here already . . . angry, shouting!

(*Enter* MASHA *carrying a pillow; she sits down on the couch.*)

VERSHININ: And when my little girls were standing in the doorway with nothing on but their night clothes, and the street was red with the glow of the fire and full of terrifying noises, it struck me that the same sort of thing used to happen years ago, when armies used to make sudden raids on towns, and plunder them and set them on fire. . . . Anyway, is there any essential difference between things as they were and as they are now? And before very long, say, in another two or three hundred years, people may be looking at our present life just as we look at the past now, with horror and scorn. Our own times may seem uncouth to them, boring and frightfully uncomfortable and strange. . . . Oh, what a great life it'll be then, what a life! (*Laughs.*) Forgive me, I'm philosophizing my head off again . . . but may I go on, please? I'm bursting to philosophize just at the moment. I'm in the mood for it. (*A pause.*) You seem as if you've all gone to sleep. As I was saying: what a great life it will be in the future! Just try to imagine it. . . . At the present time there are only three people of your intellectual calibre in the whole of this town, but future generations will be more productive of people like you. They'll go on producing more and more of the same sort until at last the time will come when everything will be just as you'd wish it yourselves. People will live their lives in your way, and then even you may be outmoded, and a new lot will come along who will be even better than you are. . . . (*Laughs.*) I'm in quite a special mood to-day. I feel full of a tremendous urge to live. . . . (*Sings.*)

> "To Love all ages are in fee,
> The passion's good for you and me." . . . (*Laughs.*)

MASHA (*sings*): Tara-tara-tara. . . .
VERSHININ: Tum-tum. . . .
MASHA: Tara-tara . . .

VERSHININ: Tum-tum, tum-tum. . . . (*Laughs.*)

(*Enter* FEDOTIK.)

FEDOTIK (*dancing about*): Burnt, burnt! Everything I've got burnt!

(*All laugh.*)

IRENA: It's hardly a joking matter. Has everything really been burnt?
FEDOTIK (*laughs*): Everything, completely. I've got nothing left. My guitar's burnt, my photographs are burnt, all my letters are burnt. Even the little note-book I was going to give you has been burnt.

(*Enter* SOLIONY.)

IRENA: No, please go away, Vassily Vassilich. You can't come in here.
SOLIONY: Can't I? Why can the Baron come in here if I can't?
VERSHININ: We really must go, all of us. What's the fire doing?
SOLIONY: It's dying down, they say. Well, I must say it's a peculiar thing that the Baron can come in here, and I can't. (*Takes a scent bottle from his pocket and sprinkles himself with scent.*)
VERSHININ: Tara-tara.
MASHA: Tum-tum, tum-tum.
VERSHININ (*laughs, to* SOLIONY): Let's go to the ballroom.
SOLIONY: Very well, we'll make a note of this. "I hardly need to make my moral yet more clear: That might be teasing geese, I fear!" [3] (*Looks at* TOOZENBACH.) Cluck, cluck, cluck! (*Goes out with* VERSHININ *and* FEDOTIK.)
IRENA: That Soliony has smoked the room out. . . . (*Puzzled.*) The Baron's asleep. Baron! Baron!
TOOZENBACH (*waking out of his doze*): I must be tired. The brick-works. . . . No, I'm not talking in my sleep. I really do intend to go to the brick-works and start working there quite soon. I've had a talk with the manager. (*To* IRENA, *tenderly.*) You are so pale, so beautiful, so fascinating. . . . Your pallor seems to light up the darkness around you, as if it were luminous, somehow. . . . You're sad, you're dissatisfied with the life you have to live. . . . Oh, come away with me, let's go away and work together!
MASHA: Nikolai Lvovich, I wish you'd go away.
TOOZENBACH (*laughs*): Oh, you're here, are you? I didn't see you. (*Kisses* IRENA's *hand.*) Good-bye, I'm going. You know as I look at you now, I keep thinking of the day — it was a long time ago, your Saint's day — when you talked to us about the joy of work. . . . You were so gay and high-spirited then. . . . And what a happy

[3] From Krylov's fable *Geese* (translated by Bernard Pares).

life I saw ahead of me! Where is it all now? (*Kisses her hand.*)
There are tears in your eyes. You should go to bed, it's beginning to
get light . . . it's almost morning. . . . Oh, if only I could give
my life for you!

MASHA: Nikolai Lvovich, please go away! Really now. . . .

TOOZENBACH: I'm going. (*Goes out.*)

MASHA (*lies down*): Are you asleep, Fiodor?

KOOLYGHIN: Eh?

MASHA: Why don't you go home?

KOOLYGHIN: My darling Masha, my sweet, my precious Masha. . . .

IRENA: She's tired. Let her rest a while, Fyedia.

KOOLYGHIN: I'll go in a moment. My wife, my dear, good wife! . . .
How I love you! . . . only you!

MASHA (*crossly*): *Amo, amas, amat, amamus, amatis, amant!*

KOOLYGHIN (*laughs*): Really, she's an amazing woman! — I've been
married to you for seven years, but I feel as if we were only married
yesterday. Yes, on my word of honour, I do! You really are amazing!
Oh, I'm so happy, happy, happy!

MASHA: And I'm so bored, bored, bored! (*Sits up.*) I can't get it out
of my head. . . . It's simply disgusting. It's like having a nail
driven into my head. No, I can't keep silent about it any more. It's
about Andrey. . . . He's actually mortgaged this house to a bank,
and his wife's got hold of all the money — and yet the house doesn't
belong to him, it belongs to all four of us! Surely, he must realize
that, if he's got any honesty.

KOOLYGHIN: Why bring all this up, Masha? Why bother about it now?
Andriusha owes money all round. . . . Leave him alone.

MASHA: Anyway, it's disgusting. (*Lies down.*)

KOOLYGHIN: Well, we aren't poor, Masha. I've got work, I teach at the
county school, I give private lessons in my spare time. . . . I'm
just a plain, honest man. . . . *Omnia mea mecum porto*, as they
say.

MASHA: I don't ask for anything, but I'm just disgusted by injustice.
(*A pause.*) Why don't you go home, Fiodor?

KOOLYGHIN (*kisses her*): You're tired. Just rest here for a while. . . .
I'll go home and wait for you. . . . Go to sleep. (*Goes to the
door.*) I'm happy, happy, happy! (*Goes out.*)

IRENA: The truth is that Andrey is getting to be shallow-minded. He's
aging and since he's been living with that woman he's lost all the
inspiration he used to have! Not long ago he was working for a
professorship, and yet yesterday he boasted of having at last been
elected a member of the County Council. Fancy him a member,
with Protopopov as chairman! They say the whole town's laughing

at him, he's the only one who doesn't know anything or see anything. And now, you see, everyone's at the fire, while he's just sitting in his room, not taking the slightest notice of it. Just playing his violin. (*Agitated.*) Oh, how dreadful it is, how dreadful, how dreadful! I can't bear it any longer, I can't, I really can't! . . .

(*Enter* OLGA. *She starts arranging things on her bedside table.*)

IRENA (*sobs loudly*): You must turn me out of here! Turn me out; I can't stand it any more!

OLGA (*alarmed*): What is it? What is it, darling?

IRENA (*sobbing*): Where. . . . Where has it all gone to? Where is it? Oh, God! I've forgotten. . . . I've forgotten everything . . . there's nothing but a muddle in my head. . . . I don't remember what the Italian for "window" is, or for "ceiling." . . . Every day I'm forgetting more and more, and life's slipping by, and it will never, never come back. . . . We shall never go to Moscow. . . . I can see that we shall never go. . . .

OLGA: Don't, my dear, don't. . . .

IRENA (*trying to control herself*): Oh, I'm so miserable! . . . I can't work, I won't work! I've had enough of it, enough! . . . First I worked on the telegraph, now I'm in the County Council office, and I hate and despise everything they give me to do there. . . . I'm twenty-three years old, I've been working all this time, and I feel as if my brain's dried up. I know I've got thinner and uglier and older, and I find no kind of satisfaction in anything, none at all. And the time's passing . . . and I feel as if I'm moving away from any hope of a genuine, fine life, I'm moving further and further away and sinking into a kind of abyss. I feel in despair, and I don't know why I'm still alive, why I haven't killed myself. . . .

OLGA: Don't cry, my dear child, don't cry. . . . It hurts me.

IRENA: I'm not crying any more. That's enough of it. Look, I'm not crying now. Enough of it, enough! . . .

OLGA: Darling, let me tell you something. . . . I just want to speak as your sister, as your friend. . . . That is, if you want my advice. . . . Why don't you marry the Baron?

IRENA (*weeps quietly.*)

OLGA: After all, you do respect him, you think a lot of him. . . . It's true, he's not good-looking, but he's such a decent, clean-minded sort of man. . . . After all, one doesn't marry for love, but to fulfil a duty. At least, I think so, and I'd marry even if I weren't in love. I'd marry anyone that proposed to me, as long as he was a decent man. I'd even marry an old man.

IRENA: I've been waiting all this time, imagining that we'd be moving to Moscow, and I'd meet the man I'm meant for there. I've dreamt about him and I've loved him in my dreams. . . . But it's all turned out to be nonsense . . . nonsense. . . .

OLGA (*embracing her*): My darling sweetheart, I understand everything perfectly. When the Baron resigned his commission and came to see us in his civilian clothes, I thought he looked so plain that I actually started to cry. . . . He asked me why I was crying. . . . How could I tell him? But, of course, if it were God's will that he should marry you, I'd feel perfectly happy about it. That's quite a different matter, quite different!

(NATASHA, *carrying a candle, comes out of the door on the right, crosses the stage and goes out through the door on the left without saying anything.*)

MASHA (*sits up*): She goes about looking as if she'd started the fire.

OLGA: You're silly, Masha. You're the stupidest person in our family. Forgive me for saying so.

(*A pause.*)

MASHA: My dear sisters, I've got something to confess to you. I must get some relief, I feel the need of it in my heart. I'll confess it to you two alone, and then never again, never to anybody! I'll tell you in a minute. (*In a low voice.*) It's a secret, but you'll have to know everything. I can't keep silent any more. (*A pause.*) I'm in love, in love. . . . I love that man. . . . You saw him here just now. . . . Well, what's the good? . . . I love Vershinin. . . .

OLGA (*goes behind her screen*): Don't say it. I don't want to hear it.

MASHA: Well, what's to be done? (*Holding her head.*) I thought he was queer at first, then I started to pity him . . . then I began to love him . . . love everything about him — his voice, his talk, his misfortunes, his two little girls. . . .

OLGA: Nevertheless, I don't want to hear it. You can say any nonsense you like, I'm not listening.

MASHA: Oh, you're stupid, Olia! If I love him, well — that's my fate! That's my destiny. . . . He loves me, too. It's all rather frightening, isn't it? Not a good thing, is it? (*Takes* IRENA *by the hand and draws her to her.*) Oh, my dear! . . . How are we going to live through the rest of our lives? What's going to become of us? When you read a novel, everything in it seems so old and obvious, but when you fall in love yourself, you suddenly discover that you don't really know anything, and you've got to make your own decisions. . . . My dear sisters, my dear sisters! . . . I've confessed it all to you, and now I'll keep quiet. . . . I'll be like that madman in the story by Gogol — silence . . . silence! . . .

(*Enter* ANDREY *followed by* FERAPONT.)

ANDREY (*crossly*): What do you want? I don't understand you.

FERAPONT (*stopping in the doorway, impatiently*): I've asked you about ten times already, Andrey Serghyeevich.

ANDREY: In the first place, you're not to call me Andrey Serghyeevich — call me "Your Honour."

FERAPONT: The firemen are asking Your Honour if they may drive through your garden to get to the river. They've been going a long way round all this time — it's a terrible business!

ANDREY: All right. Tell them it's all right. (FERAPONT *goes out.*) They keep on plaguing me. Where's Olga? (OLGA *comes from behind the screen.*) I wanted to see you. Will you give me the key to the cupboard? I've lost mine. You know the key I mean, the small one you've got. . . .

(OLGA *silently hands him the key.* IRENA *goes behind the screen on her side of the room.*)

ANDREY: What a terrific fire! It's going down though. That Ferapont annoyed me, the devil take him! Silly thing he made me say. . . . Telling him to call me "Your Honour"! . . . (*A pause.*) Why don't you say anything, Olia? (*A pause.*) It's about time you stopped this nonsense . . . sulking like this for no reason whatever. . . . You here, Masha? And Irena's here, too. That's excellent! We can talk it over then, frankly and once for all. What have you got against me? What is it?

OLGA: Drop it now, Andriusha. Let's talk it over to-morrow. (*Agitated.*) What a dreadful night!

ANDREY (*in great embarrassment*): Don't get upset. I'm asking you quite calmly, what have you got against me? Tell me frankly.

VERSHININ'S VOICE (*off stage*): Tum-tum-tum!

MASHA (*in a loud voice, getting up*): Tara-tara-tara! (*To* OLGA.) Goodbye, Olia, God bless you! (*Goes behind the screen and kisses* IRENA.) Sleep well. . . . Good-bye, Andrey. I should leave them now, they're tired . . . talk it over to-morrow. . . . (*Goes out.*)

OLGA: Really, Andriusha, let's leave it till to-morrow. . . . (*Goes behind the screen on her side of the room.*) It's time to go to bed.

ANDREY: I only want to say one thing, then I'll go. In a moment. . . . First of all, you've got something against my wife, against Natasha. I've always been conscious of it from the day we got married. Natasha is a fine woman, she's honest and straightforward and high-principled. . . . That's my opinion. I love and respect my wife. You understand that I respect her, and I expect others to respect her, too. I repeat: she's an honest, high-principled woman, and all your grievances against her — if you don't mind my saying so — are just imagination, and nothing more. . . . (*A pause.*) Secondly, you seem to be annoyed with me for not making myself a professor, and not doing any academic work. But I'm working in the Council Office, I'm a member of the County Council, and I feel my service there is just as fine and valuable as any academic work I might do. I'm a member of the County Council, and if you want to know, I'm proud of it! (*A pause.*) Thirdly . . . there's something else I must tell you. . . . I know I mortgaged the house without asking your permission. . . . That was wrong, I admit it, and I ask you to forgive me. . . . I was driven to it by my debts. . . . I'm in debt for about thirty-five thousand roubles. I don't play cards any more, I've given it up long ago. . . . The only thing I can say to justify myself is that you girls get an annuity, while I don't get anything . . . no income, I mean. . . . (*A pause.*)

KOOLYGHIN (*calling through the door*): Is Masha there? She's not there? (*Alarmed.*) Where can she be then? It's very strange. . . . (*Goes away.*)

ANDREY: So you won't listen? Natasha is a good, honest woman, I tell you. (*Walks up and down the stage, then stops.*) When I married her, I thought we were going to be happy, I thought we should all be happy. . . . But . . . oh, my God! . . . (*Weeps.*) My dear sisters, my dear, good sisters, don't believe what I've been saying, don't believe it. . . . (*Goes out.*)

KOOLYGHIN (*through the door, agitated*): Where's Masha? Isn't Masha here? Extraordinary! (*Goes away.*)

(*The alarm is heard again. The stage is empty.*)

IRENA (*speaking from behind the screen*): Olia! Who's that knocking on the floor?

OLGA: It's the doctor, Ivan Romanych. He's drunk.

IRENA: It's been one thing after another all night. (*A pause.*) Olia! (*Peeps out from behind the screen.*) Have you heard? The troops are being moved from the district . . . they're being sent somewhere a long way off.

OLGA: That's only a rumour.

IRENA: We'll be left quite alone then. . . . Olia!

OLGA: Well?

IRENA: Olia, darling, I do respect the Baron. . . . I think a lot of him, he's a very good man. . . . I'll marry him, Olia, I'll agree to marry

him, if only we can go to Moscow! Let's go, please do let's go!
There's nowhere in all the world like Moscow. Let's go, Olia! Let's
go!

ACT IV

(*The old garden belonging to the Prozorovs' house. A river is seen
at the end of a long avenue of fir-trees, and on the far bank of the
river a forest. On the right of the stage there is a verandah with
a table on which champagne bottles and glasses have been left. It
is midday. From time to time people from the street pass through
the garden to get to the river. Five or six soldiers march through
quickly.*

CHEBUTYKIN, *radiating a mood of benevolence which does not
leave him throughout the act, is sitting in a chair in the garden.
He is wearing his army cap and is holding a walking stick, as if
ready to be called away at any moment.* KOOLYGHIN, *with a decoration round his neck and with his moustache shaved off,* TOOZEN-
BACH *and* IRENA *are standing on the verandah saying good-bye to*
FEDOTIK *and* RODÉ, *who are coming down the steps. Both officers
are in marching uniform.*)

TOOZENBACH (*embracing* FEDOTIK): You're a good fellow, Fedotik;
we've been good friends! (*Embraces* RODÉ.) Once more, then. . . .
Good-bye, my dear friends!

IRENA: Au revoir!

FEDOTIK: It's not "au revoir." It's good-bye. We shall never meet
again!

KOOLYGHIN: Who knows? (*Wipes his eyes, smiling.*) There! you've
made me cry.

IRENA: We'll meet some time.

FEDOTIK: Perhaps in ten or fifteen years' time. But then we'll hardly
know one another. . . . We shall just meet and say, "How are
you?" coldly. . . . (*Takes a snapshot.*) Wait a moment. . . .
Just one more, for the last time.

RODÉ (*embraces* TOOZENBACH): We're not likely to meet again. . . .
(*Kisses* IRENA's *hand.*) Thank you for everything . . . everything!

FEDOTIK (*annoyed*): Do just wait a second!

TOOZENBACH: We'll meet again if we're fated to meet. Do write to us.
Be sure to write.

RODÉ (*glancing round the garden*): Good-bye, trees! (*Shouts.*) Heigh-
ho! (*A pause.*) Good-bye, echo!

KOOLYGHIN: I wouldn't be surprised if you got married out there, in Poland. . . . You'll get a Polish wife, and she'll put her arms round you and say: Kohane![4] (*Laughs.*)

FEDOTIK (*glances at his watch*): There's less than an hour to go. Soliony is the only one from our battery who's going down the river on the barge. All the others are marching with the division. Three batteries are leaving to-day by road and three more to-morrow — then the town will be quite peaceful.

TOOZENBACH: Yes, and dreadfully dull, too.

RODÉ: By the way, where's Maria Serghyeevna?

KOOLYGHIN: She's somewhere in the garden.

FEDOTIK: We must say good-bye to her.

RODÉ: Good-bye. I really must go, or I'll burst into tears. (*Quickly embraces* TOOZENBACH *and* KOOLYGHIN, *kisses* IRENA's *hand.*) Life's been very pleasant here. . . .

FEDOTIK (*to* KOOLYGHIN): Here's something for a souvenir for you — a note-book with a pencil. . . . We'll go down to the river through here. (*They go off, glancing back.*)

RODÉ (*shouts*): Heigh-ho!

KOOLYGHIN (*shouts*): Good-bye!

(*At the back of the stage* FEDOTIK *and* RODÉ *meet* MASHA, *and say good-bye to her; she goes off with them.*)

IRENA: They've gone. . . . (*Sits down on the bottom step of the verandah.*)

CHEBUTYKIN: They forgot to say good-bye to me.

IRENA: Well, what about you?

CHEBUTYKIN: That's true, I forgot, too. Never mind, I'll be seeing them again quite soon. I'll be leaving to-morrow. Yes . . . only one more day. And then, in a year's time I'll be retiring. I'll come back here and finish the rest of my life near you. There's just one more year to go and then I get my pension. . . . (*Puts a newspaper in his pocket and takes out another.*) I'll come back here and lead a reformed life. I'll be a nice, quiet, well-behaved little man.

IRENA: Yes, it's really time you reformed, my dear friend. You ought to live a different sort of life, somehow.

CHEBUTYKIN: Yes. . . . I think so, too. (*Sings quietly.*) Tarara-boom-di-ay. . . . I'm sitting on a tomb-di-ay. . . .

KOOLYGHIN: Ivan Romanych is incorrigible! Incorrigible!

CHEBUTYKIN: Yes, you ought to have taken me in hand. You'd have reformed me!

---

[4] A Polish word meaning "beloved."

IRENA: Fiodor's shaved his moustache off. I can't bear to look at him.

KOOLYGHIN: Why not?

CHEBUTYKIN: If I could just tell you what your face looks like now —
but I daren't.

KOOLYGHIN: Well! Such are the conventions of life! *Modus vivendi*,
you know. The director shaved his moustache off, so I shaved mine
off when they gave me an inspectorship. No one likes it, but personally I'm quite indifferent. I'm content. Whether I've got a
moustache or not, it's all the same to me. (*Sits down.*)

ANDREY (*passes across the back of the stage pushing a pram with a
child asleep in it.*)

IRENA: Ivan Romanych, my dear friend, I'm awfully worried about
something. You were out in the town garden last night — tell me
what happened there?

CHEBUTYKIN: What happened? Nothing. Just a trifling thing. (*Reads
his paper.*) It doesn't matter anyway.

KOOLYGHIN: They say that Soliony and the Baron met in the town
garden outside the theatre last night and . . .

TOOZENBACH: Don't please! What's the good? . . . (*Waves his hand
at him deprecatingly and goes into the house.*)

KOOLYGHIN: It was outside the theatre. . . . Soliony started badgering the Baron, and he lost patience and said something that offended
him.

CHEBUTYKIN: I don't know anything about it. It's all nonsense.

KOOLYGHIN: A school-master once wrote "nonsense" in Russian over
a pupil's essay, and the pupil puzzled over it, thinking it was a Latin
word. (*Laughs.*) Frightfully funny, you know! They say that Soliony's in love with Irena and that he got to hate the Baron more and
more. . . . Well, that's understandable. Irena's a very nice girl.
She's a bit like Masha, she tends to get wrapped up in her own
thoughts. (*To* IRENA.) But your disposition is more easy-going than
Masha's. And yet Masha has a very nice disposition, too. I love her,
I love my Masha.

(*From the back of the stage comes a shout: "Heigh-ho!"*)

IRENA (*starts*): Anything seems to startle me to-day. (*A pause.*) I've
got everything ready, too. I'm sending my luggage off after lunch.
The Baron and I are going to get married to-morrow, and directly
afterwards we're moving to the brick-works, and the day after tomorrow I'm starting work at the school. So our new life will begin,
God willing! When I was sitting for my teacher's diploma, I suddenly started crying for sheer joy, with a sort of feeling of blessed-

ness. . . . (*A pause.*) The carrier will be coming for my luggage in a minute. . . .

KOOLYGHIN: That's all very well, but somehow I can't feel that it's meant to be serious. All ideas and theories, but nothing really serious. Anyway, I wish you luck from the bottom of my heart.

CHEBUTYKIN (*moved*): My dearest girl, my precious child! You've gone on so far ahead of me, I'll never catch you up now. I've got left behind like a bird which has grown too old and can't keep up with the rest of the flock. Fly away, my dears, fly away, and God be with you! (*A pause.*) It's a pity you've shaved your moustache off, Fiodor Illyich.

KOOLYGHIN: Don't keep on about it, please! (*Sighs.*) Well, the soldiers will be leaving to-day, and everything will go back to what it was before. Anyway, whatever they say, Masha is a good, loyal wife. Yes, I love her dearly and I'm thankful for what God has given me. Fate treats people so differently. For instance, there's an excise clerk here called Kozyrev. He was at school with me and he was expelled in his fifth year because he just couldn't grasp the *ut consecutivum*. He's dreadfully hard up now, and in bad health, too, and whenever I meet him, I just say to him: "Hullo, *ut consecutivum!*" "Yes," he replies, "that's just the trouble — *consecutivum*" . . . and he starts coughing. Whereas I — I've been lucky all my life. I'm happy, I've actually been awarded the order of Saint Stanislav, second class — and now I'm teaching the children the same old *ut consecutivum*. Of course, I'm clever, cleverer than plenty of other people, but happiness does not consist of merely being clever. . . .

(*In the house someone plays "The Maiden's Prayer."*)

IRENA: To-morrow night I shan't have to listen to "The Maiden's Prayer." I shan't have to meet Protopopov. . . . (*A pause.*) By the way, he's in the sitting-room. He's come again.

KOOLYGHIN: Hasn't our headmistress arrived yet?

IRENA: No, we've sent for her. If you only knew how difficult it is for me to live here by myself, without Olia! She lives at the school now; she's the headmistress and she's busy the whole day. And I'm here alone, bored, with nothing to do, and I hate the very room I live in. So I've just made up my mind — if I'm really not going to be able to live in Moscow, that's that. It's my fate, that's all. Nothing can be done about it. It's God's will, everything that happens, and that's the truth. Nikolai Lvovich proposed to me. . . . Well, I thought it over, and I made up my mind. He's such a nice man, it's really extraordinary how nice he is. . . . And then suddenly I felt as though my soul had grown wings, I felt more cheerful and so re-

lieved somehow that I wanted to work again. Just to start work!
. . . Only something happened yesterday, and now I feel as though
something mysterious is hanging over me. . . .

CHEBUTYKIN: Nonsense!

NATASHA (*speaking through the window*): Our headmistress!

KOOLYGHIN: Our headmistress has arrived! Let's go indoors.

(*Goes indoors with* IRENA.)

CHEBUTYKIN (*reads his paper and sings quietly to himself*): Tarara-
boom-di-ay. . . . I'm sitting on a tomb-di-ay. . . .

(MASHA *walks up to him;* ANDREY *passes across the back of the
stage pushing the pram.*)

MASHA: You look very comfortable sitting here. . . .

CHEBUTYKIN: Well, why not? Anything happening?

MASHA (*sits down*): No, nothing. (*A pause.*) Tell me something.
Were you in love with my mother?

CHEBUTYKIN: Yes, very much in love.

MASHA: Did she love you?

CHEBUTYKIN (*after a pause*): I can't remember now.

MASHA: Is my man here? Our cook Marfa always used to call her
policeman "my man." Is he here?

CHEBUTYKIN: Not yet.

MASHA: When you have to take your happiness in snatches, in little
bits, as I do, and then lose it, as I've lost it, you gradually get
hardened and bad-tempered. (*Points at her breast.*) Something's
boiling over inside me, here. (*Looking at* ANDREY, *who again crosses
the stage with the pram.*) There's Andrey, our dear brother. . . .
All our hopes are gone. It's the same as when thousands of people
haul a huge bell up into a tower. Untold labour and money is spent
on it, and then suddenly it falls and gets smashed. Suddenly, without rhyme or reason. It was the same with Andrey. . . .

ANDREY: When are they going to settle down in the house? They're
making such a row.

CHEBUTYKIN: They will soon. (*Looks at his watch.*) This is an old-
fashioned watch: it strikes. . . . (*Winds his watch which then
strikes.*) The first, second and fifth batteries will be leaving punctually at one o'clock. (*A pause.*) And I shall leave to-morrow.

ANDREY: For good?

CHEBUTYKIN: I don't know. I may return in about a year. Although,
God knows . . . it's all the same. . . .

(*The sounds of a harp and a violin are heard.*)

ANDREY: The town will seem quite empty. Life will be snuffed out like a candle. (*A pause.*) Something happened yesterday outside the theatre; everybody's talking about it. I'm the only one that doesn't seem to know about it.

CHEBUTYKIN: It was nothing. A lot of nonsense. Soliony started badgering the Baron, or something. The Baron lost his temper and insulted him, and in the end Soliony had to challenge him to a duel. (*Looks at his watch.*) I think it's time to go. . . . At half-past twelve, in the forest over there, on the other side of the river. . . . Bang-bang! (*Laughs.*) Soliony imagines he's like Lermontov. He actually writes poems. But, joking apart, this is his third duel.

MASHA: Whose third duel?

CHEBUTYKIN: Soliony's.

MASHA: What about the Baron?

CHEBUTYKIN: Well, what about him? (*A pause.*)

MASHA: My thoughts are all in a muddle. . . . But what I mean to say is that they shouldn't be allowed to fight. He might wound the Baron or even kill him.

CHEBUTYKIN: The Baron's a good enough fellow, but what does it really matter if there's one Baron more or less in the world? Well, let it be! It's all the same. (*The shouts of "Ah-oo!" and "Heigh-ho!" are heard from beyond the garden.*) That's Skvortsov, the second, shouting from the boat. He can wait.

ANDREY: I think it's simply immoral to fight a duel, or even to be present at one as a doctor.

CHEBUTYKIN: That's only how it seems. . . . We don't exist, nothing exists, it only seems to us that we do. . . . And what difference does it make?

MASHA: Talk, talk, nothing but talk all day long! . . . (*Starts to go.*) Having to live in this awful climate with the snow threatening to fall at any moment, and then on the top of it having to listen to all this sort of talk. . . . (*Stops.*) I won't go into the house, I can't bear going in there. . . . Will you let me know when Vershinin comes? . . . (*Walks off along the avenue.*) Look, the birds are beginning to fly away already! (*Looks up.*) Swans or geese. . . . Dear birds, happy birds. . . . (*Goes off.*)

ANDREY: Our house will seem quite deserted. The officers will go, you'll go, my sister will get married, and I'll be left alone in the house.

CHEBUTYKIN: What about your wife?

(*Enter FERAPONT with some papers.*)

ANDREY: My wife is my wife. She's a good, decent sort of woman . . . she's really very kind, too, but there's something about her which pulls her down to the level of an animal . . . a sort of mean, blind, thick-skinned animal — anyway, not a human being. I'm telling you this as a friend, the only person I can talk openly to. I love Natasha, it's true. But at times she appears to me so utterly vulgar, that I feel quite bewildered by it, and then I can't understand why, for what reasons I love her — or, anyway, did love her.

CHEBUTYKIN (*gets up*): Well, dear boy, I'm going away to-morrow and it may be we shall never see each other again. So I'll give you a bit of advice. Put on your hat, take a walking stick, and go away. . . . Go away, and don't ever look back. And the further you go, the better.

(SOLIONY *passes across the back of the stage accompanied by two officers. Seeing* CHEBUTYKIN, *he turns towards him, while the officers walk on.*)

SOLIONY: It's time, Doctor. Half past twelve already. (*Shakes hands with* ANDREY.)

CHEBUTYKIN: In a moment. Oh, I'm tired of you all. (*To* ANDREY.) Andriusha, if anyone asks for me, tell them I'll be back presently. (*Sighs.*) Oh-ho-ho!

SOLIONY: "He had no time to say 'Oh, oh!'
Before that bear had struck him low." . . .

(*Walks off with him.*) What are you groaning about, old man?

CHEBUTYKIN: Oh, well!

SOLIONY: How do you feel?

CHEBUTYKIN (*crossly*): Like a last year's bird's-nest.

SOLIONY: You needn't be so agitated about it, old boy. I shan't indulge in anything much, I'll just scorch his wings a little, like a woodcock's. (*Takes out a scent bottle and sprinkles scent over his hands.*) I've used up a whole bottle to-day, but my hands still smell. They smell like a corpse. (*A pause.*) Yes. . . . Do you remember that poem of Lermontov's?

"And he, rebellious, seeks a storm,
As if in storms there were tranquillity." . . .

CHEBUTYKIN: Yes.

"He had no time to say 'Oh, oh!'
Before that bear had struck him low."

(*Goes out with* SOLIONY. *Shouts of* "Heigh-ho!" *and* "Ah-oo!" *are heard. Enter* ANDREY *and* FERAPONT.)

FERAPONT: Will you sign these papers, please?

ANDREY (*with irritation*): Leave me alone! Leave me alone, for Heaven's sake. (*Goes off with the pram.*)

FERAPONT: Well, what am I supposed to do with the papers then? They are meant to be signed, aren't they? (*Goes to back of stage.*)

(*Enter* IRENA *and* TOOZENBACH, *the latter wearing a straw hat.* KOOLYGHIN *crosses the stage, calling:* "Ah-oo! Masha! Ah-oo!")

TOOZENBACH: I think he's the only person in the whole town who's glad that the army is leaving.

IRENA: That's quite understandable, really. (*A pause.*) The town will look quite empty.

TOOZENBACH: My dear, I'll be back in a moment.

IRENA: Where are you going?

TOOZENBACH: I must slip back to the town, and then . . . I want to see some of my colleagues off.

IRENA: It's not true. . . . Nikolai, why are you so absent-minded to-day? (*A pause.*) What happened outside the theatre last night?

TOOZENBACH (*with a movement of impatience*): I'll be back in an hour. . . . I'll be back with you again. (*Kisses her hands.*) My treasure! . . . (*Gazes into her eyes.*) It's five years since I first began to love you, and still I can't get used to it, and you seem more beautiful every day. What wonderful, lovely hair! What marvellous eyes! I'll take you away to-morrow. We'll work, we'll be rich, my dreams will come to life again. And you'll be happy! But — there's only one "but," only one — you don't love me!

IRENA: I can't help that! I'll be your wife, I'll be loyal and obedient to you, but I can't love you. . . . What's to be done? (*Weeps.*) I've never loved anyone in my life. Oh, I've had such dreams about being in love! I've been dreaming about it for ever so long, day and night . . . but somehow my soul seems like an expensive piano which someone has locked up and the key's got lost. (*A pause.*) Your eyes are so restless.

TOOZENBACH: I was awake all night. Not that there's anything to be afraid of in my life, nothing threatening. . . . Only the thought of that lost key torments me and keeps me awake. Say something to me. . . . (*A pause.*) Say something!

IRENA: What? What am I to say? What?

TOOZENBACH: Anything.

IRENA: Don't, my dear, don't. . . . (*A pause.*)

TOOZENBACH: Such trifles, such silly little things sometimes become so important suddenly, for no apparent reason! You laugh at them, just as you always have done, you still regard them as trifles, and yet you suddenly find they're in control, and you haven't the power to stop them. But don't let us talk about all that! Really, I feel quite elated. I feel as if I was seeing those fir-trees and maples and birches for the first time in my life. They all seem to be looking at me with a sort of inquisitive look and waiting for something. What beautiful trees — and how beautiful, when you think of it, life ought to be with trees like these! (*Shouts of "Ah-oo! Heigh-ho!" are heard.*) I must go, it's time. . . . Look at that dead tree, it's all dried-up, but it's still swaying in the wind along with the others. And in the same way, it seems to me that, if I die, I shall still have a share in life somehow or other. Goodbye, my dear. . . . (*Kisses her hands.*) Your papers, the ones you gave me, are on my desk, under the calendar.

IRENA: I'm coming with you.

TOOZENBACH (*alarmed*): No, no! (*Goes off quickly, then stops in the avenue.*) Irena!

IRENA: What?

TOOZENBACH (*not knowing what to say*): I didn't have any coffee this morning. Will you tell them to get some ready for me? (*Goes off quickly.*)

(IRENA *stands, lost in thought, then goes to the back of the stage and sits down on a swing. Enter* ANDREY *with the pram;* FERAPONT *appears.*)

FERAPONT: Andrey Serghyeech, the papers aren't mine, you know, they're the office papers. I didn't make them up.

ANDREY: Oh, where has all my past life gone to? — the time when I was young and gay and clever, when I used to have fine dreams and great thoughts, and the present and the future were bright with hope? Why do we become so dull and commonplace and uninteresting almost before we've begun to live? Why do we get lazy, indifferent, useless, unhappy? . . . This town's been in existence for two hundred years; a hundred thousand people live in it, but there's not one who's any different from all the others! There's never been a scholar or an artist or a saint in this place, never a single man sufficiently outstanding to make you feel passionately that you wanted to emulate him. People here do nothing but eat, drink and sleep. . . . Then they die and some more take their places, and they eat, drink and sleep, too, — and just to introduce a bit of variety into their lives, so as to avoid getting completely stupid with boredom, they indulge in their disgusting gossip and vodka and gambling and law-suits. The wives deceive their husbands, and the husbands lie to their wives, and pretend they don't see anything and don't hear anything. . . . And all this overwhelming vulgarity and pettiness crushes the children and puts out any spark they might have in them, so that they, too, become miserable, half-dead creatures, just like one another and just like their parents! . . . (*To* FERAPONT, *crossly.*) What do you want?

FERAPONT: What? Here are the papers to sign.

ANDREY: What a nuisance you are!

FERAPONT (*hands him the papers*): The porter at the finance department told me just now . . . he said last winter they had two hundred degrees of frost in Petersburg.

ANDREY: I hate the life I live at present, but oh! the sense of elation when I think of the future! Then I feel so light-hearted, such a sense of release! I seem to see light ahead, light and freedom. I see myself free, and my children, too, — free from idleness, free from *kvass*, free from eternal meals of goose and cabbage, free from after-dinner naps, free from all this degrading parasitism! . . .

FERAPONT: They say two thousand people were frozen to death. They say everyone was scared stiff. It was either in Petersburg or in Moscow, I can't remember exactly.

ANDREY (*with sudden emotion, tenderly*): My dear sisters, my dear good sisters! (*Tearfully.*) Masha, my dear sister! . . .

NATASHA (*through the window*): Who's that talking so loudly there? Is that you, Andriusha? You'll wake Sofochka. *Il ne faut pas faire du bruit, la Sophie est dormie déjà. Vous êtes un ours.* (*Getting angry.*) If you want to talk, give the pram to someone else. Ferapont, take the pram from the master.

FERAPONT: Yes, Madam. (*Takes the pram.*)

ANDREY (*shamefacedly*): I was talking quietly.

NATASHA (*in the window, caressing her small son*): Bobik! Naughty Bobik! Aren't you a naughty boy!

ANDREY (*glancing through the papers*): All right, I'll go through them and sign them if they need it. You can take them back to the office later. (*Goes into the house, reading the papers.*)

(FERAPONT *wheels the pram into the garden.*)

NATASHA (*in the window*): What's Mummy's name, Bobik? You darling! And who's that lady? Auntie Olia. Say: "Hullo, Auntie Olia."

(*Two street musicians, a man and a girl, enter and begin to play on a violin and a harp;* VERSHININ, OLGA *and* ANFISA *come out of the house and listen in silence for a few moments; then* IRENA *approaches them.*)

OLGA: Our garden's like a public road; everybody goes through it. Nanny, give something to the musicians.

ANFISA (*giving them money*): Go along now, God bless you, good people! (*The musicians bow and go away.*) Poor, homeless folk! Whoever would go dragging round the streets playing tunes if he had enough to eat? (*To* IRENA.) How are you, Irenushka? (*Kisses her.*) Ah, my child, what a life I'm having! Such comfort! In a large flat at the school with Oliushka — and no rent to pay, either! The Lord's been kind to me in my old age. I've never had such a comfortable time in my life, old sinner that I am! A big flat, and no rent to pay, and a whole room to myself, with my own bed. All free. Sometimes when I wake up in the night I begin to think, and then — Oh, Lord! Oh, Holy Mother of God! — there's no one happier in the world than me!

VERSHININ (*glances at his watch*): We shall be starting in a moment, Olga Serghyeevna. It's time I went. (*A pause.*) I wish you all the happiness in the world . . . everything. . . . Where's Maria Serghyeevna?

IRENA: She's somewhere in the garden. I'll go and look for her.

VERSHININ: That's kind of you. I really must hurry.

ANFISA: I'll come and help to look for her. (*Calls out.*) Mashenka, ah-oo! (*Goes with* IRENA *towards the far end of the garden.*) Ah-oo! Ah-oo!

VERSHININ: Everything comes to an end. Well, here we are — and now it's going to be "good-bye." (*Looks at his watch.*) The city gave us a sort of farewell lunch. There was champagne, and the mayor made a speech, and I ate and listened, but in spirit I was with you here. . . . (*Glances round the garden.*) I've grown so . . . so accustomed to you.

OLGA: Shall we meet again some day, I wonder?

VERSHININ: Most likely not! (*A pause.*) My wife and the two little girls will be staying on here for a month or two. Please, if anything happens, if they need anything. . . .

OLGA: Yes, yes, of course. You needn't worry about that. (*A pause.*) To-morrow there won't be a single officer or soldier in the town. . . . All that will be just a memory, and, of course, a new life will begin for us here. . . . (*A pause.*) Nothing ever happens as we'd like it to. I didn't want to be a headmistress, and yet now I am one. It means we shan't be going to live in Moscow. . . .

VERSHININ: Well. . . . Thank you for everything. Forgive me if ever I've done anything. . . . I've talked a lot too much, far too much. . . . Forgive me for that, don't think too unkindly of me.

OLGA (*wipes her eyes*): Now . . . why is Masha so long coming?

VERSHININ: What else can I tell you now it's time to say "good-bye"? What shall I philosophize about now? . . . (*Laughs.*) Yes, life is difficult. It seems quite hopeless for a lot of us, just a kind of impasse. . . . And yet you must admit that it is gradually getting easier and brighter, and it's clear that the time isn't far off when the light will spread everywhere. (*Looks at his watch.*) Time, it's time for me to go. . . . In the old days the human race was always making war, its entire existence was taken up with campaigns, advances, retreats, victories. . . . But now all that's out of date, and in its place there's a huge vacuum, clamouring to be filled. Humanity is passionately seeking something to fill it with and, of course, it will find something some day. Oh! If only it would happen soon! (*A pause.*) If only we could educate the industrious people and make the educated people industrious. . . . (*Looks at his watch.*) I really must go. . . .

OLGA: Here she comes!

(*Enter* MASHA.)

VERSHININ: I've come to say good-bye. . . .

(OLGA *walks off and stands a little to one side so as not to interfere with their leave-taking.*)

MASHA (*looking into his face*): Good-bye! . . . (*A long kiss.*)
OLGA: That'll do, that'll do.
MASHA (*sobs loudly.*)
VERSHININ: Write to me. . . . Don't forget me! Let me go . . . it's time. Olga Serghyeevna, please take her away . . . I must go . . . I'm late already. . . . (*Deeply moved, kisses* OLGA's *hands, then embraces* MASHA *once again and goes out quickly.*)
OLGA: That'll do, Masha! Don't, my dear, don't. . . .

(*Enter* KOOLYGHIN.)

KOOLYGHIN (*embarrassed*): Never mind, let her cry, let her. . . . My dear Masha, my dear, sweet Masha. . . . You're my wife, and I'm happy in spite of everything. . . . I'm not complaining, I've no reproach to make — not a single one. . . . Olga here is my witness. . . . We'll start our life over again in the same old way, and you won't hear a word from me . . . not a hint. . . .
MASHA (*suppressing her sobs*): "A green oak grows by a curving shore, And round that oak hangs a golden chain." . . . "A golden chain round that oak." . . . Oh, I'm going mad. . . . By a curving shore . . . a green oak. . . .
OLGA: Calm yourself, Masha, calm yourself. . . . Give her some water.
MASHA: I'm not crying any more. . . .
KOOLYGHIN: She's not crying any more . . . she's a good girl.

(*The hollow sound of a gun-shot is heard in the distance.*)

MASHA: "A green oak grows by a curving shore, And round that oak hangs a golden chain." . . . A green cat . . . a green oak . . . I've got it all mixed up. . . . (*Drinks water.*) My life's messed up. . . . I don't want anything now. . . . I'll calm down in a moment. . . . it doesn't matter. . . . What *is* "the curving shore"? Why does it keep coming into my head all the time? My thoughts are all mixed up.

(*Enter* IRENA.)

OLGA: Calm down, Masha. That's right . . . good girl! . . . Let's go indoors.

MASHA (*irritably*): I'm not going in there! (*Sobs, but immediately checks herself.*) I don't go into that house now, and I'm not going to. . . .

IRENA: Let's sit down together for a moment, and not talk about anything. I'm going away to-morrow, you know. . . .

(*A pause.*)

KOOLYGHIN: Yesterday I took away a false beard and a moustache from a boy in the third form. I've got them here. (*Puts them on.*) Do I look like our German teacher? . . . (*Laughs.*) I do, don't I? The boys are funny.

MASHA: It's true, you do look like that German of yours.

OLGA (*laughs*): Yes, he does.

(MASHA *cries.*)

IRENA: That's enough, Masha!

KOOLYGHIN: Very much like him, I think!

(*Enter* NATASHA.)

NATASHA (*to the maid*): What? Oh, yes. Mr. Protopopov is going to keep an eye on Sofochka, and Andrey Serghyeevich is going to take Bobik out in the pram. What a lot of work these children make! . . . (*To* IRENA.) Irena, you're really leaving to-morrow? What a pity! Do stay just another week, won't you? (*Catching sight of* KOOLYGHIN, *shrieks; he laughs and takes off the false beard and moustache.*) Get away with you! How you scared me! (*To* IRENA.) I've grown so accustomed to you being here. . . . You mustn't think it's going to be easy for me to be without you. I'll get Andrey and his old violin to move into your room: he can saw away at it as much as he likes there. And then we'll move Sofochka into his room. She's such a wonderful child, really! Such a lovely little girl! This morning she looked at me with such a sweet expression, and then she said: "Ma-mma!"

KOOLYGHIN: It's quite true, she is a beautiful child.

NATASHA: So to-morrow I'll be alone here. (*Sighs.*) I'll have this fir-tree avenue cut down first, then that maple tree over there. It looks so awful in the evenings. . . . (*To* IRENA.) My dear, that belt you're wearing doesn't suit you at all. Not at all in good taste. You want something brighter to go with that dress. . . . I'll tell them to put flowers all round here, lots of flowers, so that we get plenty of scent from them. . . . (*Sternly.*) Why is there a fork lying on this seat? (*Going into the house, to the maid.*) Why is that fork left on the seat there? (*Shouts.*) Don't answer me back!

KOOLYGHIN: There she goes again.

(*A band plays a military march off stage; all listen.*)

OLGA: They're going.

(*Enter* CHEBUTYKIN.)

MASHA: The soldiers are going. Well. . . . Happy journey to them! (*To her husband.*) We must go home. . . . Where's my hat and cape? . . .

KOOLYGHIN: I took them indoors. I'll bring them at once.

OLGA: Yes, we can go home now. It's time.

CHEBUTYKIN: Olga Serghyeevna!

OLGA: What is it? (*A pause.*) What?

CHEBUTYKIN: Nothing. . . . I don't know quite how to tell you. . . . (*Whispers into her ear.*)

OLGA (*frightened*): It can't be true!

CHEBUTYKIN: Yes . . . a bad business. . . . I'm so tired . . . quite worn out. . . . I don't want to say another word. . . . (*With annoyance.*) Anyway, nothing matters! . . .

MASHA: What's happened?

OLGA (*puts her arms round* IRENA): What a dreadful day! . . . I don't know how to tell you, dear. . . .

IRENA: What is it? Tell me quickly, what is it? For Heaven's sake! . . . (*Cries.*)

CHEBUTYKIN: The Baron's just been killed in a duel.

IRENA (*cries quietly*): I knew it, I knew it. . . .

CHEBUTYKIN (*goes to the back of the stage and sits down*): I'm tired. . . . (*Takes a newspaper out of his pocket.*) Let them cry for a bit. . . . (*Sings quietly to himself.*) Tarara-boom-di-ay, I'm sitting on a tomb-di-ay. . . . What difference does it make? . . .

(*The three sisters stand huddled together.*)

MASHA: Oh, listen to that band! They're leaving us . . . one of them's gone for good . . . for ever! We're left alone . . . to start our lives all over again. We must go on living . . . we must go on living. . . .

IRENA (*puts her head on* OLGA's *breast*): Some day people will know why such things happen, and what the purpose of all this suffering is. . . . Then there won't be any more riddles. . . . Meanwhile we must go on living . . . and working. Yes, we must just go on working! To-morrow I'll go away alone and teach in a school somewhere; I'll give my life to people who need it. . . . It's autumn now, winter will soon be here, and the snow will cover everything . . . but I'll go on working and working! . . .

OLGA (*puts her arms round both her sisters*): How cheerfully and jauntily that band's playing — really I feel as if I wanted to live! Merciful God! The years will pass, and we shall all be gone for good and quite forgotten. . . . Our faces and our voices will be forgotten and people won't even know that there were once three of us here. . . . But our sufferings may mean happiness for the people who come after us. . . . There'll be a time when peace and happiness reign in the world, and then we shall be remembered kindly and blessed. No, my dear sisters, life isn't finished for us yet! We're going to live! The band is playing so cheerfully and joyfully — maybe, if we wait a little longer, we shall find out why we live, why we suffer. . . . Oh, if we only knew, if only we knew!

(*The music grows fainter and fainter.* KOOLYGHIN, *smiling happily, brings out the hat and the cape.* ANDREY *enters; he is pushing the pram with* BOBIK *sitting in it.*)

CHEBUTYKIN (*sings quietly to himself*): Tarara-boom-di-ay. . . . I'm sitting on a tomb-di-ay. . . . (*Reads the paper.*) What does it matter? Nothing matters!

OLGA: If only we knew, if only we knew! . . .

WHEN *Three Sisters* was first performed by the Stanislavsky ensemble at the Moscow Art Theater in 1901, even Chekhov's own friends were less than enthusiastic. One can, perhaps, understand why, for the greatness of the play may not reveal itself readily; it is achieved against such heavy odds. The play seems to lack plot, and its main characters are lethargic melancholiacs, sometimes pathetic, sometimes laughable, invariably frustrated, musing upon themselves and a vague future in rhapsodic tirades no one listens to, making ineffectual little gestures toward happiness, wasting their small lives in boredom and apathy. How can there be greatness here? One might conceive of Chekhov telling himself that life, after all, does not run in plots, but readers who have learned to admire the plot structures of *Oedipus Rex, Macbeth,* and *Tartuffe* will retort that absolute realism is an impossibility in art, that life is formless and art nothing if not form, and that realism as a literary ideal therefore should not be measured against standards of stenographic or photographic reproductions of petty life in the raw.

This is all true, but it does not finish Chekhov. He knew — the plays prove it — that a dramatist is an artist who gives form to his vision of life in scenic action. If Chekhov seems difficult or dull, it is not because his plays lack action, but because their kind of action differs from that of most other traditionally great plays. He writes not about what happens to people but about what does not happen to them (which, of course, for literary purposes is a kind of happening). In Ibsen there is a core of melodrama that makes for suspense and coherent action, in Shaw the tonic of clashing ideologies, in Strindberg the nightmarish fascination of evil ghosts. In Chekhov there are only gray little lives captured with perfect sharpness of vision. The dismal drabness, the wearying, frustrating monotony — that is life. "All I wanted to do," Chekhov wrote to a friend, "was to say to people, 'Have a look at yourselves and see how bad and dreary your lives are!' The important thing is that people should realize that, for when they do, they will certainly create a better life for themselves." Chekhov is forever staging Thoreau's "lives of quiet desperation." That nothing great happens to people who are not great is precisely the point. Chekhov was rightly irritated when he heard his plays called gloomy and tragic.

Still, one does not quite explain Chekhov's art by talking of the action of non-happening. Perhaps this is why so much has been written about mood and atmosphere in his plays: a blend of pity for good people caught in the rut of existence, of irony and gentle laughter at their absorption in their frustrations and their inability to free themselves and act on their idealism, of knowledge of the isolation of the human heart. Because there is no plot that continuously demands to be furthered, scenes and speeches can be allowed to play themselves out in the varying tempos and little irrelevancies by which life proceeds in the ordinary living room. Compared to Chekhov's, Ibsen's domestic scenes may seem crude and contrived.

But the emphasis on the delicate atmosphere that surrounds

these fragile lives has obscured Chekhov's command of action. Things, after all, do happen in his plays. In *Three Sisters* visitors call, gifts are given, lunches eaten, pictures taken, papers signed, jokes told, babies wheeled, love made, fires seen. And these little events, though not causally nor logically connected, constitute more than a random phase in an infinite progress of triviality. They make an action which points backward (life in Moscow) and forward (what will life be like for the sisters from now on?) and yet has definite beginning and end. In general terms, it is an action of good life atrophying and mean life succeeding; in specific terms, the gradual disappointment of the sisters' hope for a better life. Season and circumstance of the first and the last act not only set the limits for the action; they also define the nature of its movement.

From the mass of events that fills the interval, five main strands of action emerge. Each of the first four involves a Prozorov, and each ends in passive frustration. There is the love of Masha and Vershinin — romantic, mature, and adulterous. In double contrast, there is Toozenbach's legitimate but unreciprocated love for Irena. There is Olga's rise to the headmistress-ship she doesn't want, the making of an old maid. And there is Andrey's moral dissolution, marked by the lessening of his ambition and his surrender to his wife. The wife's, Natasha's, is the fifth, the non-Prozorov action. She is the play's antagonist, whose rise to power we see at four different stages. The coarseness of her being and the nature of her development are evident in the growing frequency of her remarks in French, the language of the gentility she makes pretense to, and by the impression she somehow gives of aging faster than her sisters-in-law. The action spans five years — long enough for Natasha to change from flustered girl to formidable matron.

Around these opposite dramatic movements Chekhov weaves the texture of his play. He juxtaposes scenes that subtly modify one another by varying in tempo and mood. Near the opening of the play Olga's passionate outburst of longing for Moscow is interrupted by Chebutykin's and Toozenbach's voices from the adjoining room: "The devil you have! — It's nonsense, I agree." We have no idea what they are talking about, but in context the seven words assume tremendous dramatic voltage. Near the end of the second act the idiotic argument between Soliony and Chebutykin is followed by a little interlude of pleasant though equally silly dancing and singing. Then comes another nonsense argument — about the number of universities in Moscow. Then there are again movement and physical activity as the entertainment is cut short by Natasha's demand that everyone leave so little Bobik can have quiet. The stage, crowded a moment ago, is empty. Then Andrey and Soliony dispiritedly discuss marriage; then Soliony tries to make love to Irena. The sequence of discordant little scenes continues till Natasha (devoted mother a few minutes ago) goes out for a sleigh ride with her admirer and Irena is left alone and the words "Moscow! Moscow! Moscow!" fall from her lips in an agony of longing. A succession of such scenes does not constitute a plot in any ordinary sense, but in the shifts from farce to pathos, from triviality to importance, from activity and dramatic progress to bickering stasis, and from ensemble scene to soliloquy, the sequence builds a scenic image that both commands instant belief as reality and embodies Chekhov's theme about the attrition of soul in the meaninglessness of everyday. "Meaning?" says Toozenbach once when Masha suggests that existence has some purpose. "Look out there, it's snowing. What's the meaning of that?"

Just beyond the pettiness on stage is the outside world, represented by the pressures of unseen characters. To list them and decide how they affect the characters we *do* see is to become aware of an added dimension in the play, a kind of natural force, built-in facts of a life that systematically defeats human happiness.

Symbolism is still another strand in the rich texture. The frequent pauses, the anecdotes nobody listens to, the philosophical discussions that end nowhere, the fragments of song and poetry that nobody understands, the way remarks have of being misunderstood or of just missing being relevant to the talk of the moment — these are eminently performable dialogue symbols of human isolation. Chebutykin's and Soliony's speeches are particularly striking instances of the way the dialogue emphasizes failure in human communication. Generally, the verbal symbolism eludes precise interpretation and is for that reason all the more effective. Specifying which characters can be considered birds of passage and in what sense is not only unnecessary but ruinous. The power of the image goes beyond any symbolic function and resists reduction to mere meaning. It carries its own weight as tonal element.

The scenic symbols are more definite in significance. The military uniforms, Chebutykin's unrelated clippings of newspaper trivia, the cards in the game of patience, Natasha's sinister appearance with a lighted candle during the fire, Soliony's ominously futile bottle of perfume — all are images of central abstracts in the play. At the same time, they are the stuff of reality: acts, facts, objects — things that *are* before they signify and that signify at all only because they so unmistakably are.

The chief symbol in the play is Moscow — the object of the sisters' dream of escape. But Moscow is a curiously indeterminate quality. Nobody seems really to know it. One of our chief informants is old, befuddled Ferapont. Is it true that a rope is stretched across the city? If so, what for? How many universities are there? Do Moscow merchants kill themselves on pancakes? It is the city where love waits for Irena and where Andrey will become a professor, but to Vershinin it is a city of gloomy bridges, without birch trees. How real is the city of the sisters' longing? To ask the question is to doubt the validity of their frustration, to suggest that they build their sorrow on an illusion and are escaping from a reality they could improve upon had they but the will and the strength to face it. The question is never answered, but in its ambivalence lies much of Chekhov's poetic realism.

Three Sisters proves nothing — except, perhaps, that life can be dreary, and we need no playwright to tell us that. Almost its last words are Chebutykin's, the chorus-like voice of total negation, whose life has become so meaningless that he denies existence itself. The only answer to his nihilistic mutter that "nothing matters" is Olga's "If only we knew, if only we knew!" Knew what? Whether Chebutykin is right, that nothing matters? Or, the meaning of suffering? The wish is cryptic, but the stage image in which it is uttered suggests that all three sisters share it.

There are people — sensible people among them — who find *Three Sisters* a big bore: "four acts about not going to Moscow." But the reader who is tempted to dismiss the play because he feels that people in reality are not so ineffectual and so passively unhappy as Chekhov's ("Why, in the name of heaven, don't they just *go!*") might keep in mind that the criterion for literary excellence is not a statistical average. Chekhov's dramatic world came into being at least partly because of his exasperation with the lack of purpose and dignity in the lives of a certain class of Russian society at a certain time (a reason which has endeared him to Soviet critics). The fact that his exasperation was justified is irrelevant here, as are the causes for the middle-class lassitude. What *is* relevant is that in recording his sympathetic-ironic attitude to its victims Chekhov created human beings whose little tragicomedies of attrition somehow resemble our own.

August Strindberg

THE GHOST SONATA

Translated by Elizabeth Sprigge

Characters

THE OLD MAN, *Hummel, a Company Director*
THE STUDENT, *Arkenholtz*
THE MILKMAID, *an apparition*
THE CARETAKER'S WIFE
THE CARETAKER
THE LADY IN BLACK, *the daughter of the Caretaker's Wife and the Dead Man. Also referred to as the Dark Lady*
THE COLONEL
THE MUMMY, *the Colonel's wife*
THE GIRL, *the Colonel's daughter, actually the daughter of the Old Man*
THE ARISTOCRAT, *Baron Skanskorg. Engaged to the Lady in Black*
JOHANSSON, *the Old Man's servant*
BENGTSSON, *the Colonel's servant*
THE FIANCÉE, *a white-haired old woman, once betrothed to the Old Man*
THE COOK
A MAIDSERVANT
BEGGARS

SCENE I

Outside the house. The corner of the façade of a modern house, showing the ground floor above, and the street in front. The ground floor terminates on the right in the Round Room, above which, on the first floor, is a balcony with a flagstaff. The windows of the Round Room face the street in front of the house, and at the corner look on to the suggestion of a side-street running toward the back. At the beginning of the scene the blinds of the Round Room are down. When, later, they are raised, the white marble statue of a young woman can be seen, surrounded with palms and brightly lighted by rays of sunshine.

To the left of the Round Room is the Hyacinth Room; its window filled with pots of hyacinths, blue, white and pink. Further left, at the back, is an imposing double front door with laurels in tubs on either side of it. The doors are wide open, showing a staircase of white marble with a banister of mahogany and brass. To the left of the front door is another ground-floor window, with a window-mirror.[1] On the balcony rail in the corner above the Round Room are a blue silk quilt and two white pillows. The windows to the left of this are hung with white sheets.[2]

In the foreground, in front of the house, is a green bench; to the right a street drinking-fountain, to the left an advertisement column.

It is a bright Sunday morning, and as the curtain rises the bells of several churches, some near, some far away, are ringing.

On the staircase the LADY IN BLACK stands motionless.

The CARETAKER'S WIFE sweeps the doorstep, then polishes the brass on the door and waters the laurels.

In a wheel-chair by the advertisement column sits the OLD MAN, reading a newspaper. His hair and beard are white and he wears spectacles.

The MILKMAID comes round the corner on the right, carrying milk bottles in a wire basket. She is wearing a summer dress with brown shoes, black stockings and a white cap. She takes off her cap and hangs it on the fountain, wipes the perspiration from her forehead, washes her hands and arranges her hair, using the water as a mirror.

A steamship bell is heard, and now and then the silence is broken by the deep notes of an organ in a nearby church.

After a few moments, when all is silent and the MILKMAID has finished her toilet, the STUDENT enters from the left. He has had a sleepless night and is unshaven. He goes straight up to the fountain. There is a pause before he speaks.

---

[1] Set at an angle inside the window, so as to show what is going on in the street.
[2] Sign of mourning.

STUDENT: May I have the cup?

(*The* MILKMAID *clutches the cup to her.*)

Haven't you finished yet?

(*The* MILKMAID *looks at him with horror.*)

OLD MAN (*to himself*): Who's he talking to? I don't see anybody. Is he crazy? (*He goes on watching them in great astonishment.*)

STUDENT (*to the* MILKMAID): What are you staring at? Do I look so terrible? Well, I've had no sleep, and of course you think I've been making a night of it . . .

(*The* MILKMAID *stays just as she is.*)

You think I've been drinking, eh? Do I smell of liquor?

(*The* MILKMAID *does not change.*)

I haven't shaved, I know. Give me a drink of water, girl. I've earned it. (*Pause.*) Oh well, I suppose I'll have to tell you. I spent the whole night dressing wounds and looking after the injured. You see, I was there when that house collapsed last night. Now you know.

(*The* MILKMAID *rinses the cup and gives him a drink.*)

Thanks.

(*The* MILKMAID *stands motionless. Slowly.*)

Will you do me a great favor? (*Pause.*) The thing is, my eyes, as you can see, are inflamed, but my hands have been touching wounds and corpses, so it would be dangerous to put them near my eyes. Will you take my handkerchief — it's quite clean — and dip it in the fresh water and bathe my eyes? Will you do this? Will you play the good Samaritan?

(*The* MILKMAID *hesitates, but does as he bids.*)

Thank you, my dear. (*He takes out his purse. She makes a gesture of refusal.*) Forgive my stupidity, but I'm only half-awake. . . .

(*The* MILKMAID *disappears.*)

OLD MAN (*to the* STUDENT): Excuse me speaking to you, but I heard you say you were at the scene of the accident last night. I was just reading about it in the paper.

STUDENT: Is it in the paper already?

OLD MAN: The whole thing, including your portrait. But they regret that they have been unable to find out the name of the splendid young student. . . .

STUDENT: Really? (*Glances at the paper.*) Yes, that's me. Well I never!

OLD MAN: Who was it you were talking to just now?

STUDENT: Didn't you see? (*Pause.*)

OLD MAN: Would it be impertinent to inquire — what in fact your name is?

STUDENT: What would be the point? I don't care for publicity. If you get any praise, there's always disapproval too. The art of running people down has been developed to such a pitch. . . . Besides, I don't want any reward.

OLD MAN: You're well off, perhaps.

STUDENT: No, indeed. On the contrary, I'm very poor.

OLD MAN: Do you know, it seems to me I've heard your voice before. When I was young I had a friend who pronounced certain words just as you do. I've never met anyone else with quite that pronunciation. Only him — and you. Are you by any chance related to Mr. Arkenholtz, the merchant?

STUDENT: He was my father.

OLD MAN: Strange are the paths of fate. I saw you when you were an infant, under very painful circumstances.

STUDENT: Yes, I understand I came into the world in the middle of a bankruptcy.

OLD MAN: Just that.

STUDENT: Perhaps I might ask your name.

OLD MAN: I am Mr. Hummel.

STUDENT: Are you the? . . . I remember that . . .

OLD MAN: Have you often heard my name mentioned in your family?

STUDENT: Yes.

OLD MAN: And mentioned perhaps with a certain aversion?

(*The* STUDENT *is silent.*)

Yes, I can imagine it. You were told, I suppose, that I was the man who ruined your father? All who ruin themselves through foolish speculations consider they were ruined by those they couldn't fool. (*Pause.*) Now these are the facts. Your father robbed me of seventeen thousand crowns — the whole of my savings at that time.

STUDENT: It's queer that the same story can be told in two such different ways.

OLD MAN: You surely don't believe I'm telling you what isn't true?

STUDENT: What am I to believe? My father didn't lie.

OLD MAN: That is so true. A father never lies. But I too am a father, and so it follows . . .

STUDENT: What are you driving at?

OLD MAN: I saved your father from disaster, and he repaid me with all the frightful hatred that is born of an obligation to be grateful. He taught his family to speak ill of me.

STUDENT: Perhaps you made him ungrateful by poisoning your help with unnecessary humiliation.

OLD MAN: All help is humiliating, sir.

STUDENT: What do you want from me?

OLD MAN: I'm not asking for the money, but if you will render me a few small services, I shall consider myself well paid. You see that I am a cripple. Some say it is my own fault; others lay the blame on my parents. I prefer to blame life itself, with its pitfalls. For if you escape one snare, you fall headlong into another. In any case, I am unable to climb stairs or ring doorbells, and that is why I am asking you to help me.

STUDENT: What can I do?

OLD MAN: To begin with, push my chair so that I can read those playbills. I want to see what is on tonight.

STUDENT (*pushing the chair*): Haven't you got an attendant?

OLD MAN: Yes, but he has gone on an errand. He'll be back soon. Are you a medical student?

STUDENT: No, I am studying languages, but I don't know at all what I'm going to do.

OLD MAN: Aha! Are you good at mathematics?

STUDENT: Yes, fairly.

OLD MAN: Good. Perhaps you would like a job.

STUDENT: Yes, why not?

OLD MAN: Splendid. (*He studies the playbills.*) They are doing *The Valkyrie* for the matinée. That means the Colonel will be there with his daughter, and as he always sits at the end of the sixth row, I'll put you next to him. Go to that telephone kiosk please and order a ticket for seat eighty-two in the sixth row.

STUDENT: Am I to go to the Opera in the middle of the day?

OLD MAN: Yes. Do as I tell you and things will go well with you. I want to see you happy, rich and honored. Your début last night as the brave rescuer will make you famous by tomorrow and then your name will be worth something.

STUDENT (*going to the telephone kiosk*): What an odd adventure!

OLD MAN: Are you a gambler?

STUDENT: Yes, unfortunately.

OLD MAN: We'll make it fortunately. Go on now, telephone.

(*The* STUDENT *goes. The* OLD MAN *reads his paper. The* LADY IN
BLACK *comes out on to the pavement and talks to the* CARE-
TAKER'S WIFE. *The* OLD MAN *listens, but the audience hears noth-
ing. The* STUDENT *returns.*)

Did you fix it up?

STUDENT: It's done.

OLD MAN: You see that house?

STUDENT: Yes, I've been looking at it a lot. I passed it yesterday when
the sun was shining on the windowpanes, and I imagined all the
beauty and elegance there must be inside. I said to my companion:
"Think of living up there in the top flat, with a beautiful young
wife, two pretty little children and an income of twenty thousand
crowns a year."

OLD MAN: So that's what you said. That's what you said. Well, well!
I too am very fond of this house.

STUDENT: Do you speculate in houses?

OLD MAN: Mm — yes. But not in the way you mean.

STUDENT: Do you know the people who live here?

OLD MAN: Every one of them. At my age one knows everybody, and
their parents and grandparents too, and one's always related to them
in some way or other. I am just eighty, but no one knows me — not
really. I take an interest in human destiny.

(*The blinds of the Round Room are drawn up. The* COLONEL *is
seen, wearing mufti. He looks at the thermometer outside one of
the windows, then turns back into the room and stands in front of
the marble statue.*)

Look, that's the Colonel, whom you will sit next to this afternoon.

STUDENT: Is he — the Colonel? I don't understand any of this, but
it's like a fairy story.

OLD MAN: My whole life's like a book of fairy stories, sir. And although
the stories are different, they are held together by one thread, and
the main theme constantly recurs.

STUDENT: Who is that marble statue of?

OLD MAN: That, naturally, is his wife.

STUDENT: Was she such a wonderful person?

OLD MAN: Er . . . yes.

STUDENT: Tell me.

OLD MAN: We can't judge people, young man. If I were to tell you that
she left him, that he beat her, that she returned to him and married him a second time, and that now she is sitting inside there like

a mummy, worshipping her own statue — then you would think me crazy.

STUDENT: I don't understand.

OLD MAN: I didn't think you would. Well, then we have the window with the hyacinths. His daughter lives there. She has gone out for a ride, but she will be home soon.

STUDENT: And who is the dark lady talking to the caretaker?

OLD MAN: Well, that's a bit complicated, but it is connected with the dead man, up there where you see the white sheets.

STUDENT: Why, who was he?

OLD MAN: A human being like you or me, but the most conspicuous thing about him was his vanity. If you were a Sunday child, you would see him presently come out of that door to look at the Consulate flag flying at half-mast. He was, you understand, a Consul, and he reveled in coronets and lions and plumed hats and colored ribbons.

STUDENT: Sunday child, you say? I'm told I was born on a Sunday.

OLD MAN: No, were you really? I might have known it. I saw it from the color of your eyes. Then you can see what others can't. Have you noticed that?

STUDENT: I don't know what others do see, but at times. . . . Oh, but one doesn't talk of such things!

OLD MAN: I was almost sure of it. But you can talk to me, because I understand such things.

STUDENT: Yesterday, for instance . . . I was drawn to that obscure little street where later on the house collapsed. I went there and stopped in front of that building which I had never seen before. Then I noticed a crack in the wall. . . . I heard the floor boards snapping. . . . I dashed over and picked up a child that was passing under the wall. . . . The next moment the house collapsed. I was saved, but in my arms, which I thought held the child, was nothing at all.

OLD MAN: Yes, yes, just as I thought. Tell me something. Why were you gesticulating that way just now by the fountain? And why were you talking to yourself?

STUDENT: Didn't you see the milkmaid I was talking to?

OLD MAN (*in horror*): Milkmaid?

STUDENT: Surely. The girl who handed me the cup.

OLD MAN: Really? So that's what was going on. Ah well, I haven't second sight, but there are things I can do.

(THE FIANCÉE *is now seen to sit down by the window which has the window-mirror.*)

Look at that old woman in the window. Do you see her? Well, she was my fiancée once, sixty years ago. I was twenty. Don't be alarmed. She doesn't recognize me. We see one another every day, and it makes no impression on me, although once we vowed to love one another eternally. Eternally!

STUDENT: How foolish you were in those days! We never talk to our girls like that.

OLD MAN: Forgive us, young man. We didn't know any better. But can you see that that old woman was once young and beautiful?

STUDENT: It doesn't show. And yet there's some charm in her looks. I can't see her eyes.

(*The* CARETAKER'S WIFE *comes out with a basket of chopped fir branches.*[3])

OLD MAN: Ah, the caretaker's wife! That dark lady is her daughter by the dead man. That's why her husband was given the job of caretaker. But the dark lady has a suitor, who is an aristocrat with great expectations. He is in the process of getting a divorce — from his present wife, you understand. She's presenting him with a stone mansion in order to be rid of him. This aristocratic suitor is the son-in-law of the dead man, and you can see his bedclothes being aired on the balcony upstairs. It is complicated, I must say.

STUDENT: It's fearfully complicated.

OLD MAN: Yes, that it is, internally and externally, although it looks quite simple.

STUDENT: But then who was the dead man?

OLD MAN: You asked me that just now, and I answered. If you were to look round the corner, where the tradesmen's entrance is, you would see a lot of poor people whom he used to help — when it suited him.

STUDENT: He was a kind man then.

OLD MAN: Yes — sometimes.

STUDENT: Not always?

OLD MAN: No-o. That's the way of people. Now, sir, will you push my chair a little, so that it gets into the sun. I'm horribly cold. When you're never able to move about, the blood congeals. I'm going to die soon, I know that, but I have a few things to do first. Take my hand and feel how cold I am.

STUDENT (*taking it*): Yes, inconceivably. (*He shrinks back, trying in vain to free his hand.*)

OLD MAN: Don't leave me. I am tired now and lonely, but I haven't always been like this, you know. I have an enormously long life be-

---

[3] It was customary in Sweden to strew the ground with these for a funeral.

hind me, enormously long. I have made people unhappy and people
have made me unhappy — the one cancels out the other — but before I die I want to see you happy. Our fates are entwined through
your father — and other things.

STUDENT: Let go of my hand. You are taking all my strength. You are
freezing me. What do you want with me?

OLD MAN (*letting go*): Be patient and you shall see and understand.
Here comes the young lady.

(*They watch the* GIRL *approaching, though the audience cannot
yet see her.*)

STUDENT: The Colonel's daughter?

OLD MAN: His daughter — yes. Look at her. Have you ever seen such a
masterpiece?

STUDENT: She is like the marble statue in there.

OLD MAN: That's her mother, you know.

STUDENT: You are right. Never have I seen such a woman of woman
born. Happy the man who may lead her to the altar and his home.

OLD MAN: You can see it. Not everyone recognizes her beauty. So,
then, it is written.

(*The* GIRL *enters, wearing an English riding habit. Without noticing anyone she walks slowly to the door, where she stops to say
a few words to the* CARETAKER'S *WIFE. Then she goes into the
house. The* STUDENT *covers his eyes with his hand.*)

OLD MAN: Are you weeping?

STUDENT: In the face of what's hopeless there can be nothing but despair.

OLD MAN: I can open doors and hearts, if only I find an arm to do my
will. Serve me and you shall have power.

STUDENT: Is it a bargain? Am I to sell my soul?

OLD MAN: Sell nothing. Listen. All my life I have *taken*. Now I have
a craving to give — give. But no one will accept. I am rich, very
rich, but I have no heirs, except for a good-for-nothing who torments the life out of me. Become my son. Inherit me while I am
still alive. Enjoy life so that I can watch, at least from a distance.

STUDENT: What am I to do?

OLD MAN: First go to *The Valkyrie*.

STUDENT: That's settled. What else?

OLD MAN: This evening you must be in there — in the Round Room.

STUDENT: How am I to get there?

OLD MAN: By way of *The Valkyrie*.

STUDENT: Why have you chosen me as your medium? Did you know me before?

OLD MAN: Yes, of course. I have had my eye on you for a long time. But now look up there at the balcony. The maid is hoisting the flag to half-mast for the Consul. And now she is turning the bedclothes. Do you see that blue quilt? It was made for two to sleep under, but now it covers only one.

(*The* GIRL, *having changed her dress, appears in the window and waters the hyacinths.*)

There is my little girl. Look at her, look! She is talking to the flowers. Is she not like that blue hyacinth herself? She gives them drink — nothing but pure water, and they transform the water into color and fragrance. Now here comes the Colonel with the newspaper. He is showing her the bit about the house that collapsed. Now he's pointing to your portrait. She's not indifferent. She's reading of your brave deed. . . .

I believe it's clouding over. If it turns to rain I shall be in a pretty fix, unless Johansson comes back soon.

(*It grows cloudy and dark. The* FIANCÉE *at the window-mirror closes her window.*)

Now my fiancée is closing the window. Seventy-nine years old. The window-mirror is the only mirror she uses, because in it she sees not herself, but the world outside — in two directions. But the world can see her; she hasn't thought of that. Anyhow she's a handsome old woman.

(*Now the* DEAD MAN, *wrapped in a winding sheet, comes out of the door.*)

STUDENT: Good God, what do I see?

OLD MAN: What do you see?

STUDENT: Don't *you* see? There, in the doorway, the dead man?

OLD MAN: I see nothing, but I expected this. Tell me.

STUDENT: He is coming out into the street. (*Pause.*) Now he is turning his head and looking up at the flag.

OLD MAN: What did I tell you? You may be sure he'll count the wreaths and read the visiting cards. Woe to him who's missing.

STUDENT: Now he's turning the corner.

OLD MAN: He's gone to count the poor at the back door. The poor are in the nature of a decoration, you see. "Followed by the blessings of many." Well, he's not going to have my blessing. Between ourselves he was a great scoundrel.

STUDENT: But charitable.

OLD MAN: A charitable scoundrel, always thinking of his grand funeral. When he knew his end was near, he cheated the State out of fifty thousand crowns. Now his daughter has relations with another woman's husband and is wondering about the Will. Yes, the scoundrel can hear every word we're saying, and he's welcome to it. Ah, here comes Johansson!

(JOHANSSON *enters.*)

Report!

(JOHANSSON *speaks, but the audience does not hear.*)

Not at home, eh? You are an ass. And the telegram? Nothing? Go on. . . . At six this evening? That's good. Special edition, you say? With his name in full. Arkenholtz, a student, born . . . parents . . . That's splendid. . . . I think it's beginning to rain. . . . What did he say about it? So — so. He wouldn't? Well, he must. Here comes the aristocrat. Push me round the corner, Johansson, so I can hear what the poor are saying. And, Arkenholtz, you wait for me here. Understand? (*To* JOHANSSON.) Hurry up now, hurry up.

(JOHANSSON *wheels the chair round the corner. The* STUDENT *remains watching the* GIRL, *who is now loosening the earth round the hyacinths. The* ARISTOCRAT, *wearing mourning, comes in and speaks to the* DARK LADY, *who has been walking to and fro on the pavement.*)

ARISTOCRAT: But what can we do about it? We shall have to wait.

LADY: I can't wait.

ARISTOCRAT: You can't? Well then, go into the country.

LADY: I don't want to do that.

ARISTOCRAT: Come over here or they will hear what we are saying.

(*They move toward the advertisement column and continue their conversation inaudibly.* JOHANSSON *returns.*)

JOHANSSON (*to the* STUDENT): My master asks you not to forget that other thing, sir.

STUDENT (*hesitating*): Look here . . . first of all tell me . . . who is your master?

JOHANSSON: Well, he's so many things, and he has been everything.

STUDENT: Is he a wise man?

JOHANSSON: Depends what that is. He says all his life he's been looking for a Sunday child, but that may not be true.

STUDENT: What does he want? He's grasping, isn't he?

JOHANSSON: It's power he wants. The whole day long he rides round in his chariot like the god Thor himself. He looks at houses, pulls them down, opens up new streets, builds squares. . . . But he breaks into houses too, sneaks through windows, plays havoc with human destinies, kills his enemies — and never forgives. Can you imagine it, sir? This miserable cripple was once a Don Juan — although he always lost his women.

STUDENT: How do you account for that?

JOHANSSON: You see he's so cunning he makes the women leave him when he's tired of them. But what he's most like now is a horse-thief in the human market. He steals human beings in all sorts of different ways. He literally stole me out of the hands of the law. Well, as a matter of fact I'd made a slip — hm, yes — and only he knew about it. Instead of getting me put in gaol, he turned me into a slave. I slave — for my food alone, and that's none of the best.

STUDENT: Then what is it he means to do in this house?

JOHANSSON: I'm not going to talk about that. It's too complicated.

STUDENT: I think I'd better get away from it all.

(*The* GIRL *drops a bracelet out the window.*)

JOHANSSON: Look! The young lady has dropped her bracelet out of the window.

(*The* STUDENT *goes slowly over, picks up the bracelet and returns it to the* GIRL, *who thanks him stiffly. The* STUDENT *goes back to* JOHANSSON.)

So you mean to get away. That's not so easy as you think, once he's got you in his net. And he's afraid of nothing between heaven and earth — yes, of one thing he is — of one person rather. . . .

STUDENT: Don't tell me. I think perhaps I know.

JOHANSSON: How can you know?

STUDENT: I'm guessing. Is it a little milkmaid he's afraid of?

JOHANSSON: He turns his head the other way whenever he meets a milk cart. Besides, he talks in his sleep. It seems he was once in Hamburg. . . .

STUDENT: Can one trust this man?

JOHANSSON: You can trust him — to do anything.

STUDENT: What's he doing now round the corner?

JOHANSSON: Listening to the poor. Sowing a little word, loosening one stone at a time, till the house falls down — metaphorically speaking. You see I'm an educated man. I was once a book-seller. . . . Do you still mean to go away?

STUDENT: I don't like to be ungrateful. He saved my father once, and now he only asks a small service in return.

JOHANSSON: What is that?

STUDENT: I am to go to *The Valkyrie.*

JOHANSSON: That's beyond me. But he's always up to new tricks. Look at him now, talking to that policeman. He is always thick with the police. He uses them, gets them involved in his interests, holds them with false promises and expectations, while all the time he's pumping them. You'll see that before the day is over he'll be received in the Round Room.

STUDENT: What does he want there? What connection has he with the Colonel?

JOHANSSON: I think I can guess, but I'm not sure. You'll see for yourself once you're in there.

STUDENT: I shall never be in there.

JOHANSSON: That depends on yourself. Go to *The Valkyrie.*

STUDENT: Is that the way?

JOHANSSON: Yes, if he said so. Look. Look at him in his war chariot, drawn in triumph by the beggars, who get nothing for their pains but the hint of a treat at his funeral.

(*The* OLD MAN *appears standing up in his wheel-chair, drawn by one of the beggars and followed by the rest.*)

OLD MAN: Hail the noble youth who, at the risk of his own life, saved so many others in yesterday's accident. Three cheers for Arkenholtz!

(*The* BEGGARS *bare their heads but do not cheer. The* GIRL *at the window waves her handkerchief. The* COLONEL *gazes from the window of the Round Room. The* OLD WOMAN *rises at her window. The* MAID *on the balcony hoists the flag to the top.*)

Clap your hands, citizens. True, it is Sunday, but the ass in the pit and the ear in the corn field will absolve us. And although I am not a Sunday child, I have the gift of prophecy and also that of healing. Once I brought a drowned person back to life. That was in Hamburg on a Sunday morning just like this. . . .

(*The* MILKMAID *enters, seen only by the* STUDENT *and the* OLD MAN. *She raises her arms like one who is drowning and gazes fixedly at the* OLD MAN. *He sits down, then crumples up, stricken with horror.*)

Johansson! Take me away! Quick! . . . Arkenholtz, don't forget *The Valkyrie.*

STUDENT: What is all this?

JOHANSSON: We shall see. We shall see.

SCENE II

Inside the Round Room. At the back is a white porcelain stove. On either side of it are a mirror, a pendulum clock and candelabra. On the right of the stove is the entrance to the hall beyond which is a glimpse of a room furnished in green and mahogany. On the left of the stove is the door to a cupboard, papered like the wall. The statue, shaded by palms, has a curtain which can be drawn to conceal it.

A door on the left leads into the Hyacinth Room, where the GIRL *sits reading.*

The back of the COLONEL *can be seen, as he sits in the Green Room, writing.*

BENGTSSON, *the Colonel's servant, comes in from the hall. He is wearing livery, and is followed by* JOHANSSON, *dressed as a waiter.*

BENGTSSON: Now you'll have to serve the tea, Johansson, while I take the coats. Have you ever done it before?

JOHANSSON: It's true I push a war chariot in the daytime, as you know, but in the evenings I go as a waiter to receptions and so forth. It's always been my dream to get into this house. They're queer people here, aren't they?

BENGTSSON: Ye-es. A bit out of the ordinary anyhow.

JOHANSSON: Is it to be a musical party or what?

BENGTSSON: The usual ghost supper, as we call it. They drink tea and don't say a word — or else the Colonel does all the talking. And they crunch their biscuits, all at the same time. It sounds like rats in an attic.

JOHANSSON: Why do you call it the ghost supper?

BENGTSSON: They look like ghosts. And they've kept this up for twenty years, always the same people saying the same things or saying nothing at all for fear of being found out.

JOHANSSON: Isn't there a mistress of the house?

BENGTSSON: Oh yes, but she's crazy. She sits in a cupboard because her eyes can't bear the light. (*He points to the papered door.*) She sits in there.

JOHANSSON: In there?

BENGTSSON: Well, I told you they were a bit out of the ordinary.

JOHANSSON: But then — what does she look like?

BENGTSSON: Like a mummy. Do you want to have a look at her? (*He opens the door.*) There she is.

(*The figure of the* COLONEL'S WIFE *is seen, white and shrivelled into a* MUMMY.)

JOHANSSON: Oh my God!

MUMMY (*babbling*): Why do you open the door? Haven't I told you to keep it closed?

BENGTSSON (*in a wheedling tone*): Ta, ta, ta, ta. Be a good girl now, then you'll get something nice. Pretty Polly.

MUMMY (*parrot-like*): Pretty Polly. Are you there, Jacob? Currrrr!

BENGTSSON: She thinks she's a parrot, and maybe she's right. (*To the* MUMMY.) Whistle for us, Polly.

(*The* MUMMY *whistles.*)

JOHANSSON: Well, I've seen a few things in my day, but this beats everything.

BENGTSSON: You see, when a house gets old, it grows moldy, and when people stay a long time together and torment each other they go mad. The mistress of the house — shut up, Polly! — that mummy there, has been living here for forty years — same husband, same furniture, same relatives, same friends. (*He closes the papered door.*) And the goings-on in this house — well, they're beyond me. Look at that statue — that's her when she was young.

JOHANSSON: Good Lord! Is that the mummy?

BENGTSSON: Yes. It's enough to make you weep. And somehow, carried away by her own imagination or something, she's got to be a bit like a parrot — the way she talks and the way she can't stand cripples or sick people. She can't stand the sight of her own daughter, because she's sick.

JOHANSSON: Is the young lady sick?

BENGTSSON: Didn't you know that?

JOHANSSON: No. And the Colonel, who is he?

BENGTSSON: You'll see.

JOHANSSON (*looking at the statue*): It's horrible to think that . . . How old is she now?

BENGTSSON: Nobody knows. But it's said that when she was thirty-five she looked nineteen, and that's what she made the Colonel believe she was — here in this very house. Do you know what that black Japanese screen by the couch is for? They call it the death-screen, and when someone's going to die, they put it round — same as in a hospital.

JOHANSSON: What a horrible house! And the student was longing to get in, as if it were paradise.

BENGTSSON: What student? Oh, I know. The one who's coming here this evening. The Colonel and the young lady happened to meet him at the Opera, and both of them took a fancy to him. Hm. Now it's my turn to ask questions. Who is your master — the man in the wheelchair?

JOHANSSON: Well, he . . . er . . . Is he coming here too?

BENGTSSON: He hasn't been invited.

JOHANSSON: He'll come uninvited — if need be.

(*The* OLD MAN *appears in the hall on crutches, wearing a frock-coat and top-hat. He steals forward and listens.*)

BENGTSSON: He's a regular old devil, isn't he?

JOHANSSON: Up to the ears.

BENGTSSON: He looks like old Nick himself.

JOHANSSON: And he must be a wizard too, for he goes through locked doors.

(*The* OLD MAN *comes forward and takes hold of* JOHANSSON *by the ear.*)

OLD MAN: Rascal — take care! (*To* BENGTSSON.) Tell the Colonel I am here.

BENGTSSON: But we are expecting guests.

OLD MAN: I know. But my visit is as good as expected, if not exactly looked forward to.

BENGTSSON: I see. What name shall I say? Mr. Hummel?

OLD MAN: Exactly. Yes.

(BENGTSSON *crosses the hall to the Green Room, the door of which he closes behind him.*)

(*To* JOHANSSON.) Get out!

(JOHANSSON *hesitates.*)

Get out!

(JOHANSSON *disappears into the hall. The* OLD MAN *inspects the room and stops in front of the statue in much astonishment.*)

Amelia! It is she — she!

MUMMY (*from the cupboard*): Prrr-etty Polly.

(*The* OLD MAN *starts.*)

OLD MAN: What was that? Is there a parrot in the room? I don't see it.

MUMMY: Are you there, Jacob?

OLD MAN: The house is haunted.

MUMMY: Jacob!

OLD MAN: I'm scared. So these are the kind of secrets they guard in this house. (*With his back turned to the cupboard he stands looking at a portrait.*) There he is — he!

(*The* MUMMY *comes out behind the* OLD MAN *and gives a pull at his wig.*)

MUMMY: Currrrr! Is it . . . ? Currrrr!

OLD MAN (*jumping out of his skin*): God in heaven! Who is it?

MUMMY (*in a natural voice*): Is it Jacob?

OLD MAN: Yes, my name is Jacob.

MUMMY (*with emotion*): And my name is Amelia.

OLD MAN: No, no, no . . . Oh my God!

MUMMY: That's how I look. Yes. (*Pointing to the statue.*) And that's how I *did* look. Life opens one's eyes, does it not? I live mostly in the cupboard to avoid seeing and being seen. . . . But, Jacob, what do you want here?

OLD MAN: My child. Our child.

MUMMY: There she is.

OLD MAN: Where?

MUMMY: There — in the Hyacinth Room.

OLD MAN (*looking at the* GIRL): Yes, that is she. (*Pause.*) And what about her father — the Colonel, I mean — your husband?

MUMMY: Once, when I was angry with him, I told him everything.

OLD MAN: Well. . . . ?

MUMMY: He didn't believe me. He just said: "That's what all wives say when they want to murder their husbands." It was a terrible crime none the less. It has falsified his whole life — his family tree too. Sometimes I take a look in the Peerage, and then I say to myself: Here she is, going about with a false birth certificate like some servant girl, and for such things people are sent to the reformatory.

OLD MAN: Many do it. I seem to remember your own date of birth was given incorrectly.

MUMMY: My mother made me do that. I was not to blame. And in our crime, *you* played the biggest part.

OLD MAN: No. Your husband caused that crime, when he took my fiancée from me. I was born one who cannot forgive until he has punished. That was to me an imperative duty — and is so still.

MUMMY: What are you expecting to find in this house? What do you want? How did you get in? Is it to do with my daughter? If you touch her, you shall die.

OLD MAN: I mean well by her.

MUMMY: Then you must spare her father.

OLD MAN: No.

MUMMY: Then you shall die. In this room, behind that screen.

OLD MAN: That may be. But I can't let go once I've got my teeth into a thing.

MUMMY: You want to marry her to that student. Why? He is nothing and has nothing.

OLD MAN: He will be rich, through me.

MUMMY: Have you been invited here tonight?

OLD MAN: No, but I propose to get myself an invitation to this ghost supper.

MUMMY: Do you know who is coming?

OLD MAN: Not exactly.

MUMMY: The Baron. The man who lives up above — whose father-in-law was buried this afternoon.

OLD MAN: The man who is getting a divorce in order to marry the daughter of the Caretaker's wife . . . The man who used to be — your lover.

MUMMY: Another guest will be your former fiancée, who was seduced by my husband.

OLD MAN: A select gathering.

MUMMY: Oh God, if only we might die, might die!

OLD MAN: Then why have you stayed together?

MUMMY: Crime and secrets and guilt bind us together. We have broken our bonds and gone our own ways, times without number, but we are always drawn together again.

OLD MAN: I think the Colonel is coming.

MUMMY: Then I will go in to Adèle. (*Pause.*) Jacob, mind what you do. Spare him. (*Pause. She goes into the Hyacinth Room and disappears.*)

(*The* COLONEL *enters, cold and reserved, with a letter in his hand.*)

COLONEL: Be seated, please.

(*Slowly the* OLD MAN *sits down. Pause. The* COLONEL *stares at him.*)

You wrote this letter, sir?

OLD MAN: I did.

COLONEL: Your name is Hummel?

OLD MAN: It is. (*Pause.*)

COLONEL: As I understand, you have bought in all my unpaid promissory notes. I can only conclude that I am in your hands. What do you want?

OLD MAN: I want payment, in one way or another.

COLONEL: In what way?

OLD MAN: A very simple one. Let us not mention the money. Just bear with me in your house as a guest.

COLONEL: If so little will satisfy you . . .

OLD MAN: Thank you.

COLONEL: What else?

OLD MAN: Dismiss Bengtsson.

COLONEL: Why should I do that? My devoted servant, who has been with me a lifetime, who has the national medal for long and faithful service — why should I do that?

OLD MAN: That's how you see him — full of excellent qualities. He is not the man he appears to be.

COLONEL: Who is?

OLD MAN (*taken aback*): True. But Bengtsson must go.

COLONEL: Are you going to run my house?

OLD MAN: Yes. Since everything here belongs to me — furniture, curtains, dinner service, linen . . . and more too.

COLONEL: How do you mean — more?

OLD MAN: Everything. I own everything here. It is mine.

COLONEL: Very well, it is yours. But my family escutcheon and my good name remain my own.

OLD MAN: No, not even those. (*Pause.*) You are not a nobleman.

COLONEL: How dare you!

OLD MAN (*producing a document*): If you read this extract from *The Armorial Gazette*, you will see that the family whose name you are using has been extinct for a hundred years.

COLONEL: I have heard rumors to this effect, but I inherited the name from my father. (*Reads.*) It is true. You are right. I am not a nobleman. Then I must take off my signet ring. It is true, it belongs to you. (*Gives it to him.*) There you are.

OLD MAN (*pocketing the ring*): Now we will continue. You are not a Colonel either.

COLONEL: I am not . . . ?

OLD MAN: No. You once held the temporary rank of Colonel in the American Volunteer Force, but after the war in Cuba and the reorganization of the Army, all such titles were abolished.

COLONEL: Is this true?

OLD MAN (*indicating his pocket*): Do you want to read it?

COLONEL: No, that's not necessary. Who are you, and what right have you to sit there stripping me in this fashion?

OLD MAN: You will see. But as far as stripping you goes . . . do you know who you are?

COLONEL: How dare you?

OLD MAN: Take off that wig and have a look at yourself in the mirror. But take your teeth out at the same time and shave off your moustache. Let Bengtsson unlace your metal stays and perhaps a certain X.Y.Z., a lackey, will recognize himself. The fellow who was a cupboard lover in a certain kitchen . . .

(*The* COLONEL *reaches for the bell on the table, but* HUMMEL *checks him.*)

Don't touch that bell, and don't call Bengtsson. If you do, I'll have him arrested. (*Pause.*) And now the guests are beginning to arrive. Keep your composure and we will continue to play our old parts for a while.

COLONEL: Who are you? I recognize your voice and eyes.

OLD MAN: Don't try to find out. Keep silent and obey.

(*The* STUDENT *enters and bows to the* COLONEL.)

STUDENT: How do you do, sir.

COLONEL: Welcome to my house, young man. Your splendid behavior at that great disaster has brought your name to everybody's lips, and I count it an honor to receive you in my home.

STUDENT: My humble descent, sir . . . Your illustrious name and noble birth. . . .

COLONEL: May I introduce Mr. Arkenholtz — Mr. Hummel. If you will join the ladies in here, Mr. Arkenholtz — I must conclude my conversation with Mr. Hummel.

(*He shows the* STUDENT *into the Hyacinth Room, where he remains visible, talking shyly to the* GIRL.)

A splendid young man, musical, sings, writes poetry. If he only had blue blood in him, if he were of the same station, I don't think I should object . . .

OLD MAN: To what?

COLONEL: To my daughter . . .

OLD MAN: Your daughter! But apropos of that, why does she spend all her time in there?

COLONEL: She insists on being in the Hyacinth Room except when she is out-of-doors. It's a peculiarity of hers. Ah, here comes Miss Beatrice von Holsteinkrona — a charming woman, a pillar of the Church, with just enough money of her own to suit her birth and position.

OLD MAN (*to himself*): My fiancée.

(*The* FIANCÉE *enters, looking a little crazy.*)

COLONEL: Miss Holsteinkrona — Mr. Hummel.

(The FIANCÉE *curtseys and takes a seat. The* ARISTOCRAT *enters and seats himself. He wears mourning and looks mysterious.*)

Baron Skanskorg . . .

OLD MAN (*aside, without rising*): That's the jewel-thief, I think. (*To the* COLONEL.) If you bring in the Mummy, the party will be complete.

COLONEL (*at the door of the Hyacinth Room*): Polly!

MUMMY (*entering*): Currrrr . . . !

COLONEL: Are the young people to come in too?

OLD MAN: No, not the young people. They shall be spared.

(*They all sit silent in a circle.*)

COLONEL: Shall we have the tea brought in?

OLD MAN: What's the use? No one wants tea. Why should we pretend about it?

COLONEL: Then shall we talk?

OLD MAN: Talk of the weather, which we know? Inquire about each other's health, which we know just as well? I prefer silence — then one can hear thoughts and see the past. Silence cannot hide anything — but words can. I read the other day that differences of language originated among savages for the purpose of keeping one tribe's secrets hidden from another. Every language therefore is a code, and he who finds the key can understand every language in the world. But this does not prevent secrets from being exposed without a key, specially when there is a question of paternity to be proved. Proof in a Court of Law is another matter. Two false witnesses suffice to prove anything about which they are agreed, but one does not take witnesses along on the kind of explorations I have in mind. Nature herself has instilled in human beings a sense of modesty which tries to hide what should be hidden, but we slip into situations unintentionally, and by chance sometimes the deepest secret is divulged — the mask torn from the impostor, the villain exposed. . . .

(*Pause. All look at each other in silence.*)

What a silence there is now!

(*Long silence.*)

Here, for instance, in this honorable house, in this elegant home, where beauty, wealth and culture are united. . . .

(*Long silence.*)

All of us now sitting here know who we are — do we not? There's no need for me to tell you. And you know me, although you pretend ignorance. (*He indicates the Hyacinth Room.*) In there is my daughter. *Mine* — you know that too. She had lost the desire to live, without knowing why. The fact is she was withering away in this air charged with crime and deceit and falseness of every kind. That is why I looked for a friend for her in whose company she might enjoy the light and warmth of noble deeds.

(*Long silence.*)

That was my mission in this house: to pull up the weeds, to expose the crimes, to settle all accounts, so that those young people might start afresh in this home, which is my gift to them.

(*Long silence.*)

Now I am going to grant safe-conduct, to each of you in his and her proper time and turn. Whoever stays I shall have arrested.

(*Long silence.*)

Do you hear the clock ticking like a death-watch beetle in the wall? Do you hear what it says? "It's time, it's time, it's time." When it strikes, in a few moments, your time will be up. Then you can go, but not before. It's raising its arm against you before it strikes. Listen! It is warning you. "The clock can strike." And I can strike too. (*He strikes the table with one of his crutches.*) Do you hear?

(*Silence. The* MUMMY *goes up to the clock and stops it, then speaks in a normal and serious voice.*)

MUMMY: But I can stop time in its course. I can wipe out the past and undo what is done. But not with bribes, not with threats — only through suffering and repentance. (*She goes up to the* OLD MAN.) We are miserable human beings, that we know. We have erred and we have sinned, we like all the rest. We are not what we seem, because at bottom we are better than ourselves, since we detest our sins. But when you, Jacob Hummel, with your false name, choose to sit in judgment over us, you prove yourself worse than us miserable sinners. For you are not the one you appear to be. You are a thief of human souls. You stole me once with false promises. You murdered the Consul who was buried today; you strangled him with debts.

You have stolen the student, binding him by the pretence of a claim on his father, who never owed you a farthing.

(*Having tried to rise and speak, the* OLD MAN *sinks back in his chair and crumples up more and more as she goes on.*)

But there is one dark spot in your life which I am not quite sure about, although I have my suspicions. I think Bengtsson knows. (*She rings the bell on the table.*)

OLD MAN: No, not Bengtsson, not him.

MUMMY: So he does know. (*She rings again.*)

(*The* MILKMAID *appears in the hallway door, unseen by all but the* OLD MAN, *who shrinks back in horror. The* MILKMAID *vanishes as* BENGTSSON *enters.*)

Do you know this man, Bengtsson?

BENGTSSON: Yes, I know him and he knows me. Life, as you are aware, has its ups and downs. I have been in his service; another time he was in mine. For two whole years he was a sponger in my kitchen. As he had to be away by three, the dinner was got ready at two, and the family had to eat the warmed-up leavings of that brute. He drank the soup stock, which the cook then filled up with water. He sat out there like a vampire, sucking the marrow out of the house, so that we became like skeletons. And he nearly got us put in prison when we called the cook a thief. Later I met this man in Hamburg under another name. He was a usurer then, a blood-sucker. But while he was there he was charged with having lured a young girl out on to the ice so as to drown her, because she had seen him commit a crime he was afraid would be discovered. . . .

(*The* MUMMY *passes her hand over the* OLD MAN's *face.*)

MUMMY: *This* is you. Now give up the notes and the Will.

(JOHANSSON *appears in the hallway door and watches the scene with great interest, knowing he is now to be freed from slavery. The* OLD MAN *produces a bundle of papers and throws it on the table. The* MUMMY *goes over and strokes his back.*)

Parrot. Are you there, Jacob?

OLD MAN (*like a parrot*): Jacob is here. Pretty Polly. Currrrr!

MUMMY: May the clock strike?

OLD MAN (*with a clucking sound*): The clock may strike. (*Imitating a cuckoo clock.*) Cuckoo, cuckoo, cuckoo. . . .

(*The* MUMMY *opens the cupboard door.*)

MUMMY: Now the clock has struck. Rise, and enter the cupboard where I have spent twenty years repenting our crime. A rope is hanging there, which you can take as the one with which you strangled the Consul, and with which you meant to strangle your benefactor. . . . Go!

(*The* OLD MAN *goes in to the cupboard. The* MUMMY *closes the door.*)

Bengtsson! Put up the screen — the death-screen.

(BENGTSSON *places the screen in front of the door.*)

It is finished. God have mercy on his soul.
ALL: Amen. (*Long silence.*)

(*The* GIRL *and the* STUDENT *appear in the Hyacinth Room. She has a harp, on which he plays a prelude, and then accompanies the* STUDENT's *recitation.*)

STUDENT: *I saw the sun. To me it seemed*
   that I beheld the Hidden.
   Men must reap what they have sown;
   blest is he whose deeds are good.
   Deeds which you have wrought in fury,
   cannot in evil find redress.
   Comfort him you have distressed
   with loving-kindness — this will heal.
   No fear has he who does no ill.
   Sweet is innocence.

SCENE III

Inside the Hyacinth Room. The general effect of the room is exotic and oriental. There are hyacinths everywhere, of every color, some in pots, some with the bulbs in glass vases and the roots going down into the water.

On top of the tiled stove is a large seated Buddha, in whose lap rests a bulb from which rises the stem of a shallot (Allium ascalonicum), bearing its globular cluster of white, starlike flowers.

On the right is an open door, leading into the Round Room, where the COLONEL *and the* MUMMY *are seated, inactive and silent. A part of the death-screen is also visible.*

On the left is a door to the pantry and kitchen.

The STUDENT *and the* GIRL *(Adèle) are beside the table; he standing, she seated with her harp.*

GIRL: Now sing to my flowers.

STUDENT: Is this the flower of your soul?

GIRL: The one and only. Do you too love the hyacinth?

STUDENT: I love it above all other flowers — its virginal shape rising straight and slender out of the bulb, resting on the water and sending its pure white roots down into the colorless fluid. I love its colors: the snow-white, pure as innocence, the yellow honey-sweet, the youthful pink, the ripe red, but best of all the blue — the dewy blue, deep-eyed and full of faith. I love them all, more than gold or pearls. I have loved them ever since I was a child, have worshipped them because they have all the fine qualities I lack. . . . And yet . . .

GIRL: Go on.

STUDENT: My love is not returned, for these beautiful blossoms hate me.

GIRL: How do you mean?

STUDENT: Their fragrance, strong and pure as the early winds of spring which have passed over melting snows, confuses my senses, deafens me, blinds me, thrusts me out of the room, bombards me with poisoned arrows that wound my heart and set my head on fire. Do you know the legend of that flower?

GIRL: Tell it to me.

STUDENT: First its meaning. The bulb is the earth, resting on the water or buried in the soil. Then the stalk rises, straight as the axis of the world, and at the top are the six-pointed star-flowers.

GIRL: Above the earth — the stars. Oh, that is wonderful! Where did you learn this? How did you find it out?

STUDENT: Let me think . . . In your eyes. And so, you see, it is an image of the Cosmos. This is why Buddha sits holding the earth-bulb, his eyes brooding as he watches it grow, outward and upward, transforming itself into a heaven. This poor earth will become a heaven. It is for this that Buddha waits.

GIRL: I see it now. Is not the snowflake six-pointed too like the hyacinth flower?

STUDENT: You are right. The snowflakes must be falling stars.

GIRL: And the snowdrop is a snow-star, grown out of snow.

STUDENT: But the largest and most beautiful of all the stars in the firmament, the golden-red Sirius, is the narcissus with its gold and red chalice and its six white rays.

GIRL: Have you seen the shallot in bloom?

STUDENT: Indeed I have. It bears its blossoms within a ball, a globe like the celestial one, strewn with white stars.

GIRL: Oh how glorious! Whose thought was that?

STUDENT: Yours.

GIRL: Yours.

STUDENT: Ours. We have given birth to it together. We are wedded.

GIRL: Not yet.

STUDENT: What's still to do?

GIRL: Waiting, ordeals, patience.

STUDENT: Very well. Put me to the test. (*Pause.*) Tell me. Why do your parents sit in there so silently, not saying a single word?

GIRL: Because they have nothing to say to each other, and because neither believes what the other says. This is how my father puts it: What's the point of talking, when neither of us can fool the other?

STUDENT: What a horrible thing to hear!

GIRL: Here comes the Cook. Look at her, how big and fat she is.

(*They watch the* COOK, *although the audience cannot yet see her.*)

STUDENT: What does she want?

GIRL: To ask me about the dinner. I have to do the housekeeping as my mother's ill.

STUDENT: What have we to do with the kitchen?

GIRL: We must eat. Look at the Cook. I can't bear the sight of her.

STUDENT: Who is that ogress?

GIRL: She belongs to the Hummel family of vampires. She is eating us.

STUDENT: Why don't you dismiss her?

GIRL: She won't go. We have no control over her. We've got her for our sins. Can't you see that we are pining and wasting away?

STUDENT: Don't you get enough to eat?

GIRL: Yes, we get many dishes, but all the strength has gone. She boils the nourishment out of the meat and gives us the fibre and water, while she drinks the stock herself. And when there's a roast, she first boils out the marrow, eats the gravy and drinks the juices herself. Everything she touches loses its savor. It's as if she sucked with her eyes. We get the grounds when she has drunk the coffee. She drinks the wine and fills the bottles up with water.

STUDENT: Send her packing.

GIRL: We can't.

STUDENT: Why not?

GIRL: We don't know. She won't go. No one has any control over her. She has taken all our strength from us.

STUDENT: May I get rid of her?

GIRL: No. It must be as it is. Here she is. She will ask me what is to be for dinner. I shall tell her. She will make objections and get her own way.

STUDENT: Let her do the ordering herself then.

GIRL: She won't do that.

STUDENT: What an extraordinary house! It is bewitched.

GIRL: Yes. But now she is turning back, because she has seen you.

THE COOK (*in the doorway*): No, that wasn't the reason. (*She grins, showing all her teeth.*)

STUDENT: Get out!

COOK: When it suits me. (*Pause.*) It does suit me now. (*She disappears.*)

GIRL: Don't lose your temper. Practice patience. She is one of the ordeals we have to go through in this house. You see, we have a housemaid too, whom we have to clean up after.

STUDENT: I am done for. *Cor in æthere.* Music!

GIRL: Wait.

STUDENT: Music!

GIRL: Patience. This room is called the room of ordeals. It looks beautiful, but it is full of defects.

STUDENT: Really? Well, such things must be seen to. It is very beautiful, but a little cold. Why don't you have a fire?

GIRL: Because it smokes.

STUDENT: Can't you have the chimney swept?

GIRL: It doesn't help. You see that writing-desk there?

STUDENT: An unusually fine piece.

GIRL: But it wobbles. Every day I put a piece of cork under that leg, and every day the housemaid takes it away when she sweeps and I have to cut a new piece. The penholder is covered with ink every morning and so is the inkstand. I have to clean them up every morning after that woman, as sure as the sun rises. (*Pause.*) What's the worst job you can think of?

STUDENT: To count the washing. Ugh!

GIRL: That I have to do. Ugh!

STUDENT: What else?

GIRL: To be waked in the middle of the night and have to get up and see to the window, which the housemaid has left banging.

STUDENT: What else?

GIRL: To get up on a ladder and tie the cord on the damper[4] which the housemaid has torn off.

---

[4] Damper to the big stove.

STUDENT: What else?

GIRL: To sweep after her, to dust after her, to light the fire in the stove when all she's done is throw in some wood. To see to the damper, to wipe the glasses, to lay the table over again, to open the bottles, to see that the rooms are aired, to remake my bed, to rinse the water-bottle when it's green with sediment, to buy matches and soap which are always lacking, to wipe the chimneys and trim the wicks to keep the lamps from smoking — and so that they don't go out when we have company, I have to fill them myself. . . .

STUDENT: Music!

GIRL: Wait. The labor comes first. The labor of keeping the dirt of life at a distance.

STUDENT: But you are wealthy and have two servants.

GIRL: It doesn't help. Even if we had three. Living is hard work, and sometimes I grow tired. (*Pause.*) Think then if there were a nursery as well.

STUDENT: The greatest of joys.

GIRL: And the costliest. Is life worth so much hardship?

STUDENT: That must depend on the reward you expect for your labors. I would not shrink from anything to win your hand.

GIRL: Don't say that. You can never have me.

STUDENT: Why not?

GIRL: You mustn't ask. (*Pause.*)

STUDENT: You dropped your bracelet out of the window. . . .

GIRL: Because my hand has grown so thin. (*Pause.*)

(*The* COOK *appears with a Japanese bottle in her hand.*)

There she is — the one who devours me and all of us.

STUDENT: What has she in her hand?

GIRL: It is the bottle of coloring matter that has letters like scorpions on it. It is the soy which turns water into soup and takes the place of gravy. She makes cabbage soup with it — and mock-turtle soup too.

STUDENT (*to* COOK): Get out!

COOK: You drain us of sap, and we drain you. We take the blood and leave you the water, but colored . . . colored. I am going now, but all the same I shall stay, as long as I please. (*She goes out.*)

STUDENT: Why did Bengtsson get a medal?

GIRL: For his great merits.

STUDENT: Has he no defects?

GIRL: Yes, great ones. But you don't get a medal for them.

(*They smile.*)

STUDENT: You have many secrets in this house.

GIRL: As in all others. Permit us to keep ours.

STUDENT: Don't you approve of candor?

GIRL: Yes — within reason.

STUDENT: Sometimes I'm seized with a raging desire to say all I think. But I know the world would go to pieces if one were completely candid. (*Pause.*) I went to a funeral the other day . . . in church. It was very solemn and beautiful.

GIRL: Was it Mr. Hummel's?

STUDENT: My false benefactor's — yes. At the head of the coffin stood an old friend of the deceased. He carried the mace. I was deeply impressed by the dignified manner and moving words of the clergyman. I cried. We all cried. Afterwards we went to a tavern, and there I learned that the man with the mace had been in love with the dead man's son. . . .

(*The* GIRL *stares at him, trying to understand.*)

And that the dead man had borrowed money from his son's admirer. (*Pause.*) Next day the clergyman was arrested for embezzling the church funds. A pretty story.

GIRL: Oh . . . ! (*Pause.*)

STUDENT: Do you know how I am thinking about you now?

GIRL: Don't tell me, or I shall die.

STUDENT: I must, or I shall die.

GIRL: It is in asylums that people say everything they think.

STUDENT: Exactly. My father finished up in an asylum.

GIRL: Was he ill?

STUDENT: No, he was well, but he was mad. You see, he broke out once — in these circumstances. Like all of us, he was surrounded with a circle of acquaintances; he called them friends for short. They were a lot of rotters, of course, as most people are, but he had to have some society — he couldn't get on all alone. Well, as you know, in everyday life no one tells people what he thinks of them, and he didn't either. He knew perfectly well what frauds they were — he'd sounded the depths of their deceit — but as he was a wise and well-bred man, he was always courteous to them. Then one day he gave a big party. It was in the evening and he was tired by the day's work and by the strain of holding his tongue and at the same time talking rubbish with his guests. . . .

(*The* GIRL *is frightened.*)

Well, at the dinner table he rapped for silence, raised his glass, and began to speak. Then something loosed the trigger. He made an enormous speech in which he stripped the whole company naked, one after the other, and told them of all their treachery. Then, tired out, he sat down on the table and told them all to go to hell.

GIRL: Oh!

STUDENT: I was there, and I shall never forget what happened then. Father and Mother came to blows, the guests rushed for the door . . . and my father was taken to a madhouse, where he died. (*Pause.*) Water that is still too long stagnates, and so it is in this house too. There is something stagnating here. And yet I thought it was paradise itself that first time I saw you coming in here. There I stood that Sunday morning, gazing in. I saw a Colonel who was no Colonel. I had a benefactor who was a thief and had to hang himself. I saw a mummy who was not a mummy and an old maid — what of the maidenhood, by the way? Where is beauty to be found? In nature, and in my own mind, when it is in its Sunday clothes. Where are honor and faith? In fairy-tales and children's fancies. Where is anything that fulfills its promise? In my imagination. Now your flowers have poisoned me and I have given the poison back to you. I asked you to become my wife in a home full of poetry and song and music. Then the Cook came. . . . *Sursum Corda!* Try once more to strike fire and glory out of the golden harp. Try, I beg you, I implore you on my knees. (*Pause.*) Then I will do it myself. (*He picks up the harp, but the strings give no sound.*) It is dumb and deaf. To think that the most beautiful flowers are so poisonous, are the most poisonous. The curse lies over the whole of creation, over life itself. Why will you not be my bride? Because the very life-spring within you is sick . . . now I can feel that vampire in the kitchen beginning to suck me. I believe she is a Lamia, one of those that suck the blood of children. It is always in the kitchen quarters that the seed-leaves of the children are nipped, if it has not already happened in the bedroom. There are poisons that destroy the sight and poisons that open the eyes. I seem to have been born with the latter kind, for I cannot see what is ugly as beautiful, nor call evil good. I cannot. Jesus Christ descended into hell. That was His pilgrimage on earth — to this madhouse, this prison, this charnel-house, this earth. And the madmen killed Him when He wanted to set them free; but the robber they let go. The robber always gets the sympathy. Woe! Woe to us all. Saviour of the world, save us! We perish.

(*And now the* GIRL *has drooped, and it is seen that she is dying. She rings.* BENGTSSON *enters.*)

GIRL: Bring the screen. Quick. I am dying.

(BENGTSSON *comes back with the screen, opens it and arranges it in front of the* GIRL.)

STUDENT: The Liberator is coming. Welcome, pale and gentle one. Sleep, you lovely, innocent, doomed creature, suffering for no fault of your own. Sleep without dreaming, and when you wake again . . . may you be greeted by a sun that does not burn, in a home without dust, by friends without stain, by a love without flaw. You wise and gentle Buddha, sitting there waiting for a Heaven to sprout from the earth, grant us patience in our ordeal and purity of will, so that this hope may not be confounded.

(*The strings of the harp hum softly and a white light fills the room.*)

> I saw the sun. To me it seemed
> that I beheld the Hidden.
> Men must reap what they have sown;
> blest is he whose deeds are good.
> Deeds which you have wrought in fury,
> cannot in evil find redress.
> Comfort him you have distressed
> with loving-kindness — this will heal.
> No fear has he who does no ill.
> Sweet is innocence.

(*A faint moaning is heard behind the screen.*)

You poor little child, child of this world of illusion, guilt, suffering, and death, this world of endless change, disappointment, and pain. May the Lord of Heaven be merciful to you upon your journey.

(*The room disappears. Böcklin's picture* The Island of the Dead *is seen in the distance, and from the island comes music, soft, sweet, and melancholy.*)

WHEN Strindberg wrote *The Ghost Sonata* (in 1907) his Intimate Theater in Stockholm had just opened and he was worried about its success, his domestic arrangements were made trying by problems with servants (one reason, perhaps, for the prominent and rather obtusely ridiculed "kitchen imagery" in the play), and he suffered from a severe attack of psoriasis (a painful skin disease) of the hands. *The Ghost Sonata*, he wrote to his German translator, had been written "with bleeding hands."

The difficulties one experiences with *The Ghost Sonata* could be due to something we might call the inertia of literary taste. Perhaps the play baffles because it seems so unlike the kind of plays with which we are familiar, plays like *The Wild Duck*, *Three Sisters*, and *A View From the Bridge*, in which people much like ourselves suffer and triumph, are good and evil, sick and sane, noble and ignoble, act or fail to act, in a world much like our own. If we get past our initial sense of being lost among incoherent and inexplicable events, we may begin to recognize familiar themes. Strindberg, too, looks behind the façade of middle-class life and uncovers its moral iniquities. Like Ibsen's, his characters are guilt-haunted captives of their past. And his picture of life stagnating and rotting in a petty and sordid everyday — where people torture one another with silences, and where "the labor of keeping the dirt of life at a distance" saps the good and the young — is close to Chekhov's.

Still, the differences between *The Ghost Sonata* and naturalistic plays are obvious. Strindberg's play is not an authentic image of what actual life appears to be. It deals with the irrational, the mystical, in human life; it is scarcely a coincidence that it is roughly contemporary with the birth of psychoanalysis. Strindberg's stage is more than a setting for the action. It is plastic and fluid, responsive to the playwright's shifting phantasmagoria, an integral part of the play. To move from *Three Sisters* to *The Ghost Sonata* is to leave the familiar living room, drab, perhaps, and stifling, but safely *real*, and to enter a nightmare where ordinary realities appear in new and changing shapes and grotesque combinations, all the more disturbing for being recognizable as their ordinary selves behind the distortions. Clocks and screens and a bottle of soya sauce loom larger than life in Strindberg's ghostly dream. And yet, they are not symbols. They are nothing but themselves, only, somehow, more frighteningly so than in real life; they are solidly there, as things, but imbued with more than thing-like power. And *as* things they will not allow us to think the nightmare unreal. Here horror is a commonplace, normality a dread beyond comprehension and remedy. It is of the essence of Strindberg's art that his ultimate "ghost" is a lazy and impudent cook. The ordinary is both ordinary and supernatural, both tiresome and terrifying.

The reader who still feels that the play "doesn't make sense" may take the dream metaphor a step further. If in Ibsen, Shaw, Chekhov, and Miller our position as audience is that of unobserved observer, fly on the living room wall, in *The Ghost Sonata* it may be thought of as that of troubled dreamer. And dreams are not required to make sense. That they do not is often what makes them most compelling.

The Ghost Sonata has come to be regarded as a pioneer specimen of a kind of drama that has been given the name *expressionistic*. The term is not Strindberg's, it is unlikely that he ever heard it applied to his plays, but it is as meaningful as such labels ever are. Expressionists do not try to copy nature, don't care to make a cow look like a cow. They express themselves, turn reality inside out, fragmentize it, bring its meaning (to them) to the surface, record the feel of experience in bone and nerve. They claim for their subjectivity as much reality as does the scientist for his objectivity. Suppose you don't like liver or colonial furniture (the expressionist may say). What is for you the truer statement about these things: that liver has a certain color, texture, chemical composition, nutritional value, price per pound? Or that it makes you sick? That American colonial is characterized by certain lines and shapes and finishes, a certain use of maple wood? Or that it is ugly? Isn't the second statement in each case as true as the first? Isn't it as important, since it takes account of your feelings? Isn't it at any rate worth expressing?

The distortions of objective reality in this art — sometimes to the point of the unrecognizability of pure abstractionism — serve to universalize it. The emphasis is on the feeling rather than on the real-life object that happens to occasion the feeling. "Abstractionism," says a modern practitioner, "can touch many springs in the human spirit, whereas reality can touch only one." The same premise underlies expressionism — though it is surrealistic rather than non-realistic, like abstractionism. In expressing himself the artist expresses every man's subjectivity, articulates the inarticulate, helps us for the moment exercise our human potential. "We don't live in reality," says Strindberg, "but in what we take reality to be." Perhaps the theory of expressionism is best summed up in the answer a painter acquaintance of Strindberg's gave to a technology-minded friend's suggestion that in an age of photography paint and brush were old-fashioned and inaccurate tools for recording truth: "As long as the camera can't enter heaven and hell," said Edvard Munch, "people will keep on painting and other people keep on looking at what they paint." In *The Ghost Sonata* Strindberg enters hell.

Hell (in this connection) is a state of mind, a climate of the soul, something experienced rather than understood. The musical term "sonata" in the title suggests a work that calls for a sensory and emotional response to its evocation of evil — not for explanation.

The play's theme is the universality of evil, the suffering of the in-nocent, the ambiguity of human motives. The Old Man seems to be a satanic figure — the Mummy calls him "a thief of human souls" — but we cannot really be sure that he is not also the would-be redeemer of his natural daughter and the benefactor of the young man whose father he once wronged (or did he?). The anguish of sin and shame that constitutes the human condition in this most mercilessly dark of all Strindberg's plays is expressed in personal re-lationships seen as a vast and complicated network of mutual guilt and recrimination.* This is the master image of the play, and it ex-plains why some of the structurally most important characters are little more than names. Their function is to be strands in the web of universal sin. Their anonymity furthers that function.

The play's world is a world of deceptions. Act I begins in hope and promise as a penniless young hero is befriended by a wealthy old man on a bright Sunday morning. But the sun disappears, the kindly benefactor appears as a stricken Thor, the blustering heathen god of wrath and war, and the blessing of being a Sunday child amounts only to seeing ghosts from the Old Man's evil past. The second "movement" of the sonata marks the seeming fulfillment of the Student's hopes. He enters the elegant apartment house and meets his beloved. But the remainder of the act disillusions hope in a sequence of disclosure and counter-disclosure. The Old Man's ex-posure of his victims and the purgation of his sinful past are frus-trated at their moment of apparent fruition in a dramatization of something close to Christ's "Judge not, that ye be not judged." Act-ing outside of time, the insane Mummy suddenly turns sane savior, and the wise benefactor hangs himself — the unmasker unmasked.

---

* It may be as well to clarify those relationships here. To do so is not to "get" the play; it is not even a necessary step toward adequate response. But the re-lationships are so involved and so implausible (as realism) that they are likely to be obstacles to enjoyment if left unclarified.

There are two sets of relationships, both adulterous and both involving an illegitimate daughter. (1) The Janitor's Wife is the mother of the Dark Lady by the Dead Man (the Consul). The Dark Lady is engaged to be married to Baron Skanskorg (the Aristocrat) and is apparently pregnant with his child. The Baron is getting a divorce from another daughter (presumably legitimate) of the Dead Man. (2) The Mummy is the wife of the Colonel and the mother of the Girl by the Old Man (Hummel). The Old Man seduced the Mummy in revenge for the Colonel's seduction of the Old Man's Fiancée. The two sets of relationships are linked by still another illicit affair: that between the Mummy and the Baron. (The Old Man's relationship with the Student and the Student's father, with Johansson and Bengtsson, and with the Milkmaid, while part of the general mesh of past and hidden crimes, do not concern these love entanglements.)

But the company stands revealed: a seduced virgin; a jewel thief turned baron about to enter a mésalliance; a host who is fake father, fake officer, fake nobleman, whose very appearance is faked by means of wig, false teeth, and iron corset; an adulterous wife; a master who once was servant and a servant who once was master.

In the third movement, the house of promised happiness has shrunk to a room of desperate but passive suffering, the Hyacinth room of ordeals, beautiful but fatal, where the mysterious poetry of love decays to complaints about servants and housekeeping, where flowers sicken and the Girl dies. Here rules the same vampire evil that had seemed to die with the Old Man, and the suffering of the beautiful and the innocent is presided over by a statue of Buddha, incarnating that infinite patience with which weary mankind must await the miraculous liberation from the curse of life.

Anticipation, disillusionment, suffering — these are the phases of life. Existence, poisoned at the roots, is paralysis in the contemplation of one's own damnation or slow dystrophy in the endless execution of small and distasteful domestic tasks. The kitchen is in charge of a giant, undismissible slattern, whose actions contradict her calling: she grows fat on the food she should serve others. There is no restoration of the ruined house, no atonement for the Old Man, the Mummy, or the Colonel. Salvation is hardly more than a pious hope and a prayer set to soft music before a sentimental picture. The action does not include the Christian redemption the ending hints at. The burden of life is too heavy to bear; blessed are those who, like the Girl, find release in death. "Oh God, if only we might die, might die!" cries the Mummy. But the sleep of death is denied these tormented souls. They are ghosts, miserably, hopelessly, immortal.

Philosophically, the pervasive gloom of *The Ghost Sonata* may not survive scrutiny. The play is not, as far as reader or spectator can discover, based on any rational, coherent system of thought. It asserts, or, rather, it shows — it does not prove. On the other hand, that Strindberg has not philosophized his vision renders it immune to rational criticism. It does not presume to conform to its tenets and can refuse to be judged on its terms. That may be its strength. Its sense-defying manipulation of fragments of reality weaves a spell for those who once have shared, if only in a dream, the awareness of evil at the very core of human existence. It haunts our imagination long after our daylight minds have granted or refused to grant assent to its ghastly judgment.)⟍⟋

W. B. Yeats
PURGATORY

Characters

   A BOY
   AN OLD MAN

SCENE: *A ruined house and a bare tree in the background.*

BOY: Half-door, hall door,
   Hither and thither day and night,
   Hill or hollow, shouldering this pack,
   Hearing you talk.
OLD MAN: Study that house.
   I think about its jokes and stories;
   I try to remember what the butler
   Said to a drunken gamekeeper
   In mid-October, but I cannot.
   If I cannot, none living can.
   Where are the jokes and stories of a house,
   Its threshold gone to patch a pig-sty?
BOY: So you have come this path before?
OLD MAN: The moonlight falls upon the path,
   The shadow of a cloud upon the house,
   And that's symbolical; study that tree,
   What is it like?

BOY: A silly old man.

OLD MAN: It's like — no matter what it's like.
    I saw it a year ago stripped bare as now,
    So I chose a better trade.
    I saw it fifty years ago
    Before the thunderbolt had riven it,
    Green leaves, ripe leaves, leaves thick as butter,
    Fat, greasy life. Stand there and look,
    Because there is somebody in that house.

(*The* BOY *puts down pack and stands in the doorway.*)

BOY: There's nobody here.

OLD MAN: There's somebody there.

BOY: The floor is gone, the window's gone,
    And where there should be roof there's sky,
    And here's a bit of an egg-shell thrown
    Out of a jackdaw's nest.

OLD MAN: But there are some
    That do not care what's gone, what's left:
    The souls of Purgatory that come back
    To habitations and familiar spots.

BOY: Your wits are out again.

OLD MAN: Re-live
    Their transgressions, and that not once
    But many times; they know at last
    The consequence of those trangressions
    Whether upon others or upon themselves;
    Upon others, others may bring help,
    For when the consequence is at an end
    The dream must end; if upon themselves,
    There is no help but in themselves
    And in the mercy of God.

BOY: I have had enough!
    Talk to the jackdaws, if talk you must.

OLD MAN: Stop! Sit there upon that stone.
    That is the house where I was born.

BOY: The big old house that was burnt down?

OLD MAN: My mother that was your grand-dam owned it,
    This scenery and this countryside,
    Kennel and stable, horse and hound —
    She had a horse at the Curragh, and there met
    My father, a groom in the training stable,
    Looked at him and married him.

Her mother never spoke to her again,
And she did right.

BOY: What's right and wrong?
My grand-dad got the girl and the money.

OLD MAN: Looked at him and married him,
And he squandered everything she had.
She never knew the worst, because
She died in giving birth to me,
But now she knows it all, being dead.
Great people lived and died in this house;
Magistrates, colonels, members of Parliament,
Captains and Governors, and long ago
Men that had fought at Aughrim and the Boyne.
Some that had gone on Government work
To London or to India came home to die,
Or came from London every spring
To look at the may-blossom in the park.
They had loved the trees that he cut down
To pay what he had lost at cards
Or spent on horses, drink and women;
Had loved the house, had loved all
The intricate passages of the house,
But he killed the house; to kill a house
Where great men grew up, married, died,
I here declare a capital offence.

BOY: My God, but you had luck! Grand clothes,
And maybe a grand horse to ride.

OLD MAN: That he might keep me upon his level
He never sent me to school, but some
Half-loved me for my half of her:
A gamekeeper's wife taught me to read,
A Catholic curate taught me Latin.
There were old books and books made fine
By eighteenth-century French binding, books
Modern and ancient, books by the ton.

BOY: What education have you given me?

OLD MAN: I gave the education that befits
A bastard that a pedlar got
Upon a tinker's daughter in a ditch.
When I had come to sixteen years old
My father burned down the house when drunk.

BOY: But that is my age, sixteen years old,
At the Puck Fair.

OLD MAN: And everything was burnt;
Books, library, all were burnt.

BOY: Is what I have heard upon the road the truth,
That you killed him in the burning house?

OLD MAN: There's nobody here but our two selves?

BOY: Nobody, Father.

OLD MAN: I stuck him with a knife,
That knife that cuts my dinner now,
And after that I left him in the fire.
They dragged him out, somebody saw
The knife-wound but could not be certain
Because the body was all black and charred.
Then some that were his drunken friends
Swore they would put me upon trial,
Spoke of quarrels, a threat I had made.
The gamekeeper gave me some old clothes,
I ran away, worked here and there
Till I became a pedlar on the roads,
No good trade, but good enough
Because I am my father's son,
Because of what I did or may do.
Listen to the hoof-beats! Listen, listen!

BOY: I cannot hear a sound.

OLD MAN: Beat! Beat!
This night is the anniversary
Of my mother's wedding night,
Or of the night wherein I was begotten.
My father is riding from the public-house,
A whiskey-bottle under his arm.

(A *window is lit showing a young girl.*)

Look at the window; she stands there
Listening, the servants are all in bed,
She is alone, he has stayed late
Bragging and drinking in the public-house.

BOY: There's nothing but an empty gap in the wall.
You have made it up. No, you are mad!
You are getting madder every day.

OLD MAN: It's louder now because he rides
Upon a gravelled avenue
All grass to-day. The hoof-beat stops,
He has gone to the other side of the house,

Gone to the stable, put the horse up.
She has gone down to open the door.
This night she is no better than her man
And does not mind that he is half drunk,
She is mad about him. They mount the stairs.
She brings him into her own chamber.
And that is the marriage-chamber now.
The window is dimly lit again.

Do not let him touch you! It is not true
That drunken men cannot beget,
And if he touch he must beget
And you must bear his murderer.
Deaf! Both deaf! If I should throw
A stick or a stone they would not hear;
And that's a proof my wits are out.
But there's a problem: she must live
Through everything in exact detail,
Driven to it by remorse, and yet
Can she renew the sexual act
And find no pleasure in it, and if not,
If pleasure and remorse must both be there,
Which is the greater?
                    I lack schooling.
Go fetch Tertullian; he and I
Will ravel all that problem out
Whilst those two lie upon the mattress
Begetting me.
               Come back! Come back!
And so you thought to slip away,
My bag of money between your fingers,
And that I could not talk and see!
You have been rummaging in the pack.

(*The light in the window has faded out.*)

BOY: You never gave me my right share.
OLD MAN: And had I given it, young as you are,
   You would have spent it upon drink.
BOY: What if I did? I had a right
   To get it and spend it as I chose.
OLD MAN: Give me that bag and no more words.
BOY: I will not.
OLD MAN: I will break your fingers.

(They struggle for the bag. In the struggle it drops, scattering the money. The OLD MAN *staggers but does not fall. They stand looking at each other. The window is lit up. A man is seen pouring whiskey into a glass.)*

BOY: What if I killed you? You killed my grand-dad,
Because you were young and he was old.
Now I am young and you are old.

OLD MAN *(staring at window)*: Better-looking, those sixteen years ——

BOY: What are you muttering?

OLD MAN: Younger — and yet
She should have known he was not her kind.

BOY: What are you saying? Out with it!

(OLD MAN *points to window.)*

My God! The window is lit up
And somebody stands there, although
The floorboards are all burnt away.

OLD MAN: The window is lit up because my father
Has come to find a glass for his whiskey.
He leans there like some tired beast.

BOY: A dead, living, murdered man!

OLD MAN: "Then the bride-sleep fell upon Adam":
Where did I read those words?

                                        And yet
There's nothing leaning in the window
But the impression upon my mother's mind;
Being dead she is alone in her remorse.

BOY: A body that was a bundle of old bones
Before I was born. Horrible! Horrible!

(He covers his eyes.)

OLD MAN: That beast there would know nothing, being nothing,
If I should kill a man under the window
He would not even turn his head.

(He stabs the BOY*.)*

My father and my son on the same jack-knife!
That finishes — there — there — there —

(He stabs again and again. The window grows dark.)

"Hush-a-bye baby, thy father's a knight,
Thy mother a lady, lovely and bright."

No, that is something that I read in a book,
And if I sing it must be to my mother,
And I lack rhyme.

(*The stage has grown dark except where the tree stands in white light.*)

        Study that tree.
It stands there like a purified soul,
All cold, sweet, glistening light.
Dear mother, the window is dark again,
But you are in the light because
I finished all that consequence.
I killed that lad because had he grown up
He would have struck a woman's fancy,
Begot, and passed pollution on.

I am a wretched foul old man
And therefore harmless. When I have stuck
This old jack-knife into a sod
And pulled it out all bright again,
And picked up all the money that he dropped,
I'll to a distant place, and there
Tell my old jokes among new men.

(*He cleans the knife and begins to pick up money.*)

Hoof-beats! Dear God,
How quickly it returns — beat — beat — !

Her mind cannot hold up that dream.
Twice a murderer and all for nothing,
And she must animate that dead night
Not once but many times!

        O God,
Release my mother's soul from its dream!
Mankind can do no more. Appease
The misery of the living and the remorse of the dead.

PURGATORY was written in 1938 and produced at the Abbey Theater in Dublin in the same year, a few months before Yeats's death.

An old pedlar and his bastard son arrive at the ruins of a country house that once belonged to the old man's mother. As, in a ghostly return of the past, the drunken sexual revelry in which the old man was begotten repeats itself behind the lighted windows, the pedlar stabs his son to death with the same knife he killed his father with years before. But discontinuing the befouled family line has not "finished all that consequence": the drunken groom once more rides home, the debased union is about to recur, and the pedlar realizes that only God's mercy can release his mother from the purgatory of endlessly repeating her sin.

There are affinities here both with *Oedipus Rex* (which Yeats translated) — the family tragedy, the parricide motif, the return of the past — and with the form and mood of a play like *The Ghost Sonata*. It dramatizes a conflict between values, the aristocratic idealism of the middle generation (the pedlar) against the materialism of grandfather and grandson. The idealism issues in a futile murder and in awareness of endless suffering. Its religious implications do not, in spite of the play's title, seem particularly Catholic in postulating purgatory as a reliving of past transgression. But — again like *The Ghost Sonata* — *Purgatory* cannot really be explained. To read it as thesis, religious or otherwise, is to violate its integrity as image, single, simple, brief, a tableau of two men, a bare tree, and a ruined house.

The tree, looking like "a silly old man," suggests the sterility of the pedlar's life. He has been reduced to trade, an occupation antithetical to that of his ancestors:

> Great people lived and died in this house;
> Magistrates, colonels, members of Parliament,
> Captains and Governors, and long ago
> Men that had fought at Aughrim and the Boyne.
> Some that had gone on government work
> To London or to India came home to die,
> Or came from London every spring
> To look at the may-blossom in the park.

The groom, his father, had ruined all that, wasted his wife's wealth, and, in a fire suggestive of the lust that drove him and his wife together, destroyed the house itself. For this he died:

> to kill a house
> Where great men grew up, married, died,
> I here declare a capital offence.

After the pedlar has killed his son, he thinks he will have cancelled the past when he has

> stuck
> This old jack-knife into a sod
> And pulled it out all bright again.

But the soil does not purge. It is rather as if the cleansing of the knife is a third stabbing, compounded, perhaps, by the stabber's picking up the money that represents the values by which his two earlier victims lived. At any rate, it is just at this moment that the fired house, the symbol of ruined tradition, proves stronger than the expiatory act.

Yeats was opposed to the contemporary drama of naturalism, the Ibsen school of play-writing. With its emphasis on character and on real-life problems and its commitment to a dialogue that reproduced as faithfully as possible the inarticulateness of ordinary people, it seemed to him like a stale, ugly, soul-starving, unimaginative "mimicry of the restless surface of reality." He wanted a spiritual drama, a pure form that would be an end in itself because it would tap the roots of man's primeval consciousness, a dance-like ritual, deliberately distancing itself from the beholder, a symbolic, characterless, nonpopular drama for small and select audiences. In the aristocratic plays of the traditional Japanese Noh theater, highly stylized and formalized in gesture and chant, using masks rather than mimicry and make-up, Yeats found inspiration for his own nonrealistic, esoteric plays of the later part of his career. Of these plays, *Purgatory*, the next to the last, is perhaps the most immediately meaningful to an audience uninitiate in Yeats's symbolism and mysticism. No arcane, extraneous knowledge is required to respond to its supernatural sights and sounds, to the almost colloquial terseness of its free and flexible four-beat lines, in which the irregular sequence of iambs and trochees suggests the pedlar's tenseness, to the poignant drama represented by the old lullaby he sings after he has killed his son, and to its reverberating relevance to the whole play:

> "Hush-a-bye baby, thy father's a knight,
> Thy mother a lady, lovely and bright."

Bertolt Brecht

THE GOOD WOMAN
OF SETZUAN

An English Version by Eric Bentley

Characters

WONG, *a water seller*

THREE GODS

SHEN TE, *a prostitute, later a shopkeeper*

MRS. SHIN, *former owner of Shen Te's shop*

A FAMILY OF EIGHT (*husband, wife, brother, sister-in-law, grand-father, nephew, niece, boy*)

AN UNEMPLOYED MAN

A CARPENTER

MRS. MI TZU, *Shen Te's landlady*

YANG SUN, *an unemployed pilot, later a factory manager*

AN OLD WHORE

A POLICEMAN

AN OLD MAN

AN OLD WOMAN, *his wife*

MR. SHU FU, *a barber*

MRS. YANG, *mother of Yang Sun*

GENTLEMEN, VOICES, CHILDREN (3), etcetera.

PROLOGUE

(*At the gates of the half-westernized city of Setzuan.** Evening.* WONG *the Water Seller introduces himself to the audience.*)

WONG: I sell water here in the city of Setzuan. It isn't easy. When water is scarce, I have long distances to go in search of it, and when it is plentiful, I have no income. But in our part of the world there is nothing unusual about poverty. Many people think only the gods can save the situation. And I hear from a cattle merchant — who travels a lot — that some of the highest gods are on their way here at this very moment. Informed sources have it that heaven is quite disturbed at all the complaining. I've been coming out here to the city gates for three days now to bid these gods welcome. I want to be the first to greet them. What about those fellows over there? No, no, they *work*. And that one there has ink on his fingers, he's no god, he must be a clerk from the cement factory. *Those* two are another story. They look as though they'd like to beat you. But gods don't need to beat you, do they? (*Enter* THREE GODS.) What about those three? Old-fashioned clothes — dust on their feet — they *must* be gods! (*He throws himself at their feet.*) Do with me what you will, illustrious ones!

FIRST GOD (*with an ear trumpet*): Ah! (*He is pleased.*) So we were expected?

WONG (*giving them water*): Oh, yes. And I *knew* you'd come.

FIRST GOD: We need somewhere to stay the night. You know of a place?

WONG: The whole town is at your service, illustrious ones! What sort of a place would you like?

(*The* GODS *eye each other.*)

FIRST GOD: Just try the first house you come to, my son.

WONG: That would be Mr. Fo's place.

FIRST GOD: Mr. Fo.

WONG: One moment! (*He knocks at the first house.*)

VOICE FROM MR. FO'S: No!

(WONG *returns a little nervously.*)

---

* So Brecht's first MS. Brecht must later have learned that Setzuan (usually spelled Szechwan) is not a city but a province and he adjusted the printed German text. I have kept the earlier reading as such mythology seems to me more Brechtian than Brecht's own second thoughts. — E.B.

WONG: It's too bad. Mr. Fo isn't in. And his servants don't dare do a thing without his consent. He'll have a fit when he finds out who they turned away, won't he?

FIRST GOD (*smiling*): He will, won't he?

WONG: One moment! The next house is Mr. Cheng's. Won't he be thrilled?

FIRST GOD: Mr. Cheng.

(WONG *knocks.*)

VOICE FROM MR. CHENG'S: Keep your gods. We have our own troubles!

WONG (*back with the* GODS): Mr. Cheng is very sorry, but he has a houseful of relations. I think some of them are a bad lot, and naturally, he wouldn't like you to see them.

THIRD GOD: Are we so terrible?

WONG: Well, only with bad people, of course. Everyone knows the province of Kwan is always having floods.

SECOND GOD: Really? How's *that*?

WONG: Why, because they're so irreligious.

SECOND GOD: Rubbish. It's because they neglected the dam.

FIRST GOD (*to* SECOND): Sh! (*To* WONG.) You're still in hopes, aren't you, my son?

WONG: Certainly. All Setzuan is competing for the honor! What happened up to now is pure coincidence. I'll be back. (*He walks away, but then stands undecided.*)

SECOND GOD: What did I tell you?

THIRD GOD: It *could* be pure coincidence.

SECOND GOD: The same coincidence in Shun, Kwan, and Setzuan? People just aren't religious any more, let's face the fact. Our mission has failed!

FIRST GOD: Oh come, we might run into a good person any minute.

THIRD GOD: How did the resolution read? (*Unrolling a scroll and reading from it.*) "The world can stay as it is if enough people are found living lives worthy of human beings." Good people, that is. Well, what about this Water Seller himself? *He's* good, or I'm very much mistaken.

SECOND GOD: You're very much mistaken. When he gave us a drink, I had the impression there was something odd about the cup. Well, look! (*He shows the cup to the* FIRST GOD.)

FIRST GOD: A false bottom!

SECOND GOD: The man is a swindler.

FIRST GOD: Very well, count *him* out. That's one man among millions. And as a matter of fact, we only need one on *our* side. These atheists are saying, "The world must be changed because no one can *be* good and *stay* good." No one, eh? I say: let us find one — just one — and we have those fellows where we want them!

THIRD GOD (*to* WONG): Water Seller, is it so hard to find a place to stay?

WONG: Nothing could be easier. It's just me. I don't go about it right.

THIRD GOD: Really? (*He returns to the others. A* GENTLEMAN *passes by.*)

WONG: Oh dear, they're catching on. (*He accosts the* GENTLEMAN.) Excuse the intrusion, dear sir, but three gods have just turned up. Three of the very highest. They need a place for the night. Seize this rare opportunity — to have real gods as your guests!

GENTLEMAN (*laughing*): A new way of finding free rooms for a gang of crooks.

(*Exit* GENTLEMAN.)

WONG (*shouting at him*): Godless rascal! Have you no religion, gentlemen of Setzuan? (*Pause.*) Patience, illustrious ones! (*Pause.*) There's only one person left. Shen Te, the prostitute. She *can't* say no. (*Calls up to a window.*) Shen Te!

(SHEN TE *opens the shutters and looks out.*)

WONG: *They're* here, and nobody wants them. Will you take them?

SHEN TE: Oh, no, Wong, I'm expecting a gentleman.

WONG: Can't you forget about him for tonight?

SHEN TE: The rent has to be paid by tomorrow or I'll be out on the street.

WONG: This is no time for calculation, Shen Te.

SHEN TE: Stomachs rumble even on the Emperor's birthday, Wong.

WONG: Setzuan is one big dung hill!

SHEN TE: Oh, very well! I'll hide till my gentleman has come and gone. Then I'll take them. (*She disappears.*)

WONG: They mustn't see her gentleman or they'll know what she is.

FIRST GOD (*who hasn't heard any of this*): I think it's hopeless.

(*They approach* WONG.)

WONG (*jumping, as he finds them behind him*): A room has been found, illustrious ones! (*He wipes sweat off his brow.*)

SECOND GOD: Oh, good.

THIRD GOD: Let's see it.

WONG (*nervously*): Just a minute. It has to be tidied up a bit.

THIRD GOD: Then we'll sit down here and wait.

WONG (*still more nervous*): No, no! (*Holding himself back.*) Too much traffic, you know.

THIRD GOD (*with a smile*): Of course, if you *want* us to move.

(*They retire a little. They sit on a doorstep.* WONG *sits on the ground.*)

WONG (*after a deep breath*): You'll be staying with a single girl — the finest human being in Setzuan!

THIRD GOD: That's nice.

WONG (*to the audience*): They gave me such a look when I picked up my cup just now.

THIRD GOD: You're worn out, Wong.

WONG: A little, maybe.

FIRST GOD: Do people here have a hard time of it?

WONG: The good ones do.

FIRST GOD: What about yourself?

WONG: You mean I'm not good. That's true. And I don't have an easy time either!

(*During this dialogue, a* GENTLEMAN *has turned up in front of* SHEN TE'S *house, and has whistled several times. Each time* WONG *has given a start.*)

THIRD GOD (*to* WONG, *softly*): Psst! I think he's gone now.

WONG (*confused and surprised*): Ye-e-es.

(*The* GENTLEMAN *has left now, and* SHEN TE *has come down to the street.*)

SHEN TE (*softly*): Wong!

(*Getting no answer, she goes off down the street.* WONG *arrives just too late, forgetting his carrying pole.*)

WONG (*softly*): Shen Te! Shen Te! (*To himself.*) So she's gone off to earn the rent. Oh dear, I can't go to the gods *again* with no room to offer them. Having failed in the service of the gods, I shall run to my den in the sewer pipe down by the river and hide from their sight!

(*He rushes off.* SHEN TE *returns, looking for him, but finding the gods. She stops in confusion.*)

SHEN TE: You are the illustrious ones? My name is Shen Te. It would please me very much if my simple room could be of use to you.

THIRD GOD: Where is the Water Seller, Miss . . . Shen Te?

SHEN TE: I missed him, somehow.

FIRST GOD: Oh, he probably thought you weren't coming, and was afraid of telling us.

THIRD GOD (*picking up the carrying pole*): We'll leave this with you. He'll be needing it.

(*Led by* SHEN TE, *they go into the house. It grows dark, then light. Dawn. Again escorted by* SHEN TE, *who leads them through the half-light with a little lamp, the* GODS *take their leave.*)

FIRST GOD: Thank you, thank you, dear Shen Te, for your elegant hospitality! We shall not forget! And give our thanks to the Water Seller — he showed us a good human being.

SHEN TE: Oh, I'*m* not good. Let me tell you something: when Wong asked me to put you up, I hesitated.

FIRST GOD: It's all right to hesitate if you then go ahead! And in giving us that room you did much more than you knew. You proved that good people still exist, a point that has been disputed of late — even in heaven. Farewell!

SECOND GOD: Farewell!

THIRD GOD: Farewell!

SHEN TE: Stop, illustrious ones! I'm not sure you're right. I'd like to be good, it's true, but there's the rent to pay. And that's not all: I sell myself for a living. Even so I can't make ends meet, there's too much competition. I'd like to honor my father and mother and speak nothing but the truth and not covet my neighbor's house. I should love to stay with one man. But how? How is it done? Even breaking only a *few* of your commandments, I can hardly manage.

FIRST GOD (*clearing his throat*): These thoughts are but, um, the misgivings of an unusually good woman!

THIRD GOD: Goodbye, Shen Te! Give our regards to the Water Seller!

SECOND GOD: And above all: be good! Farewell!

FIRST GOD: Farewell!

THIRD GOD: Farewell!

(*They start to wave goodbye.*)

SHEN TE: But everything is so expensive, I don't feel sure I can do it!

SECOND GOD: That's not in our sphere. We never meddle with economics.

THIRD GOD: One moment.

(*They stop.*)

Isn't it true she might do better if she had more money?

SECOND GOD: Come, come! How could we ever account for it Up Above?

FIRST GOD: Oh, there are ways.

(*They put their heads together and confer in dumb show.*)

(*To* SHEN TE, *with embarrassment.*) As you say you can't pay your rent, well, um, we're not paupers, so of course we *insist* on paying for our room. (*Awkwardly thrusting money into her hands.*) There! (*Quickly.*) But don't tell anyone! The incident is open to misinterpretation.

SECOND GOD: It certainly is!

FIRST GOD (*defensively*): But there's no law against it! It was never decreed that a god mustn't pay hotel bills!

(*The* GODS *leave.*)

SCENE 1

(*A small tobacco shop. The shop is not as yet completely furnished and hasn't started doing business.*)

SHEN TE (*to the audience*): It's three days now since the gods left. When they said they wanted to pay for the room, I looked down at my hand, and there was more than a thousand silver dollars! I bought a tobacco shop with the money, and moved in yesterday. I don't own the building, of course, but I can pay the rent, and I hope to do a lot of good here. Beginning with Mrs. Shin, who's just coming across the square with her pot. She had the shop before me, and yesterday she dropped in to ask for rice for her children.

(*Enter* MRS. SHIN. *Both women bow.*)

How do you do, Mrs. Shin.

MRS. SHIN: How do you do, Miss Shen Te. You like your new home?

SHEN TE: Indeed, yes. Did your children have a good night?

MRS. SHIN: In that hovel? The youngest is coughing already.

SHEN TE: Oh, dear!

MRS. SHIN: You're going to learn a thing or two in these slums.

SHEN TE: Slums? That's not what you said when you sold me the shop!

MRS. SHIN: Now don't start nagging! Robbing me and my innocent children of their home and then calling it a slum! That's the limit! (*She weeps.*)

SHEN TE (*tactfully*): I'll get your rice.

MRS. SHIN: And a little cash while you're at it.

SHEN TE: I'm afraid I haven't sold anything yet.

MRS. SHIN (*screeching*): I've got to have it. Strip the clothes from my back and then cut my throat, will you? I know what I'll do: I'll leave my children on your doorstep! (*She snatches the pot out of* SHEN TE's *hands.*)

SHEN TE: Please don't be angry. You'll spill the rice.

(*Enter an elderly* HUSBAND *and* WIFE *with their shabbily-dressed* NEPHEW.)

WIFE: Shen Te, dear! You've come into money, they tell me. And we haven't a roof over our heads! A tobacco shop. We had one too. But it's gone. Could we spend the night here, do you think?

NEPHEW (*appraising the shop*): Not bad!

WIFE: He's our nephew. We're inseparable!

MRS. SHIN: And who are these . . . ladies and gentlemen?

SHEN TE: They put me up when I first came in from the country. (*To the audience.*) Of course, when my small purse was empty, they put me out on the street, and they may be afraid I'll do the same to them. (*To the newcomers, kindly.*) Come in, and welcome, though I've only one little room for you — it's behind the shop.

HUSBAND: That'll do. Don't worry.

WIFE (*bringing* SHEN TE *some tea*): We'll stay over here, so we won't be in your way. Did you make it a tobacco shop in memory of your first real home? We can certainly give you a hint or two! That's one reason we came.

MRS. SHIN (*to* SHEN TE): Very nice! As long as you have a few customers too!

HUSBAND: Sh! A customer!

(*Enter an* UNEMPLOYED MAN, *in rags.*)

UNEMPLOYED MAN: Excuse me. I'm unemployed.

(MRS. SHIN *laughs.*)

SHEN TE: Can I help you?

UNEMPLOYED MAN: Have you any damaged cigarettes? I thought there might be some damage when you're unpacking.

WIFE: What nerve, begging for tobacco! (*Rhetorically.*) Why don't they ask for bread?

UNEMPLOYED MAN: Bread is expensive. One cigarette butt and I'll be a new man.

SHEN TE (*giving him cigarettes*): That's very important — to be a new man. You'll be my first customer and bring me luck.

(*The* UNEMPLOYED MAN *quickly lights a cigarette, inhales, and goes off, coughing.*)

WIFE: Was that right, Shen Te, dear?

MRS. SHIN: If this is the opening of a shop, you can hold the closing at the end of the week.

HUSBAND: I bet he had money on him.

SHEN TE: Oh, no, he said he hadn't!

NEPHEW: How d'you know he wasn't lying?

SHEN TE (*angrily*): How do you know he was?

WIFE (*wagging her head*): You're too good, Shen Te, dear. If you're going to keep this shop, you'll have to learn to say No.

HUSBAND: Tell them the place isn't yours to dispose of. Belongs to . . . some relative who insists on all accounts being strictly in order . . .

MRS. SHIN: That's right! What do you think you are — a philanthropist?

SHEN TE (*laughing*): Very well, suppose I ask you for my rice back, Mrs. Shin?

WIFE (*combatively, at* MRS. SHIN): So that's *her* rice?

(*Enter the* CARPENTER, *a small man.*)

MRS. SHIN (*who, at the sight of him, starts to hurry away*): See you tomorrow, Miss Shen Te! (*Exit* MRS. SHIN.)

CARPENTER: Mrs. Shin, it's you I want!

WIFE (*to* SHEN TE): Has she some claim on you?

SHEN TE: She's hungry. That's a claim.

CARPENTER: Are you the new tenant? And filling up the shelves already? Well, they're not yours, till they're paid for, ma'am. I'm the carpenter, so I should know.

SHEN TE: I took the shop "furnishings included."

CARPENTER: You're in league with that Mrs. Shin, of course. All right: I demand my hundred silver dollars.

SHEN TE: I'm afraid I haven't got a hundred silver dollars.

CARPENTER: Then you'll find it. Or I'll have you arrested.

WIFE (*whispering to* SHEN TE): That relative: make it a cousin.

SHEN TE: Can't it wait till next month?

CARPENTER: No!

SHEN TE: Be a little patient, Mr. Carpenter, I can't settle all claims at once.

CARPENTER: Who's patient with me? (*He grabs a shelf from the wall.*) Pay up — or I take the shelves back!

WIFE: Shen Te! Dear! Why don't you let your . . . cousin settle this affair? (*To* CARPENTER.) Put your claim in writing. Shen Te's cousin will see you get paid.

CARPENTER (*derisively*): Cousin, eh?

HUSBAND: Cousin, yes.

CARPENTER: I know these cousins!

NEPHEW: Don't be silly. He's a personal friend of mine.

HUSBAND: What a man! Sharp as a razor!

CARPENTER: All right. I'll put my claim in writing. (*Puts shelf on floor, sits on it, writes out bill.*)

WIFE (*to* SHEN TE): He'd tear the dress off your back to get his shelves. Never recognize a claim! That's my motto.

SHEN TE: He's done a job, and wants something in return. It's shameful that I can't give it to him. What will the gods say?

HUSBAND: You did your bit when you took *us* in.

(*Enter the* BROTHER, *limping, and the* SISTER-IN-LAW, *pregnant.*)

BROTHER (*to* HUSBAND *and* WIFE): So this is where you're hiding out! There's family feeling for you! Leaving us on the corner!

WIFE (*embarrassed, to* SHEN TE): It's my brother and his wife. (*To them.*) Now stop grumbling, and sit quietly in that corner. (*To* SHEN TE.) It can't be helped. She's in her fifth month.

SHEN TE: Oh yes. Welcome!

WIFE (*to the couple*): Say thank you.

(*They mutter something.*)

The cups are there. (*To* SHEN TE.) Lucky you bought this shop when you did!

SHEN TE (*laughing and bringing tea*): Lucky indeed!

(*Enter* MRS. MI TZU, *the landlady.*)

MRS. MI TZU: Miss Shen Te? I am Mrs. Mi Tzu, your landlady. I hope our relationship will be a happy one? I like to think I give my tenants modern, personalized service. Here is your lease. (*To the others, as* SHEN TE *reads the lease.*) There's nothing like the opening of a little shop, is there? A moment of true beauty! (*She is looking around.*) Not very much on the shelves, of course. But everything in the gods' good time! Where are your references, Miss Shen Te?

SHEN TE: Do I *have* to have references?

MRS. MI TZU: After all, I haven't a notion who you are!

HUSBAND: Oh, *we'd* be glad to vouch for Miss Shen Te! We'd go through fire for her!

MRS. MI TZU: And who may *you* be?

HUSBAND (*stammering*): Ma Fu, tobacco dealer.

MRS. MI TZU: Where is your shop, Mr. . . . Ma Fu?

HUSBAND: Well, um, I haven't a shop — I've just sold it.

MRS. MI TZU: I see. (*To* SHEN TE.) Is there no one else that knows you?

WIFE (*whispering to* SHEN TE): Your cousin! Your cousin!

MRS. MI TZU: This is a respectable house, Miss Shen Te. I never sign a lease without certain assurances.

SHEN TE (*slowly, her eyes downcast*): I have . . . a cousin.

MRS. MI TZU: On the square? Let's go over and see him. What does he do?

SHEN TE (*as before*): He lives . . . in another city.

WIFE (*prompting*): Didn't you say he was in Shung?

SHEN TE: That's right. Shung.

HUSBAND (*prompting*): I had his name on the tip of my tongue. Mr. . . .

SHEN TE (*with an effort*): Mr. . . . Shui . . . Ta.

HUSBAND: That's it! Tall, skinny fellow!

SHEN TE: Shui Ta!

NEPHEW (*to* CARPENTER): *You* were in touch with him, weren't you? About the shelves?

CARPENTER (*surlily*): Give him this bill. (*He hands it over.*) I'll be back in the morning. (*Exit* CARPENTER.)

NEPHEW (*calling after him, but with his eyes on* MRS. MI TZU): Don't worry! Mr. Shui Ta pays on the nail!

MRS. MI TZU (*looking closely at* SHEN TE): I'll be happy to make his acquaintance, Miss Shen Te. (*Exit* MRS. MI TZU.)

(*Pause.*)

WIFE: By tomorrow morning she'll know more about you than you do yourself.

SISTER-IN-LAW (*to* NEPHEW): This thing isn't built to last.

(*Enter* GRANDFATHER.)

WIFE: It's Grandfather! (*To* SHEN TE.) Such a good old soul!

(*The* BOY *enters.*)

BOY (*over his shoulder*): Here they are!

WIFE: And the boy, how he's grown! But he always could eat enough for ten.

(*Enter the* NIECE.)

WIFE (*to* SHEN TE): Our little niece from the country. There are more of us now than in your time. The less we had, the more there were of us; the more there were of us, the less we had. Give me the key.

We must protect ourselves from unwanted guests. (*She takes the key and locks the door.*) Just make yourself at home. I'll light the little lamp.

NEPHEW (*a big joke*): I hope her cousin doesn't drop in tonight! The strict Mr. Shui Ta!

(SISTER-IN-LAW *laughs.*)

BROTHER (*reaching for a cigarette*): One cigarette more or less . . .
HUSBAND: One cigarette more or less.

(*They pile into the cigarettes. The* BROTHER *hands a jug of wine round.*)

NEPHEW: Mr. Shui Ta'll pay for it!
GRANDFATHER (*gravely, to* SHEN TE): How do you do?

(SHEN TE, *a little taken aback by the belatedness of the greeting, bows. She has the* CARPENTER'S *bill in one hand, the landlady's lease in the other.*)

WIFE: How about a bit of a song? To keep Shen Te's spirits up?
NEPHEW: Good idea. Grandfather: you start!

Song of the Smoke

GRANDFATHER:
I used to think (before old age beset me)
    That brains could fill the pantry of the poor.
But where did all my cerebration get me?
    I'm just as hungry as I was before.
                    So what's the use?
                        See the smoke float free
                    Into ever colder coldness!
                        It's the same with me.

HUSBAND:
The straight and narrow path leads to disaster
    And so the crooked path I tried to tread.
That got me to disaster even faster.
    (They say we shall be happy when we're dead.)
                        So what's the use, etc.

NIECE:
You older people, full of expectation,
    At any moment now you'll walk the plank!
The future's for the younger generation!
    Yes, even if that future is a blank.
                        So what's the use, etc.

NEPHEW (*to the* BROTHER): Where'd you get that wine?

SISTER-IN-LAW (*answering for the* BROTHER): He pawned the sack of tobacco.

HUSBAND (*stepping in*): What? That tobacco was all we had to fall back on! You pig!

BROTHER: *You'd* call a man a pig because your wife was frigid! Did you refuse to drink it?

(*They fight. The shelves fall over.*)

SHEN TE (*imploringly*): Oh, don't! Don't break everything! Take it, take it all, but don't destroy a gift from the gods!

WIFE (*disparagingly*): This shop isn't big enough. I should never have mentioned it to Uncle and the others. When *they* arrive, it's going to be disgustingly overcrowded.

SISTER-IN-LAW: And did you hear our gracious hostess? She cools off quick!

(*Voices outside. Knocking at the door.*)

UNCLE'S VOICE: Open the door!

WIFE: Uncle? Is that you, Uncle?

UNCLE'S VOICE: Certainly, it's me. Auntie says to tell you she'll have the children here in ten minutes.

WIFE (*to* SHEN TE): I'll have to let him in.

SHEN TE (*who scarcely hears her*):
The little lifeboat is swiftly sent down
Too many men too greedily
Hold on to it as they drown.

Scene 1A

(WONG'S *den in a sewer pipe.*)

WONG (*crouching there*): All quiet! It's four days now since I left the city. The gods passed this way on the second day. I heard their steps on the bridge over there. They must be a long way off by this time, so I'm safe.

(*Breathing a sigh of relief, he curls up and goes to sleep. In his dream the pipe becomes transparent, and the* GODS *appear.*)

(*Raising an arm, as if in self-defense.*) I know, I know, illustrious ones! I found no one to give you a room — not in all Setzuan! There, it's out. Please continue on your way!

FIRST GOD (*mildly*): But you did find someone. Someone who took us in for the night, watched over us in our sleep, and in the early morning lighted us down to the street with a lamp.

WONG: It was . . . Shen Te, that took you in?

THIRD GOD: Who else?

WONG: And I ran away! "She isn't coming," I thought, "she just can't afford it."

GODS (*singing*):
O you feeble, well-intentioned, and yet feeble chap!
Where there's need the fellow thinks there is no goodness!
When there's danger he thinks courage starts to ebb away!
Some people only see the seamy side!
What hasty judgment! What premature desperation!

WONG: I'm *very* ashamed, illustrious ones.

FIRST GOD: Do us a favor, Water Seller. Go back to Setzuan. Find Shen Te, and give us a report on her. We hear that she's come into a little money. Show interest in her goodness — for no one can be good for long if goodness is not in demand. Meanwhile we shall continue the search, and find other good people. After which, the idle chatter about the impossibility of goodness will stop!

(*The* GODS *vanish.*)

SCENE 2

(*A knocking.*)

WIFE: Shen Te! Someone at the door. Where is she anyway?

NEPHEW: She must be getting the breakfast. Mr. Shui Ta will pay for it.

(*The* WIFE *laughs and shuffles to the door. Enter* MR. SHUI TA *and the* CARPENTER.)

WIFE: Who is it?

SHUI TA: I am Miss Shen Te's cousin.

WIFE: What?

SHUI TA: My name is Shui Ta.

WIFE: Her cousin?

NEPHEW: Her cousin?

NIECE: But that was a joke. She hasn't got a cousin.

HUSBAND: So early in the morning?

BROTHER: What's all the noise?

SISTER-IN-LAW: This fellow says he's her cousin.

BROTHER: Tell him to prove it.

NEPHEW: Right. If you're Shen Te's cousin, prove it by getting the breakfast.

SHUI TA (*whose regime begins as he puts out the lamp to save oil. Loudly, to all present, asleep or awake*): Would you all please get dressed! Customers will be coming! I wish to open my shop!

HUSBAND: *Your* shop? Doesn't it belong to our good friend Shen Te?

(SHUI TA *shakes his head.*)

SISTER-IN-LAW: So we've been cheated. Where *is* the little liar?

SHUI TA: Miss Shen Te has been delayed. She wishes me to tell you there will be nothing she can do — now I am here.

WIFE (*bowled over*): I thought she was *good!*

NEPHEW: Do you have to believe *him?*

HUSBAND: *I* don't.

NEPHEW: Then do something.

HUSBAND: Certainly! I'll send out a search party at once. You, you, you, and you, go out and look for Shen Te.

(*As the* GRANDFATHER *rises and makes for the door.*)

Not you, Grandfather, you and I will hold the fort.

SHUI TA: You won't find Miss Shen Te. She has suspended her hospitable activity for an unlimited period. There are too many of you. She asked me to say: this is a tobacco shop, not a gold mine.

HUSBAND: Shen Te never said a thing like that. Boy, food! There's a bakery on the corner. Stuff your shirt full when they're not looking!

SISTER-IN-LAW: Don't overlook the raspberry tarts.

HUSBAND: And don't let the policeman see you.

(*The* BOY *leaves.*)

SHUI TA: Don't you depend on this shop now? Then why give it a bad name, by stealing from the bakery?

NEPHEW: Don't listen to him. Let's find Shen Te. She'll give him a piece of her mind.

SISTER-IN-LAW: Don't forget to leave us some breakfast.

(BROTHER, SISTER-IN-LAW, *and* NEPHEW *leave.*)

SHUI TA (*to the* CARPENTER): You see, Mr. Carpenter, nothing has changed since the poet, eleven hundred years ago, penned these lines:

A governor was asked what was needed
To save the freezing people in the city.

He replied:
"A blanket ten thousand feet long
To cover the city and all its suburbs."

(*He starts to tidy up the shop.*)

CARPENTER: Your cousin owes me money. I've got witnesses. For the shelves.

SHUI TA: Yes, I have your bill. (*He takes it out of his pocket.*) Isn't a hundred silver dollars rather a lot?

CARPENTER: No deductions! I have a wife and children.

SHUI TA: How many children?

CARPENTER: Three.

SHUI TA: I'll make you an offer. Twenty silver dollars.

(*The* HUSBAND *laughs.*)

CARPENTER: You're crazy. Those shelves are real walnut.

SHUI TA: Very well. Take them away.

CARPENTER: What?

SHUI TA: They cost too much. Please take them away.

WIFE: Not bad! (*And she, too, is laughing.*)

CARPENTER (*a little bewildered*): Call Shen Te, someone! (*To* SHUI TA.) She's *good!*

SHUI TA: Certainly. She's ruined.

CARPENTER (*provoked into taking some of the shelves*): All right, you can keep your tobacco on the floor.

SHUI TA (*to the* HUSBAND): Help him with the shelves.

HUSBAND (*grins and carries one shelf over to the door where the* CARPENTER *now is*): Goodbye, shelves!

CARPENTER (*to the* HUSBAND): You dog! You want my family to starve?

SHUI TA: I repeat my offer. I have no desire to keep my tobacco on the floor. Twenty silver dollars.

CARPENTER (*with desperate aggressiveness*): One hundred!

(SHUI TA *shows indifference, looks through the window. The* HUSBAND *picks up several shelves.*)

(*To* HUSBAND.) You needn't smash them against the doorpost, you idiot! (*To* SHUI TA.) These shelves were made to measure. They're no use anywhere else!

SHUI TA: Precisely.

(*The* WIFE *squeals with pleasure.*)

CARPENTER (*giving up, sullenly*): Take the shelves. Pay what you want to pay.

SHUI TA (*smoothly*): Twenty silver dollars.

(*He places two large coins on the table. The* CARPENTER *picks them up.*)

HUSBAND (*brings the shelves back in*): And quite enough too!

CARPENTER (*slinking off*): Quite enough to get drunk on.

HUSBAND (*happily*): Well, we got rid of *him*!

WIFE (*weeping with fun, gives a rendition of the dialogue just spoken*): "Real walnut," says he. "Very well, take them away," says his lordship. "I have children," says he. "Twenty silver dollars," says his lordship. "They're no use anywhere else," says he. "Precisely," said his lordship! (*She dissolves into shrieks of merriment.*)

SHUI TA: And now: go!

HUSBAND: What's that?

SHUI TA: You're thieves, parasites. I'm giving you this chance. Go!

HUSBAND (*summoning all his ancestral dignity*): That sort deserves no answer. Besides, one should never shout on an empty stomach.

WIFE: Where's that boy?

SHUI TA: Exactly. The boy. I want no stolen goods in this shop. (*Very loudly.*) I strongly advise you to leave! (*But they remain seated, noses in the air. Quietly.*) As you wish.

(SHUI TA *goes to the door. A* POLICEMAN *appears.* SHUI TA *bows.*)

I am addressing the officer in charge of this precinct?

POLICEMAN: That's right, Mr., um . . . what was the name, sir?

SHUI TA: Mr. Shui Ta.

POLICEMAN: Yes, of course, sir.

(*They exchange a smile.*)

SHUI TA: Nice weather we're having.

POLICEMAN: A little on the warm side, sir.

SHUI TA: Oh, a little on the warm side.

HUSBAND (*whispering to the* WIFE): If he keeps it up till the boy's back, we're done for. (*Tries to signal* SHUI TA.)

SHUI TA (*ignoring the signal*): Weather, of course, is one thing indoors, another out on the dusty street!

POLICEMAN: Oh, quite another, sir!

WIFE (*to the* HUSBAND): It's all right as long as he's standing in the doorway — the boy will see him.

SHUI TA: Step inside for a moment! It's quite cool indoors. My cousin and I have just opened the place. And we attach the greatest importance to being on good terms with the, um, authorities.

POLICEMAN (*entering*): Thank you, Mr. Shui Ta. It *is* cool!

HUSBAND (*whispering to the* WIFE): And now the boy *won't* see him.

SHUI TA (*showing* HUSBAND *and* WIFE *to the* POLICEMAN): Visitors, I think my cousin knows them. They were just leaving.

HUSBAND (*defeated*): Ye-e-es, we were . . . just leaving.

SHUI TA: I'll tell my cousin you couldn't wait.

(*Noise from the street. Shouts of* "Stop, thief!")

POLICEMAN: What's that?

(*The* BOY *is in the doorway with cakes and buns and rolls spilling out of his shirt. The* WIFE *signals desperately to him to leave. He gets the idea.*)

No, you don't! (*He grabs the* BOY *by the collar.*) Where's all this from?

BOY (*vaguely pointing*): Down the street.

POLICEMAN (*grimly*): So that's it. (*Prepares to arrest the* BOY.)

WIFE (*stepping in*): And *we* knew nothing about it. (*To the* BOY.) Nasty little thief!

POLICEMAN (*dryly*): Can you clarify the situation, Mr. Shui Ta?

(SHUI TA *is silent.*)

POLICEMAN (*who understands silence*): Aha. You're all coming with me — to the station.

SHUI TA: I can hardly say how sorry I am that *my* establishment . . .

WIFE: Oh, he saw the boy leave not ten minutes ago!

SHUI TA: And to conceal the theft asked a policeman in?

POLICEMAN: Don't listen to her, Mr. Shui Ta, I'll be happy to relieve you of their presence one and all! (*To all three.*) Out! (*He drives them before him.*)

GRANDFATHER (*leaving last. Gravely*): Good morning!

POLICEMAN: Good morning!

(SHUI TA, *left alone, continues to tidy up.* MRS. MI TZU *breezes in.*)

MRS. MI TZU: *You're* her cousin, are you? Then have the goodness to explain what all this means — police dragging people from a respectable house! By what right does your Miss Shen Te turn my property into a house of assignation? — Well, as you see, I know all!

SHUI TA: Yes. My cousin has the worst possible reputation: that of being poor.

MRS. MI TZU: No sentimental rubbish, Mr. Shui Ta. Your cousin was a common . . .

SHUI TA: Pauper. Let's use the uglier word.

MRS. MI TZU: I'm speaking of her conduct, not her earnings. But there must have *been* earnings, or how did she buy all this? Several elderly gentlemen took care of it, I suppose. I repeat: this is a respectable house! I have tenants who prefer not to live under the same roof with such a person.

SHUI TA (*quietly*): How much do you want?

MRS. MI TZU (*he is ahead of her now*): I beg your pardon.

SHUI TA: To reassure yourself. To reassure your tenants. How much will it cost?

MRS. MI TZU: You're a cool customer.

SHUI TA (*picking up the lease*): The rent is high. (*He reads on.*) I assume it's payable by the month?

MRS. MI TZU: Not in her case.

SHUI TA (*looking up*): What?

MRS. MI TZU: Six months rent payable in advance. Two hundred silver dollars.

SHUI TA: Six . . . ! Sheer usury! And where am I to find it?

MRS. MI TZU: You should have thought of that before.

SHUI TA: Have you no heart, Mrs. Mi Tzu? It's true Shen Te acted foolishly, being kind to all those people, but she'll improve with time. I'll see to it she does. She'll work her fingers to the bone to pay her rent, and all the time be as quiet as a mouse, as humble as a fly.

MRS. MI TZU: Her social background . . .

SHUI TA: Out of the depths! She came out of the depths! And before she'll go back there, she'll work, sacrifice, shrink from nothing. . . . Such a tenant is worth her weight in gold, Mrs. Mi Tzu.

MRS. MI TZU: It's silver we were talking about, Mr. Shui Ta. Two hundred silver dollars or . . .

(*Enter the* POLICEMAN.)

POLICEMAN: Am I intruding, Mr. Shui Ta?

MRS. MI TZU: This tobacco shop is well-known to the police, I see.

POLICEMAN: Mr. Shui Ta has done us a service, Mrs. Mi Tzu. I am here to present our official felicitations!

MRS. MI TZU: That means less than nothing to me, sir. Mr. Shui Ta, all I can say is: I hope your cousin will find my terms acceptable. Good day, gentlemen. (*Exit.*)

SHUI TA: Good day, ma'am.

(*Pause.*)

POLICEMAN: Mrs. Mi Tzu a bit of a stumbling block, sir?

SHUI TA: She wants six months' rent in advance.

POLICEMAN: And you haven't got it, eh?

(SHUI TA *is silent.*)

But surely you can get it, sir? A man like you?

SHUI TA: What about a woman like Shen Te?

POLICEMAN: You're not staying, sir?

SHUI TA: No, and I won't be back. Do you smoke?

POLICEMAN (*taking two cigars, and placing them both in his pocket*): Thank you, sir — I see your point. Miss Shen Te — let's mince no words — Miss Shen Te lived by selling herself. "What else could she have done?" you ask. "How else was she to pay the rent?" True. But the fact remains, Mr. Shui Ta, it is not respectable. Why not? A very deep question. But, in the first place, love — love isn't bought and sold like cigars, Mr. Shui Ta. In the second place, it isn't respectable to go waltzing off with someone that's paying his way, so to speak — it must be for love! Thirdly and lastly, as the proverb has it: not for a handful of rice but for love! (*Pause. He is thinking hard.*) "Well," you may say, "and what good is all this wisdom if the milk's already spilt?" Miss Shen Te is what she is. Is *where* she is. We have to face the fact that if she doesn't get hold of six months' rent pronto, she'll be back on the streets. The question then as I see it — everything in this world is a matter of opinion — the question as I see it is: *how* is she to get hold of this rent? How? Mr. Shui Ta: I don't know. (*Pause.*) I take that back, sir. It's just come to me. A husband. We must find her a husband!

(*Enter a little* OLD WOMAN.)

OLD WOMAN: A good cheap cigar for my husband, we'll have been married forty years tomorrow and we're having a little celebration.

SHUI TA: Forty years? And you still want to celebrate?

OLD WOMAN: As much as we can afford to. We have the carpet shop across the square. We'll be good neighbors, I hope?

SHUI TA: I hope so too.

POLICEMAN (*who keeps making discoveries*): Mr. Shui Ta, you know what we need? We need capital. And how do we acquire capital? We get married.

SHUI TA (*to* OLD WOMAN): I'm afraid I've been pestering this gentleman with my personal worries.

POLICEMAN (*lyrically*): We can't pay six months' rent, so what do we do? We marry money.

SHUI TA: That might not be easy.

POLICEMAN: Oh, I don't know. She's a good match. Has a nice, growing business. (*To the* OLD WOMAN.) What do you think?

OLD WOMAN (*undecided*): Well —

POLICEMAN: Should she put an ad in the paper?

OLD WOMAN (*not eager to commit herself*): Well, if *she* agrees —

POLICEMAN: I'll write it for her. *You* lend us a hand, and *we* write an ad for you! (*He chuckles away to himself, takes out his notebook, wets the stump of a pencil between his lips, and writes away.*)

SHUI TA (*slowly*): Not a bad idea.

POLICEMAN: "What . . . respectable . . . man . . . with small capital . . . widower . . . not excluded . . . desires . . . marriage . . . into flourishing . . . tobacco shop?" And now let's add: "am . . . pretty . . ." No! . . . "Prepossessing appearance."

SHUI TA: If you don't think that's an exaggeration?

OLD WOMAN: Oh, not a bit. I've seen her.

(*The* POLICEMAN *tears the page out of his notebook, and hands it over to* SHUI TA.)

SHUI TA (*with horror in his voice*): How much luck we need to keep our heads above water! How many ideas! How many friends! (*To the* POLICEMAN.) Thank you, sir. I think I see my way clear.

SCENE 3

(*Evening in the municipal park. Noise of a plane overhead.* YANG SUN, *a young man in rags, is following the plane with his eyes: one can tell that the machine is describing a curve above the park.* YANG SUN *then takes a rope out of his pocket, looking anxiously about him as he does so. He moves toward a large willow. Enter* TWO PROSTITUTES, *one old, the other the* NIECE *whom we have already met.*)

NIECE: Hello. Coming with me?

YANG SUN (*taken aback*): If you'd like to buy me a dinner.

OLD WHORE: Buy you a dinner! (*To the* NIECE.) Oh, we know him — it's the unemployed pilot. Waste no time on him!

NIECE: But he's the only man left in the park. And it's going to rain.

OLD WHORE: Oh, how do you know?

(*And they pass by.* YANG SUN *again looks about him, again takes his rope, and this time throws it round a branch of the willow tree. Again he is interrupted. It is the* TWO PROSTITUTES *returning — and in such a hurry they don't notice him.*)

NIECE: It's going to pour!

(*Enter* SHEN TE.)

OLD WHORE: There's that *gorgon* Shen Te! That *drove* your family out into the cold!

NIECE: It wasn't her. It was that cousin of hers. She offered to *pay* for the cakes. I've nothing against her.

OLD WHORE: I have, though. (*So that* SHEN TE *can hear.*) Now where could the little lady be off to? She may be rich now but that won't stop her snatching our young men, will it?

SHEN TE: I'm going to the tearoom by the pond.

NIECE: Is it true what they say? You're marrying a widower — with three children?

SHEN TE: Yes. I'm just going to see him.

YANG SUN (*his patience at breaking point*): Move on there! This is a park, not a whorehouse!

OLD WHORE: Shut your mouth!

(*But the* TWO PROSTITUTES *leave.*)

YANG SUN: Even in the farthest corner of the park, even when it's raining, you can't get rid of them! (*He spits.*)

SHEN TE (*overhearing this*): And what right have you to scold them? (*But at this point she sees the rope.*) Oh!

YANG SUN: Well, what are you staring at?

SHEN TE: That rope. What is it for?

YANG SUN: Think! Think! I haven't a penny. Even if I had, I wouldn't spend it on you. I'd buy a drink of water.

(*The rain starts.*)

SHEN TE (*still looking at the rope*): What is the rope for? You mustn't!

YANG SUN: What's it to you? Clear out!

SHEN TE (*irrelevantly*): It's raining.

YANG SUN: Well, don't try to come under this tree.

SHEN TE: Oh, no. (*She stays in the rain.*)

YANG SUN: Now go away. (*Pause.*) For one thing, I don't like your looks, you're bow-legged.

SHEN TE (*indignantly*): That's not true!

YANG SUN: Well, don't show 'em to me. Look, it's raining. You better come under this tree.

(*Slowly, she takes shelter under the tree.*)

SHEN TE: Why did you want to do it?

YANG SUN: You really want to know? (*Pause.*) To get rid of you! (*Pause.*) You know what a flyer is?

SHEN TE: Oh yes, I've met a lot of pilots. At the tearoom.

YANG SUN: You call *them* flyers? Think they know what a machine *is*? Just 'cause they have leather helmets? They gave the airfield director a bribe, that's the way *those* fellows got up in the air! Try one of them out sometime. "Go up to two thousand feet," tell him, "then let it fall, then pick it up again with a flick of the wrist at the last moment." Know what he'll say to that? "It's not in my contract." Then again, there's the landing problem. It's like landing on your own backside. It's no different, planes are human. Those fools don't understand. (*Pause.*) And I'm the biggest fool for reading the book on flying in the Peking school and skipping the page where it says: "we've got enough flyers and we don't need you." I'm a mail pilot and no mail. You understand that?

SHEN TE (*shyly*): Yes. I do.

YANG SUN: No, you don't. You'd never understand that.

SHEN TE: When we were little we had a crane with a broken wing. He made friends with us and was very good-natured about our jokes. He would strut along behind us and call out to stop us going too fast for him. But every spring and autumn when the cranes flew over the villages in great swarms, he got quite restless. (*Pause.*) I understood that. (*She bursts out crying.*)

YANG SUN: Don't!

SHEN TE (*quieting down*): No.

YANG SUN: It's bad for the complexion.

SHEN TE (*sniffing*): I've stopped.

(*She dries her tears on her big sleeve. Leaning against the tree, but not looking at her, he reaches for her face.*)

YANG SUN: You can't even wipe your own face. (*He is wiping it for her with his handkerchief. Pause.*)

SHEN TE (*still sobbing*): I don't know *anything*!

YANG SUN: You interrupted me! What for?

SHEN TE: It's such a rainy day. You only wanted to do . . . *that* because it's such a rainy day.

(*To the audience.*)

In our country
The evenings should never be somber
High bridges over rivers
The grey hour between night and morning
And the long, long winter:
Such things are dangerous
For, with all the misery,

A very little is enough
And men throw away an unbearable life.

(*Pause.*)

YANG SUN: Talk about yourself for a change.

SHEN TE: What about me? I have a shop.

YANG SUN (*incredulous*): You have a shop, do you? Never thought of walking the streets?

SHEN TE: I *did* walk the streets. Now I have a shop.

YANG SUN (*ironically*): A gift of the gods, I suppose!

SHEN TE: How did you know?

YANG SUN (*even more ironical*): One fine evening the gods turned up saying: here's some money!

SHEN TE (*quickly*): One fine morning.

YANG SUN (*fed up*): This isn't much of an entertainment.

(*Pause.*)

SHEN TE: I can play the zither a little. (*Pause.*) And I can mimic men. (*Pause.*) I got the shop, so the first thing I did was to give my zither away. I can be as stupid as a fish now, I said to myself, and it won't matter.

I'm rich now, I said
I walk alone, I sleep alone
For a whole year, I said
I'll have nothing to do with a man.

YANG SUN: And now you're marrying one! The one at the tearoom by the pond?

(SHEN TE *is silent.*)

YANG SUN: What do you know about love?

SHEN TE: Everything.

YANG SUN: Nothing. (*Pause.*) Or d'you just mean you enjoyed it?

SHEN TE: No.

YANG SUN (*again without turning to look at her, he strokes her cheek with his hand*): You like that?

SHEN TE: Yes.

YANG SUN (*breaking off*): You're easily satisfied, I must say. (*Pause.*) What a town!

SHEN TE: You have no friends?

YANG SUN (*defensively*): Yes, I have! (*Change of tone.*) But they don't want to hear I'm still unemployed. "What?" they ask. "Is there still water in the sea?" You have friends?

SHEN TE (*hesitating*): Just a . . . cousin.

YANG SUN: Watch him carefully.

SHEN TE: He only came once. Then he went away. He won't be back.

(YANG SUN *is looking away.*)

But to be without hope, they say, is to be without goodness!

(*Pause.*)

YANG SUN: Go on talking. A voice is a voice.

SHEN TE: Once, when I was a little girl, I fell, with a load of brushwood. An old man picked me up. He gave me a penny too. Isn't it funny how people who don't have very much like to give some of it away? They must like to show what they can do, and how could they show it better than by being kind? Being wicked is just like being clumsy. When we sing a song, or build a machine, or plant some rice, we're being kind. You're kind.

YANG SUN: You make it sound easy.

SHEN TE: Oh, no. (*Little pause.*) Oh! A drop of rain!

YANG SUN: Where'd you feel it?

SHEN TE: Between the eyes.

YANG SUN: Near the right eye? Or the left?

SHEN TE: Near the left eye.

YANG SUN: Oh, good. (*He is getting sleepy.*) So you're through with men, eh?

SHEN TE (*with a smile*): But I'm not bow-legged.

YANG SUN: Perhaps not.

SHEN TE: Definitely not.

(*Pause.*)

YANG SUN (*leaning wearily against the willow*): I haven't had a drop to drink all day, I haven't eaten anything for *two* days. I couldn't love you if I tried.

(*Pause.*)

SHEN TE: I like it in the rain.

(*Enter* WONG *the Water Seller, singing.*)

The Song of the Water Seller in the Rain

"Buy my water," I am yelling
And my fury restraining

For no water I'm selling
'Cause it's raining, 'cause it's raining!
　　　I keep yelling: "Buy my water!"
　　　But no one's buying
　　　Athirst and dying
　　　And drinking and paying!
　　　Buy water!
　　　Buy water, you dogs!

Nice to dream of lovely weather!
Think of all the consternation
Were there no precipitation
Half a dozen years together!
Can't you hear them shrieking: "Water!"
Pretending they adore me!
They all would go down on their knees before me!
Down on your knees!
Go down on your knees, you dogs!

What are lawns and hedges thinking?
What are fields and forests saying?
"At the cloud's breast we are drinking!
And we've no idea who's paying!"
　　　I keep yelling: "Buy my water!"
　　　But no one's buying
　　　Athirst and dying
　　　And drinking and paying!
　　　Buy water!
　　　Buy water, you dogs!

(*The rain has stopped now.* SHEN TE *sees* WONG *and runs toward him.*)

SHEN TE: Wong! You're back! Your carrying pole's at the shop.
WONG: Oh, thank you, Shen Te. And how is life treating *you?*
SHEN TE: I've just met a brave and clever man. And I want to buy him a cup of your water.
WONG (*bitterly*): Throw back your head and open your mouth and you'll have all the water you need —
SHEN TE (*tenderly*):
　　　I want *your* water, Wong
　　　The water that has tired you so
　　　The water that you carried all this way
　　　The water that is hard to sell because it's been raining

I need it for the young man over there — he's a flyer!
    A flyer is a bold man:
    Braving the storms
    In company with the clouds
    He crosses the heavens
    And brings to friends in far-away lands
    The friendly mail!

(*She pays* WONG, *and runs over to* YANG SUN *with the cup. But* YANG SUN *is fast asleep.*)

(*Calling to* WONG, *with a laugh.*) He's fallen asleep! Despair and rain and I have worn him out!

Scene 3A

(WONG's *den. The sewer pipe is transparent, and the* GODS *again appear to* WONG *in a dream.*)

WONG (*radiant*): I've seen her, illustrious ones! And she hasn't changed!

FIRST GOD: That's good to hear.

WONG: She loves someone.

FIRST GOD: Let's hope the experience gives her the strength to stay good!

WONG: It does. She's doing good deeds all the time.

FIRST GOD: Ah? What sort? What sort of good deeds, Wong?

WONG: Well, she has a kind word for everybody.

FIRST GOD (*eagerly*): And then?

WONG: Hardly anyone leaves her shop without tobacco in his pocket — even if he can't pay for it.

FIRST GOD: Not bad at all. Next?

WONG: She's putting up a family of eight.

FIRST GOD (*gleefully, to the* SECOND GOD): Eight! (*To* WONG.) And that's not all, of course!

WONG: She bought a cup of water from me even though it was raining.

FIRST GOD: Yes, yes, yes, all these smaller good deeds!

WONG: Even they run into money. A little tobacco shop doesn't make so much.

FIRST GOD (*sententiously*): A prudent gardener works miracles on the smallest plot.

WONG: She hands out rice every morning. That eats up half her earnings.

FIRST GOD (*a little disappointed*): Well, as a beginning . . .

WONG: They call her the Angel of the Slums — whatever the Carpenter may say!

FIRST GOD: What's this? A carpenter speaks ill of her?

WONG: Oh, he only says her shelves weren't paid for in full.

SECOND GOD (*who has a bad cold and can't pronounce his n's and m's*): What's this? Not paying a carpenter? Why was that?

WONG: I suppose she didn't have the money.

SECOND GOD (*severely*): One pays what one owes, that's in our book of rules! First the letter of the law, then the spirit!

WONG: But it wasn't Shen Te, illustrious ones, it was her cousin. She called *him* in to help.

SECOND GOD: Then her cousin must never darken her threshold again!

WONG: Very well, illustrious ones! But in fairness to Shen Te, let me say that her cousin is a businessman.

FIRST GOD: Perhaps we should inquire what is customary? I find business quite unintelligible. But everybody's doing it. Business! Did the Seven Good Kings do business? Did Kung the Just sell fish?

SECOND GOD: In any case, such a thing must not occur again!

(*The* GODS *start to leave.*)

THIRD GOD: Forgive us for taking this tone with you, Wong, we haven't been getting enough sleep. The rich recommend us to the poor, and the poor tell us they haven't enough room.

SECOND GOD: Feeble, feeble, the best of them!

FIRST GOD: No great deeds! No heroic daring!

THIRD GOD: On such a *small* scale!

SECOND GOD: Sincere, yes, but what is actually *achieved*?

(*One can no longer hear them.*)

WONG (*calling after them*): I've thought of something, illustrious ones: Perhaps you shouldn't ask — too — much — all — at — once!

SCENE 4

(*The square in front of* SHEN TE'S *tobacco shop. Beside* SHEN TE'S *place, two other shops are seen: the carpet shop and a barber's. Morning. Outside* SHEN TE'S *the* GRANDFATHER, *the* SISTER-IN-LAW, *the* UNEMPLOYED MAN, *and* MRS. SHIN *stand waiting.*)

SISTER-IN-LAW: She's been out all night again.

MRS. SHIN: No sooner did we get rid of that crazy cousin of hers than

Shen Te herself starts carrying on! Maybe she does give us an ounce of rice now and then, but can you depend on her? Can you depend on her?

(*Loud voices from the Barber's.*)

VOICE OF SHU FU: What are you doing in my shop? Get out — at once!
VOICE OF WONG: But sir. They all let me sell . . .

(WONG *comes staggering out of the barber's shop pursued by* MR. SHU FU, *the barber, a fat man carrying a heavy curling iron.*)

SHU FU: Get out, I said! Pestering my customers with your slimy old water! Get out! Take your cup!

(*He holds out the cup.* WONG *reaches out for it.* MR. SHU FU *strikes his hand with the curling iron, which is hot.* WONG *howls.*)

You had it coming, my man!

(*Puffing, he returns to his shop. The* UNEMPLOYED MAN *picks up the cup and gives it to* WONG.)

UNEMPLOYED MAN: You can report that to the police.
WONG: My hand! It's smashed up!
UNEMPLOYED MAN: Any bones broken?
WONG: I can't move my fingers.
UNEMPLOYED MAN: Sit down. I'll put some water on it.

(WONG *sits.*)

MRS. SHIN: The water won't cost you anything.
SISTER-IN-LAW: You might have got a bandage from Miss Shen Te till she took to staying out all night. It's a scandal.
MRS. SHIN (*despondently*): If you ask me, she's forgotten we ever existed!

(*Enter* SHEN TE *down the street, with a dish of rice.*)

SHEN TE (*to the audience*): How wonderful to see Setzuan in the early morning! I always used to stay in bed with my dirty blanket over my head afraid to wake up. This morning I saw the newspapers being delivered by little boys, the streets being washed by strong men, and fresh vegetables coming in from the country on ox carts. It's a long walk from where Yang Sun lives, but I feel lighter at every step. They say you walk on air when you're in love, but it's even better walking on the rough earth, on the hard cement. In the early morning, the old city looks like a great rubbish heap. Nice, though — with all its little lights. And the sky, so pink, so transparent, before the dust comes and muddies it! What a lot you miss if you never see your city rising from its slumbers like an honest old crafts-man pumping his lungs full of air and reaching for his tools, as the poet says! (*Cheerfully, to her waiting guests.*) Good morning, every-one, here's your rice! (*Distributing the rice, she comes upon* WONG.) Good morning, Wong, I'm quite lightheaded today. On my way over, I looked at myself in all the shop windows. I'd love to be beautiful.

(*She slips into the carpet shop.* MR. SHU FU *has just emerged from his shop.*)

SHU FU (*to the audience*): It surprises me how beautiful Miss Shen Te is looking today! I never gave her a passing thought before. But now I've been gazing upon her comely form for exactly three minutes! I begin to suspect I am in love with her. She is overpoweringly attrac-tive! (*Crossly, to* WONG.) Be off with you, rascal!

(*He returns to his shop.* SHEN TE *comes back out of the carpet shop with the* OLD MAN *its proprietor and his wife — whom we have already met — the* OLD WOMAN. SHEN TE *is wearing a shawl. The* OLD MAN *is holding up a looking glass for her.*)

OLD WOMAN: Isn't it lovely? We'll give you a reduction because there's a little hole in it.

SHEN TE (*looking at another shawl on the* OLD WOMAN's *arm*): The other one's nice too.

OLD WOMAN (*smiling*): Too bad there's no hole in that!

SHEN TE: That's right. My shop doesn't make very much.

OLD WOMAN: And your good deeds eat it all up! Be more careful, my dear . . .

SHEN TE (*trying on the shawl with the hole*): Just now, I'm light-headed! Does the color suit me?

OLD WOMAN: You'd better ask a man.

SHEN TE (*to the* OLD MAN): Does the color suit me?

OLD MAN: You'd better ask your young friend.

SHEN TE: I'd like to have your opinion.

OLD MAN: It suits you, very well. But wear it this way: the dull side out.

(SHEN TE *pays up.*)

OLD WOMAN: If you decide you don't like it, you can exchange it. (*She pulls* SHEN TE *to one side.*) Has he got money?

SHEN TE (*with a laugh*): Yang Sun? Oh, no.

OLD WOMAN: Then how're you going to pay your rent?

SHEN TE: I'd forgotten about that.

OLD WOMAN: And next Monday is the first of the month! Miss Shen Te, I've got something to say to you. After we (*indicating her husband*) got to know you, we had our doubts about that marriage ad. We thought it would be better if you'd let *us* help you. Out of our savings. We reckon we could lend you two hundred silver dollars. We don't need anything in writing — you could pledge us your tobacco stock.

SHEN TE: You're prepared to lend money to a person like me?

OLD WOMAN: It's folks like you that need it. We'd think twice about lending anything to your cousin.

OLD MAN (*coming up*): All settled, my dear?

SHEN TE: I wish the gods could have heard what your wife was just saying, Mr. Ma. They're looking for good people who're happy — and helping me makes you happy because you know it was love that got me into difficulties!

(*The old couple smile knowingly at each other.*)

OLD MAN: And here's the money, Miss Shen Te.

(*He hands her an envelope.* SHEN TE *takes it. She bows. They bow back. They return to their shop.*)

SHEN TE (*holding up her envelope*): Look, Wong, here's six months' rent! Don't you believe in miracles now? And how do you like my new shawl?

WONG: For the young fellow I saw you with in the park?

(SHEN TE *nods.*)

MRS. SHIN: Never mind all that. It's time you took a look at his hand!

SHEN TE: Have you hurt your hand?

MRS. SHIN: That barber smashed it with his hot curling iron. Right in front of our eyes.

SHEN TE (*shocked at herself*): And I never noticed! We must get you to a doctor this minute or who knows what will happen?

UNEMPLOYED MAN: It's not a doctor he should see, it's a judge. He can ask for compensation. The barber's filthy rich.

WONG: You think I have a chance?

MRS. SHIN (*with relish*): If it's really good and smashed. But is it?

WONG: I think so. It's very swollen. Could I get a pension?

MRS. SHIN: You'd need a witness.

WONG: Well, you all saw it. You could all testify.

(*He looks round. The* UNEMPLOYED MAN, *the* GRANDFATHER, *and the* SISTER-IN-LAW *are all sitting against the wall of the shop eating rice. Their concentration on eating is complete.*)

SHEN TE (*to* MRS. SHIN): You saw it yourself.

MRS. SHIN: I want nothin' to do with the police. It's against my principles.

SHEN TE (*to* SISTER-IN-LAW): What about you?

SISTER-IN-LAW: Me? I wasn't looking.

SHEN TE (*to the* GRANDFATHER, *coaxingly*): Grandfather, *you'll* testify, won't you?

SISTER-IN-LAW: And a lot of good that will do. He's simple-minded.

SHEN TE (*to the* UNEMPLOYED MAN): You seem to be the only witness left.

UNEMPLOYED MAN: My testimony would only hurt him. I've been picked up twice for begging.

SHEN TE: Your brother is assaulted, and you shut your eyes?
      He is hit, cries out in pain, and you are silent?
      The beast prowls, chooses and seizes his victim, and you say:
      "Because we showed no displeasure, he has spared us."
If no one present will be a witness, I will. I'll say *I* saw it.

MRS. SHIN (*solemnly*): The name for that is perjury.

WONG: I don't know if I can accept that. Though maybe I'll have to. (*Looking at his hand.*) Is it swollen enough, do you think? The swelling's not going down?

UNEMPLOYED MAN: No, no, the swelling's holding up well.

WONG: Yes. It's *more* swollen if anything. Maybe my wrist is broken after all. I'd better see a judge at once.

(*Holding his hand very carefully, and fixing his eyes on it, he runs off.* MRS. SHIN *goes quickly into the barber's shop.*)

UNEMPLOYED MAN (*seeing her*): She is getting on the right side of Mr. Shu Fu.

SISTER-IN-LAW: You and I can't change the world, Shen Te.

SHEN TE: Go away! Go away all of you!

(*The* UNEMPLOYED MAN, *the* SISTER-IN-LAW, *and the* GRANDFATHER *stalk off, eating and sulking.*)

(*To the audience.*)

They've stopped answering
They stay put
They do as they're told
They don't care

Nothing can make them look up
But the smell of food.

(*Enter* MRS. YANG, YANG SUN'S *mother, out of breath.*)

MRS. YANG: Miss. Shen Te. My son has told me everything. I am Mrs. Yang, Sun's mother. Just think. He's got an offer. Of a job as a pilot. A letter has just come. From the director of the airfield in Peking!

SHEN TE: So he can fly again? Isn't that wonderful!

MRS. YANG (*less breathlessly all the time*): They won't give him the job for nothing. They want five hundred silver dollars.

SHEN TE: We can't let money stand in his way, Mrs. Yang!

MRS. YANG: If only you could help him out!

SHEN TE: I have the shop. I can try! (*She embraces* MRS. YANG.) I happen to have two hundred with me now. Take it. (*She gives her the old couple's money.*) It was a loan but they said I could repay it with my tobacco stock.

MRS. YANG: And they were calling Sun the Dead Pilot of Setzuan! A friend in need!

SHEN TE: We must find another three hundred.

MRS. YANG: How?

SHEN TE: Let me think. (*Slowly.*) I know someone who can help. I didn't want to call on his services again, he's hard and cunning. But a flyer must fly. And I'll make this the last time.

(*Distant sound of a plane.*)

MRS. YANG: If the man you mentioned can do it. . . . Oh, look, there's the morning mail plane, heading for Peking!

SHEN TE: The pilot can see us, let's wave!

(*They wave. The noise of the engine is louder.*)

MRS. YANG: You know that pilot up there?

SHEN TE: Wave, Mrs. Yang! I know the pilot who *will* be up there. He gave up hope. But he'll do it now. One man to raise himself above the misery, above us all.

(*To the audience.*)

Yang Sun, my lover:
Braving the storms
In company with the clouds
Crossing the heavens
And bringing to friends in far-away lands
The friendly mail!

Scene 4A

(*In front of the inner curtain. Enter* SHEN TE, *carrying* SHUI TA'S *mask. She sings.*)

The Song of Defenselessness

In our country
A useful man needs luck
Only if he finds strong backers can he prove himself useful
The good can't defend themselves and
Even the gods are defenseless.

Oh, why don't the gods have their own ammunition
And launch against badness their own expedition
Enthroning the good and preventing sedition
And bringing the world to a peaceful condition?

Oh, why don't the gods do the buying and selling
Injustice forbidding, starvation dispelling
Give bread to each city and joy to each dwelling?
Oh, why don't the gods do the buying and selling?

(*She puts on* SHUI TA'S *mask and sings in his voice.*)

You can only help one of your luckless brothers
By trampling down a dozen others

Why is it the gods do not feel indignation
And come down in fury to end exploitation
Defeat all defeat and forbid desperation
Refusing to tolerate such toleration?

Why is it?

SCENE 5

(SHEN TE'S *tobacco shop. Behind the counter,* MR. SHUI TA, *reading the paper.* MRS. SHIN *is cleaning up. She talks and he takes no notice.*)

MRS. SHIN: And when certain rumors get about, what *happens* to a little place like this? It goes to pot. I know. So, if you want my advice, Mr. Shui Ta, find out just what exactly has been going on between Miss Shen Te and that Yang Sun from Yellow Street. And remember: a certain interest in Miss Shen Te has been expressed by the barber next door, a man with twelve houses and only one wife, who, for that matter, is likely to drop off at any time. A certain interest has been expressed. (*She relishes the phrase.*) He was even inquiring about her means and, if *that* doesn't prove a man is getting serious, what would? (*Still getting no response, she leaves with her bucket.*)

YANG SUN'S VOICE: Is that Miss Shen Te's tobacco shop?

MRS. SHIN'S VOICE: Yes, it is, but it's Mr. Shui Ta who's here today.

(SHUI TA *runs to the looking glass with the short, light steps of* SHEN TE, *and is just about to start primping, when he realizes his mistake, and turns away, with a short laugh. Enter* YANG SUN. MRS. SHIN *enters behind him and slips into the back room to eavesdrop.*)

YANG SUN: I am Yang Sun.

(SHUI TA *bows.*)

Is Miss Shen Te in?

SHUI TA: No.

YANG SUN: I guess you know our relationship? (*He is inspecting the stock.*) Quite a place! And I thought she was just talking big. I'll be flying again, all right. (*He takes a cigar, solicits and receives a light from* SHUI TA.) You think we can squeeze the other three hundred out of the tobacco stock?

SHUI TA: May I ask if it is your intention to sell at once?

YANG SUN: It was decent of her to come out with the two hundred but they aren't much use with the other three hundred still missing.

SHUI TA: Shen Te was overhasty promising so much. She might have to sell the shop itself to raise it. Haste, they say, is the wind that blows the house down.

YANG SUN: Oh, she isn't a girl to keep a man waiting. For one thing or the other, if you take my meaning.

SHUI TA: I take your meaning.

YANG SUN (*leering*): Uh, huh.

SHUI TA: Would you explain what the five hundred silver dollars are for?

YANG SUN: Trying to sound me out? Very well. The director of the Peking airfield is a friend of mine from flying school. I give him five hundred: he gets me the job.

SHUI TA: The price is high.

YANG SUN: Not as these things go. He'll have to fire one of the present pilots — for negligence. Only the man he has in mind isn't negligent. Not easy, you understand. You needn't mention that part of it to Shen Te.

SHUI TA (*looking intently at* YANG SUN): Mr. Yang Sun, you are asking my cousin to give up her possessions, leave her friends, and place her entire fate in your hands. I presume you intend to marry her?

YANG SUN: I'd be prepared to.

(*Slight pause.*)

SHUI TA: Those two hundred silver dollars would pay the rent here for six months. If you were Shen Te wouldn't you be tempted to continue in business?

YANG SUN: What? Can you imagine Yang Sun the Flyer behind a counter? (*In an oily voice.*) "A strong cigar or a mild one, worthy sir?" Not in this century!

SHUI TA: My cousin wishes to follow the promptings of her heart, and, from her own point of view, she may even have what is called the right to love. Accordingly, she has commissioned me to help you to this post. There is nothing here that I am not empowered to turn immediately into cash. Mrs. Mi Tzu, the landlady, will advise me about the sale.

(*Enter* MRS. MI TZU.)

MRS. MI TZU: Good morning, Mr. Shui Ta, you wish to see me about the rent? As you know it falls due the day after tomorrow.

SHUI TA: Circumstances have changed, Mrs. Mi Tzu: my cousin is getting married. Her future husband here, Mr. Yang Sun, will be taking her to Peking. I am interested in selling the tobacco stock.

MRS. MI TZU: How much are you asking, Mr. Shui Ta?

YANG SUN: Three hundred sil —

SHUI TA: Five hundred silver dollars.

MRS. MI TZU: How much did she pay for it, Mr. Shui Ta?

SHUI TA: A thousand. And very little has been sold.

MRS. MI TZU: She was robbed. But I'll make you a special offer if you'll promise to be out by the day after tomorrow. Three hundred silver dollars.

YANG SUN (*shrugging*): Take it, man, take it.

SHUI TA: It is not enough.

YANG SUN: Why not? Why not? Certainly, it's enough.

SHUI TA: Five hundred silver dollars.

YANG SUN: But why? We only need three!

SHUI TA (*to* MRS. MI TZU): Excuse me. (*Takes* YANG SUN *on one side.*)

The tobacco stock is pledged to the old couple who gave my cousin the two hundred.

YANG SUN: Is it in writing?

SHUI TA: No.

YANG SUN (*to* MRS. MI TZU): Three hundred will do.

MRS. MI TZU: Of course, I need an assurance that Miss Shen Te is not in debt.

YANG SUN: Mr. Shui Ta?

SHUI TA: She is not in debt.

YANG SUN: When can you let us have the money?

MRS. MI TZU: The day after tomorrow. And remember: I'm doing this because I have a soft spot in my heart for young lovers! (*Exit.*)

YANG SUN (*calling after her*): Boxes, jars and sacks — three hundred for the lot and the pain's over! (*To* SHUI TA.) Where else can we raise money by the day after tomorrow?

SHUI TA: Nowhere. Haven't you enough for the trip and the first few weeks?

YANG SUN: Oh, certainly.

SHUI TA: How much, exactly?

YANG SUN: Oh, I'll dig it up, if I have to steal it.

SHUI TA: I see.

YANG SUN: Well, don't fall off the roof. I'll get to Peking somehow.

SHUI TA: Two people can't travel for nothing.

YANG SUN (*not giving* SHUI TA *a chance to answer*): I'm leaving *her* behind. No millstones round *my* neck!

SHUI TA: Oh.

YANG SUN: Don't look at me like that!

SHUI TA: How precisely is my cousin to live?

YANG SUN: Oh, you'll think of something.

SHUI TA: A small request, Mr. Yang Sun. Leave the two hundred silver dollars here until you can show me two tickets for Peking.

YANG SUN: You learn to mind your own business, Mr. Shui Ta.

SHUI TA: I'm afraid Miss Shen Te may not wish to sell the shop when she discovers that . . .

YANG SUN: You don't know women. She'll want to. Even then.

SHUI TA (*a slight outburst*): She is a human being, sir! And not devoid of common sense!

YANG SUN: Shen Te is a woman: she *is* devoid of common sense. I only have to lay my hand on her shoulder, and church bells ring.

SHUI TA (*with difficulty*): Mr. Yang Sun!

YANG SUN: Mr. Shui Whatever-it-is!

SHUI TA: My cousin is devoted to you . . . because . . .

YANG SUN: Because I have my hands on her breasts. Give me a cigar.

(*He takes one for himself, stuffs a few more in his pocket, then changes his mind and takes the whole box.*) Tell her I'll marry her, then bring me the three hundred. Or let her bring it. One or the other. (*Exit.*)

MRS. SHIN (*sticking her head out of the back room*): Well, he has your cousin under his thumb, and doesn't care if all Yellow Street knows it!

SHUI TA (*crying out*): I've lost my shop! And he doesn't love me! (*He runs berserk through the room, repeating these lines incoherently. Then stops suddenly, and addresses* MRS. SHIN.) Mrs. Shin, you grew up in the gutter, like me. Are we lacking in hardness? I doubt it. If you steal a penny from me, I'll take you by the throat till you spit it out! You'd do the same to me. The times are bad, this city is hell, but we're like ants, we keep coming, up and up the walls, however smooth! Till bad luck comes. Being in love, for instance. One weakness is enough, and love is the deadliest.

MRS. SHIN (*emerging from the back room*): You should have a little talk with Mr. Shu Fu the Barber. He's a real gentleman and just the thing for your cousin. (*She runs off.*)

SHUI TA:

A caress becomes a stranglehold
A sigh of love turns to a cry of fear
Why are there vultures circling in the air?
A girl is going to meet her lover.

(SHUI TA *sits down and* MR. SHU FU *enters with* MRS. SHIN.)

Mr. Shu Fu?

SHU FU: Mr. Shui Ta.

(*They both bow.*)

SHUI TA: I am told that you have expressed a certain interest in my cousin Shen Te. Let me set aside all propriety and confess: she is at this moment in grave danger.

SHU FU: Oh, dear!

SHUI TA: She has lost her shop, Mr. Shu Fu.

SHU FU: The charm of Miss Shen Te, Mr. Shui Ta, derives from the goodness, not of her shop, but of her heart. Men call her the Angel of the Slums.

SHUI TA: Yet her goodness has cost her two hundred silver dollars in a single day: we must put a stop to it.

SHU FU: Permit me to differ, Mr. Shui Ta. Let us rather, open wide the gates to such goodness! Every morning, with pleasure tinged by affection, I watch her charitable ministrations. For they are hungry, and she giveth them to eat! Four of them, to be precise. Why only four? I ask. Why not four hundred? I hear she has been seeking shelter for the homeless. What about my humble cabins behind the cattle run? They are at her disposal. And so forth. And so on. Mr. Shui Ta, do you think Miss Shen Te could be persuaded to listen to certain ideas of mine? Ideas like these?

SHUI TA: Mr. Shu Fu, she would be honored.

(*Enter* WONG *and the* POLICEMAN. MR. SHU FU *turns abruptly away and studies the shelves.*)

WONG: Is Miss Shen Te here?

SHUI TA: No.

WONG: I am Wong the Water Seller. You are Mr. Shui Ta?

SHUI TA: I am.

WONG: I am a friend of Shen Te's.

SHUI TA: An intimate friend, I hear.

WONG (*to the* POLICEMAN): You see? (*To* SHUI TA.) It's because of my hand.

POLICEMAN: He hurt his hand, sir, that's a fact.

SHUI TA (*quickly*): You need a sling, I see. (*He takes a shawl from the back room, and throws it to* WONG.)

WONG: But that's her new shawl!

SHUI TA: She has no more use for it.

WONG: But she bought it to please someone!

SHUI TA: It happens to be no longer necessary.

WONG (*making the sling*): She is my only witness.

POLICEMAN: Mr. Shui Ta, your cousin is supposed to have seen the Barber hit the Water Seller with a curling iron.

SHUI TA: I'm afraid my cousin was not present at the time.

WONG: But she was, sir! Just ask her! Isn't she in?

SHUI TA (*gravely*): Mr. Wong, my cousin has her own troubles. You wouldn't wish her to add to them by committing perjury?

WONG: But it was she that told me to go to the judge!

SHUI TA: Was the judge supposed to heal your hand?

(MR. SHU FU *turns quickly around.* SHUI TA *bows to* SHU FU, *and vice versa.*)

WONG (*taking the sling off, and putting it back*): I see how it is.

POLICEMAN: Well, I'll be on my way. (*To* WONG.) And you be careful. If Mr. Shu Fu wasn't a man who tempers justice with mercy, as the saying is, you'd be in jail for libel. Be off with you!

(*Exit* WONG, *followed by* POLICEMAN.)

SHUI TA: Profound apologies, Mr. Shu Fu.

SHU FU: Not at all, Mr. Shui Ta. (*Pointing to the shawl.*) The episode is over?

SHUI TA: It may take her time to recover. There are some fresh wounds.

SHU FU: We shall be discreet. Delicate. A short vacation could be arranged . . .

SHUI TA: First, of course, you and she would have to talk things over.

SHU FU: At a small supper in a small, but high-class, restaurant.

SHUI TA: I'll go and find her. (*Exit into back room.*)

MRS. SHIN (*sticking her head in again*): Time for congratulations, Mr. Shu Fu?

SHU FU: Ah, Mrs. Shin! Please inform Miss Shen Te's guests they may take shelter in the cabins behind the cattle run!

(MRS. SHIN *nods, grinning.*)

(*To the audience.*) Well? What do you think of me, ladies and gentlemen? What could a man do more? Could he be less selfish? More farsighted? A small supper in a small but . . . Does that bring rather vulgar and clumsy thoughts into your mind? Ts, ts, ts. Nothing of the sort will occur. She won't even be touched. Not even accidentally while passing the salt. An exchange of ideas only. Over the flowers on the table — white chrysanthemums, by the way (*He writes down a note of this.*) — yes, over the white chrysanthemums, two young souls will . . . shall I say "find each other"? We shall NOT exploit the misfortune of others. Understanding? Yes. An offer of assistance? Certainly. But quietly. Almost inaudibly. Perhaps with a single glance. A glance that could also — mean more.

MRS. SHIN (*coming forward*): Everything under control, Mr. Shu Fu?

SHU FU: Oh, Mrs. Shin, what do you know about this worthless rascal Yang Sun?

MRS. SHIN: Why, he's the most worthless rascal . . .

SHU FU: Is he really? You're sure? (*As she opens her mouth.*) From now on, he doesn't exist! Can't be found anywhere!

(*Enter* YANG SUN.)

YANG SUN: What's been going on here?

MRS. SHIN: Shall I call Mr. Shui Ta, Mr. Shu Fu? He wouldn't want strangers in here!

SHU FU: Mr. Shui Ta is in conference with Miss Shen Te. Not to be disturbed!

YANG SUN: Shen Te here? I didn't see her come in. What kind of conference?

SHU FU (*not letting him enter the back room*): Patience, dear sir! And if by chance I have an inkling who you are, pray take note that Miss Shen Te and I are about to announce our engagement.

YANG SUN: What?

MRS. SHIN: You didn't expect that, did you?

(YANG SUN *is trying to push past the barber into the back room when* SHEN TE *comes out.*)

SHU FU: My dear Shen Te, ten thousand apologies! Perhaps you . . .

YANG SUN: What is it, Shen Te? Have you gone crazy?

SHEN TE (*breathless*): My cousin and Mr. Shu Fu have come to an understanding. They wish me to hear Mr. Shu Fu's plans for helping the poor.

YANG SUN: Your cousin wants to part us.

SHEN TE: Yes.

YANG SUN: And you've agreed to it?

SHEN TE: Yes.

YANG SUN: They told you I was bad.

(SHEN TE *is silent.*)

And suppose I am. Does that make me need you less? I'm low, Shen Te, I have no money, I don't do the right thing but at least I put up a fight! (*He is near her now, and speaks in an undertone.*) Have you no eyes? Look at him. Have you forgotten already?

SHEN TE: No.

YANG SUN: How it was raining?

SHEN TE: No.

YANG SUN: How you cut me down from the willow tree? Bought me water? Promised me money to fly with?

SHEN TE (*shakily*): Yang Sun, what do you want?

YANG SUN: I want you to come with me.

SHEN TE (*in a small voice*): Forgive me, Mr. Shu Fu, I want to go with Mr. Yang Sun.

YANG SUN: We're lovers you know. Give me the key to the shop.

(SHEN TE *takes the key from around her neck.* YANG SUN *puts it on the counter. To* MRS. SHIN.)

Leave it under the mat when you're through. Let's go, Shen Te.

SHU FU: But this is rape! Mr. Shui Ta!!

YANG SUN (*to* SHEN TE): Tell him not to shout.

SHEN TE: Please don't shout for my cousin, Mr. Shu Fu. He doesn't agree with me, I know, but he's wrong. (*To the audience.*)

I want to go with the man I love

I don't want to count the cost

I don't want to consider if it's wise
I don't want to know if he loves me
I want to go with the man I love.

YANG SUN: That's the spirit.

(*And the couple leave.*)

Scene 5A

(*In front of the inner curtain.* SHEN TE *in her wedding clothes, on the way to her wedding.*)

SHEN TE: Something terrible has happened. As I left the shop with Yang Sun, I found the old carpet dealer's wife waiting in the street, trembling all over. She told me her husband had taken to his bed — sick with all the worry and excitement over the two hundred silver dollars they lent me. She said it would be best if I gave it back now. Of course, I had to say I would. She said she couldn't quite trust my cousin Shui Ta or even my fiancé Yang Sun. There were tears in her eyes. With my emotions in an uproar, I threw myself into Yang Sun's arms, I couldn't resist him. The things he'd said to Shui Ta had taught Shen Te nothing. Sinking into his arms, I said to myself:

To let no one perish, not even oneself
To fill everyone with happiness, even oneself
Is so good

How could I have forgotten those two old people? Yang Sun swept me away like a small hurricane. But he's not a bad man, and he loves me. He'd rather work in the cement factory than owe his flying to a crime. Though, of course, flying *is* a great passion with Sun. Now, on the way to my wedding, I waver between fear and joy.

SCENE 6

(*The "private dining room" on the upper floor of a cheap restaurant in a poor section of town. With* SHEN TE: *the* GRANDFATHER, *the* SISTER-IN-LAW, *the* NIECE, MRS. SHIN, *the* UNEMPLOYED MAN. *In a corner, alone, a* PRIEST. *A* WAITER *pouring wine. Downstage,* YANG SUN *talking to his mother. He wears a dinner jacket.*)

YANG SUN: Bad news, Mamma. She came right out and told me she can't sell the shop for me. Some idiot is bringing a claim because he lent her the two hundred she gave you.

MRS. YANG: What did *you* say? Of course, you can't marry her now.

YANG SUN: It's no use saying anything to *her*. I've sent for her cousin, Mr. Shui Ta. He said there was nothing in writing.

MRS. YANG: Good idea. I'll go out and look for him. Keep an eye on things.

(*Exit* MRS. YANG. SHEN TE *has been pouring wine.*)

SHEN TE (*to the audience, pitcher in hand*): I wasn't mistaken in him. He's bearing up well. Though it must have been an awful blow — giving up flying. I do love him so. (*Calling across the room to him.*) Sun, you haven't drunk a toast with the bride!

YANG SUN: What do we drink to?

SHEN TE: Why, to the future!

YANG SUN: When the bridegroom's dinner jacket won't be a hired one!

SHEN TE: But when the bride's dress will still get rained on sometimes!

YANG SUN: To everything we ever wished for!

SHEN TE: May all our dreams come true!

(*They drink.*)

YANG SUN (*with loud conviviality*): And now, friends, before the wedding gets under way, I have to ask the bride a few questions. I've no idea what kind of a wife she'll make, and it worries me. (*Wheeling on* SHEN TE.) For example. Can you make five cups of tea with three tea leaves?

SHEN TE: No.

YANG SUN: So I won't be getting very much tea. Can you sleep on a straw mattress the size of that book? (*He points to the large volume the* PRIEST *is reading.*)

SHEN TE: The two of us?

YANG SUN: The one of you.

SHEN TE: In that case, no.

YANG SUN: What a wife! I'm shocked!

(*While the audience is laughing, his mother returns. With a shrug of her shoulders, she tells* YANG SUN *the expected guest hasn't arrived. The* PRIEST *shuts the book with a bang, and makes for the door.*)

MRS. YANG: Where are *you* off to? It's only a matter of minutes.

PRIEST (*watch in hand*): Time goes on, Mrs. Yang, and I've another wedding to attend to. Also a funeral.

MRS. YANG (*irately*): D'you think we planned it this way? I was hoping to manage with one pitcher of wine, and we've run through two already. (*Points to empty pitcher. Loudly.*) My dear Shen Te, I don't know where your cousin can be keeping himself!

SHEN TE: My cousin?

MRS. YANG: Certainly. I'm old fashioned enough to think such a close relative should attend the wedding.

SHEN TE: Oh, Sun, is it the three hundred silver dollars?

YANG SUN (*not looking her in the eye*): Are you deaf? Mother says she's old fashioned. And I say I'm considerate. We'll wait another fifteen minutes.

HUSBAND: Another fifteen minutes.

MRS. YANG (*addressing the company*): Now you all know, don't you, that my son is getting a job as a mail pilot?

SISTER-IN-LAW: In Peking, too, isn't it?

MRS. YANG: In Peking, too! The two of us are moving to Peking!

SHEN TE: Sun, tell your mother Peking is out of the question now.

YANG SUN: Your cousin'll tell her. If he agrees. I don't agree.

SHEN TE (*amazed, and dismayed*): Sun!

YANG SUN: I hate this godforsaken Setzuan. What people! Know what they look like when I half close my eyes? Horses! Whinnying, fretting, stamping, screwing their necks up! (*Loudly.*) And what is it the thunder says? They are su-per-flu-ous! (*He hammers out the syllables.*) They've run their last race! They can go trample themselves to death! (*Pause.*) I've got to get out of here.

SHEN TE: But I've promised the money to the old couple.

YANG SUN: And since you always do the wrong thing, it's lucky your cousin's coming. Have another drink.

SHEN TE (*quietly*): My cousin can't be coming.

YANG SUN: How d'you mean?

SHEN TE: My cousin can't be where I am.

YANG SUN: Quite a conundrum!

SHEN TE (*desperately*): Sun, I'm the one that loves you. Not my cousin. He was thinking of the job in Peking when he promised you the old couple's money —

YANG SUN: Right. And that's why he's bringing the three hundred silver dollars. Here — to my wedding.

SHEN TE: He is not bringing the three hundred silver dollars.

YANG SUN: Huh? What makes you think that?

SHEN TE (*looking into his eyes*): He says you only bought one ticket to Peking.

(*Short pause.*)

YANG SUN: That was yesterday. (*He pulls two tickets part way out of his inside pocket, making her look under his coat.*) Two tickets. I don't want Mother to know. She'll get left behind. I sold her furniture to buy these tickets, so you see . . .

SHEN TE: But what's to become of the old couple?

YANG SUN: What's to become of me? Have another drink. Or do you believe in moderation? If I drink, I fly again. And if you drink, you may learn to understand me.

SHEN TE: You want to fly. But I can't help you.

YANG SUN: "Here's a plane, my darling — but it's only got one wing!"

(*The* WAITER *enters.*)

WAITER: Mrs. Yang! Mrs. Yang!

MRS. YANG: Yes?

WAITER: Another pitcher of wine, ma'am?

MRS. YANG: We have enough, thanks. Drinking makes me sweat.

WAITER: Would you mind paying, ma'am?

MRS. YANG (*to everyone*): Just be patient a few moments longer, everyone, Mr. Shui Ta is on his way over! (*To the* WAITER.) Don't be a spoilsport.

WAITER: I can't let you leave till you've paid your bill, ma'am.

MRS. YANG: But they know me here!

WAITER: That's just it.

PRIEST (*ponderously getting up*): I humbly take my leave. (*And he does.*)

MRS. YANG (*to the others, desperately*): Stay where you are, everybody! The priest says he'll be back in two minutes!

YANG SUN: It's no good, Mamma. Ladies and gentlemen, Mr. Shui Ta still hasn't arrived and the priest has gone home. We won't detain you any longer.

(*They are leaving now.*)

GRANDFATHER (*in the doorway, having forgotten to put his glass down*): To the bride! (*He drinks, puts down the glass, and follows the others.*)

(*Pause.*)

SHEN TE: Shall I go too?

YANG SUN: You? Aren't you the bride? Isn't this your wedding? (*He drags her across the room, tearing her wedding dress.*) If we can wait, you can wait. Mother calls me her falcon. She wants to see me in the clouds. But I think it may be St. Nevercome's Day before she'll go to the door and see my plane thunder by. (*Pause. He pretends the guests are still present.*) Why such a lull in the conversation, ladies and gentlemen? Don't you like it here? The ceremony is only slightly postponed — because an important guest is expected at any moment. Also because the bride doesn't know what love is. While we're waiting, the bridegroom will sing a little song. (*He does so.*)

The Song of St. Nevercome's Day

On a certain day, as is generally known,
    One and all will be shouting: Hooray, hooray!
For the beggar maid's son has a solid-gold throne
    And the day is St. Nevercome's Day
On St. Nevercome's, Nevercome's, Nevercome's Day
    He'll sit on his solid-gone throne

Oh, hooray, hooray! That day goodness will pay!
    That day badness will cost you your head!
And merit and money will smile and be funny
    While exchanging salt and bread
On St. Nevercome's, Nevercome's, Nevercome's Day
    While exchanging salt and bread

And the grass, oh, the grass will look down at the sky
    And the pebbles will roll up the stream
And all men will be good without batting an eye
    They will make of our earth a dream
On St. Nevercome's, Nevercome's, Nevercome's Day
    They will make of our earth a dream

And as for me, that's the day I shall be
    A flyer and one of the best
Unemployed man, you will have work to do
    Washerwoman, you'll get your rest
On St. Nevercome's, Nevercome's, Nevercome's Day
    Washerwoman, you'll get your rest.

MRS. YANG: It looks like he's not coming.

(*The three of them sit looking at the door.*)

Scene 6A

(WONG's *den. The sewer pipe is again transparent and again the* GODS *appear to* WONG *in a dream.*)

WONG: I'm so glad you've come, illustrious ones. It's Shen Te. She's in great trouble from following the rule about loving thy neighbor. Perhaps she's *too* good for this world!

FIRST GOD: Nonsense! You are eaten up by lice and doubts!

WONG: Forgive me, illustrious one, I only meant you might deign to intervene.

FIRST GOD: Out of the question! My colleague here intervened in some squabble or other only yesterday. (*He points to the* THIRD GOD *who has a black eye.*) The results are before us!

WONG: She had to call on her cousin again. But not even he could help. I'm afraid the shop is done for.

THIRD GOD (*a little concerned*): Perhaps we should help after all?

FIRST GOD: The gods help those that help themselves.

WONG: What if we *can't* help ourselves, illustrious ones?

(*Slight pause.*)

SECOND GOD: Try, anyway! Suffering ennobles!

FIRST GOD: Our faith in Shen Te is unshaken!

THIRD GOD: We certainly haven't found any *other* good people. You can see where we spend our nights from the straw on our clothes.

WONG: You might help her find her way by —

FIRST GOD: The good man finds his own way here below!

SECOND GOD: The good woman too.

FIRST GOD: The heavier the burden, the greater her strength!

THIRD GOD: We're only onlookers, you know.

FIRST GOD: And everything will be all right in the end, O ye of little faith!

(*They are gradually disappearing through these last lines.*)

SCENE 7

(*The yard behind* SHEN TE's *shop. A few articles of furniture on a cart.* SHEN TE *and* MRS. SHIN *are taking the washing off the line.*)

MRS. SHIN: If you ask me, you should fight tooth and nail to keep the shop.

SHEN TE: How can I? I have to sell the tobacco to pay back the two hundred silver dollars today.

MRS. SHIN: No husband, no tobacco, no house and home! What are you going to live on?

SHEN TE: I can work. I can sort tobacco.

MRS. SHIN: Hey, look, Mr. Shui Ta's trousers! He must have left here stark naked!

SHEN TE: Oh, he may have another pair, Mrs. Shin.

MRS. SHIN: But if he's gone for good as you say, why has he left his pants behind?

SHEN TE: Maybe he's thrown them away.

MRS. SHIN: Can I take them?

SHEN TE: Oh, no.

(*Enter* MR. SHU FU, *running.*)

SHU FU: Not a word! Total silence! I know all. You have sacrificed your own love and happiness so as not to hurt a dear old couple who had put their trust in you! Not in vain does this district — for all its malevolent tongues! — call you the Angel of the Slums! That young man couldn't rise to your level, so you left him. And now, when I see you closing up the little shop, that veritable haven of rest for the multitude, well, I cannot, I cannot let it pass. Morning after morning I have stood watching in the doorway not unmoved — while you graciously handed out rice to the wretched. Is that never to happen again? Is the good woman of Setzuan to disappear? If only you would allow *me* to assist you! Now don't say anything! No assurances, no exclamations of gratitude! (*He has taken out his check book.*) Here! A blank check. (*He places it on the cart.*) Just my signature. Fill it out as you wish. Any sum in the world. I herewith retire from the scene, quietly, unobtrusively, making no claims, on tiptoe, full of veneration, absolutely selflessly . . . (*He has gone.*)

MRS. SHIN: Well! You're saved. There's always some idiot of a man . . . Now hurry! Put down a thousand silver dollars and let me fly to the bank before he comes to his senses.

SHEN TE: I can pay you for the washing without any check.

MRS. SHIN: What? You're not going to cash it just because you might have to marry him? Are you crazy? Men like him *want* to be led by the nose! Are you still thinking of that flyer? All Yellow Street knows how he treated you!

SHEN TE:

When I heard his cunning laugh, I was afraid

But when I saw the holes in his shoes, I loved him dearly.

MRS. SHIN: Defending that good for nothing after all that's happened!

SHEN TE (*staggering as she holds some of the washing*): Oh!

MRS. SHIN (*taking the washing from her, dryly*): So you feel dizzy when you stretch and bend? There couldn't be a little visitor on the way? If that's it, you can forget Mr. Shu Fu's blank check: it wasn't meant for a christening present!

(*She goes to the back with a basket.* SHEN TE's *eyes follow* MRS. SHIN *for a moment. Then she looks down at her own body, feels her stomach, and a great joy comes into her eyes.*)

SHEN TE: O joy! A new human being is on the way. The world awaits him. In the cities the people say: he's got to be reckoned with, this new human being! (*She imagines a little boy to be present, and introduces him to the audience.*)

This is my son, the well-known flyer!
Say: Welcome
To the conqueror of unknown mountains and unreachable regions
Who brings us our mail across the impassable deserts!

(*She leads him up and down by the hand.*) Take a look at the world, my son. That's a tree. Tree, yes. Say: "Hello, tree!" And bow. Like this. (*She bows.*) Now you know each other. And, look, here comes the Water Seller. He's a friend, give him your hand. A cup of fresh water for my little son, please. Yes, it *is* a warm day. (*Handing the cup.*) Oh dear, a policeman, we'll have to make a circle round *him*. Perhaps we can pick a few cherries over there in the rich Mr. Pung's garden. But we mustn't be seen. You want cherries? Just like children with fathers. No, no, you can't go straight at them like that. Don't pull. We must learn to be reasonable. Well, have it your own way. (*She has let him make for the cherries.*) Can you reach? Where to put them? Your mouth is the best place. (*She tries one herself.*) Mmm, they're good. But the policeman, we must run! (*They run.*) Yes, back to the street. Calm now, so no one will notice us. (*Walking the street with her child, she sings.*)

Once a plum — 'twas in Japan —
Made a conquest of a man
But the man's turn soon did come
For he gobbled up the plum

(*Enter* WONG, *with a* CHILD *by the hand. He coughs.*)

SHEN TE: Wong!

WONG: It's about the Carpenter, Shen Te. He's lost his shop, and he's been drinking. His children are on the streets. This is one. Can you help?

SHEN TE (*to the child*): Come here, little man. (*Takes him down to the footlights. To the audience.*)

You there! A man is asking you for shelter!
A man of tomorrow says: what about today?
His friend the conqueror, whom you know,
Is his advocate!

(*To* WONG.) He can live in Mr. Shu Fu's cabins. I may have to go there myself. I'm going to have a baby. That's a secret — don't tell

Yang Sun — we'd only be in his way. Can you find the Carpenter for me?

WONG: I knew you'd think of something. (*To the* CHILD.) Goodbye, son, I'm going for your father.

SHEN TE: What about your hand, Wong? I wanted to help, but my cousin . . .

WONG: Oh, I can get along with one hand, don't worry. (*He shows how he can handle his pole with his left hand alone.*)

SHEN TE: But your right hand! Look, take this cart, sell everything that's on it, and go to the doctor with the money . . .

WONG: She's still good. But first I'll bring the Carpenter. I'll pick up the cart when I get back. (*Exit* WONG.)

SHEN TE (*to the* CHILD): Sit down over here, son, till your father comes.

(*The* CHILD *sits crosslegged on the ground. Enter the* HUSBAND *and* WIFE, *each dragging a large, full sack.*)

WIFE (*furtively*): You're alone, Shen Te, dear?

(SHEN TE *nods. The* WIFE *beckons to the* NEPHEW *offstage. He comes on with another sack.*)

Your cousin's away?

(SHEN TE *nods.*)

He's not coming back?

SHEN TE: No. I'm giving up the shop.

WIFE: That's why we're here. We want to know if we can leave these things in your new home. Will you do us this favor?

SHEN TE: Why, yes, I'd be glad to.

HUSBAND (*cryptically*): And if anyone asks about them, say they're yours.

SHEN TE: Would anyone ask?

WIFE (*with a glance back at her* HUSBAND): Oh, someone might. The police, for instance. They don't seem to like us. Where can we put it?

SHEN TE: Well, I'd rather not get in any more trouble . . .

WIFE: Listen to her! The good woman of Setzuan!

(SHEN TE *is silent.*)

HUSBAND: There's enough tobacco in those sacks to give us a new start in life. We could have our own tobacco factory!

SHEN TE (*slowly*): You'll have to put them in the back room.

(*The sacks are taken offstage, where the* CHILD *is left alone. Shyly glancing about him, he goes to the garbage can, starts playing with the contents, and eating some of the scraps. The others return.*)

WIFE: We're counting on you, Shen Te!

SHEN TE: Yes. (*She sees the* CHILD *and is shocked.*)

HUSBAND: We'll see you in Mr. Shu Fu's cabins.

NEPHEW: The day after tomorrow.

SHEN TE: Yes. Now, go. Go! I'm not feeling well.

(*Exeunt all three, virtually pushed off.*)

He is eating the refuse in the garbage can!
Only look at his little grey mouth!

(*Pause. Music.*)

As this is the world *my* son will enter
I will study to defend him.
To be good to you, my son,
I shall be a tigress to all others
If I have to.
And I shall have to.

(*She starts to go.*) One more time, then. I hope really the last.

(*Exit* SHEN TE, *taking* SHUI TA'S *trousers.* MRS. SHIN *enters and watches her with marked interest. Enter the* SISTER-IN-LAW *and the* GRANDFATHER.)

SISTER-IN-LAW: So it's true, the shop has closed down. And the furniture's in the back yard. It's the end of the road!

MRS. SHIN (*pompously*): The fruit of high living, selfishness, and sensuality! Down the primrose path to Mr. Shu Fu's cabins — with you!

SISTER-IN-LAW: Cabins? Rat holes! He gave them to us because his soap supplies only went mouldy there!

(*Enter the* UNEMPLOYED MAN.)

UNEMPLOYED MAN: Shen Te is moving?

SISTER-IN-LAW: Yes. She was sneaking away.

MRS. SHIN: She's ashamed of herself, and no wonder!

UNEMPLOYED MAN: Tell her to call Mr. Shui Ta or she's done for this time!

SISTER-IN-LAW: Tell her to call Mr. Shui Ta or *we're* done for this time!

(*Enter* WONG *and* CARPENTER, *the latter with a* CHILD *on each hand.*)

CARPENTER: So we'll have a roof over our heads for a change!

MRS. SHIN: Roof? Whose roof?

CARPENTER: Mr. Shu Fu's cabins. And we have little Feng to thank for it. (FENG, *we find, is the name of the child already there; his* FATHER *now takes him. To the other two.*) Bow to your little brother, you two! (*The* CARPENTER *and the two new arrivals bow to* FENG.)

(*Enter* SHUI TA.)

UNEMPLOYED MAN: Sst! Mr. Shui Ta!

(*Pause.*)

SHUI TA: And what is this crowd here for, may I ask?

WONG: How do you do, Mr. Shui Ta? This is the Carpenter. Miss Shen Te promised him space in Mr. Shu Fu's cabins.

SHUI TA: That will not be possible.

CARPENTER: We can't go there after all?

SHUI TA: All the space is needed for other purposes.

SISTER-IN-LAW: You mean we have to get out? But we've got nowhere to go.

SHUI TA: Miss Shen Te finds it possible to provide employment. If the proposition interests you, you may stay in the cabins.

SISTER-IN-LAW (*with distaste*): You mean *work*? Work for Miss Shen Te?

SHUI TA: Making tobacco, yes. There are three bales here already. Would you like to get them?

SISTER-IN-LAW (*trying to bluster*): We have our own tobacco! We were in the tobacco business before you were born!

SHUI TA (*to the* CARPENTER *and the* UNEMPLOYED MAN): You *don't* have your own tobacco. What about you?

(*The* CARPENTER *and the* UNEMPLOYED MAN *get the point, and go for the sacks. Enter* MRS. MI TZU.)

MRS. MI TZU: Mr. Shui Ta? I've brought you your three hundred silver dollars.

SHUI TA: I'll sign your lease instead. I've decided not to sell.

MRS. MI TZU: What? You don't need the money for that flyer?

SHUI TA: No.

MRS. MI TZU: And you can pay six months' rent?

SHUI TA (*takes the barber's blank check from the cart and fills it out*): Here is a check for ten thousand silver dollars. On Mr. Shu Fu's account. Look! (*He shows her the signature on the check.*) Your six months' rent will be in your hands by seven this evening. And now, if you'll excuse me.

MRS. MI TZU: So it's Mr. Shu Fu now. The flyer has been given his walking papers. These modern girls! In my day they'd have said she was flighty. That poor, deserted Mr. Yang Sun!

(*Exit* MRS. MI TZU. *The* CARPENTER *and the* UNEMPLOYED MAN *drag the three sacks back on the stage.*)

CARPENTER (*to* SHUI TA): I don't know why I'm doing this for you.

SHUI TA: Perhaps your children want to eat, Mr. Carpenter.

SISTER-IN-LAW (*catching sight of the sacks*): Was my brother-in-law here?

MRS. SHIN: Yes, he was.

SISTER-IN-LAW: I thought as much. I know those sacks! That's our tobacco!

SHUI TA: Really? I thought it came from my back room? Shall we consult the police on the point?

SISTER-IN-LAW (*defeated*): No.

SHUI TA: Perhaps you will show me the way to Mr. Shu Fu's cabins?

(SHUI TA *goes off, followed by the* CARPENTER *and his two older children, the* SISTER-IN-LAW, *the* GRANDFATHER, *and the* UNEMPLOYED MAN. *Each of the last three drags a sack. Enter* OLD MAN *and* OLD WOMAN.)

MRS. SHIN: A pair of pants — missing from the clothes line one minute — and next minute on the honorable backside of Mr. Shui Ta!

OLD WOMAN: We thought Miss Shen Te was here.

MRS. SHIN (*preoccupied*): Well, she's not.

OLD MAN: There was something she was going to give us.

WONG: She was going to help me too. (*Looking at his hand.*) It'll be too late soon. But she'll be back. This cousin has never stayed long.

MRS. SHIN (*approaching a conclusion*): No, he hasn't, has he?

Scene 7A

(*The sewer pipe:* WONG *asleep. In his dream, he tells the* GODS *his fears. The* GODS *seem tired from all their travels. They stop for a moment and look over their shoulders at the Water Seller.*)

WONG: Illustrious ones, I've been having a bad dream. Our beloved Shen Te was in great distress in the rushes down by the rivers — the spot where the bodies of suicides are washed up. She kept staggering and holding her head down as if she was carrying something and it was dragging her down into the mud. When I called out to her, she said she had to take your Book of Rules to the other side, and not get it wet, or the ink would all come off. You had talked to her about the virtues, you know, the time she gave you shelter in Setzuan.

THIRD GOD: Well, but what do you suggest, my dear Wong?

WONG: Maybe a little relaxation of the rules, Benevolent One, in view of the bad times.

THIRD GOD: As for instance?

WONG: Well, um, good-will, for instance, might do instead of love?

THIRD GOD: I'm afraid that would create new problems.

WONG: Or, instead of justice, good sportsmanship?

THIRD GOD: That would only mean more work.

WONG: Instead of honor, outward propriety?

THIRD GOD: Still more work! No, no! The rules will have to stand, my dear Wong!

(*Wearily shaking their heads, all three journey on.*)

SCENE 8

(SHUI TA's *tobacco factory in* SHU FU's *cabins. Huddled together behind bars, several families, mostly women and children. Among these people the* SISTER-IN-LAW, *the* GRANDFATHER, *the* CARPENTER, *and his three children. Enter* MRS. YANG *followed by* YANG SUN.)

MRS. YANG (*to the audience*): There's something I just *have* to tell you: strength and wisdom are wonderful things. The strong and wise Mr. Shui Ta has transformed my son from a dissipated good-for-nothing into a model citizen. As you may have heard, Mr. Shui Ta opened a small tobacco factory near the cattle runs. It flourished. Three months ago — I shall never forget it — I asked for an appointment, and Mr. Shui Ta agreed to see us — me and my son. I can see him now as he came through the door to meet us . . .

(*Enter* SHUI TA, *from a door.*)

SHUI TA: What can I do for you, Mrs. Yang?

MRS. YANG: This morning the police came to the house. We find you've brought an action for breach of promise of marriage. In the name of Shen Te. You also claim that Sun came by two hundred silver dollars by improper means.

SHUI TA: That is correct.

MRS. YANG: Mr. Shui Ta, the money's all gone. When the Peking job didn't materialize, he ran through it all in three days. I know he's a good-for-nothing. He sold my furniture. He was moving to Peking without me. Miss Shen Te thought highly of him at one time.

SHUI TA: What do *you* say, Mr. Yang Sun?

YANG SUN: The money's gone.

SHUI TA (*to* MRS. YANG): Mrs. Yang, in consideration of my cousin's incomprehensible weakness for your son, I am prepared to give him another chance. He can have a job — here. The two hundred silver dollars will be taken out of his wages.

YANG SUN: So it's the factory or jail?

SHUI TA: Take your choice.

YANG SUN: May I speak with Shen Te?

SHUI TA: You may not.

(*Pause.*)

YANG SUN (*sullenly*): Show me where to go.

MRS. YANG: Mr. Shui Ta, you are kindness itself: the gods will reward you! (*To* YANG SUN.) And honest work will make a man of you, my boy.

(YANG SUN *follows* SHUI TA *into the factory.* MRS. YANG *comes down again to the footlights.*)

Actually, honest work didn't agree with him — at first. And he got no opportunity to distinguish himself till — in the third week — when the wages were being paid. . . .

(SHUI TA *has a bag of money. Standing next to his foreman — the former* UNEMPLOYED MAN — *he counts out the wages. It is* YANG SUN's *turn.*)

UNEMPLOYED MAN (*reading*): Carpenter, six silver dollars. Yang Sun, six silver dollars.

YANG SUN (*quietly*): Excuse me, sir. I don't think it can be more than five. May I see? (*He takes the foreman's list.*) It says six working days. But that's a mistake, sir. I took a day off for court business. And I won't take what I haven't earned, however miserable the pay is!

UNEMPLOYED MAN: Yang Sun. Five silver dollars. (*To* SHUI TA.) A rare case, Mr. Shui Ta!

SHUI TA: How is it the book says six when it should say five?

UNEMPLOYED MAN: I must've made a mistake, Mr. Shui Ta. (*With a look at* YANG SUN.) It won't happen again.

SHUI TA (*taking* YANG SUN *aside*): You don't hold back, do you? You give your all to the firm. You're even honest. Do the foreman's mistakes always favor the workers?

YANG SUN: He does have . . . friends.

SHUI TA: Thank you. May I offer you any little recompense?

YANG SUN: Give me a trial period of one week, and I'll prove my intelligence is worth more to you than my strength.

MRS. YANG (*still down at the footlights*): Fighting words, fighting words! That evening, I said to Sun: "If you're a flyer, then fly, my falcon! Rise in the world!" And he got to be foreman. Yes, in Mr. Shui Ta's tobacco factory, he worked real miracles.

(*We see* YANG SUN *with his legs apart standing behind the workers who are handing along a basket of raw tobacco above their heads.*)

YANG SUN: Faster! Faster! You, there, d'you think you can just stand around now you're not foreman any more? It'll be your job to lead us in song. Sing!

(UNEMPLOYED MAN *starts singing. The others join in the refrain.*)

Song of the Eighth Elephant

Chang had seven elephants — all much the same —
  But then there was Little Brother
The seven, they were wild, Little Brother, he was tame
  And to guard them Chang chose Little Brother
    Run faster!
    Mr. Chang has a forest park
    Which must be cleared before tonight
    And already it's growing dark!

When the seven elephants cleared that forest park
  Mr. Chang rode high on Little Brother
While the seven toiled and moiled till dark
  On his big behind sat Little Brother
    Dig faster!
    Mr. Chang has a forest park
    Which must be cleared before tonight
    And already it's growing dark!

And the seven elephants worked many an hour
  Till none of them could work another
Old Chang, he looked sour, on the seven, he did glower
  But gave a pound of rice to Little Brother
    What was that?
    Mr. Chang has a forest park
    Which must be cleared before tonight
    And already it's growing dark!

And the seven elephants hadn't any tusks
    The one that had the tusks was Little Brother!
Seven are no match for one, if the one has a gun!
    How old Chang did laugh at Little Brother!
      Keep on digging!
      Mr. Chang has a forest park
      Which must be cleared before tonight
      And already it's growing dark!

(*Smoking a cigar,* SHUI TA *strolls by.* YANG SUN, *laughing, has joined in the refrain of the third stanza and speeded up the tempo of the last stanza by clapping his hands.*)

MRS. YANG: And that's why I say: strength and wisdom are wonderful things. It took the strong and wise Mr. Shui Ta to bring out the best in Yang Sun. A real superior man is like a bell. If you ring it, it rings, and if you don't, it don't, as the saying is.

SCENE 9

(SHEN TE'S *shop, now an office with club chairs and fine carpets. It is raining.* SHUI TA, *now fat, is just dismissing the* OLD MAN *and* OLD WOMAN. MRS. SHIN, *in obviously new clothes, looks on, smirking.*)

SHUI TA: No! I can NOT tell you when we expect her back.

OLD WOMAN: The two hundred silver dollars came today. In an envelope. There was no letter, but it must be from Shen Te. We want to write and thank her. May we have her address?

SHUI TA: I'm afraid I haven't got it.

OLD MAN (*pulling* OLD WOMAN'S *sleeve*): Let's be going.

OLD WOMAN: She's got to come back some time! (*They move off, uncertainly, worried.* SHUI TA *bows.*)

MRS. SHIN: They lost the carpet shop because they couldn't pay their taxes. The money arrived too late.

SHUI TA: They could have come to me.

MRS. SHIN: People don't like coming to you.

SHUI TA (*sits suddenly, one hand to his head*): I'm dizzy.

MRS. SHIN: After all, you *are* in your seventh month. But old Mrs. Shin will be there in your hour of trial! (*She cackles feebly.*)

SHUI TA (*in a stifled voice*): Can I count on that?

MRS. SHIN: We all have our price, and mine won't be too high for the great Mr. Shui Ta! (*She opens* SHUI TA'S *collar.*)

SHUI TA: It's for the child's sake. All of this.

MRS. SHIN: "All for the child," of course.

SHUI TA: I'm so fat. People must notice.

MRS. SHIN: Oh no, they think it's 'cause you're rich.

SHUI TA (*more feelingly*): What will happen to the child?

MRS. SHIN: You ask that nine times a day. Why, it'll have the best that money can buy!

SHUI TA: He must never see Shui Ta.

MRS. SHIN: Oh, no. Always Shen Te.

SHUI TA: What about the neighbors? There are rumors, aren't there?

MRS. SHIN: As long as Mr. Shu Fu doesn't find out, there's nothing to worry about. Drink this.

(*Enter* YANG SUN *in a smart business suit, and carrying a business-man's brief case.* SHUI TA *is more or less in* MRS. SHIN'S *arms.*)

YANG SUN (*surprised*): I seem to be in the way.

SHUI TA (*ignoring this, rises with an effort*): Till tomorrow, Mrs. Shin.

(MRS. SHIN *leaves with a smile, putting her new gloves on.*)

YANG SUN: Gloves now! She couldn't be fleecing you? And since when did *you* have a private life? (*Taking a paper from the brief case.*) You haven't been at your best lately, and things are getting out of hand. The police want to close us down. They say that at the most they can only permit twice the lawful number of workers.

SHUI TA (*evasively*): The cabins are quite good enough.

YANG SUN: For the workers maybe, not for the tobacco. They're too damp. We must take over some of Mrs. Mi Tzu's buildings.

SHUI TA: Her price is double what I can pay.

YANG SUN: Not unconditionally. If she has me to stroke her knees she'll come down.

SHUI TA: I'll never agree to that.

YANG SUN: What's wrong? Is it the rain? You get so irritable whenever it rains.

SHUI TA: Never! I will never . . .

YANG SUN: Mrs. Mi Tzu'll be here in five minutes. *You* fix it. And Shu Fu will be with her. . . . What's all that noise?

(*During the above dialogue,* WONG *is heard off stage calling:* "The good Shen Te, where is she? Which of you has seen Shen Te, good people? Where is Shen Te?" *A knock. Enter* WONG.)

WONG: Mr. Shui Ta, I've come to ask when Miss Shen Te will be back, it's six months now . . . There are rumors. People say something's happened to her.

SHUI TA: I'm busy. Come back next week.

WONG (*excited*): In the morning there was always rice on her doorstep — for the needy. It's been there again lately!

SHUI TA: And what do people conclude from this?

WONG: That Shen Te is still in Setzuan! She's been . . . (*He breaks off.*)

SHUI TA: She's been what? Mr. Wong, if you're Shen Te's friend, talk a little less about her, that's my advice to you.

WONG: I don't want your advice! Before she disappeared, Miss Shen Te told me something very important — she's pregnant!

YANG SUN: What? What was that?

SHUI TA (*quickly*): The man is lying.

WONG: A good woman isn't so easily forgotten, Mr. Shui Ta.

(*He leaves.* SHUI TA *goes quickly into the back room.*)

YANG SUN (*to the audience*): Shen Te pregnant? So that's why. Her cousin sent her away, so I wouldn't get wind of it. I have a son, a Yang appears on the scene, and what happens? Mother and child vanish into thin air! That scoundrel, that unspeakable . . . (*The sound of sobbing is heard from the back room.*) What was that? Someone sobbing? Who was it? Mr. Shui Ta the Tobacco King doesn't weep his heart out. And where does the rice come from that's on the doorstep in the morning?

(SHUI TA *returns. He goes to the door and looks out into the rain.*)

Where is she?

SHUI TA: Sh! It's nine o'clock. But the rain's so heavy, you can't hear a thing.

YANG SUN: What do you want to hear?

SHUI TA: The mail plane.

YANG SUN: What?

SHUI TA: I've been told *you* wanted to fly at one time. Is that all forgotten?

YANG SUN: Flying mail is night work. I prefer the daytime. And the firm is very dear to me — after all it belongs to my ex-fiancée, even if she's not around. And she's not, is she?

SHUI TA: What do you mean by that?

YANG SUN: Oh, well, let's say I haven't altogether — lost interest.

SHUI TA: My cousin might like to know that.

YANG SUN: I might not be indifferent — if I found she was being kept under lock and key.

SHUI TA: By whom?

YANG SUN: By you.

SHUI TA: What could you do about it?

YANG SUN: I could submit for discussion — my position in the firm.

SHUI TA: You are now my Manager. In return for a more appropriate position, you might agree to drop the enquiry into your ex-fiancée's whereabouts?

YANG SUN: I might.

SHUI TA: What position *would* be more appropriate?

YANG SUN: The one at the top.

SHUI TA: My own? (*Silence.*) And if I preferred to throw you out on your neck?

YANG SUN: I'd come back on my feet. With suitable escort.

SHUI TA: The police?

YANG SUN: The police.

SHUI TA: And when the police found no one?

YANG SUN: I might ask them not to overlook the back room. (*Ending the pretense.*) In short, Mr. Shui Ta, my interest in this young woman has not been officially terminated. I should like to see more of her. (*Into* SHUI TA's *face.*) Besides, she's pregnant and needs a friend. (*He moves to the door.*) I shall talk about it with the Water Seller. (*Exit.*)

(SHUI TA *is rigid for a moment, then he quickly goes into the back room. He returns with* SHEN TE's *belongings: underwear, etc. He takes a long look at the shawl of the previous scene. He then wraps the things in a bundle which, upon hearing a noise, he hides under the table. Enter* MRS. MI TZU *and* MR. SHU FU. *They put away their umbrellas and galoshes.*)

MRS. MI TZU: I thought your manager was here, Mr. Shui Ta. He combines charm with business in a way that can only be to the advantage of all of us.

SHU FU: You sent for us, Mr. Shui Ta?

SHUI TA: The factory is in trouble.

SHU FU: It always is.

SHUI TA: The police are threatening to close us down unless I can show that the extension of our facilities is imminent.

SHU FU: Mr. Shui Ta, I'm sick and tired of your constantly expanding projects. I place cabins at your cousin's disposal; you make a factory of them. I hand your cousin a check; you present it. Your cousin disappears and you find the cabins too small and talk of yet more . . .

SHUI TA: Mr. Shu Fu, I'm authorized to inform you that Miss Shen Te's return is now imminent.

SHU FU: Imminent? It's becoming his favorite word.

MRS. MI TZU: Yes, what does it mean?

SHUI TA: Mrs. Mi Tzu, I can pay you exactly half what you asked for your buildings. Are you ready to inform the police that I am taking them over?

MRS. MI TZU: Certainly, if I can take over your manager.

SHU FU: What?

MRS. MI TZU: He's so efficient.

SHUI TA: I'm afraid I need Mr. Yang Sun.

MRS. MI TZU: So do I.

SHUI TA: He will call on you tomorrow.

SHU FU: So much the better. With Shen Te likely to turn up at any moment, the presence of that young man is hardly in good taste.

SHUI TA: So we have reached a settlement. In what was once the good Shen Te's little shop we are laying the foundations for the great Mr. Shui Ta's twelve magnificent super tobacco markets. You will bear in mind that though they call me the Tobacco King of Setzuan, it is my cousin's interests that have been served . . .

VOICES (*off*): The police, the police! Going to the tobacco shop! Something must have happened! (*etcetera.*)

(*Enter* YANG SUN, WONG, *and the* POLICEMAN.)

POLICEMAN: Quiet there, quiet, quiet! (*They quiet down.*) I'm sorry, Mr. Shui Ta, but there's a report that you've been depriving Miss Shen Te of her freedom. Not that I believe all I hear, but the whole city's in an uproar.

SHUI TA: That's a lie.

POLICEMAN: Mr. Yang Sun has testified that he heard someone sobbing in the back room.

SHU FU: Mrs. Mi Tzu and myself will testify that no one here has been sobbing.

MRS. MI TZU: We have been quietly smoking our cigars.

POLICEMAN: Mr. Shui Ta, I'm afraid I shall have to take a look at that room. (*He does so. The room is empty.*) No one there, of course, sir.

YANG SUN: But I heard sobbing. What's that? (*He finds the clothes.*)

WONG: Those are Shen Te's things. (*To crowd.*) Shen Te's clothes are here!

VOICES (*Off. In sequence*): Shen Te's clothes! They've been found under the table! Body of murdered girl still missing! Tobacco King suspected!

POLICEMAN: Mr. Shui Ta, unless you can tell us where the girl is, I'll have to ask you to come along.

SHUI TA: I do not know.

POLICEMAN: I can't say how sorry I am, Mr. Shui Ta. (*He shows him the door.*)

SHUI TA: Everything will be cleared up in no time. There are still judges in Setzuan.

YANG SUN: I heard sobbing!

Scene 9A

(WONG'S *den. For the last time, the* GODS *appear to the Water Seller in his dream. They have changed and show signs of a long journey, extreme fatigue, and plenty of mishaps. The* FIRST *no longer has a hat; the* THIRD *has lost a leg; all* THREE *are barefoot.*)

WONG: Illustrious ones, at last you're here. Shen Te's been gone for months and today her cousin's been arrested. They think he murdered her to get the shop. But I had a dream and in this dream Shen Te said her cousin was keeping her prisoner. You must find her for us, illustrious ones!

FIRST GOD: We've found very few good people anywhere, and even they didn't keep it up. Shen Te is still the only one that stayed good.

SECOND GOD: If she *has* stayed good.

WONG: Certainly she has. But she's vanished.

FIRST GOD: That's the last straw. All is lost!

SECOND GOD: A little moderation, dear colleague!

FIRST GOD (*plaintively*): What's the good of moderation now? If she can't be found, we'll have to resign! The world is a terrible place! Nothing but misery, vulgarity, and waste! Even the countryside isn't what it used to be. The trees are getting their heads chopped off by telephone wires, and there's such a noise from all the gunfire, and I can't stand those heavy clouds of smoke, and —

THIRD GOD: The place is absolutely unlivable! Good intentions bring people to the brink of the abyss, and good deeds push them over the edge. I'm afraid our book of rules is destined for the scrap heap —

SECOND GOD: It's people! They're a worthless lot!

THIRD GOD: The world is too cold!

SECOND GOD: It's people! They are too weak!

FIRST GOD: Dignity, dear colleagues, dignity! Never despair! As for this world, didn't we agree that we only have to find one human being who can stand the place? Well, we found her. True, we lost her again. We must find her again, that's all! And at once!

(*They disappear.*)

SCENE 10

(*Courtroom. Groups:* SHU FU *and* MRS. MI TZU; YANG SUN *and* MRS. YANG; WONG, *the* CARPENTER, *the* GRANDFATHER, *the* NIECE, *the* OLD MAN, *the* OLD WOMAN; MRS. SHIN, *the* POLICEMAN; *the* UNEMPLOYED MAN, *the* SISTER-IN-LAW.)

OLD MAN: So much power isn't good for one man.

UNEMPLOYED MAN: And he's going to open twelve super tobacco markets!

WIFE: One of the judges is a friend of Mr. Shu Fu's.

SISTER-IN-LAW: Another one accepted a present from Mr. Shui Ta only last night. A great fat goose.

OLD WOMAN (*to* WONG): And Shen Te is nowhere to be found.

WONG: Only the gods will ever know the truth.

POLICEMAN: Order in the court! My lords the judges!

(*Enter the* THREE GODS *in judges' robes. We overhear their conversation as they pass along the footlights to their bench.*)

THIRD GOD: We'll never get away with it, our certificates were so badly forged.

SECOND GOD: My predecessor's "sudden indigestion" will certainly cause comment.

FIRST GOD: But he *had* just eaten a whole goose.

UNEMPLOYED MAN: Look at that! *New* judges!

WONG: New judges. And what good ones!

(*The* THIRD GOD *hears this, and turns to smile at* WONG. *The* GODS *sit. The* FIRST GOD *beats on the bench with his gavel. The* POLICEMAN *brings in* SHUI TA *who walks with lordly steps. He is whistled at.*)

POLICEMAN (*to* SHUI TA): Be prepared for a surprise. The judges have been changed.

(SHUI TA *turns quickly round, looks at them, and staggers.*)

NIECE: What's the matter now?

WIFE: The great Tobacco King nearly fainted.

HUSBAND: Yes, as soon as he saw the new judges.

WONG: Does *he* know who they are?

(SHUI TA *picks himself up, and the proceedings open.*)

FIRST GOD: Defendant Shui Ta, you are accused of doing away with your cousin Shen Te in order to take possession of her business. Do you plead guilty or not guilty?

SHUI TA: Not guilty, my lord.

FIRST GOD (*thumbing through the documents of the case*): The first witness is the Policeman. I shall ask him to tell us something of the respective reputations of Miss Shen Te and Mr. Shui Ta.

POLICEMAN: Miss Shen Te was a young lady who aimed to please, my lord. She liked to live and let live, as the saying goes. Mr. Shui Ta, on the other hand, is a man of principle. Though the generosity of Miss Shen Te forced him at times to abandon half measures, unlike the girl, he was always on the side of the law, my lord. One time, he even unmasked a gang of thieves to whom his too trustful cousin had given shelter. The evidence, in short, my lord, proves that Mr. Shui Ta was *incapable* of the crime of which he stands accused!

FIRST GOD: I see. And are there others who could testify along, shall we say, the same lines?

(SHU FU *rises.*)

POLICEMAN (*whispering to* GODS): Mr. Shu Fu — a very important person.

FIRST GOD (*inviting him to speak*): Mr. Shu Fu!

SHU FU: Mr. Shui Ta is a businessman, my lord. Need I say more?

FIRST GOD: Yes.

SHU FU: Very well, I will. He is Vice President of the Council of Commerce and is about to be elected a Justice of the Peace. (*He returns to his seat.*)

WONG: Elected! He gave him the job!

(*With a gesture the* FIRST GOD *asks who* MRS. MI TZU *is.*)

POLICEMAN: Another very important person. Mrs. Mi Tzu.

FIRST GOD (*inviting her to speak*): Mrs. Mi Tzu!

MRS. MI TZU: My lord, as Chairman of the Committee on Social Work, I wish to call attention to just a couple of eloquent facts: Mr. Shui Ta not only has erected a model factory with model housing in our city, he is a regular contributor to our home for the disabled. (*She returns to her seat.*)

POLICEMAN (*whispering*): And she's a great friend of the judge that ate the goose!

FIRST GOD (*to the* POLICEMAN): Oh, thank you. What next? (*To the Court, genially.*) Oh, yes. We should find out if any of the evidence is less favorable to the Defendant.

(WONG, *the* CARPENTER, *the* OLD MAN, *the* OLD WOMAN, *the* UN-EMPLOYED MAN, *the* SISTER-IN-LAW, *and the* NIECE *come forward.*)

POLICEMAN (*whispering*): Just the riff raff, my lord.

FIRST GOD (*addressing the* "*riff raff*"): Well, um, riff raff — do you know anything of the Defendant, Mr. Shui Ta?

WONG: Too much, my lord.

UNEMPLOYED MAN: What don't we know, my lord?

CARPENTER: He ruined us.

SISTER-IN-LAW: He's a cheat.

NIECE: Liar.

WIFE: Thief.

BOY: Blackmailer.

BROTHER: Murderer.

FIRST GOD: Thank you. We should now let the Defendant state his point of view.

SHUI TA: I only came on the scene when Shen Te was in danger of losing what I had understood was a gift from the gods. Because I did the filthy jobs which someone had to do, they hate me. My activities were held down to the minimum, my lord.

SISTER-IN-LAW: He had us arrested!

SHUI TA: Certainly. You stole from the bakery!

SISTER-IN-LAW: Such concern for the bakery! You didn't want the shop for yourself, I suppose!

SHUI TA: I didn't want the shop overrun with parasites.

SISTER-IN-LAW: We had nowhere else to go.

SHUI TA: There were too many of you.

WONG: What about this old couple: Were *they* parasites?

OLD MAN: We lost our shop because of you!

SISTER-IN-LAW: And we gave your cousin money!

SHUI TA: My cousin's fiancé was a flyer. The money had to go to *him.*

WONG: Did you care whether he flew or not? Did you care whether she married him or not? You wanted her to marry someone else! (*He points at* SHU FU.)

SHUI TA: The flyer unexpectedly turned out to be a scoundrel.

YANG SUN (*jumping up*): Which was the reason you made him your Manager?

SHUI TA: Later on he improved.

WONG: And when he improved, you sold him to her? (*He points out* MRS. MI TZU.)

SHUI TA: She wouldn't let me have her premises unless she had him to stroke her knees!

MRS. MI TZU: What? The man's a pathological liar. (*To him.*) Don't mention my property to me as long as you live! Murderer! (*She rustles off, in high dudgeon.*)

YANG SUN (*pushing in*): My lord, I wish to speak for the Defendant.

SISTER-IN-LAW: Naturally. He's your employer.

UNEMPLOYED MAN: And the worst slave driver in the country.

MRS. YANG: That's a lie! My lord, Mr. Shui Ta is a great man. He . . .

YANG SUN: He's this and he's that, but he is not a murderer, my lord. Just fifteen minutes before his arrest I heard Shen Te's voice in his own back room.

FIRST GOD: Oh? Tell us more!

YANG SUN: I heard sobbing, my lord!

FIRST GOD: But lots of women sob, we've been finding.

YANG SUN: Could I fail to recognize her voice?

SHU FU: No, you made her sob so often yourself, young man!

YANG SUN: Yes. But I also made her happy. Till he (*pointing at* SHUI TA) decided to sell her to you!

SHUI TA: Because you didn't love her.

WONG: Oh, no: it was for the money, my lord!

SHUI TA: And what was the money for, my lord? For the poor! And for Shen Te so she could go on being good!

WONG: For the poor? That he sent to his sweatshops? And why didn't you let Shen Te be good when you signed the big check?

SHUI TA: For the child's sake, my lord.

CARPENTER: What about *my* children? What did he do about them?

(SHUI TA *is silent.*)

WONG: The shop was to be a fountain of goodness. That was the gods' idea. You came and spoiled it!

SHUI TA: If I hadn't, it would have run dry!

MRS. SHIN: There's a lot in that, my lord.

WONG: What have you done with the good Shen Te, bad man? She *was* good, my lords, she was, I swear it! (*He raises his hand in an oath.*)

THIRD GOD: What's happened to your hand, Water Seller?

WONG (*pointing to* SHUI TA): It's all his fault, my lord, *she* was going to send me to a doctor — (*To* SHUI TA.) You were her worst enemy!

SHUI TA: I was her only friend!

WONG: Where is she then? Tell us where your good friend is!

(*The excitement of this exchange has run through the whole crowd.*)

all: Yes, where is she? Where is Shen Te? (*etcetera.*)

shui ta: Shen Te had to go.

wong: Where? Where to?

shui ta: I cannot tell you! I cannot tell you!

all: Why? Why did she have to go away? (*etcetera.*)

wong (*into the din with the first words, but talking on beyond the others*): Why not, why not? Why did she have to go away?

shui ta (*shouting*): Because you'd all have torn her to shreds, that's why! My lords, I have a request. Clear the court! When only the judges remain, I will make a confession.

all (*except* wong, *who is silent, struck by the new turn of events*): So he's guilty? He's confessing! (*etcetera.*)

first god (*using the gavel*): Clear the court!

policeman: Clear the court!

wong: Mr. Shui Ta has met his match this time.

mrs. shin (*with a gesture toward the judges*): You're in for a little surprise.

(*The court is cleared. Silence.*)

shui ta: Illustrious ones!

(*The* gods *look at each other, not quite believing their ears.*)

shui ta: Yes, I recognize you!

second god (*taking matters in hand, sternly*): What have you done with our good woman of Setzuan?

shui ta: I have a terrible confession to make: I am she! (*He takes off his mask, and tears away his clothes.* shen te *stands there.*)

second god: Shen Te!

shen te: Shen Te, yes. Shui Ta *and* Shen Te. Both.

Your injunction
To be good and yet to live
Was a thunderbolt:
It has torn me in two
I can't tell how it was
But to be good to others
And myself at the same time
I could not do it
Your world is not an easy one, illustrious ones!
When we extend our hand to a beggar, he tears it off for us
When we help the lost, we are lost ourselves.
And so
Since not to eat is to die

Who can long refuse to be bad?
As I lay prostrate beneath the weight of good intentions
Ruin stared me in the face
It was when I was unjust that I ate good meat
And hobnobbed with the mighty
Why?
Why are bad deeds rewarded?
Good ones punished?
I enjoyed giving
I truly wished to be the Angel of the Slums
But washed by a foster-mother in the water of the gutter
I developed a sharp eye
The time came when pity was a thorn in my side
And, later, when kind words turned to ashes in my mouth
And anger took over
I became a wolf
Find me guilty, then, illustrious ones,
But know:
All that I have done I did
To help my neighbor
To love my lover
And to keep my little one from want
For your great, godly deeds, I was too poor, too small.

(*Pause.*)

FIRST GOD (*shocked*): Don't go on making yourself miserable, Shen Te! We're overjoyed to have found you!

SHEN TE: I'm telling you I'm the bad man who committed all those crimes!

FIRST GOD (*using — or failing to use — his ear trumpet*): The good woman who did all those good deeds?

SHEN TE: Yes, but the bad man too!

FIRST GOD (*as if something had dawned*): Unfortunate coincidences! Heartless neighbors!

THIRD GOD (*shouting in his ear*): But how is she to continue?

FIRST GOD: Continue? Well, she's a strong, healthy girl . . .

SECOND GOD: You didn't hear what she said!

FIRST GOD: I heard every word! She is confused, that's all! (*He begins to bluster.*) And what about this book of rules — we can't renounce our rules, can we? (*More quietly.*) Should the world be changed? How? By whom? The world should *not* be changed! (*At a sign from him, the lights turn pink, and music plays.*)

And now the hour of parting is at hand.
Dost thou behold, Shen Te, yon fleecy cloud?
It is our chariot. At a sign from me
'Twill come and take us back from whence we came
Above the azure vault and silver stars . . .

SHEN TE: No! Don't go, illustrious ones!
FIRST GOD:

Our cloud has landed now in yonder field
From whence it will transport us back to heaven.
Farewell, Shen Te, let not thy courage fail thee . . .

(*Exeunt* GODS.)

SHEN TE: What about the old couple? They've lost their shop! What about the Water Seller and his hand? And I've got to defend myself against the barber, because I don't love him! And against Sun, because I do love him! How? How?

(SHEN TE'S *eyes follow the* GODS *as they are imagined to step into a cloud which rises and moves forward over the orchestra and up beyond the balcony.*)

FIRST GOD (*from on high*): We have faith in you, Shen Te!
SHEN TE: There'll be a child. And he'll have to be fed. I can't stay here. Where shall I go?
FIRST GOD: Continue to be good, good woman of Setzuan!
SHEN TE: I need my bad cousin!
FIRST GOD: But not very often!
SHEN TE: Once a week at least!
FIRST GOD: Once a month will be quite enough!
SHEN TE (*shrieking*): No, no! Help!

(*But the cloud continues to recede as the* GODS *sing.*)

Valedictory Hymn

What rapture, oh, it is to know
   A good thing when you see it
And having seen a good thing, oh,
   What rapture 'tis to flee it

Be good, sweet maid of Setzuan
   Let Shui Ta be clever
Departing, we forget the man
   Remember your endeavor

Because through all the length of days
   Her goodness faileth never

Sing hallelujah! May Shen Te's
Good name live on forever!

SHEN TE: Help!

◖◗ BRECHT WROTE *The Good Woman of Setzuan* between 1938
and 1941. Directly, the play does not reflect the momentous political
and military events contemporary with its genesis, but its underlying
cynicism and flippant, almost gay, despair may perhaps be said to be
typical of at least one side of the modern temper. For all its quaint
and charming Chinese ways, its humor of incident and character, its
verbal high spirits, it is an acid rather than a pleasant play. Its issues
are ultimately metaphysical and deadly serious. If we do not sense
this, it may be because we are misled by the play's form.

Brecht's dramatic art differs from all the three main styles of
modern drama. It does not belong with the tight and tidy catas-
trophe-centered drama of the Greeks, reintroduced in modern times
by Ibsen; nor with the plotless and apparently diffuse plays of mood
and atmosphere that characterize the school of Chekhov; nor with
the fluid theatricality and surrealistic fantasies of Strindbergian expressionism. It has more in common with Shakespearean drama, developing its plot on a broad and crowded canvas and by a time
scheme unconfined by the rigors of the retrospective technique and
unities. Since telling a story is the chief artistic end of this drama it
has been called (by Brecht himself) the "epic" theater — epic in
the sense not of nobly heroic and magnificent but simply of "narrative." It breaks with Ibsenite naturalism also in its frank disavowal
of illusionism. The spectator, says Brecht, should not watch a play in
a trance of gripping make-believe; the play has a social function to
perform, and to that end it must engage the spectator's mind as well
as his senses and his emotions. The superbly simple expository device of Wang's opening speech, the characters' direct address to the
audience, the spontaneous songs, the flashbacks and the "A" scenes,
the quick sequence of scenes, all these remind us we are watching
a spectacle that tells a story for our thoughtful enjoyment and moral
benefit, and not life being lived. Life-likeness and plausibility are
not esthetic issues. The argument that it is psychologically uncon-
vincing that a character as good as Shen Te at will can assume and
maintain the attitudes and practices of hard and unscrupulous Shui
Ta refuses to take the play on Brecht's terms. In order to preserve
the sovereignty of our reason Brecht wants us *not* to "identify"
with the characters. Though the two playwrights certainly have

little enough in common in most other respects, Brecht and Yeats share a belief in the value of establishing esthetic distance between play and spectator.

All this is not to deny *The Good Woman of Setzuan* a quality of realism obviously lacking in Strindberg's nightmare and in Yeats's emblematic tableau. Brecht's Setzuan may be visited by traveling gods, but it is also a town of heat and stench, pilferers and prostitutes, unpaid bills and unfed children. And what happens in it, despite its unusualness, has the austere coherence of causality in the real world.

Perhaps the best term for such a play is Brecht's own. He called it "a parable play," that is, a kind of fable, a story that insists less on being true in any literal sense than on having significance and hence truth beyond its surface facts. It is neither symbolical nor allegorical, for we are not expected to transliterate people and events back into another level or dimension of meaning, in which concretes return to the abstracts that bred them. It may be possible to do so (perhaps rain stands for love, flying for free and noble service of one's fellow men, Yang Sun for ruthless careerism, Shu Fu and Mrs. Mi Tzu for capitalism, etc.), but the play's meaning does not depend on such symbol-finding. Rather, the story is representative, archetypal. Its meaning is the sum and meaning of its events, but the events constitute a pattern shared by other events. A law of life emerges. The plot bears testimony to a general rule.

The rule is simply that the world is so arranged that the good can't win. Goodness and success are mutually exclusive.

> Goodness will pay,
> And merit and money will smile and be funny
> While exchanging salt and bread

— only on St. Nevercome's Day. Only a gift of the gods can make goodness affluent, and no sooner has it become so than it is taken advantage of by parasites and capitalists. For goodness not only to continue to be good but even to survive, it has to sprout a second, antithetical personality; Shen Te must disappear in Shui Ta. (One wonders if the change of sex implies a comment on the ethics of men and women.) There is a profound and sad sense in which the charge against Shui Ta is true: he has indeed "imprisoned" or "done away with" Shen Te. And when Shen Te tells Yang Sun that "My cousin can't be where I am," she is stating the bitter truth about human existence. The waterseller Wong has a chorus-like function in the play, and his opening soliloquy anticipates this truth in the paradox that points up man's hopeless entrapment: "When water is scarce, I have long distances to go in search of it, and when it is plentiful, I have no income." The world is so rigged that man suffers and fails unless he submerges his natural goodness and becomes a businessman like Shui Ta, paying starvation wages to his employees and housing them in damp river-bank hovels. You can't win on other terms.

This, perhaps, is no more than a cynical lesson of life. The play's metaphysical acerbity, its challenge of the cosmic order, enters when we consider the role of the three gods. They are kindly personages, but they are stuffily fatuous and ineffectual. The First God's ear trumpet is relevant in this connection. The nature of their very divinity becomes suspect in their opening dialogue with Wong:

WONG: . . . Everyone knows the province of Kwan is always having floods.
SECOND GOD: Really? How's *that?*
WONG: Why, because they're so irreligious.
SECOND GOD: Rubbish. It's because they neglected the dam.

But it is this same Second God who admonishes Shen Te to "Be good" and who, when she pleads, "But everything is so expensive. I don't feel sure I can do it!" loftily answers, "That's not in our sphere. We never meddle with economics." It is quite in character when the gods are delighted to learn at the end that defendant and alleged victim are identical, brush aside Shen Te's confession of the inhumanities she committed as Shui Ta, and vanish on a pink cloud, deaf to Shen Te's final desperate "Help!" The divine order, Brecht seems to suggest, is at fault precisely because it does *not* meddle in economics. We recall his Marxism.

The premise for the whole plot is that "the rules" will have to be changed if the gods fail to find a person who is and remains good. It is even suggested in one speech (by the First God, in the Prologue) that the gods' own existence depends on such a person. At any rate, they are clearly delighted with Shen Te. They are so delighted, in fact, that the cruelest paradox of all turns out to be that it is Shen Te's own goodness that keep things as they are, bad rules and all. It is as if the parable means not only that goodness is continually being defeated, but that it defeats itself. Shen Te versus the world order — the issue is not without its ironic ambiguities. Is goodness goodness only in a fallen world? Would it be meaningless if the rules were changed, making things easier for man? Who, in the end, has the best of the argument: the benign but foolish gods, the atheists whom they set out to confute, or embattled Shen Te? Where the grandeur lies is obvious.

Eugène Ionesco

THE LESSON

Translated by Donald M. Allen

The Characters

THE PROFESSOR, *aged 50 to 60*
THE YOUNG PUPIL, *aged 18*
THE MAID, *aged 45 to 50*

SCENE: *The office of the old professor, which also serves as a dining room. To the left, a door opens onto the apartment stairs; upstage, to the right, another door opens onto a corridor of the apartment. Upstage, a little left of center, a window, not very large, with plain curtains; on the outside sill of the window are ordinary potted plants. The low buildings with red roofs of a small town can be seen in the distance. The sky is grayish-blue. On the right stands a provincial buffet. The table doubles as a desk, it stands at stage center. There are three chairs around the table, and two more stand on each side of the window. Light-colored wallpaper, some shelves with books.*

(*When the curtain rises the stage is empty, and it remains so for a few moments. Then we hear the doorbell ring.*)

VOICE OF THE MAID (*from the corridor*): Yes. I'm coming.

(THE MAID *comes in, after having run down the stairs. She is stout, aged 45 to 50, red-faced, and wears a peasant woman's cap. She rushes in, slamming the door to the right behind her, and dries her hands on her apron as she runs towards the door on the left. Meanwhile we hear the doorbell ring again.*)

Originally published by Grove Press, Inc., in *Four Plays* by Eugène Ionesco, translated by Donald M. Allen. Copyright © 1958, by Grove Press, Inc. Reprinted by permission.

549

MAID: Just a moment, I'm coming.

(*She opens the door. A* YOUNG PUPIL, *aged 18, enters. She is wearing a gray student's smock, a small white collar, and carries a student's satchel under her arm.*)

MAID: Good morning, miss.

PUPIL: Good morning, madam. Is the Professor at home?

MAID: Have you come for the lesson?

PUPIL: Yes, I have.

MAID: He's expecting you. Sit down for a moment. I'll tell him you're here.

PUPIL: Thank you.

(*She seats herself near the table, facing the audience; the hall door is to her left; her back is to the other door, through which* THE MAID *hurriedly exits, calling.*)

MAID: Professor, come down please, your pupil is here.

VOICE OF THE PROFESSOR (*rather reedy*): Thank you. I'm coming . . . in just a moment . . .

(THE MAID *exits;* THE PUPIL *draws in her legs, holds her satchel on her lap, and waits demurely. She casts a glance or two around the room, at the furniture, at the ceiling too. Then she takes a notebook out of her satchel, leafs through it, and stops to look at a page for a moment as though reviewing a lesson, as though taking a last look at her homework. She seems to be a well-brought-up girl, polite, but lively, gay, dynamic; a fresh smile is on her lips. During the course of the play she progressively loses the lively rhythm of her movement and her carriage, she becomes withdrawn. From gay and smiling she becomes progressively sad and morose; from very lively at the beginning, she becomes more and more fatigued and somnolent. Towards the end of the play her face must clearly express a nervous depression; her way of speaking shows the effects of this, her tongue becomes thick, words come to her memory with difficulty and emerge from her mouth with as much difficulty; she comes to have a manner vaguely paralyzed, the beginning of aphasia. Firm and determined at the beginning, so much so as to appear to be almost aggressive, she becomes more and more passive, until she is almost a mute and inert object, seemingly inanimate in* THE PROFESSOR'S *hands, to such an extent that when he makes his final gesture, she no longer reacts. Insensible, her reflexes deadened, only her eyes in*) *an expressionless face will show inexpressible astonishment and fear. The transition from one manner to the other must of course be made imperceptibly.*

THE PROFESSOR *enters. He is a little old man with a little white beard. He wears pince-nez, a black skull cap, a long black schoolmaster's coat, trousers and shoes of black, detachable white collar, a black tie. Excessively polite, very timid, his voice deadened by his timidity, very proper, very much the teacher. He rubs his hands together constantly; occasionally a lewd gleam comes into his eyes and is quickly repressed.*

During the course of the play his timidity will disappear progressively, imperceptibly; and the lewd gleams in his eyes will become a steady devouring flame in the end. From a manner that is inoffensive at the start, THE PROFESSOR *becomes more and more sure of himself, more and more nervous, aggressive, dominating, until he is able to do as he pleases with* THE PUPIL, *who has become, in his hands, a pitiful creature. Of course, the voice of* THE PROFESSOR *must change too, from thin and reedy, to stronger and stronger, until at the end it is extremely powerful, ringing, sonorous, while* THE PUPIL'S *voice changes from the very clear and ringing tones that she has at the beginning of the play until it is almost inaudible. In these first scenes* THE PROFESSOR *might stammer very slightly.*)

PROFESSOR: Good morning, young lady. You . . . I expect that you . . . that you are the new pupil?

PUPIL (*turns quickly with a lively and self-assured manner; she gets up, goes towards* THE PROFESSOR, *and gives him her hand*): Yes, Professor. Good morning, Professor. As you see, I'm on time. I didn't want to be late.

PROFESSOR: That's fine, miss. Thank you, you didn't really need to hurry. I am very sorry to have kept you waiting . . . I was just finishing up . . . well . . . I'm sorry . . . You will excuse me, won't you? . . .

PUPIL: Oh, certainly, Professor. It doesn't matter at all, Professor.

PROFESSOR: Please excuse me . . . Did you have any trouble finding the house?

PUPIL: No . . . Not at all. I just asked the way. Everybody knows you around here.

PROFESSOR: For thirty years I've lived in this town. You've not been here for long? How do you find it?

PUPIL: It's all right. The town is attractive and even agreeable, there's a nice park, a boarding school, a bishop, nice shops and streets . . .

PROFESSOR: That's very true, young lady. And yet, I'd just as soon live somewhere else. In Paris, or at least Bordeaux.

PUPIL: Do you like Bordeaux?

PROFESSOR: I don't know. I've never seen it.

PUPIL: But you know Paris?

PROFESSOR: No, I don't know it either, young lady, but if you'll permit me, can you tell me, Paris is the capital city of . . . miss?

PUPIL (*searching her memory for a moment, then, happily guessing*): Paris is the capital city of . . . France?

PROFESSOR: Yes, young lady, bravo, that's very good, that's perfect. My congratulations. You have your French geography at your finger tips. You know your chief cities.

PUPIL: Oh! I don't know them all yet, Professor, it's not quite that easy, I have trouble learning them.

PROFESSOR: Oh! it will come . . . you mustn't give up . . . young lady . . . I beg your pardon . . . have patience . . . little by little . . . You will see, it will come in time . . . What a nice day it is today . . . or rather, not so nice . . . Oh! but then yes it is nice. In short, it's not too bad a day, that's the main thing . . . ahem . . . ahem . . . it's not raining and it's not snowing either.

PUPIL: That would be most unusual, for it's summer now.

PROFESSOR: Excuse me, miss, I was just going to say so . . . but as you will learn, one must be ready for anything.

PUPIL: I guess so, Professor.

PROFESSOR: We can't be sure of anything, young lady, in this world.

PUPIL: The snow falls in the winter. Winter is one of the four seasons. The other three are . . . uh . . . spr . . .

PROFESSOR: Yes?

PUPIL: . . . ing, and then summer . . . and . . . uh . . .

PROFESSOR: It begins like "automobile," miss.

PUPIL: Ah, yes, autumn . . .

PROFESSOR: That's right, miss. That's a good answer, that's perfect. I am convinced that you will be a good pupil. You will make real progress. You are intelligent, you seem to me to be well informed, and you've a good memory.

PUPIL: I know my seasons, don't I, Professor?

PROFESSOR: Yes, indeed, miss . . . or almost. But it will come in time. In any case, you're coming along. Soon you'll know all the seasons, with your eyes closed. Just as I do.

PUPIL: It's hard.

PROFESSOR: Oh, no. All it takes is a little effort, a little good will, miss. You will see. It will come, you may be sure of that.

PUPIL: Oh, I do hope so, Professor. I have a great thirst for knowledge. My parents also want me to get an education. They want me to specialize. They consider a little general culture, even if it is solid, is no longer enough, in these times.

PROFESSOR: Your parents, miss, are perfectly right. You must go on with your studies. Forgive me for saying so, but it is very necessary. Our contemporary life has become most complex.

PUPIL: And so very complicated too . . . My parents are fairly rich, I'm lucky. They can help me in my work, help me in my very advanced studies.

PROFESSOR: And you wish to qualify for . . . ?

PUPIL: Just as soon as possible, for the first doctor's orals. They're in three weeks' time.

PROFESSOR: You already have your high school diploma, if you'll pardon the question?

PUPIL: Yes, Professor, I have my science diploma and my arts diploma, too.

PROFESSOR: Ah, you're very far advanced, even perhaps too advanced for your age. And which doctorate do you wish to qualify for? In the physical sciences or in moral philosophy?

PUPIL: My parents are very much hoping — if you think it will be possible in such a short time — they very much hope that I can qualify for the total doctorate.

PROFESSOR: The total doctorate? . . . You have great courage, young lady, I congratulate you sincerely. We will try, miss, to do our best. In any case, you already know quite a bit, and at so young an age too.

PUPIL: Oh, Professor.

PROFESSOR: Then, if you'll permit me, pardon me, please, I do think that we ought to get to work. We have scarcely any time to lose.

PUPIL: Oh, but certainly, Professor, I want to. I beg you to.

PROFESSOR: Then, may I ask you to sit down . . . there . . . Will you permit me, miss, that is if you have no objections, to sit down opposite you?

PUPIL: Oh, of course, Professor, please do.

PROFESSOR: Thank you very much, miss. (*They sit down facing each other at the table, their profiles to the audience.*) There we are. Now have you brought your books and notebooks?

PUPIL (*taking notebooks and books out of her satchel*): Yes, Professor. Certainly, I have brought all that we'll need.

PROFESSOR: Perfect, miss. This is perfect. Now, if this doesn't bore you . . . shall we begin?

PUPIL: Yes, indeed, Professor, I am at your disposal.

PROFESSOR: At my disposal? (*A gleam comes into his eyes and is quickly extinguished; he begins to make a gesture that he suppresses at once.*) Oh, miss, it is I who am at *your* disposal. I am only your humble servant.

PUPIL: Oh, Professor . . .

PROFESSOR: If you will . . . now . . . we . . . we . . . I . . . I will begin by making a brief examination of your knowledge, past and present, so that we may chart our future course . . . Good. How is your perception of plurality?

PUPIL: It's rather vague . . . confused.

PROFESSOR: Good. We shall see.

(*He rubs his hands together.* THE MAID *enters, and this appears to irritate* THE PROFESSOR. *She goes to the buffet and looks for something, lingering.*)

PROFESSOR: Now, miss, would you like to do a little arithmetic, that is if you want to . . .

PUPIL: Oh, yes, Professor. Certainly, I ask nothing better.

PROFESSOR: It is rather a new science, a modern science, properly speaking, it is more a method than a science . . . And it is also a therapy. (*To* THE MAID:) Have you finished, Marie?

MAID: Yes, Professor, I've found the plate. I'm just going . . .

PROFESSOR: Hurry up then. Please go along to the kitchen, if you will.

MAID: Yes, Professor, I'm going. (*She starts to go out.*) Excuse me, Professor, but take care, I urge you to remain calm.

PROFESSOR: You're being ridiculous, Marie. Now, don't worry.

MAID: That's what you always say.

PROFESSOR: I will not stand for your insinuations. I know perfectly well how to comport myself. I am old enough for that.

MAID: Precisely, Professor. You will do better not to start the young lady on arithmetic. Arithmetic is tiring, exhausting.

PROFESSOR: Not at my age. And anyhow, what business is it of yours? This is my concern. And I know what I'm doing. This is not your department.

MAID: Very well, Professor. But you can't say that I didn't warn you.

PROFESSOR: Marie, I can get along without your advice.

MAID: As you wish, Professor. (*She exits.*)

PROFESSOR: Miss, I hope you'll pardon this absurd interruption . . . Excuse this woman . . . She is always afraid that I'll tire myself. She fusses over my health.

PUPIL: Oh, that's quite all right, Professor. It shows that she's very devoted. She loves you very much. Good servants are rare.

PROFESSOR: She exaggerates. Her fears are stupid. But let's return to our arithmetical knitting.

PUPIL: I'm following you, Professor.

PROFESSOR (*wittily*): Without leaving your seat!

PUPIL (*appreciating his joke*): Like you, Professor.

PROFESSOR: Good. Let us arithmetize a little now.

PUPIL: Yes, gladly, Professor.

PROFESSOR: It wouldn't be too tiresome for you to tell me . . .

PUPIL: Not at all, Professor, go on.

PROFESSOR: How much are one and one?

PUPIL: One and one make two.

PROFESSOR (*marveling at* THE PUPIL's *knowledge*): Oh, but that's very good. You appear to me to be well along in your studies. You should easily achieve the total doctorate, miss.

PUPIL: I'm so glad. Especially to have someone like you tell me this.

PROFESSOR: Let's push on: how much are two and one?

PUPIL: Three.

PROFESSOR: Three and one?

PUPIL: Four.

PROFESSOR: Four and one?

PUPIL: Five.

PROFESSOR: Five and one?

PUPIL: Six.

PROFESSOR: Six and one?

PUPIL: Seven.

PROFESSOR: Seven and one?

PUPIL: Eight.

PROFESSOR: Seven and one?

PUPIL: Eight again.

PROFESSOR: Very well answered. Seven and one?

PUPIL: Eight once more.

PROFESSOR: Perfect. Excellent. Seven and one?

PUPIL: Eight again. And sometimes nine.

PROFESSOR: Magnificent. You are magnificent. You are exquisite. I congratulate you warmly, miss. There's scarcely any point in going on. At addition you are a past master. Now, let's look at subtraction. Tell me, if you are not exhausted, how many are four minus three?

PUPIL: Four minus three? . . . Four minus three?

PROFESSOR: Yes. I mean to say: subtract three from four.

PUPIL: That makes . . . seven?

PROFESSOR: I am sorry but I'm obliged to contradict you. Four minus three does not make seven. You are confused: four plus three makes seven, four minus three does not make seven . . . This is not addition anymore, we must subtract now.

PUPIL (*trying to understand*): Yes . . . yes . . .

PROFESSOR: Four minus three makes . . . How many? . . . How many?

PUPIL: Four?

PROFESSOR: No, miss, that's not it.

PUPIL: Three, then.

PROFESSOR: Not that either, miss . . . Pardon, I'm sorry . . . I ought to say, that's not it . . . excuse me.

PUPIL: Four minus three . . . Four minus three . . . Four minus three? . . . But now doesn't that make ten?

PROFESSOR: Oh, certainly not, miss. It's not a matter of guessing, you've got to think it out. Let's try to deduce it together. Would you like to count?

PUPIL: Yes, Professor. One . . . two . . . uh . . .

PROFESSOR: You know how to count? How far can you count up to?

PUPIL: I can count to . . . to infinity.

PROFESSOR: That's not possible, miss.

PUPIL: Well then, let's say to sixteen.

PROFESSOR: That is enough. One must know one's limits. Count then, if you will, please.

PUPIL: One . . . two . . . and after two, comes three . . . then four . . .

PROFESSOR: Stop there, miss. Which number is larger? Three or four?

PUPIL: Uh . . . three or four? Which is the larger? The larger of three or four? In what sense larger?

PROFESSOR: Some numbers are smaller and others are larger. In the larger numbers there are more units than in the smaller . . .

PUPIL: Than in the small numbers?

PROFESSOR: Unless the small ones have smaller units. If they are very small, then there might be more units in the small numbers than in the large . . . if it is a question of other units . . .

PUPIL: In that case, the small numbers can be larger than the large numbers?

PROFESSOR: Let's not go into that. That would take us much too far. You must realize simply that more than numbers are involved here . . . there are also magnitudes, totals, there are groups, there are heaps, heaps of such things as plums, trucks, geese, prune pits, etc. To facilitate our work, let's merely suppose that we have only equal numbers, then the bigger numbers will be those that have the most units.

PUPIL: The one that has the most is the biggest? Ah, I understand, Professor, you are identifying quality with quantity.

PROFESSOR: That is too theoretical, miss, too theoretical. You needn't concern yourself with that. Let us take an example and reason from a definite case. Let's leave the general conclusions for later. We have the number four and the number three, and each has always the same number of units. Which number will be larger, the smaller or the larger?

PUPIL: Excuse me, Professor . . . What do you mean by the larger number? Is it the one that is not so small as the other?

PROFESSOR: That's it, miss, perfect. You have understood me very well.

PUPIL: Then, it is four.

PROFESSOR: What is four — larger or smaller than three?

PUPIL: Smaller . . . no, larger.

PROFESSOR: Excellent answer. How many units are there between three and four? . . . Or between four and three, if you prefer?

PUPIL: There aren't any units, Professor, between three and four. Four comes immediately after three; there is nothing at all between three and four!

PROFESSOR: I haven't made myself very well understood. No doubt, it is my fault. I've not been sufficiently clear.

PUPIL: No, Professor, it's my fault.

PROFESSOR: Look here. Here are three matches. And here is another one, that makes four. Now watch carefully — we have four matches. I take one away, now how many are left?

(*We don't see the matches, nor any of the objects that are mentioned.* THE PROFESSOR *gets up from the table, writes on the imaginary blackboard with an imaginary piece of chalk, etc.*)

PUPIL: Five. If three and one make four, four and one make five.

PROFESSOR: That's not it. That's not it at all. You always have a tendency to add. But one must be able to subtract too. It's not enough to integrate, you must also disintegrate. That's the way life is. That's philosophy. That's science. That's progress, civilization.

PUPIL: Yes, Professor.

PROFESSOR: Let's return to our matches. I have four of them. You see, there are really four. I take one away, and there remain only . . .

PUPIL: I don't know, Professor.

PROFESSOR: Come now, think. It's not easy, I admit. Nevertheless, you've had enough training to make the intellectual effort required to arrive at an understanding. So?

PUPIL: I can't get it, Professor. I don't know, Professor.

PROFESSOR: Let us take a simpler example. If you had two noses, and I pulled one of them off . . . how many would you have left?

PUPIL: None.

PROFESSOR: What do you mean, none?

PUPIL: Yes, it's because you haven't pulled off any, that's why I have one now. If you had pulled it off, I wouldn't have it anymore.

PROFESSOR: You've not understood my example. Suppose that you have only one ear.

PUPIL: Yes, and then?

PROFESSOR: If I gave you another one, how many would you have then?

PUPIL: Two.

PROFESSOR: Good. And if I gave you still another ear. How many would you have then?

PUPIL: Three ears.

PROFESSOR: Now, I take one away . . . and there remain . . . how many ears?

PUPIL: Two.

PROFESSOR: Good. I take away still another one, how many do you have left?

PUPIL: Two.

PROFESSOR: No. You have two, I take one away, I eat one up, then how many do you have left?

PUPIL: Two.

PROFESSOR: I eat one of them . . . one.

PUPIL: Two.

PROFESSOR: One.

PUPIL: Two.

PROFESSOR: One!

PUPIL: Two!

PROFESSOR: One!!!

PUPIL: Two!!!

PROFESSOR: One!!!

PUPIL: Two!!!

PROFESSOR: One!!!

PUPIL: Two!!!

PROFFESSOR: No. No. That's not right. The example is not . . . it's not convincing. Listen to me.

PUPIL: Yes, Professor.

PROFESSOR: You've got . . . you've got . . . you've got . . .

PUPIL: Ten fingers!

PROFESSOR: If you wish. Perfect. Good. You have then ten fingers.

PUPIL: Yes, Professor.

PROFESSOR: How many would you have if you had only five of them?

PUPIL: Ten, Professor.

PROFESSOR: That's not right!

PUPIL: But it is, Professor.

PROFESSOR: I tell you it's not!

PUPIL: You just told me that I had ten . . .

PROFESSOR: I also said, immediately afterwards, that you had five!

PUPIL: I don't have five, I've got ten!

PROFESSOR: Let's try another approach . . . for purposes of subtraction let's limit ourselves to the numbers from one to five . . . Wait now, miss, you'll soon see. I'm going to make you understand.

(THE PROFESSOR *begins to write on the imaginary blackboard. He moves it closer to* THE PUPIL, *who turns around in order to see it.*)

PROFESSOR: Look here, miss . . . (*He pretends to draw a stick on the blackboard and the number 1 below the stick; then two sticks and the number 2 below, then three sticks and the number 3 below, then four sticks with the number 4 below.*) You see . . .

PUPIL: Yes, Professor.

PROFESSOR: These are sticks, miss, sticks. This is one stick, these are two sticks, and three sticks, then four sticks, then five sticks. One stick, two sticks, three sticks, four and five sticks, these are numbers. When we count the sticks, each stick is a unit, miss . . . What have I just said?

PUPIL: "A unit, miss! What have I just said?"

PROFESSOR: Or a figure! Or a number! One, two, three, four, five, these are the elements of numeration, miss.

PUPIL (*hesitant*): Yes, Professor. The elements, figures, which are sticks, units and numbers . . .

PROFESSOR: At the same time . . . that's to say, in short — the whole of arithmetic is there.

PUPIL: Yes, Professor. Good, Professor. Thanks, Professor.

PROFESSOR: Now, count, if you will please, using these elements . . . add and subtract . . .

PUPIL (*as though trying to impress them on her memory*): Sticks are really figures and numbers are units?

PROFESSOR: Hmm . . . so to speak. And then?

PUPIL: One could subtract two units from three units, but can one subtract two twos from three threes? And two figures from four numbers? And three numbers from one unit?

PROFESSOR: No, miss.

PUPIL: Why, Professor?

PROFESSOR: Because, miss.

PUPIL: Because why, Professor? Since one is the same as the other?

PROFESSOR: That's the way it is, miss. It can't be explained. This is only comprehensible through internal mathematical reasoning. Either you have it or you don't.

PUPIL: So much the worse for me.

PROFESSOR: Listen to me, miss, if you don't achieve a profound understanding of these principles, these arithmetical archetypes, you will never be able to perform correctly the functions of a polytechnician. Still less will you be able to teach a course in a polytechnical school . . . or the primary grades. I realize that this is not easy, it is very, very abstract . . . obviously . . . but unless you can comprehend the primary elements, how do you expect to be able to calculate mentally — and this is the least of the things that even an ordinary engineer must be able to do — how much, for example, are three billion seven hundred fifty-five million nine hundred ninety-eight thousand two hundred fifty-one, multiplied by five billion one hundred sixty-two million three hundred and three thousand five hundred and eight?

PUPIL (*very quickly*): That makes nineteen quintillion three hundred ninety quadrillion two trillion eight hundred forty-four billion two hundred nineteen million one hundred sixty-four thousand five hundred and eight . . .

PROFESSOR (*astonished*): No. I don't think so. That must make nineteen quintillion three hundred ninety quadrillion two trillion eight hundred forty-four billion two hundred nineteen million one hundred sixty-four thousand five hundred and nine . . .

PUPIL: . . . No . . . five hundred and eight . . .

PROFESSOR (*more and more astonished, calculating mentally*): Yes . . . you are right . . . the result is indeed . . . (*He mumbles unintelligibly:*) . . . quintillion, quadrillion, trillion, billion, million . . . (*Clearly:*) one hundred sixty-four thousand five hundred and eight . . . (*Stupefied:*) But how did you know that, if you don't know the principles of arithmetical reasoning?

PUPIL: It's easy. Not being able to rely on my reasoning, I've memorized all the products of all possible multiplications.

PROFESSOR: That's pretty good . . . However, permit me to confess to you that that doesn't satisfy me, miss, and I do not congratulate you: in mathematics and in arithmetic especially, the thing that counts — for in arithmetic it is always necessary to count — the thing that counts is, above all, understanding . . . It is by mathematical reasoning, simultaneously inductive and deductive, that you ought to arrive at this result — as well as at any other result. Mathematics is the sworn enemy of memory, which is excellent otherwise,

The Lesson

but disastrous, arithmetically speaking! . . . That's why I'm not happy with this . . . this won't do, not at all . . .

PUPIL (*desolated*): No, Professor.

PROFESSOR: Let's leave it for the moment. Let's go on to another exercise . . .

PUPIL: Yes, Professor.

MAID (*entering*): Hmm, hmm, Professor . . .

PROFESSOR (*who doesn't hear her*): It is unfortunate, miss, that you aren't further along in specialized mathematics . . .

MAID (*taking him by the sleeve*): Professor! Professor!

PROFESSOR: I hear that you will not be able to qualify for the total doctor's orals . . .

PUPIL: Yes, Professor, it's too bad!

PROFESSOR: Unless you . . . (*To* THE MAID:) Let me be, Marie . . . Look here, why are you bothering me? Go back to the kitchen! To your pots and pans! Go away! Go away! (*To* THE PUPIL:) We will try to prepare you at least for the partial doctorate . . .

MAID: Professor! . . . Professor! . . . (*She pulls his sleeve.*)

PROFESSOR (*to* THE MAID): Now leave me alone! Let me be! What's the meaning of this? . . . (*To* THE PUPIL:) I must therefore teach you, if you really do insist on attempting the partial doctorate . . .

PUPIL: Yes, Professor.

PROFESSOR: . . . The elements of linguistics and of comparative philology . . .

MAID: No, Professor, no! . . . You mustn't do that! . . .

PROFESSOR: Marie, you're going too far!

MAID: Professor, especially not philology, philology leads to calamity . . .

PUPIL (*astonished*): To calamity? (*Smiling, a little stupidly.*) That's hard to believe.

PROFESSOR (*to* THE MAID): That's enough now! Get out of here!

MAID: All right, Professor, all right. But you can't say that I didn't warn you! Philology leads to calamity!

PROFESSOR: I'm an adult, Marie!

PUPIL: Yes, Professor.

MAID: As you wish. (*She exits.*)

PROFESSOR: Let's continue, miss.

PUPIL: Yes, Professor.

PROFESSOR: I want you to listen now with the greatest possible attention to a lecture I have prepared . . .

PUPIL: Yes, Professor!

PROFESSOR: . . . Thanks to which, in fifteen minutes' time, you will be able to acquire the fundamental principles of the linguistic and comparative philology of the neo-Spanish languages.

PUPIL: Yes, Professor, oh good! (*She claps her hands.*)

PROFESSOR (*with authority*): Quiet! What do you mean by that?

PUPIL: I'm sorry, Professor. (*Slowly, she replaces her hands on the table.*)

PROFESSOR: Quiet! (*He gets up, walks up and down the room, his hands behind his back; from time to time he stops at stage center or near* THE PUPIL, *and underlines his words with a gesture of his hand; he orates, but without being too emotional.* THE PUPIL *follows him with her eyes, occasionally with some difficulty, for she has to turn her head far around; once or twice, not more, she turns around completely.*) And now, miss, Spanish is truly the mother tongue which gave birth to all the neo-Spanish languages, of which Spanish, Latin, Italian, our own French, Portuguese, Romanian, Sardinian or Sardanapalian, Spanish and neo-Spanish — and also, in certain of its aspects, Turkish which is otherwise very close to Greek, which is only logical, since it is a fact that Turkey is a neighbor of Greece and Greece is even closer to Turkey than you are to me — this is only one more illustration of the very important linguistic law which states that geography and philology are twin sisters . . . You may take notes, miss.

PUPIL (*in a dull voice*): Yes, Professor!

PROFESSOR: That which distinguishes the neo-Spanish languages from each other and their idioms from the other linguistic groups, such as the group of languages called Austrian and neo-Austrian or Hapsburgian, as well as the Esperanto, Helvetian, Monacan, Swiss, Andorran, Basque, and jai alai groups, and also the groups of diplomatic and technical languages — that which distinguishes them, I repeat, is their striking resemblance which makes it so hard to distinguish them from each other — I'm speaking of the neo-Spanish languages which one is able to distinguish from each other, however, only thanks to their distinctive characteristics, absolutely indisputable proofs of their extraordinary resemblance, which renders indisputable their common origin, and which, at the same time, differentiates them profoundly — through the continuation of the distinctive traits which I've just cited.

PUPIL: Oooh! Ye-e-e-s-s-s, Professor!

PROFESSOR: But let's not linger over generalities . . .

PUPIL (*regretfully, but won over*): Oh, Professor . . .

PROFESSOR: This appears to interest you. All the better, all the better

PUPIL: Oh, yes, Professor . . .

PROFESSOR: Don't worry, miss. We will come back to it later . . . That is if we come back to it at all. Who can say?

PUPIL (*enchanted in spite of everything*): Oh, yes, Professor.

PROFESSOR: Every tongue — you must know this, miss, and remember it *until the hour of your death* . . .

PUPIL: Oh! yes, Professor, until the hour of my death . . . Yes, Professor . . .

PROFESSOR: . . . And this, too, is a fundamental principle, every tongue is at bottom nothing but language, which necessarily implies that it is composed of sounds, or . . .

PUPIL: Phonemes . . .

PROFESSOR: Just what I was going to say. Don't parade your knowledge. You'd do better to listen.

PUPIL: All right, Professor. Yes, Professor.

PROFESSOR: The sounds, miss, must be seized on the wing as they fly so that they'll not fall on deaf ears. As a result, when you set out to articulate, it is recommended, insofar as possible, that you lift up your neck and chin very high, and rise up on the tips of your toes, you see, this way . . .

PUPIL: Yes, Professor.

PROFESSOR: Keep quiet. Remain seated, don't interrupt me . . . And project the sounds very loudly with all the force of your lungs in conjunction with that of your vocal cords. Like this, look: "Butterfly," "Eureka," "Trafalgar," "Papaya." This way, the sounds become filled with a warm air that is lighter than the surrounding air so that they can fly without danger of falling on deaf ears, which are veritable voids, tombs of sonorities. If you utter several sounds at an accelerated speed, they will automatically cling to each other, constituting thus syllables, words, even sentences, that is to say groupings of various importance, purely irrational assemblages of sounds, denuded of all sense, but for that very reason the more capable of maintaining themselves without danger at a high altitude in the air. By themselves, words charged with significance will fall, weighted down by their meaning, and in the end they always collapse, fall . . .

PUPIL: . . . On deaf ears.

PROFESSOR: That's it, but don't interrupt . . . and into the worst confusion . . . Or else burst like balloons. Therefore, miss . . . (THE PUPIL *suddenly appears to be unwell.*) What's the matter?

PUPIL: I've got a toothache, Professor.

PROFESSOR: That's not important. We're not going to stop for anything so trivial. Let us go on . . .

PUPIL (*appearing to be in more and more pain*): Yes, Professor.

PROFESSOR: I draw your attention in passing to the consonants that change their nature in combinations. In this case *f* becomes *v*, *d* becomes *t*, *g* becomes *k*, and vice versa, as in these examples that I will cite for you: "That's all right," "hens and chickens," "Welsh rabbit," "lots of nothing," "not at all." *

PUPIL: I've got a toothache.

PROFESSOR: Let's continue.

PUPIL: Yes.

PROFESSOR: To resume: it takes years and years to learn to pronounce. Thanks to science, we can achieve this in a few minutes. In order to project words, sounds and all the rest, you must realize that it is necessary to pitilessly expel air from the lungs, and make it pass delicately, caressingly, over the vocal cords, which, like harps or leaves in the wind, will suddenly shake, agitate, vibrate, vibrate, vibrate or uvulate, or fricate or jostle against each other, or sibilate, sibilate, placing everything in movement, the uvula, the tongue, the palate, the teeth . . .

PUPIL: I have a toothache.

PROFESSOR: . . . And the lips . . . Finally the words come out through the nose, the mouth, the ears, the pores, drawing along with them all the organs that we have named, torn up by the roots, in a powerful, majestic flight, which is none other than what is called, improperly, the voice, whether modulated in singing or transformed into a terrible symphonic storm with a whole procession . . . of garlands of all kinds of flowers, of sonorous artifices: labials, dentals, occlusives, palatals, and others, some caressing, some bitter or violent.

PUPIL: Yes, Professor, I've got a toothache.

PROFESSOR: Let's go on, go on. As for the neo-Spanish languages, they are closely related, so closely to each other, that they can be considered as true second cousins. Moreover, they have the same mother: Spanishe, with a mute *e*. That is why it is so difficult to distinguish them from one another. That is why it is so useful to pronounce carefully, and to avoid errors in pronunciation. Pronunciation itself is worth a whole language. A bad pronunciation can get you into trouble. In this connection, permit me, parenthetically, to share a personal experience with you. (*Slight pause.* THE PROFESSOR *goes over his memories for a moment; his features mellow, but he recovers at once.*) I was very young, little more than a child. It was during my military service. I had a friend in the regiment, a vicomte,

---

* All to be heavily elided. [Translator's note.]

who suffered from a rather serious defect in his pronunciation: he could not pronounce the letter *f*. Instead of *f*, he said *f*. Thus, instead of "Birds of a feather flock together," he said: "Birds of a feather flock together." He pronounced filly instead of filly, Firmin instead of Firmin, French bean instead of French bean, go frig yourself instead of go frig yourself, farrago instead of farrago, fee fi fo fum instead of fee fi fo fum, Philip instead of Philip, fictory instead of fictory, February instead of February, March-April instead of March-April, Gerard de Nerval and not as is correct — Gerard de Nerval, Mirabeau instead of Mirabeau, etc., instead of etc., and thus instead of etc., instead of etc., and thus and so forth. However, he managed to conceal his fault so effectively that, thanks to the hats he wore, no one ever noticed it.

PUPIL: Yes, I've got a toothache.

PROFESSOR (*abruptly changing his tone, his voice hardening*): Let's go on. We'll first consider the points of similarity in order the better to apprehend, later on, that which distinguishes all these languages from each other. The differences can scarcely be recognized by people who are not aware of them. Thus, all the words of all the languages . . .

PUPIL: Uh, yes? . . . I've got a toothache.

PROFESSOR: Let's continue . . . are always the same, just as all the suffixes, all the prefixes, all the terminations, all the roots . . .

PUPIL: Are the roots of words square?

PROFESSOR: Square or cube. That depends.

PUPIL: I've got a toothache.

PROFESSOR: Let's go on. Thus, to give you an example which is little more than an illustration, take the word "front" . . .

PUPIL: How do you want me to take it?

PROFESSOR: However you wish, so long as you take it, but above all do not interrupt.

PUPIL: I've got a toothache.

PROFESSOR: Let's continue . . . I said: Let's continue. Take now the word "front." Have you taken it?

PUPIL: Yes, yes, I've got it. My teeth, my teeth . . .

PROFESSOR: The word "front" is the root of "frontispiece." It is also to be found in "affronted." "Ispiece" is the suffix, and "af" the prefix. They are so called because they do not change. They don't want to.

PUPIL: I've got a toothache.

PROFESSOR: Let's go on. (*Rapidly:*) These prefixes are of Spanish origin. I hope you noticed that, did you?

PUPIL: Oh, how my tooth aches.

PROFESSOR: Let's continue. You've surely also noticed that they've not changed in French. And now, young lady, nothing has succeeded in changing them in Latin either, nor in Italian, nor in Portuguese, nor in Sardanapalian, nor in Sardanapali, nor in Romanian, nor in neo-Spanish, nor in Spanish, nor even in the Oriental: front, frontispiece, affronted, always the same word, invariably with the same root, the same suffix, the same prefix, in all the languages I have named. And it is always the same for all words.

PUPIL: In all languages, these words mean the same thing? I've got a toothache.

PROFESSOR: Absolutely. Moreover, it's more a notion than a word. In any case, you have always the same signification, the same composition, the same sound structure, not only for this word, but for all conceivable words, in all languages. For one single notion is expressed by one and the same word, and its synonyms, in all countries. Forget about your teeth.

PUPIL: I've got a toothache. Yes, yes, yes.

PROFESSOR: Good, let's go on. I tell you, let's go on . . . How would you say, for example, in French: the roses of my grandmother are as yellow as my grandfather who was Asiatic?

PUPIL: My teeth ache, ache, ache.

PROFESSOR: Let's go on, let's go on, go ahead and answer, anyway.

PUPIL: In French?

PROFESSOR: In French.

PUPIL: Uhh . . . I should say in French: the roses of my grandmother are . . . ?

PROFESSOR: As yellow as my grandfather who was Asiatic . . .

PUPIL: Oh well, one would say, in French, I believe, the roses . . . of my . . . how do you say "grandmother" in French?

PROFESSOR: In French? Grandmother.

PUPIL: The roses of my grandmother are as yellow — in French, is it "yellow"?

PROFESSOR: Yes, of course!

PUPIL: Are as yellow as my grandfather when he got angry.

PROFESSOR: No . . . who was A . . .

PUPIL: . . . siatic . . . I've got a toothache.

PROFESSOR: That's it.

PUPIL: I've got a tooth . . .

PROFESSOR: Ache . . . so what . . . let's continue! And now translate the same sentence into Spanish, then into neo-Spanish . . .

PUPIL: In Spanish . . . this would be: the roses of my grandmother are as yellow as my grandfather who was Asiatic.

PROFESSOR: No. That's wrong.

PUPIL: And in neo-Spanish: the roses of my grandmother are as yellow as my grandfather who was Asiatic.

PROFESSOR: That's wrong. That's wrong. That's wrong. You have inverted it, you've confused Spanish with neo-Spanish, and neo-Spanish with Spanish . . . Oh . . . no . . . it's the other way around . . .

PUPIL: I've got a toothache. You're getting mixed up.

PROFESSOR: You're the one who is mixing me up. Pay attention and take notes. I will say the sentence to you in Spanish, then in neo-Spanish, and finally, in Latin. You will repeat after me. Pay attention, for the resemblances are great. In fact, they are identical resemblances. Listen, follow carefully . . .

PUPIL: I've got a tooth . . .

PROFESSOR: . . . Ache.

PUPIL: Let us go on . . . Ah! . . .

PROFESSOR: . . . In Spanish: the roses of my grandmother are as yellow as my grandfather who was Asiatic; in Latin: the roses of my grandmother are as yellow as my grandfather who was Asiatic. Do you detect the differences? Translate this into . . . Romanian.

PUPIL: The . . . how do you say "roses" in Romanian?

PROFESSOR: But "roses," what else?

PUPIL: It's not "roses"? Oh, how my tooth aches!

PROFESSOR: Certainly not, certainly not, since "roses" is a translation in Oriental of the French word "roses," in Spanish "roses," do you get it? In Sardanapali, "roses" . . .

PUPIL: Excuse me, Professor, but . . . Oh, my toothache! . . . I don't get the difference.

PROFESSOR: But it's so simple! So simple! It's a matter of having a certain experience, a technical experience and practice in these diverse languages, which are so diverse in spite of the fact that they present wholly identical characteristics. I'm going to try to give you a key . . .

PUPIL: Toothache . . .

PROFESSOR: That which differentiates these languages, is neither the words, which are absolutely the same, nor the structure of the sentence which is everywhere the same, nor the intonation, which does not offer any differences, nor the rhythm of the language . . . that which differentiates them . . . are you listening?

PUPIL: I've got a toothache.

PROFESSOR: Are you listening to me, young lady? Aah! We're going to lose our temper.

PUPIL: You're bothering me, Professor. I've got a toothache.

PROFESSOR: Son of a cocker spaniel! Listen to me!

PUPIL: Oh well . . . yes . . . yes . . . go on . . .

PROFESSOR: That which distinguishes them from each other, on the one hand, and from their mother, Spanishe with its mute *e*, on the other hand . . . is . . .

PUPIL (*grimacing*): Is what?

PROFESSOR: Is an intangible thing. Something intangible that one is able to perceive only after very long study, with a great deal of trouble and after the broadest experience . . .

PUPIL: Ah?

PROFESSOR: Yes, young lady. I cannot give you any rule. One must have a feeling for it, and well, that's it. But in order to have it, one must study, study, and then study some more.

PUPIL: Toothache.

PROFESSOR: All the same, there are some specific cases where words differ from one language to another . . . but we cannot base our knowledge on these cases, which are, so to speak, exceptional.

PUPIL: Oh, yes? . . . Oh, Professor, I've got a toothache.

PROFESSOR: Don't interrupt! Don't make me lose my temper! I can't answer for what I'll do. I was saying, then . . . Ah, yes, the exceptional cases, the so-called easily distinguished . . . or facilely distinguished . . . or conveniently . . . if you prefer . . . I repeat, if you prefer, for I see that you're not listening to me . . .

PUPIL: I've got a toothache.

PROFESSOR: I say then: in certain expressions in current usage, certain words differ totally from one language to another, so much so that the language employed is, in this case, considerably easier to identify. I'll give you an example: the neo-Spanish expression, famous in Madrid: "My country is the new Spain," becomes in Italian: "My country is . . .

PUPIL: The new Spain.

PROFESSOR: No! "My country is Italy." Tell me now, by simple deduction, how do you say "Italy" in French?

PUPIL: I've got a toothache.

PROFESSOR: But it's so easy: for the word "Italy," in French we have the word "France," which is an exact translation of it. My country is France. And "France" in Oriental: "Orient!" My country is the Orient. And "Orient" in Portuguese: "Portugal!" The Oriental expression: My country is the Orient is translated then in the same fashion into Portuguese: My country is Portugal! And so on . . .

PUPIL: Oh, no more, no more. My teeth . . .

PROFESSOR: Ache! ache! ache! . . . I'm going to pull them out, I will! One more example. The word "capital" — it takes on, according to

the language one speaks, a different meaning. That is to say that
when a Spaniard says: "I reside in the capital," the word "capital"
does not mean at all the same thing that a Portuguese means when
he says: "I reside in the capital." All the more so in the case of a
Frenchman, a neo-Spaniard, a Romanian, a Latin, a Sardanapali
. . . Whenever you hear it, young lady — young lady, I'm saying
this for you! Pooh! Whenever you hear the expression: "I reside in
the capital," you will immediately and easily know whether this is
Spanish or Spanish, neo-Spanish, French, Oriental, Romanian, or
Latin, for it is enough to know which metropolis is referred to by
the person who pronounces the sentence . . . at the very moment
he pronounces it . . . But these are almost the only precise examples that I can give you . . .

PUPIL: Oh dear! My teeth . . .

PROFESSOR: Silence! Or I'll bash in your skull!

PUPIL: Just try to! Skulldugger!

(*The Professor seizes her wrist and twists it.*)

PUPIL: Oww!

PROFESSOR: Keep quiet now! Not a word!

PUPIL (*whimpering*): Toothache . . .

PROFESSOR: One thing that is the most . . . how shall I say it? . . .
the most paradoxical . . . yes . . . that's the word . . . the most
paradoxical thing, is that a lot of people who are completely illiterate speak these different languages . . . do you understand? What
did I just say?

PUPIL: . . . "Speak these different languages! What did I just say?"

PROFESSOR: You were lucky that time! . . . The common people
speak a Spanish full of neo-Spanish words that they are entirely unaware of, all the while believing that they are speaking Latin . . .
or they speak Latin, full of Oriental words, all the while believing
that they're speaking Romanian . . . or Spanish, full of neo-Spanish, all the while believing that they're speaking Sardanapali, or
Spanish . . . Do you understand?

PUPIL: Yes! yes! yes! yes! What more do you want . . . ?

PROFESSOR: No insolence, my pet, or you'll be sorry . . . (*In a rage:*)
But the worst of all, young lady, is that certain people, for example,
in a Latin that they suppose is Spanish, say: "Both my kidneys are
of the same kidney," in addressing themselves to a Frenchman who
does not know a word of Spanish, but the latter understands it as if
it were his own language. For that matter he thinks it is his own
language. And the Frenchman will reply, in French: "Me too, sir,

mine are too," and this will be perfectly comprehensible to a Spaniard, who will feel certain that the reply is in pure Spanish and that Spanish is being spoken . . . when, in reality, it was neither Spanish nor French, but Latin in the neo-Spanish dialect . . . Sit still, young lady, don't fidget, stop tapping your feet . . .

PUPIL: I've got a toothache.

PROFESSOR: How do you account for the fact that, in speaking without knowing which language they speak, or even while each of them believes that he is speaking another, the common people understand each other at all?

PUPIL: I wonder.

PROFESSOR: It is simply one of the inexplicable curiosities of the vulgar empiricism of the common people — not to be confused with experience! — a paradox, a non-sense, one of the aberrations of human nature, it is purely and simply instinct — to put it in a nutshell . . . That's what is involved here.

PUPIL: Hah! hah!

PROFESSOR: Instead of staring at the flies while I'm going to all this trouble . . . you would do much better to try to be more attentive . . . it is not I who is going to qualify for the partial doctor's orals . . . I passed mine a long time ago . . . and I've won my total doctorate, too . . . and my supertotal diploma . . . Don't you realize that what I'm saying is for your own good?

PUPIL: Toothache!

PROFESSOR: Ill-mannered . . . It can't go on like this, it won't do, it won't do, it won't do . . .

PUPIL: I'm . . . listening . . . to you . . .

PROFESSOR: Ahah! In order to learn to distinguish all the different languages, as I've told you, there is nothing better than practice . . . Let's take them up in order. I am going to try to teach you all the translations of the word "knife."

PUPIL: Well, all right . . . if you want . . .

PROFESSOR (*calling* THE MAID): Marie! Marie! She's not there . . . Marie! Marie! . . . Marie, where are you? (*He opens the door on the right.*) Marie! . . . (*He exits.*)

(THE PUPIL *remains alone several minutes, staring into space, wearing a stupefied expression.*)

PROFESSOR (*offstage, in a shrill voice*): Marie! What are you up to? Why don't you come! When I call you, you must come! (*He reenters, followed by* THE MAID.) It is I who gives the orders, do you hear? (*He points at* THE PUPIL:) She doesn't understand anything, that girl. She doesn't understand!

MAID: Don't get into such a state, sir, you know where it'll end! You're going to go too far, you're going to go too far.

PROFESSOR: I'll be able to stop in time.

MAID: That's what you always say. I only wish I could see it.

PUPIL: I've got a toothache.

MAID: You see, it's starting, that's the symptom!

PROFESSOR: What symptom? Explain yourself? What do you mean?

PUPIL (*in a spiritless voice*): Yes, what do you mean? I've got a toothache.

MAID: The final symptom! The chief symptom!

PROFESSOR: Stupid! stupid! stupid! (THE MAID *starts to exit.*) Don't go away like that! I called you to help me find the Spanish, neo-Spanish, Portuguese, French, Oriental, Romanian, Sardanapali, Latin and Spanish knives.

MAID (*severely*): Don't ask me. (*She exits.*)

PROFESSOR (*makes a gesture as though to protest, then refrains, a little helpless. Suddenly, he remembers*): Ah! (*He goes quickly to the drawer where he finds a big knife, invisible or real according to the preference of the director. He seizes it and brandishes it happily.*) Here is one, young lady, here is a knife. It's too bad that we only have this one, but we're going to try to make it serve for all the languages, anyway! It will be enough if you will pronounce the word "knife" in all the languages, while looking at the object, very closely, fixedly, and imagining that it is in the language that you are speaking.

PUPIL: I've got a toothache.

PROFESSOR (*almost singing, chanting*): Now, say "kni," like "kni," "fe," like "fe" . . . And look, look, look at it, watch it . . .

PUPIL: What is this one in? French, Italian or Spanish?

PROFESSOR: That doesn't matter now . . . That's not your concern. Say: "kni."

PUPIL: "Kni."

PROFESSOR: . . . "fe" . . . Look. (*He brandishes the knife under* THE PUPIL's *eyes.*)

PUPIL: "fe" . . .

PROFESSOR: Again . . . Look at it.

PUPIL: Oh, no! My God! I've had enough. And besides, I've got a toothache, my feet hurt me, I've got a headache.

PROFESSOR (*abruptly*): Knife . . . look . . . knife . . . look . . . knife . . . look . . .

PUPIL: You're giving me an earache, too. Oh, your voice! It's so piercing!

PROFESSOR: Say: knife . . . kni . . . fe . . .

PUPIL: No! My ears hurt, I hurt all over . . .

PROFESSOR: I'm going to tear them off, your ears, that's what I'm going to do to you, and then they won't hurt you anymore, my pet.

PUPIL: Oh . . . you're hurting me, oh, you're hurting me . . .

PROFESSOR: Look, come on, quickly, repeat after me: "kni" . . .

PUPIL: Oh, since you insist . . . knife . . . knife . . . (*In a lucid moment, ironically:*) Is that neo-Spanish . . . ?

PROFESSOR: If you like, yes, it's neo-Spanish, but hurry up . . . we haven't got time . . . And then, what do you mean by that insidious question? What are you up to?

PUPIL (*becoming more and more exhausted, weeping, desperate, at the same time both exasperated and in a trance*): Ah!

PROFESSOR: Repeat, watch. (*He imitates a cuckoo:*) Knife, knife . . . knife, knife . . . knife, knife . . . knife, knife . . .

PUPIL: Oh, my head . . . aches . . . (*With her hand she caressingly touches the parts of her body as she names them:*) . . . My eyes . . .

PROFESSOR (*like a cuckoo*): Knife, knife . . . knife, knife . . .

(*They are both standing.* THE PROFESSOR *still brandishes his invisible knife, nearly beside himself, as he circles around her in a sort of scalp dance, but it is important that this not be exaggerated and that his dance steps be only suggested.* THE PUPIL *stands facing the audience, then recoils in the direction of the window, sickly, languid, victimized.*)

PROFESSOR: Repeat, repeat: knife . . . knife . . . knife . . .

PUPIL: I've got a pain . . . my throat, neck . . . oh, my shoulders . . . my breast . . . knife . . .

PROFESSOR: Knife . . . knife . . . knife . . .

PUPIL: My hips . . . knife . . . my thighs . . . kni . . .

PROFESSOR: Pronounce it carefully . . . knife . . . knife . . .

PUPIL: Knife . . . my throat . . .

PROFESSOR: Knife . . . knife . . .

PUPIL: Knife . . . my shoulders . . . my arms, my breast, my hips . . . knife . . . knife . . .

PROFESSOR: That's right . . . Now, you're pronouncing it well . . .

PUPIL: Knife . . . my breast . . . my stomach . . .

PROFESSOR (*changing his voice*): Pay attention . . . don't break my window . . . the knife kills . . .

PUPIL (*in a weak voice*): Yes, yes . . . the knife kills?

PROFESSOR (*striking* THE PUPIL *with a very spectacular blow of the knife*): Aaah! That'll teach you!

(THE PUPIL *also cries "Aaah!" then falls, flopping in an immodest position onto a chair which, as though by chance, is near the window. The murderer and his victim shout "Aaah!" at the same moment. After the first blow of the knife,* THE PUPIL *flops onto the chair, her legs spread wide and hanging over both sides of the chair.* THE PROFESSOR *remains standing in front of her, his back to the audience. After the first blow, he strikes her dead with a second slash of the knife, from bottom to top. After that blow a noticeable convulsion shakes his whole body.*)

PROFESSOR (*winded, mumbling*): Bitch . . . Oh, that's good, that does me good . . . Ah! Ah! I'm exhausted . . . I can scarcely breathe . . . Aah! (*He breathes with difficulty; he falls — fortunately a chair is there; he mops his brow, mumbles some incomprehensible words; his breathing becomes normal. He gets up, looks at the knife in his hand, looks at the young girl, then as though he were waking up, in a panic:*) What have I done! What's going to happen to me now! What's going to happen! Oh! dear! Oh dear, I'm in trouble! Young lady, young lady, get up! (*He is agitated, still holding onto the invisible knife, which he doesn't know what to do with.*) Come now, young lady, the lesson is over . . . you may go . . . you can pay another time . . . Oh! she is dead . . . dea-ead . . . And by my knife . . . She is dea-ead . . . It's terrible. (*He calls* THE MAID:) Marie! Marie! My good Marie, come here! Ah! ah! (*The door on the right opens a little and* THE MAID *appears.*) No . . . don't come in . . . I made a mistake . . . I don't need you, Marie . . . I don't need you anymore . . . do you understand? . . .

(THE MAID *enters wearing a stern expression, without saying a word. She sees the corpse.*)

PROFESSOR (*in a voice less and less assured*): I don't need you, Marie . . .

MAID (*sarcastic*): Then, you're satisfied with your pupil, she's profited by your lesson?

PROFESSOR (*holding the knife behind his back*): Yes, the lesson is finished . . . but . . . she . . . she's still there . . . she doesn't want to leave . . .

MAID (*very harshly*): Is that a fact? . . .

PROFESSOR (*trembling*): It wasn't I . . . it wasn't I . . . Marie . . . No . . . I assure you . . . it wasn't I, my little Marie . . .

MAID: And who was it? Who was it then? Me?

PROFESSOR: I don't know . . . maybe . . .

MAID: Or the cat?

PROFESSOR: That's possible . . . I don't know . . .

MAID: And today makes it the fortieth time! . . . And every day it's the same thing! Every day! You should be ashamed, at your age . . . and you're going to make yourself sick! You won't have any pupils left. That will serve you right.

PROFESSOR (*irritated*): It wasn't my fault! She didn't want to learn! She was disobedient! She was a bad pupil! She didn't want to learn!

MAID: Liar! . . .

PROFESSOR (*craftily approaching* THE MAID, *holding the knife behind his back*): It's none of your business! (*He tries to strike her with a blow of the knife;* THE MAID *seizes his wrist in mid-gesture and twists it;* THE PROFESSOR *lets the knife fall to the floor*): . . . I'm sorry!

MAID (*gives him two loud, strong slaps;* THE PROFESSOR *falls onto the floor, on his prat; he sobs*): Little murderer! bastard! You're disgusting! You wanted to do that to me? I'm not one of your pupils, not me! (*She pulls him up by the collar, picks up his skullcap and puts it on his head; he's afraid she'll slap him again and holds his arm up to protect his face, like a child.*) Put the knife back where it belongs, go on! (THE PROFESSOR *goes and puts it back in the drawer of the buffet, then comes back to her.*) Now didn't I warn you, just a little while ago: arithmetic leads to philology, and philology leads to crime . . .

PROFESSOR: You said "to calamity"!

MAID: It's the same thing.

PROFESSOR: I didn't understand you. I thought that "calamity" was a city and that you meant that philology leads to the city of Calamity . . .

MAID: Liar! Old fox! An intellectual like you is not going to make a mistake in the meanings of words. Don't try to pull the wool over my eyes.

PROFESSOR (*sobbing*): I didn't kill her on purpose!

MAID: Are you sorry at least?

PROFESSOR: Oh, yes, Marie, I swear it to you!

MAID: I can't help feeling sorry for you! Ah! you're a good boy in spite of everything! I'll try to fix this. But don't start it again . . . It could give you a heart attack . . .

PROFESSOR: Yes, Marie! What are we going to do, now?

MAID: We're going to bury her . . . along with the thirty-nine others . . . that will make forty coffins . . . I'll call the undertakers and my lover, Father Auguste . . . I'll order the wreaths . . .

PROFESSOR: Yes, Marie, thank you very much.

MAID: Well, that's that. And perhaps it won't be necessary to call Auguste, since you yourself are something of a priest at times, if one can believe the gossip.

PROFESSOR: In any case, don't spend too much on the wreaths. She didn't pay for her lesson.

MAID: Don't worry . . . The least you can do is cover her up with her smock, she's not decent that way. And then we'll carry her out . . .

PROFESSOR: Yes, Marie, yes. (*He covers up the body.*) There's a chance that we'll get pinched . . . with forty coffins . . . Don't you think . . . people will be surprised . . . Suppose they ask us what's inside them?

MAID: Don't worry so much. We'll say that they're empty. And besides, people won't ask questions, they're used to it.

PROFESSOR: Even so . . .

MAID (*she takes out an armband with an insignia, perhaps the Nazi swastika*): Wait, if you're afraid, wear this, then you won't have anything more to be afraid of. (*She puts the armband around his arm.*) . . . That's good politics.

PROFESSOR: Thanks, my little Marie. With this, I won't need to worry . . . You're a good girl, Marie . . . very loyal . . .

MAID: That's enough. Come on, sir. Are you all right?

PROFESSOR: Yes, my little Marie. (THE MAID *and* THE PROFESSOR *take the body of the young girl, one by the shoulders, the other by the legs, and move towards the door on the right.*) Be careful. We don't want to hurt her. (*They exit.*)

(*The stage remains empty for several moments. We hear the doorbell ring at the left.*)

VOICE OF THE MAID: Just a moment, I'm coming!

(*She appears as she was at the beginning of the play, and goes towards the door. The doorbell rings again.*)

MAID (*aside*): She's certainly in a hurry, this one! (*Aloud:*) Just a moment! (*She goes to the door on the left, and opens it.*) Good morning, miss! You are the new pupil? You have come for the lesson? The Professor is expecting you. I'll go tell him that you've come. He'll be right down. Come in, miss, come in!

⌐◯⌐ THE LESSON, first performed in Paris in 1951, is the product of an age that can dispassionately contemplate its own wounds, derive a grim pleasure from philosophical nihilism, and produce literature that honestly seeks neither to please nor to instruct. Instead, it reflects reality in a shattered mirror — as bizarre and macabre and incoherent but sharply etched scenes of infinite suggestiveness — "open" parables that puzzle, tease, and elude interpretation. If one insists — it is hard to say how well or ill advised such an effort is — on relating a play like *The Lesson* to other areas of the contemporary intellectual scene, existentialism comes to mind, with its godless universe and its doctrine that man is what man does. But neither philosophy nor psychology nor any other rational discipline is likely to explain *The Lesson*. By the same token, one can have no argument with those who find its absurdities uninteresting or even offensive, or with the naive sophisticates who "refuse to be taken in" by something that is "obviously meant as a joke." But whether callous or gullible, one *can* try to record one's own unmistakable sense of dramatic power in the play.

It begins normally enough. Its stage picture and its opening action — the drab, professorial dining room-office, the small town glimpsed beyond the potted plants in the window, the red-faced maid rushing to answer the door — are the paraphernalia of straightforward, humdrum naturalism. The long stage direction near the beginning anticipates queerer developments to come as well as a patterned action,* but the Professor's and the Pupil's opening speeches seem to promise nothing more extraordinary than a satirical farce on timid pedantry and brash young ignorance. The satire grows more hilarious as the arithmetic lesson proceeds, but there is also Marie's ominous interruption, and we begin to be aware of speeches that touch on more than just the idiocies of the learning process:

PROFESSOR: . . . If they are very small, then there might be more units in the small numbers than in the large . . . if it is a question of other units . . .

PUPIL: In that case, the small numbers can be larger than the large numbers?

Still, what seems to be happening is that the lesson is turning into a clash of impeccable mathematical theory and common sense. The farce comes to a climax when the girl, earlier lavishly complimented

---

* Since the stage direction is not available to the theater audience, *reading The Lesson* — like reading a play by Shaw — clearly differs from *seeing* it in a way fundamentally different in kind from that in which reading and seeing any play can be said to differ. In the stage direction, Ionesco, as it were, tells all, and if he does not eliminate suspense, he substitutes one kind of suspense for another: we wonder not what will happen but how and why it happens and what the Professor's "final gesture" will be.

for knowing the name of the capital of France, suddenly proves to possess a brain like an electric computer in answering the Professor's preposterous problem in multiplication and the Professor sullenly rejects the answer — not because it is not correct (it is), but because it has not been arrived at by the proper method. And yet, there is an element of reasonableness in the Professor's attitude: the girl's triumph is due to rote learning, not to grasp of mathematics. On the other hand (the ironies flicker in all directions), *what* rote learning!

But we are also becoming aware of the two opposite movements announced in the long stage direction, and as the movements intersect and draw, respectively, toward frenzy and trance, we find it increasingly difficult to reduce their significance to a satirical allegory of how old teacher saps and absorbs young pupil's vitality until learning conquers and kills life. The double movement gives the play structure, but the allegory cannot contain its ending. It is both too ritualistic and too raw to be simply satirical. Satire does not account for the obvious sexual implications of the murder scene or for Marie's role as habitual accomplice. It does not answer the questions about the plot. What about the other thirty-nine victims? Where are the coffins? Why isn't the town alarmed, why are no inquiries made? Why the cyclical nature of the action? What about the nice young girl, all vivacity and thirst for knowledge, who is about to become still another victim of the total doctorate? For that matter, is there a sense in which the dead Pupil may be said to have reached her ambition?

Answers are not forthcoming. We may refuse to take the play seriously — but if we do, we have not come to terms with it; we have only refused to consider it worth bothering about. But the play remains — with the sharp solidity of its setting, the unambiguity of its events, its penetration of the rationalities with which we invest our experience of ourselves and our world. Even a prank — particularly a prank — has the power to embody Ionesco's conviction that "comic and tragic are merely two aspects of the same situation," that "there are no alternatives: if man is not tragic, he is ridiculous and painful, 'comic,' in fact" and that "by revealing his absurdity one can achieve a sort of tragedy.")

Arthur Miller

A VIEW
FROM THE BRIDGE

Characters

LOUIS	RODOLPHO
MIKE	FIRST IMMIGRATION OFFICER
ALFIERI	SECOND IMMIGRATION OFFICER
EDDIE	MR. LIPARI
CATHERINE	MRS. LIPARI
BEATRICE	TWO "SUBMARINES"
MARCO	NEIGHBORS
TONY	

ACT I

(The street and house front of a tenement building. The front is skeletal entirely. The main acting area is the living room-dining room of EDDIE's apartment. It is a worker's flat, clean, sparse, homely. There is a rocker down front; a round dining table at center, with chairs; and a portable phonograph.

At back are a bedroom door and an opening to the kitchen; none of these interiors are seen.

At the right, forestage, a desk. This is MR. ALFIERI's *law office.*

There is also a telephone booth. This is not used until the last scenes, so it may be covered or left in view.

A stairway leads up to the apartment, and then farther up to the next story, which is not seen.

Ramps, representing the street, run upstage and off to right and left.

As the curtain rises, LOUIS *and* MIKE, *longshoremen, are pitching coins against the building at left.*

A distant foghorn blows.

Enter ALFIERI, *a lawyer in his fifties turning gray; he is portly, good-humored, and thoughtful. The two pitchers nod to him as he passes. He crosses the stage to his desk, removes his hat, runs his fingers through his hair, and grinning, speaks to the audience.*)

ALFIERI: You wouldn't have known it, but something amusing has just happened. You see how uneasily they nod to me? That's because I am a lawyer. In this neighborhood to meet a lawyer or a priest on the street is unlucky. We're only thought of in connection with disasters, and they'd rather not get too close.

I often think that behind that suspicious little nod of theirs lie three thousand years of distrust. A lawyer means the law, and in Sicily, from where their fathers came, the law has not been a friendly idea since the Greeks were beaten.

I am inclined to notice the ruins in things, perhaps because I was born in Italy. . . . I only came here when I was twenty-five. In those days, Al Capone, the greatest Carthaginian of all, was learning his trade on these pavements, and Frankie Yale himself was cut precisely in half by a machine gun on the corner of Union Street, two blocks away. Oh, there were many here who were justly shot by unjust men. Justice is very important here.

But this is Red Hook, not Sicily. This is the slum that faces the bay on the seaward side of Brooklyn Bridge. This is the gullet of New York swallowing the tonnage of the world. And now we are quite civilized, quite American. Now we settle for half, and I like it better. I no longer keep a pistol in my filing cabinet.

And my practice is entirely unromantic.

My wife has warned me, so have my friends; they tell me the people in this neighborhood lack elegance, glamour. After all, who have I dealt with in my life? Longshoremen and their wives, and fathers and grandfathers, compensation cases, evictions, family squabbles — the petty troubles of the poor — and yet . . . every few years there is still a case, and as the parties tell me what the trouble is, the flat air in my office suddenly washes in with the green scent of the sea, the dust in this air is blown away and the thought comes that in some Caesar's year, in Calabria perhaps or on the cliff at Syracuse, another lawyer, quite differently dressed, heard the same complaint and sat there as powerless as I, and watched it run its bloody course.

(EDDIE *has appeared and has been pitching coins with the men and is highlighted among them. He is forty — a husky, slightly overweight longshoreman.*)

This one's name was Eddie Carbone, a longshoreman working the docks from Brooklyn Bridge to the breakwater where the open sea begins. (ALFIERI *walks into darkness.*)

EDDIE (*moving up steps into doorway*): Well, I'll see ya, fellas.

(CATHERINE *enters from kitchen, crosses down to window, looks out.*)

LOUIS: You workin' tomorrow?

EDDIE: Yeah, there's another day yet on that ship. See ya, Louis. (EDDIE *goes into the house, as light rises in the apartment.*)

(CATHERINE *is waving to* LOUIS *from the window and turns to him.*)

CATHERINE: Hi, Eddie!

(EDDIE *is pleased and therefore shy about it; he hangs up his cap and jacket.*)

EDDIE: Where you goin' all dressed up?

CATHERINE (*running her hands over her skirt*): I just got it. You like it?

EDDIE: Yeah, it's nice. And what happened to your hair?

CATHERINE: You like it? I fixed it different. (*Calling to kitchen.*) He's here, B.!

EDDIE: Beautiful. Turn around, lemme see in the back. (*She turns for him.*) Oh, if your mother was alive to see you now! She wouldn't believe it.

CATHERINE: You like it, huh?

EDDIE: You look like one of them girls that went to college. Where you goin'?

CATHERINE (*taking his arm*): Wait'll B. comes in, I'll tell you some-thing. Here, sit down. (*She is walking him to the armchair. Calling offstage.*) Hurry up, will you, B.?

EDDIE (*sitting*): What's goin' on?

CATHERINE: I'll get you a beer, all right?

EDDIE: Well, tell me what happened. Come over here, talk to me.

CATHERINE: I want to wait till B. comes in. (*She sits on her heels beside him.*) Guess how much we paid for the skirt.

EDDIE: I think it's too short, ain't it?

CATHERINE (*standing*): No! not when I stand up.

EDDIE: Yeah, but you gotta sit down sometimes.

CATHERINE: Eddie, it's the style now. (*She walks to show him.*) I mean, if you see me walkin' down the street —

EDDIE: Listen, you been givin' me the willies the way you walk down the street, I mean it.

CATHERINE: Why?

EDDIE: Catherine, I don't want to be a pest, but I'm tellin' you you're walkin' wavy.

CATHERINE: I'm walkin' wavy?

EDDIE: Now don't aggravate me, Katie, you are walkin' wavy! I don't like the looks they're givin' you in the candy store. And with them new high heels on the sidewalk — clack, clack, clack. The heads are turnin' like windmills.

CATHERINE: But those guys look at all the girls, you know that.

EDDIE: You ain't "all the girls."

CATHERINE (*almost in tears because he disapproves*): What do you want me to do? You want me to —

EDDIE: Now don't get mad, kid.

CATHERINE: Well, I don't know what you want from me.

EDDIE: Katie, I promised your mother on her deathbed. I'm respon-sible for you. You're a baby, you don't understand these things. I mean like when you stand here by the window, wavin' outside.

CATHERINE: I was wavin' to Louis!

EDDIE: Listen, I could tell you things about Louis which you wouldn't wave to him no more.

CATHERINE (*trying to joke him out of his warning*): Eddie, I wish there was one guy you couldn't tell me things about!

EDDIE: Catherine, do me a favor, will you? You're gettin' to be a big girl now, you gotta keep yourself more, you can't be so friendly, kid. (*Calls.*) Hey, B., what're you doin' in there? (*To* CATHERINE.) Get her in here, will you? I got news for her.

CATHERINE (*starting out*): What?

EDDIE: Her cousins landed.

CATHERINE (*clapping her hands together*): No! (*She turns instantly and starts for the kitchen.*) B.! Your cousins!

(BEATRICE *enters, wiping her hands with a towel.*)

BEATRICE (*in the face of* CATHERINE's *shout*): What?

CATHERINE: Your cousins got in!

BEATRICE (*astounded, turns to* EDDIE): What are you talkin' about? Where?

EDDIE: I was just knockin' off work before and Tony Bereli come over to me; he says the ship is in the North River.

BEATRICE (*her hands are clasped at her breast; she seems half in fear, half in unutterable joy*): They're all right?

EDDIE: He didn't see them yet, they're still on board. But as soon as they get off he'll meet them. He figures about ten o'clock they'll be here.

BEATRICE (*sits, almost weak from tension*): And they'll let them off the ship all right? That's fixed, heh?

EDDIE: Sure, they give them regular seamen papers and they walk off with the crew. Don't worry about it, B., there's nothin' to it. Couple of hours they'll be here.

BEATRICE: What happened? They wasn't supposed to be till next Thursday.

EDDIE: I don't know; they put them on any ship they can get them out on. Maybe the other ship they was supposed to take there was some danger — What you cryin' about?

BEATRICE (*astounded and afraid*): I'm — I just — I can't believe it! I didn't even buy a new tablecloth; I was gonna wash the walls —

EDDIE: Listen, they'll think it's a millionaire's house compared to the way they live. Don't worry about the walls. They'll be thankful. (*To* CATHERINE.) Whyn't you run down buy a tablecloth. Go ahead, here. (*He is reaching into his pocket.*)

CATHERINE: There's no stores open now.

EDDIE (*to* BEATRICE): You was gonna put a new cover on the chair.

BEATRICE: I know — well, I thought it was gonna be next week! I was gonna clean the walls, I was gonna wax the floors. (*She stands disturbed.*)

CATHERINE (*pointing upward*): Maybe Mrs. Dondero upstairs —

BEATRICE (*of the tablecloth*): No, hers is worse than this one. (*Suddenly.*) My God, I don't even have nothin' to eat for them! (*She starts for the kitchen.*)

EDDIE (*reaching out and grabbing her arm*): Hey, hey! Take it easy.

BEATRICE: No, I'm just nervous, that's all. (*To* CATHERINE.) I'll make the fish.

EDDIE: You're savin' their lives, what're you worryin' about the table-cloth? They probably didn't see a tablecloth in their whole life where they come from.

BEATRICE (*looking into his eyes*): I'm just worried about you, that's all I'm worried.

EDDIE: Listen, as long as they know where they're gonna sleep.

BEATRICE: I told them in the letters. They're sleepin' on the floor.

EDDIE: Beatrice, all I'm worried about is you got such a heart that I'll end up on the floor with you, and they'll be in our bed.

BEATRICE: All right, stop it.

EDDIE: Because as soon as you see a tired relative, I end up on the floor.

BEATRICE: When did you end up on the floor?

EDDIE: When your father's house burned down I didn't end up on the floor?

BEATRICE: Well, their house burned down!

EDDIE: Yeah, but it didn't keep burnin' for two weeks!

BEATRICE: All right, look, I'll tell them to go someplace else. (*She starts into the kitchen.*)

EDDIE: Now wait a minute. Beatrice! (*She halts. He goes to her.*) I just don't want you bein' pushed around, that's all. You got too big a heart. (*He touches her hand.*) What're you so touchy?

BEATRICE: I'm just afraid if it don't turn out good you'll be mad at me.

EDDIE: Listen, if everybody keeps his mouth shut, nothin' can happen. They'll pay for their board.

BEATRICE: Oh, I told them.

EDDIE: Then what the hell. (*Pause. He moves.*) It's an honor, B. I mean it. I was just thinkin' before, comin' home, suppose my father didn't come to this country, and I was starvin' like them over there . . . and I had people in America could keep me a couple of months? The man would be honored to lend me a place to sleep.

BEATRICE (*there are tears in her eyes. She turns to* CATHERINE): You see what he is? (*She turns and grabs* EDDIE's *face in her hands.*) Mmm! You're an angel! God'll bless you. (*He is gratefully smiling.*) You'll see, you'll get a blessing for this!

EDDIE (*laughing*): I'll settle for my own bed.

BEATRICE: Go, Baby, set the table.

CATHERINE: We didn't tell him about me yet.

BEATRICE: Let him eat first, then we'll tell him. Bring everything in. (*She hurries* CATHERINE *out.*)

EDDIE (*sitting at the table*): What's all that about? Where's she goin'?

BEATRICE: Noplace. It's very good news, Eddie. I want you to be happy.

EDDIE: What's goin' on?

(CATHERINE *enters with plates, forks.*)

BEATRICE: She's got a job.

(*Pause.* EDDIE *looks at* CATHERINE, *then back to* BEATRICE.)

EDDIE: What job? She's gonna finish school.

CATHERINE: Eddie, you won't believe it —

EDDIE: No — no, you gonna finish school. What kinda job, what do you mean? All of a sudden you —

CATHERINE: Listen a minute, it's wonderful.

EDDIE: It's not wonderful. You'll never get nowheres unless you finish school. You can't take no job. Why didn't you ask me before you take a job?

BEATRICE: She's askin' you now, she didn't take nothin' yet.

CATHERINE: Listen a minute! I came to school this morning and the principal called me out of the class, see? To go to his office.

EDDIE: Yeah?

CATHERINE: So I went in and he says to me he's got my records, y'know? And there's a company wants a girl right away. It ain't exactly a secretary, it's a stenographer first, but pretty soon you get to be secretary. And he says to me that I'm the best student in the whole class —

BEATRICE: You hear that?

EDDIE: Well why not? Sure she's the best.

CATHERINE: I'm the best student, he says, and if I want, I should take the job and the end of the year he'll let me take the examination and he'll give me the certificate. So I'll save practically a year!

EDDIE (*strangely nervous*): Where's the job? What company?

CATHERINE: It's a big plumbing company over Nostrand Avenue.

EDDIE: Nostrand Avenue and where?

CATHERINE: It's someplace by the Navy Yard.

BEATRICE: Fifty dollars a week, Eddie.

EDDIE (*to* CATHERINE, *surprised*): Fifty?

CATHERINE: I swear.

(*Pause.*)

EDDIE: What about all the stuff you wouldn't learn this year, though?

CATHERINE: There's nothin' more to learn, Eddie, I just gotta practice from now on. I know all the symbols and I know the keyboard. I'll just get faster, that's all. And when I'm workin' I'll keep gettin' better and better, you see?

BEATRICE: Work is the best practice anyway.

EDDIE: That ain't what I wanted, though.

CATHERINE: Why! It's a great big company —

EDDIE: I don't like that neighborhood over there.

CATHERINE: It's a block and half from the subway, he says.

EDDIE: Near the Navy Yard plenty can happen in a block and a half. And a plumbin' company! That's one step over the water front. They're practically longshoremen.

BEATRICE: Yeah, but she'll be in the office, Eddie.

EDDIE: I know she'll be in the office, but that ain't what I had in mind.

BEATRICE: Listen, she's gotta go to work sometime.

EDDIE: Listen, B., she'll be with a lotta plumbers? And sailors up and down the street? So what did she go to school for?

CATHERINE: But it's fifty a week, Eddie.

EDDIE: Look, did I ask you for money? I supported you this long I support you a little more. Please, do me a favor, will ya? I want you to be with different kind of people. I want you to be in a nice office. Maybe a lawyer's office someplace in New York in one of them nice buildings. I mean if you're gonna get outa here then get out; don't go practically in the same kind of neighborhood.

(*Pause.* CATHERINE *lowers her eyes.*)

BEATRICE: Go, Baby, bring in the supper. (CATHERINE *goes out.*) Think about it a little bit, Eddie. Please. She's crazy to start work. It's not a little shop, it's a big company. Some day she could be a secretary. They picked her out of the whole class. (*He is silent, staring down at the tablecloth, fingering the pattern.*) What are you worried about? She could take care of herself. She'll get out of the subway and be in the office in two minutes.

EDDIE (*somehow sickened*): I know that neighborhood, B., I don't like it.

BEATRICE: Listen, if nothin' happened to her in this neighborhood it ain't gonna happen noplace else. (*She turns his face to her.*) Look, you gotta get used to it, she's no baby no more. Tell her to take it. (*He turns his head away.*) You hear me? (*She is angering.*) I don't understand you; she's seventeen years old, you gonna keep her in the house all her life?

EDDIE (*insulted*): What kinda remark is that?

BEATRICE (*with sympathy but insistent force*): Well, I don't understand when it ends. First it was gonna be when she graduated high school, so she graduated high school. Then it was gonna be when she learned stenographer, so she learned stenographer. So what're we gonna wait for now? I mean it, Eddie, sometimes I don't understand you; they picked her out of the whole class, it's an honor for her.

(CATHERINE *enters with food, which she silently sets on the table. After a moment of watching her face,* EDDIE *breaks into a smile, but it almost seems that tears will form in his eyes.*)

EDDIE: With your hair that way you look like a madonna, you know that? You're the madonna type. (*She doesn't look at him, but continues ladling out food onto the plates.*) You wanna go to work, heh, Madonna?

CATHERINE (*softly*): Yeah.

EDDIE (*with a sense of her childhood, her babyhood, and the years*): All right, go to work. (*She looks at him, then rushes and hugs him.*) Hey, hey! Take it easy! (*He holds her face away from him to look at her.*) What're you cryin' about? (*He is affected by her, but smiles his emotion away.*)

CATHERINE (*sitting at her place*): I just — (*Bursting out.*) I'm gonna buy all new dishes with my first pay! (*They laugh warmly.*) I mean it. I'll fix up the whole house! I'll buy a rug!

EDDIE: And then you'll move away.

CATHERINE: No, Eddie!

EDDIE (*grinning*): Why not? That's life. And you'll come visit on Sundays, then once a month, then Christmas and New Year's, finally.

CATHERINE (*grasping his arm to reassure him and to erase the accusation*): No, please!

EDDIE (*smiling but hurt*): I only ask you one thing — don't trust nobody. You got a good aunt but she's got too big a heart, you learned bad from her. Believe me.

BEATRICE: Be the way you are, Katie, don't listen to him.

EDDIE (*to* BEATRICE — *strangely and quickly resentful*): You lived in a house all your life, what do you know about it? You never worked in your life.

BEATRICE: She likes people. What's wrong with that?

EDDIE: Because most people ain't people. She's goin' to work; plumbers; they'll chew her to pieces if she don't watch out. (*To* CATHERINE.) Believe me, Katie, the less you trust, the less you be sorry.

(EDDIE *crosses himself and the women do the same, and they eat.*)

CATHERINE: First thing I'll buy is a rug, heh, B.?

BEATRICE: I don't mind. (*To* EDDIE.) I smelled coffee all day today. You unloadin' coffee today?

EDDIE: Yeah, a Brazil ship.

CATHERINE: I smelled it too. It smelled all over the neighborhood.

EDDIE: That's one time, boy, to be a longshoreman is a pleasure. I could work coffee ships twenty hours a day. You go down in the hold, y'know? It's like flowers, that smell. We'll bust a bag tomorrow, I'll bring you some.

BEATRICE: Just be sure there's no spiders in it, will ya? I mean it. (*She directs this to* CATHERINE, *rolling her eyes upward.*) I still remember that spider coming out of that bag he brung home. I nearly died.

EDDIE: You call that a spider? You oughta see what comes outa the bananas sometimes.

BEATRICE: Don't talk about it!

EDDIE: I seen spiders could stop a Buick.

BEATRICE (*clapping her hands over her ears*): All right, shut up!

EDDIE (*laughing and taking a watch out of his pocket*): Well, who started with spiders?

BEATRICE: All right, I'm sorry, I didn't mean it. Just don't bring none home again. What time is it?

EDDIE: Quarter nine. (*Puts watch back in his pocket. They continue eating in silence.*)

CATHERINE: He's bringin' them ten o'clock, Tony?

EDDIE: Around, yeah. (*He eats.*)

CATHERINE: Eddie, suppose somebody asks if they're livin' here. (*He looks at her as though already she had divulged something publicly. Defensively.*) I mean if they ask.

EDDIE: Now look, Baby, I can see we're gettin' mixed up again here.

CATHERINE: No, I just mean . . . people'll see them goin' in and out.

EDDIE: I don't care who sees them goin' in and out as long as you don't see them goin' in and out. And this goes for you too, B. You don't see nothin' and you don't know nothin'.

BEATRICE: What do you mean? I understand.

EDDIE: You don't understand; you still think you can talk about this to somebody just a little bit. Now lemme say it once and for all, because you're makin' me nervous again, both of you. I don't care if somebody comes in the house and sees them sleepin' on the floor, it never comes out of your mouth who they are or what they're doin' here.

BEATRICE: Yeah, but my mother'll know —

EDDIE: Sure she'll know, but just don't you be the one who told her, that's all. This is the United States government you're playin' with now, this is the Immigration Bureau. If you said it you knew it, if you didn't say it you didn't know it.

CATHERINE: Yeah, but Eddie, suppose somebody —

EDDIE: I don't care what question it is. You — don't — know — nothin'. They got stool pigeons all over this neighborhood they're payin' them every week for information, and you don't know who they are. It could be your best friend. You hear? (*To* BEATRICE.) Like Vinny Bolzano, remember Vinny?

BEATRICE: Oh, yeah. God forbid.

EDDIE: Tell her about Vinny. (*To* CATHERINE.) You think I'm blowin' steam here? (*To* BEATRICE.) Go ahead, tell her. (*To* CATHERINE.) You was a baby then. There was a family lived next door to her mother, he was about sixteen —

BEATRICE: No, he was no more than fourteen, cause I was to his confirmation in Saint Agnes. But the family had an uncle that they were hidin' in the house, and he snitched to the Immigration.

CATHERINE: The kid snitched?

EDDIE: On his own uncle!

CATHERINE: What, was he crazy?

EDDIE: He was crazy after, I tell you that, boy.

BEATRICE: Oh, it was terrible. He had five brothers and the old father. And they grabbed him in the kitchen and pulled him down the stairs — three flights his head was bouncin' like a coconut. And they spit on him in the street, his own father and his brothers. The whole neighborhood was cryin'.

CATHERINE: Ts! So what happened to him?

BEATRICE: I think he went away. (*To* EDDIE.) I never seen him again, did you?

EDDIE (*rises during this, taking out his watch*): Him? You'll never see him no more, a guy do a thing like that? How's he gonna show his face? (*To* CATHERINE, *as he gets up uneasily.*) Just remember, kid, you can quicker get back a million dollars that was stole than a word that you gave away. (*He is standing now, stretching his back.*)

CATHERINE: Okay, I won't say a word to nobody, I swear.

EDDIE: Gonna rain tomorrow. We'll be slidin' all over the decks. Maybe you oughta put something on for them, they be here soon.

BEATRICE: I only got fish, I hate to spoil it if they ate already. I'll wait, it only takes a few minutes; I could broil it.

CATHERINE: What happens, Eddie, when that ship pulls out and they ain't on it, though? Don't the captain say nothin'?

EDDIE (*slicing an apple with his pocket knife*): Captain's pieced off, what do you mean?

CATHERINE: Even the captain?

EDDIE: What's the matter, the captain don't have to live? Captain gets a piece, maybe one of the mates, piece for the guy in Italy who fixed the papers for them, Tony here'll get a little bite. . . .

BEATRICE: I just hope they get work here, that's all I hope.

EDDIE: Oh, the syndicate'll fix jobs for them; till they pay 'em off they'll get them work every day. It's after the pay-off, then they'll have to scramble like the rest of us.

BEATRICE: Well, it be better than they got there.

EDDIE: Oh sure, well, listen. So you gonna start Monday, heh, Madonna?

CATHERINE (*embarrassed*): I'm supposed to, yeah.

(EDDIE *is standing facing the two seated women. First* BEATRICE *smiles, then* CATHERINE, *for a powerful emotion is on him, a childish one and a knowing fear, and the tears show in his eyes — and they are shy before the avowal.*)

EDDIE (*sadly smiling, yet somehow proud of her*): Well . . . I hope you have good luck. I wish you the best. You know that, kid.

CATHERINE (*rising, trying to laugh*): You sound like I'm goin' a million miles!

EDDIE: I know. I guess I just never figured on one thing.

CATHERINE (*smiling*): What?

EDDIE: That you would ever grow up. (*He utters a soundless laugh at himself, feeling his breast pocket of his shirt.*) I left a cigar in my other coat, I think. (*He starts for the bedroom.*)

CATHERINE: Stay there! I'll get it for you.

(*She hurries out. There is a slight pause, and* EDDIE *turns to* BEATRICE, *who has been avoiding his gaze.*)

EDDIE: What are you mad at me lately?

BEATRICE: Who's mad? (*She gets up, clearing the dishes.*) I'm not mad. (*She picks up the dishes and turns to him.*) You're the one is mad. (*She turns and goes into the kitchen as* CATHERINE *enters from the bedroom with a cigar and a pack of matches.*)

CATHERINE: Here! I'll light it for you! (*She strikes a match and holds it to his cigar. He puffs. Quietly.*) Don't worry about me, Eddie, heh?

EDDIE: Don't burn yourself. (*Just in time she blows out the match.*) You better go in help her with the dishes.

CATHERINE (*turns quickly to the table, and, seeing the table cleared, she says, almost guiltily*): Oh! (*She hurries into the kitchen, and as she exits there.*) I'll do the dishes, B.!

(*Alone,* EDDIE *stands looking toward the kitchen for a moment. Then he takes out his watch, glances at it, replaces it in his pocket, sits in the armchair, and stares at the smoke flowing out of his mouth.*

The lights go down, then come up on ALFIERI, *who has moved onto the forestage.*)

ALFIERI: He was as good a man as he had to be in a life that was hard and even. He worked on the piers when there was work, he brought home his pay, and he lived. And toward ten o'clock of that night, after they had eaten, the cousins came.

(*The lights fade on* ALFIERI *and rise on the street. Enter* TONY, *escorting* MARCO *and* RODOLPHO, *each with a valise.* TONY *halts, indicates the house. They stand for a moment looking at it.*)

MARCO (*he is a square-built peasant of thirty-two, suspicious, tender, and quiet-voiced*): Thank you.
TONY: You're on your own now. Just be careful, that's all. Ground floor.
MARCO: Thank you.
TONY (*indicating the house*): I'll see you on the pier tomorrow. You'll go to work.

(MARCO *nods.* TONY *continues on walking down the street.*)

RODOLPHO: This will be the first house I ever walked into in America! Imagine! She said they were poor!
MARCO: Ssh! Come. (*They go to door.*)

(MARCO *knocks. The lights rise in the room.* EDDIE *goes and opens the door. Enter* MARCO *and* RODOLPHO, *removing their caps.* BEATRICE *and* CATHERINE *enter from the kitchen. The lights fade in the street.*)

EDDIE: You Marco?
MARCO: Marco.
EDDIE: Come on in! (*He shakes* MARCO's *hand.*)
BEATRICE: Here, take the bags!
MARCO (*nods, looks to the women and fixes on* BEATRICE. *Crosses to* BEATRICE): Are you my cousin? (*She nods. He kisses her hand.*)
BEATRICE (*above the table, touching her chest with her hand*): Beatrice. This is my husband, Eddie. (*All nod.*) Catherine, my sister Nancy's daughter. (*The brothers nod.*)
MARCO (*indicating* RODOLPHO): My brother. Rodolpho. (RODOLPHO

nods. MARCO *comes with a certain formal stiffness to* EDDIE.) I
want to tell you now Eddie — when you say go, we will go.

EDDIE: Oh, no . . . (*Takes* MARCO's *bag.*)

MARCO: I see it's a small house, but soon, maybe, we can have our own
house.

EDDIE: You're welcome, Marco, we got plenty of room here. Katie, give
them supper, heh? (*Exits into bedroom with their bags.*)

CATHERINE: Come here, sit down. I'll get you some soup.

MARCO (*as they go to the table*): We ate on the ship. Thank you. (*To*
EDDIE, *calling off to bedroom.*) Thank you.

BEATRICE: Get some coffee. We'll all have coffee. Come sit down.

(RODOLPHO *and* MARCO *sit, at the table.*)

CATHERINE (*wondrously*): How come he's so dark and you're so light,
Rodolpho?

RODOLPHO (*ready to laugh*): I don't know. A thousand years ago, they
say, the Danes invaded Sicily.

(BEATRICE *kisses* RODOLPHO. *They laugh as* EDDIE *enters.*)

CATHERINE (*to* BEATRICE): He's practically blond!

EDDIE: How's the coffee doin'?

CATHERINE (*brought up*): I'm gettin' it. (*She hurries out to kitchen.*)

EDDIE (*sits on his rocker*): Yiz have a nice trip?

MARCO: The ocean is always rough. But we are good sailors.

EDDIE: No trouble gettin' here?

MARCO: No. The man brought us. Very nice man.

RODOLPHO (*to* EDDIE): He says we start to work tomorrow. Is he
honest?

EDDIE (*laughing*): No. But as long as you owe them money, they'll get
you plenty of work. (*To* MARCO.) Yiz ever work on the piers in
Italy?

MARCO: Piers? Ts! — no.

RODOLPHO (*smiling at the smallness of his town*): In our town there
are no piers, only the beach, and little fishing boats.

BEATRICE: So what kinda work did yiz do?

MARCO (*shrugging shyly, even embarrassed*): Whatever there is, anything.

RODOLPHO: Sometimes they build a house, or if they fix the bridge —
Marco is a mason and I bring him the cement. (*He laughs.*) In harvest time we work in the fields . . . if there is work. Anything.

EDDIE: Still bad there, heh?

MARCO: Bad, yes.

RODOLPHO (*laughing*): It's terrible! We stand around all day in the piazza listening to the fountain like birds. Everybody waits only for the train.

BEATRICE: What's on the train?

RODOLPHO: Nothing. But if there are many passengers and you're lucky you make a few lire to push the taxi up the hill.

(*Enter* CATHERINE; *she listens.*)

BEATRICE: You gotta push a taxi?

RODOLPHO (*laughing*): Oh, sure! It's a feature in our town. The horses in our town are skinnier than goats. So if there are too many passengers we help to push the carriages up to the hotel. (*He laughs.*) In our town the horses are only for show.

CATHERINE: Why don't they have automobile taxis?

RODOLPHO: There is one. We push that too. (*They laugh.*) Everything in our town, you gotta push!

BEATRICE (*to* EDDIE): How do you like that!

EDDIE (*to* MARCO): So what're you wanna do, you gonna stay here in this country or you wanna go back?

MARCO (*surprised*): Go back?

EDDIE: Well, you're married, ain't you?

MARCO: Yes. I have three children.

BEATRICE: Three! I thought only one.

MARCO: Oh, no. I have three now. Four years, five years, six years.

BEATRICE: Ah . . . I bet they're cryin' for you already, heh?

MARCO: What can I do? The older one is sick in his chest. My wife — she feeds them from her own mouth. I tell you the truth, if I stay there they will never grow up. They eat the sunshine.

BEATRICE: My God. So how long you want to stay?

MARCO: With your permission, we will stay maybe a —

EDDIE: She don't mean in this house, she means in the country.

MARCO: Oh. Maybe four, five, six years, I think.

RODOLPHO (*smiling*): He trusts his wife.

BEATRICE: Yeah, but maybe you'll get enough, you'll be able to go back quicker.

MARCO: I hope. I don't know. (*To* EDDIE.) I understand it's not so good here either.

EDDIE: Oh, you guys'll be all right — till you pay them off, anyway. After that, you'll have to scramble, that's all. But you'll make better here than you could there.

RODOLPHO: How much? We hear all kinds of figures. How much can a man make? We work hard, we'll work all day, all night —

(MARCO *raises a hand to hush him.*)

EDDIE (*he is coming more and more to address* MARCO *only*): On the average a whole year? Maybe — well, it's hard to say, see. Sometimes we lay off, there's no ships three four weeks.

MARCO: Three, four weeks! — Ts!

EDDIE: But I think you could probably — thirty, forty a week, over the whole twelve months of the year.

MARCO (*rises, crosses to* EDDIE): Dollars.

EDDIE: Sure dollars.

(MARCO *puts an arm round* RODOLPHO *and they laugh.*)

MARCO: If we can stay here a few months, Beatrice —

BEATRICE: Listen, you're welcome, Marco —

MARCO: Because I could send them a little more if I stay here.

BEATRICE: As long as you want, we got plenty a room.

MARCO (*his eyes are showing tears*): My wife — (*To* EDDIE.) My wife — I want to send right away maybe twenty dollars —

EDDIE: You could send them something next week already.

MARCO (*he is near tears*): Eduardo . . . (*He goes to* EDDIE, *offering his hand.*)

EDDIE: Don't thank me. Listen, what the hell, it's no skin off me. (*To* CATHERINE.) What happened to the coffee?

CATHERINE: I got it on. (*To* RODOLPHO.) You married too? No.

RODOLPHO (*rises*): Oh, no . . .

BEATRICE (*to* CATHERINE): I told you he —

CATHERINE: I know, I just thought maybe he got married recently.

RODOLPHO: I have no money to get married. I have a nice face, but no money. (*He laughs.*)

CATHERINE (*to* BEATRICE): He's a real blond!

BEATRICE (*to* RODOLPHO): You want to stay here too, heh? For good?

RODOLPHO: Me? Yes, forever! Me, I want to be an American. And then I want to go back to Italy when I am rich, and I will buy a motorcycle. (*He smiles.* MARCO *shakes him affectionately.*)

CATHERINE: A motorcycle!

RODOLPHO: With a motorcycle in Italy you will never starve any more.

BEATRICE: I'll get you coffee. (*She exits to the kitchen.*)

EDDIE: What you do with a motorcycle?

MARCO: He dreams, he dreams.

RODOLPHO (*to Marco*): Why? (*To Eddie.*) Messages! The rich people in the hotel always need someone who will carry a message. But quickly, and with a great noise. With a blue motorcycle I would station myself in the courtyard of the hotel, and in a little while I would have messages.

MARCO: When you have no wife you have dreams.

EDDIE: Why can't you just walk, or take a trolley or sump'm?

(*Enter* BEATRICE *with coffee.*)

RODOLPHO: Oh, no, the machine, the machine is necessary. A man comes into a great hotel and says, I am a messenger. Who is this man? He disappears walking, there is no noise, nothing. Maybe he will never come back, maybe he will never deliver the message. But a man who rides up on a great machine, this man is responsible, this man exists. He will be given messages. (*He helps* BEATRICE *set out the coffee things.*) I am also a singer, though.

EDDIE: You mean a regular — ?

RODOLPHO: Oh, yes. One night last year Andreola got sick. Baritone. And I took his place in the garden of the hotel. Three arias I sang without a mistake! Thousand-lire notes they threw from the tables, money was falling like a storm in the treasury. It was magnificent. We lived six months on that night, eh, Marco?

(MARCO *nods doubtfully.*)

MARCO: Two months.

(EDDIE *laughs.*)

BEATRICE: Can't you get a job in that place?

RODOLPHO: Andreola got better. He's a baritone, very strong.

(BEATRICE *laughs.*)

MARCO (*regretfully, to* BEATRICE): He sang too loud.

RODOLPHO: Why too loud?

MARCO: Too loud. The guests in that hotel are all Englishmen. They don't like too loud.

RODOLPHO (*to* CATHERINE): Nobody ever said it was too loud!

MARCO: I say. It was too loud. (*To* BEATRICE.) I knew it as soon as he started to sing. Too loud.

RODOLPHO: Then why did they throw so much money?

MARCO: They paid for your courage. The English like courage. But once is enough.

RODOLPHO (*to all but* MARCO): I never heard anybody say it was too loud.

CATHERINE: Did you ever hear of jazz?

RODOLPHO: Oh, sure! I *sing* jazz.

CATHERINE (*rises*): You could sing jazz?

RODOLPHO: Oh, I sing Napolidan, jazz, bel canto — I sing "Paper Doll," you like "Paper Doll"?

CATHERINE: Oh, sure, I'm crazy for "Paper Doll." Go ahead, sing it.

RODOLPHO (*takes his stance after getting a nod of permission from* MARCO, *and with a high tenor voice begins singing*):
"I'll tell you boys it's tough to be alone,
And it's tough to love a doll that's not your own.
I'm through with all of them,
I'll never fall again,
Hey, boy, what you gonna do?
I'm gonna buy a paper doll that I can call my own,
A doll that other fellows cannot steal.

(EDDIE *rises and moves upstage.*)

And then those flirty, flirty guys
With their flirty, flirty eyes
Will have to flirt with dollies that are real —"
EDDIE: Hey, kid — hey, wait a minute —
CATHERINE (*enthralled*): Leave him finish, it's beautiful! (*To* BEATRICE.) He's terrific! It's terrific, Rodolpho.
EDDIE: Look, kid; you don't want to be picked up, do ya?
MARCO: No — no! (*He rises.*)
EDDIE (*indicating the rest of the building*): Because we never had no singers here . . . and all of a sudden there's a singer in the house, y'know what I mean?
MARCO: Yes, yes. You'll be quiet, Rodolpho.
EDDIE (*he is flushed*): They got guys all over the place, Marco. I mean.
MARCO: Yes. He'll be quiet. (*To* RODOLPHO.) You'll be quiet.

(RODOLPHO *nods.* EDDIE *has risen, with iron control, even a smile. He moves to* CATHERINE.)

EDDIE: What's the high heels for, Garbo?
CATHERINE: I figured for tonight —
EDDIE: Do me a favor, will you? Go ahead.

(*Embarrassed now, angered,* CATHERINE *goes out into the bedroom.* BEATRICE *watches her go and gets up; in passing, she gives* EDDIE *a cold look, restrained only by the strangers, and goes to the table to pour coffee.*)

EDDIE (*striving to laugh, and to* MARCO, *but directed as much to* BEATRICE): All actresses they want to be around here.
RODOLPHO (*happy about it*): In Italy too! All the girls.

(CATHERINE *emerges from the bedroom in low-heel shoes, comes to the table.* RODOLPHO *is lifting a cup.*)

EDDIE (*he is sizing up* RODOPHLO, *and there is a concealed suspicion*):
Yeah, heh?

RODOLPHO: Yes! (*Laughs, indicating* CATHERINE.) Especially when
they are so beautiful!

CATHERINE: You like sugar?

RODOLPHO: Sugar? Yes! I like sugar very much!

(EDDIE *is downstage, watching as she pours a spoonful of sugar
into his cup, his face puffed with trouble, and the room dies.
Lights rise on* ALFIERI.)

ALFIERI: Who can ever know what will be discovered? Eddie Carbone
had never expected to have a destiny. A man works, raises his family,
goes bowling, eats, gets old, and then he dies. Now, as the weeks
passed, there was a future, there was a trouble that would not go
away.

(*The lights fade on* ALFIERI, *then rise on* EDDIE *standing at the
doorway of the house.* BEATRICE *enters on the street. She sees*
EDDIE, *smiles at him. He looks away. She starts to enter the house
when* EDDIE *speaks.*)

EDDIE: It's after eight.

BEATRICE: Well, it's a long show at the Paramount.

EDDIE: They must've seen every picture in Brooklyn by now. He's supposed to stay in the house when he ain't working. He ain't supposed
to go advertising himself.

BEATRICE: Well that's his trouble, what do you care? If they pick him
up they pick him up, that's all. Come in the house.

EDDIE: What happened to the stenography? I don't see her practice no
more.

BEATRICE: She'll get back to it. She's excited, Eddie.

EDDIE: She tell you anything?

BEATRICE (*comes to him, now the subject is opened*): What's the matter with you? He's a nice kid, what do you want from him?

EDDIE: That's a nice kid? He gives me the heeby-jeebies.

BEATRICE (*smiling*): Ah, go on, you're just jealous.

EDDIE: Of *him*? Boy, you don't think much of me.

BEATRICE: I don't understand you. What's so terrible about him?

EDDIE: You mean it's all right with you? That's gonna be her husband?

BEATRICE: Why? He's a nice fella, hard workin', he's a good-lookin'
fella.

EDDIE: He sings on the ships, didja know that?

BEATRICE: What do you mean, he sings?

EDDIE: Just what I said, he sings. Right on the deck, all of a sudden, a whole song comes out of his mouth — with motions. You know what they're callin' him now? Paper Doll they're callin' him, Canary. He's like a weird. He comes out on the pier, one-two-three, it's a regular free show.

BEATRICE: Well, he's a kid; he don't know how to behave himself yet.

EDDIE: And with that wacky hair; he's like a chorus girl or sump'm.

BEATRICE: So he's blond, so —

EDDIE: I just hope that's his regular hair, that's all I hope.

BEATRICE: You crazy or sump'm? (*She tries to turn him to her.*)

EDDIE (*he keeps his head turned away*): What's so crazy? I don't like his whole way.

BEATRICE: Listen, you never seen a blond guy in your life? What about Whitey Balso?

EDDIE (*turning to her victoriously*): Sure, but Whitey don't sing; he don't do like that on the ships.

BEATRICE: Well, maybe that's the way they do in Italy.

EDDIE: Then why don't his brother sing? Marco goes around like a man; nobody kids Marco. (*He moves from her, halts. She realizes there is a campaign solidified in him.*) I tell you the truth I'm surprised I have to tell you all this. I mean I'm surprised, B.

BEATRICE (*she goes to him with purpose now*): Listen, you ain't gonna start nothin' here.

EDDIE: I ain't startin' nothin', but I ain't gonna stand around lookin' at that. For that character I didn't bring her up. I swear, B., I'm surprised at you; I sit there waitin' for you to wake up but everything is great with you.

BEATRICE: No, everything ain't great with me.

EDDIE: No?

BEATRICE: No. But I got other worries.

EDDIE: Yeah. (*He is already weakening.*)

BEATRICE: Yeah, you want me to tell you?

EDDIE (*in retreat*): Why? What worries you got?

BEATRICE: When am I gonna be a wife again, Eddie?

EDDIE: I ain't been feelin' good. They bother me since they came.

BEATRICE: It's almost three months you don't feel good; they're only here a couple of weeks. It's three months, Eddie.

EDDIE: I don't know, B. I don't want to talk about it.

BEATRICE: What's the matter, Eddie, you don't like me, heh?

EDDIE: What do you mean, I don't like you? I said I don't feel good, that's all.

BEATRICE: Well, tell me, am I doing something wrong? Talk to me.

EDDIE (*Pause. He can't speak, then*): I can't. I can't talk about it.

BEATRICE: Well tell me what —
EDDIE: I got nothin' to say about it!

(*She stands for a moment; he is looking off; she turns to go into the house.*)

EDDIE: I'll be all right, B.; just lay off me, will ya? I'm worried about her.
BEATRICE: The girl is gonna be eighteen years old, it's time already.
EDDIE: B., he's taking her for a ride!
BEATRICE: All right, that's her ride. What're you gonna stand over her till she's forty? Eddie, I want you to cut it out now, you hear me? I don't like it! Now come in the house.
EDDIE: I want to take a walk, I'll be in right away.
BEATRICE: They ain't goin' to come any quicker if you stand in the street. It ain't nice, Eddie.
EDDIE: I'll be in right away. Go ahead. (*He walks off.*)

(*She goes into the house.* EDDIE *glances up the street, sees* LOUIS *and* MIKE *coming, and sits on an iron railing.* LOUIS *and* MIKE *enter.*)

LOUIS: Wanna go bowlin' tonight?
EDDIE: I'm too tired. Goin' to sleep.
LOUIS: How's your two submarines?
EDDIE: They're okay.
LOUIS: I see they're gettin' work allatime.
EDDIE: Oh yeah, they're doin' all right.
MIKE: That's what we oughta do. We oughta leave the country and come in under the water. Then we get work.
EDDIE: You ain't kiddin'.
LOUIS: Well, what the hell. Y'know?
EDDIE: Sure.
LOUIS (*sits on railing beside* EDDIE): Believe me, Eddie, you got a lotta credit comin' to you.
EDDIE: Aah, they don't bother me, don't cost me nutt'n.
MIKE: That older one, boy, he's a regular bull. I seen him the other day liftin' coffee bags over the Matson Line. They leave him alone he woulda load the whole ship by himself.
EDDIE: Yeah, he's a strong guy, that guy. Their father was a regular giant, supposed to be.
LOUIS: Yeah, you could see. He's a regular slave.
MIKE (*grinning*): That blond one, though — (EDDIE *looks at him.*) He's got a sense of humor. (LOUIS *snickers.*)
EDDIE (*searchingly*): Yeah. He's funny —

MIKE (*starting to laugh*): Well he ain't exackly funny, but he's always like makin' remarks like, y'know? He comes around, everybody's laughin'. (LOUIS *laughs*.)

EDDIE (*uncomfortably, grinning*): Yeah, well . . . he's got a sense of humor.

MIKE (*laughing*): Yeah, I mean, he's always makin' like remarks, like, y'know?

EDDIE: Yeah, I know. But he's a kid yet, y'know? He — he's just a kid, that's all.

MIKE (*getting hysterical with* LOUIS): I know. You take one look at him — everybody's happy. (LOUIS *laughs*.) I worked one day with him last week over the Moore-MacCormack Line, I'm tellin' you they was all hysterical. (LOUIS *and he explode in laughter*.)

EDDIE: Why? What'd he do?

MIKE: I don't know . . . he was just humorous. You never can remember what he says, y'know? But it's the way he says it. I mean he gives you a look sometimes and you start laughin'!

EDDIE: Yeah. (*Troubled.*) He's got a sense of humor.

MIKE (*gasping*): Yeah.

LOUIS (*rising*): Well, we see ya, Eddie.

EDDIE: Take it easy.

LOUIS: Yeah. See ya.

MIKE: If you wanna come bowlin' later we're goin' Flatbush Avenue.

(*Laughing, they move to exit, meeting* RODOLPHO *and* CATHERINE *entering on the street. Their laughter rises as they see* RODOLPHO, *who does not understand but joins in.* EDDIE *moves to enter the house as* LOUIS *and* MIKE *exit.* CATHERINE *stops him at the door.*)

CATHERINE: Hey, Eddie — what a picture we saw! Did we laugh!

EDDIE (*he can't help smiling at sight of her*): Where'd you go?

CATHERINE: Paramount. It was with those two guys, y'know? That —

EDDIE: Brooklyn Paramount?

CATHERINE (*with an edge of anger, embarrassed before* RODOLPHO): Sure, the Brooklyn Paramount. I told you we wasn't goin' to New York.

EDDIE (*retreating before the threat of her anger*): All right, I only asked you. (*To* RODOLPHO.) I just don't want her hangin' around Times Square, see? It's full of tramps over there.

RODOLPHO: I would like to go to Broadway once, Eddie. I would like to walk with her once where the theaters are and the opera. Since I was a boy I see pictures of those lights.

EDDIE (*his little patience waning*): I want to talk to her a minute, Rodolpho. Go inside, will you?

RODOLPHO: Eddie, we only walk together in the streets. She teaches me.

CATHERINE: You know what he can't get over? That there's no fountains in Brooklyn!

EDDIE (*smiling unwillingly*): Fountains? (RODOLPHO *smiles at his own naïveté.*)

CATHERINE: In Italy he says, every town's got fountains, and they meet there. And you know what? They got oranges on the trees where he comes from, and lemons. Imagine — on the trees? I mean it's interesting. But he's crazy for New York.

RODOLPHO (*attempting familiarity*): Eddie, why can't we go once to Broadway — ?

EDDIE: Look, I gotta tell her something —

RODOLPHO: Maybe you can come too. I want to see all those lights. (*He sees no response in* EDDIE'S *face. He glances at* CATHERINE.) I'll walk by the river before I go to sleep. (*He walks off down the street.*)

CATHERINE: Why don't you talk to him, Eddie? He blesses you, and you don't talk to him hardly.

EDDIE (*eneveloping her with his eyes*): I bless you and you don't talk to me. (*He tries to smile.*)

CATHERINE: *I* don't talk to you? (*She hits his arm.*) What do you mean?

EDDIE: I don't see you no more. I come home you're runnin' around someplace —

CATHERINE: Well, he wants to see everything, that's all, so we go. . . . You mad at me?

EDDIE: No. (*He moves from her, smiling sadly.*) It's just I used to come home, you was always there. Now, I turn around, you're a big girl. I don't know how to talk to you.

CATHERINE: Why?

EDDIE: I don't know, you're runnin', you're runnin', Katie. I don't think you listening any more to me.

CATHERINE (*going to him*): Ah, Eddie, sure I am. What's the matter? You don't like him?

(*Slight pause.*)

EDDIE (*turns to her*): You like him, Katie?

CATHERINE (*with a blush but holding her ground*): Yeah. I like him.

EDDIE (*his smile goes*): You like him.

CATHERINE (*looking down*): Yeah. (*Now she looks at him for the consequences, smiling but tense. He looks at her like a lost boy.*)

What're you got against him? I don't understand. He only blesses you.

EDDIE (*turns away*): He don't bless me, Katie.

CATHERINE: He does! You're like a father to him!

EDDIE (*turns to her*): Katie.

CATHERINE: What, Eddie?

EDDIE: You gonna marry him?

CATHERINE: I don't know. We just been . . . goin' around, that's all. (*Turns to him.*) What're you got against him, Eddie? Please, tell me. What?

EDDIE: He don't respect you.

CATHERINE: Why?

EDDIE: Katie . . . if you wasn't an orphan, wouldn't he ask your father's permission before he run around with you like this?

CATHERINE: Oh, well, he didn't think you'd mind.

EDDIE: He knows I mind, but it don't bother him if I mind, don't you see that?

CATHERINE: No, Eddie, he's got all kinds of respect for me. And you too! We walk across the street he takes my arm — he almost bows to me! You got him all wrong, Eddie; I mean it, you —

EDDIE: Katie, he's only bowin' to his passport.

CATHERINE: His passport!

EDDIE: That's right. He marries you he's got the right to be an American citizen. That's what's goin' on here.

(*She is puzzled and surprised.*)

You understand what I'm tellin' you? The guy is lookin' for his break, that's all he's lookin' for.

CATHERINE (*pained*): Oh, no, Eddie, I don't think so.

EDDIE: You don't think so! Katie, you're gonna make me cry here. Is that a workin' man? What does he do with his first money? A snappy new jacket he buys, records, a pointy pair new shoes and his brother's kids are starvin' over there with tuberculosis? That's a hit-and-run guy, baby; he's got bright lights in his head, Broadway. Them guys don't think of nobody but theirself! You marry him and the next time you see him it'll be for divorce!

CATHERINE (*steps toward him*): Eddie, he never said a word about his papers or —

EDDIE: You mean he's supposed to tell you that?

CATHERINE: I don't think he's even thinking about it.

EDDIE: What's better for him to think about! He could be picked up any day here and he's back pushin' taxis up the hill!

CATHERINE: No, I don't believe it.

EDDIE: Katie, don't break my heart, listen to me.

CATHERINE: I don't want to hear it.

EDDIE: Katie, listen . . .

CATHERINE: He loves me!

EDDIE (*with deep alarm*): Don't say that, for God's sake! This is the oldest racket in the country —

CATHERINE (*desperately, as though he had made his imprint*): I don't believe it! (*She rushes to the house.*)

EDDIE (*following her*): They been pullin' this since the Immigration Law was put in! They grab a green kid that don't know nothin' and they —

CATHERINE (*sobbing*): I don't believe it and I wish to hell you'd stop it!

EDDIE: Katie!

(*They enter the apartment. The lights in the living room have risen and* BEATRICE *is there. She looks past the sobbing* CATHERINE *at* EDDIE, *who, in the presence of his wife, makes an awkward gesture of eroded command, indicating* CATHERINE.)

EDDIE: Why don't you straighten her out?

BEATRICE (*inwardly angered at his flowing emotion, which in itself alarms her*): When are you going to leave her alone?

EDDIE: B., the guy is no good!

BEATRICE (*suddenly, with open fright and fury*): You going to leave her alone? Or you gonna drive me crazy?

(*He turns, striving to retain his dignity, but nevertheless in guilt walks out of the house, into the street and away.* CATHERINE *starts into a bedroom.*)

Listen, Catherine.

(CATHERINE *halts, turns to her sheepishly.*)

What are you going to do with yourself?

CATHERINE: I don't know.

BEATRICE: Don't tell me you don't know; you're not a baby any more, what are you going to do with yourself?

CATHERINE: He won't listen to me.

BEATRICE: I don't understand this. He's not your father, Catherine. I don't understand what's going on here.

CATHERINE (*as one who herself is trying to rationalize a buried impulse*): What am I going to do, just kick him in the face with it?

BEATRICE: Look, honey, you wanna get married, or don't you wanna get married? What are you worried about, Katie?

CATHERINE (*quietly, trembling*): I don't know B. It just seems wrong if he's against it so much.

BEATRICE (*never losing her aroused alarm*): Sit down, honey, I want to tell you something. Here, sit down. Was there ever any fella he liked for you? There wasn't, was there?

CATHERINE: But he says Rodolpho's just after his papers.

BEATRICE: Look, he'll say anything. What does he care what he says? If it was a prince came here for you it would be no different. You know that, don't you?

CATHERINE: Yeah, I guess.

BEATRICE: So what does that mean?

CATHERINE (*slowly turns her head to* BEATRICE): What?

BEATRICE: It means you gotta be your own self more. You still think you're a little girl, honey. But nobody else can make up your mind for you any more, you understand? You gotta give him to understand that he can't give you orders no more.

CATHERINE: Yeah, but how am I going to do that? He thinks I'm a baby.

BEATRICE: Because *you* think you're a baby. I told you fifty times already, you can't act the way you act. You still walk around in front of him in your slip —

CATHERINE: Well I forgot.

BEATRICE: Well you can't do it. Or like you sit on the edge of the bathtub talkin' to him when he's shavin' in his underwear.

CATHERINE: When'd I do that?

BEATRICE: I seen you in there this morning.

CATHERINE: Oh . . . well, I wanted to tell him something and I —

BEATRICE: I know, honey. But if you act like a baby and he be treatin' you like a baby. Like when he comes home sometimes you throw yourself at him like when you was twelve years old.

CATHERINE: Well I like to see him and I'm happy so I —

BEATRICE: Look, I'm not tellin' you what to do honey, but —

CATHERINE: No, you could tell me, B.! Gee, I'm all mixed up. See, I — He looks so sad now and it hurts me.

BEATRICE: Well look Katie, if it's goin' to hurt you so much you're gonna end up an old maid here.

CATHERINE: No!

BEATRICE: I'm tellin' you, I'm not makin' a joke. I tried to tell you a couple of times in the last year or so. That's why I was so happy you were going to go out and get work, you wouldn't be here so much, you'd be a little more independent. I mean it. It's wonderful for a whole family to love each other, but you're a grown woman and you're in the same house with a grown man. So you'll act different now, heh?

CATHERINE: Yeah, I will. I'll remember.

BEATRICE: Because it ain't only up to him, Katie, you understand? I told him the same thing already.

CATHERINE (*quickly*): What?

BEATRICE: That he should let you go. But, you see, if only I tell him, he thinks I'm just bawlin' him out, or maybe I'm jealous or somethin', you know?

CATHERINE (*astonished*): He said you was jealous?

BEATRICE: No, I'm just sayin' maybe that's what he thinks. (*She reaches over to* CATHERINE'*s hand; with a strained smile.*) You think I'm jealous of you, honey?

CATHERINE: No! It's the first I thought of it.

BEATRICE (*with a quiet sad laugh*): Well you should have thought of it before . . . but I'm not. We'll be all right. Just give him to understand; you don't have to fight, you're just — You're a woman, that's all, and you got a nice boy, and now the time came when you said good-by. All right?

CATHERINE (*strangely moved at the prospect*): All right. . . . If I can.

BEATRICE: Honey . . . you gotta.

(CATHERINE, *sensing now an imperious demand, turns with some fear, with a discovery, to* BEATRICE. *She is at the edge of tears, as though a familiar world had shattered.*)

CATHERINE: Okay.

(*Lights out on them and up on* ALFIERI, *seated behind his desk.*)

ALFIERI: It was at this time that he first came to me. I had represented his father in an accident case some years before, and I was acquainted with the family in a casual way. I remember him now as he walked through my doorway —

(*Enter* EDDIE *down right ramp.*)

His eyes were like tunnels; my first thought was that he had committed a crime.

(EDDIE *sits beside the desk, cap in hand, looking out.*)

But soon I saw it was only a passion that had moved into his body, like a stranger. (ALFIERI *pauses, looks down at his desk, then to* EDDIE *as though he were continuing a conversation with him.*) I don't quite understand what I can do for you. Is there a question of law somewhere?

EDDIE: That's what I want to ask you.

ALFIERI: Because there's nothing illegal about a girl falling in love with an immigrant.

EDDIE: Yeah, but what about it if the only reason for it is to get his papers?

ALFIERI: First of all you don't know that.

EDDIE: I see it in his eyes; he's laughin' at her and he's laughin' at me.

ALFIERI: Eddie, I'm a lawyer. I can only deal in what's provable. You understand that, don't you? Can you prove that?

EDDIE: *I know what's in his mind, Mr. Alfieri!*

ALFIERI: Eddie, even if you could prove that —

EDDIE: Listen . . . will you listen to me a minute? My father always said you was a smart man. I want you to listen to me.

ALFIERI: I'm only a lawyer, Eddie.

EDDIE: Will you listen a minute? I'm talkin' about the law. Lemme just bring out what I mean. A man, which he comes into the country illegal, don't it stand to reason he's gonna take every penny and put it in the sock? Because they don't know from one day to another, right?

ALFIERI: All right.

EDDIE: He's spendin'. Records he buys now. Shoes. Jackets. Y'understand me? This guy ain't worried. This guy is *here*. So it must be that he's got it all laid out in his mind already — he's stayin'. Right?

ALFIERI: Well? What about it?

EDDIE: All right. (*He glances at* ALFIERI, *then down to the floor.*) I'm talking to you confidential, ain't I?

ALFIERI: Certainly.

EDDIE: I mean it don't go no place but here. Because I don't like to say this about anybody. Even my wife I didn't exactly say this.

ALFIERI: What is it?

EDDIE (*takes a breath and glances briefly over each shoulder*): The guy ain't right, Mr. Alfieri.

ALFIERI: What do you mean?

EDDIE: I mean he ain't right.

ALFIERI: I don't get you.

EDDIE (*shifts to another position in the chair*): Dja ever get a look at him?

ALFIERI: Not that I know of, no.

EDDIE: He's a blond guy. Like . . . platinum. You know what I mean?

ALFIERI: No.

EDDIE: I mean if you close the paper fast — you could blow him over.

ALFIERI: Well that doesn't mean —

EDDIE: Wait a minute, I'm tellin' you sump'm. He sings, see. Which is — I mean it's all right, but sometimes he hits a note, see. I turn around. I mean — high. You know what I mean?

ALFIERI: Well, that's a tenor.

EDDIE: I know a tenor, Mr. Alfieri. This ain't no tenor. I mean if you came in the house and you didn't know who was singin', you wouldn't be lookin' for him you be lookin' for her.

ALFIERI: Yes, but that's not —

EDDIE: I'm tellin' you sump'm, wait a minute. Please, Mr. Alfieri. I'm tryin' to bring out my thoughts here. Couple of nights ago my niece brings out a dress which it's too small for her, because she shot up like a light this last year. He takes the dress, lays it on the table, he cuts it up; one-two-three, he makes a new dress. I mean he looked so sweet there, like an angel — you could kiss him he was so sweet.

ALFIERI: Now look, Eddie —

EDDIE: Mr. Alfieri, they're laughin' at him on the piers. I'm ashamed. Paper Doll they call him. Blondie now. His brother thinks it's because he's got a sense of humor, see — which he's got — but that ain't why they're laughin'. Which they're not goin' to come out with it because they know he's my relative, which they have to see me if they make a crack, y'know? But I know what they're laughin' at, and when I think of that guy layin' his hands on her I could — I mean it's eatin' me out, Mr. Alfieri, because I struggled for that girl. And now he comes in my house and —

ALFIERI: Eddie, look — I have my own children. I understand you. But the law is very specific. The law does not . . .

EDDIE (*with a fuller flow of indignation*): You mean to tell me that there's no law that a guy which he ain't right can go to work and marry a girl and — ?

ALFIERI: You have no recourse in the law, Eddie.

EDDIE: Yeah, but if he ain't right, Mr. Alfieri, you mean to tell me —

ALFIERI: There is nothing you can do, Eddie, believe me.

EDDIE: Nothin'.

ALFIERI: Nothing at all. There's only one legal question here.

EDDIE: What?

ALFIERI: The manner in which they entered the country. But I don't think you want to do anything about that, do you?

EDDIE: You mean — ?

ALFIERI: Well, they entered illegally.

EDDIE: Oh, Jesus, no, I wouldn't do nothin' about that, I mean —

ALFIERI: All right, then, let me talk now, eh?

EDDIE: Mr. Alfieri, I can't believe what you tell me. I mean there must be some kinda law which —

ALFIERI: Eddie, I want you to listen to me. (*Pause.*) You know, sometimes God mixes up the people. We all love somebody, the wife, the kids — every man's got somebody that he loves, heh? But sometimes . . . there's too much. You know? There's too much, and it goes where it mustn't. A man works hard, he brings up a child, sometimes it's a niece, sometimes even a daughter, and he never realizes it, but through the years — there is too much love for the daughter, there is too much love for the niece. Do you understand what I'm saying to you?

EDDIE (*sardonically*): What do you mean, I shouldn't look out for her good?

ALFIERI: Yes, but these things have to end, Eddie, that's all. The child has to grow up and go away, and the man has to learn to forget. Because after all, Eddie — what other way can it end? (*Pause.*) Let her go. That's my advice. You did your job, now it's her life; wish her luck, and let her go. (*Pause.*) Will you do that? Because there's no law, Eddie; make up your mind to it; the law is not interested in this.

EDDIE: You mean to tell me, even if he's a punk? If he's —

ALFIERI: There's nothing you can do.

(EDDIE *stands.*)

EDDIE: Well, all right, thanks. Thanks very much.

ALFIERI: What are you going to do?

EDDIE (*with a helpless but ironic gesture*): What can I do? I'm a patsy, what can a patsy do? I worked like a dog twenty years so a punk could have her, so that's what I done. I mean, in the worst times, in the worst, when there wasn't a ship comin' in the harbor, I didn't stand around lookin' for relief — I hustled. When there was empty piers in Brooklyn I went to Hoboken, Staten Island, the West Side, Jersey, all over — because I made a promise. I took out of my own mouth to give to her. I took out of my wife's mouth. I walked hungry plenty days in this city! (*It begins to break through.*) And now I gotta sit in my own house and look at a son-of-a-bitch punk like that — which he came out of nowhere! I give him my house to sleep! I take the blankets off my bed for him, and he takes and puts his dirty filthy hands on her like a goddam thief!

ALFIERI (*rising*): But, Eddie, she's a woman now.

EDDIE: He's stealing from me!

ALFIERI: She wants to get married, Eddie. She can't marry you, can she?

EDDIE (*furiously*): What're you talkin' about, marry me! I don't know what the hell you're talkin' about!

(*Pause.*)

ALFIERI: I gave you my advice, Eddie. That's it.

(EDDIE *gathers himself. A pause.*)

EDDIE: Well, thanks. Thanks very much. It just — it's breakin' my heart, y'know. I —

ALFIERI: I understand. Put it out of your mind. Can you do that?

EDDIE: I'm — (*He feels the threat of sobs, and with a helpless wave.*) I'll see you around. (*He goes out up the right ramp.*)

ALFIERI (*sits on desk*): There are times when you want to spread an alarm, but nothing has happened. I knew, I knew then and there — I could have finished the whole story that afternoon. It wasn't as though there was a mystery to unravel. I could see every step coming, step after step, like a dark figure walking down a hall toward a certain door. I knew where he was heading for, I knew where he was going to end. And I sat here many afternoons asking myself why, being an intelligent man, I was so powerless to stop it. I even went to a certain old lady in the neighborhood, a very wise old woman, and I told her, and she only nodded, and said, "Pray for him . . ." And so I — waited here.

(*As lights go out on* ALFIERI, *they rise in the apartment where all are finishing dinner.* BEATRICE *and* CATHERINE *are clearing the table.*)

CATHERINE: You know where they went?

BEATRICE: Where?

CATHERINE: They went to Africa once. On a fishing boat.

(EDDIE *glances at her.*)

It's true, Eddie.

(BEATRICE *exits into the kitchen with dishes.*)

EDDIE: I didn't say nothin'. (*He goes to his rocker, picks up a news-paper.*)

CATHERINE: And I was never even in Staten Island.

EDDIE (*sitting with the paper*): You didn't miss nothin'.

(*Pause.* CATHERINE *takes dishes out.*)

How long that take you, Marco — to get to Africa?

MARCO (*rising*): Oh . . . two days. We go all over.

RODOLPHO (*rising*): Once we went to Yugoslavia.

EDDIE (*to* MARCO): They pay all right on them boats?

(BEATRICE *enters. She and* RODOLPHO *stack the remaining dishes.*)

MARCO: If they catch fish they pay all right. (*Sits on a stool.*)

RODOLPHO: They're family boats, though. And nobody in our family owned one. So we only worked when one of the families was sick.

BEATRICE: Y'know, Marco, what I don't understand — there's an ocean full of fish and yiz are all starvin'.

EDDIE: They gotta have boats, nets, you need money.

(CATHERINE *enters.*)

BEATRICE: Yeah, but couldn't they like fish from the beach? You see them down Coney Island —

MARCO: Sardines.

EDDIE: Sure. (*Laughing.*) How you gonna catch sardines on a hook?

BEATRICE: Oh, I didn't know they're sardines. (*To* CATHERINE.) They're sardines!

CATHERINE: Yeah, they follow them all over the ocean, Africa, Yugoslavia . . . (*She sits and begins to look through a movie magazine.* RODOLPHO *joins her.*)

BEATRICE (*to* EDDIE): It's funny, y'know. You never think of it, that sardines are swimming in the ocean! (*She exits to kitchen with dishes.*)

CATHERINE: I know. It's like oranges and lemons on a tree. (*To* EDDIE.) I mean you ever think of oranges and lemons on a tree?

EDDIE: Yeah, I know. It's funny. (*To* MARCO.) I heard that they paint the oranges to make them look orange.

(BEATRICE *enters.*)

MARCO (*he has been reading a letter*): Paint?

EDDIE: Yeah, I heard that they grow like green.

MARCO: No, in Italy the oranges are orange.

RODOLPHO: Lemons are green.

EDDIE (*resenting his instruction*): I know lemons are green, for Christ's sake, you see them in the store they're green sometimes. I said oranges they paint, I didn't say nothin' about lemons.

BEATRICE (*sitting; diverting their attention*): Your wife is gettin' the money all right, Marco?

MARCO: Oh, yes. She bought medicine for my boy.

BEATRICE: That's wonderful. You feel better, heh?

MARCO: Oh, yes! But I'm lonesome.

BEATRICE: I just hope you ain't gonna do like some of them around here. They're here twenty-five years, some men, and they didn't get enough together to go back twice.

MARCO: Oh, I know. We have many families in our town, the children never saw the father. But I will go home. Three, four years, I think.

BEATRICE: Maybe you should keep more here. Because maybe she thinks it comes so easy you'll never get ahead of yourself.

MARCO: Oh, no, she saves. I send everything. My wife is very lonesome. (*He smiles shyly.*)

BEATRICE: She must be nice. She pretty? I bet, heh?

MARCO (*blushing*): No, but she understand everything.

RODOLPHO: Oh, he's got a clever wife!

EDDIE: I betcha there's plenty surprises sometimes when those guys get back there, heh?

MARCO: Surprises?

EDDIE (*laughing*): I mean, you know — they count the kids and there's a couple extra than when they left?

MARCO: No — no . . . The women wait, Eddie. Most. Most. Very few surprises.

RODOLPHO: It's more strict in our town.

(EDDIE *looks at him now.*)

It's not so free.

EDDIE (*rises, paces up and down*): It ain't so free here either, Rodolpho, like you think. I seen greenhorns sometimes get in trouble that way — they think just because a girl don't go around with a shawl over her head that she ain't strict, y'know? Girl don't have to wear black dress to be strict. Know what I mean?

RODOLPHO: Well, I always have respect —

EDDIE: I know, but in your town you wouldn't just drag off some girl without permission, I mean. (*He turns.*) You know what I mean, Marco? It ain't that much different here.

MARCO (*cautiously*): Yes.

BEATRICE: Well, he didn't exactly drag her off though, Eddie.

EDDIE: I know, but I seen some of them get the wrong idea sometimes. (*To* RODOLPHO.) I mean it might be a little more free here but it's just as strict.

RODOLPHO: I have respect for her, Eddie. I do anything wrong?

EDDIE: Look, kid, I ain't her father, I'm only her uncle —

BEATRICE: Well then, be an uncle then.

(EDDIE *looks at her, aware of her criticizing force.*)

I *mean.*

MARCO: No, Beatrice, if he does wrong you must tell him. (*To* EDDIE.) What does he do wrong?

EDDIE: Well, Marco, till he came here she was never out on the street twelve o'clock at night.

MARCO (*to* RODOLPHO): You come home early now.

BEATRICE (*to* CATHERINE): Well, you said the movie ended late, didn't you?

CATHERINE: Yeah.

BEATRICE: Well, tell him, honey. (*To* EDDIE.) The movie ended late.

EDDIE: Look, B., I'm just sayin' — he thinks she always stayed out like that.

MARCO: You come home early now, Rodolpho.

RODOLPHO (*embarrassed*): All right, sure. But I can't stay in the house all the time, Eddie.

EDDIE: Look, kid, I'm not only talkin' about her. The more you run around like that the more chance you're takin'. (*To* BEATRICE.) I mean suppose he gets hit by a car or something. (*To* MARCO.) Where's his papers, who is he? Know what I mean?

BEATRICE: Yeah, but who is he in the daytime, though? It's the same chance in the daytime.

EDDIE (*holding back a voice full of anger*): Yeah, but he don't have to go lookin' for it, Beatrice. If he's here to work, then he should work; if he's here for a good time then he could fool around! (*To* MARCO.) But I understood, Marco, that you was both comin' to make a livin' for your family. You understand me, don't you, Marco? (*He goes to his rocker.*)

MARCO: I beg your pardon, Eddie.

EDDIE: I mean, that's what I understood in the first place, see.

MARCO: Yes. That's why we came.

EDDIE (*sits on his rocker*): Well, that's all I'm askin'.

(EDDIE *reads his paper. There is a pause, an awkwardness. Now* CATHERINE *gets up and puts a record on the phonograph — "Paper Doll."*)

CATHERINE (*flushed with revolt*): You wanna dance, Rodolpho?

(EDDIE *freezes.*)

RODOLPHO (*in deference to* EDDIE): No, I — I'm tired.

BEATRICE: Go ahead, dance, Rodolpho.

CATHERINE: Ah, come on. They got a beautiful quartet, these guys. Come.

(She has taken his hand and he stiffly rises, feeling EDDIE'S *eyes on his back, and they dance.)*

EDDIE *(to* CATHERINE*)*: What's that, a new record?

CATHERINE: It's the same one. We bought it the other day.

BEATRICE *(to* EDDIE*)*: They only bought three records. *(She watches them dance;* EDDIE *turns his head away.* MARCO *just sits there, waiting. Now* BEATRICE *turns to* EDDIE*.)* Must be nice to go all over in one of them fishin' boats. I would like that myself. See all them other countries?

EDDIE: Yeah.

BEATRICE *(to* MARCO*)*: But the women don't go along, I bet.

MARCO: No, not on the boats. Hard work.

BEATRICE: What're you got, a regular kitchen and everything?

MARCO: Yes, we eat very good on the boats — especially when Rodolpho comes along; everybody gets fat.

BEATRICE: Oh, he cooks?

MARCO: Sure, very good cook. Rice, pasta, fish, everything.

*(*EDDIE *lowers his paper.)*

EDDIE: He's a cook, too! *(Looking at* RODOLPHO*.)* He sings, he cooks . . .

*(*RODOLPHO *smiles thankfully.)*

BEATRICE: Well it's good, he could always make a living.

EDDIE: It's wonderful. He sings, he cooks, he could make dresses . . .

CATHERINE: They get some high pay, them guys. The head chefs in all the big hotels are men. You read about them.

EDDIE: That's what I'm sayin'.

*(*CATHERINE *and* RODOLPHO *continue dancing.)*

CATHERINE: Yeah, well, I mean.

EDDIE *(to* BEATRICE*)*: He's lucky, believe me. *(Slight pause. He looks away, then back to* BEATRICE*.)* That's why the water front is no place for him. *(They stop dancing.* RODOLPHO *turns off phonograph.)* I mean like me — I can't cook, I can't sing, I can't make dresses, so I'm on the water front. But if I could cook, if I could sing, if I could make dresses, I wouldn't be on the water front. *(He has been unconsciously twisting the newspaper into a tight roll. They are all regarding him now; he senses he is exposing the issue and he is driven on.)* I would be someplace else. I would be like in a dress store. (*He has bent the rolled paper and it suddenly tears in two. He suddenly gets up and pulls his pants up over his belly and goes to* MARCO.) What do you say, Marco, we go to the bouts next Saturday night. You never seen a fight, did you?

MARCO (*uneasily*): Only in the moving pictures.

EDDIE (*going to* RODOLPHO): I'll treat yiz. What do you say, Danish? You wanna come along? I'll buy the tickets.

RODOLPHO: Sure. I like to go.

CATHERINE (*goes to* EDDIE; *nervously happy now*): I'll make some coffee, all right?

EDDIE: Go ahead, make some! Make it nice and strong. (*Mystified, she smiles and exits to kitchen. He is weirdly elated, rubbing his fists into his palms. He strides to* MARCO.) You wait, Marco, you see some real fights here. You ever do any boxing?

MARCO: No, I never.

EDDIE (*to* RODOLPHO): Betcha you have done some, heh?

RODOLPHO: No.

EDDIE: Well, come on, I'll teach you.

BEATRICE: What's he got to learn that for?

EDDIE: Ya can't tell, one a these days somebody's liable to step on his foot or sump'm. Come on, Rodolpho, I show you a couple a passes. (*He stands below table.*)

BEATRICE: Go ahead, Rodolpho. He's a good boxer, he could teach you.

RODOLPHO (*embarrassed*): Well, I don't know how to — (*He moves down to* EDDIE.)

EDDIE: Just put your hands up. Like this, see? That's right. That's very good, keep your left up, because you lead with the left, see, like this. (*He gently moves his left into* RODOLPHO's *face.*) See? Now what you gotta do is you gotta block me, so when I come in like that you — (RODOLPHO *parries his left.*) Hey, that's very good! (RODOLPHO *laughs.*) All right, now come into me. Come on.

RODOLPHO: I don't want to hit you, Eddie.

EDDIE: Don't pity me, come on. Throw it, I'll show you how to block it. (RODOLPHO *jabs at him, laughing. The others join.*) 'At's it. Come on again. For the jaw right here. (RODOLPHO *jabs with more assurance.*) Very good!

BEATRICE (*to* MARCO): He's very good!

(EDDIE *crosses directly upstage of* RODOLPHO.)

EDDIE: Sure, he's great! Come on, kid, put sump'm behind it, you can't hurt me. (RODOLPHO, *more seriously, jabs at* EDDIE's *jaw and grazes it.*) Attaboy.

(CATHERINE *comes from the kitchen, watches.*)

Now I'm gonna hit you, so block me, see?

CATHERINE (*with beginning alarm*): What are they doin'?

(*They are lightly boxing now.*)

BEATRICE (*she senses only the comradeship in it now*): He's teachin' him; he's very good!

EDDIE: Sure, he's terrific! Look at him go! (RODOLPHO *lands a blow.*) 'At's it! Now, watch out, here I come, Danish! (*He feints with his left hand and lands with his right. It mildly staggers* RODOLPHO. MARCO *rises.*)

CATHERINE (*rushing to* RODOLPHO): Eddie!

EDDIE: Why? I didn't hurt him. Did I hurt you, kid? (*He rubs the back of his hand across his mouth.*)

RODOLPHO: No, no, he didn't hurt me. (*To* EDDIE *with a certain gleam and a smile.*) I was only surprised.

BEATRICE (*pulling* EDDIE *down into the rocker*): That's enough, Eddie; he did pretty good, though.

EDDIE: Yeah. (*Rubbing his fists together.*) He could be very good, Marco. I'll teach him again.

(MARCO *nods at him dubiously.*)

RODOLPHO: Dance, Catherine. Come. (*He takes her hand; they go to phonograph and start it. It plays "Paper Doll."*)

(RODOLPHO *takes her in his arms. They dance.* EDDIE *in thought sits in his chair, and* MARCO *takes a chair, places it in front of* EDDIE, *and looks down at it.* BEATRICE *and* EDDIE *watch him.*)

MARCO: Can you lift this chair?

EDDIE: What do you mean?

MARCO: From here. (*He gets on one knee with one hand behind his back, and grasps the bottom of one of the chair legs but does not raise it.*)

EDDIE: Sure, why not? (*He comes to the chair, kneels, grasps the leg, raises the chair one inch, but it leans over to the floor.*) Gee, that's hard, I never knew that. (*He tries again, and again fails.*) It's on an angle, that's why, heh?

MARCO: Here.

(MARCO *kneels, grasps, and with strain slowly raises the chair higher and higher, getting to his feet now.* RODOLPHO *and* CATHERINE *have stopped dancing as* MARCO *raises the chair over his head.*

MARCO *is face to face with* EDDIE, *a strained tension gripping his eyes and jaw, his neck stiff, the chair raised like a weapon over* EDDIE's *head — and he transforms what might appear like a glare of warning into a smile of triumph, and* EDDIE's *grin vanishes as he absorbs his look.*)

CURTAIN

ACT II

(*Light rises on* ALFIERI *at his desk.*)

ALFIERI: On the twenty-third of that December a case of Scotch whisky slipped from a net while being unloaded — as a case of Scotch whisky is inclined to do on the twenty-third of December on Pier Forty-one. There was no snow, but it was cold, his wife was out shopping. Marco was still at work. The boy had not been hired that day; Catherine told me later that this was the first time they had been alone together in the house.

(*Light is rising on* CATHERINE *in the apartment.* RODOLPHO *is watching as she arranges a paper pattern on cloth spread on the table.*)

CATHERINE: You hungry?

RODOLPHO: Not for anything to eat. (*Pause.*) I have nearly three hundred dollars. Catherine?

CATHERINE: I heard you.

RODOLPHO: You don't like to talk about it any more?

CATHERINE: Sure, I don't mind talkin' about it.

RODOLPHO: What worries you, Catherine?

CATHERINE: I been wantin' to ask you about something. Could I?

RODOLPHO: All the answers are in my eyes, Catherine. But you don't look in my eyes lately. You're full of secrets. (*She looks at him. She seems withdrawn.*) What is the question?

CATHERINE: Suppose I wanted to live in Italy.

RODOLPHO (*smiling at the incongruity*): You going to marry somebody rich?

CATHERINE: No, I mean live there — you and me.

RODOLPHO (*his smile vanishing*): When?

CATHERINE: Well . . . when we get married.

RODOLPHO (*astonished*): You want to be an Italian?

CATHERINE: No, but I could live there without being Italian. Americans live there.

RODOLPHO: Forever?

CATHERINE: Yeah.

RODOLPHO (*crosses to rocker*): You're fooling.

CATHERINE: No, I mean it.

RODOLPHO: Where do you get such an idea?

CATHERINE: Well, you're always saying it's so beautiful there, with the mountains and the ocean and all the —

RODOLPHO: You're fooling me.

CATHERINE: I mean it.

RODOLPHO (*goes to her slowly*): Catherine, if I ever brought you home with no money, no business, nothing, they would call the priest and the doctor and they would say Rodolpho is crazy.

CATHERINE: I know, but I think we would be happier there.

RODOLPHO: Happier! What would you eat? You can't cook the view!

CATHERINE: Maybe you could be a singer, like in Rome or —

RODOLPHO: Rome! Rome is full of singers.

CATHERINE: Well, I could work then.

RODOLPHO: Where?

CATHERINE: God, there must be jobs somewhere!

RODOLPHO: There's nothing! Nothing, nothing, nothing. Now tell me what you're talking about. How can I bring you from a rich country to suffer in a poor country? What are you talking about? (*She searches for words.*) I would be a criminal stealing your face. In two years you would have an old, hungry face. When my brother's babies cry they give them water, water that boiled a bone. Don't you believe that?

CATHERINE (*quietly*): I'm afraid of Eddie here.

(*Slight pause.*)

RODOLPHO (*steps closer to her*): We wouldn't live here. Once I am a citizen I could work anywhere and I would find better jobs and we would have a house, Catherine. If I were not afraid to be arrested I would start to be something wonderful here!

CATHERINE (*steeling herself*): Tell me something. I mean just tell me, Rodolpho — would you still want to do it if it turned out we had to go live in Italy? I mean just if it turned out that way.

RODOLPHO: This is your question or his question?

CATHERINE: I would like to know, Rodolpho. I mean it.

RODOLPHO: To go there with nothing.

CATHERINE: Yeah.

RODOLPHO: No. (*She looks at him wide-eyed.*) No.

CATHERINE: You wouldn't?

RODOLPHO: No; I will not marry you to live in Italy. I want you to be my wife, and I want to be a citizen. Tell him that, or I will. Yes. (*He moves about angrily.*) And tell him also, and tell yourself, please, that I am not a beggar, and you are not a horse, a gift, a favor for a poor immigrant.

CATHERINE: Well, don't get mad!

RODOLPHO: I am furious! (*Goes to her.*) Do you think I am so desperate? My brother is desperate, not me. You think I would carry on my back the rest of my life a woman I didn't love just to be an American? It's so wonderful? You think we have no tall buildings in Italy? Electric lights? No wide streets? No flags? No automobiles? Only work we don't have. I want to be an American so I can work, that is the only wonder here — work! How can you insult me, Catherine?

CATHERINE: I didn't mean that —

RODOLPHO: My heart dies to look at you. Why are you so afraid of him?

CATHERINE (*near tears*): I don't know!

RODOLPHO: Do you trust me, Catherine? You?

CATHERINE: It's only that I — He was good to me, Rodolpho. You don't know him; he was always the sweetest guy to me. Good. He razzes me all the time but he don't mean it. I know. I would — just feel ashamed if I made him sad. 'Cause I always dreamt that when I got married he would be happy at the wedding, and laughin' — and now he's — mad all the time and nasty — (*She is weeping.*) Tell him you'd live in Italy — just tell him, and maybe he would start to trust you a little, see? Because I want him to be happy; I mean — I like him, Rodolpho — and I can't stand it!

RODOLPHO: Oh, Catherine — oh, little girl.

CATHERINE: I love you, Rodolpho, I love you.

RODOLPHO: Then why are you afraid? That he'll spank you?

CATHERINE: Don't, don't laugh at me! I've been here all my life. . . . Every day I saw him when he left in the morning and when he came home at night. You think it's so easy to turn around and say to a man he's nothin' to you no more?

RODOLPHO: I know, but —

CATHERINE: You don't know; nobody knows! I'm not a baby, I know a lot more than people think I know. Beatrice says to be a woman, but —

RODOLPHO: Yes.

CATHERINE: Then why don't she be a woman? If I was a wife I would make a man happy instead of goin' at him all the time. I can tell a block away when he's blue in his mind and just wants to talk to somebody quiet and nice. . . . I can tell when he's hungry or wants a beer before he even says anything. I know when his feet hurt him, I mean I *know* him and now I'm supposed to turn around and make a stranger out of him? I don't know why I have to do that, I mean.

RODOLPHO: Catherine. If I take in my hands a little bird. And she grows and wishes to fly. But I will not let her out of my hands because I love her so much, is that right for me to do? I don't say you must hate him; but anyway you must go, mustn't you? Catherine?

CATHERINE (*softly*): Hold me.

RODOLPHO (*clasping her to him*): Oh, my little girl.

CATHERINE: Teach me. (*She is weeping.*) I don't know anything, teach me, Rodolpho, hold me.

RODOLPHO: There's nobody here now. Come inside. Come. (*He is leading her toward the bedrooms.*) And don't cry any more.

(*Light rises on the street. In a moment* EDDIE *appears. He is unsteady, drunk. He mounts the stairs. He enters the apartment, looks around, takes out a bottle from one pocket, puts it on the table. Then another bottle from another pocket, and a third from an inside pocket. He sees the pattern and cloth, goes over to it and touches it, and turns toward upstage.*)

EDDIE: Beatrice? (*He goes to the open kitchen door and looks in.*) Beatrice? Beatrice?

(CATHERINE *enters from bedroom; under his gaze she adjusts her dress.*)

CATHERINE: You got home early.

EDDIE: Knocked off for Christmas early. (*Indicating the pattern.*) Rodolpho makin' you a dress?

CATHERINE: No. I'm makin' a blouse.

(RODOLPHO *appears in the bedroom doorway.* EDDIE *sees him and his arm jerks slightly in shock.* RODOLPHO *nods to him testingly.*)

RODOLPHO: Beatrice went to buy presents for her mother.

(*Pause.*)

EDDIE: Pack it up. Go ahead. Get your stuff and get outa here. (CATHERINE *instantly turns and walks toward the bedroom, and* EDDIE *grabs her arm.*) Where you goin'?

CATHERINE (*trembling with fright*): I think I have to get out of here, Eddie.

EDDIE: No, you ain't goin' nowheres, he's the one.

CATHERINE: I think I can't stay here no more. (*She frees her arm, steps back toward the bedroom.*) I'm sorry, Eddie. (*She sees the tears in his eyes.*) Well, don't cry. I'll be around the neighborhood; I'll see you. I just can't stay here no more. You know I can't. (*Her sobs of pity and love for him break her composure.*) Don't you know I can't? You know that, don't you? (*She goes to him.*) Wish me luck. (*She clasps her hands prayerfully.*) Oh, Eddie, don't be like that!

EDDIE: You ain't goin' nowheres.

CATHERINE: Eddie, I'm not gonna be a baby any more! You —

(*He reaches out suddenly, draws her to him, and as she strives to free herself he kisses her on the mouth.*)

RODOLPHO: Don't! (*He pulls on* EDDIE's *arm.*) Stop that! Have respect for her!

EDDIE (*spun round by* RODOLPHO): You want something?

RODOLPHO: Yes! She'll be my wife. That is what I want. My wife!

EDDIE: But what're you gonna be?

RODOLPHO: I show you what I be!

CATHERINE: Wait outside; don't argue with him!

EDDIE: Come on, show me! What're you gonna be? Show me!

RODOLPHO (*with tears of rage*): Don't say that to me!

(RODOLPHO *flies at him in attack.* EDDIE *pins his arms, laughing, and suddenly kisses him.*)

CATHERINE: Eddie! Let go, ya hear me! I'll kill you! Leggo of him!

(*She tears at* EDDIE's *face and* EDDIE *releases* RODOLPHO. EDDIE *stands there with tears rolling down his face as he laughs mockingly at* RODOLPHO. *She is staring at him in horror.* RODOLPHO *is rigid. They are like animals that have torn at one another and broken up without a decision, each waiting for the other's mood.*)

EDDIE (*to* CATHERINE): You see? (*To* RODOLPHO.) I give you till to-morrow, kid. Get outa here. Alone. You hear me? Alone.

CATHERINE: I'm going with him, Eddie. (*She starts toward* RODOLPHO.)

EDDIE (*indicating* RODOLPHO *with his head*): Not with that. (*She halts, frightened. He sits, still panting for breath, and they watch him helplessly as he leans toward them over the table.*) Don't make me do nuttin', Catherine. Watch your step, submarine. By rights they oughta throw you back in the water. But I got pity for you. (*He moves unsteadily toward the door, always facing* RODOLPHO.)

Just get outa here and don't lay another hand on her unless you wanna go out feet first. (*He goes out of the apartment.*)

(*The lights go down, as they rise on* ALFIERI.)

ALFIERI: On December twenty-seventh I saw him next. I normally go home well before six, but that day I sat around looking out my window at the bay, and when I saw him walking through my doorway, I knew why I had waited. And if I seem to tell this like a dream, it was that way. Several moments arrived in the course of the two talks we had when it occurred to me how — almost transfixed I had come to feel. I had lost my strength somewhere. (EDDIE *enters, removing his cap, sits in the chair, looks thoughtfully out.*) I looked in his eyes more than I listened — in fact, I can hardly remember the conversation. But I will never forget how dark the room became when he looked at me; his eyes were like tunnels. I kept wanting to call the police, but nothing had happened. Nothing at all had really happened. (*He breaks off and looks down at the desk. Then he turns to* EDDIE.) So in other words, he won't leave?

EDDIE: My wife is talkin' about renting a room upstairs for them. An old lady on the top floor is got an empty room.

ALFIERI: What does Marco say?

EDDIE: He just sits there. Marco don't say much.

ALFIERI: I guess they didn't tell him, heh? What happened?

EDDIE: I don't know; Marco don't say much.

ALFIERI: What does your wife say?

EDDIE (*unwilling to pursue this*): Nobody's talkin' much in the house. So what about that?

ALFIERI: But you didn't prove anything about him. It sounds like he just wasn't strong enough to break your grip.

EDDIE: I'm tellin' you I know — he ain't right. Somebody that don't want it can break it. Even a mouse, if you catch a teeny mouse and you hold it in your hand, that mouse can give you the right kind of fight. He didn't give me the right kind of fight, I know it, Mr. Alfieri, the guy ain't right.

ALFIERI: What did you do that for, Eddie?

EDDIE: To show her what he is! So she would see, once and for all! Her mother'll turn over in the grave! (*He gathers himself almost peremptorily.*) So what do I gotta do now? Tell me what to do.

ALFIERI: She actually said she's marrying him?

EDDIE: She told me, yeah. So what do I do?

(*Slight pause.*)

ALFIERI: This is my last word, Eddie, take it or not, that's your business. Morally and legally you have no rights, you cannot stop it; she is a free agent.

EDDIE (*angering*): Didn't you hear what I told you?

ALFIERI (*with a tougher tone*): I heard what you told me, and I'm telling you what the answer is. I'm not only telling you now, I'm warning you — the law is nature. The law is only a word for what has a right to happen. When the law is wrong it's because it's unnatural, but in this case it is natural and a river will drown you if you buck it now. Let her go. And bless her. (*A phone booth begins to glow on the opposite side of the stage; a faint, lonely blue.* EDDIE *stands up, jaws clenched.*) Somebody had to come for her, Eddie, sooner or later. (EDDIE *starts turning to go and* ALFIERI *rises with new anxiety.*) You won't have a friend in the world, Eddie! Even those who understand will turn against you, even the ones who feel the same will despise you! (EDDIE *moves off.*) Put it out of your mind! Eddie! (*He follows into the darkness, calling desperately.*)

(EDDIE *is gone. The phone is glowing in light now. Light is out on* ALFIERI. EDDIE *has at the same time appeared beside the phone.*)

EDDIE: Give me the number of the Immigration Bureau. Thanks. (*He dials.*) I want to report something. Illegal immigrants. Two of them. That's right. Four-forty-one Saxon Street, Brooklyn, yeah. Ground floor. Heh? (*With greater difficulty.*) I'm just around the neighborhood, that's all. Heh?

(*Evidently he is being questioned further, and he slowly hangs up. He leaves the phone just as* LOUIS *and* MIKE *come down the street.*)

LOUIS: Go bowlin', Eddie?

EDDIE: No, I'm due home.

LOUIS: Well, take it easy.

EDDIE: I'll see yiz.

(*They leave him, exiting right, and he watches them go. He glances about, then goes up into the house. The lights go on in the apartment.* BEATRICE *is taking down Christmas decorations and packing them in a box.*)

EDDIE: Where is everybody? (BEATRICE *does not answer.*) I says where is everybody?

BEATRICE (*looking up at him, wearied with it, and concealing a fear of him*): I decided to move them upstairs with Mrs. Dondero.

EDDIE: Oh, they're all moved up there already?

BEATRICE: Yeah.

EDDIE: Where's Catherine? She up there?

BEATRICE: Only to bring pillow cases.

EDDIE: She ain't movin' in with them.

BEATRICE: Look, I'm sick and tired of it. I'm sick and tired of it!

EDDIE: All right, all right, take it easy.

BEATRICE: I don't wanna hear no more about it, you understand? Nothin'!

EDDIE: What're you blowin' off about? Who brought them in here?

BEATRICE: All right, I'm sorry; I wish I'd a drop dead before I told them to come. In the ground I wish I was.

EDDIE: Don't drop dead, just keep in mind who brought them in here, that's all. (*He moves about restlessly.*) I mean I got a couple of rights here. (*He moves, wanting to beat down her evident disapproval of him.*) This is my house here not their house.

BEATRICE: What do you want from me? They're moved out; what do you want now?

EDDIE: I want my respect!

BEATRICE: So I moved them out, what more do you want? You got your house now, you got your respect.

EDDIE (*he moves about biting his lip*): I don't like the way you talk to me, Beatrice.

BEATRICE: I'm just tellin' you I done what you want!

EDDIE: I don't like it! The way you talk to me and the way you look at me. This is my house. And she is my niece and I'm responsible for her.

BEATRICE: So that's why you done that to him?

EDDIE: I done what to him?

BEATRICE: What you done to him in front of her; you know what I'm talkin' about. She goes around shakin' all the time, she can't go to sleep! That's what you call responsible for her?

EDDIE (*quietly*): The guy ain't right, Beatrice. (*She is silent.*) Did you hear what I said?

BEATRICE: Look, I'm finished with it. That's all. (*She resumes her work.*)

EDDIE (*helping her to pack the tinsel*): I'm gonna have it out with you one of these days, Beatrice.

BEATRICE: Nothin' to have out with me, it's all settled. Now we gonna be like it never happened, that's all.

EDDIE: I want my respect, Beatrice, and you know what I'm talkin' about.

BEATRICE: What?

(*Pause.*)

EDDIE (*finally his resolution hardens*): What I feel like doin' in the bed and what I don't feel like doin'. I don't want no —

BEATRICE: When'd I say anything about that?

EDDIE: You said, you said, I ain't deaf. I don't want no more conversations about that, Beatrice. I do what I feel like doin' or what I don't feel like doin'.

BEATRICE: Okay.

(*Pause.*)

EDDIE: You used to be different, Beatrice. You had a whole different way.

BEATRICE: *I'm* no different.

EDDIE: You didn't used to jump me all the time about everything. The last year or two I come in the house I don't know what's gonna hit me. It's a shootin' gallery in here and I'm the pigeon.

BEATRICE: Okay, okay.

EDDIE: Don't tell me okay, okay, I'm tellin' you the truth. A wife is supposed to believe the husband. If I tell you that guy ain't right don't tell me he is right.

BEATRICE: But how do you know?

EDDIE: Because I know. I don't go around makin' accusations. He give me the heeby-jeebies the first minute I seen him. And I don't like you sayin' I don't want her marryin' anybody. I broke my back payin' her stenography lessons so she could go out and meet a better class of people. Would I do that if I didn't want her to get married? Sometimes you talk like I was a crazy man or sump'm.

BEATRICE: But she likes him.

EDDIE: Beatrice, she's a baby, how is she gonna know what she likes?

BEATRICE: Well, you kept her a baby, you wouldn't let her go out. I told you a hundred times.

(*Pause.*)

EDDIE: All right. Let her go out, then.

BEATRICE: She don't wanna go out now. It's too late, Eddie.

(*Pause.*)

EDDIE: Suppose I told her to go out. Suppose I —

BEATRICE: They're going to get married next week, Eddie.

EDDIE (*his head jerks around to her*): She said that?

BEATRICE: Eddie, if you want my advice, go to her and tell her good luck. I think maybe now that you had it out you learned better.

EDDIE: What's the hurry next week?

BEATRICE: Well, she's been worried about him bein' picked up; this way he could start to be a citizen. She loves him, Eddie. (*He gets up, moves about uneasily, restlessly.*) Why don't you give her a good word? Because I still think she would like you to be a friend, y'know? (*He is standing, looking at the floor.*) I mean like if you told her you'd go to the wedding.

EDDIE: She asked you that?

BEATRICE: I know she would like it. I'd like to make a party here for her. I mean there oughta be some kinda send-off. Heh? I mean she'll have trouble enough in her life, let's start it off happy. What do you say? Cause in her heart she still loves you, Eddie. I know it. (*He presses his fingers against his eyes.*) What're you, cryin'? (*She goes to him, holds his face.*) Go . . . whyn't you go tell her you're sorry?

(CATHERINE *is seen on the upper landing of the stairway, and they hear her descending.*)

There . . . she's comin' down. Come on, shake hands with her.

EDDIE (*moving with suppressed suddenness*): No, I can't, I can't talk to her.

BEATRICE: Eddie, give her a break; a wedding should be happy!

EDDIE: I'm goin', I'm goin' for a walk.

(*He goes upstage for his jacket.* CATHERINE *enters and starts for the bedroom door.*)

BEATRICE: Katie? . . . Eddie, don't go, wait a minute. (*She embraces* EDDIE's *arm with warmth.*) Ask him, Katie. Come on, honey.

EDDIE: It's all right, I'm — (*He starts to go and she holds him.*)

BEATRICE: No, she wants to ask you. Come on, Katie, ask him. We'll have a party! What're we gonna do, hate each other? Come on!

CATHERINE: I'm gonna get married, Eddie. So if you wanna come, the wedding be on Saturday.

(*Pause.*)

EDDIE: Okay. I only wanted the best for you, Katie. I hope you know that.

CATHERINE: Okay. (*She starts out again.*)

EDDIE: Catherine? (*She turns to him.*) I was just tellin' Beatrice . . . if you wanna go out, like . . . I mean I realize maybe I kept you home too much. Because he's the first guy you ever knew, y'know? I mean now that you got a job, you might meet some fellas, and you get a different idea, y'know? I mean you could always come back to him, you're still only kids, the both of yiz. What's the hurry? Maybe you'll get around a little bit, you grow up a little more, maybe you'll see different in a couple of months. I mean you be surprised, it don't have to be him.

CATHERINE: No, we made it up already.

EDDIE (*with increasing anxiety*): Katie, wait a minute.

CATHERINE: No, I made up my mind.

EDDIE: But you never knew no other fella, Katie! How could you make up your mind?

CATHERINE: Cause I did. I don't want nobody else.

EDDIE: But, Katie, suppose he gets picked up.

CATHERINE: That's why we gonna do it right away. Soon as we finish the wedding he's goin' right over and start to be a citizen. I made up my mind, Eddie. I'm sorry. (*To* BEATRICE.) Could I take two more pillow cases for the other guys?

BEATRICE: Sure, go ahead. Only don't let her forget where they came from.

(CATHERINE *goes into a bedroom.*)

EDDIE: She's got other boarders up there?

BEATRICE: Yeah, there's two guys that just came over.

EDDIE: What do you mean, came over?

BEATRICE: From Italy. Lipari the butcher — his nephew. They come from Bari, they just got here yesterday. I didn't even know till Marco and Rodolpho moved up there before.

(CATHERINE *enters, going toward exit with two pillow cases.*)

It'll be nice, they could all talk together.

EDDIE: Catherine! (*She halts near the exit door. He takes in* BEATRICE *too.*) What're you, got no brains? You put them up there with two other submarines?

CATHERINE: Why?

EDDIE (*in a driving fright and anger*): Why! How do you know they're not trackin' these guys? They'll come up for them and find Marco and Rodolpho! Get them out of the house!

BEATRICE: But they been here so long already —

EDDIE: How do you know what enemies Lipari's got? Which they'd love to stab him in the back?

CATHERINE: Well what'll I do with them?

EDDIE: The neighborhood is full of rooms. Can't you stand to live a couple of blocks away from him? Get them out of the house!

CATHERINE: Well maybe tomorrow night I'll —

EDDIE: Not tomorrow, do it now. Catherine, you never mix yourself with somebody else's family! These guys get picked up, Lipari's liable to blame you or me and we got his whole family on our head. They got a temper, that family.

(*Two men in overcoats appear outside, start into the house.*)

CATHERINE: How'm I gonna find a place tonight?

EDDIE: Will you stop arguin' with me and get them out! You think I'm always tryin' to fool you or sump'm? What's the matter with you, don't you believe I could think of your good? Did I ever ask sump'm for myself? You think I got no feelin's? I never told you nothin' in my life that wasn't for your good. Nothin'! And look at the way you talk to me! Like I was an enemy! Like I — (*A knock on the door. His head swerves. They all stand motionless. Another knock.* EDDIE, *in a whisper, pointing upstage.*) Go up the fire escape, get them out over the back fence.

(CATHERINE *stands motionless, uncomprehending.*)

FIRST OFFICER (*in the hall*): Immigration! Open up in there!

EDDIE: Go, go. Hurry up! (*She stands a moment staring at him in a realized horror.*) Well, what're you lookin' at!

FIRST OFFICER: Open up!

EDDIE (*calling toward door*): Who's that there?

FIRST OFFICER: Immigration, open up.

(EDDIE *turns, looks at* BEATRICE. *She sits. Then he looks at* CATHERINE. *With a sob of fury* CATHERINE *streaks into a bedroom. Knock is repeated.*)

EDDIE: All right, take it easy, take it easy. (*He goes and opens the door. The* OFFICER *steps inside.*) What's all this?

FIRST OFFICER: Where are they?

(SECOND OFFICER *sweeps past and, glancing about, goes into the kitchen.*)

EDDIE: Where's who?

FIRST OFFICER: Come on, come on, where are they? (*He hurries into the bedrooms.*)

EDDIE: Who? We got nobody here. (*He looks at* BEATRICE, *who turns her head away. Pugnaciously, furious, he steps toward* BEATRICE.) What's the matter with *you*?

(FIRST OFFICER *enters from the bedroom, calls to the kitchen.*)

FIRST OFFICER: Dominick?

(*Enter* SECOND OFFICER *from kitchen.*)

SECOND OFFICER: Maybe it's a different apartment.

FIRST OFFICER: There's only two more floors up there. I'll take the front, you go up the fire escape. I'll let you in. Watch your step up there.

SECOND OFFICER: Okay, right, Charley. (FIRST OFFICER *goes out apartment door and runs up the stairs.*) This is Four-forty-one, isn't it?

EDDIE: That's right.

(SECOND OFFICER *goes out into the kitchen.* EDDIE *turns to* BEATRICE. *She looks at him now and sees his terror.*)

BEATRICE (*weakened with fear*): Oh, Jesus, Eddie.

EDDIE: What's the matter with you?

BEATRICE (*pressing her palms against her face*): Oh, my God, my God.

EDDIE: What're you, accusin' me?

BEATRICE (*her final thrust is to turn toward him instead of running from him*): My God, what did you do?

(*Many steps on the outer stair draw his attention. We see the* FIRST OFFICER *descending, with* MARCO, *behind him* RODOLPHO, *and* CATHERINE *and the two strange immigrants, followed by* SECOND OFFICER. BEATRICE *hurries to door.*)

CATHERINE (*backing down stairs, fighting with* FIRST OFFICER; *as they appear on the stairs*): What do yiz want from them? They work, that's all. They're boarders upstairs, they work on the piers.

BEATRICE (*to* FIRST OFFICER): Ah, Mister, what do you want from them, who do they hurt?

CATHERINE (*pointing to* RODOLPHO): They ain't no submarines, he was born in Philadelphia.

FIRST OFFICER: Step aside, lady.

CATHERINE: What do you mean? You can't just come in a house and —

FIRST OFFICER: All right, take it easy. (*To* RODOLPHO.) What street were you born in Philadelphia?

CATHERINE: What do you mean, what street? Could you tell me what street you were born?

FIRST OFFICER: Sure. Four blocks away, One-eleven Union Street. Let's go fellas.

CATHERINE (*fending him off* RODOLPHO): No, you can't! Now, get outa here!

FIRST OFFICER: Look, girlie, if they're all right they'll be out tomorrow. If they're illegal they go back where they came from. If you want, get yourself a lawyer, although I'm tellin' you now you're wasting your money. Let's get them in the car, Dom. (*To the men.*) Andiamo, Andiamo, let's go.

(*The men start, but* MARCO *hangs back.*)

BEATRICE (*from doorway*): Who're they hurtin', for God's sake, what do you want from them? They're starvin' over there, what do you want! Marco!

(MARCO *suddenly breaks from the group and dashes into the room and faces* EDDIE; BEATRICE *and* FIRST OFFICER *rush in as* MARCO *spits into* EDDIE's *face.*

CATHERINE *runs into hallway and throws herself into* RODOL-PHO's *arms.* EDDIE, *with an enraged cry, lunges for* MARCO.)

EDDIE: Oh, you mother's — !

(FIRST OFFICER *quickly intercedes and pushes* EDDIE *from* MARCO, *who stands there accusingly.*)

FIRST OFFICER (*between them, pushing* EDDIE *from* MARCO): Cut it out!

EDDIE (*over the* FIRST OFFICER's *shoulder, to* MARCO): I'll kill you for that, you son of a bitch!

FIRST OFFICER: Hey! (*Shakes him.*) Stay in here now, don't come out, don't bother him. You hear me? Don't come out, fella.

(*For an instant there is silence. Then* FIRST OFFICER *turns and takes* MARCO's *arm and then gives a last, informative look at* EDDIE. *As he and* MARCO *are going out into the hall,* EDDIE *erupts.*)

EDDIE: I don't forget that, Marco! You hear what I'm sayin'?

(*Out in the hall,* FIRST OFFICER *and* MARCO *go down the stairs. Now, in the street,* LOUIS, MIKE, *and several neighbors including the butcher,* LIPARI — *a stout, intense, middle-aged man — are gathering around the stoop.*

LIPARI, *the butcher, walks over to the two strange men and kisses them. His wife, keening, goes and kisses their hands.* EDDIE *is emerging from the house shouting after* MARCO. BEATRICE *is trying to restrain him.*)

EDDIE: That's the thanks I get? Which I took the blankets off my bed for yiz? You gonna apologize to me, Marco! *Marco!*

FIRST OFFICER (*in the doorway with* MARCO): All right, lady, let them go. Get in the car, fellas, it's over there.

(RODOLPHO *is almost carrying the sobbing* CATHERINE *off up the street, left.*)

CATHERINE: He was born in Philadelphia! What do you want from him?

FIRST OFFICER: Step aside, lady, come on now . . .

(*The* SECOND OFFICER *has moved off with the two strange men.* MARCO, *taking advantage of the* FIRST OFFICER'S *being occupied with* CATHERINE, *suddenly frees himself and points back at* EDDIE.)

MARCO: That one! I accuse that one!

(EDDIE *brushes* BEATRICE *aside and rushes out to the stoop.*)

FIRST OFFICER (*grabbing him and moving him quickly off up the left street*): Come on!

MARCO (*as he is taken off, pointing back at* EDDIE): That one! He killed my children! That one stole the food from my children!

(MARCO *is gone. The crowd has turned to* EDDIE.)

EDDIE (*to* LIPARI *and wife*): He's crazy! I give them the blankets off my bed. Six months I kept them like my own brothers!

(LIPARI, *the butcher, turns and starts up left with his arm around his wife.*)

EDDIE: Lipari! (*He follows* LIPARI *up left.*) For Christ's sake, I kept them, I give them the blankets off my bed!

(LIPARI *and wife exit.* EDDIE *turns and starts crossing down right to* LOUIS *and* MIKE.)

EDDIE: Louis! *Louis!*

(LOUIS *barely turns, then walks off and exits down right with* MIKE. *Only* BEATRICE *is left on the stoop.* CATHERINE *now returns, blank-eyed, from offstage and the car.* EDDIE *calls after* LOUIS *and* MIKE.)

EDDIE: He's gonna take that back. He's gonna take that back or I'll kill him! You hear me? I'll kill him! I'll kill him! (*He exits up street calling.*)

(*There is a pause of darkness before the lights rise, on the reception room of a prison.* MARCO *is seated;* ALFIERI, CATHERINE, *and* RODOLPHO *standing.*)

ALFIERI: I'm waiting, Marco, what do you say?

RODOLPHO: Marco never hurt anybody.

ALFIERI: I can bail you out until your hearing comes up. But I'm not going to do it, you understand me? Unless I have your promise. You're an honorable man, I will believe your promise. Now what do you say?

MARCO: In my country he would be dead now. He would not live this long.

ALFIERI: All right, Rodolpho — you come with me now.

RODOLPHO: No! Please, mister. Marco — promise the man. Please, I want you to watch the wedding. How can I be married and you're in here? Please, you're not going to do anything; you know you're not.

(MARCO *is silent.*)

CATHERINE (*kneeling left of* MARCO): Marco, don't you understand? He can't bail you out if you're gonna do something bad. To hell with Eddie. Nobody is gonna talk to him again if he lives to a hundred. Everybody knows you spit in his face, that's enough, isn't it? Give me the satisfaction — I want you at the wedding. You got a wife and kids, Marco. You could be workin' till the hearing comes up, instead of layin' around here.

MARCO (*to* ALFIERI): I have no chance?

ALFIERI (*crosses to behind* MARCO): No, Marco. You're going back. The hearing is a formality, that's all.

MARCO: But him? There is a chance, eh?

ALFIERI: When she marries him he can start to become an American. They permit that, if the wife is born here.

MARCO (*looking at* RODOLPHO): Well — we did something. (*He lays a palm on* RODOLPHO's *arm and* RODOLPHO *covers it.*)

RODOLPHO: Marco, tell the man.

MARCO (*pulling his hand away*): What will I tell him? He knows such a promise is dishonorable.

ALFIERI: To promise not to kill is not dishonorable.

MARCO (*looking at* ALFIERI): No?

ALFIERI: No.

MARCO (*gesturing with his head — this is a new idea*): Then what is done with such a man?

ALFIERI: Nothing. If he obeys the law, he lives. That's all.

MARCO (*rises, turns to* ALFIERI): The law? All the law is not in a book.

ALFIERI: Yes. In a book. There is no other law.

MARCO (*his anger rising*): He degraded my brother. My blood. He robbed my children, he mocks my work. I work to come here, mister!

ALFIERI: I know, Marco —

MARCO: There is no law for that? Where is the law for that?

ALFIERI: There is none.

MARCO (*shaking his head, sitting*): I don't understand this country.

ALFIERI: Well? What is your answer? You have five or six weeks you could work. Or else you sit here. What do you say to me?

MARCO (*lowers his eyes. It almost seems he is ashamed*): All right.

ALFIERI: You won't touch him. This is your promise.

(*Slight pause.*)

MARCO: Maybe he wants to apologize to me.

(MARCO *is staring away.* ALFIERI *takes one of his hands.*)

ALFIERI: This is not God, Marco. You hear? Only God makes justice.

MARCO: All right.

ALFIERI (*nodding, not with assurance*): Good! Catherine, Rodolpho, Marco, let us go.

(CATHERINE *kisses* RODOLPHO *and* MARCO, *then kisses* ALFIERI'S *hand.*)

CATHERINE: I'll get Beatrice and meet you at the church. (*She leaves quickly.*)

(MARCO *rises.* RODOLPHO *suddenly embraces him.* MARCO *pats him on the back and* RODOLPHO *exits after* CATHERINE. MARCO *faces* ALFIERI.)

ALFIERI: Only God, Marco.

(MARCO *turns and walks out.* ALFIERI *with a certain processional tread leaves the stage. The lights dim out.*

The lights rise in the apartment. EDDIE *is alone in the rocker, rocking back and forth in little surges. Pause. Now* BEATRICE *emerges from a bedroom. She is in her best clothes, wearing a hat.*)

BEATRICE (*with fear, going to* EDDIE): I'll be back in about an hour, Eddie. All right?

EDDIE (*quietly, almost inaudibly, as though drained*): What, have I been talkin' to myself?

BEATRICE: Eddie, for God's sake, it's her wedding.

EDDIE: Didn't you hear what I told you? You walk out that door to that wedding you ain't comin' back here, Beatrice.

BEATRICE: Why! What do you want?

EDDIE: I want my respect. Didn't you ever hear of that? From my wife?

(CATHERINE *enters from bedroom.*)

CATHERINE: It's after three; we're supposed to be there already, Beatrice. The priest won't wait.

BEATRICE: Eddie. It's her wedding. There'll be nobody there from her family. For my sister let me go. I'm goin' for my sister.

EDDIE (*as though hurt*): Look, I been arguin' with you all day already, Beatrice, and I said what I'm gonna say. He's gonna come here and apologize to me ɔr nobody from this house is goin' into that church today. Now if that's more to you than I am, then go. But don't come back. You be on my side or on their side, that's all.

CATHERINE (*suddenly*): Who the hell do you think you are?

BEATRICE: Sssh!

CATHERINE: You got no more right to tell nobody nothin'! Nobody! The rest of your life, nobody!

BEATRICE: Shut up, Katie! (*She turns* CATHERINE *around.*)

CATHERINE: You're gonna come with me!

BEATRICE: I can't Katie, I can't . . .

CATHERINE: How can you listen to him? This rat!

BEATRICE (*shaking* CATHERINE): Don't you call him that!

CATHERINE (*clearing from* BEATRICE): What're you scared of? He's a rat! He belongs in the sewer!

BEATRICE: Stop it!

CATHERINE (*weeping*): He bites people when they sleep! He comes when nobody's lookin' and poisons decent people. In the garbage he belongs!

(EDDIE *seems about to pick up the table and fling it at her.*)

BEATRICE: No, Eddie! Eddie! (*To* CATHERINE.) Then we all belong in the garbage. You, and me too. Don't say that. Whatever happened we all done it, and don't you ever forget it, Catherine. (*She goes to* CATHERINE.) Now go, go to your wedding, Katie, I'll stay home. Go. God bless you, God bless your children.

(*Enter* RODOLPHO.)

RODOLPHO: Eddie?

EDDIE: Who said you could come in here? Get outa here!

RODOLPHO: Marco is coming, Eddie.

(*Pause.* BEATRICE *raises her hands in terror.*)

He's praying in the church. You understand? (*Pause.* RODOLPHO *advances into the room.*) Catherine, I think it is better we go. Come with me.

CATHERINE: Eddie, go away, please.

BEATRICE (*quietly*): Eddie. Let's go someplace. Come. You and me.

(*He has not moved.*)

I don't want you to be here when he comes. I'll get your coat.

EDDIE: Where? Where am I goin'? This is my house.

BEATRICE (*crying out*): What's the use of it! He's crazy now, you know the way they get, what good is it! You got nothin' against Marco, you always liked Marco!

EDDIE: I got nothin' against Marco? Which he called me a rat in front of the whole neighborhood? Which he said I killed his children! Where you been?

RODOLPHO (*quite suddenly, stepping up to* EDDIE): It is my fault, Eddie. Everything. I wish to apologize. It was wrong that I do not ask your permission. I kiss your hand. (*He reaches for* EDDIE's *hand, but* EDDIE *snaps it away from him.*)

BEATRICE: Eddie, he's apologizing!

RODOLPHO: I have made all our troubles. But you have insult me too. Maybe God understand why you did that to me. Maybe you did not mean to insult me at all —

BEATRICE: Listen to him! Eddie, listen what he's tellin' you!

RODOLPHO: I think, maybe when Marco comes, if we can tell him we are comrades now, and we have no more argument between us. Then maybe Marco will not —

EDDIE: Now, listen —

CATHERINE: Eddie, give him a chance!

BEATRICE: What do you want! Eddie, what do you want!

EDDIE: I want my name! He didn't take my name; he's only a punk. Marco's got my name — (*to* RODOLPHO) and you can run tell him, kid, that he's gonna give it back to me in front of this neighborhood, or we have it out. (*Hoisting up his pants.*) Come on, where is he? Take me to him.

BEATRICE: Eddie, listen —

EDDIE: I heard enough! Come on, let's go!

BEATRICE: Only blood is good? He kissed your hand!

EDDIE: What he does don't mean nothin' to nobody! (*To* RODOLPHO.) Come on!

BEATRICE (*barring his way to the stairs*): What's gonna mean somethin'? Eddie, listen to me. Who could give you your name? Listen to me, I love you, I'm talkin' to you, I love you; if Marco'll kiss your hand outside, if he goes on his knees, what is he got to give you? That's not what you want.

EDDIE: Don't bother me!

BEATRICE: You want somethin' else, Eddie, and you can never have her!

CATHERINE (*in horror*): B.!

EDDIE (*shocked, horrified, his fists clenching*): Beatrice!

(MARCO *appears outside, walking toward the door from a distant point.*)

BEATRICE (*crying out, weeping*): The truth is not as bad as blood, Eddie! I'm tellin' you the truth — tell her good-by forever!

EDDIE (*crying out in agony*): That's what you think of me — that I would have such a thought? (*His fists clench his head as though it will burst.*)

MARCO (*calling near the door outside*): Eddie Carbone!

(EDDIE *swerves about; all stand transfixed for an instant. People appear outside.*)

EDDIE (*as though flinging his challenge*): Yeah, Marco! Eddie Carbone. Eddie Carbone. Eddie Carbone. (*He goes up the stairs and emerges from the apartment.* RODOLPHO *streaks up and out past him and runs to* MARCO.)

RODOLPHO: No, Marco, please! Eddie, please, he has children! You will kill a family!

BEATRICE: Go in the house! Eddie, go in the house!

EDDIE (*he gradually comes to address the people*): Maybe he come to apologize to me. Heh, Marco? For what you said about me in front of the neighborhood? (*He is incensing himself and little bits of laughter even escape him as his eyes are murderous and he cracks his knuckles in his hands with a strange sort of relaxation.*) He knows that ain't right. To do like that? To a man? Which I put my roof over their head and my food in their mouth? Like in the Bible? Strangers I never seen in my whole life? To come out of the water and grab a girl for a passport? To go and take from your own family like from the stable — and never a word to me? And now accusations in the bargain! (*Directly to* MARCO.) Wipin' the neighborhood with my name like a dirty rag! I want my name, Marco. (*He is moving now, carefully, toward* MARCO.) Now gimme my name and we go together to the wedding.

BEATRICE *and* CATHERINE (*keening*): Eddie! Eddie, don't! Eddie!

EDDIE: No, Marco knows what's right from wrong. Tell the people, Marco, tell them what a liar you are! (*He has his arms spread and* MARCO *is spreading his.*) Come on, liar, you know what you done! (*He lunges for* MARCO *as a great hushed shout goes up from the people.*)

(MARCO *strikes* EDDIE *beside the neck.*)

MARCO: Animal! You go on your knees to me!

(EDDIE *goes down with the blow and* MARCO *starts to raise a foot to stomp him when* EDDIE *springs a knife into his hand and* MARCO *steps back.* LOUIS *rushes in toward* EDDIE.)

LOUIS: Eddie, for Christ's sake!

(EDDIE *raises the knife and* LOUIS *halts and steps back.*)

EDDIE: You lied about me, Marco. Now say it. Come on now, say it!
MARCO: Anima-a-a-l!

(EDDIE *lunges with the knife.* MARCO *grabs his arm, turning the blade inward and pressing it home as the women and* LOUIS *and* MIKE *rush in and separate them, and* EDDIE, *the knife still in his hand, falls to his knees before* MARCO. *The two women support him for a moment, calling his name again and again.*)

CATHERINE: Eddie I never meant to do nothing bad to you.
EDDIE: Then why — Oh, B.!
BEATRICE: Yes, yes!
EDDIE: My B.!

(*He dies in her arms, and* BEATRICE *covers him with her body.* ALFIERI, *who is in the crowd, turns out to the audience. The lights have gone down, leaving him in a glow, while behind him the dull prayers of the people and the keening of the women continue.*)

ALFIERI: Most of the time now we settle for half and I like it better. But the truth is holy, and even as I know how wrong he was, and his death useless, I tremble, for I confess that something perversely pure calls to me from his memory — not purely good, but himself purely, for he allowed himself to be wholly known and for that I think I will love him more than all my sensible clients. And yet, it is better to settle for half, it must be! And so I mourn him — I admit it — with a certain . . . alarm.

CURTAIN

MILLER first wrote A *View from the Bridge* as a one-acter that played with only moderate success (as part of a two-part bill) on Broadway in 1955. The two-act version, published in 1957, has had successful runs both abroad and in the United States, but so far Miller has not given it a New York production.

A *View from the Bridge* is tragic in theme; naturalistic in setting, plot, and language; and epic in stage technique. Like Miller's earlier plays, it is a "tragedy of the common man," but despite the obvious differences in the protagonists' social station and significance, the fatality of Eddie Carbone's psychic make-up echoes the tragedy of character in the aristocratic tradition of the genre. For all his commonness, there is nothing common about Eddie's uncompromising commitment to his single passion. He even has his moment of Sophoclean irony when he warns Catherine that with the two submarines in the house she cannot be careful enough: "They got stool pigeons all over this neighborhood . . . , and you don't know who they are. It could be your best friend. You hear?"

The setting is contemporary and realistic, and the conflict grows out of one of those tense family situations that have furnished naturalistic plots since Ibsen's days (though the particular tensions of Miller's play would have been out of bounds for a playwright of a genteel age). And Miller has learned the Ibsenite technique of dialogue of implication, of expository hints almost but not quite submerged in the small talk. Within minutes of Eddie's return home from work in the first scene we sense there is something unwholesome in his attitude to Catherine, the Madonna reference strengthens our suspicions, and they are confirmed in the little scene right after dinner whence we gather that Eddie's secret passion keeps him away from Beatrice's bed. The faithful reproduction of the flat slovenliness of lower-class speech ("They wasn't supposed to be till next Thursday." "Maybe the other ship they was supposed to take there was some danger"), at times barely articulate ("Yeah, I mean, he's always makin' like remarks, like, y'know?"), is phonetically authentic to a degree beyond anything Ibsen or Chekhov attempted, but then their characters were middle-class, not lower-class, nor had it yet become naturalistic fashion to reflect nonstandard usage in spelling and typography. In fact, Eddie's, Catherine's, and Beatrice's speeches seem so true to life that we may be bothered by Miller's use of convention in Marco's and Rodolpho's. He skillfully suggests their unidiomatic flavor ("The older one is sick in the chest. My wife — she feeds them from her own mouth. I tell you the truth, if I stay there they will never grow up"), but it hardly seems plausible that two presumably uneducated Sicilian fishermen, fresh off the boat, are able to speak fluent English at all.*

---

* To argue that *all* the characters (including the Carbones) speak Italian is only to raise other, more serious problems. It is part of the play's irony that

Miller departs from naturalism only in his narrative manner, including the modern theatricality of the spare and flexible staging that permits nonrealistic effects (as in the phone-booth scene) as well as easy transitions from exterior to interior scenes and from one point of time to another. Alfieri, Miller's narrator, is simultaneously chorus — sympathetic and understanding spectator and commentator, the audience representative in the play — and a device for "framing" Eddie's story, distancing us from it and providing us with a point of view. But though, technically, we see the play through the lawyer's eyes, the drama about Eddie exists independent of its presumed presenter. The direct realism, the irresistible intimacy of the Carbone household, constantly leap across the esthetic distance that Alfieri's presence in theory insures, and only when he speaks are we aware of him as a prism through which we see the play.

Alfieri's limited function as technical device affects the success of his thematic function and takes us back to considering the nature of the play's tragic effect. He just is not a big enough character in the play to enforce the tragic meaning he sees in the story. Almost by definition, naturalistic tragedy deals with the suffering of unimportant people. Whether the downfall of a longshoreman can ever seem as significant or as cathartic as the fall of the great heroes of Greek and Shakespearean tragedy is debatable. The gain in ease of identification for a democratic audience, the almost automatic sympathy and empathy that come from recognizing as familiar the protagonist's circumstance, speech, and attitudes, must be set against the loss in magnitude of language and action. Naturalism has cut itself off from the drama of heightened human utterance. All Scotland is involved in Macbeth's evil, not only because he has the power of a king, but because to Shakespeare's time a king was, ideally, the embodiment of his people, the nation incarnate; Thebes' survival depends on the removal of Oedipus, her hidden cancer; but Eddie Carbone's death is only the unavoidable and violent end of a sick man. His suffering is a painful case history, and Eddie himself is pathetic because he is so thoroughly commonplace and likable, "as good a man as he had to be in a life that was hard and even," but he lives and dies in a spiritual darkness that renders his fate ultimately meaningless. What he does to himself, to his wife, to Catherine, to Rodolpho and Marco, and — worst of all — to Marco's wife and children is terrible, but the terror cannot issue in the catharsis of

---

Eddie considers himself wholly American; the irony would be blurred or gone if we assume that Italian is his natural language. Besides, the distinction in tone, idiom, and social level between the speech of the Carbones and that of the two brothers, which Miller observes throughout, would be meaningless.

expiated guilt, for he does not understand what he does; there is no recognition. Hence there *is* no guilt. There is not even any real struggle, because he does not recognize his true antagonist: not Rodolpho's "homosexuality" but his own illicit passion. In the preface to the play Miller writes that "the basic feeling" he was trying to create in his audience was "the desire to stop this man and tell him what he was really doing to his life." But can we feel it is he who is doing it? — not rather forces within him, beyond his comprehension and control? And if Eddie is not a free agent, then nothing anyone could have told him would have stopped his progress toward disaster.

But Alfieri's epitaph on Eddie claims a kind of greatness for him. Though Eddie was wrong,

". . . something perversely pure calls to me from his memory — not purely good, but himself purely, for he allowed himself to be wholly known and for that I think I will love him more than all my sensible clients."

To Alfieri, Eddie is memorable because he did not play it safe, did not "settle for half," did not compromise his dream. And because he didn't, he fulfilled his destiny, became completely what he was, in all its horror. But since it is impossible for us to feel that *not* to follow his destructive impulses was an alternative open to Eddie, the merit of his reckless pursuit of his obsession becomes questionable, and Alfieri's final speech seems less alarming than sentimental. What happens to Eddie affects us, but not as classical tragedy affects us. There is intensity in him, but it is the intensity of psychosis rather than of tragic greatness. He dies because of the irrationality and passion for which the idea of Sicily stands in the play; it makes symbolic sense that it is Marco who kills him. He dies for the delusion that Catherine "ain't all the girls," that he can, somehow, keep her virginity perpetually available to his dream of love.

APPENDIX

Biographical Notes and Suggested Reading

SOPHOCLES (496-406 B.C.) was born in Colonus, near Athens, and his home town is the setting for *Oedipus at Colonus*, the last of the nearly 120 plays he wrote. Only seven of them are extant today. They are, in the order in which they probably were written, *Antigone, Oedipus Rex, Electra, Ajax, Trachiniae, Philoctetes, Oedipus at Colonus*. In the annual competition among playwrights writing for the Dionysiac festival, Sophocles won the prize eighteen times. He innovated the use of three characters (in addition to the chorus) on stage simultaneously.

Chronologically, Sophocles is the second of the three great Athenian tragedians — some thirty years younger than Aeschylus, some fifteen years older than Euripides. His manhood coincides with the cultural flowering of Athens in the age of Pericles. Sophocles is said to have been a handsome, charming, well-to-do man. His civic employments appear to have been given him as the result of his fame as playwright. Aristophanes, the great writer of comedies and Sophocles' younger contemporary, summed up the tenor of his life in calling him "contented among the living, contented among the dead" — a curious but provocative judgment in view of the fact that it concerns one of the world's greatest tragic poets.

Suggested Reading

Brooks, Cleanth, and Robert B. Heilman, *Understanding Drama: Twelve Plays*. New York: Henry Holt and Company, 1948.

Butcher, S. H., *Aristotle's Theory of Poetry and Fine Art*. New York: Dover Publications, 1951.

Fergusson, Francis, *The Idea of a Theater*. Garden City, N.Y.: Doubleday & Company (Anchor Book), 1949.

Kitto, H. D. F., *Greek Tragedy: A Literary Study*. Garden City, N.Y.: Doubleday & Company (Anchor Book), 1954.

Knox, Bernard, "Sophocles' Oedipus," in *Tragic Themes in West-ern Literature*, ed. Cleanth Brooks. New Haven: Yale University Press, 1955.

Whitman, Cedric H., *Sophocles: A Study in Heroic Humanism.* Cambridge, Mass.: Harvard University Press, 1951.

Nothing is known about the author of *Everyman* and next to nothing about Peter Dorland of Diest, who possibly is the author of the Flem-ish play *Elckerlijk* (printed in 1495), on which *Everyman* may have been based.

Suggested Reading

Chambers, E. K., *English Literature at the Close of the Middle Ages.* New York: Oxford University Press, 1947.

Cormican, L. A., "Morality Tradition and the Interludes," in *The Age of Chaucer*, ed. Boris Ford. London: Penguin Books, 1954.

WILLIAM SHAKESPEARE (1564-1616). Enough is known about Shake-speare, both as man and as playwright, to refute all hypotheses that he was not the author of the plays ascribed to him. The evidence consists of legal documents and contemporary references, both friendly and unfriendly. He was the son of a substantial tradesman in Stratford-on-Avon, presumably received a good grammar-school education (includ-ing training in Latin) till the age of sixteen, and two years later mar-ried Anne Hathaway, who was eight years older than he, and with whom he had three children. In the early 1590's he turns up in London as a rising young poet and playwright-actor, a member of the Lord Chamberlain's Company, later (1603) known as the King's Servants. When the Globe theater was built in 1599, Shakespeare was listed as the second of nine shareholders. He retired to Stratford some time be-fore 1612, apparently a prosperous man.

His thirty-seven plays are traditionally divided into three groups: comedies (such as *A Midsummer-Night's Dream*, 1594;* *Much Ado About Nothing*, 1597; *As You Like It*, 1597; *Twelfth Night*, 1601), histories (such as *Richard III*, 1591; *Richard II*, 1594; *Henry IV*, parts 1 and 2, *Henry V*, all 1597), and tragedies (such as *Romeo and Juliet*, 1594; *Julius Cæsar*, 1597; *Hamlet*, 1601; *Othello*, 1601; *King Lear*,

---

* The dates are from G. B. Harrison's *Introducing Shakespeare* (pp. 115-116), where they are given as "approximate."

1606; *Macbeth*, 1606; *Coriolanus*, 1606). "Comedy," however, is a label that hardly fits farces like *The Comedy of Errors* (1591) and *The Merry Wives of Windsor* (1597), the darkly tinged romantic melodrama of *The Merchant of Venice* (1594), the ambiguous moral issues of *Measure for Measure* (1601) and *All's Well That Ends Well* (1601), or the poetic-philosophical fantasy of *The Tempest* (1611).

Suggested Reading

Bradley, A. C., *Shakespearean Tragedy*. New York: Meridian Books, 1955 (first published in 1904).

Brooks, Cleanth, "The Naked Babe and the Cloak of Manliness," in *The Well Wrought Urn*. New York: Harcourt, Brace and World (Harvest Book), 1947.

Chute, Marchette, *Shakespeare of London*. New York: E. P. Dutton & Co., 1949.

Fergusson, Francis, *The Human Image in Dramatic Literature*. Garden City, N.Y.: Doubleday & Company (Anchor Book), 1957.

Granville-Barker, H., and G. B. Harrison, eds., *A Companion to Shakespeare Studies*. Garden City, N.Y.: Doubleday & Company (Anchor Book), 1960.

Halliday, F. B., *Shakespeare: A Pictorial Biography*. New York: Thomas Y. Crowell Co., 1956.

Harrison, G. B., *Introducing Shakespeare*. London: Penguin Books, 1954.

Van Doren, Mark, *Shakespeare*. Garden City, N.Y.: Doubleday & Company (Anchor Book), 1939.

Webster, Margaret, *Shakespeare Without Tears*, rev. ed. Cleveland: World Publishing Company, 1955.

JEAN BAPTISTE POQUELIN (MOLIÈRE) (1622-1673) was the son of a well-to-do upholsterer attached to the royal court. Both upholstering and law studies proved abortive, and in 1643 young Poquelin co-founded a theater and took the name Molière (its significance is un-known) as a stage name. Unsuccessful in Paris, the theater toured the provinces between 1645 and 1658 — Molière's years of apprenticeship. In 1659 Molière had his first success as playwright with the satire *The Affected Ladies*. In 1661 the company, enjoying royal patronage, estab-lished itself in its own theater, the Palais Royal, in Paris. Until his death Molière continued to write comedies for his company and to act, mainly in comic parts. As man of the theater he was eminently successful, but his marriage to a much younger woman, the sister or possibly the daughter of his one-time mistress, appears to have been unhappy. Grim irony attended his death: he suffered a hemorrhage while performing the title role of his own comedy *The Hypochondriac* and died a few hours afterward.

Molière is generally recognized as the greatest of French writers of comedy. Like Shakespeare's, his best works belong to world literature. Among them are (in addition to *Tartuffe*), *School for Wives* (1662), *The Misanthrope* (1666), *The Miser* (1668), *The Gentleman Burgher* (1670), *The Learned Ladies* (1672), and *The Hypochondriac* (1673).

Suggested Reading

Chapman, Percy Addison, *The Spirit of Molière*. Princeton, N.J.: Princeton University Press, 1940.

Fernandez, Ramon, *Molière: The Man Seen Through His Plays*. New York: Hill and Wang, 1958.

Palmer, John, *Molière*. New York: Brown & Warren, 1930.

HENRIK IBSEN (1828-1906) was born in Skien, a small town in southern Norway. His father, a merchant, went bankrupt when the boy was eight. At sixteen he was apprenticed to a druggist. Two years later a maid in the household gave birth to his illegitimate child. These early events may have conditioned his later reticence and excessive outer propriety. Both financial ruin and bastardy are recurrent motifs in his plays. He wrote his first play in 1848, under the influence of the liberalism of the February revolution of that year. In the 1850's and early 1860's he held positions as salaried playwright and director at theaters in Bergen and Christiania (Oslo). Norway's failure to help Denmark in her war against Prussia in 1864 disillusioned him deeply (though he did not himself volunteer), and he and his wife and son left Norway for twenty-seven years of self-imposed exile in Italy and Germany. He died in Christiania after several years' illness.

Ibsen's iconoclasm, naturalistic symbolism, and novel and influential dramaturgy have earned him the label "father of modern drama." His canon, however, is more varied than the label suggests. His early plays dealt with saga and peasant subject matter. His first popular success was the philosophical dramatic poem *Brand* (1866), followed by the complementary, antithetical *Peer Gynt* (1867). His third period comprises the so-called social thesis plays on which his world fame largely rests. The main ones are: *A Doll's House* (1879), *Ghosts* (1881), *An Enemy of the People* (1882), *Rosmersholm* (1886), and *Hedda Gabler* (1890), though the last two are only incidentally thesis plays at all.

His last plays are heavily symbolic and interiorized and partly of autobiographical import, such as *The Master Builder* (1892) and *When We Dead Awaken* (1899).

Suggested Reading

Downs, Brian W., *A Study of Six Plays by Ibsen*. Cambridge: Cambridge University Press, 1950.

McFarlane, James W., *Ibsen and the Temper of Norwegian Literature*. London: Oxford University Press, 1960.

Northam, John, *Ibsen's Dramatic Method*. London: Faber and Faber, 1953.

Tennant, P., *Ibsen's Dramatic Technique*. Cambridge: Bowes & Bowes, 1948.

Weigand, Hermann, *The Modern Ibsen*. New York: E. P. Dutton & Co., 1960 (first published in 1925).

(GEORGE) BERNARD SHAW (1856-1950) was born in Dublin of impoverished English parents. His formal education ended when he was fifteen. In 1876 he arrived in London, entered journalism, wrote five unsuccessful novels, and joined the Fabian Society, a group of radical socialist intellectuals. His political views, however, never became the orthodoxy of any ideological camp. Between 1886 and 1898 he wrote art, music, and drama criticism for leading periodicals. *The Quintessence of Ibsenism*, which he published in 1891, is enthusiastic propaganda for Ibsen as a playwright of liberal ideas, but it says perhaps more about Shaw himself than about Ibsen. The long series of his plays began in 1891 with *Widowers' Houses*, a play of social criticism, and ended only in 1947. Shaw's prefaces to his plays, in impeccably lucid, incisive prose, are often as good clues to his thought as the plays themselves. In 1905 he bought the house at Ayot St. Lawrence in Hertfordshire in which he lived till his death. He received the Nobel Prize in 1925. He was a life-long vegetarian and teetotaller, was against vivisection and vaccination, and willed the bulk of his fortune to a project for reforming English spelling.

Shaw's plays are drama of dialectics rather than of character — brilliant and caustic exposures of sham and nonsense, more serious than their flamboyant wit immediately suggests. The following are among his best and most representative: *Candida* (1894), *Caesar and Cleopatra* (1898), *Man and Superman* (1903), *Major Barbara* (1905), *The Doctor's Dilemma* (1906), *Pygmalion* (1912), *Heartbreak House* (1916), *Back to Methuselah* (1921), *Saint Joan* (1923).

Suggested Reading

Bentley, Eric, *Bernard Shaw*, rev. ed. New York: New Directions, 1957.

————, *The Playwright as Thinker*. New York: Meridian Books, 1957.

Henderson, Archibald, *George Bernard Shaw: Man of the Century*. New York: Appleton-Century-Crofts, 1956.

Kronenberger, Louis, ed., *George Bernard Shaw: A Critical Survey*. Cleveland: World Publishing Company, 1953.

Nethercot, Arthur H., *Men and Supermen*. Cambridge, Mass.: Harvard University Press, 1954.

Shaw, Bernard, *Shaw on Theatre*, ed. E. J. West. New York: Hill and Wang, 1958.

ANTON PAVLOVICH CHEKHOV (1860-1904) was born in Taganrog on the Sea of Azov in southern Russia, the grandson of a serf. A harsh boyhood was followed by medical studies in Moscow. He received his degree in 1884, but he never practiced medicine regularly and during his last years not at all. While he was still a student he began to write — and to get published — small, comical sketches. In 1886 a successful collection of short stories, somewhat in the manner of de Maupassant, brought him acceptance in leading literary circles. His early plays failed on the stage, but in 1898 *The Seagull*, which had been a humiliating fiasco in St. Petersburg two years earlier, was a brilliant success in the newly opened Moscow Art Theater, under the direction of Konstantin Stanislavsky. *The Seagull* established Chekhov's reputation as playwright, the success of the "Stanislavsky method" of naturalistic acting, and the finances of the new theater. During the few remaining years of his life, Chekhov, already desperately ill with tuberculosis, spent his winters in Yalta on the Crimea. He wrote three additional plays for the Moscow Art Theater: *Uncle Vanya* (1899), *Three Sisters* (1901), and his greatest success, *The Cherry Orchard* (1904). In 1901 he married one of the Theater's leading actresses. He died at a sanatorium in southern Germany.

Suggested Reading

Magarshack, David, *Chekhov the Dramatist*. New York: Hill and Wang, 1960.

Toumanova, Princess Nina Andronikova, *Anton Chekhov: The Voice of Twilight Russia*. New York: Columbia University Press, 1960.

AUGUST STRINDBERG (1849-1912) was born in Stockholm, the son of a stolid, middle-class father and a working-class mother. The couple had children together before their marriage, but the future playwright was born in wedlock. Strindberg unsuccessfully tried for an advanced university degree and a career in acting. The eight years of his young manhood when he worked as a librarian, became a scholar of some note, and wrote his earliest plays and tales, may have been the happiest in his restless, tragic life. In 1877 he married for the first time. Two years later he made a name for himself with the satiric, realistic novel *The Red Room* and left Sweden to live by his pen abroad. In 1884 he was acquitted of a charge of blasphemy, but the affair strained his hypersensitive nerves. There followed a period of frenetic literary activity, partly in Sweden, partly on the Continent. His autobiographical writing from the 1880's and the naturalistic plays *The Father* (1887), *Miss Julie* (1888), and *Creditors* (1888) reflect the growth of the mysogyny which contributed to the dissolution of his marriage in 1891. Through most of the 1890's Strindberg suffered from a persecution complex attended by hallucinations, though authorities disagree as to whether he ever actually became what should be called insane. Between voluntary stays at mental hospitals he studied and wrote on botany and chemistry — but also alchemy, occultism, and demonology. A second marriage failed in 1894. The autobiographical narrative *Inferno* (1897) records the critical years of his psychopathy. From 1902 till his death Strindberg lived in Stockholm, indubitably sane though hardly serene. His third marriage ended in divorce in 1904, but his amazing literary creativity never again left him: novels, tales, short stories, historical writings, philological, anthropological, and political essays, and plays, poured from his pen. Among the last were religious dramas: *To Damascus* (1898); *Dance of Death* (1901), another play about married horrors; *The Dream Play* (1901), an early example of expressionism; a long series of plays with subjects from Swedish history; and, finally, a group of esoteric, often fantastic "chamber plays," performed at the Intimate Theater, Strindberg's own stage, managed by a younger friend. *The Storm* and *The Pelican* (like *The Ghost Sonata* written in 1907) are the most significant of these last plays.

Suggested Reading

Bentley, Eric, *The Playwright as Thinker*. New York: Meridian Books, 1957.

Dahlström, C. E. W. L., *Strindberg's Dramatic Expressionism*. Ann Arbor, Mich.: University of Michigan Press, 1930.

Mortensen, Brita M. E., and Brian W. Downs, *Strindberg: An Introduction to His Life and Work*. Cambridge: Cambridge University Press, 1949.

Sprigge, Elizabeth, *The Strange Life of August Strindberg*. London: Hamish Hamilton, 1949.

WILLIAM BUTLER YEATS (1865-1939) was the son of a distinguished Dublin portrait painter, and he, too, for a time practiced painting. His childhood was divided between London and his mother's home in Sligo county in western Ireland, a country that influenced motif and imagery in his poetry. His early verse was in the contemporary manner of the pre-Raphaelites and their successors — sensuously romantic, rich, a little soft and vague. In 1899 he was one of the founders of the Irish Literary Theater and was for many years its leader. He dreamed of making it a center for the revival of a mystical, poetic theater, but though several of his own plays were performed there and he brought to the theater John Millington Synge, perhaps the greatest dramatic talent of the Irish literary renaissance, and though the Abbey Theater (as it came to be known) became one of modern Europe's great stages, Yeats never realized his dream of a poetic Irish theater. In the 1920's and '30's Yeats's poems gained in depth and in taut, sparse strength, but his growing reliance on a semi-private stock of metaphors and symbols derived from his reading in mysticism and occultism often made them difficult. For some years after 1922 he was a member of the Senate of the newly independent Irish republic, though many aspects of politics in a modern democracy were distasteful to his aristocratic, tradition-oriented, non-pragmatic loyalties. In 1923 he received the Nobel Prize.

Yeats's early, most popular plays are based on themes from Irish folklore: *The Countess Kathleen* (1889-1892), *The Land of Heart's Desire* (1894), *Cathleen ni Houlihan* (1902), *The Hour Glass* (1902). *At the Hawk's Well* (1914) and *The Death of Cuchulain* (1938-1939) are early and late examples of his later, terse and emblematic manner.

Suggested Reading

Ellis-Fermor, Una, *The Irish Dramatic Movement*. London: Methuen & Co., 1954.

Ellmann, Richard, *Yeats, the Man and the Masks*. New York: E. P. Dutton & Co., 1948.

Wilson, F. A. C., *W. B. Yeats and Tradition*. London: Victor Gollancz, 1958.

BERTOLT BRECHT (1898-1956) was born in the south German town of Augsburg in Bavaria. He studied medicine, served in World War I, began writing plays and in the 1920's was part of a group of avant-garde and leftist poets, playwrights, actors, and artists in Berlin. He fled Germany when Hitler came to power, lived in Denmark during the late '30's and in California from 1941 to 1947. For a while he worked in Hollywood. For two years after his return to Europe after the war he wrote and produced plays for the National Theater in Zürich, Switzerland. He moved to East Berlin in 1949, where he worked with his own ensemble till his death, staunchly supporting the Communist régime. Some of his anti-war poems are modern classics in Germany, but abroad he is most famous for his dramas: *The Three-Penny Opera* (1928) with music by Kurt Weill (a modern version of the early eighteenth century *Beggar's Opera* by John Gay); *The Private Life of the Master Race* (1937), an anti-Nazi play; *Mother Courage* (1941); *Galileo* (1943, 1947); *The Caucasian Chalk Circle* (1948). Brecht has been influential not only as playwright and director but also as theorist of the theater.

Suggested Reading

Bentley, Eric, *The Playwright as Thinker*. New York: Meridian Books, 1957.

Esslin, Martin, *Brecht, the Man and His Work*. Garden City, N.Y.: Doubleday & Company, 1960.

Willett, John, *The Theatre of Bertolt Brecht*. London: Methuen & Co., 1959.

EUGÈNE IONESCO (1912-   ), though Romanian by birth, has lived most of his life in France and writes in French. For a few years he taught French in Bucharest; later he worked in a Paris publishing house. He started writing plays, he says, because he disliked the theater. Whether this means that he hoped to improve upon an unsatisfactory dramatic repertory or is simply another Ionescian paradox is hard to say. During the 1950's he became one of the most publicized and controversial of contemporary playwrights. Like the Irishman Samuel Beckett, Ionesco represents the "absurd" theater, and like Beckett he is almost constantly preoccupied with the failure of human communication, specifically with the disjunction of speech and meaning. Critical opinion about him ranges from the charge that his plays are "hollow and pretentious fakery" to enthusiastic approval of his cultivation of "pure" theater and comparisons with such diverse figures as Molière,

Lewis Carroll, and Strindberg. Besides *The Lesson*, his best known plays are *The Bald Soprano* (1950) and *The Chairs* (1952).

Suggested Reading

Fowler, W., "New French Theater," *Sewanee Review*, LXVII (Autumn, 1959), 643-657.

Grossvogel, David I., *The Self-Conscious Stage in Modern French Drama*. New York: Columbia University Press, 1958.

Ionesco, Eugène, "The World of Ionesco," *Tulane Drama Review*, III (Oct., 1958), 45-47.

Watson, Donald, "The Plays of Ionesco," *Tulane Drama Review*, III (Oct., 1958), 48-53.

ARTHUR MILLER (1915-   ) was born in New York. In 1938 he graduated from the University of Michigan. After a succession of odd jobs, he became associated with the Federal Theater in New York. In 1944 he wrote the script for the movie "The Story of G.I. Joe." *Focus*, a novel about anti-Semitism, was a success in 1945. An early play failed on the stage, but in 1947 he scored a hit with *All My Sons*. *Death of a Salesman* (1949) received the Pulitzer Prize. *The Crucible* (1953), a play about the Salem witch trials, with fairly obvious reference to the contemporary political scene in the United States, was less well received.

Suggested Reading

Driver, Tom, "Strength and Weakness in Arthur Miller," *Tulane Drama Review*, IV (Summer, 1960), 45-52.

Miller, Arthur, "Introduction," *Collected Plays*. New York: Viking Press, 1957.

Popkin, Henry, "Arthur Miller: The Strange Encounter," *Sewanee Review*, LXVIII (Winter, 1960), 34-60.

SUGGESTED GENERAL READING ON DRAMA

Theory

Brooks, Cleanth, and Robert B. Heilman, *Understanding Drama: Twelve Plays*. New York: Henry Holt and Company, 1948.

Butcher, S. H., *Aristotle's Theory of Poetry and Fine Art*. New York: Dover Publications, 1951.

Clark, Barrett H., ed., *European Theories of Drama, with a Supplement on the American Drama.* New York: Crown Publishers, 1947.

Downer, Alan S., *The Art of the Play: An Anthology of Nine Plays.* New York: Henry Holt and Company, 1955.

Drew, Elizabeth, *Discovering Drama.* New York: W. W. Norton & Co., 1937.

Eliot, T. S., *Poetry and Drama.* Cambridge, Mass.: Harvard University Press, 1951.

Fergusson, Francis, *The Idea of a Theater.* Garden City, N.Y.: Doubleday & Company (Anchor Book), 1949.

Nicoll, Allardyce, *The Theory of Drama.* London: G. G. Harrap & Company, 1937.

Sewall, Richard B., *The Vision of Tragedy.* New Haven, Conn.: Yale University Press, 1959.

Thompson, Alan R., *The Anatomy of Drama,* 2nd ed. Berkeley, Calif.: University of California Press, 1946.

History and Criticism

Bentley, Eric, *In Search of Theater.* New York: Alfred A. Knopf, 1953.

———, *The Playwright as Thinker.* New York: Meridian Books, 1957.

Gassner, John, *Form and Idea in Modern Theatre.* New York: Dryden Press, 1956.

———, *Masters of the Drama,* 3rd rev. ed. New York: Dover Publications, 1954.

———, *The Theatre in Our Times.* New York: Crown Publishers, 1954.

Nicoll, Allardyce, *World Drama from Aeschylus to Anouilh.* London: G. G. Harrap & Company, 1949.

Theater Arts

Cole, Toby, and Helen Krich Chinoy, eds., *Actors on Acting.* New York: Crown Publishers, 1949.

Gorelik, Mordecai, *New Theatres for Old.* New York: S. French, 1940.

Macgowan, Kenneth, and William Melnitz, *The Living Stage: A History of the World Theater.* New York: Prentice-Hall, Inc., 1955. (A shorter version is *The Golden Ages of the Theater,* 1959.)

Stanislavsky, Constantin, *An Actor Prepares,* tr. Elizabeth Reynolds Hapgood. New York: Theatre Arts Books, 1936.

Reference

Hartnoll, Phyllis, ed., *The Oxford Companion to the Theatre,* 2nd ed. London: Oxford University Press, 1957.

Some Useful Collections of Plays

Bentley, Eric, ed., *The Play: A Critical Anthology.* New York: Prentice-Hall, 1951.

————, *The Modern Theatre,* I-VI. Garden City, N.Y.: Doubleday & Company (Anchor Books), 1955-1960.

Gassner, John, ed., *Treasury of the Theatre,* I-II. New York: Simon and Schuster, 1950-1951.

Grene, David and Richmond Lattimore, eds., *The Complete Greek Tragedies,* I-IV. Chicago: University of Chicago Press, 1959.

Watson, E. Bradlee and Benfield Pressey, eds., *Contemporary Drama, 11 Plays.* New York: Charles Scribner's Sons, 1956.

————, *Contemporary Drama, 15 Plays.* New York: Charles Scribner's Sons, 1959.